D1470383

TALES
of the
WEST

Compiled by Frank Oppel

CASTLE

TABLE
OF
CONTENTS

1

Little Big Horn Medicine

OWEN WISTER

LITTLE BIG HORN MEDICINE.

BY OWEN WISTER.

OMETHING new was
happening among the
Crow Indians. A
young pretender had
appeared in the tribe.
What this might lead
to was unknown
alike to white
man and to red;
but the old Crow chiefs
discussed it in their coun-
cils, and the soldiers at
Fort Custer, and the ci-
vilians at the agency
twelve miles up the river, and all the
white settlers in the valley, discussed it
also. Lieutenants Stirling and Haines,
of the First Cavalry, were speculating
upon it as they rode one afternoon.

"Can't tell about Indians," said Stirling. "But I think the Crows are too
reasonable to go on the war-path."

"Reasonable!" said Haines. He was
young, and new to Indians.

"Just so. Until you come to his super-
stitions, the Indian can reason as straight
as you or I. He's perfectly logical."

"Logical!" echoed Haines again. He
held the regulation Eastern view that the
Indian knows nothing but the three blind
appetites.

"You'd know better," remarked Stirling, "if you'd been fighting 'em for fifteen years. They're as shrewd as Æsop's
fables."

Just then two Indians appeared round
a bluff—one old and shabby, the other
young and very gaudy—riding side by
side.

"That's Cheschapah," said Stirling.
"That's the agitator in all his feathers.
His father, you see, dresses more conser-
vatively."

The feathered dandy now did a singular thing. He galloped towards the two
officers almost as if to bear them down,
and steering much too close, flashed by
yelling, amid a clatter of gravel.

"Nice manners," commented Haines.
"Seems to have a chip on his shoulder."

But Stirling looked thoughtful. "Yes,"
he muttered, "he has a chip."

Meanwhile the shabby father was approaching. His face was mild and sad,
and he might be seventy. He made a

gesture of greeting. "How!" he said,
pleasantly, and ambled on his way.

"Now there you have an object-lesson," said Stirling. "Old Pounded Meat
has no chip. The question is, are the
fathers or the sons going to run the Crow
Nation?"

"Why did the young chap have a dog
on his saddle?" inquired Haines.

"I didn't notice it. For his supper,
probably — probably he's getting up a
dance. He is scheming to be a chief.
Says he is a medicine-man, and can make
water boil without fire; but the big men
of the tribe take no stock in him—not
yet. They've seen soda-water before.
But I'm told this water-boiling astonishes
the young."

"You say the old chiefs take no stock
in him yet?"

"Ah, that's the puzzle. I told you just
now Indians could reason."

"And I was amused."

"Because you're an Eastern man. I
tell you, Haines, if it wasn't my business
to shoot Indians I'd study them."

"You're a crank," said Haines.

But Stirling was not a crank. He
knew that so far from being a mere animal, the Indian is of a subtlety more ancient than the Sphinx. In his primal
brain—nearer nature than our own—the
directness of a child mingles with the
profoundest cunning. He believes easily
in powers of light and darkness, yet is a
sceptic all the while. Stirling knew this;
but he could not know just when, if ever,
the young charlatan Cheschapah would
succeed in cheating the older chiefs; just
when, if ever, he would strike the chord
of their superstition. Till then they would
reason that the white man was more comfortable as a friend than as a foe, that
rations and gifts of clothes and farming
implements were better than battles and
prisons. Once their superstition was set
alight, these three thousand Crows might
suddenly follow Cheschapah to burn and
kill and destroy.

"How does he manage his soda-water,
do you suppose?" inquired Haines.

"That's mysterious. He has never
been known to buy drugs, and he's careful where he does his trick. He's still a
little afraid of his father. All Indians

3

are. It's queer where he was going with that dog."

Hard galloping sounded behind them, and a courier from the Indian agency overtook and passed them, hurrying to Fort Custer. The officers hurried too, and arriving, received news and orders. Forty Sioux were reported up the river coming to visit the Crows. It was peaceable, but untimely. The Sioux agent over at Pine Ridge had given these forty permission to go, without first finding out if it would be convenient to the Crow agent to have them come. It is a rule of the Indian Bureau that if one tribe desire to visit another, the agents of both must consent. Now, most of the Crows were farming and quiet, and it was not wise that a visit from the Sioux and a season of feasting should tempt their hearts and minds away from the tilling of the soil. The visitors must be taken charge of and sent home.

"Very awkward, though," said Stirling to Haines. He had been ordered to take two troops and arrest the unoffending visitors on their way. "The Sioux will be mad, and the Crows will be madder. What a bungle! and how like the way we manage Indian affairs!" And so they started.

Thirty miles away, by a stream towards which Stirling with his command was steadily marching through the night, the visitors were gathered. There was a cook-fire and a pot, and a stewing dog leaped in the froth. Old men in blankets and feathers sat near it, listening to young Cheschapah's talk in the flighty lustre of the flames. An old squaw acted as interpreter between Crow and Sioux. Round about, at a certain distance, the figures of the crowd lounged at the edge of the darkness. Two grizzled squaws stirred the pot, spreading a clawed fist to their eyes against the red heat of the coals, while young Cheschapah harangued the older chiefs.

"And more than that I, Cheschapah, can do," said he, boasting in Indian fashion. "I know how to make the white man's heart soft so he cannot fight." He paused for effect, but his hearers seemed uninterested. "You have come pretty

"BOASTING IN INDIAN FASHION."

far to see us," resumed the orator, "and I, and my friend Two Whistles, and my father, Pounded Meat, have come a day to meet you and bring you to our place. I have brought you a fat dog. I say it is good the Crow and the Sioux shall be friends. All the Crow chiefs are glad. Pretty Eagle is a big chief, and he will tell you what I tell you. But I am bigger than Pretty Eagle. I am a medicine-man."

He paused again; but the grim old chiefs were looking at the fire, and not at him. He got a friendly glance from his henchman, Two Whistles, but he heard his father give a grunt.

That enraged him. "I am a medicine-man," he repeated, defiantly. "I have been in the big hole in the mountains where the river goes, and spoken there with the old man who makes the thunder. I talked with him as one chief to another. I am going to kill all the white men."

At this old Pounded Meat looked at his son angrily, but the son was not afraid of his father just then. "I can make medicine to bring the rain," he continued. "I can make water boil when it is cold. With this I can strike the white man blind when he is so far that his eyes do not show in his face."

He swept out from his blanket an old cavalry sabre painted scarlet. Young Two Whistles made a movement of awe, but Pounded Meat said, "My son's tongue has grown longer than his sword."

Laughter sounded among the old chiefs. Cheschapah turned his impudent yet somewhat visionary face upon his father. "What do you know of medicine?" said he. "Two sorts of Indians are among the Crows to-day," he continued to the chiefs. "One sort are the fathers, and the sons are the other. The young warriors are not afraid of the white man. The old plant corn with the squaws. Is this the way with the Sioux?"

"With the Sioux," remarked a grim visitor, "no one fears the white man. But the young warriors do not talk much in council."

Pounded Meat put out his hand gently, as if in remonstrance. Other people must not chide his son.

"You say you can make water boil with no fire?" pursued the Sioux, who was named Young-man-afraid-of-his-horses, and had been young once.

Pounded Meat came between. "My son is a good man," said he. "These words of his are not made in the heart, but are head words you need not count. Cheschapah does not like peace. He has heard us sing our wars and the enemies we have killed, and he remembers that he has no deeds, being young. When he thinks of this sometimes he talks words without sense. But my son is a good man."

The father again extended his hand, which trembled a little. The Sioux had listened, looking at him with respect, and forgetful of Cheschapah, who now stood before them with a cup of cold water.

"You shall see," he said, "who it is that talks words without sense."

Two Whistles and the young bucks crowded to watch, but the old men sat where they were. As Cheschapah stood relishing his audience, Pounded Meat stepped up suddenly and upset the cup. He went to the stream and refilled it himself. "Now make it boil," said he.

Cheschapah smiled, and as he spread his hand quickly over the cup, the water foamed up.

"Huh!" said Two Whistles, startled.

The medicine-man quickly seized his moment. "What does Pounded Meat know of my medicine?" said he. "The dog is cooked. Let the dance begin."

The drums set up their dull blunt beating, and the crowd of young and less important bucks came from the outer circle nearer to the council. Cheschapah set the pot in the midst of the flat camp, to be the centre of the dance. None of the old chiefs said more to him, but sat apart with the empty cup, having words among themselves. The flame reared high into the dark, and showed the rock wall towering close, and at its feet the light lay red on the streaming water. The young Sioux stripped naked of their blankets, hanging them in a screen against the wind from the jaws of the cañon, with more constant shouts as the drumming beat louder, and strokes of echo fell from the black cliffs. The figures twinkled across each other in the glare, drifting and alert, till the dog-dance shaped itself into twelve dancers with a united sway of body and arms, one and another singing his song against the lifted sound of the drums. The twelve sank crouching in simulated hunt for an enemy back and forth over the same space, swinging together.

Presently they sprang with a shout

upon their feet, for they had taken the enemy. Cheschapah, leading the line closer to the central pot, began a new figure, dancing the pursuit of the bear. This went faster; and after the bear was taken, followed the elk-hunt, and a new sway and crouch of the twelve gesturing bodies. The thudding drums were ceaseless; and as the dance went always faster and always nearer the dog-pot, the steady blows of sound inflamed the dancers; their chests heaved, and their arms and bodies swung alike as the excited crew filed and circled closer to the pot, following Cheschapah, and shouting uncontrollably. They came to firing pistols and slashing the air with knives, when suddenly Cheschapah caught up a piece of steaming dog from the pot, gave it to his best friend, and the dance was done. The dripping figures sat quietly, shining and smooth with sweat, eating their dog-flesh in the ardent light of the fire and the cold splendor of the moon. By-and-by they lay in their blankets to sleep at ease.

The elder chiefs had looked with distrust at Cheschapah as he led the dance; now that the entertainment was over, they rose with gravity to go to their beds.

"It is good for the Sioux and the Crows to be friends," said Pounded Meat to Young-man-afraid-of-his-horses. "But we want no war with the white man. It is a few young men who say that war is good now."

"We have not come for war," replied the Sioux. "We have come to eat much meat together, and remember that day when war was good on the Little Horn, and our warriors killed Yellow Hair and all his soldiers."

Pounded Meat came to where he and Cheschapah had their blankets.

"We shall have war," said the confident son to his father. "My medicine is good."

"Peace is also pretty good," said Pounded Meat. "Get new thoughts. My son, do you not care any more for my words?"

Cheschapah did not reply.

"I have lived a long while. Yet one man may be wrong. But all cannot be. The other chiefs say what I say. The white men are too strong."

"They would not be too strong if the old men were not cowards."

"Have done," said the father, sternly. "If you are a medicine-man, do not talk like a light fool."

The Indian has an "honor thy father" deep in his religion too, and Cheschapah was silent. But after he was asleep, Pounded Meat lay brooding. He felt himself dishonored, and his son to be an evil in the tribe. With these sore notions keeping him awake, he saw the night wane into gray, and then he heard the distant snort of a horse. He looked, and started from his blankets, for the soldiers had come, and he ran to wake the sleeping Indians. Frightened, and ignorant why they should be surrounded, the Sioux leaped to their feet; and Stirling, from where he sat on his horse, saw their rushing, frantic figures.

"Go quick, Kinney," he said to the interpreter, "and tell them it's peace, or they'll be firing on us."

Kinney rode forward alone, with one hand raised; and seeing that sign, they paused, and crept nearer like crafty rabbits, while the sun rose and turned the place pink. And then came the parley, and the long explanation; and Stirling thanked his stars to see they were going to allow themselves to be peaceably arrested. Bullets you get used to; but after the firing's done, you must justify it to important personages who live comfortably in Eastern towns and have never seen an Indian in their lives, and are rancid with philanthropy and ignorance.

Stirling would sooner have faced Sioux than sentimentalists, and he was fervently grateful to these savages for coming with him quietly without obliging him to shoot them. Cheschapah was not behaving so nicely; and recognizing him, Stirling understood about the dog. The medicine-man, with his faithful Two Whistles, was endeavoring to excite the prisoners as they were marched down the river to the Crow Agency.

Stirling sent for Kinney. "Send that rascal away," he said. "I'll not have him bothering here."

The interpreter obeyed, but with a singular smile to himself. When he had ordered Cheschapah away, he rode so as to overhear Stirling and Haines talking. When they speculated about the soda-water, Kinney smiled again. He was a quiet sort of man. The people in the valley admired his business head. He supplied grain and steers to Fort Custer, and used to say that business was always slow in time of peace.

By evening Stirling had brought his

prisoners to the agency, and there was the lieutenant of Indian police of the Sioux come over from Pine Ridge to bring them home. There was restlessness in the air as night fell round the prisoners and their guard. It was Cheschapah's hour, and the young Crows listened while he declaimed against the white man for thwarting their hospitality. The strong chain of sentinels was kept busy preventing these hosts from breaking through to fraternize with their guests. Cheschapah did not care that the old Crow chiefs would not listen. When Pretty Eagle remarked laconically that peace was good, the agitator laughed; he was gaining a faction, and the faction was feeling its oats. Accordingly, next morning, though the prisoners were meek on being started home by Stirling with twenty soldiers, and the majority of the Crows were meek at seeing them thus started, this was not all. Cheschapah, with a yelling swarm of his young friends, began to buzz about the column as it marched up the river. All had rifles.

"It's an interesting state of affairs," said Stirling to Haines. "There are at least fifty of these devils at our heels now, and more coming. We've got twenty men. Haines, your Indian experiences may begin quite early in your career."

"Yes, especially if our prisoners take to kicking."

"Well, to compensate for spoiling their dinner party, the agent gave them some rations and his parting blessing. It may suffice."

The line of march had been taken up by ten men in advance, followed in the usual straggling fashion by the prisoners, and the rear-guard was composed of the other ten soldiers under Stirling and Haines. With them rode the chief of the Crow police and the lieutenant of the Sioux. This little band was, of course, far separated from the advance-guard, and it listened to the young Crow bucks yelling at its heels. They yelled in English. Every Indian knows at least two English words; they are pungent, and far from complimentary.

"It's got to stop here," said Stirling, as they came to a ford known as Reno's Crossing. "They've got to be kept on this side."

"Can it be done without gunpowder?" Haines asked.

"If a shot is fired now, my friend, it's war, and a court of inquiry in Washington for you and me, if we're not buried here. Sergeant, you will take five men and see the column is kept moving. The rest remain with me. The prisoners must be got across and away from their friends."

The fording began, and the two officers went over to the east bank to see that the instructions were carried out.

"See that?" observed Stirling. As the last of the rear-guard stepped into the stream, the shore they were leaving filled instantly with the Crows. "Every man jack of them is armed. And here's an interesting development," he continued.

It was Cheschapah riding out into the water, and with him Two Whistles. The rear-guard passed up the trail, and the little knot of men with the officers stood halted on the bank. They were nine — the two Indian police, the two lieutenants, and five long muscular boys of K troop of the First Cavalry. They remained on the bank, looking at the thick painted swarm that yelled across the ford.

"Bet you there's a hundred," remarked Haines.

"You forget I never gamble," murmured Stirling. Two of the five long boys overheard this and grinned at each other, which Stirling noted; and he loved them. It was curious to mark the two shores; the feathered multitude and its yells and its fifty yards of rifles that fronted a small spot of white men sitting easily in the saddle; and the clear, pleasant water speeding between. Cheschapah and Two Whistles came tauntingly towards this spot, and the mass of Crows on the other side drew forward a little.

"You tell them," said Stirling to the chief of the Crow police, "that they must go back."

Cheschapah came nearer, by way of obedience.

"Take them over, then," the officer ordered.

The chief of Crow police rode to Cheschapah, speaking and pointing. His horse drew close, shoving the horse of the medicine-man, who now launched an insult that with Indians calls for blood. He struck the man's horse with his whip, and at that a volume of yells chorussed from the other bank.

"Looks like the court of inquiry," re-

"HIS HORSE DREW CLOSE, SHOVING THE HORSE OF THE MEDICINE-MAN."

marked Stirling. "Don't shoot, boys," he commanded aloud.

The amazed Sioux policeman gasped. "You not shoot?" he said. "But he hit that man's horse, all the same hit your horse, all the same hit you."

"Right. Quite right," growled Stirling. "All the same hit Uncle Sam. But we soldier devils have orders to temporize." His eye rested hard and serious on the party in the water as he went on speaking with jocular unconcern. "Temporize, Johnny," said he. "You savvy temporize?"

"Ump! Me no savvy."

"Bully for you, Johnny. Too many syllables. Well, now! he's hit that horse again. One more for the court of inquiry. Steady, boys! There's Two Whistles switching now. They ought to call that lad Young Dog Tray. And there's a chap in paint fooling with his gun. If any more do that—it's very catching— Yes, we're going to have a circus. Attention! Now what's that, do you suppose?"

An apparition, an old chief, came suddenly on the other bank, pushing through the crowd, grizzled and little and lean, among the smooth, full-limbed young blood. They turned and saw him, and slunk from the tones of his voice and the light in his ancient eye. They swerved and melted among the cottonwoods, so the ford's edge grew bare of dusky bodies and looked sandy and green again. Cheschapah saw the wrinkled figure coming, and his face sank tame. He stood uncertain in the stream, seeing his banded companions gone and the few white soldiers firm on the bank. The old chief rode to him through the water, his face brightened with a last flare of command.

"Make your medicine!" he said. "Why are the white men not blind? Is the medicine bad to-day?" And he whipped his son's horse to the right, and to the left he slashed the horse of Two Whistles, and whirling the leather quirt, drove them cowed before him and out of the stream, with never a look or word to the white men. He crossed the sandy margin, and as a man drives steers to the corral, striking spurs to his horse and following the frightened animals close when they would twist aside, so did old Pounded Meat herd his son down the valley.

"Useful old man," remarked Stirling;

"and brings up his children carefully. Let's get these prisoners along."

"How rural the river looks now!" Haines said, as they left the deserted banks.

So the Sioux went home in peace, the lieutenants, with their command of twenty, returned to the post, and all white people felt much obliged to Pounded Meat for his act of timely parental discipline— all except one white person.

Sol Kinney sauntered into the agency store one evening. "I want ten pounds of sugar," said he, "and navy plug as usual. And say, I'll take another bottle of them Seltzer fizz salts. Since I quit whiskey," he explained, "my liver's poorly."

He returned with his purchase to his cabin, and set a lamp in the window. Presently the door opened noiselessly, and Cheschapah came in.

"Maybe you got that now?" he said, in English.

The interpreter fumbled among bottles of liniment and vaseline, and from among these household remedies brought the blue one he had just bought. Cheschapah watched him like a child, following his steps round the cabin. Kinney tore a half-page from an old Sunday *World*, and poured a little heap of the salts into it. The Indian touched the heap timidly with his finger. "Maybe no good," he suggested.

"Heap good!" said the interpreter, throwing a pinch into a glass. When Cheschapah saw the water effervesce, he folded his newspaper with the salt into a tight lump, stuck the talisman into his clothes, and departed, leaving Mr. Kinney well content. He was doing his best to nourish the sinews of war, for business in the country was discouragingly slack.

Now the Crows were a tribe that had never warred with us, but only with other tribes; they had been valiant enough to steal our cattle, but sufficiently discreet to stop there; and Kinney realized that he had uphill work before him. His dearest hopes hung upon Cheschapah, in whom he thought he saw a development. From being a mere humbug, the young Indian seemed to be getting a belief in himself as something genuinely out of the common. His success in creating a party had greatly increased his conceit, and he walked with a strut, and his face was more unsettled and visionary than ever.

One clear sign of his mental change was that he no longer respected his father at all, though the lonely old man looked at him often with what in one of our race would have been tenderness. Cheschapah had been secretly maturing a plot ever since his humiliation at the crossing, and now he was ready. With his lump of newspaper carefully treasured, he came to Two Whistles.

"Now we go," he said. "We shall fight with the Piegans. I will make big medicine, so that we shall get many of their horses and women. Then Pretty Eagle will be afraid to go against me in the council. Pounded Meat whipped my horse. Pounded Meat can cut his hay without Cheschapah, since he is so strong."

But little Two Whistles wavered. "I will stay here," he ventured to say to the prophet.

"Does Two Whistles think I cannot do what I say?"

"I think you make good medicine."

"You are afraid of the Piegans."

"No, I am not afraid. I have hay the white man will pay me for. If I go, he will not pay me. If I had a father, I would not leave him." He spoke pleadingly, and his prophet bore him down by ridicule. Two Whistles believed, but he did not want to lose the money the agent was to pay for his hay. And so, not so much because he believed as because he was afraid, he resigned his personal desires.

The next morning the whole band had disappeared with Cheschapah. The agent was taken aback at this marked challenge to his authority—of course they had gone without permission—and even the old Crow chiefs held a council.

Pretty Eagle resorted to sarcasm. "He has taken his friends to the old man who makes the thunder," he said. But others did not feel sarcastic, and one observed, "Cheschapah knows more than we know."

"Let him make rain, then," said Pretty Eagle. "Let him make the white man's heart soft."

The situation was assisted by a step of the careful Kinney. He took a private journey to Junction City, through which place he expected Cheschapah to return, and there he made arrangements to have as much whiskey furnished to the Indian and his friends as they should ask for. It was certainly a good stroke of business.

The victorious raiders did return that way, and Junction City was most hospitable to their thirst. The valley of the Big Horn was resonant with their homeward yells. They swept up the river, and the agent heard them coming, and he locked his door immediately. He listened to their descent upon his fold, and he peeped out and saw them ride round the tightly shut buildings in their war-paint and the pride of utter success. They had taken booty from the Piegans, and now, knocking at the store, they demanded ammunition, proclaiming at the same time in English that Cheschapah was a big man, and knew a "big heap medicine." The agent told them from inside that they could not have any ammunition. He also informed them that he knew who they were, and that they were under arrest. This touched their primitive sense of the incongruous. On the buoyancy of the whiskey they rode round and round the store containing the agent, and then rushed away, firing shots at the buildings and shots in the air, and so gloriously home among their tribe, while the agent sent a courier packing to Fort Custer.

The young bucks who had not gone on the raid to the Piegans thronged to hear the story, and the warriors told it here and there, walking in their feathers among a knot of friends, who listened with gay exclamations of pleasure and envy. Great was Cheschapah, who had done all this! And one and another told exactly and at length how he had seen the cold water rise into foam beneath the medicine-man's hand; it could not be told too often; not every companion of Cheschapah's had been accorded the privilege of witnessing this miracle, and each narrator in his circle became a wonder himself to the bold boyish faces that surrounded him. And after the miracle he told how the Piegans had been like a flock of birds before the medicine-man. Cheschapah himself passed among the groups, alone and aloof; he spoke to none, and he looked at none, and he noted how their voices fell to whispers as he passed; his ear caught the magic words of praise and awe; he felt the gaze of admiration follow him away, and a mist rose like incense in his brain. He wandered among the scattered tepees, and turning came along the same paths again that he might once more overhear his worshippers. Great was Cheschapah!

His heart beat, a throb of power passed through his body, and "Great is Cheschapah!" said he, aloud; for the fumes of hallucination wherewith he had drugged others had begun to make him drunk also. He sought a tepee where the wife of another chief was alone, and at his light call she stood at the entrance and heard him longer than she had ever listened to him before. But she withstood the temptation that was strong in the young chief's looks and words. She did not speak much, but laughed unsteadily, and shaking her head with averted eyes, left him, and went where several women were together, and sat among them.

Cheschapah told his victory to the council, with many sentences about himself, and how his medicine had fended all hurt from the Crows. The elder chiefs sat cold.

"Ump!" said one at the close of the oration, and "Heh!" remarked another. The sounds were of assent without surprise.

"It is good," said Pretty Eagle. His voice seemed to enrage Cheschapah.

"Heh! it is always pretty good!" remarked Spotted Horse.

"I have done this too," said Pounded Meat to his son, simply. "Once, twice, three times. The Crows have always been better warriors than the Piegans."

"Have you made water boil like me?" Cheschapah said.

"I am not a medicine-man," replied his father. "But I have taken horses and squaws from the Piegans. You make good medicine, maybe; but a cup of water will not kill many white men. Can you make the river boil? Let Cheschapah make bigger medicine, so the white man shall fear him as well as the Piegans, whose hearts are well known to us."

Cheschapah scowled. "Pounded Meat shall have this," said he. "I will make medicine to-morrow, old fool!"

"Drive him from the council!" said Pretty Eagle.

"Let him stay," said Pounded Meat. "His bad talk was not to the council, but to me, and I do not count it."

But the medicine-man left the presence of the chiefs, and came to the cabin of Kinney.

"Hello!" said the white man. "Sit down."

"You got that?" said the Indian, standing.

"More water medicine? I guess so. Take a seat."

"No, not boil any more. You got that other?"

"That other, eh? Well, now, you're not going to blind them yet? What's your hurry?"

"Yes. Make blind to-morrow. Me great chief!"

A slight uneasiness passed across the bantering face of Kinney. His Seltzer salts performed what he promised, but he had mentioned another miracle, and he did not want his dupe to find him out until a war was thoroughly set agoing. He looked at the young Indian, noticing his eyes.

"What's the matter with you, anyway, Cheschapah?"

"Me great chief!" The raised voice trembled with unearthly conviction.

"Well, I guess you are. I guess you've got pretty far along," said the frontier cynic. He tilted his chair back and smiled at the child whose primitive brain he had tampered with so easily. The child stood looking at him with intent black eyes. "Better wait, Cheschapah. Come again. Medicine heap better after a while."

The Indian's quick ear caught the insincerity without understanding it. "You give me that quick!" he said, suddenly terrible.

"Oh, all right, Cheschapah. You know more medicine than me."

"Yes, I know more."

The white man brought a pot of scarlet paint, and the Indian's staring eyes contracted. Kinney took the battered cavalry sabre in his hand, and set its point in the earth floor of the cabin. "Stand back," he said, in mysterious tones, and Cheschapah shrank from the impending sorcery. Now Kinney had been to school once, in his Eastern childhood, and there had committed to memory portions of Shakespeare, Mrs. Hemans, and other poets out of a Reader. He had never forgotten a single word of any of them, and it now occurred to him that for the purposes of an incantation it would be both entertaining for himself and impressive to Cheschapah if he should recite "The Battle of Hohenlinden." He was drawing squares and circles with the point of the sabre.

"No," he said to himself, "that piece won't do. He knows too much English.

Some of them words might strike him as bein' too usual, and he'd start to kill me, and spoil the whole thing. 'Munich' and 'chivalry' are snortin', but 'sun was low' ain't worth a d——. I guess—"

He stopped guessing, for the noon recess at school came in his mind, like a picture, and with it certain old-time preliminaries to the game of tag.

"'Eeny, meeny, money, my,'"

said Kinney, tapping himself, the sabre, the paint-pot, and Cheschapah in turn, one for each word. The incantation was begun. He held the sabre solemnly upright, while Cheschapah tried to control his excited breathing where he stood flattened against the wall.

"'Butter, leather, boney, stry;
  Hare-bit, frost-neck,
  Harrico, barrico, whee, why, whoa, whack!'

You're it, Cheschapah." After that the weapon was given its fresh coat of paint, and Cheschapah went away with his new miracle in the dark.

"He is it," mused Kinney, grave, but inwardly lively. He was one of those sincere artists who need no popular commendation. "And whoever he does catch, it won't be me," he concluded. He felt pretty sure there would be war now.

Dawn showed the summoned troops near the agency at the corral, standing to horse. Cheschapah gathered his hostiles along the brow of the ridge in the rear of the agency buildings, and the two forces watched each other across the intervening four hundred yards.

"There they are," said the agent, jumping about. "Shoot them, colonel; shoot them!"

"You can't do that, you know," said the officer, "without an order from the President, or an overt act from the Indians."

So nothing happened, and Cheschapah told his friends the white men were already afraid of him. He saw more troops arrive, water their horses in the river, form line outside the corral, and dismount. He made ready at this movement, and all Indian on-lookers scattered from the expected fight. Yet the white man staid quiet. It was issue day, but no families remained after drawing their rations. They had had no dance the night before, as was usual, and they did not linger a moment now, but came and departed with their beef and flour at once.

"I have done all this," said Cheschapah to Two Whistles.

"Cheschapah is a great man," assented the friend and follower. He had gone at once to his hay-field on his return from the Piegans, but some one had broken the little Indian's fence, and cattle were wandering in what remained of his crop.

"Our nation knows I will make a war, and therefore they do not stay here," said the medicine-man, caring nothing what Two Whistles might have suffered. "And now they will see that the white soldiers dare not fight with Cheschapah. The sun is high now, but they have not moved because I have stopped them. Do you not see it is my medicine?"

"We see it." It was the voice of the people.

But a chief spoke. "Maybe they wait for us to come."

Cheschapah answered. "Their eyes shall be made sick. I will ride among them, but they will not know it." He galloped away alone, and lifted his red sword as he sped along the ridge of the hills, showing against the sky. Below at the corral the white soldiers waited ready, and heard him chanting his war-song through the silence of the day. He turned in a long curve, and came in near the watching troops and through the agency, and then, made bolder by their motionless figures and guns held idle, he turned again and flew singing along close to the line, so they saw his eyes; and a few that had been talking low as they stood side by side fell silent at the spectacle. They could not shoot until some Indian should shoot. They watched him and the gray pony pass and return to the hostiles on the hill. Then they saw the hostiles melt away like magic. Their prophet had told them to go to their tepees and wait for the great rain he would now bring. It was noon, and the sky utterly blue over the bright valley. The sun rode a space nearer the west, and thick black clouds assembled in the mountains and descended; their shadow flooded the valley with a lake of slatish blue, and presently the sudden torrents sluiced down with flashes and the ample thunder of Montana. Thus not alone the law against our soldiers' firing the first shot in an Indian excitement, but now also the elements coincided to help the medicine-man's destiny.

Cheschapah sat in a tepee with his

father, and as the rain splashed heavily on the earth the old man gazed at the young one.

"Why do you tremble, my son? You have made the white soldier's heart soft," said Pounded Meat. "You are indeed a great man, my son."

Cheschapah rose. "Do not call me your son," said he. "That is a lie." He went out into the fury of the rain, lifting his face against the drops, and exultingly calling out at each glare of the lightning. He went to Pretty Eagle's young squaw, who held off from him no longer, but got on a horse, and the two rode into the mountains. Before the sun had set, the sky was again utterly blue, and a cool scent rose everywhere in the shining valley.

The Crows came out of their tepees, and there were the white soldiers obeying orders and going away. They watched the column slowly move across the flat land below the bluffs, where the road led down the river twelve miles to the post.

"They are afraid," said new converts. "Cheschapah's rain has made their hearts soft."

"They have not all gone," said Pretty Eagle. "Maybe he did not make enough rain." But even Pretty Eagle began to be shaken, and he heard several of his brother chiefs during the next few days openly declare for the medicine-man. Cheschapah with his woman came from the mountains, and Pretty Eagle did not dare to harm him. Then another coincidence followed that was certainly most reassuring to the war party. Some of them had no meat, and told Cheschapah they were hungry. With consummate audacity he informed them he would give them plenty at once. On the same day another timely electric storm occurred up the river, and six steers were struck by lightning.

When the officers at Fort Custer heard of this they became serious.

"If this was not the nineteenth century," said Haines, "I should begin to think the elements were deliberately against us."

"It's very careless of the weather," said Stirling. "Very inconsiderate, at such a juncture."

Yet nothing more dangerous than red-tape happened for a while. There was a beautiful quantity of investigation from Washington, and this gave the hostiles

time to increase both in faith and numbers.

Among the excited Crows only a few wise old men held out. As for Cheschapah himself, ambition and success had brought him to the weird enthusiasm of a fanatic. He was still a charlatan, but a charlatan who believed utterly in his star. He moved among his people with growing mystery, and his hapless adjutant, Two Whistles, rode with him, slaved for him, abandoned the plans he had for making himself a farm, and desiring peace in his heart, weakly cast his lot with war. Then one day there came an order from the agent to all the Indians: they were to come in by a certain fixed day. The department commander had assembled six hundred troops at the post, and these moved up the river and went into camp. The usually empty ridges, and the bottom where the road ran, filled with white and red men. Half a mile to the north of the buildings, on the first rise from the river, lay the cavalry, and some infantry above them with a howitzer, while across the level, three hundred yards opposite, along the river-bank, was the main Indian camp. Even the hostiles had obeyed the agent's order; and come in close to the troops, totally unlike hostiles in general; for Cheschapah had told them he would protect them with his medicine, and they shouted and sang all through this last night. The women joined with harsh cries and shriekings, and a scalp-dance went on, besides lesser commotions and gatherings, with the throbbing of drums everywhere. Through the sleepless din ran the barking of a hundred dogs, that herded and hurried in crowds of twenty at a time, meeting, crossing from fire to fire among the tepees. Their yelps rose to the high bench of land, summoning a horde of coyotes. These cringing nomads gathered from the desert in a tramp army, and skulking down the bluffs, sat in their outer darkness and ceaselessly howled their long shrill greeting to the dogs that sat in the circle of light. The general sent scouts to find the nature of the dance and hubbub, and these brought word it was peaceful; and in the morning another scout summoned the elder chiefs to a talk with the friend who had come from the Great Father at Washington to see them and find if their hearts were good.

"Our hearts are good," said Pretty

Eagle. " We do not want war. If you want Cheschapah, we will drive him out from the Crows to you."

" There are other young chiefs with bad hearts," said the commissioner, naming the ringleaders that were known. He made a speech, but Pretty Eagle grew sullen. " It is well," said the commissioner; " you will not help me to make things smooth, and now I step aside and the war chief will talk."

" If you want any other chiefs," said Pretty Eagle, " come and take them."

" Pretty Eagle shall have an hour and a half to think on my words," said the general. " I have plenty of men behind me to make my words good. You must send me all those Indians who fired at the agency."

The Crow chiefs returned to the council, which was apart from the war party's camp; and Cheschapah walked in among them, and after him, slowly, old Pounded Meat, to learn how the conference had gone.

" You have made a long talk with the white man," said Cheschapah. " Talk is pretty good for old men. I and the young chiefs will fight now and kill our enemies."

" Cheschapah," said Pounded Meat, " if your medicine is good, it may be the young chiefs will kill our enemies to-day. But there are other days to come, and after them still others; there are many, many days. My son, the years are a long road. The life of one man is not long, but enough to learn this thing truly: the white man will always return. There was a day on this river when the dead soldiers of Yellow Hair lay in hills, and the squaws of the Sioux warriors climbed among them with their knives. What do the Sioux warriors do now when they meet the white man on this river? Their hearts are on the ground, and they go home like children when the white man says, ' You shall not visit your friends.' My son, I thought war was good once. I have kept you from the arrows of our enemies on many trails when you were so little that my blankets were enough for both. Your mother was not here any more, and the chiefs laughed because I carried you. Oh, my son, I have seen the hearts of the Sioux broken by the white man, and I do not think war is good."

" The talk of Pounded Meat is very good," said Pretty Eagle. " If Chescha-

pah were wise like his father, this trouble would not have come to the Crows. But we could not give the white chief so many of our chiefs that he asked for to-day."

Cheschapah laughed. " Did he ask for so many? He wanted only Cheschapah, who is not wise like Pounded Meat."

" You would have been given to him," said Pretty Eagle.

" Did Pretty Eagle tell the white chief that? Did he say he would give Cheschapah? How would he give me? In one hand or two? Or would the old warrior take me to the white man's camp on the horse his young squaw left?"

Pretty Eagle raised his rifle, and Pounded Meat, quick as a boy, seized the barrel and pointed it up among the poles of the tepee, where the quiet black fire smoke was oozing out into the air. " Have you lived so long," said Pounded Meat to his ancient comrade, " and do this in the council?" His wrinkled head and hands shook, the sudden strength left him, and the rifle fell free.

" Let Pretty Eagle shoot," said Cheschapah, looking at the council. He stood calm, and the seated chiefs turned their grim eyes upon him. Certainty was in his face, and doubt in theirs. " Let him send his bullet five times—ten times. Then I will go and let the white soldiers shoot at me until they all lie dead."

" It is heavy for me," began Pounded Meat, " that my friend should be the enemy of my son."

" Tell that lie no more," said Cheschapah. " You are not my father. I have made the white man blind, and I have softened his heart with the rain. I will call the rain to-day." He raised his red sword, and there was a movement among the sitting figures. " The clouds will come from my father's place, where I have talked with him as one chief to another. My mother went into the mountains to gather berries. She was young, and the thunder-maker saw her face. He brought the black clouds, so her feet turned from home, and she walked where the river goes into the great walls of the mountain, and that day she was stricken fruitful by the lightning. You are not the father of Cheschapah." He dealt Pounded Meat a blow, and the old man fell. But the council sat still until the sound of Cheschapah's galloping horse died away. They were ready now to risk everything. Their scepticism was conquered.

"THE HEAD LAY IN THE WATER."

The medicine-man galloped to his camp of hostiles, and seeing him, they yelled and quickly finished plaiting their horses' tails. Cheschapah had accomplished his wish; he had become the prophet of all the Crows, and he led the armies of the faithful. Each man stripped his blanket off and painted his body for the fight. The forms slipped in and out of the brush, buckling their cartridge-belts, bringing their ponies, while many families struck their tepees and moved up nearer the agency. The spare horses were run across the river into the hills, and through the yelling that shifted and swept like flames along the wind the hostiles made ready and gathered, their crowds quivering with motion, and changing place and shape as more mounted riders appeared.

"Are the holes dug deep as I marked them on the earth?" said Cheschapah to Two Whistles. "That is good. We shall soon have to go into them from the great rain I will bring. Make these strong, to stay as we ride. They are good medicine, and with them the white soldiers will not see you any more than they saw me when I rode among them that day."

He had strips and capes of red flannel, and he and Two Whistles fastened them to their painted bodies.

"You will let me go with you?" said Two Whistles.

"You are my best friend," said Cheschapah, "and to-day I will take you. You shall see my great medicine when I make the white man's eyes grow sick."

The two rode forward, and one hundred and fifty followed them, bursting from their tepees like an explosion, and rushing along quickly in skirmish-line. Two Whistles rode beside his speeding prophet, and saw the red sword waving near his face, and the sun in the great still sky, and the swimming, fleeting earth. His superstition and the fierce ride put him in a sort of trance.

"The medicine is beginning," shouted Cheschapah; and at that Two Whistles saw the day grow large with terrible shining, and heard his own voice calling and could not stop it. They left the hundred and fifty behind, he knew not where or when. He saw the line of troops ahead change to separate waiting shapes of men, and their legs and arms become plain; then all the guns took clear form in lines of steady glitter. He seemed suddenly alone far ahead of the band, but the voice of Cheschapah spoke close by his ear through the singing wind, and he repeated each word without understanding; he was watching the ground rush by, lest it might rise against his face, and all the while he felt his horse's motion under him, smooth and perpetual. Something weighed against his leg, and there was Cheschapah he had forgotten, always there at his side, veering him round somewhere. But there was no red sword waving. Then the white men must be blind already, wherever they were, and Cheschapah, the only thing he could see, sat leaning one hand on his horse's rump firing a pistol. The ground came swimming towards his eyes always, smooth and wide like a gray flood, but Two Whistles knew that Cheschapah would not let it sweep him away. He saw a horse without a rider floated out of blue smoke, and floated in again with a cracking noise; white soldiers moved in a row across his eyes, very small and clear, and broke into a blurred eddy of shapes which the flood swept away clean and empty. Then a dead white man came by on the quick flood. Two Whistles saw the yellow stripe on his sleeve; but he was gone, and there was nothing but sky and blaze, with Cheschapah's head-dress in the middle. The horse's even motion continued beneath him, when suddenly the head-dress fell out of Two Whistles' sight, and the earth returned. They were in brush, with his horse standing and breathing, and a dead horse on the ground with Cheschapah, and smoke and moving people everywhere outside. He saw Cheschapah run from the dead horse and jump on a gray pony and go. Somehow he was on the ground too, looking at a red sword lying beside his face. He stared at it a long while, then took it in his hand, still staring; all at once he rose and broke it savagely, and fell again. His faith was shivered to pieces like glass. But he got on his horse, and the horse moved away. He was looking at the blood running on his body. The horse moved always, and Two Whistles followed with his eye a little deeper gush of blood along a crease in his painted skin, noticed the flannel, and remembering the lie of his prophet, instantly began tearing the red rags from his body, and flinging them to the ground with cries of scorn. Presently he heard some voices, and soon one voice much nearer, and saw he had come to a new place, where there were white soldiers looking at him quietly. One was riding up and telling him to give up his pistol. Two Whistles got off and stood behind his horse, looking at the pistol. The white soldier came quite near, and at his voice Two Whistles moved slowly out from behind the horse, and listened to the cool words as the soldier repeated his command. The Indian was pointing his pistol uncertainly, and he looked at the soldier's coat and buttons, and the straps on the shoulders, and the bright steel sabre, and the white man's blue eyes; then Two Whistles looked at his own naked, clotted body, and turning the pistol against himself, fired it into his breast.

Far away up the river, on the right of the line, a lieutenant with two men was wading across after some hostiles that had been skirmishing with his troop. The hostiles had fallen back after some hot shooting, and had dispersed among the brush and tepees on the further shore, picking up their dead, as Indians do. It was interesting work this splashing breast-high through a river into a concealed hornets'-nest, and the lieutenant thought a little on his unfinished plans and duties in life; he noted one dead Indian left on the shore, and went steadfastly in among the half-seen tepees, rummaging and beating in the thick brush to be sure no hornets remained. Finding them gone, and their dead spirited away, he came back on the bank to the one dead Indian, who had a fine head-dress, and was still ribanded with gay red streamers of flannel, and was worth all the rest of the dead put together, and much more. The head lay in the water, and one hand held the rope of the gray pony, who stood quiet and uninterested over his fallen rider. They began carrying the prize across to the other bank, where many had now collected, among others Kinney, and the lieutenant's captain, who subsequently said, "I found the body of Cheschapah"; and,

indeed, it was a very good thing to be able to say.

"This busts the war," said Kinney to the captain, as the body was being lifted over the Little Horn. "They know he's killed, and they've all quit. I was up by the tepees near the agency just now, and I could see the hostiles jamming back home for dear life. They was chucking their rifles to the squaws, and jumping in the river—ha! ha!—to wash off their war-paint, and each son of a —— would crawl out and sit innercint in the family blanket his squaw had ready. If you was to go there now, cap'n, you'd find just a lot of harmless Injuns eatin' supper like all the year round. Let me help you, boys, with that carcass."

Kinney gave a hand to the lieutenant and boys of G troop, First United States Cavalry, and they lifted Cheschapah up the bank. In the tilted position of the body the cartridge-belt slid a little, and a lump of newspaper fell into the stream. Kinney watched it open and float away with a momentary effervescence. The dead medicine-man was laid between the white and red camps, that all might see he could be killed like other people; and this wholesome discovery brought the Crows to terms at once. Pretty Eagle had displayed a flag of truce, and now he surrendered the guilty chiefs whose hearts had been bad. Every one came where the dead prophet lay to get a look at him. For a space of hours Pretty Eagle and the many other Crows he had deceived rode by in single file, striking him with their whips; after them came a young squaw, and she also lashed the upturned face.

This night was untroubled at the agency, and both camps and the valley lay quiet in the peaceful dark. Only Pounded Meat, alone on the top of a hill, mourned for his son; and his wailing voice sounded through the silence until the new day came. Then the general had him stopped and brought in, for it might be that the old man's noise would unsettle the Crows again.

2

Salvation Gap

OWEN WISTER

SALVATION GAP.

BY OWEN WISTER.

AFTER cutting the Gazelle's throat, Drylyn had gone out of her tent, secure and happy in choosing the skilful moment. They would think it was the other man—the unknown one. There were his boot-prints this fine morning, marking his way from the tent down the hill into the trees. He was not an inhabitant of the camp. This was his first visit, cautiously made, and nobody had seen him come or go except Drylyn.

The woman was proprietor of the dance-hall at Salvation Gap, and on account of her beauty and habits had been named the American Beer Gazelle by a travelling naturalist who had education, and was interested in the wild animals of all countries. Drylyn's relations with the Gazelle were colored with sentiment. The sentiment on his part was genuine; so genuine that the shrewd noticing camp joked Drylyn, telling him he had grown to look young again under the elixir of romance. One of the prospectors had remarked fancifully that Drylyn's "rusted mustache hed livened up; same ez flow'rs ye've kerried a long ways when yer girl puts 'em in a pitcher o' water." Being the sentiment of a placer miner, the lover's feeling took no offence or wound at any conduct of the Gazelle's that was purely official; it was for him that she personally cared. He never

thought of suspecting anything when, after one of her trips to Folsom, she began to send away some of the profits—gold, coined sometimes, sometimes raw dust—that her hall of entertainment earned for her. She mentioned to him that her mother in San Anton' needed it, and simple-minded Drylyn believed. It did not occur to him to ask, or even wonder, how it came that this mother had never needed money until so lately, or why the trips to Folsom became so constant. Counting her middle-aged adorer a fool, the humorous Gazelle had actually once, on being prevented from taking the journey herself, asked him to carry the package to Folsom for her, and deliver it there to a certain shot-gun messenger of the express company, who would see that it went to the right place. A woman's name and an address at San Antonio were certainly scrawled on the parcel. The faithful Drylyn waited till the stage came in, and handed over his treasure to the messenger, who gave him one amazed look that he did not notice. He ought to have seen that young man awhile afterwards, the package torn open, a bag of dust on his knee, laughing almost to tears over a letter he had found with the gold inside the wrapping. But Drylyn was on the road up to Salvation Gap at that time. The shot-gun messenger was twenty-three;

21

Drylyn was forty-five. Gazelles are apt to do this sort of thing. After all, though, it was silly, just for the sake of a laugh, to let the old lover learn the face of his secret rival. It was one of those early unimagined nails people sometimes drive in their own coffins. An ancient series of events followed: continued abject faith and passion on the miner's part; continued presents of dust from him to the lady; on her part continued trips to Folsom, a lessened caution, and a brag of manner based upon her very just popularity at the Gap; next, Drylyn's first sickening dawn of doubt, jealousy equipping him with a new and alien slyness; the final accident of his seeing the shot-gun messenger on his very first visit to the Gap come out of the Gazelle's tent so early in the morning; the instant blaze of truth and fury that turned Drylyn to a clever calculating wild beast. So now her throat was cut, and she was good and dead. He had managed well. The whole game had shown instantly like a picture on his brain, complete at a stroke, with every move clear. He had let the man go down the hill—just for the present. The camp had got up, eaten its breakfast, and gone out to the ditches, Drylyn along with the rest. Owing to its situation, neighbors could not see him presently leave his claim and walk back quickly to the Gap at an hour when the dance-hall was likely to be lonely. He had ready what to say if the other women should be there; but they were away at the creek below, washing, and the luxurious, unsuspecting Gazelle was in bed in her own tent, not yet disturbed. The quiet wild beast walked through the deserted front entrance of the hall in the most natural manner, and so behind among the empty bottles, and along the plank into the tent; then, after a while, out again. She would never be disturbed now, and the wild beast was back at his claim, knee-deep, and busy among the digging and the wetness, in another pair of overalls just like the ones that were now under some stones at the bottom of a mud-puddle. And then one very bad long scream came up to the ditches, and Drylyn knew the women had returned from their washing.

He raised his head mechanically to listen. He had never been a bad man; had never wished to hurt anybody in his life before that he could remember; but as he pondered upon it in his slow, sure brain he knew that he was glad he had done this, and was going to do more. He was going to follow those tracks pretty soon, and finish the whole job with his own hand. They had fooled him, and had taken trouble to do it; gone out of their way, made game of him to the quick; and when he remembered, for the twentieth time this morning, that day he had carried the package of gold-dust—some of it very likely his own—to the smooth-faced messenger at Folsom, Drylyn's stolid body trembled from head to foot, and he spoke blind, inarticulate words.

But down below there the screams were sounding. A brother miner came running by. Drylyn realized that he ought to be running too, of course, and so he ran. All the men were running from their various scattered claims, and Salvation Gap grew noisy and full of people at once. There was the sheriff also, come up last evening on the track of some stage-robbers, and quite opportune for this, he thought. He liked things to be done legally. The turmoil of execration and fierce curiosity thrashed about for the right man to pitch on for this crime. The murdered woman had been such good company, so hearty a wit, such a robust songstress, so tireless a dancer, so thoroughly everybody's friend, that it was inconceivable to the mind of Salvation Gap that anybody there had done it. The women were crying and wringing their hands—the Gazelle had been good to them too—the men were talking and cursing, all but Drylyn there among them, serious and strange-looking; so silent that the sheriff eyed him once or twice, though he knew nothing of the miner's infatuation. And then some woman shrieked out the name of Drylyn, and the crowd had him gripped in a second, to let him go the next, laughing at the preposterous idea. Saying nothing? Of course he didn't feel like talking. To be sure he looked dazed. It was hard luck on him. They told the sheriff about him and the Gazelle. They explained that Drylyn was "sort of loony, anyway," and the sheriff said, "Oh!" and began to wonder and surmise in this half-minute they had been now gathered, when suddenly the inevitable boot-prints behind the tent down the hill were found. The shout of discovery startled Drylyn as genuinely as if he had

THE SHOT-GUN MESSENGER.

never known, and he joined the wild rush of people to the hill. Nor was this acting. The violence he had set going, and in which he swam like a straw, made him forget, or for the moment drift away from, his arranged thoughts, and the tracks on the hill had gone clean out of his head. He was become a mere blank spectator in the storm, incapable of calculation. His own handiwork had stunned him, for he had not foreseen that consequences were going to rise and burst like this. The next thing he knew he was in a pursuit, with pine-trees passing, and the hurrying sheriff remarking to the band that he proposed to maintain order. Drylyn heard his neighbor, a true Californian, whose words were lightest when his purpose was most serious, telling the sheriff that order was certainly Heaven's first law, and an elegant thing anywhere. But the anxious officer made no retort in kind, and only said that irregularities were damaging to the county's good name, and would keep settlers from moving in. So the neighbor turned to Drylyn and asked him when he was intending to wake up, as sleep-walking was considered to be unhealthy. Drylyn gave a queer, almost wistful, smile, and so they went along; the chatty neighbor spoke low to another man, and said he had never sized up the true state of Drylyn's feeling for the Gazelle, and that the sheriff might persuade some people to keep regular, when they found the man they were hunting, but he doubted if the sheriff would be persuading enough for Drylyn. They came out on a road, and the sleep-walker recognized a rock and knew how far they had gone, and that this was the stage road between Folsom and Surprise Springs. They followed the road, and round a bend came on the man. He had been taking it easily, being in no hurry. He had come to this point by the stage the night before, and now he was waiting for its return to take him back to Folsom. He had been lunching, and was seated on a stone by a small creek. He looked up and saw them, and their gait, and ominous compactness. What he did was not the thing for him to do. He leaped into cover and drew his revolver. This attempt at defence and escape was really for the sake of the gold-dust he had in his pocket. But when he recognized the sheriff's voice, telling him it would go better with him

if he did not try to kill any more people, he was greatly relieved that it was not highwaymen after him and his little gold, and he put up his pistol and waited for them, smiling, secure in his identity; and when they drew nearer he asked them how many people he had killed already. They came up and caught him and found the gold in a moment, ripping it from his pocket; and the yell they gave at that stopped his smiling entirely. When he found himself in irons and hurried along, he began to explain that there was some mistake, and was told by the chatty neighbor that maybe killing a woman was always a mistake, certainly one this time. As they walked him among them they gave small notice to his growing fright and bewilderment, but when he appealed to the sheriff on the score of old acquaintanceship, and pitifully begged to know what they supposed he had done, the miners laughed curiously. That brought his entreating back to them, and he assured them, looking in their faces, that he truly did need to be told why they wanted him. So they held up the gold and asked him whose that had been, and he made a wretched hesitation in answering. If anything was needed to clinch their certainty, that did. They could not know that the young successful lover had recognized Drylyn's strange face, and did not want to tell the truth before him, and hence was telling an unskilful lie instead. A rattle of wheels sounded among the pines ahead, and the stage came up and stopped. Only the driver and a friend were on it, and both of them knew the shot-gun messenger and the sheriff, and they asked in some astonishment what the trouble was. It had been stage-robbers the sheriff had started after, the driver thought. And—as he commented in friendly tones—to turn up with Wells and Fargo's messenger was the neatest practical joke that had occurred in the county for some time. The always serious and anxious sheriff told the driver the accusation, and it was a genuine cry of horror that the young lover gave at hearing the truth at last, and at feeling the ghastly chain of probability that had wound itself about him.

The sheriff wondered if there were a true ring in the man's voice. It certainly sounded so. He was talking with rapid agony, and it was the whole true story that was coming out now. But the chatty neighbor nudged another neighbor at the new explanation about the gold-dust. That there was no great quantity of it after all, weighed little against this double accounting for one simple fact; moreover, the new version did not do the messenger credit in the estimation of the miners, but gave them a still worse opinion of him. It is scarcely fair to disbelieve what a man says he did, and at the same time despise him for having done it. Miners, however, are rational rather than logical; while the listening sheriff grew more determined there should be a proper trial, the deputation from the Gap made up its mind more inexorably the other way. It had even been in the miners' heads to finish the business here on the Folsom road, and get home for supper; pine-trees were handy, and there was rope in the stage. They were not much moved by the sheriff's plea that something further might have turned up at the Gap, but at the driver's more forcible suggestion that the Gap would feel disappointed at being left out, they consented to take the man back there. Drylyn never offered any opinion, or spoke at all. It was not necessary that he should, and they forgot about him. It was time to be getting along, they said. What was the good in standing in the road here? They nodded good-day to the stage-driver, and took themselves and the prisoner into the pines. Once the sheriff had looked at the driver and his friend perched on the halted stage, but he immediately saw too much risk in his half-formed notion of an alliance with them to gallop off with the prisoner; his part must come later, if at all.

But the driver had perfectly understood the sheriff's glance, and he was on the sheriff's side, though he showed no sign. As he drove along he began thinking about the way the prisoner had cried out just now, and the inconsiderable value of the dust, and it became clear in his mind that this was a matter for a court and twelve quiet men. The friend beside him was also intent upon his own thoughts, and neither said a word to the other along the lonely road. The horses soon knew that they were not being driven any more, and they slackened their pace, and finding no reproof came for this, they fell to a comfortable walk. Presently several had snatched a branch in passing, and it waved from their mouths as they nibbled.

After that they gave up all pretence at being stage-horses, and the driver noticed them. From habit he whipped them up into shape and gait, and the next moment pulled them in short, at the thought that had come to him. The prisoner must be got away from the Gap. The sheriff was too single-handed among such a crowd as that, and the driver put a question to his friend. It could be managed by taking a slight liberty with other people's horses; but Wells and Fargo would not find fault with this when the case was one of their own servants, hitherto so well thought of. The stage, being empty and light, could spare two horses and go on, while those two horses, handled with discretion and timeliness, might be very useful at the Gap. The driver had best not depart from rule so far as to leave his post and duty; one man would be enough. The friend thought well of this plan, and they climbed down into the road from opposite sides and took out the wheelers. To be sure these animals were heavy, and not of the sort best for escaping on, but better than walking; and timeliness and discretion can do a great deal. So in a little while the driver and his stage were gone on their way, the friend with the two horses had disappeared in the wood, and the road was altogether lonely.

The sheriff's brain was hard at work, and he made no protest now as he walked along, passive in the company of the miners and their prisoner. The prisoner had said all that he had to say, and his man's firmness, which the first shock and amazement had wrenched from him, had come to his help again, bringing a certain shame at having let his reserve and bearing fall to pieces, and at having made himself a show; so he spoke no more than his grim captors did, as they took him swiftly through the wood. The sheriff was glad it was some miles they had to go; for though they went very fast, the distance and the time, and even the becoming tired in body, might incline their minds to more deliberation. He could think yet of nothing new to urge. He had seen and heard only the same things that all had, and his present hopes lay upon the Gap and what more might have come to light there since his departure. He looked at Drylyn, but the miner's serious and massive face gave him no suggestion; and the sheriff's reason again destroyed the germ of suspicion that some-

"I'D LIKE TO HAVE IT OVER."

thing plainly against reason had several times put in his thoughts. Yet it stuck with him that they had hold of the wrong man.

When they reached the Gap, and he found the people there as he had left them, and things the same way, with nothing new turned up to help his theory, the sheriff once more looked round; but Drylyn was not in the crowd. He had gone, they told him, to look at *her;* he had set a heap of store by her, they repeated.

"A heap of store," said the sheriff, thinking. "Where is she now?"

"On her bed," said a woman, "same as ever, only we've fixed her up some."

"Then I'll take a look at her—and him. You boys won't do anything till I come back, will you?"

"Why, if ye're so anxious to see us do it, sheriff," said the chatty neighbor, "I guess we can wait that long fer ye."

The officer walked to the tent. Drylyn was standing over the body, quiet and dumb. He was safe for the present the sheriff knew, and so he left him without speaking and returned to the prisoner and his guard in front of the dance-hall. He found them duly waiting, the only change was that they had a rope there.

"Once upon a time," said the sheriff, "there was a man in Arkansaw that had no judgment."

"They raise 'em that way in Arkansaw," said the chatty neighbor, as the company made a circle to hear the story —a tight, cautious circle—with the prisoner and the officer beside him standing in the centre.

"The man's wife had good judgment," continued the narrator, "but she went and died on him."

"Well, I guess that *was* good judgment," said the neighbor.

"So the man, he had to run the farm alone. Now they raised poultry, which his wife had always attended to. And he knew she had a habit of setting hens on duck eggs. He had never inquired her reasons, being shiftless, but that fact he knew. Well, come to investigate the hen-house, there was duck eggs, and hens on 'em, and also a heap of hens' eggs, but no more hens wishing to set. So the man, having no judgment, persuaded a duck to stay with those eggs. Now it's her I'm chiefly interested in. She was a good enough duck, but hasty. When the eggs hatched out, she didn't stop to notice, but up and takes them down to the pond, and gets mad with them, and shoves them in, and they drowns. Next day or two a lot of the young ducks, they hatched out and come down with the hen and got in the water all right, and the duck figured out she'd made some mistake, and she felt distressed. But the chickens were in heaven."

The sheriff studied his audience and saw that he had lulled their rage a little. "Now," said he, "ain't you boys just a trifle like that duck? I don't know as I can say much to you more than what I have said, and I don't know as I can do anything, fixed as I am. This thing looks bad for him we've got here. Why, I can see that as well as you. But, boys! it's an awful thing to kill an innocent man! I saw that done once, and—God forgive me!—I was one of them. I'll tell you how that was. He looked enough like the man we wanted. We were certainly on the right trail. We came on a cabin we'd never known of before, pretty far up in the hills—a strange cabin, you see. That seemed just right; just where a man would hide. We were mad at the crime committed, and took no thought. We knew we had caught him—that's the way we felt. So we got our guns ready, and crept up close through the trees, and surrounded that cabin. We called him to come out, and he came with a book in his hand he'd been reading. He did look like the man, and boys!—we gave him no time! He never knew why we fired. He was a harmless old prospector who had got tired of poor luck and knocking around, and over his door he had painted some words : ' Where the wicked cease from troubling.' He had figured that up there by that mountain stream the world would let him alone. And ever since then I have thought my life belonged to him first, and me second. Now this afternoon I'm alone here. You know I can't do much. And I'm going to ask you to help me respect the law. I don't say that in this big country there may not be places, and there may not be times, when the law is too young or else too rotten to take care of itself, and when the American citizen must go back to bed-rock principles. But is that so in our valley? Why, if this prisoner is guilty, you can't name me one man of your acquaintance who would want him to live. And that being so, don't we owe him the chance to clear himself if he can? I can see that prospector now at his door, old, harmless, coming fearless at our call, because he had no guilt upon his conscience—and we shot him down without a word. Boys! he has the call on me now; and if you insist—"

The sheriff paused, satisfied with what he saw on the faces around him. Some of the men knew the story of the prospector—it had been in the papers—but of his part in it they had not known. They understood quite well the sacrifice he stood ready to make now in defending the prisoner. The favorable silence was broken by the sound of horses. Timeliness and discretion were coming up the hill. Drylyn at the same moment came out of the dead woman's tent, and looking down, realized the intended rescue. With his mind waked suddenly from its dull dream and opened with a human impulse, he ran to help; but the sheriff saw him, and thought he was trying to escape.

"That's the man!" he shouted savagely to the ring.

Some of the Gap ran to the edge of the hill, and seeing the hurrying Drylyn and the horses below, also realized the rescue. Putting the wrong two and two together, they instantly saw in all this a well-devised scheme of delay and collusion. They came back, running through the dance-hall to the front, and the sheriff was pinioned from behind, thrown down, and held.

"So ye were alone, were ye?" said the chatty neighbor. "Well, ye made a good talk. Keep quiet—we don't want to hurt ye."

At this supposed perfidy the Gap's rage was at white heat again; the men massed together, and fierce and quick as lightning the messenger's fate was wrought. The work of adjusting the rope and noose was complete and death going on in the air when Drylyn, meaning to look the ground over for the rescue, came cautiously back up the hill and saw the body, black against the clear sunset sky. At his outcry they made ready for him, and when he blindly rushed among them they held him, and paid no attention to his ravings. Then, when the rope had finished its work, they let him go, and the sheriff too. The driver's friend had left his horses among the pines, and had come up to see what was going on at the Gap. He now joined the crowd.

"You meant well," the sheriff said to him. "I wish you would tell the boys how you come to be here. They're thinking I lied to them."

"Maybe I can change their minds." It was Drylyn's deep voice. "I am the man you were hunting," he said.

They looked at him seriously, as one looks at a friend whom an illness has seized. The storm of feeling had spent itself, the mood of the Gap was relaxed and torpid, and the serenity of coming dusk began to fill the mountain air.

"You boys think I'm touched in the head," said Drylyn, and paused. "This knife done it," said he. "This one I'm showing you."

They looked at the knife in his hand.

"He come between me and her," Drylyn pursued. "I was aiming to give him his punishment myself. That would have been square." He turned the knife over in his hand, and glancing up from it, caught the look in their eyes. "You don't believe me!" he exclaimed, savagely. "Well, I'm going to make you. Sheriff, I'll bring you some evidence."

He walked to the creek, and they stood idle and dull till he returned. Then they

fell back from him and his evidence, leaving him standing beneath the dead man.

"Does them look like being touched in the head?" inquired Drylyn, and he threw down the overalls, which fell with a damp slap on the ground. "I don't seem to mind telling you," he said. "I feel as quiet--as quiet as them tall pines the sun's just quittin' for the night." He looked at the men expectantly, but none of them stirred. "I'd like to have it over," said he.

Still no one moved.

"I have a right to ask it shall be quick," he repeated. "You were quick enough with him." And Drylyn lifted his hand towards the messenger.

They followed his gesture, staring up at the wrong man, then down at the right one. The chatty neighbor shook his head. "Seems curious," he said, slowly. "It ought to be done. But I couldn't no more do it—gosh! how *can* a man fire his gun right after it's been discharged?"

The heavy Drylyn looked at his comrades of the Gap. "You won't?" he said.

"You better quit us," suggested the neighbor. "Go somewheres else."

Drylyn's eyes ran painfully over ditch and diggings, the near cabins and the distant hills, then returned to the messenger. "Him and me," he muttered. "It ain't square. Him and me—" Suddenly he broke out, "I don't choose him to think I was that kind of man!"

Before they could catch him he fell, and the wet knife slid from his fingers. "Sheriff," he began, but his tone changed. "I'm overtakin' him!" he said. "He's going to know now. Put me alongside—" And they were able to fill in the rest.

3

The Shake-up at the Y-Bar-T

BEN BLOW

THE SHAKE-UP AT THE Y-BAR-T

BY BEN BLOW

DRAWING BY J. N. MARCHAND

THE Foreman of the Jack Hall outfit lit a cigar—one of the huge Maduros that he smokes when peace and plenty are upon him—and smiled. The smoke curled up into fantastic pictures, mountains, gleam-capped, and valleys; snow water streams with whirls where lurk the trout. The smile revealed content.

"Out there," he said, "the man inside the clothes wuz all that counted in the general round-up an' the feller that tried to run a blazer most always got a call. I've seen a heap o' men come out there from a heap o' different places, an' some o' them found out that they wuz mighty far from home, but now an' then one drifted in and found his place a-waitin', an' it wuz thataway with Van Renzler of the Y-Bar-T. He'd come out for the company which owned the outfit, people back East that wouldn't know a pinto from a Rocky Mountain goat, but which had sense enough not to throw away their money like they wuz pourin' water in a rat hole, which they wuz sure a-doin', for their foreman wuz as crooked as a sack of snakes.

"Van Renzler comes a-ridin' up to Jack Hall one noon when things ain't none too busy with us, an' when he slides off from his horse an' makes hisself acquainted I says to myself, 'he sure is green, but what he don't know he's soon a-goin' to learn, for he's got a square jaw an' he kind o' bites his words off when he speaks like he knows that what he says is what he meant to say.' 'My name's Van Renzler,' he says, 'an' I'm a-lookin' for the foreman of the Jack Hall outfit.'

"'Which is named Bill Winters,' I says, a-wishin' to be polite an' friendly. 'Set down an' make yourself at home.'

"He grins wide an' shows a heap o' teeth an' stretches out his hand an' we shakes, an' from the feel of his grip I knows plumb well that he's a square, white man. He don't give me none o' these clammy-handed-limp-finger-just-from-the-grave hand shakes nor none o' these shake-quick-an'-get-done-with-it-or-you'll-get-your-hands-dirty kind, but he grabs my hand plumb honest an' open an' holds it tight an' steady an' looks me straight in the eyes when he does it, an' I says to myself without no further consultation that him an' me is goin' to be friends.

"'Delighted,' he says, 'that's what I wanted to hear, but I ought to put my horse away before I rests myself, bein' as we've rode over from Buenavista this mornin'.'

"'Plumb right you are,' I says, 'you've learned lessons number one to forty-seven in the cow business, I kin see that.'

"He grins again.

"'A man that don't take care of his horse ain't entitled to a horse, accordin' to my way o' thinkin',' he says, 'an' I like horses too well to be without one,' an' then he gets up an' uncinches an' hangs up his saddle, which is a Mayne an' Winchester, plumb stylish, with hawk-bill taps an' silver conchas, an' then we goes back to the house an' introduces Cook, which puffs up like a hop-toad, proud an' happy to meet up with him.

"'Everything tastes mighty good,' said Van Renzler, seein' Cook kind o' lookin' anxious; which ain't no lie, judgin' by the way he eats. 'I'm beginnin' to think I'll get reel heavy if I stay out here long enough, an' from the looks o' things I've got to camp here quite a while.'

"'You ain't ben here long, then?' says Cook, kind o' inquisitive like.

"'Bout a week,' says Van Renzler 'an' in that time I've found that what I don't know about the cattle business 'd make a large thick book.'

"'That's a good sign,' I says, 'you kin learn it plenty soon. If you get started right it's hop-scotch, but you bog quick if you set off on the wrong trail.'

"'Which ain't no lie,' says Cook. 'Anything that Bill tells you is thick woolen goods three foot wide, as me an' Bull kin true swear to, bein' intimate acquainted with him an' sure conscious of his good points. If you want to learn anything about the cattle business all you got to do is ask Bill Winters an' he'll sure head you right an' give you a boost to start with.'

"'Cook,' I says, bein' some took aback before a stranger. 'You reminds me of a man from Kansas which I use to know which stepped so high that he had to walk backward to keep from puttin' his feet plumb into his own mouth; can't you go fry some cakes an' hush your talk?' Then Van Renzler laughs like he wuz tickled to death an' sticks his hand out an' says, 'Shake! You're the man I'm lookin' for.'

"I kind o' felt upset a little by the way Cook 'd let his tongue run off, but we shook, an' then when we gets through we goes outside an' lights our pipes.

"'I come out here to kind o' look things over at the Y-Bar-T outfit,' he says, wadin' in waist deep at the first jump, 'an' if I ain't away off from the truth we've got a foreman that's got a deeper interest in hisself than is right.'

"'Maybe so,' I says, 'an' maybe not, but thinkin' a thing an' provin' it is different some.'

"'Right you are,' he says, 'but if they's anything wrong I'm a-goin' to find it sooner or later, an' when I find it out I'm a-goin' to get a square deal or know the reason why.' When he says this he kind o' shakes his head an' bites the words off sharp an' spits them out, an' I says to myself that the Y-Bar-T outfit is goin' to be plumb shook up to the roots, for I knows that the foreman is as crooked as a snake track on a dusty trail. 'We own twenty-five hundred acres,' he says, 'an' we've got close to twenty thousand o' Government land under lease an' fence. A couple o' years ago we bought thirty-five hundred head o' cattle, range delivery, which, allowin' for a five per cent. loss, 'd make us have close on to thirty-three.'

"'Five per cent. ain't enough,' I says to him; 'if you got 'em from Texas in the shape I heard you did fifteen wouldn't be none extravagant, maybe too little if you count 'em up.'

"'Well, then, fifteen,' he says, 'which 'd make three thousand not countin' in the increase, an' if we've got a "cow" over two thousand I'm dead wrong an' ain't no judge.'

"'From what I hear you ain't none wrong,' I says, 'not that it's any of my funeral, but I don't believe in bein' crooked myself an' if they's any way I kin help you get things straightened out I'm a-goin' to do it. If I wuz in your place I'd have a round-up an' count the cattle an' satisfy myself just how bad things had got to be, an' then when I wuz dead sure I'd located the guilty party I'd hop on him so hard that he'd think the moon 'd worked loose an' fell on his head. But I'd be mighty careful how I talked, for like as not they's more than one mixed up if stealin' 's goin' on.'

"'That's right,' he says, 'speak low, step soft, an' carry a great big stick an' you kin travel far,' which is sure good sense an' mighty good advice.

"'Round your cattle up,' I says, 'throw 'em and brand 'em if you ain't got a corral; run 'em through a chute an' mark them if you has, an' let your boys sweep the range up pretty clean an' the count, if made honest, 'll come close to showin' exactly what you've got on hand.'

"'We paid taxes on thirty-six fifty last year,' he says, kind o' studyin' the matter over in his mind.

"'In which cases,' I says, 'the State of Colraydo, an' more particular Chaffee County, owes the Y-Bar-T a drawback of close to fifty cents on the dollar by the 'rithmatics that use to be my school books when I wuz a boy, an' if I kin help you in any way you go ahead an' holler.'

"'Well,' he says, 'the way to do a thing is to go ahead an' do it; if you'll let me have a couple of good square boys to kind o' overlook the count I'll see they don't lose anything by it, an' if you feel that you kin spare the time to come along and sort o' act as a board o' directors an' give me a bit of advice when I need it I'll be delighted, an' I want to say to you, Mr. Winters——'

"'Mister be damned,' I says, 'so fur as I'm concerned titles an' nightshirts ain't none needed out in this country; my friends kin call me Bill an' them that ain't my friends don't need to waste their breath on me.'

"'All right, Bill,' he says, 'that's the way I feel about it; Bill it is, an' you an' me 'll set things straight at-Y-Bar-T before a bear kin wag his tail.'" The Foreman paused and blew a cloud of blue-tinged smoke and smiled.

"He sure wuz hell on bears," he said, "but that wuz him. Ready to size a man up quick an' take or leave him; slow to think bad of anybody an' square enough to see that even the devil got his due."

"'Well,' I says, 'that bein' settled, what's the first step in the clean-up?'

"'How'm I goin' to start?' he says, reel thoughtful. 'I'm a-goin' to fire that damned foreman, that's how I'm goin' to start.'

"'You're hollerin' out loud when you states that,' I says; 'that's the medicine the Y-Bar-T needs to set it straight; give the head rustler the grand bounce an' the little taggers-on-after 'll trot up to you waggin' their tails. Then if you kin prove they's anything crooked you kin blame soon get a square deal, for if this country is kind o' rough an' tumbly, the right is the right an' it's spelled with a big R.'

"'Shake,' he says; 'you make me sure I've met a man that'll do to tie up with,' an' we shakes.

"'Mr. Van Renzler,' I says, but he chops me off short an' gives me a slap on the shoulder that drove my boot heels a inch an' a half into the solid ground, an' grins till he shows a gold back tooth.

"'Mister be damned,' he says, 'here's where I get even. On nightshirts I differs with you, but on titles you called the turn.'

"'Van,' I says, 'I've got a bottle of dog bite in the house that's ten years old an' so thick that you c'd blow soap bubbles with it if you wanted; let's licker an' then I'll call in Short Leg Dwyer an' one o' my other best boys, which we calls Ugly Anderson becuz he's so blame good-lookin' that the girls won't give him no peace. Them boys kin round up an' tally-brand a bunch before a flea kin hop out o' danger, an' that's some less than two years.'

"Then we goes into the house an lickers plum sedate an' joyful, an' at supper when the boys comes in they cottons to Van an' we gets to talkin' about huntin', which sure

pleases an' delights him, an' when we rolls in for the night he sets on the edge of his bunk an' looks at me an' says, 'Bill, when this here Y-Bar-T matter is all settled you an' me is goin' to load a camp kit on a couple o' pack horses an' we're goin' way up toward the Elk mountins an' get a grizzly bear skin if they's any one a-walkin' so heavy that he leaves a track.'

"Well, when mornin' come I calls up Short Leg an' Ugly an' tells 'em how the land lays over at the Y-Bar-T, an' them an' me an' Van rides over thataway an' when we gets there Van calls the foreman in an' says he's goin' to let him out becuz he kind o' thinks he'll take things in charge hisself.

"The foreman, which is a ugly critter named Wilkins, with little near-set eyes, begins to kick a rumpus an' in the end gets fired off the place an' goes, an' then we starts the tally, an' havin' a corral we fixes up a chute an' tally-brands them quick an' easy, an' in the end we finds that all we counts is something over eighteen hundred head. There sure has been some reckless stealin' goin' on, an' we gets plumb industrious an' finds that Wilkins is been runnin' off the calves an' brandin' them with his own mark, which is a B. T. branded on the side, an' if they's any way o' stealin' that he ain't tried it's becuz he ain't had brains enough to think it up.

"'It's a dirty mix-up,' Van says to me when we gets most of Wilkins' tracks uncovered; 'we've treated him too white, lettin' him use the range for a herd o' his own, which most like he's stole from us. But anyway,' he says, 'I'm a-goin' to keep them to kind o' square things up,' which is sure wise an' just what I'd a done. We rounds up somethin' over a hundred head an' puts them up where no one can't bother them an' then sets down an' waits for Wilkins to deal the cards, hearin' that he's a-goin' round the country makin' brags that he's goin' to get even with the Y-Bar-T if he has to burn some buildin's.

"But Van stands pat an' when we gets things fixed I sends Short Leg an' Ugly back to Jack Hall, givin' them good advice an' tellin' them that they better ride back home a-lookin' at their horses' ears an' not get festive or cut up becuz they has a little money picked kind o' easy on the side, an' I stays on at Y-Bar-T to kind o' see that Van gets things runnin' right, the which it's well I does, for Wilkins comes back with the two rustlers that's been let out an' tries to run a sandy on Van so that he kin get the cattle which he claims, but which ain't his by common sense or law.

"'I ain't anxious for no lawsuits,' says Van, 'nor I ain't borrowin' trouble, but you ain't dealt fair with this outfit an' I'm a-goin' to keep the cattle to kind o' square us up.' Which sure is right, only I says to Van the cheapest way is to let this here Wilkins party know he's gettin' off mighty easy, which Van does an' tells him to get a move on an' never come back. Wilkins is kind o' surly an' if he had the sand to push his blaze reel hard they'd been some shootin' on the spot, but he backs down an' starts away, but stops down at the bunk house an' goes inside to try 'n raise some trouble with the boys, which makes Van mad for sure, an' as I looks at him I says that Wilkins 'd be heaps better off if he'd a rode on off the place an' not delayed.

"'I'm a-goin' down there,' says Van, 'an' end this thing right now.'

"'I'll come along,' I says, 'to kind o' help if things gets smoky.' Which I does, an' we walks down to the bunk house an' finds Wilkins an' his two rustlers in there tryin' to win away the boys, but when he sees us he gets kind o' shaky an' starts to leave, but we shuts the door an' I kin see that Van is mad clean through. His face is turkey red, an' he kind o' squints an' his mustache is reel bristly an' I kin see a little spot in the side of his neck beatin' like his blood is runnin' fast. He goes up close to Wilkins, which gets kind o' pale. 'I've told you to keep off this place twice now,' he says, an' bites the words off worse than ever, an' I sees he ain't a-goin' to hold in much longer an' prepares to burn some powder on the Wilkins party if they gives me a chance. 'You've run this thing to suit yourself too long an' now I've said the last I'm goin' to say, you thief.'

"As he says this I see Wilkins kind o' move his hand toward his gun, but before you'd a thought it could be did I sees the muscles on Van's back knot up an' then uncoil an' he reaches around short-armed an' hits Wilkins on the side of his face, an' I ain't a-lyin' none when I says it sounded like a mule kickin' an oak post. Down goes Wilkins like a brick fallin' off a chimley, an' I produces my gun an' says 'hands up'

to the two rustlers, which they does, not wantin' to bat an eye, or breathe for fear the boys 'll hop them. When Wilkins drops he loses his gun, which Van gets, an' as his head has whacked the boards considerable when he fell he goes to sleep plumb peaceful on the floor.

"'Is he dead?' I says, 'which I hope he is, the low-down pup, tryin' to smoke this room up.'

"Van shakes his head. 'No, he ain't dead,' he says, 'only shook up; he'll come around all right.'

"An' while we're waitin' the boys gets the guns of the two I'm holdin' up an' then we sets them over against the wall on a bench an' tells them to be quiet, an' then Wilkins kind o' rolls uneasy from side to side a couple o' times like a seasick ship an' opens his eyes an' sets up, kind o' wonderin' if he's the only survivor left.

"'You low-lived pup,' I says to him, plumb mad. 'Tryin' to follow up your blazer with a gun play, you cattle-stealin' son-of-a-gun,' an' then I calls him all the names I kin remember an' cusses him till it looks to me like I ain't left no room for any more, an' when I gets through an' stops to kind o' breathe Van gets a hold of Wilkins an' jerks him up an' slaps him across the face, flat-handed, so good an' hard it popped.

"'That's the way we does things back East,' he says, 'you thief. If Bill's forgot to call you anything, you're it.' An' I looks at him an' I sees that he's got over bein' mad an' is beginnin' to grin, but Wilkins never peeps an' we takes the three an' loads them on their horses an' shoos them off, but has some trouble a-holdin' down the boys, which wants to shoot them up to show they're glad they're gone. An' then I says: 'Van, why in the name of Cotopaxi didn't you plug him or let me plug him; reachin' for a gun in this country is disturbin' the peace an' quiet of the neighbors an' the state.'

"He kind o' laughs. 'Bill,' he says, 'I hit that feller a half a ton worth on the jaw an' it 'll be at least a day or two before he kin smile without the earache. No good a-killin' him; we've fixed him so he's goin' to stay away from here for good.' An blame me if every puncher in the lot didn't take sides with him against me, which wuz a sign that the Y-Bar-T has got a boss at

"He stands up there and dares them to come and take the man
away from him."

Drawing by J. N. Marchand.

last that the boys 'll ride their best horse gant fur.

"'Bill,' he says, when we gets up to the house, 'how about that bear hunt, it's gettin' close, ain't it?'

"'It's none too close,' I says. 'It 'll snow in a couple of days if I know the sign, an' when it does we'll have to wait a while, but sooner or later we'll go out an' assassinate the biggest rooster of a grizzly that you ever heard of.'

"'That's what,' he says, 'I'm a-goin' to get some trophies before I get done with it.'

"'You've got a starter,' I says; 'these here three guns which we've just took so ladylike an' peaceable 'll do to build on, an' if you're thataway inclined you ought to get a right smart lot o' things.' Which he allows is true, tickled to death an' plumb delighted, which he says.

"Well, the next day it sets in to snow, an' we builds up a roarin' big fire to go to bed by an' in the night I has a dream that I'm a-gettin' close to hell, which it turns out to be that the house has caught on fire, an' durn me if it don't burn plumb level with the ground. We saves what we kin, which is a good deal considerin', an' Van gets his three guns, which he is tickled over doin'. There's considerable whisperin' around that night an' the boys seems to have been made restless by the fire an' kind o' excited about somethin', an' the next mornin' they gets out plumb early, an' when we misses them it strikes me that they has remembered what Wilkins said about there goin' to be some burnin' an' is goin' to ride over an' see if they couldn't hold an inquest on his worthless skin.

"'Van,' I says, 'I kind o' smell a lynchin' in the air.'

"'By God,' he says, 'we've got to stop it. Wilkins ain't guilty; there wasn't a track around the house after it burned, an' if he'd been there the snow 'd showed it. Where d'you reckon we can find the boys in time to put a stop to them?'

"'Let 'em go ahead an' hold their party,' I says. 'If this here Wilkins don't need it now it's likely that he'll get it later, so let 'em go.'

"'Bill,' he says, 'if you're the friend I think you are you'll help me stop the boys. I believe in livin' by the law an' ain't a-goin' to see it broke if I kin help it.'

"'You're right,' I says. An' he wuz right, but it wouldn't a done no harm in the least to hang Wilkins. 'You saddle up quick,' I says, 'an' we'll ride over Harvard Mountin way, where the critter's got a kind of house, an' most like unless we proceed over there hell bent for election we'll get there after the party is over, which 'd be a awful shame, for if they do lift him I sure 'd like to see the way he acts.' But we don't, we gets there in time to see the Y-Bar-T punchers draggin' Wilkins around plumb crazy with a rope around his neck, huntin' for a tree to swing him from, which it's a good thing for him is some difficult to find close by, an' if ever I see a full-growed man or heard one talk I heard one when Van busts right into the middle of the crowd an' grabs a hold o' Wilkins, which is cryin' an' prayin' like most crooked people does when things gets wild. He takes the rope off Wilkins' neck an' grabs a hold of him an' the way he talks to them boys on law an' order an' argues with them an' shows them that Wilkins is low-down enough to burn a house but lacks the sand, an' then he kind o'. gets excited an' stands up there before them an' dares them to come an' take the man away from him, which gets the boys, who sure goes plumb crazy from joy at havin' a reel man talk to them, an' they can't yell loud enough for him.

"An' then we goes on home, an' blame me if Van ain't swung on to the rope, which wuz Wilkins' own, for another trophy, an' I'm a son-of-a-gun if we don't get the bear hunt, an' he kills the granddaddy of all the bears in the Elk mountins, if he don't I'm a lyin' pup; an' right now he's got the skin made up into a rug an' sets with his feet on it like as not an' thinks about the time he use to be at Y-Bar-T in the good old days. An' the last time he come out there I wuz about the first one he made tracks for, an' he wuz the same old Van, even if he is a big man now, an' when I calls him Mister he says, 'Bill, what wuz that you use to say about nightshirts an' titles?' an' I says, 'Van, do you remember that ten-year-old dog bite?' an' he laughs an' grabs my hand an' squeezes it, a-showin' that he ain't lost his grip none, an' says, 'Lord bless you, Bill. I wish I could live out here right now.'"

4

Only the Master Shall Praise

JOHN M. OSKISON

THE CENTURY MAGAZINE

JANUARY, 1900.

"ONLY THE MASTER SHALL PRAISE."

THE PRIZE STORY IN "THE CENTURY'S" COMPETITION FOR COLLEGE GRADUATES OF 1898.

BY JOHN M. OSKISON, B. A.,
Leland Stanford Junior University.

ON the cattle ranges of the Indian Territory ten years ago he was known as "the Runt," because he was several inches shorter than the average puncher. His other title of "Hanner" had been fastened upon him by a ludicrous incident in his youth. "Hanner the Runt" was a half-breed Cherokee cowboy, who combined with the stoicism of the Indian something of the physical energy and mental weakness of his white father. One of his shoulders was knocked down a quarter of a foot lower than the other, two ribs had been "caved in" on his left side, and a scar high up on his cheek-bone indicated a stormy life. It was a matter of speculation in the cow-camps as to the number of times Hanner had been thrown from horses and discharged by his employers; he would have been called the foot-ball of fate had these cow-boys been modern and college-bred.

No trick that was ever perpetrated upon him, no service that another imposed upon him, no jeer flung straight in his face, could destroy the innocent trust he felt in humanity. Bill Seymour had caused him to break his ribs by falling from a wild pony, and had then thrashed the puncher who laughed at the fall. In this way Hanner had become the slave of Seymour.

The two, Seymour and Hanner, now rode for Colonel Clarke, and were generally together. It was convenient for Seymour to have his "vallet" to do his work, and it was the chief joy of Hanner's uncolored existence to do something for the man who had fought for him. The grotesque little figure never stopped to ask whether his friend were worthy of his devotion. Bill Seymour was a short, athletic fellow, and good to look upon, but he bore in his nature a too large share of the devil to be dependable. Silent, gruff, and capable when sober, he became a laughing, steel-hearted fury when drunk, and he got drunk as often as he could reach liquor. More than Hanner had felt the sting of his quirt as Bill reeled laughing and jesting on the streets, and had feared to show the anger that rose in their hearts. He made enemies when drunk, and gravely apologized to them in his sober days. One man, a traveling cattle-buyer, braver than most, and not knowing his man, had drawn a small pistol and shot the puncher in the body. Bill, who was not hurt at all seriously, laughingly strode up to the shooter, seized the weapon, and pointing at his feet, said:

"Now dance for me, you impident son of a mosquito! Dance till you drop! Tryin' to plug me with a toy like that—a cursèd little thirty-two!" He flung the pistol noisily into the street, caught the man by one ear, and slapped his face.

There is one time in the year when the cow-puncher feels that he must get away from his work and indulge in a "good time." He does not know the significance of the Fourth of July except in a hazy way, but he does know that on that day he may have abundant whisky for the buying, even though its sale be prohibited by law. He knows, too, that he will find at the big celebrations in the Territory all his friends and enemies worth meeting and fighting; and this meeting of friends and fighting of enemies gives the spice of variety to his life.

As the two companions rode to the largest town in the Territory on the morning of the Fourth, one could see that their outfits were typical of themselves. Bill Seymour rode the best and fastest horse on the ranch; his saddle was new and modern in make, his spurs rare and shanked long—only a leader of cow-boy fashions had dared to wear them; his hat was a Stetson, and hardly discolored by the weather. Hanner might have fitted himself up from the ranch dump-heap. Two old, unmated spurs dangled from a pair of "run-over" boot-heels, the patched corduroy trousers he wore had been traded to him long ago by his champion, and between the bottom of a dirty waistcoat and the top of his trousers there showed a greasy cartridge-belt, with scattering cartridges stuck in it. A "floppy" black hat, which almost concealed his dark, pinched features, completed the queer figure. The pony he rode was called "Pignuts," and was knotty and scrubby and tough enough to deserve the title.

"Bill, ye ain't a-goin' to git drunk to-day, are ye? They say they 's goin' to be a lot of extra marshals 'at ain't lettin' any drunk walk the streets to-day. I wish ye would n't drink too much, Bill!" Remembering other celebrations, Hanner wished to get through the day with as little trouble on Bill's account as possible.

"Oh, go to the devil, you old woman! Who said I was goin' to get drunk? Somethin' I never do. Come on; let 's ride up," Bill replied shortly; and the two galloped into town through a cloud of dust raised by many incoming wagons.

"Hello, Lem! How 's the Convict? Keepin' healthy now, Smear? What 's the show and the price?" Bill greeted the punchers from the ranches in all parts of the country with a familiarity possible only to one who knows and does and dares as much as the best of them.

"Got the dangdest mule fer buckin' down here they 's goin' to have rode to-day ye ever seen. Five dollars in it fer the man that rides it. Why don't ye try, Hanner?" The Convict winked at Bill, and insinuatingly confronted the Runt with the question.

"I don't hardly think this here saddle of mine 'u'd stand it," the Runt returned, after glancing at Seymour. "Think I 'd better try it, Bill?"

"Get your bloomin' neck broke if you do, but I expect it 'u'd be good for you. Yes, go ahead and ride it, and I 'll lend you this saddle."

Bill's words were spoken in jest, but Hanner meditated upon them seriously during the day, and when the vicious mule was led out for its first trial, Seymour noted with some anxiety that his own saddle was buckled upon it. He was careless with drink now, and grinned in anticipation of the sorry figure the Runt would present astride the mule. He made a foolish drunken wager that "Hanner 'll stay with that there mule till its tongue sticks out and it can't hump its back any more."

The bucking mule was the closing scene in the day's spectacle. The high-heeled, stiff-muscled cow-boys had chased a greased pig over a fifty-acre field, and been sadly beaten by the street boys of the town; they had pitched rings at the heads of canes over the handles of cheap penknives, and wasted their efforts trying for a gilded watch pegged down with a large-handled awl; they had ridden in the tourney, flying past rings hung in the air, and picking them off with wooden spears, causing strangers to gaze with open-eyed wonder at their dash and recklessness; they had bucked the scores of games which gamblers had devised to part the fool and his money, and were gathered now to watch a game they could understand and appreciate.

Out of a knot of excited men Hanner went straight to the waiting, restless mule. With a mock air of bravado he struck the excited mule across the flank with his sombrero, after roughly seizing the reins. No one who has not learned by experience how to mount a plunging horse can understand how Hanner lifted himself out of the chaos of rearing mule and struggling attendants into the saddle before he signed to the men to turn the animal loose.

When the mule found itself free to act there was a momentary pause. Then began the short, nasty jumps straight into the air, buster's life shorter. Hanner was bleeding at the nose in half a minute. The twisting jumps were continued until the strength of the mule was almost exhausted, and as yet only the hat of the puncher had been dislodged. A short pause followed, during which the mule changed its tactics, and Hanner thwacked its sweaty neck with his

GOING TO THE CELEBRATION.

with the animal's back bowed, its legs stiff, and its head lowered. It was the first powerful effort of the angered beast, made with devilish confidence. Hanner was scarcely shaken by these first straight jumps, but then began the twisting series, which is the second expedient of a bucking animal. A jump high into the air, with a seemingly impossible twist to the side, landed the mule with its head turned almost half round. Before the rider caught his breath another jump and another half-turn were made. These are the motions that make a bronco-open hand. The next motion was a sudden rearing by the mule. As it rose on its hind legs the rider yanked fiercely on the reins, and, slipping to the ground on one side, allowed the brute to fall on its back. The saddle-horn buried itself in the earth, and the mule's hoofs beat the air a moment before it scrambled to its feet.

Hanner was cooler than the mule now, and swung himself back into the saddle with the first long leap of the desperate animal. This was the easy part of the trial for the rider, and the spectacular part for the world.

The mule ran straight away for the opposite fence of the fair-grounds with long, lunging jumps, rising and pitching forward with the speed of a racing yacht. Hanner brought his craft about before it sailed into the fence, and beat it fore and aft with a flourishing hand. He was wild with triumph now, his hair blowing in the wind. He leaned forward as in a race, urging the thoroughly tired and conquered mule straight for the crowd. A particularly vicious dig with the spurs made the beast plunge into the scattering knot of spectators and rise to a four-barred gate. At the opposite side of the track no fence barred its way, and it ran, frightened and quivering, under the awning of a lemonade-vender's stand, scattering glasses and confections to the winds, and wrecking the stand. Hanner slowly dismounted, stroked the sweaty flank of the subdued mule, then turning and picking up an unbroken bottle of soda, proposed a toast "to our gentle old family-buggy hoss!"

The punchers cheered Hanner with the heartiness of men who can appreciate the feat.

"Hanner, you 're all right. I knowed you could do it." Bill's praise fell sweetly upon the Runt's ears. "Where 's that wooley I made the bet with? Hanner, we 'll drink; yes, sir, we 'll liquor up now and have a good time. I won the bet and you won the five for ridin' the mule. We 'll drink, Hanner." Seymour slapped Hanner's shoulder in a cruelly hearty fashion.

"No, Bill; let 's not drink any more to-day," Hanner protested, though he had not drunk anything.

"Hanner, I don't understand you; blast me if I do." Bill was argumentative. "Here you are, just rode the buckinest mule in the Territory, and you won't take a drink with your best friend! Now, if anybody else 'u'd refuse to drink with Bill Seymour I think they 'd have trouble. But you, Hanner, I reckon I 'll just have to pour it down you." The drunken puncher tried to carry out his plan, but changed his mind at Hanner's appeal.

"Don't, Bill; fer God's sake, Bill, I 'm too sick to drink! Let 's go home, Bill. I 'm shore sick. Won't ye come on home with me?"

"I believe the darn little skunk is sick," muttered Bill to himself. Then aloud: "If you want to go home with me you 'll have to come along pretty quick. I 'm tired of this show, and, anyway, I 've got to get over to the round-up on Big Creek to-morrow.

Get your horse and wait for me here; I 'm goin' to see Smear before I go home."

Hanner knew that his companion went for another bottle of whisky, but knew also the futility of protesting.

They rode out of the tired, dirty, and heated crowd, where the dance-platforms were beginning to fill up, and where the owner of the two-headed calf, the five-legged mule, and the biggest steer in the world, was beseeching everybody to come and view his collection. Bill rode at a gallop, with his companion spurring at his heels, until they passed quite out of sight of the revelers. Then he turned with an air of real concern to the Runt, and asked:

"You shore 'nough sick, Hanner? That mule shore put up a stiff article."

Hanner was not diplomatic, and spoke out truthfully: "Sick? No, I ain't sick. What 'u'd I want to see ye get drunk an' run in for? They 'd 'a' run ye in to-night, Bill, I know. Did ye ever notice the color of the sky this time a day, Bill? Seems to me it ain't so darn purty as some people think." The sun was setting in a dull, coppery sky, the air was sultry, and the dust rose in thick clouds.

For a minute Bill did not reply, but looked at his companion with a half-puzzled expression. Then he broke out:

"Well, you 're a nice one, ain't you? Do you know what I 'm a mind to do to you for this dirty trick? You think I 'm a darn kid to sneak like this to keep from gettin' run in? Oh, you baby! For a cent I 'd make you walk all the way home, and lay this quirt over your shoulders every step of the way."

"Oh, no, Bill; ye would n't think o' doin' that. D' ye want to go back? I did n't know ye cared to stay so bad."

"Go back? You think I 'm crazy? What 'u'd the punchers say? No, curse you; you've robbed me of my fun. That mule ought to 'a' killed you!"

Hanner had learned long before the value of silence, and rode beside his morose companion with now and then an anxious glance at him. Bill was meditative, and quite forgot the rider at his side. The pale light of a young moon deepened the shadows and illuminated the heavy, sluggish dust-clouds that rose in the wake of the riders. Hungry calves, neglected at the ranches since early morning by the celebrating ranchmen, bawled in useless appeal; scurrying, skulking coyotes answered with their threatening cries the challenge of the ranch-dogs. A mile away, and coming toward them with rhythmic hoof-beat and noisy rattle of hub on axle, the two riders heard a wagon and team.

"Who do ye reckon kin be goin' into town this time o' night, Bill?" asked Hanner.

"Hold on here, Hanner; we'll stop." Bill meditated a moment, then went on: "You know what that team is? It's the mail-stage from Coffeyville to Vinita. Darn old rattle-trap; it's a disgrace to the country. Ought to have a railroad through this God-forsaken land. That driver's a fool, and you know what I'm goin' to do? Darn your skin, Hanner, you made me miss the fun at Vinita; now I'm goin' to have some fun of my own. We'll rob the stage! Ever hear about the road-agents, the James boys and the Younger gang? Well, they robbed overland stages and trains for swag; but we won't get anything here, only some fun, and scare the fool driver. Stage-robbers always jump out and grab the horses' heads and poke a gun in the driver's face. We'll tie our horses over there in the gully, and hide in the grass here by the road. You jump out and get the horses, and I'll fix the driver. See? Come on; tie up over here!"

"Ye don't mean that, do ye, Bill? Oh, come on and let's go home." Hanner detected a determined ring in the puncher's voice, and he dared not protest more.

"You don't have to get in on this unless you want to. I can do it myself." Bill considered the plan a good joke, being drunk enough to forget that robbing the mails is a very serious crime in the eyes of the law, and the most serious in the eyes of citizen posses, who sometimes take the law into their hands. He galloped down the rain-washed gully and tied his horse out of sight of travelers on the road. Hanner, expecting an end of the joke, rode with him; but when Bill turned to go back to the road on foot, the little puncher announced his intention of having nothing to do with it.

"Then give me that floppy old hat. I got to wear some kind of a mask. Let me have that old red handkerchief round your neck, too. Now I look like a shore-'nough stage-robber—or like you, and that's worse. Well, ride out of the way if you ain't goin' to help." The amateur highwayman half stumbled, chuckling at the prospect of fun, to a place in the long grass at the roadside.

Hanner rode far down the dry wash, and waited in anxious silence. He heard the scarcely understood command of Bill Seymour to the driver. The rattling of the wagon suddenly ceased. There was a brief moment of absolute silence, and a pistol cracked. Another shot from the same gun rang out. In a short moment an answering shot was heard. Hanner could have sworn that it was the bark of Bill's revolver. An angry shout from Bill was followed by a fusillade of shots. The rattling of harness indicated a struggle with the horses. Then a yell from the driver started the stage-team at a gallop. The firing ceased, and trembling with fright, Hanner heard the noisy wagon pass on toward Vinita.

Thoroughly sobered now, Bill ran to his horse, mounted, and rode to meet his companion. The two galloped on their way for five minutes before Seymour trusted his voice to explain. After breaking into a string of furious oaths, he said:

"What a fool I was! Softy Sam wasn't drivin' the blanked wagon at all. When I got holt of the horses they shot at me. I yelled to 'em to stop, that I was only jokin', but the fools kept on pluggin' away at me. I got behind the horses and yelled again. Then I had to shoot. One of 'em fell back off the seat, and then the other one whipped up the horses. I let 'em go quick. That unshot fool plugged at me till he got out of sight. No, I did n't get hurt, but your hat got a hole in it all right."

"Ye did n't kill one of 'em, did ye, Bill? Ye don't think ye did? That would n't do, ye know, at all."

"Kill one? Hit one, all right; maybe killed him. The fool! Oh, that's just my luck. Curse you, Hanner, it was your fault, you cur, takin' me away from the fair-grounds with your old-granny tale about bein' sick. Say, what we goin' to do about it now, eh? We got to get out of this, or we'll get strung up, shore—I will, I mean. We'll ride for the Verdigris River timber and hide there. Well, have you got anything better?"

"Bill, could n't we explain, tell the marshals it was a mistake, and—"

"Get strung up to a limb before we got through tellin' that, you darn fool! But it ain't a question of 'we'; I'm the only one in this. You kept out of it, you cowardly skunk, and you're safe. You want to run away now, and keep your skin whole?" Bill grew incoherent, scarcely retaining sense enough to spur on toward his destination.

Meanwhile the stage had reached Vinita, with the wounded man at the point of dying, and the driver too much confused to do anything to help him. Quite by chance, a considerable sum of money had been sent through the mails that day, and the regular

"THESE ARE THE MOTIONS THAT MAKE A BRONCO-BUSTER'S LIFE SHORTER."

driver had been replaced by two well-known deputy sheriffs. After the driver had finished telling of the attack made by a short man wearing a big, floppy black hat, and with a dirty red handkerchief tied over his lower face, a posse was immediately formed to hunt the bandit down. No one could guess who the guilty one might be.

Dick Brewer, the leader of the party, questioned minutely: "Would you know the hat if you saw it?"

"Yes," the driver answered; "Tom Forbes put a hole through it before he got shot. I saw it nearly fall off his head—a great, big, wide-brimmed, floppy thing, with what looked like a piece of rope for a band."

"Somethin' like the hat that Hanner the Runt wore to-day, was n't it, Smear?" the Convict commented. Then he asked: "Where is Bill Seymour and Hanner, anyway? You seen 'em last, did n't you, Smear?"

"They started home an hour ago. Bill said he had to get over to the Big Creek round-up to-morrow, an' he got a bottle of my whisky before he went." Smear remembered the unusual incident of Bill's early departure; ordinarily, duty was not allowed to interfere with the puncher's pleasure.

To Smear, who made one of the pursuing party, the words "a big, floppy black hat and a dirty red handkerchief" kept repeating themselves in his mind. At each repetition he recalled with distinctness the appearance of the Runt as he had gone out to ride the wild mule. No other puncher in the country would wear that hat, and none would feel quite respectable with that dirty red rag about his neck at a Fourth of July celebration.

"But, shucks!" Smear muttered to himself, "it can't be him. But he's got nerve, the little devil, ridin' that mule the way he did! He ought to 'a' been with Bill Seymour, though; could n't tear the cuss away from him. Well, we'll see."

Hanner and Bill rode at a steady gallop until, in the middle of the night, they plunged into the Verdigris River timber. No definite plan of action had been formed; they felt only a strong desire to get away out of sight. The horses must rest, and, overcome by fatigue, Bill dropped asleep. The consciousness of a crime done did not disturb him; in his mind it was an accident, the unfortunate result of a joke. Hanner did not sleep. He stared up through the tree-tops into the starlit sky, and pondered the significance of the deed. The course he had suggested to Bill, that of confessing and

explaining the matter, still seemed to be the wisest one to him. "Surely," he thought, "they would understand, for they all know Bill's nature. Did n't everybody know that he must indulge in a joke whenever he could?" A plan began to form in his mind.

"I kin sneak away before Bill wakes up, an' go explain to the marshals. They'll let Bill go, I know they will. I kin do this fer ye, Bill, an' ye'll be glad of it. I don't want to have ye scoutin' round the country; I want ye here, so we kin still ride together. I made ye come away from the fair, an' I got to git ye out of the trouble I got ye into." Hanner scarcely spoke his thoughts. He waited undecided for two or three hours. The dawn was just beginning to filter in to the hiding-place as he stole forth quietly to his horse and rode to find the posse.

More than one gang of outlaws had made the river-bottom their headquarters and been captured there. The pursuers of the lonely mail-robber inferred that he was one of a number, and that he was very likely to be heard of in the old haunts. So early morning found the posse scouring the country outside the timber, inquiring of ranchmen and the women of the houses for a trace of the man they sought. It would do little good to try to rout him out of the great forest of brush and swamp until some trace of his location had been found.

Dick Brewer and Smear were riding together near the road that plunges through the thickest of the timber when Hanner rode out. They stopped, attracted by his action. The little puncher looked anxiously about until he saw the waiting horsemen, then galloped toward them. Smear felt sick at heart on seeing the floppy hat and the dirty red handkerchief that he wore. Brewer saw them, too, and his hand flew to his revolver. He had not voiced his suspicions before, but now Smear exclaimed with excitement:

"If that there hat's got a hole in it, we've got the man!"

"It's the Runt!" Brewer had not heard the insinuations which were made before the posse started.

The appearance of the bullet-hole in the crown of the old hat sufficed to make Brewer and Smear bring Hanner to a halt before their pointed pistols. At sight of their stern faces and threatening weapons Hanner's power of speech was gone. He tried to say that he wanted to explain, and grew quite incoherent.

"'I RECKON YE GOT THE MAN ALL RIGHT.'"

"Never mind; explain when you get up before all of us," the leader commanded.

Half an hour of scurrying about by Smear and vigorous blowing of signal-calls brought the party together. Everything was extremely orderly and businesslike. A man who robbed mails and killed drivers had no claim on their consideration; the only question was, to be sure of the man. When they were sure of him, no matter what his former standing, he must be hanged straightway. The effect of a lynching they felt to be good. Dick Brewer called upon the driver of the mail-wagon to step forth and declare truthfully whether or not he recognized the prisoner.

"Yes, sir; I can swear that that hat is the one the robber wore, and allowing for the difference between daylight and moonlight, I 'd say that handkerchief was around the robber's face."

"Is he of the same size and build?" asked the leader.

"About the same; but I won't swear to anything but the hat. I know that."

It grew clear to the mind of the confused little puncher that if he told the story which he had planned to tell, Bill Seymour would be caught and hanged within the day. No excuse that he had perfected would stand for an instant against the plain fact that an attempt to rob the mails had been made and a man murdered. He saw, too, just as plainly, that if he did not tell the truth concerning Bill, he, as the owner of the hat, would suffer the penalty. He knew that very soon he would be asked to tell his story, to clear up the evidence against him. There was none of the great excitement present that nerves men to self-sacrifice. The day was young yet, and the air was chilling. The legs of the horses and the boots of the men were dew-splashed and dripping. It was not pleasant to die now, even though life had been hard and mean to him. He felt a shudder of repulsion when he thought of the mode of death.

On the other side he considered what he owed to Bill. Out of a host of cow-boys he had known, Bill was the only one who had ever recognized the fierce desire for comradeship that had consumed him, the only one who had not passed him by in open ridicule.

"Bill fought fer me when I was down," Hanner whispered to himself. "He knowed I was human. An' I brought this on to him. He come away yesterday because he thought I was sick. He 'd 'a' got away, maybe, if I had n't left him asleep to explain. If he had to go I would n't have nobody to ride with, an' if I take his place—if I go he 'll know an'—" Hanner did not trust himself to go on, but turned to the leader and said:

"I reckon ye got the man all right."

Under the misshapen body and the half-foolish features there was a stoic in Hanner. To save the life of his friend, the man whom he worshiped and the other punchers respected, was the one great service he could render. He died there with a blind terror in his heart at the blackness of the unknown, and with the thought of Bill Seymour in his mind. The men who hanged him felt no exultation at having avenged a crime, but only a nameless pity for the poor fellow.

A day later Bill Seymour, while dodging about in the timber, learned from a chance-met friend of Hanner's fate. Looking this friend full in the face, he said:

"The poor little fool, to do a thing like that!"

5

A Samaritan of the "L-Bar"

R.L. KETCHUM

A SAMARITAN OF THE "L-BAR"
By R·L·KETCHUM.

Drawn by Dan Smith.

"HEN HAWK" was in great spirits. He had been bubbling with good humor for two weeks, and every day the springs increased. Only ten days more, and then for "the States." We of the "L-Bar," who had known him for two years almost, were at a loss to account for this sudden rise in Hen's mental temperature, and probably showed it. Indeed, there were several of the boys who hinted that an explanation from him would be gratefully received by his curiosity-beset co-workers; but Hen merely widened his grin, and said nothing. But just before Christmas he let the secret out.

"Boys," said he, in a muffled voice, caused by a knife-load of potato in his mouth, "I'm goin' back to th' States!"

Open-eyed astonishment all around the breakfast table.

"That's what, boys, I'm goin' right after New-Year's, tew."

"The dooce, ye say! Must've lost a rich r'lation 'r b'en doin' a little rustlin' on th' side. Now I think of 't, they was some talk 'bout thar bein' some inside 'sistance t' th' Baldy Stites gang w'en they honored this hyar vicinity wi' th'r 'tentions last year," volunteered "Red" Posey. Hen, having joined liberally in the smiles that followed this remark, went on:

"I cast th' insinerations back intuh th' teeth o' th' red-nosed gent wi' th' fragrant name. No, sir! 'Taint neither one n'r t'other. Mebbe 'fore I go I'll tell ye—an' mebbe I won't."

51

And Mr. Hawkins again smiled, knowing that the boys would suffer immeasurably until they knew whence came the "stake" on which he was going home.

Next day, immediately after breakfast, Hen rode off in the direction of Brownsville, the nearest town on the west, about thirty miles away, and we saw nothing of him until Friday, when he returned, whistling cheerfully. The boys were very keen to know what his errand had been, for they were sure he had not gone merely to get a few things from the grocers and harness-makers, but Hen did not enlighten them.

That night, however, in the boss's room, he told the story to a select audience, consisting of the boss and the scribe.

"I b'en kinder holdin' off, ye see, 'cause a feller haint no ways certain 'bout savin' 'is milk t'll he gets the pail out f'm under the caow; but now, bein's I've got it O. K., I may's well tell ye, on'y I don't want th' boys t' knaow.

"Ye see, 'twas this a-way. 'Bout five years ago, back in Maine I c'cluded t' come out hyar an' grow up wi' th' kentry a hull lot. 'Twasn't 'cause I wanted t' dew it, but ye see, I sort o' hed tuh."

"Ah, yes," observed the boss, dryly. "I believe the late Mr. Stites began his brilliant career in somewhat the same way. Was your difficulty about a horse, too?"

Hen's laugh over, he proceeded, somewhat blushingly.

"No, 'twar'nt that, hardly. But they wan't no chance thar for a poor cuss, an' so I pulled out. Ye see, me 'n Molly Hopkins hed 'bout made up aour min's to git spliced, an' ev'rythin' was goin' jig-step, w'en in steps ol' George Hopkins an' takes a han' hisself. Ol' Hop was a high-toned stallion, an' put on heaps o' airs, 'cause he was the best fixed man in taown, an' hed b'en s'lectman an' member o' th' legislater, w'ile I was only a carpenter an' hadn't ary red. Th' ol' egiot might've saw haow things was goin' on—I reckon he did—but he never let on t'll one night he come home f'm taown an' heerd me 'n Molly talkin' in th' sittin'-room.

"Then he jes' plowed in brash. Gosh! how he did lay it all over me. Went on ter give me th' devil fer my 'dacity in persoomin' t' th' han' o' his, George

Hopkins', darter. 'Th' idee! I want ye t' understan', young man,' says he, 'th't I have better plans for her th'n lettin' 'er marry a penniless carpenter.' 'N he went on an' tore 'round fer a while thet style; but I stood my groun' t'll finally he says, 'Young man, when you can show a bank 'count o' ten thaousan' dollars, she's yourn, an' not b'fore.' Then he grins a hull lot, thinkin' haow I'd hev t' hustle a consid'ble speck 'fore I got that in my corral.

"Wa-al, me 'n Molly talked it over a lot 'n fin'lly concluded th't I'd hev t' go sommers else, ef ever I got forehanded; so one day we says good-by, daown in the medder lot, an' I pulled out fer Californy.

"Sence then I've b'en knockin' 'raound all over th' kentry, trying one thing 'n 'nother. Purty hard luck most o' th' time, tew; but just 'fore I come hyar, I located a claim, me 'n 'nother feller, over in Colorado, an' worked it some. It didn't pan out none, so we hed t' try somethin' else, an hyar I come, leavin' Peters t' keep up work on the claim, him havin' a job clus by. Wa-al, th' other day, Peters he saold aout tew a Boston comp'ny fer twenty-five thaousand—an' my half's what I went to Braownsville fer. That's all."

There wasn't a man on the ranch who wasn't torn up a little about the heart at the prospect of Hen's going, and who wasn't honestly glad at his good fortune. Even the misanthropic Posey evinced not a little regret as he said good-by to him, when, the morning after New-Year's, Hen sat on his bronco all ready to start for Jersey, the railroad town to the east of us.

It was a beautiful morning, almost like spring, and Hen couldn't have wished for a better day to start on. The last good-by said, he straightened up, sniffed the cold wind, looked to see that everything was all right, and with an "Adios, boys," was off, waving his hand in acknowledgment of the rousing cheer we gave him as he reached the top of the hill.

Jersey was only twenty-odd miles away, and Hen expected to arrive there at noon, in time to get his dinner, dispose of his bronco, and make the two o'clock train east. There was plenty of time, so he let his horse take its own gait, and gave himself up to his thoughts.

Drawn by Frederic Remington.
"IT WAS ONE OF THESE . . . . . THAT CAUSED HIM TO REIN UP HIS HORSE SO SUDDENLY."

Going home! Home! How sweet the word sounded! Five years—only five, but they seemed twice as many. He wondered how he had ever managed to live through them. The first two had not been so hard. He had been full of hope and vigor, and had told himself that it was only a little while—only a little while. Then when the reward for all his toil seemed to be no less distant than at first, it was hard. Sometimes he had thought that he would give it up and go home to confess himself beaten; then the picture of the little brown-eyed girl, who through her tears had told him to be brave and patient and all would be well, would come before him, and he would set his teeth hard and "pitch in" again. Maybe it had soured him a bit. He wondered if sometimes he had not been rather unsociable and rather poor company for his companions, and concluded he had.

His thoughts turned again to Molly. How pretty and sad she had looked with the tears on her pink cheeks that day—for somehow he couldn't for the life of him think of her except as he saw her last, watching him as he went down the road. And just to think! Only a few days more, and—"Hullo! Wa-al, I'll be tee-totally doggoned!"

The wind had shifted around into the north; dull, gray clouds hid the blue and gold that had made the early day so fair. Two or three flakes of snow were visible now and then. It was one of these striking Hen on the cheek that had caused him to rein up his horse so suddenly and make the able remark just recited.

Not a living creature was in sight on all the broad plain. Hen and his horse were as much alone as if they had been on the open sea. Human habitation between the "L-Bar" and Jersey, there was none. Hen dismounted and laid his ear to the ground, listening intently for a few seconds. Yes—there it was—that dull, whispering, indistinct roar, which the plainsman knows and fears, the voice of the coming blizzard. The horse heard it, or felt it, and turned his head, whinnying softly.

"Yes, ol' pony, it's comin' all right 'nough," said Hen, as he rose from the ground, "an' me 'n you's got to hustle a hull lot, Mister Pokey. Let 'er slide."

Only twelve miles or so, and yet Hen knew that the blizzard might overtake him before he had traveled four. He urged his horse faster, knowing that the faithful animal could easily stand the work.

It was growing rapidly colder, and the few flakes of snow were being rapidly followed by thousands. The wind was increasing in velocity and Hen, bending low over his horse's neck, could hear the vicious "swish-swish" of the snow as it was hurled through the grass and along the ground. Very soon it was impossible to see more than a hundred yards or so ahead, but Hen knew the general direction and for safety's sake was heading for the stage road leading into Jersey from the southwest.

On and on they went, Pokey, alive to the situation, pounding along at his top traveling speed, steady as a clock. On and on came the storm, covering horse and rider with snow as fine as flour until they looked like ghosts. Hen, leaning back to get his overcoat, lost the direction, but he knew Pokey would do better without his piloting.

How cold it was. Hen's hands and toes were like lumps of ice—worse, they had hardly any feeling in them. His ear and cheek on the side exposed to the storm were getting nipped. Well, he would soon strike the stage road, and then, if he had not miscalculated, there would be only five or six miles——

"Great Scott!"

For Pokey had given a sudden, high leap and stood still, panting. Almost under his feet lay a snow-covered object with a strange look about it. Hen leaned down from the saddle and turned it over. It was a dead man, holding tight, in the stiff right hand, a whip such as stage-drivers use.

"Stage-driver, deader'n Tom Jefferson. Drunk, likely, an' fell off, poor cuss!" But there was no time to stop and investigate. In another second Pokey was turned to the left and pounding along the road.

A dark object loomed up suddenly as they shot past, and a sudden thrill sent the sluggish blood coursing through Hen's veins. He halted and turned Pokey's unwilling head on the back course.

Sure enough, it was the stage; but there were no horses attached. Hen felt around and reached the door-handle. A cry—a child's cry—came from within. Hen tied Pokey firmly to a wheel, found the door again and entered.

"Thank God!" It was a woman's voice "Oh, sir, have you come to take us away? The driver fell off, I think, and the horses broke loose somehow, and we're almost frozen." Hen could see her

now. It was a young, good-looking
woman, and she clasped tight to her breast
a child about three years old. Neither
was clad for such awful weather.

Hen's heart stood still for a moment.
If that woman and child remained here
it was almost certain death. It might be
days before help could reach them, and
even if aid could come to them to-morrow,
they would have frozen meanwhile. On
the other hand——

"Can you ride, missis?"

"Yes, indeed."

"Wa-al, come then, quick."

In another minute——

"Ride straddle, so. Naow, hold th'
kid, an' let th' hoss take 'is own road."

"But what are you going to——"

Hen was fastening the driver's robe
about her.

"I'm all right. Naow hang on an'
keep holt o' th' kid. Go on, Pokey.
Good-by, missis."

He was alone on the prairie in a deserted
stage-coach, with the storm howling about
him and his thoughts were of other things
for a long time before he remembered
that his money was in his saddle-bags.

"Wa-al, chances is purty nigh agin my
ever needin' it," he muttered, in his quaint
way. " 'Taint like I had a stove an' a
hull lot o' grub. She'll save it for me
likely, anyhaow."

It was two days later that the stage,
coming down from Jersey with several
Samaritans aboard found him. It was two
weeks and more before he came to himself
in the hotel, where he had had every possible attention. He was, as he himself
remarked, "Dern glad t' be alive, an' find
I hedn't los' no han's n'r feet."

But the woman and child had gone—
they left Jersey the very day that Hen's
half-dead form had been brought in by
the relief party—and with them went
Hen's money; for the saddle-bags had
been taken to the woman's room by the
hostler, and no one else had had possession of them, besides which, much to
the landlord's surprise, she had paid
her bill with a one-hundred dollar
greenback when she left. Hen's
money had been mostly in bills of that
denomination.

The boys gave Hen all the sympathy
that was com-
ing to him,
and through
the smoke rings
the boss allowed
that Hen "ought
to have put that
money in the
safe up at Bran-
nagan's saloon.
Saddle-bags
were only for
whiskey and to-
bacco and grub
and sich like."

Drawn by Frederic Remington.
"LEANED DOWN FROM THE SADDLE AND TURNED IT OVER."

6

The Mule Driver and the Garrulous Mute

REX E. BEACH

"AN AMICABLE SETTLEMENT"

THE MULE DRIVER AND THE GARRULOUS MUTE

BY

REX E. BEACH

ILLUSTRATED BY ROLLIN Y. KIRBY

BILL had finished panning the concentrates from our last clean-up, and now the silver ball of amalgam sizzled and fried on the shovel over the little chip-fire, while we smoked in the sun before the cabin. Removed from the salivating fumes of the quicksilver, we watched the yellow tint grow and brighten in the heat.

"There's two diseases which the doctors ain't got any license to monkey with," began Bill, chewing out blue smoke from his lungs with each word, "and they're both fevers. After they butt into your system they stick crossways, like a swallered toothpick; there ain't any patent medicine that can bust their holt."

I settled against the door-jamb and nodded.

"I've had them both, acute and continuous, since I was old enough to know my own mind and the taste of tobacco; I hold them mainly responsible for my present condition." He mournfully viewed his fever-ridden frame which sprawled a pitiful six-feet-two from the heels of his

59

gum-boots to the grizzled hair beneath his white Stetson.

"The first and most rabid," he continued, "is horse-racing — and t'other is the mining fever, which last is a heap insidiouser in its action and more lingering in its effect.

"It wasn't long after that deal in the Territory that I felt the symptoms coming on agin, and this time they pinted most emphatic toward prospecting, so me and 'Kink' Martin loaded our kit onto the burros and hit West.

"'Kink' was a terrible good prospector, though all-fired unlucky and peculiar. Most people called him crazy, 'cause he had fits of goin' for days without a peep.

"Hosstyle and ornery to the whole world; sort of bulging out and exploding with silence, as it were.

"We'd been out in the hills for a week on our first trip before he got one of them death-watch faces on him, and boycotted the English langwidge. I stood for it three days, trying to jolly a grin on to him or rattle a word loose, but he just wouldn't jolt.

"One night we packed into camp tired, hungry, and dying for a good feed.

"I hustled around and produced a supper fit for old Mr. Eppycure. Knowing that 'Kink' had a weakness for strong coffee

that was simply a hinge in him, I pounded up about a quart of coffee beans in the corner of a blanket and boiled out a South American liquid that was nothing but the real Arbuckle mud.

"This wasn't no chafing-dish party either, because the wood was wet and the smoke chased me round the fire. Then it blazed up in spurts and fired the bacon-grease, so that when I grabbed the skillet the handle sizzled the life all out of my callouses. I kicked the fire down to a nice bed of coals and then the coffee-pot upset and put it out. Ashes got into the bacon, and —Oh! you know how joyful it is to cook on a green fire when you're dead tired and your hoodoo's on vicious.

"When the 'scoffings' were finally ready, I wasn't in what you might exactly call a mollyfying and tactful mood nor exuding genialness and enthusiasms anyways noticeable."

"I herded the best in camp towards him, watching for a benevolent symptom, but he just dogged it in silence and never changed a hair. That was the limit, so I inquired sort of ominous and gentle, 'Is that coffee strong enough for ye, Mr. Martin?'

"He give a little impecunious grunt, implying, 'Oh! it'll do,' and with that I

"'I'M DURNED IF MY GUN DIDN'T GO OFF ACCIDENTAL AN PLUMB RUIN ONE OF 'EM'"

seen little green specks begin to buck and wing in front of my eyes; reaching back of me, I grabbed the Winchester and throwed it down on him.

" 'Now, you laugh, darn you,' I says, 'in a hurry. Just turn it out gleeful and infractious.'

" He stared into the nozzle of that Krupp for a minute, then swallered twice to tune up his reeds, and says, friendly and perlite, but serious and wheezy:

" 'Why, what in hell ails you, William?'

" 'Laugh, you old dong-beater,' I yells, rising gradually to the occasion, 'or I'll bust your cupola like a blue-rock.'

" 'I've got to have merriment,' I says. 'I pine for warmth and genial smiles, and you're due to furnish the sunshine. You emit a few shreds of mirth with expedition or the upper end of your spinal-cord is going to catch cold.'

" Say! his jaws squeaked like a screen door when he loosened, but he belched up a beauty, sort of stagy and artificial it was, but a great help. After that we got to know each other a heap better. Yes, sir; soon after that we got real intimate. He knocked the gun out of my hands, and we began to arbitrate. We plumb ruined that spot for a camping place; rooted it up in furrows, and tramped each other's stummicks out of shape. We finally reached an amicable settlement by me getting him agin a log where I could brand him with the coffee-pot.

" Right there we drawed up a protoplasm, by the terms of which he was to laugh anyways twice at meal-times.

" He told me that he reckoned he was locoed, and always had been since a youngster, when the Injuns run in on them down at Frisbee, the time of the big 'killing.' 'Kink' saw his mother and father both murdered, and other things, too, which was impressive, but not agreeable for a growing child. He had formed a sort of antipathy for Injuns at that time, which he confessed he hadn't rightly been able to overcome.

" Now, he allus found himself planning how to hand Mr. Lo the double cross and avoid complications.

" We worked down into South Western Arizony to a spot about thirty-five miles back of Fort Walker and struck a prospect. Sort of a teaser it was, but worth working on. We'd just got nicely started when

'Kink' comes into camp one day after taking a passiar around the butte for game, and says:

" 'The queerest thing happened to me just now, Kid.'

" 'Well, scream it at me,' I says, sort of smelling trouble in the air.

" 'Oh! It wasn't much,' says he. 'I was just working down the big canyon over there after a deer when I seen two feather-dusters coming up the trail. I hid behind a rock, watching 'em go past, and I'm durned if my gun didn't go off accidental and plumb ruin one of 'em. Then I looks carefuller and seen it wasn't no feather-duster at all — nothing but an Injun.'

" 'What about the other one?'

" 'That's the strangest part,' says 'Kink.' 'Pretty soon the other one turns and hits the back-trail like he'd forgot something; then I seen him drop off his horse, too, sudden and all togetherish. I'm awful careless with this here gun,' he says. 'I hate to see a man laugh from his tonsils forrard, the way he did. It ain't humorous.'

" 'See here,' I says, 'I ain't the kind that finds fault with my pardner, nor saying this to be captious and critical of your play; but don't you know them Cochises ain't on the war-path? Them Injuns has been on their reservation for five years, peaceable, domesticated, and eating from the hand. This means trouble.'

" 'My old man didn't have no war paint on him one day back at Frisbee,' whispers 'Kink,' and his voice sounded puckered up and dried, 'and my mother wasn't so darned quarrelsome, either.'

" Then I says, 'Well! them bodies has got to be hid, or we'll have the tribe and the blue-bellies from the fort a scouring these hills till a red-bug couldn't hide.'

" 'To hell with 'em,' says 'Kink.' 'I've done all I'm going to for 'em. Let the coyotes finish the job.'

" 'No, siree,' I replies. 'I don't blame you for having a prejudice agin savages, but my parents is still robust and husky, and I have an idea that they'd rather see me back on the ranch than glaring through the bars for life. I'm going over to bury the meat.'

" Off I went, but when I slid down the gulch, I only found one body. T'other had disappeared. You can guess how much time I lost getting back to camp.

" ' " Kink," ' I says, 'we're a straddle of the raggedest proposition in this country. One of your dusters at this moment is jamming his cayuse through the horizon between here and the post. Pretty soon things is going to bust loose. 'Bout tomorrer evening we'll be eating hog-bosom on Uncle Sam.'

" ' Well ! Well ! ' says 'Kink,' ' ain't that a pity. Next time I'll conquer my natural shyness and hold a post-mortem with a rock.'

" ' There won't be no next time, I reckon,' I says, ' 'cause we can't make it over appeal to me. I may get raised out before the draw, but the percentage is just as strong agin your game as mine.'

" ' Boy, if I was backing your system,' says 'Kink,' 'I'd shore copper this move and play her to lose. You come on with me, and we'll make it through — mebbe.'

" ' No,' I says ; ' here I sticks.'

" I made up a pack-strap out of my extry overhalls while he got grub together, to start south through one hundred miles of the ruggedest and barrenest country that was ever left unfinished.

" Next noon I was parching some coffee-

"I JUMPED CLEAN OVER THE FIRE"

into Mexico without being caught up. They'll nail us sure, seeing as we're the only white men for twenty-five miles around.'

" ' I'd rather put up a good run than a bad stand, anyhow,' says he, ' and I allows, furthermore, there's going to be some hard trails to foller and a tolable disagreeable fight before I pleads "not guilty" to the Colonel. We'll both duck over into the Santa —— '

" ' Now, don't tell me what route you're going,' I interrupts, ' 'cause I believe I'll stay and bluff it through, rather than sneak for it, though neither proposition don't

beans in the frying-pan, when I heard hoofs down the gully back of me. I never looked up when they come into the open nor when I heard a feller say ' Halt !'

" ' Hello there !' somebody yells. ' You there at the fire.' I kept on shaking the skillet over the camp-fire.

" ' What's the matter with him ?' somebody said. A man got off and walked up behind me.

" ' See here, brother,' he says, tapping me on the shoulder ; 'this don't go.'

" I jumped clean over the fire, dropped the pan, and let out a deaf and dumb holler, ' Ee ! Ah !'

"'YES, SIR. . . . IT CAME BACK UNEXPECTED, REGULAR MIRACLE'"

"The men began to laugh; it seemed to rile the little leftenant.

"'Cut this out,' says he. 'You can talk as well as I can, and you're a going to tell us about this Injun killin'. Don't try any fake business, or I'll roast your little heels over that fire like yams.'

"I just acted the dummy, wiggled my fingers, and handed him the joyful gaze, heliographing with my teeth as though I was glad to see visitors. However, I wondered if that runt would really give my chilblains a treat. He looked like a West Pointer, and I didn't know but he'd try to haze me.

"Well! they 'klow-towed' around there for an hour looking for clues, but I'd hid all the signs of 'Kink,' so finally they strapped me onto a horse and we hit back for the fort.

"The little man tried all kinds of tricks to make me loosen on the way down, but I just acted wounded innocence and 'Ee'd' and 'Ah'd' at him till he let me alone.

"When we rode up to the post he says to the Colonel:

"'We've got the only man there is in the mountains back there, sir, but he's playing dumb. I don't know what his game is.'

"'Dumb, eh?' says the old man, looking me over pretty keen. 'Well! I guess we'll find his voice if he's got one.'

"He took me inside, and, speaking of examinations, probably I didn't get one. He kept looking at me like he wanted to place me, but I give him the 'Ee! Ah!' till everybody began to laugh. They tried me with a pencil and paper, but I balked, laid my ears back, and buck-jumped. That made the old man sore, and he says: 'Lock him up! Lock him up; I'll make him talk if I have to skin him.' So I was dragged to the 'skookum-house,' where I spent the night figuring out my finish.

"I could feel it coming just as plain, and I begun to see that when I did open up and prattle after 'Kink' was safe nobody wouldn't believe my little story. I had sized the Colonel up as a dead stringy old proposition, too. He was one of these big-chopped fellers with a mouth set more'n half way up from his chin and little thin lips like the edge of a knife blade, and just as full of blood — face, big and rustic-finished.

"I says to myself, 'Bud, it looks like you wouldn't be forced to prospect for a living any more this season. If that old sport turns himself loose you're going to get "life" three times and a holdover.'

"Next morning they tried every way to make me talk. Once in a while the old man looked at me puzzled and searching, but I didn't know him from a sweat-pad, and just paid strict attention to being dumb.

"It was mighty hard, too. I got so nervous my mouth simply ached to let out a cayoodle. The words kept trying to crawl through my æsophagus, and when I backed 'em up, they slid down and stood around in groups, hanging onto the straps, gradually filling me with witful gems of thought.

"The Colonel talked to me serious and quiet, like I had good ears, and says, 'My man, you can understand every word I say, I'm sure, and what your object is in maintaining this ridiculous silence, I don't know. You're accused of a crime, and it looks serious for you.'

"Then he gazes at me queer and intent, and says, 'If you only knew how bad you are making your case you'd make a clean breast of it. Come now, let's get at the truth.'

"Them thought jewels and wads of repartee was piling up in me fast, like tailings from a ground-sluice, till I could feel myself getting bloated and pussy with langwidge.

"But I thought, 'No! to-morrow "Kink" 'll be safe, and then I'll throw a jolt into this man's camp that'll go down in history. They'll think some Chinaman's been thawing out a box of giant powder when I let out my roar.'

"I goes to the guard-house again, with a soldier at my back. Everything would have been all right if we hadn't run into a mule team.

"They had been freighting from the railroad, and as we left the barracks we ran afoul of four outfits, three span to the wagon, with the loads piled on till the teams was all lather and the wheels complainin' to the gods, trying to pass the corner of the barracks where there was a narrow opening between the buildings.

"Now a good mule-driver is the littlest, orneriest speck in the human line that's known to the microscope, but when you get a poor one, he'd spoil one of them cholera germs you read about just by contact. The leader of this bunch was worse than the worst; strong on whip-arm, but surprising weak on judgment. He tried to make the turn, run plump into the corner

of the building, stopped, backed, swung, and proceeded to get into grief.

"The mules being hot and nervous, he sent them all to the loco patch instanter. They began to plunge and turn and back and snarl. Before you could say 'Craps! you lose,' them shave-tails was giving the grandest exhibition of animal idiocy in the Territory, barring the teamster. He follered their trail to the madhouse, yanking the mouths out of them, cruel and vicious.

"Now, one mule can cause a heap of tribulation, and six mules can break a man's heart, but there wasn't no excuse for that driver to stand upon his hind legs, close his eyes, and throw thirty foot of lash into that plungin', buckin', white-eyed mess. When he did it, all the little words inside of me began to foam and fizzle like sedlitz; out they came, biling, in mouthfuls, and streams, and squirts, backwards, sideways, and through my nose.

"'Here! you infernal half-spiled, dog-robbing walloper,' I says; 'you don't know enough to drive puddle ducks to a pond. You quit heaving that quirt or I'll harm you past healing.'

"He turned his head and grit out something through his teeth that stimulated my circulation. I skipped over the wheels and put my left onto his neck, fingering the keys on his blow-pipe like a flute. Then I give him a toss and gathered up the lines. Say! it was like the smell of grease-paint to an actor man for me to feel the ribbons again, and them mules knew they had a chair-man who savvied 'em too, and had mule talk pat, from soda to hock.

"I just intimated things over them with that whip, and talked to them like they was my own flesh and blood. I starts at the worst words the English langwidge and the range had produced, to date, and got steadily and rapidly worse as long as I talked.

"Arizony may be slow in the matter of standing collars and rag-time, but she leads the world in profanity. Without being swelled on myself, I'll say, too, that I once had more'n a local reputation in that line, having originated some quaint and feeling conceits which has won modest attention, and this day I was certainly trained to the minute.

"I addressed them brutes fast and earnest for five minutes steady, and never crossed my trail or repeated a thought.

"It must have been sacred and beautiful. Anyhow, it was strong enough to soak into their pores so that they strung out straight as a chalk-line. Then I lifted them into the collars, and we rumbled past the building, swung in front of the commissary door, cramped and stopped. With the wheelers on their haunches, I backed up to the door square as a die.

"I wiped the sweat out of my eyes and looked up into the grinning face of about fifty swatties, realizing I was a mute — and a prisoner.

"I heard a voice say, 'Bring me that man.' There stood the Colonel oozing out wrath at every pore.

"I parted from that wagon hesitating and reluctant, but two soldiers to each leg will bust any man's grip. I lost some clothes, too, after we hit the ground, but I needed the exercise.

"The old man was alone in his office when they dragged me in, and he sent my guards out.

"'So you found your voice, did you?' he says.

"'Yes, sir,' I answers. 'It came back unexpected, regular miracle.'

"He drummed on the table for a long time, and then says, sort of immaterial and irreverent, 'You're a pretty good mule puncher, eh?'

"'It ain't for me to say I'm the best in the Territory,' I says ; 'but I'm curious to meet the feller that claims the title.'

"He continues, 'It reminds me of an exhibition I saw once, back in New Mexico,

"I HATED TO SELL HIM"

long time ago, at the little Flatwater Canyon.'

"'Maybe you've heard tell of the fight there when the Apaches were up? Yes? Well, I happened to be in that scrimmage.'

"'I was detailed with ten men to convoy a wagon train through to Fort Lewis. We had no trouble till we came to the end of that canyon, just where she breaks out onto the flats. There we got it. They were hidden up on the ridges ; we lost two men and one wagon before we could get out onto the prairie.

"'I got touched up in the neck, first clatter, and was bleeding pretty badly; still I hung to my horse, and we stood 'em off till the teams made it out of the gulch ; but just as we came out my horse fell and threw me — broke his leg. I yelled to the boys :

"'"Go on ! For God's sake, go on !"' Any delay there meant loss of the whole outfit. Besides, the boys had more than they could manage, Injuns on three sides.

"'We had a young Texan driving the last wagon. When I went down he swung those six mules of his and came back up that trail into the gut, where the bullets snapped like grasshoppers.

"'It was the prettiest bit of driving I ever saw, not to mention nerve. He whirled the outfit between me and the bluff on two wheels, yelling, "Climb on ! Climb on ! We ain't going to stay long !" I was just able to make it onto the seat. In the turn they dropped one of his wheelers. He ran out on the tongue and cut the brute loose. We went rattling down the gulch behind five mules. All the time there came out of that man's lungs the fiercest stream of profanity my ears ever burned under. I was pretty sick for a few weeks, so I never got a chance to thank that teamster. He certainly knew the mind of an army mule, though. His name was — let me see — Wiggins — yes, Wiggins.'

"'Oh, no, it wasn't,' I breaks in, foolish ; 'it was Joyce.'

"Then I stopped and felt like a kid, for the Colonel comes up and shuts the circulation out of both my hands.

"'I wasn't sure of you, Bill,' he says, 'till I saw you preside over those mules out there and heard your speech — then I recognized the gift.' He laughed like a boy, still making free with my hands. 'I'm darn glad to see you, Bill Joyce. Now then,' he says, 'tell me all about this killing up in the hills,' and I done so.

"After I finished he never said anything for a long time, just drummed the desk again and looked thoughtful.

" 'It's too bad you didn't speak out, Bill, when you first came in. Now, you've showed everybody that you can talk — just a little, anyhow,' and he smiles, 'and they all think you're the man caused the trouble. I don't see but that you've got to stand trial. I wish I could help you, Bill.'

" 'But see here, Colonel,' I says; 'I couldn't squeal on "Kink." We're pardners. I just had to give him a chance to cut. I played dumb 'cause I knew if I talked at all, being simple and guileless, you all would twist me up and have the whole thing in a jiffy. That man give me the last drop of water in his canteen on the Mojave, and him with his own tongue swelled clean out of his mouth, too. When we was snowed in, up in the Bitter Roots, with me snow-blind and starving, he crawled from Sheeps-Horn clean to Miller's — snow twelve foot deep, too, and nary a snow-shoe in miles, but he brought the outfit in to where I was lyin' 'bout gone in. He lost some fingers and more toes wallering through them mountain drifts that day, but he never laid down till he brought the boys back.

" ' Colonel ! we've slept on the same blanket, we've et the same grub, we've made and lost together, and I *had* to give him a show, that's all. I'm into this here trouble now. Tell me how I'm going to get out. What would you do ?'

" He turns to the open window and says : ' Partners are partners ! That's my horse out there at that post. If I were you I'd run like hell.'

" That was the willingest horse I ever rode, and I hated to sell him, but he was tolable used up when I got across the line."

7

The Fight at Buckskin

CLARENCE EDWARD MULFORD

Hopalong takes command.

THE
OUTING
MAGAZINE

DECEMBER, 1905

THE FIGHT AT BUCKSKIN

By CLARENCE EDWARD MULFORD

ILLUSTRATED   BY F. E. SCHOONOVER

BUCKSKIN was a town of one hundred inhabitants. The census claimed two hundred, but it was a well-known fact that it was exaggerated. One instance of this is shown at the name of Tom Flynn. Those who once knew Tom Flynn, alias Johnny Redmond, alias Bill Sweeney, alias Chuck Mullen, by all four names, could find them in the census list. Furthermore, he had been shot and killed in the March of the year preceding the census, and now occupied a grave in the young but flourishing cemetery. Perry's Bend, twenty miles up the river, was cognizant of this and other facts, and, laughing in open derision at the padded list, claimed to be the better town in all ways, including marksmanship.

One year before this tale opens, Buck Peters, an example for the more recent Billy the Kid, had paid Perry's Bend a short but busy visit. He had ridden in at the north end of Main Street and out at the south. As he came in, he was fired at by a group of ugly cowboys from a ranch known as the C 80. He was hit twice, but he unlimbered his artillery and before his horse had carried him, half dead, out on the prairie, he had killed four of the group. Several citizens had joined the cowboys and added their bullets against Buck. Two of these were dead. One had been the best bartender in the county, and the rage of the suffering citizens can well be imagined. They swore vengeance on Buck, his ranch, and his stamping-ground, Buckskin.

The difference between Buck and Billy the Kid is that the former never shot a man who wasn't trying to shoot him or who hadn't been warned by some action against Buck that would call for it. He minded his own business and never picked a quarrel, but a list of the men he had assisted over the Great Divide is too long to appear here. He was quiet and pacific up to a certain point. After that had been passed he became a raging cyclone in a tenement house and storm-cellars were much in demand.

"Fanning" is the name of a certain style of gun-play and was universal among the bad-men of the West. While Buck was not a bad-man he had to rub elbows with them frequently and he believed that the sauce for the goose was the sauce for the gander. So he had removed the trigger of his revolver and worked the hammer with the thumb of the "gun-hand" or the thumb of the unencumbered hand. The speed thus acquired was greater than that of the more modern double-action weapon. Six shots in three seconds was his average speed when that number were required, and when it is thoroughly understood that at least five of them found their intended billets it is not difficult to realize that fanning was an operation of danger when Buck was doing it.

He was a good rider, as all cowboys are, and was not afraid of anything that lived. At one time he and his chums, Red Connors and Hopalong Cassidy, had successfully routed a band of fifteen Apaches who wanted their scalps. Of these, twelve never hunted scalps again nor anything else on this earth, and the other three returned to their tribe with the report that three evil-spirits had chased them with "wheel-guns" (cannons).

So now, since his visit to Perry's Bend the rivalry of the two towns had turned to hatred and an alert and eager readiness to increase the inhabitants of each other's graveyard. A state of war existed which for a time resulted in nothing worse than acrimonious suggestions. But the time came when the score was settled to the satisfaction of one side, at least.

Four ranches were also concerned in the trouble. Buckskin was surrounded by two, the Bar 20 and the Three Triangle. Perry's Bend was the common point for the C 80 and the Double Arrow. Each of the two ranch contingents accepted the feud as a matter of course, and as a matter of course took sides with their respective towns. As no better class of fighters ever lived, the trouble assumed Homeric proportions and insured a danger zone well worth watching.

Bar 20's northern line was C 80's southern one, and Skinny Thompson took his turn at out-riding one morning after the season's round-up. He was to follow the boundary and turn back stray cattle. When he had covered the greater part of his journey he saw Shorty Jones riding toward him on a course parallel to his own and about long revolver range away. Shorty and he had "crossed trails" the year before and the best of feelings did not exist between them.

Shorty stopped and stared at Skinny, who did likewise at Shorty. Shorty turned his mount around and applied the spurs, thereby causing his indignant horse to raise both heels at Skinny. The latter took it all in gravely and, as Shorty faced him again, placed his left thumb to his nose, wiggling his fingers suggestively. Shorty took no apparent notice of this but began to shout:

"Yu wants to keep yore busted-down cows on yore own side. They was all over us day afore yesterday. I'm goin' to salt any more what comes over, an' don't yu fergit it, neither."

Thompson wig-wagged with his fingers again and shouted in reply: "Yu' c'n salt all yu wants to, but if I ketch yu adoin' it yu won't have to work no more. An' I kin say right here thet they's more C 80 cows over here than they's Bar 20's over there."

Shorty reached for his revolver and yelled, "Yore a liar!"

Among the cowboys in particular and the Westerners in general at that time, the three suicidal terms, unless one was an expert in drawing quick and shooting straight with one movement, were the words "liar," "coward," and "thief." Any man who was called one of these in earnest, and he was the judge, was expected to shoot if he could and save his life, for the words were seldom used without a gun coming with them. The movement of Shorty's hand toward his belt before the appellation reached him was enough for Skinny, who let go at long range—and missed.

The two reports were as one. Both urged their horses nearer and fired again. This time Skinny's sombrero gave a sharp jerk and a hole appeared in the crown. The third shot of Skinny's sent the horse of the other to its knees and then over on its side. Shorty very promptly crawled behind it and, as he did so, Skinny began a wide circle, firing at intervals as Shorty's smoke cleared away.

Shorty had the best position for defense as he was in a shallow coulée, but he knew that he could not leave it until his opponent had either grown tired of the affair or had used up his ammunition. Skinny knew it, too. Skinny also knew that he could get back to the ranch-house and lay in a supply of food and ammunition and return before Shorty could cover the twelve miles he had to go on foot.

Finally Thompson began to head for home. He had carried the matter as far as he could without it being murder. Too much time had elapsed now, and, besides, it was before breakfast and he was hungry. He would go away and settle the score at some time when they would be on equal terms.

He rode along the line for a mile and chanced to look back. Two C 80 punchers were riding after him, and, as they saw him turn and discover them, they fired at him and yelled. He rode on for some distance and cautiously drew his rifle out of its long holster at his right leg. Suddenly he turned around in the saddle and fired twice. One of his pursuers fell forward on the neck of his horse, and his comrade turned to help him. Thompson wigwagged again and rode on. He reached the ranch as the others were finishing their breakfast.

At the table Red Connors remarked that the tardy one had a hole in his sombrero, and asked its owner how and where he had received it.

"Had a argument with C 80 out'n th' line."

"Go 'way! Ventilate enny?"

"One."

"Good boy, sonny! Hey, Hopalong, Skinny perforated C 80 this mawnin'!"

Hopalong Cassidy was struggling with a mouthful of beef. He turned his eyes toward Red without ceasing, and grinning as well as he could under the circumstances managed to grunt out "Gu—," which was as near to "Good" as the beef would allow.

Lanky Smith now chimed in as he repeatedly stuck his knife into a reluctant boiled potato, "How'd yu do it, Skinny?"

"Bet he sneaked up on him," joshed Buck Peters; "did yu ask his pardin, Skinny?"

"Ask nothin'," remarked Red, "he jest nachurly walks up to C 80 an' sez, 'Kin I have the pleasure of ventilatin' yu?' an' C 80 he sez, 'If yu do it easy like,' sez he. Didn't he, Thompson?"

"They'll be some ventilatin' under th' table if yu fellows don't lemme alone; I'm hungry," complained Skinny.

"Say, Hopalong, I bets yu I kin clean up C 80 all by my lonesome," announced Buck, winking at Red.

"Yah! Yu onct tried to clean up the Bend, Buckie, an' if Pete an' Billy hadn't afound yu when they come by Eagle Pass that night, yu wouldn't be here eatin' beef by th' pound," glancing at the hard-working Hopalong. "It wuz plum' lucky fer yu that they wuz acourtin' that time, wasn't it, Hopalong?" suddenly asked Red. Hopalong nearly strangled in his efforts to speak. He gave it up and nodded his head.

"Why cayn't yu git it straight, Connors? I wasn't doin' no courtin', it was Pete. I runned into him on th' other side o' th' pass. I'd look fine acourtin', wouldn't I?" asked the downtrodden Williams.

Pete Wilson skillfully flipped a potato into that worthy's coffee, spilling the beverage of the questionable name over a large expanse of blue flannel shirt. "Yu's all right, yu are. Why, when I meets yu, yu was lost in th' arms of yore lady-love. All I could see was yore feet. Go an' git tangled up with a two hundred and forty pound half-breed squaw an' then try to lay it onter me! When I proposed drownin' yore troubles over at Cowan's, yu went an' got mad over what yu called th' insinooation. An' yu shore didn't look enny too blamed fine, neither."

"All th' same," volunteered Thompson, who had taken the edge from his appetite, "we better go over an' pay C 80 a call. I don't like what Shorty said about saltin' our cattle. He'll shore do it, unless I camps on th' line, which same I ain't hankerin' after."

"Oh, he wouldn't stop th' cows that way, Skinny; he wuz only afoolin'," exclaimed Connors meekly.

"Foolin' yore gran'mother! That there bunch'll do ennything if we wasn't lookin'," hotly replied Skinny.

"That's shore nuff gospel, Thomp. They's sore fer mor'n one thing. They lost two of their most promising members when Buck went on th' war-path, an' they's hankerin' to git square," remarked Johnny Nelson, stealing the pie, a rare treat, of his neighbor when that unfortunate individual was not looking. He had it half-way to his mouth when its former owner, Jimmy Price, a boy of eighteen, turned his head and saw it going.

"Hi-yi! Yu clay-bank coyote, drap thet pie! Did yu ever see such a son-of-a-gun fer pie?" he plaintively asked Red Connors as he grabbed a mighty handful of apples and crust. "Pie 'll kill yu some day, yu bob-tailed jack! I had an uncle that died onct. He et too much pie an' he went an' turned green, an' so 'll yu if yu don't let it alone."

"Yu ought'r seed th' pie Johnny had down in Eagle Flat," murmured Lanky Smith reminiscently. "She had feet that 'd stop a stam*pede*. Johnny wuz shore loco about her. Swore she wuz th' finest blossom what ever growed." Here he choked and tears of laughter coursed down his weather-beaten face as he pictured her. "She wuz a dainty Greaser about fifteen han's high an' about sixteen han's around. Johnny used to chalk off when he hugged her, usen't yu, Johnny? One night when he had got purty well around on th' second lap he run inter a Greaser jest startin' out on his fust. They hain't caught that Mexican yet."

Nelson was pelted with everything in sight. He slowly wiped off the pie-crust and bread and potatoes. "Enny-body 'd think I wuz a busted grub-wagon," he grumbled. When he had fished the last piece of beef out of his ear he went out and offered to stand treat. As the round-up was over, they slid into their saddles and raced for Cowan's saloon at Buckskin.

Buckskin was very hot, in fact, it was never anything else. Few people were on the streets and the town was quiet. Over in the Houston Hotel a crowd of cowboys were lounging in the bar-room. They were very quiet—a condition as rare as it was ominous. Their mounts, twelve in all, were switching flies from their quivering skins in the corral at the rear. Eight of these had a large C 80 branded on their flanks; the other four, a Double Arrow.

In the bar-room a slim, wiry man was looking out of the dirty window up the street at Cowan's saloon. Shorty was complaining, "They shore oughter be here now. They rounded up last week." The man nearest assured him that they would come. The man at the window turned and said, "They's yer now."

In front of Cowan's a crowd of nine happy-go-lucky, dare-devil riders were sliding from their saddles. They threw the reins over the heads of their mounts and filed in to the bar. Laughter issued from the open door and the clink of glasses could be heard. They stood in picturesque groups, strong, self-reliant, humorous, virile. Their expensive sombreros were pushed far back on their heads, and their hairy chaps were covered with the alkali dust from their ride.

Cowan, bottle in hand, pushed out several more glasses. He kicked a dog from under his feet and looked at Buck. "Rounded up yet?" he inquired.

"Shore, day afore yisterday," came the reply. The rest were busy removing the dust from their throats, and gradually drifted into groups of two or three. One of these groups strolled over to the solitary card table, and found Jimmy Price resting in a cheap chair, his legs on the table.

"I wisht yu'd extricate yore delicate feet from off'n this hyar table, James," humbly requested Lanky Smith, morally backed up by those with him.

"Ya-as, they shore is delicate, Mr. Smith," responded Jimmy without moving.

"We wants to play draw, Jimmy," explained Pete.

"Yore shore welcome to play if yu wants to. Didn't I tell yu when yu growed that mustache that yu didn't have to ask me enny more?" queried the placid James, paternally.

"Call 'em off, Sonny. Pete sez he kin clean me out. Ennyhow, yu kin have th' fust deàl," compromised Lanky.

"I'm shore sorry fer Pete if he cayn't. Yu don't reckon I has to have fust deal to beat yu fellers, do yu? Go way an' lemme alone; I never seed such a bunch fer buttin' in as yu fellers."

Billy Williams returned to the bar. Then he walked along it until he was behind the recalcitrant possessor of the table. While his aggrieved friends shuffled their feet uneasily to cover his approach, he, tip-toed up behind Jimmy, and, with a nod, grasped that indignant individual firmly by the neck while the others grabbed his feet. They carried him, twisting and bucking, to the middle of the street and deposited him in the dust, returning to the now vacant table.

Jimmy rested quietly for a few seconds and then slowly arose, dusting the alkali from him. "Th' wall-eyed piruts," he muttered, and then scratched his head for a way to "play hunk." As he gazed sorrowfully at the saloon he heard a snicker from behind him. He, thinking it was one of his late tormentors, paid no attention to it. Then a cynical, biting laugh stung him. He wheeled to see Shorty leaning against a tree, a sneering leer on his flushed face. Shorty's right hand was suspended above his holster, hooked to his belt by the thumb—a favorite position of his when expecting trouble.

"One of yore reg'lar habits?" he drawled.

Jimmy began to dust himself in silence, but his lips were compressed to a thin white line.

"Does they hurt yu?" pursued the onlooker.

Jimmy looked up. "I heard tell that they make glue outen cayuses, sometimes," he remarked. Shorty's eyes flashed. The loss of the horse had been rankling in his heart all day.

"Does they git yu frequent?" he asked. His voice sounded hard.

"Oh, 'bout as frequent as yu lose a cayuse, I reckon," replied Jimmy hotly.

Shorty's hand streaked to his holster and Jimmy followed his lead. Jimmy's Colt was caught. He had bucked too much. As he fell Shorty ran for the Houston House.

Pistol shots were common for they were the universal method of expressing emotions. The poker players grinned, thinking their victim was letting off his indignation. Lanky sized up his hand and remarked half audibly, "He's a shore good kid."

The bartender, fearing for his new beveled, gilt-framed mirror, gave a hasty glance out the window. He turned around, made change, and remarked to Buck, "Yore kid, Jimmy, is plugged." Several of the more credulous craned their necks to see, Buck being the first. "H—l!" he shouted, and ran out to where Jimmy lay coughing, his toes twitching. The saloon was deserted and a crowd of angry cowboys surrounded their chum—a boy. Buck had seen Shorty enter the door of the Houston House and he swore. "Chase them —— —— cayuses behind th' saloon, Pete, an' git under cover."

Jimmy was choking and he coughed up blood. "He's shore—got me. My—gun stuck," he added apologetically. He tried

to sit up, but was not able and he looked surprised. "It's purty—damn hot—out here," he suggested. Johnny and Billy carried him in the saloon and placed him by the table, in the chair he had previously vacated. As they stood up he fell across the table and died.

Billy placed the dead boy's sombrero on his head and laid the refractory six-shooter on the table. "I wonder who th' —— —— was." He looked at the slim figure and started to go out, followed by Johnny. As he reached the threshold a bullet zipped past him and thudded into the frame of the door. He backed away and looked surprised. "That's Shorty's shootin'—he allus misses 'bout that much." He looked out and saw Buck standing behind the live-oak that Shorty had leaned against, firing at the hotel. Turning around, he made for the rear, remarking to Johnny that "they's in th' Houston." Johnny looked at the quiet figure in the chair and swore softly. He followed Billy. Cowan, closing the door and taking a .70 caliber buffalo gun from under the bar, went out also and slammed the rear door forcibly.

Up the street two hundred yards from the Houston House Skinny and Pete lay hidden behind a bowlder. Three hundred yards on the other side of the hotel Johnny and Billy were stretched out in an arroyo. Buck was lying down now, and Hopalong, from his position in the barn belonging to the Hotel, was methodically dropping the horses of the besieged, a job he hated as much as he hated poison. The corral was their death trap. Red and Lanky were emitting clouds of smoke from behind the store, immediately across the street from the bar-room. A .70 caliber buffalo gun roared down by the plaza, and several Sharps cracked a protest from different points. The town had awakened and the shots were dropping steadily.

Strange noises filled the air. They grew in tone and volume and then dwindled away to nothing. The hum of the buffalo gun and the sobbing *pi-in-in-ing* of the Winchesters were liberally mixed with the sharp whines of the revolvers.

There were no windows in the hotel now. Raw furrows in the bleached wood showed yellow, and splinters mysteriously sprang from the casings. The panels of the door were producing cracks and the cheap door handle flew many ways at once. An empty whiskey keg on the stoop boomed out mournfully at intervals and finally rolled down the steps with a rumbling protest. Wisps of smoke slowly climbed up the walls and seemed to be waving defiance to the curling wisps in the open.

Pete raised his shoulder to refill the magazine of his smoking rifle and dropped the cartridges all over his lap. He looked sheepishly at Skinny and began to load with his other hand.

"Yore plum' loco, yu air. Don't yu reckon they kin hit a blue shirt at two hundred?" Skinny cynically inquired. "Got one that time," he announced a second later.

"I wonder who's got th' buffalo," grunted Pete. "Mus' be Cowan," he replied to his own question and settled himself to use his left hand.

"Don't yu git Shorty, he's my meat," suggested Skinny.

"Yu better tell Buck—he ain't got no love fer Shorty," replied Pete, aiming carefully.

The panic in the corral ceased and Hopalong was now sending his regrets against the panels of the rear door. He had cut his last initial in the near panel and was starting a wobbly "H" in its neighbor. He was in a good position. There were no windows in the rear wall and, as the door was a very dangerous place, he was not fired at.

He began to get tired of this one-sided business and crawled up on the window ledge, dangling his feet on the outside. He occasionally sent a bullet at a different part of the door, but amused himself by annoying Buck.

"Plenty hot down there?" he pleasantly inquired, and, as he received no answer, he tried again. "Better save some of them catridges fer some other time, Buck."

Buck was sending .45 Winchesters into the shattered window with a precision that presaged evil to any of the defenders who were rash enough to try to gain the other end of the room.

Hopalong bit off a chew of tobacco and drowned a green fly that was crawling up the side of the barn. The yellow liquid streaked downward a short distance and was eagerly sucked up by the warped boards.

A spurt of smoke leaped from the battered door and the bored Hopalong promptly tumbled back inside. He felt of his arm, and then, delighted at the notice taken of his artistic efforts, shot several times from a crack on his right. "This yer's shore gittin' like home," he gravely remarked to the splinter that whizzed past his head. He shot again at the door and it sagged outward accompanied by the thud of a falling body. "Pies like mother used to make," he announced to the empty loft as he slipped the magazine full of .45's. "An' pills like popper used to take," he continued when he had lowered the level of the liquor in his flask.

He rolled a cigarette and tossed the match into the air, extinguishing it by a shot from his "fanner."

"Got enny cigarettes, Hoppy?" said a voice from below.

"Shore," replied the joyous puncher, recognizing Pete; "how'd yu git hyar?"

"Like a cow. Busy?"

"None whatever. Comin' up?"

"Nope. Skinny wants a smoke too."

Hopalong handed tobacco and papers down the hole. "So long."

"So long," replied the daring Pete, who risked death twice for a smoke.

The hot afternoon dragged along and about three o'clock Buck held up an empty cartridge belt to the gaze of the curious Hopalong. That observant worthy nodded and threw a double handful of cartridges, one by one, to the patient and unrelenting Buck, who filled his gun and piled the few remaining ones up at his side. "Th' lives of mice and men gang aft all wrong," he remarked at random.

"Th' son-of-a-gun's talkin' Shakespeare," marveled Hopalong.

"Satiate enny, Buck?" he asked as that worthy settled down to await his chance.

"Two," he replied, "Shorty an' another. Plenty damn hot down here," he complained. A spurt of alkali dust stung his face, but the hand that made it never made another. "Three," he called. "How many, Hoppy?"

"One. That's four. Wonder if th' others got enny?"

"Pete said Skinny got one," replied the intent Buck.

"Th' son-of-a-gun, he never said nothin'

about it, an' me a fillin' his ornery paws with smokin'." Hopalong was indignant.

"Bet yu ten we don't git 'em afore dark," he announced.

"Got yu. Go yu ten more I gits another," promptly responded Buck.

"That's a shore cinch. Make her twenty."

"She is."

"Yu'll have to square it with Skinny, he shore wanted Shorty plum' bad," Hopalong informed the unerring marksman.

"Why didn't he say suthin' about it? Anyhow, Jimmy was my bunkie."

Hopalong's cigarette disintegrated and the board at his left received a hole. He promptly disappeared and Buck laughed. He sat up in the hay and angrily spat the soaked paper out from between his lips.

"All that trouble fer nothin', th' white-eyed coyote," he muttered. Then he crawled around to one side and fired at the center of his "C." Another shot hurtled at him and his left arm fell to his side. "That's funny—wonder where th' damn pirut is?" He looked out cautiously and saw a cloud of smoke over a knothole which was situated close up under the eaves of the bar-room; and it was being agitated. Some one was blowing at it to make it disappear. He aimed very carefully at the knot and fired. He heard a sound between a curse and a squawk and was not molested any further from that point.

"I knowed he'd git hurt," he explained to the bandage, torn from the edge of his kerchief, that he bound around his last wound.

Down in the arroyo Johnny was complaining.

"This yer's a no good bunk," he plaintively remarked.

"It shore ain't—but it's th' best we kin find," apologized Billy.

"That's th' sixth that feller sent up there. He's a damn poor shot," observed Johnny; "must be Shorty."

"Shorty kin shoot plum' good—tain't him," contradicted Billy.

"Yas—with a six-shooter. He's off'n his feed with a rifle," explained Johnny.

"Yu wants to stay down from up there, yu ijit," warned Billy as the disgusted Johnny crawled up the bank. He slid down again with a welt on his neck.

"That's somebody else now. He oughter a done better'n that," he said.

Billy had fired as Johnny started to slide and he smoothed his aggrieved chum. "He could onct, yu means."

"Did yu git him?" asked the anxious Johnny, rubbing his welt.

"Plum' center," responded the business-like Billy. "Go up agin, mebby I kin git another," he suggested, tentatively.

"Mebby yu kin go to h—l. I ain't no gallery," grinned the now exuberant owner of the welt.

"Who's got th' buffalo?" he inquired as the .70 caliber roared.

"Mus' be Cowan. He's shore all right. Sounds like a bloomin' cannon," replied Billy. "Lemme alone with yore fool questions, I'm busy," he complained as his talkative partner started to ask another. "Go an' git me some water—I'm alkalied. An' git some .45's, mine's purty near gone."

Johnny crawled down the arroyo and reappeared at Hopalong's barn.

As he entered the door a handful of empty shells fell on his hat and dropped to the floor. He shook his head and remarked, "That mus' be that fool Hopalong."

"Yore shore right. How's business?" inquired the festive Cassidy.

"Purty fair. Billy's got one. How many's gone?"

"Buck's got three, I got two an' Skinny's got one. That's six, an' Billy's is seven. They's five more," he replied.

"How'd yu know?" queried Johnny as he filled his flask at the horse trough.

"They's twelve cayuses behind th' hotel."

"They might git away on 'em," suggested the practical Johnny.

"Cayn't. They's all cashed in."

"Yu said that they's five left," ejaculated the puzzled water-carrier.

"Yah, yore a smart cuss, ain't yu?"

Johnny grinned and then said, "Got enny smokin'?"

Hopalong looked grieved. "I ain't no store. Why don't yu git generous an' buy some?"

He partially filled Johnny's hand, and as he put the sadly depleted bag away he inquired, "Got enny papers?"

"Nope."

"Got enny matches?" he asked, cynically.

"Nope."

"Kin yu smoke 'em?" he yelled, indignantly.

"Shore nuff," placidly replied the unruffled Johnny. "Billy wants some .45's."

Hopalong gasped. "Don't he want my gun, too?"

"Nope. Got a better one. Hurry up, he'll git mad."

Hopalong was a very methodical person. He was the only one of his crowd to carry a second cartridge strap. It hung over his right shoulder and rested on his left hip, holding one hundred cartridges and his second Colt. His waist belt held fifty cartridges and all would fit both the rifle and revolvers. He extracted twenty from that part of the shoulder strap hardest to get at, the back, by simply pulling it over his shoulder and plucking out the bullets as they came into reach.

"That's all yu kin have. I'm *Buck's* ammernition jackass," he explained. "Bet yu ten we gits 'em afore dark"—he was hedging.

"Enny fool knows that. I'll take yu if yu bets the other way," responded Johnny, grinning. He knew Hopalong's weak spot.

"Yore on," promptly responded Hopalong, who would bet on anything.

"Well, so long," said Johnny as he crawled away.

"Hey, yu, Johnny!" called out Hopalong, "don't yu go an' tell ennybody I got enny pills left. I ain't no ars'nal."

Johnny replied by elevating one foot and waving it. Then he disappeared.

Behind the store, the most precarious position among the besiegers, Red Connors and Lanky Smith were ensconced and commanded a view of the entire length of the bar-room. They could see the dark mass they knew to be the rear door and derived a great amount of amusement from the spots of light that were appearing in it. They watched the "C" (reversed to them) appear and be completed. When the wobbly "H" grew to completion they laughed heartily. Then the hardwood bar had been dragged across their field of vision and up to the front windows, and they could only see the indiscriminate holes that appeared in the upper panels at frequent intervals.

Every time they fired they had to expose a part of themselves to a return shot, with the result that Lanky's ear and cheek showed furrows and blood, while his forearm was seared its entire length. Red had been more fortunate and only had a hole through his ear. The butt of his gun was marred and he had a piece of lead in his jaw.

They laboriously rolled several large rocks out in the open, pushing them beyond the shelter of the store with their rifles. When they had crawled behind them they each had another wound. From their new position they could see Hopalong sitting in his window. He promptly waved his sombrero and grinned.

They were the most experienced fighters of all except Buck, and were saving their shots. When they did shoot they always had some portion of a man's body to aim at, and the damage they inflicted was considerable. They said nothing, being older than the rest and more taciturn, and they were not reckless. Although Hopalong's antics made them laugh, they grumbled at his recklessness and were not tempted to emulate him. It was noticeable, too, that they shoved their rifles out simultaneously, and, although both were aiming, only one fired.

Lanky's gun cracked so close to the enemy's that the whirl of the bullet over Red's head was merged in the crack of his partner's reply. The portion of a face that for one bare second showed above the bar disappeared and they knew that Lanky had got his man.

When Hopalong saw the rocks roll out from behind the store he grew very curious. Then he saw a flash, followed instantly by another from the second rifle. He saw several of these follow shots and could sit in silence no longer. He waved his hat to attract attention and then shouted "How many?" A shot was sent straight up in the air and he notified Buck that there were only four left.

The fire of these four grew less rapid— they were saving their ammunition. A pot shot at Hopalong sent that gentleman's rifle hurtling to the ground. Another tore through his hat, removing a neat amount of skin and hair and giving him a life-long part. He fell back inside and proceeded to shoot fast and straight with his revolvers, his head burning as though on fire.

"Shorty had the best position for defense."

From a painting by Frank E. Schoonover.

When he had vented the dangerous pressure of his anger he went below and tried to fish the rifle in with a long stick. It was obdurate, so he sent three more shots into the door, and, receiving no reply, ran out around the corner of his shelter and grasped the weapon. When half way back he sank to the ground. Before another shot could be fired at him with any judgment, a ripping, spitting rifle was being frantically worked from the barn. The bullets tore the door into seams and gaps; the lowest panel, the one having the "H" in it, fell inward in chunks. Johnny had returned for another smoke.

Hopalong, still grasping the rifle, rolled rapidly around the corner of the barn. He endeavored to stand, but could not. He had been shot in the muscles of his right thigh. Johnny, hearing rapid and fluent swearing, came out.

"Where'd they git yu?" he asked.

"In th' off leg. Hurts like h—l. Did yu git him?"

"Nope. I jest come fer another cig; got enny left?"

"Up above. Yore gall is shore appallin'. Help me in, yu two-laigged jackass."

"Shore. We'll shore pay our 'tentions to that door. She'll go purty soon—she's as full of holes as th' bad lan's," replied Johnny. "Git aholt an' hop along, Hopalong."

He helped the swearing Hopalong inside, and then the lead they pumped into the wrecked door was scandalous. Another panel fell in and Hopalong's "C" was destroyed. A wide crack appeared in the one above it and grew rapidly. Its mate began to gape and finally both were driven in. The increase in the light caused by these openings allowed Red and Lanky to secure better aim and soon the fire of the defenders died out.

Johnny dropped his rifle and, drawing his six-shooter, ran out and dashed for the dilapidated door, while Hopalong covered that opening with a fusilade.

As Johnny's shoulder sent the framework flying inward he narrowly missed sudden death. As it was he staggered to the side, out of range, and dropped full length to the ground, flat on his face. Hopalong's rifle cracked incessantly, but to no avail. The man who had fired the shot was dead. Buck got him immediately after he had shot Johnny.

Calling to Skinny and Red to cover him, Buck sprinted to where Johnny lay gasping. The bullet had entered his breast, just missed his lungs, and had passed out his back. Buck, Colt in hand, leaped through the door, but met with no resistance. He signaled to Hopalong, who yelled, "They's none left."

The trees and rocks and gulleys and buildings yielded men who soon crowded around the hotel. A young doctor, lately graduated, appeared. It was his first case, but he eased Johnny and saved his life. Then he went over to Hopalong, who was now raving, and attended to him. The others were patched up and the struggling young physician had his pockets crammed full of gold and silver coins.

The scene of the wrecked bar-room was indescribable. Holes, furrows, shattered glass and bottles, the liquor oozing down the walls of the shelves and running over the floor; the ruined furniture, a wrecked bar, seared and shattered and covered with blood; bodies as they had been piled in the corners; ropes, shells, hats; and liquor everywhere, over everything, met the gaze of those who had caused the chaos.

Perry's Bend had failed to wipe out the score.

8

The Vagrant Sioux

CLARENCE EDWARD MULFORD

BAR 20 RANGE YARNS

II.—THE VAGRANT SIOUX

BY CLARENCE EDWARD MULFORD

PAINTING BY FRANK E. SCHOONOVER

I

THE town lay sprawled over half a square mile of alkali plain, its main street depressing in its width, for those who were responsible for its inception had worked with a generosity born of the knowledge that they had at their immediate and unchallenged disposal the broad lands of Texas and New Mexico, on which to assemble a grand total of twenty buildings, four of which were of wood. As this material was scarce and had to be brought from where the waters of the Gulf lapped against the flat coast, the last-mentioned buildings were a matter of local pride as indicating the progressiveness of their owners. These creations of hammer and saw were of one story, crude and unpainted; their cheap weather-sheathing, warped and shrunken by the pitiless sun, curled back on itself and allowed unrestricted entrance to alkali dust and air. The other shacks were of adobe, and reposed in that magnificent squalor dear to their owners, Indians and "Greasers."

Such was the town of Buckskin, located in the valley of the Rio Pecos, fifty miles south of the Texas-New Mexico line. It was an incident of the Cattle Trail, that most unique and stupendous of all modern migrations, and its founders must have been inspired with a malicious desire to perpetrate a crime against geography, or else they reveled in a perverse cussedness, for within a mile on every side lay broad prairies, and two miles to the east flowed the indolent waters of the Rio Pecos itself. The distance separating the town from the river was excusable, for at certain seasons of the year the placid stream swelled mightily and swept down in a broad expanse of turbulent, yellow flood.

On the afternoon of one August day the town seemed desolated, and the earth and the buildings thereon were as huge furnaces radiating a visible heat; but when the blazing sun had begun to settle in the west, it awoke with a clamor that might have been laid to the efforts of a zealous Satan. At this time it became the Mecca of two-score or more joyous cowboys from the neighboring ranches, who livened things as those knights of the saddle could.

In the scant but heavy shadow of Cowan's saloon sat a picturesque figure, from whom came guttural, resonant rumblings which mingled in a spirit of loneliness with the fretful sighs of a flea-tormented dog. Both dog and master were vagrants, and they were tolerated because it was a matter of supreme indifference as to who came or how long they stayed, as long as the ethics and the unwritten law of the cow country were inviolate. And the breaking of these caused no unnecessary anxiety, for justice was both speedy and sure.

When the outcast Sioux and his yellow dog had drifted into town some few months before, they had caused neither expostulation nor inquiry, as the cardinal virtue of that whole broad land was to ask a man no questions which might prove embarrassing to all concerned; judgment was of observation, not of history, and a man's past would reveal itself through his actions.

It mattered little whether he was an embezzler or the wild chip from some prosperous eastern block, as men came to the range to forget and to lose touch with the pampered East; and the range absorbed them as its own. A man was only a man as his skin contained the qualities necessary; and the illiterate who could ride and shoot and live to himself was far more esteemed than the educated who could not do those things. The more a man depends upon himself and the closer is his contact to a quick judgment, the more laconic and even-poised he becomes. And the knowledge that he is himself a judge, tends to create caution and judgment. He has no court to uphold his honor and to offer him protection, so he must be quick to protect himself and to maintain his own standing. His nature saved him, or it executed; and the range absolved him of all unpaid penalties of a careless past. He became a man born again and he took up his burden, the exactions of a new environment, and he lived as long as those exactions gave him the right to live. He must tolerate no restrictions of his natural rights, and he must not restrict; for the one would proclaim him a coward; the other, a bully; and both received short shifts in that land of the self-protected. The basic law of nature is, the survival of the fittest.

So, when the wanderers found their level in Buckskin, they were not even asked by what name men knew them. Not caring to hear a name which might not harmonize with their idea of the fitness of things, the cowboys of the Bar 20 had, with a freedom born of excellent livers and fearless temperaments, bestowed names befitting their sense of humor and adaptability. The official title of the Sioux was By-and-by; the dog was known as Fleas. Never had names more clearly described the objects to be represented, for they were excellent examples of cowboy discernment and aptitude.

In their eyes By-and-by was a man. He could feel and he could resent insults. They did not class him as one of themselves because he did not have energy enough to demand and justify such classification. With them he had a right to enjoy his life as he saw fit, so long as he did not trespass on or restrict the rights of others. They

were not analytic in temperament, neither were they moralists. He was not a menace to society, because society had superb defenses. So they vaguely recognized his many poor qualities and clearly saw his few good ones. He could shoot, when permitted, with the best; no horse, however refractory, had ever been known to throw him; he was an adept at following the trails left by rustlers, and that was an asset; he became of value to the community; he was an economic factor. His ability to consume liquor with indifferent effects raised him another notch in their estimation. He was not always talking when some one else wished to—another count. There remained about him that stoical indifference to the petty; that observant nonchalance of the Indian; and there was a suggestion, faint, it was true, of a dignity common to chieftains. He was a log of grave deference that tossed on their sea of mischievous hilarity.

He wore a pair of corduroy trousers, known to the care-free as "pants," which were held together by numerous patches of what had once been brilliantly colored calico. A pair of suspenders, torn into two separate straps, made a belt for himself and a collar for his dog. The trousers had probably been secured during a fit of absent-mindedness on his part when their former owner had not been looking. Tucked at intervals in the top of the corduroys (the exceptions making convenient shelves for alkali dust) was what at one time had been a stiff-bosomed shirt. This was open down the front and back, the weight of the trousers on the belt holding it firmly on the square shoulders of the wearer, thus precluding the necessity of collar buttons. A pair of moccasins, beautifully worked with wampum, protected his feet from the onslaughts of cacti and the inquisitive and pugnacious sand-flies; and lying across his lap was a repeating Winchester rifle, not dangerous because it was empty, a condition due to the wisdom of the citizens in forbidding any one to sell, trade or give to him those tubes of concentrated trouble, because he *could* get drunk.

The two were contented and happy. They had no cares nor duties, and their pleasures were simple and easily secured, as they consisted of sleep and a proneness avoid moving. Like the untrammeled coyote, their bed was where sleep overtook them; their food, what the night wrapped in a sense of security, or the generosity of the cowboys of the Bar 20. No tub-ridden Diogenes ever knew so little of responsibility or as much unadulterated content. There is a penalty even to civilization and ambition.

When the sun had cast its shadows beyond By-and-by's feet, the air became charged with noise; shouts, shots and the rolling thunder of madly pounding hoofs echoed flatly throughout the town. By-and-by yawned, stretched and leaned back, reveling in the semi-conscious ecstasy of the knowledge that he did not have to immediately get up. Fleas opened one eye and cocked an ear in inquiry, and then rolled over on his back, squirmed and sighed contentedly and long. The outfit of the Bar 20 had come to town.

The noise came rapidly nearer and increased in volume as the riders turned the corner and drew rein suddenly, causing their mounts to slide on their haunches in ankle-deep dust.

"Hullo, old Buck-with-th'-pants, how's yore liver?"

"Come up an' irrigate, old tank!"

"Chase th' flea ranch an' trail along!"

These were a few of the salutations discernible among the medley of playful yells, the safety valves of supercharged goodnature.

"Skr-e-e!" yelled Hopalong Cassidy, letting off a fusillade of shots in the vicinity of Fleas, who rapidly retreated around the corner, where he wagged his tail in eager expectation. He was not disappointed, for a cow pony tore around in pursuit and Hopalong leaned over and scratched the yellow back, thumping it heartily, and, tossing a chunk of beef into the open jaws of the delighted dog, departed as he had come. The advent of the outfit meant a square meal and the dog knew it.

In Cowan's, lined up against the bar, the others were earnestly and assiduously endeavoring, with a promise of success, to get By-and-by drunk, which endeavors coincided perfectly with By-and-by's idea of the fitness of things. The fellowship and the liquor combined to thaw out his reserve and to loosen his tongue. After gazing with an air of injured surprise at the genial loosening of his knees, he gravely

handed his rifle, with an exaggerated sweep of his arm, to the cowboy nearest to him, and wrapped his arms around the recipient to insure his balance. The rifle was passed from hand to hand until it came to Buck Peters, who gravely presented it to its owner as a new gun.

By-and-by threw out his stomach in an endeavor to keep his head in line with his heels, and, grasping the weapon with both hands, turned to Cowan, to whom he gave it.

"Yu hab this un. Me got two. Me keep new un, mebbyso." Then he loosened his belt and drank long and deep.

A shadow darkened the doorway and Hopalong limped in. Spying By-and-by pushing the bottle into his mouth, while Red Connors propped him up, he grinned and took out five silver dollars, which he jingled under By-and-by's eyes, causing that worthy to lay aside the liquor and erratically grab for the tantalizing fortune.

"Not yet, sabe?" said Hopalong, changing the position of the money. "If yu wants to corral this here herd of simoleons yu has to ride a cayuse what Red bet me yu can't ride. Yu has got to grow on that there saddle an' stay growed for five whole minutes by Buck's ticker. I ain't a-goin' to tell yu he's any saw-horse, for yu'd know better, as yu reckons Red wouldn't bet on no losin' proposition if he knowed better, which same he don't. Yu straddles that four-laigged cloud-burst an' yu gets these, sabe? I ain't seen th' cayuse yet that yu couldn't freeze to, an' I'm backin' my opinions with my moral support an' one month's pay."

By-and-by's eyes began to glitter as the meaning of the words sifted through his befuddled mind. Ride a horse—five dollars—ride a five—dollars horse—horses ride dollars—then he straightened up and began to speak in an incoherent jumble of Sioux and bad English. He, the mighty rider of the Sioux; he, the bravest warrior and the greatest hunter; could he ride a horse for five dollars? Well, he rather thought he could. Grasping Red by the shoulder, he tacked for the door and narrowly missed hitting the bottom step first, landing, as it happened, in the soft dust with Red's leg around his neck. Somewhat sobered by the jar, he stood up and apologized to the crowd for Red getting in the way, declaring that Red was a "Heap good un," and that he didn't mean to do it.

The outfit of the Bar 20 was, perhaps, the most famous of all from Canada to the Rio Grande. The foreman, Buck Peters, controlled a crowd of men (who had all the instincts of boys) that had shown no quarter to many rustlers, and who, while always care-free and easy-going (even fighting with great good humor and carelessness), had established the reputation of being the most reckless gang of daredevil gunfighters that ever pounded leather. Crooked gaming houses, from El Paso to Cheyenne and from Phœnix to Leavenworth, unanimously and enthusiastically damned them from their boots to their sombreros, and the sheriffs and marshals of many localities had received from their hands most timely assistance —and some trouble. Wiry, indomitable, boyish and generous, they were splendid examples of virile manhood; and, surrounded as they were with great dangers and a unique civilization, they should not, in justice, be judged by opinions born of the commonplace.

They were real cowboys, which means, public opinion to the contrary notwithstanding, that they were not lawless, nor drunken, shooting bullies who held life cheaply, as their kin has been unjustly pictured; but, while these men were naturally peaceable, they had to continually rub elbows with men who were not. Gamblers, criminals, bullies and the riff-raff that fled from the protected East, had drifted among them in great numbers and it was this class that caused the trouble. The hard-working "cow punchers" lived according to the law of the land, a land farther from Broadway than China was, and they obeyed that greatest of all laws, that of self-preservation. Their fun was boisterous, but they paid for all the damage they inflicted; their work was one continual hardship, and the reaction of one extreme swings far toward the limit of its antithesis. Go back to the Apple if you would trace the beginning of self-preservation and the need.

There were, at this time, eight in the outfit, Jimmy Price (a boy of eighteen) having been wantonly shot and killed the year before by a cowboy of the C 80, a neighboring ranch; and in the battle that followed between the respective outfits his

passing had been paid for. His surviving friends seldom mentioned him, but on the pegs above his vacant bunk hung his Cheyenne saddle and all of his effects; and woe to the man or men who spoke of him in an unjust or insulting manner!

Buck Peters was a man of mild appearance, somewhat slow of speech and correspondingly quick of action, who never became flurried. His was the master hand that controlled, and his Colts enjoyed the reputation of never missing when a hit could have been expected with reason. Many floods, stampedes and blizzards had assailed his nerves, but he yet could pour a glass of liquor, held at arm's length, through a knothole in the floor without wetting the wood.

Next in age came Lanky Smith, a small, undersized man of retiring disposition. Then came Skinny Thompson, six feet four on his bared soles, and true to his name; Hopalong described him as "th' shadow of a chalk mark." Pete Wilson, the slow-witted and very taciturn, and Billy Williams, the wavering pessimist, were of ordinary height and appearance. Red Connors, with hair that shamed the name, was the possessor of a temper that was as dry as tinder; his greatest weakness was his regard for the rifle as a means of preserving peace. Johnny Nelson had taken the place formerly occupied by Jimmy Price, that of the protégé, and he could do no wrong. The last, Hopalong Cassidy, was a combination of irresponsibility, humor, good nature, love of fighting, and nonchalance when face to face with danger. His most prominent attribute was that of always getting into trouble without any intention of so doing; in fact, he was much aggrieved and surprised when it came. It seemed as though when any "bad-man" desired to add to his reputation he invariably selected Hopalong as the means (a fact due, perhaps, to the perversity of things in general). Bad-men became scarce soon after Hopalong became a fixture in any locality. He had been crippled some years before in a successful attempt to prevent the assassination of a friend, Sheriff Harris, of Albuquerque, and he still possessed a limp.

When Red had relieved his feelings and had dug the alkali out of his ears and eyes, he led the Sioux to the rear of the saloon, where a "pinto" was busily engaged in endeavoring to pitch a saddle from his back, employing the intervals in trying to see how much of the picket rope he could wrap around his legs.

When By-and-by saw what he was expected to ride he felt somewhat relieved, for the pony did not appear to have more than the ordinary amount of cussedness. He waved his hand, and Johnny and Red bandaged the animal's eyes, which quieted him at once, and then they untangled the rope from around his legs and saw that the cinches were secure. Motioning to By-and-by that all was ready, they jerked the bandage off as the Indian settled himself in the saddle.

Had By-and-by been really sober he would have taken the conceit out of that pony in chunks, and as it was, he experienced no great difficulty in holding his seat; but in his addled state of mind he grasped the end of the cinch strap in such a way that when the pony jumped forward in its last desperate effort the buckle slipped and the cinch became unfastened; and By-and-by, still seated in the saddle, flew headforemost into the horse trough, where he spilled much water.

As this happened Cowan turned the corner, and when he saw the wasted water (which he had to carry, bucketful at a time, from the wells a good quarter of a mile away) his anger blazed forth, and yelling, he ran for the drenched Sioux who was just crawling out of his bath. When the unfortunate saw the irate man bearing down on him, he sputtered in rage and fear, and, turning, he ran down the street with Cowan thundering flat footedly behind on a fat man's gallop, to the hysterical cheers of the delighted outfit, who saw in it nothing but a good joke.

When Cowan returned from his hopeless task, blowing and wheezing, he heard sundry remarks, *sotto voce*, which were not calculated to increase his opinion of his physical condition.

"Seems to me," remarked the irrepressible Hopalong, "that one of those cayuses has got th' heaves."

"It shore sounds like it," acquiesced Johnny, red in the face from holding in his laughter, "an' say, somebody interferes."

"All knock-kneed animals do, yu heathen," supplied Red.

"Sounded like thunder a short time past, an' from th' dust it must be sort of windy out," drawled Buck.

"Hey, yu, let up on that an' have a drink on th' house," invited Cowan. "If I gits that d—n warwhoop I'll make yu think there's been a cyclone. I'll see how long that bum hangs around this here burg, I will."

Red's eyes narrowed and his temper got the upper hand. "He ain't no bum when yu gives him rotgut at a quarter of a dollar a glass, is he? Any time that 'bum' gits razzled out for nothin' more 'n this, why, I goes too; an' I ain't sayin' nothin' about goin' peaceable-like, neither."

"I knowed somethin' like this 'ud happen," dolefully sang out Billy Williams, strong on the side of his pessimism.

"For th' Lord's sake, have yu broke out?" asked Red, disgustedly. "I'm goin' to hit th' trail—but just keep this afore yore mind: if By-an'-by gits in any accidents or ain't in sight when I comes to town again, this here climate 'll be a d—n sight hotter 'n it is now. No hard feelings, sabe? It's just a casual bit of advice. Come on, fellows, let's amble—I'm hungry."

As they raced across the plain toward the ranch, a pair of beady eyes, snapping with a drunken rage, watched them from an arroyo; and when Cowan entered the saloon the next morning he could not find By-and-by's rifle, which he had placed behind the bar. He also missed a handful of cartridges from the box near the cash drawer; and had he looked closely at his bottled whiskey he would have noticed a loss there. A horse was missing from a Mexican's corral and there were rumors that several Indians had been seen far out on the plain.

II

"Phew! I'm shore hungry," said Hopalong, as he and Red dismounted at the ranch the next morning for breakfast. "Wonder what's good for it?"

"They's three things that's good for famine," said Red, leading the way to the bunk-house. "Yu can pull in yore belt, yu can drink, an' yu can eat. Yore getting as bad as Johnny—but he's young yet."

The others met their entrance with a

volley of good-humored banter, some of which was so personal and evoked such responses that it sounded like the preliminary skirmish to a fight. But under all was that soft accent, that drawl of humorous appreciation and eyes twinkling in suppressed merriment. Here they were thoroughly at home and the spirit of comradeship manifested itself in many subtle ways; the wit became more daring and sharp, Billy lost some of his pessimism, and the alertness disappeared from their manner.

Skinny left off romping with Red and yawned. "I wish that cook 'ud wake up an' git breakfast. He's th' cussedest Greaser I ever saw—he kin go to sleep standin' up an' not know it. *Johnny's th'* boy that worries *him*—th' kid comes in an' whoops things up till he's gorged himself."

"Johnny's got th' most appallin' feel for grub of anybody I knows," added Red. "I wonder what's keepin' him—he's usually hangin' around here bawlin' for his grub like a spoiled calf, long afore cookie's got th' fire goin'."

"Mebby he rustled some grub out with him — I saw him tiptoin' out of th' gallery this mornin' when I come back for my cigs," remarked Hopalong, glancing at Billy.

Billy groaned and made for the gallery. Emerging half a minute later he blurted out his tale of woe: "Every time I blows myself an' don't drink it all in town, some slab-sided maverick freezes to it. It's gone," he added, dismally.

"Too bad, Billy—but what is it?" asked Skinny.

"What is it? Wha'd yu think it was, yu emaciated match? *Jewelry? Cayuses?* It's whiskey—two simoleons worth. Somethin's allus wrong. This here whole yearth's wrong, just like that cross-eyed sky-pilot said over to——"

"Will yu let up?" yelled Red, throwing a sombrero at the grumbling unfortunate. "Yu ask Buck where yore tanglefoot is."

"I'd shore look nice askin' th' *boss* if he'd rustled my whiskey, *wouldn't I?* An' would yu mind throwin' somebody else's hat? I paid twenty wheels for that, eight years ago, an' I don't want it mussed none."

"Gee, yore easy! Why, Ah Sing, over at Albuquerque, gives them away every

time yu gits yore shirt washed," gravely interposed Hopalong as he went out to cuss the cook.

"Well, what 'd yu think of that?" exclaimed Billy in an injured tone.

"Oh, yu needn't be hikin' for Albuquerque—Washee-Washee 'ud charge yu double for washin' yore shirt. Yu ought to fall in th' river some day—then he might talk business," called Hopalong over his shoulder, as he heaved an old boot into the gallery. "Hey, yu hibernatin' son of morphine, if yu don't git them flapjacks in here pretty sudden-like, I'll scatter yu all over th' landscape, sabe? Yu just wait till Johnny comes!"

"Wonder where th' kid is?" asked Lanky, rolling a cigarette.

"Off somewhere lookin' at th' sun through th' bottom of my bottle," grumbled Billy.

Hopalong started to go out, but halted on the sill and looked steadily off toward the northwest. "That's funny. Hey, fellows, here comes Buck an' Johnny ridin' double—on a walk, too!" he exclaimed. "Wonder what th'—thunder! Red, Buck's carryin' him! Somethin's busted!" he yelled, as he dashed for his pony and made for the newcomers.

"I told yu he was hittin' my bottle," pertly remarked Billy, as he followed the rest outside.

"Did yu ever see Johnny drunk? Did yu ever see him drink more 'n two glasses? Shut yore wailin' face—they's somethin' worse 'n that in this here," said Red, his temper rising. "Hopalong an' me took yore cheap liquor—it's under Pete's bunk," he added.

The trio approached on a walk and Johnny, delirious and covered with blood, was carried into the bunk house. Buck waited until all had assembled again and then, his face dark with anger, spoke sharply and without the usual drawl: "Skragged from behind, d—n them! Get some grub an' water an' be quick. We'll see who th' gent with th' grudge is."

At this point the expostulations of the indignant cook, who, not understanding the cause, regarded the invasion of china-shop bulls as sacrilegious, came to his ears. Striding quickly to the door, he grabbed the pan the Mexican was about to throw, and, turning the now frightened man around, thundered, "Keep quiet an' get 'em some grub."

When rifles and ammunition had been secured they mounted and followed him at a hard gallop along the back trail. No words were spoken, for none were necessary. All knew that they would not return until they had found the man for whom they were looking, even if the chase led to Canada. They did not ask Buck for any of the particulars, for the foreman was not in the humor to talk, and all, save Hopalong, whose curiosity was always on edge, recognized only two facts and cared for nothing else: Johnny had been ambushed and they were going to get the one who was responsible. They did not even conjecture as to who it might be, because the trail would lead them to the man himself, and it mattered nothing who or what he was—there was only one course to take with an assassin. So they said nothing, but rode on with squared jaws and set lips, the seven ponies breast to breast in a close arc.

Soon they came to an arroyo which they took at a leap. As they approached it they saw signs in the dust which told them that a body had lain there huddled up; and there were brown spots on the baked alkali. The trail they followed was now single, Buck having ridden along the bank of the arroyo when hunting for Johnny, for whom he had orders. This trail was very irregular, as if the horse had wandered at will. Suddenly they came upon five tracks all pointing one way, and four of these turned abruptly and disappeared in the northwest. Half a mile beyond the point of separation was a chaparral, which was an important factor to them.

Each man knew just what had taken place as if he had been an eye-witness, for the trail was plain. The assassins had waited in the chaparral for Johnny to pass, probably having seen him riding that way. When he had passed and his back had been turned to them they had fired and wounded him severely at the first volley, for Johnny was of the stuff that fights back and his revolvers had showed full chambers and clean barrels when Red had examined them in the bunk house. Then they had given chase for a short distance, and, from some inexplicable motive, probably fear, they had turned and ridden off without

knowing how bad he was hit. It was this trail that led to the northwest, and it was this trail that they followed without pausing; and four men suited them better than one, for there would be a fight and a good one.

When they had covered fifty miles they sighted the Cross Bar O ranch, where they hoped to secure fresh mounts. As they rode up to the ranch house the owner, Bud Wallace, came around the corner and saw them.

"Hullo, boys! What deviltry are yu up to now?" he asked.

Buck leaped from his mount, followed by the others, and shoved his sombrero back on his head as he started to remove the saddle.

"We're trailin' a bunch of murderers. They ambushed Johnny an' d—n near killed him. I stopped here to get fresh cayuses."

"Yu did right!" replied Wallace heartily. Then raising his voice, he shouted to some of his men who were near the corral to bring up the seven best horses they could rope. Then he told the cook to bring out plenty of food and drink.

"I got four punchers what ain't doin' nothin' but eat," he suggested.

"Much obliged, Wallace, but there's only four of 'em an' we'd rather get 'em ourselves—Johnny 'ud feel better," replied Buck, throwing his saddle on the horse that was led up to him.

"How's yore catridges—got plenty?" persisted Wallace.

"Two hundred apiece," responded Buck, springing into his saddle and riding off. "So long," he called.

"So long, an' plug h—l out of them," shouted Wallace as the dust swept over him.

At five in the afternoon they forded the Black River at a point where it crossed the state line from New Mexico, and at dusk camped at the base of the Guadaloupe Mountains. At daybreak they took up the chase, grim and merciless, and shortly afterward they passed the smouldering remains of a camp fire, showing that the pursued had been in a great hurry, for it should have been put out and masked. At noon they left the mountains to the rear and sighted the Barred Horseshoe, which they approached.

The owner of the ranch saw them coming, and from their appearance surmised that something was wrong.

"What is it?" he shouted. "Rustlers?"

"Nope. Murderers. I wants to swap cayuses quick," answered Buck.

"There they are. Th' boys just brought 'em in. Anything else I can let yu have?"

"Nope," shouted Buck as they galloped off.

"Somebody's goin' to get plugged full of holes," murmured the ranch owner as he watched them kicking up the dust in huge clouds.

After they had forded a tributary of the Rio Penasco near the Sacramento Mountains and had surmounted the opposite bank, Hopalong spurred his horse to the top of a hummock and swept the plain with Pete's field glasses, which he had borrowed for the occasion, and returned to the rest, who had kept on without slacking the pace. As he took up his former position he grunted "War-whoops," and unslung his rifle, an example followed by the others. The ponies were now running at top speed, and as they shot over a rise their riders saw their quarry a mile and a half in advance. One of the Indians looked back and discharged his rifle in defiance, and it now became a race worthy of the name —Death fled from Death. The fresher mounts of the cowboys steadily cut down the distance, and as the rifles of the pursuers began to speak, the hard-pressed Indians made for the smaller of two knolls, the plain leading to the larger one being too heavily strewn with bowlders to permit speed.

As the fugitives settled down behind the rocks that fringed the edge of their elevation a shot from one of them disabled Billy's arm, but had no other effect than to increase the score to be settled. The pursuers rode behind a rise and dismounted, from where, leaving their mounts protected, they scattered out to surround the knoll.

Hopalong, true to his curiosity, finally turned up on the highest point of the other knoll, a spur to the range in the west, for he always wanted to see all he could. Skinny, due to his fighting instinct, settled one hundred yards to the north and on the same spur. Buck lay hidden behind an enormous bowlder eight hundred yards to the

northeast of Skinny, and the same distance southeast of Buck was Red Connors, who was crawling up the bed of an arroyo. Billy, nursing his arm, lay in front of the horses, and Pete, from his position between Billy and Hopalong, was crawling from rock to rock in an endeavor to get near enough to use his Colts, his favorite and most effective weapons. Intermittent puffs of smoke arising from a point between Skinny and Buck showed where Lanky Smith was improving each shining hour.

There had been no directions given, each man choosing his own position, yet each was of strategic worth. Billy protected the horses, Hopalong and Skinny swept the knoll with a plunging fire, and Lanky and Buck lay in the course the besieged would most likely take if they tried a dash. Off to the east Red barred them from creeping down the arroyo, and from where Pete was he could creep up to within sixty yards if he chose the right rocks. The ranges varied from four hundred yards for Buck to sixty for Pete, and the others averaged close to three hundred, which allowed very good shooting on both sides.

Hopalong and Skinny moved nearer to each other for companionship, and as the former raised his head to see what the others were doing he received a graze on the ear.

"Wow!" he yelled, rubbing the tingling member.

Two puffs of smoke floated up from the knoll, and Skinny swore.

"Where'd he get yu, Fat?" asked Hopalong.

"G'wan, don't get funny, son," replied Skinny.

Jets of smoke arose from the north and east, where Buck and Red were stationed, and Pete was half way to the knoll. So far he hadn't been hit as he dodged in and out, and, emboldened by his luck, he made a run of five yards and his sombrero was shot from his head. Another dash and his empty holster was ripped from its support. As he crouched behind a rock he heard a yell from Hopalong, and saw that interested individual waving his sombrero to cheer him on. An angry *pang!* from the knoll caused that enthusiastic rooter to drop for safety.

"Locoed son-of-a-gun," complained Pete. "He'll shore git potted." Then he glanced at Billy, who was the center of several successive spurts of dust.

"How's business, Billy?" he called pleasantly.

"Oh, they'll git me yet," responded the pessimist. "Yu needn't git anxious. If that off buck wasn't so green he'd a had me long ago."

"Ya-*hoo*! Pete! Oh, Pete!" called Hopalong, sticking his head out at one side and grinning as the wondering object of his hail craned his neck to see what the matter was.

"Huh?" grunted Pete, and then remembering the distance he shouted, "What's th' matter?"

"Got any cigarettes?" asked Hopalong.

"Yu d—n sheep!" said Pete, and turning back to work, he drove a .44 into a yellow moccasin.

Hopalong began to itch and he saw that he was near an ant-hill. Then the cactus at his right boomed out mournfully and a hole appeared in it. He fired at the smoke and a yell informed him that he had made a hit. "Go 'way!" he complained as a green fly buzzed past his nose. Then he scratched each leg with the foot of the other and squirmed incessantly, kicking out with both feet at once. A warning, metallic *whir-r-r!* on his left caused him to yank them in again, and, turning his head quickly, he had the pleasure of lopping off the head of a rattlesnake with his Colt's.

"Glad yu wasn't a copperhead," he exclaimed. "Somebody had ought a shot that fool Noah. D—n th' ants!" He drowned, with a jet of tobacco juice, a Gila monster that was staring at him, and took a savage delight in its frantic efforts to bury itself.

Soon he heard Skinny swear and he sung out: "What's th' matter, Skinny? Git plugged again?"

"Naw, bugs—ain't they h—l?" plaintively asked his friend.

"They ain't none over here. What kind of bugs?"

"Sufferin' Moses, I ain't no bugologist! All kinds!"

But Hopalong got it at last. He had found tobacco and rolled a cigarette and, in reaching for a match, exposed his shoulder to a shot that broke his collar bone. Skinny's rifle cracked in reply, and the offending brave rolled out from behind a rock. From the fuss emanating from Hopalong's direction Skinny knew that his neighbor had been hit.

"Don't yu care, Hoppy. I got th' cuss," he said consolingly. "Where'd he git yu?" he asked.

"In th' heart, yu pie-faced nuisance. Come over here an' corral this cussed bandage, an' gimme some water," snapped the injured man.

Skinny wormed his way through the thorny chaparral and bound up the shoulder. "Anything else?" he asked.

"Yes. Shoot that bunch of warts an' blow that tobacco-eyed Gila to Cheyenne. This here's worse than the time we cleaned oùt th' C 80 outfit!" Then he kicked the dead toad and swore at the sun.

"Close yore yap; yore worse than a kid! Anybody'd think yu never got plugged afore," said Skinny indignantly.

"I can cuss all I wants," replied Hopalong, proving his assertion as he grabbed his gun and fired at the dead Indian. A bullet whined above his head and Skinny fired at the smoke. He peeped out and saw that his friends were getting nearer to the knoll.

"They's closin' in now. We'll soon be gittin' home," he reported.

Hopalong looked out in time to see Buck make a dash for a bowlder that lay ten yards in front of him, which he reached in safety. Lanky also ran in and Pete added five more yards to his advance. Buck made another dash, but leaped into the air, and, coming down as if from an intentional high jump, staggered and stumbled for a few paces and then fell flat, rolling over and over toward the shelter of a split rock, where he lay quiet. A leering red face peered over the rocks on the knoll, but the whoop of exultation was cut short, for Red's rifle cracked and the warrior rolled down the steep bank, where another shot from the same gun settled him beyond question.

Hopalong choked and, turning his face away, angrily dashed his knuckles into his eyes. "D—n 'em! D—n 'em! They've got Buck! They've got Buck, d—n 'em! They've got Buck, Skinny! Good old Buck! They've got him! Jimmy's gone, Johnny's plugged and now Buck's gone! Come on!" he sobbed in a frenzy of vengeance. "Come on, Skinny! We'll tear their cussed hides into a deeper red than they are now! Oh, d—n it, I can't see—where's my gun?" He groped for the rifle and fought Skinny when the latter, red-eyed but cool, endeavored to restrain him. "Lemme go, curse yu! Don't yu know they got Buck? Lemme go!"

"Down! Red's got th' skunk. *Yu* can't do nothin'—they'd drop yu afore yu took five steps! *Red's* got him, I tell yu! Do yu want me to lick yu! We'll pay 'em with th' coals of h—l if you'll keep yore head!" exclaimed Skinny, throwing the crazed man heavily.

Musical tones, rising and falling in weird octaves, whining pityingly, diabolically; sobbing in a fascinating monotone and slobbering in ragged chords; calling as they swept over the plain, always calling and exhorting, they mingled in barbaric discord with the defiant barks of the six-shooters and the inquiring cracks of the Winchesters. High up in the air several specks sailed and drifted, more coming up rapidly from all directions. Buzzards know well where food can be found.

As Hopalong leaned back against a rock he was hit in the thigh by a ricochet that tore its way out, whirling like a circular saw, a span above where it entered. The wound was very nasty, being ripped twice the size made by an ordinary shot, and it bled profusely. Skinny crawled over and attended to it, making a tourniquet of his neck-kerchief and bandaging it with a strip torn from his shirt.

"Yore shore lucky, yu are," he grumbled as he made his way back to his post, where he vented his rancor by emptying the semi-depleted magazine of his Winchester at the knoll.

Hopalong began to sing and shout and he talked of Jimmy and his childhood, interspersing the broken narrative with choice selections as sung in the music halls of Leavenworth and Abilene. He wound up by yelling and struggling, and Skinny had his hands full in holding him.

"Hopalong! Cassidy! Come out of that! Keep quiet—yu'll shore get plugged if yu don't stop that plungin'. For God's sake, did yu hear that?" A bullet viciously hissed between them and flattened out on a near-by rock; others cut their way through the chaparral to the sound of falling twigs, and Skinny threw himself on the struggling man and strapped Hopalong with his belt to the base of a honey-mesquite that grew at his side.

"Hold still now, an' let that bandage alone. Yu allus goes off th' range when yu gets plugged," he complained. He cut down a cactus and poured the sap over the wounded man's face, causing him to gurgle and look around. His eyes had a sane look now and Skinny slid off his chest.

"Git that—belt loose; I ain't—no cow," brokenly blazed out the picketed Hopalong. Skinny did so, handed the irate man his Colts and returned to his own post, from where he fired twice, reporting the shots.

"I'm tryin' to get him on th' glance—th' first one went high an' th' other fell flat," he explained.

Hopalong listened eagerly, for this was shooting that he could appreciate. "Lemme see," he commanded. Skinny dragged him over to a crack and settled down for another try.

"Where is he, Skinny?" asked Hopalong.

"Behind that second big one. No, over on this here side. See that smooth granite? If I can get her there on th' right spot he'll shore know it." He aimed carefully and fired.

Through Pete's glasses Hopalong saw a leaden splotch appear on the rock and he notified the marksman that he was shooting high. "Put her on that bump closer down," he suggested. Skinny did so and another yell reached their ears.

"That's a dandy. Yore shore all right, yu old cuss," complimented Hopalong, elated at the success of the experiment.

Skinny fired again and a brown arm flopped out into sight. Another shot struck it and it jerked as though it were lifeless.

"He's cashed. See how she jumped? Like a rope," remarked Skinny with a grin. The arm lay quiet.

Pete had gained his last cover and was all eyes and Colts. Lanky was also very close in and was intently watching one particular rock. Several shots echoed from the far side of the knoll and they knew that Red was all right. Billy was covering a cluster of rocks that protruded above the others and, as they looked, his rifle rang out and the last defender leaped down and disappeared in the chaparral.

He wore yellow trousers and an old boiled shirt.

"By-an'-by, by all that's bad!" yelled Hopalong. "Th' measly coyote! An' me a-fillin' his ornery hide with liquor. Well, they'll have to find him all over again, now," he complained, astounded by the revelation. He fired into the chaparral to express his pugnacious disgust and scared out a huge tarantula, which alighted on Skinny's chaps, crawling rapidly toward the unconscious man's neck. Hopalong's face hardened and he slowly covered the insect and fired, driving it into the sand, torn and lifeless. The bullet touched the leathern garment and Skinny remonstrated, knowing that Hopalong was in no condition for fancy shooting.

"Huh!" exclaimed Hopalong. "That was a tarantula what I plugged. He was headin' for yore neck," he explained, watching the chaparral with apprehension.

"Go 'way, was it? Bully for yu!" exclaimed Skinny, tarantulas being placed at par with rattlesnakes, and he considered that he had been saved from a horrible death. "Thought yu said they wasn't no bugs over here," he added in an aggrieved tone.

"They wasn't none. Yu brought 'em. I only had th' main show—Gilas, rattlers an' toads," he replied, and then added, "Ain't it cussed hot up here?"

"She is. Yu won't have no cinch ridin' home with that leg. Yu better take my cayuse—he's busted more 'n yourn," responded Skinny.

"Yore cayuse is at th' Cross Bar O, yu wall-eyed pirute."

"Shore 'nuff. Funny how a feller forgets sometimes. Lemme alone now, they's goin' to git By-an'-by. Pete an' Lanky has just went in after him."

That was what had occurred. The two impatient punchers had grown tired of waiting, and risked what might easily have been death in order to hasten matters. The others kept up a rapid fire, directed at the far end of the chaparral on the knoll, in order to mask the movements of their venturesome friends, intending, also, to drive By-and-by toward them so that he would be the one to get picked off as he advanced.

Several shots rang out in quick succession on the knoll and the chaparral became agitated. Several more shots sounded from the depths of the thicket, and a mounted Indian dashed out of the northern edge and headed in Buck's direction. His course would take him close to Buck, whom he had seen fall, and would let him escape at a point midway between Red and Skinny, as Lanky was on the knoll, and the range was very far to allow effective shooting by these two.

Red saw him leave the chaparral, and in his haste to reload jammed the cartridge, and By-and-by swept on toward temporary safety, with Red dancing in a paroxysm of rage, swelling his vocabulary with words he had forgotten existed.

By-and-by, rising to his full height in the saddle, turned and wiggled his fingers at the frenzied Red and made several other signs that the cowboy was in the humor to appreciate to the fullest extent. Then he turned and shook his rifle at the marksmen on the larger knoll, whose best shots kicked up the dust full fifty yards too short. The pony was sweeping toward the reservation and friends only fifteen miles away, and By-and-by knew that once among the mountains he would be on equal footing, at least, with his enemies. As he passed the rock behind which Buck lay sprawled on his face, he uttered a piercing whoop of triumph and leaned forward on his pony's neck. Twenty leaps farther, and the spiteful crack of an unerring rifle echoed from where the foreman was painfully supporting himself on his elbows. The pony swept on in a spurt of nerve-racking speed, but alone. By-and-by shrieked again and crashed heavily to the ground, where he rolled inertly and then lay still. Men like Buck are dangerous until their hearts have ceased to beat.

9

Trials of a Peaceful Puncher

CLARENCE EDWARD MULFORD

BAR 20 RANGE YARNS

III.—TRIALS OF A PEACEFUL PUNCHER

BY CLARENCE EDWARD MULFORD

PAINTING BY N. C. WYETH

MOKE drifted over the table in an agitated cloud and dribbled lazily upward from the muzzle of a six-shooter. The man who held it looked searchingly at those around him. Strained and eager faces peered at his opponent, who was sliding slowly forward in his chair. His head rolled inertly on his shoulder and the edge of his half-open shirt showed a purplish spot on its faded blue surface. For the length of a minute no sound but the guarded breathing of the onlookers could be heard. This was broken by the thud of the falling body and a nervous cough from the rear of the room. The faces assumed their ordinary nonchalant expressions, their rugged lines heavily shadowed in the light of the flickering oil lamps. Two men carried the body from the room, and the shuffling of cards and the clink of silver became audible. "Hopalong" Cassidy had objected to insulting remarks about his affliction.

Hopalong was very sensitive about his crippled leg, and was always prompt to resent any scorn or curiosity directed at it, especially when emanating from strangers. A young man of twenty-three years, when surrounded by nearly perfect specimens of physical manhood, is apt to be painfully self-conscious of any such defect, and it reacted on his nature at times, even though he was well known for his happy-go-lucky disposition and playfulness. He consoled himself with the knowledge that what he lost in symmetry was more than balanced by the celerity and certainty of his gun hand, which was right or left, or both, as the occasion demanded.

Hopalong was an active member of the outfit representing the Bar 20, a ranch of the Pecos valley, Texas, and adjoining the town of Buckskin. He was well known throughout the cattle country, as were his chums. Many stories of him were in circulation, the morals of which were calculated to inspire respect and deference; and the reputation of his outfit was also established. Buck Peters, the foreman, Red Connors and the others were famed for their sand, marksmanship and humor. They had been tried many times and were labeled "O. K."

At the present time Hopalong was drifting home from one of his nomadic trips, and he had left his card at almost every place he had visited. There was that affair in Red-Hot Gulch, Colorado, where, under pressure, he had invested sundry pieces of lead in the persons of several obstreperous citizens, and then had paced the zealous and excitable sheriff to the state line.

He next was noticed in Cheyenne, where his deformity was vividly dwelt upon, to the extent of six words, by one Tarantula Charley, the aforesaid Charley not being able to proceed to greater length on account of heart failure. As Charley had been an ubiquitous nuisance, there were no objections as to the manner of his going, and those present availed themselves of the opportunity offered by Hopalong to indulge in a free drink.

Laramie was his next stopping place, and shortly after his arrival he was requested to sing and dance by a local terror, who informed all present that he was the only

95

"Sitting up cross-legged, with each hand holding a gun
from which came thin wisps of smoke."

Painting by N. C. Wyeth.

seventeen-buttoned rattlesnake in the cow country. Hopalong, hurt and indignant at being treated like a common tenderfoot, promptly knocked the terror down, which forced him, later in the day, to separate His Snakeship from his "buttons" with a .45 caliber slug. After he had irrigated several square feet of parched throats belonging to the audience, he again took up his journey and spent a day at Denver, where he managed to avoid any further trouble.

Santa Fé loomed up before him several days later and he entered it shortly before noon. At this time the old Spanish city was a bundle of high-strung nerves, and certain parts of it were calculated to furnish any and all kinds of excitement except revival meetings and church fairs. Hopalong straddled a lively nerve before he had been in the city an hour. Two local bad men, Slim Travennes and Tex Ewalt, desiring to establish the fact that they were roaring prairie fires, attempted to consume the placid and innocent stranger as he limped across the plaza in search of a game of draw poker at the Black Hills Emporium, with the result that they were extinguished, to the chagrin and disgust of their immediate acquaintances, who endeavored to drown their mortification and sorrow in rapid but somewhat wild gunplay. After they had collected several ounces of lead apiece they had pressing engagements elsewhere, with the exception of one who remained to mark the spot.

Hopalong reloaded his guns and proceeded to the Emporium, where he found a game all prepared for him in every sense of the word. On the third deal he objected to the way in which the dealer manipulated the cards, and when the smoke cleared away he was the only occupant of the room, except a man who lay face down on the other side of the table, and a dog, belonging to the bartender, that had intercepted a stray bullet.

Hunting up the owner of the hound, he apologized for being the indirect cause of the animal's death, deposited a sum of Mexican dollars in that gentleman's palm, and went on his way to Alameda, which he entered shortly after dark and where the opening event took place.

Several hours later, as his luck was vacillating, he felt a heavy hand on his shoulder, and missed Buck Peter's head by the breadth of a razor's edge in his belief that it belonged to the partner of the man he had just shot. He was overjoyed at seeing Buck and Red, the latter grinning as only Red could grin, and he withdrew from the game to enjoy his good fortune.

While Hopalong had been wandering over the country the two friends had been hunting for him and had traced him successfully, that being due to the trail he had blazed with his six-shooters. This they had accomplished without harm to themselves, as those of whom they inquired thought that they must want Hopalong "bad," and cheerfully gave the information required.

They had started out more for the purpose of accompanying him for pleasure, but that had changed to an urgent necessity in the following manner:

While on the way from Denver to Santa Fé they had met Pie Willis of the "Three-Triangle," a ranch that adjoined their own, and they paused to pass the compliments of the season.

"Purty far from th' grub wagon, Pie," remarked Buck.

"Oh, I'm only goin' to Denver," responded Pie.

"Purty hot," suggested Red.

"She shore is. Seen anybody yu knows?" Pie asked.

"One or two—Billy of th' Star Crescent an' Panhandle Lukins," answered Buck.

"That so? Panhandle's goin' to punch for us next year. I'll hunt him up. I heard down south of Albuquerque that Thirsty Jones an' his brothers are lookin' for trouble," offered Pie.

"Yah! They ain't lookin' for no trouble —they just goes around blowin' off. Trouble? Why, they don't know what she is," remarked Red contemptuously.

"Well, they's been dodgin' th' sheriff purty lively lately, an' if that ain't trouble I don't know what is," said Pie.

"It shore is, an' hard to dodge," acquiesced Buck.

"Well, I has to amble. Is Panhandle in Denver? Yes? I calculates as how me an' him 'll buck th' tiger for a whirl—he's shore lucky. Well, so long," said Pie as he moved on.

"So long," responded the two.

"Hey, wait a minute," yelled Pie after

he had ridden a hundred yards. "If yu sees Hopalong yu might tell him that th' Joneses are goin' to hunt him up when they gits to Albuquerque. They's shore sore on him. 'Tain't none of my funeral, only they ain't always a-carin' how they goes after a feller. So long," and soon he was a cloud of dust on the horizon.

"Trouble!" snorted Red; "well, between dodgin' Harris an' huntin' Hopalong I reckons they'll shore find her." Then to himself he murmured, "Funny how everythin' comes his way."

"That's gospel shore enough, but as Pie said, they ain't a whole lot particular as how they deals th' cards. We better get a move on an' find that ornery little cuss," replied Buck.

"O. K., only I ain't losin' no sleep about Hoppy. His gun's too lively fer me to do any worryin'," asserted Red.

"They'll get lynched some time, shore," declared Buck.

"Not if they find Hoppy," grimly replied Red.

They tore through Santa Fé, only stopping long enough to wet their throats, and after several hours of hard riding entered Alameda, where they found Hopalong in the manner narrated.

After some time the three left the room and headed for Albuquerque, twelve miles to the south. At ten o'clock they dismounted before the Nugget and Rope, an unpainted wooden building supposed to be a clever combination of barroom, dance and gambling hall and hotel. The cleverness lay in the man who could find the hotel part.

The proprietor of the Nugget and Rope, a German named Baum, not being troubled with police rules, kept the door wide open for the purpose of inviting trade, a proceeding not to the liking of his patrons for obvious reasons. Probably not one man in ten was fortunate enough to have no one "looking for him," and the lighted interior assured good hunting to any one in the dark street. He was continually opening the door, which every newcomer promptly and forcibly slammed shut. When he saw men walk across the room for the express purpose of slamming it he began to cherish the idea that there was a conspiracy on foot to anger him and thus force him to bring about his own death. After the door had been slammed three times in one evening by one man, the last slam being so forcible as to shake two bottles from the shelf and to crack the door itself, he became positive that his suspicions were correct, and so was very careful to smile and take it as a joke. Finally, wearied by his vain efforts to keep it open and fearing for the door, he hit upon a scheme, the brilliancy of which inflated his chest and gave him the appearance of a prize-winning bantam. When his patrons strolled in that night there was no door to slam, as it lay behind the bar.

When Buck and Red entered, closely followed by Hopalong, they elbowed their way to the rear of the room, where they could see before being seen. As yet they had said nothing to Hopalong about Pie's warning, and were debating in their minds whether they should do so or not, when Hopalong interrupted their thoughts by laughing. They looked up and he nodded toward the front, where they saw that anxious eyes from all parts of the room were focused on the open door. Then they noticed that it had been removed. The air of semi-hostile, semi-anxious inquiry of the patrons and the smile of satisfaction covering the face of Baum appealed to them as the most ludicrous sight their eyes had seen for months, and they leaned back and roared with laughter, thus calling forth sundry looks of disapproval from the innocent causers of their merriment. But they were too well known in Albuquerque to allow the disapproval to approach a serious end, and finally, as the humorous side of the situation dawned on the crowd, they joined in the laugh and all went merrily.

At the psychologic moment some one shouted for a dance and the suggestion met with uproarious approval. At that moment Harris, the sheriff, came in and volunteered to supply the necessary music if the crowd would pay the fine against a straying fiddler he had corraled the day before. A hat was quickly passed and a sum was realized which would pay several fines to come and Harris departed for the music.

A chair was placed on the bar for the musician and, to the tune of "Old Dan Tucker" and an assortment of similar airs, the board floor shook and trembled. It was a comical sight and Hopalong, the only wall-flower besides Baum and the sheriff, laughed until he became weak. Cow-punchers play as they work, hard and earnestly, and there was plenty of action. Sombreros flapped like huge wings and the baggy chaps looked like small, distorted balloons.

The Virginia reel was a marvel of supple, exaggerated grace and the quadrille looked like a free-for-all for unbroken colts. The honor of prompter was conferred upon the sheriff, and he gravely called the changes as they were usually called in that section of the country:

"Oh, th' ladies trail in
    An' th' gents trail out,
An' all stampede down th' middle.
If yu ain't got th' tin
    Yu can dance an' shout,
But yu must keep up with th' fiddle."

As the dance waxed faster and the dancers grew hotter, Hopalong, feeling lonesome because he wouldn't face ridicule, even if it was not expressed, went over and stood by the sheriff. He and Harris were good friends, for he had received the wound that crippled him in saving the sheriff from assassination. Harris killed the man who had fired that shot, and from this episode on the burning desert grew a friendship that was as strong as their own natures.

Harris was very well liked by the majority and feared by the rest, for he was a "square" man and the best sheriff the county had ever known. Quiet and un-assuming, small of stature, and with a kind word for every one, he was a universal favorite among the better class of citizens. Quick as a flash and unerring in his shooting, he was a nightmare to the "bad men." No profane word had ever been known to leave his lips, and he was the possessor of a widespread reputation for generosity. His face was naturally frank and open; but when his eyes narrowed with deter-mination it became blank and cold. When he saw his young friend sidle over to him he smiled and nodded a hearty welcome.

"They's shore cuttin' her loose," re-marked Hopalong.

"First two pairs forward an' back!— they shore is," responded the prompter.

"Who's th' gent playin' lady to Buck?" queried Hopalong.

"Forward again an' ladies change!— Billy Jordan."

Hopalong watched the couple until they swung around and then he laughed silently. "Buck's got too many feet," he seriously remarked to his friend.

"Swing th' girl yu loves th' best!—he ain't lonesome, look at that——"

Two shots rang out in quick succession and Harris stumbled, wheeled and pitched forward on his face as Hopalong's som-brero spun across his body. For a second there was an intense silence, heavy, strained and sickening. Then a roar broke forth and the crowd of frenzied merry-makers, headed by Hopalong, poured out into the street and spread out to search the town. As daylight dawned the searchers began to straggle back with the same report of failure. Buck and Red met on the street near the door and each looked questioningly at the other. Each shook his head and looked around, their fingers toying absent-mindedly at their belts. Finally Buck cleared his throat and remarked casually, "Mebby he's following 'em."

Red nodded and they went over toward their horses. As they were hesitating which route to take, Billy Jordan came up.

"Mebby yu'd like to see yore pardner— he's out by Buzzard's Spring. We'll take care of *him*," jerking his thumb over his shoulder toward the saloon where Harris's body lay. "And we'll *all* git th' oth'rs later. They can't git away for long."

Buck and Red nodded and headed for Buzzard's Spring. As they neared the water hole they saw Hopalong sitting on a rock, his head resting in one hand while the other hung loosely from his knee. He did not notice them when they arrived, and with a ready tact they sat quietly on their horses and looked in every direction except toward him. The sun became a ball of molten fire and the sand flies annoyed them incessantly, but still they sat and waited, silent and apologetic.

Hopalong finally arose, reached for his sombrero, and, finding it gone, swore long and earnestly at the scene its loss brought before him. He walked over to his horse and, leaping into the saddle, turned and faced his friends. "Yu old sons-of-guns," he said. They looked sheepish and nodded negatively in answer to the look of inquiry in his eyes. "They ain't got 'em yet," remarked Red slowly. Hopalong straight-ened up, his eyes narrowed and his face became hard and resolute as he led the way back toward the town.

Buck rode up beside him and, wiping his face with his shirt sleeve, began to speak to Red. "We *might* look up th' Joneses, Red. They had been dodgin' th' sheriff purty lively lately, an' they was huntin' Hopalong. Ever since we had to kill their brother in Buckskin they has been yappin' as how they was goin' to wipe us out. Hopalong an' Harris was standin' clost together an' they tried for both. They shot twice, one for Harris an' one for Hopalong, an' what more do yu want?"

"It shore looks thataway, Buck," replied Red, biting into a huge plug of tobacco which he produced from his chaps. "Anyhow, they wouldn't be no loss if they didn't. 'Member what Pie said?"

Hopalong looked straight ahead, and when he spoke the words sounded as though he had bitten them off: "Yore right, Buck, but I gits first try at Thirsty. He's my meat an' I'll plug th' fellow what says he ain't. Damn him!"

The others replied by applying their spurs, and in a short time they dismounted before the Nugget and Rope. Thirsty wouldn't have a chance to not care how he dealt the cards.

Buck and Red moved quickly through the crowd, speaking fast and earnestly. When they returned to where they had left their friend they saw him half a block away and they followed slowly, one on either side of the street. There would be no bullets in his back if they knew what they were about, and they usually did.

As Hopalong neared the corner, Thirsty and his two brothers turned it and saw him. Thirsty said something in a low voice, and the other two walked across the street and disappeared behind the store. When assured that they were secure, Thirsty walked up to a huge bowlder on the side of the street farthest from the store and turned and faced his enemy, who approached rapidly until about five paces away, when he slowed up and finally stopped.

For a number of seconds they sized each other up, Hopalong quiet and deliberate with a deadly hatred; Thirsty pale and furtive with a sensation hitherto unknown to him. It was Right meeting Wrong, and Wrong lost confidence. Often had Thirsty Jones looked death in the face and laughed, but there was something in Hopalong's eyes that made his flesh creep. "As ye sow, so shall ye reap."

He glanced quickly past his foe and took in the scene with one flash of his eyes. There was the crowd, eager, expectant, scowling. There were Buck and Red, each lounging against a bowlder, Buck on his right, Red on his left. Before him stood the only man he had ever feared. Hopalong shifted his feet and Thirsty, coming to himself with a start, smiled. His nerve had been shaken, but he was master of himself once more.

"Well!" he snarled, scowling.

Hopalong made no response, but stared him in the eyes.

Thirsty expected action, and the deadly quiet of his enemy oppressed him. He stared in turn, but the insistent searching of his opponent's eyes scorched him and he shifted his gaze to Hopalong's neck.

"Well!" he repeated uneasily.

"Did yu have a nice time at th' dance last night?" asked Hopalong, still searching the face before him.

"Was there a dance? I was over in Alameda," replied Thirsty shortly.

"Ya-as, there was a dance, an' yu can shoot purty damn far if yu was in Alameda," responded Hopalong, his voice low and monotonous.

Thirsty shifted his feet and glanced around. Buck and Red were still lounging against their bowlders and apparently were not paying any attention to the proceedings. His fickle nerve came back again, for he knew he would receive fair play. So he faced Hopalong once more and regarded him with a cynical smile.

"Yu seems to worry a whole lot about me. Is it because yu has a tender feelin', or because it's none of yore damn business?" he asked aggressively.

Hopalong paled with sudden anger, but controlled himself.

"It's because yu murdered Harris," he replied.

"Shoo! An' how does yu figger it out?" asked Thirsty, jauntily.

"He was huntin' yu hard an' yu thought yu'd stop it, so yu came in to lay for him. When yu saw me an' him together yu saw th' chance to wipe out another score. That's how I figger it out," replied Hopalong quietly.

"Yore a reg'lar 'tective, ain't yu?" Thirsty asked ironically.

"I've got common sense," responded Hopalong.

"Yu has? Yu better tell th' rest that, too," replied Thirsty.

"I know yu shot Harris, an' yu can't get out of it by making funny remarks. Anyhow, yu won't be much loss, an' th' stage company 'll feel better, too."

"Shoo! An' suppose I did shoot him, I done a good job, didn't I?"

"Yu did th' worst job yu could do, yu highway robber," softly said Hopalong, at the same time moving nearer. "Harris knew yu stopped th' stage last month, an' that's why yu've been dodgin' him."

"Yore a liar!" shouted Thirsty, reaching for his gun.

The movement was fatal, for before he could draw, the Colt in Hopalong's holster leaped out and flashed from its owner's hip and Thirsty fell sideways, face down in the dust of the street.

Hopalong started toward the fallen man, but as he did so a shot rang out from behind the store and he pitched forward, stumbled and rolled behind the bowlder. As he stumbled his left hand streaked to his hip, and when he fell he had a gun in each hand.

As he disappeared from sight Goodeye and Bill Jones stepped from behind the store and started to run away. Not able to resist the temptation to look again, they stopped and turned and Bill laughed.

"Easy as h—l," he said.

"Run, yu fool—Red an' Buck'll be here. Want to git plugged?" shouted Goodeye, angrily.

They turned and started for a group of ponies twenty yards away, and as they leaped into the saddles two shots were fired and they crashed headlong to the ground, Bill over the body of his brother. As the reports died away Buck and Red turned the corner of the store, Colts in hand, and, checking their rush as they saw the saddles emptied, they turned toward the street and saw Hopalong, with blood oozing from an abrasion on his cheek, sitting up cross-legged, with each hand holding a gun, from which came thin wisps of smoke.

"Th' son-of-a-gun!" said Buck, proud and delighted.

"Th' son-of-a-gun!" echoed Red, grinning.

10

Hopalong Keeps His Word

CLARENCE EDWARD MULFORD

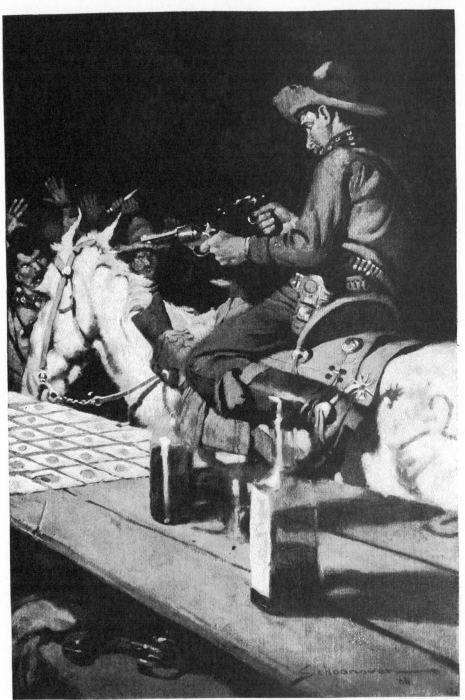

Drawing by Frank E. Schoonover.

"Hopalong's Colts peeped over the ears of his horse,
and he backed into a corner near the bar."

BAR 20 RANGE YARNS

IV.—HOPALONG KEEPS HIS WORD

BY CLARENCE EDWARD MULFORD

THE waters of the Rio Grande slid placidly toward the Gulf, the hot sun branding the sleepy waters with streaks of molten fire. To the north arose from the gray sandy plain the Quitman Mountains, and beyond them lay Bass Cañon. From the latter emerged a solitary figure astride a broncho, and, as he ascended the topmost rise, he glanced below him at the placid stream and beyond it into Mexico. As he sat quietly in his saddle he smiled and laughed gently to himself. The trail he had just followed had been replete with trouble which had suited the state of his mind, and he now felt humorous, having cleaned up a pressing debt with his six-shooter. Surely there ought to be a mild sort of excitement in the land he faced, something picturesque and out of the ordinary. This was to be the finishing touch to his trip, and he had left his two companions at Albuquerque in order that he might have to himself all that he could find.

Not many miles to the south of him lay the town which had been the rendezvous of Tamale José, whose weakness had been a liking for other people's cattle. Well he remembered his first man hunt: the discovery of the theft, the trail and pursuit and—the ending. He was scarcely eighteen years of age when that event took place, and the wisdom he had absorbed then had stood him in good stead many times since. He had even now a touch of pride at the recollection how, when his older companions had failed to get Tamale José, he with his undeveloped strategy had gained that end. The fight would never be forgotten, as it was his first, and no sight of wounds would ever affect him as did those of Red Connors as he lay huddled up in the dark corner of that old adobe hut.

He came to himself and laughed again as he thought of Carmencita, the first girl he had ever known—and the last. With a boy's impetuosity he had wooed her in a manner far different from that of the peons who sang beneath her window and talked to her mother. He had boldly scaled the wall and did his courting in her house, trusting to luck and to his own ability to avoid being seen. No hidden meaning lay in his words; he spoke from his heart and with no concealment. And he remembered the treachery that had forced him, fighting, to the camp of his outfit; and when he had returned with his friends she had disappeared. To this day he hated that mud-walled convent and those sisters who so easily forgot how to talk. The fragrance of the old days wrapped themselves around him, and although he had ceased to pine for his black-eyed Carmencita — well, it would be nice if he chanced to see her again. Spurring his mount into an easy canter he swept down to and across the river, fording it where he had crossed it when pursuing Tamale José.

The town lay indolent under the Mexican night, and the strumming of guitars and the tinkle of spurs and tiny bells softly echoed from several houses. The convent of St. Maria lay indistinct in its heavy shadows, and the little church farther up the dusty street showed dim lights in its stained windows. Off to the north became audible the rhythmic beat of a horse, and soon a cowboy swept past the convent with a mocking bow. He clattered across the stone-paved plaza and threw his mount back on its haunches as he stopped before a house. Glancing around and determining to find out a few facts as soon as possible, he rode up to the low door and pounded upon it with the butt of his Colt. After waiting for possibly half a minute and receiving no response, he hammered a tune upon it with two Colts, and had the satisfaction of seeing half a score of heads protrude from the windows in the near-by houses.

"If I could scare up another gun I might get th' whole blamed town up," he grumbled whimsically, and fell on the door with another tune.

"Who is it?" came from within. The voice was distinctly feminine and Hopalong winked to himself in congratulation.

"Me," he replied, twirling his fingers from his nose at the curious, forgetting that the darkness hid his actions from sight.

"Yes, I know; but who is 'me'?" came from the house.

"Ain't I a fool!" he complained to himself, and raising his voice he replied coaxingly, "Open th' door a bit an' see. Are yu Carmencita?"

"O–o–o! But you must tell me who it is first."

"Mr. Cassidy," he replied, flushing at the 'mister,' "an' I wants to see Carmencita."

"Carmencita who?" teasingly came from behind the door.

Hopalong scratched his head. "Gee, yu've roped me—I suppose she has got another handle. Oh, yu know—she used to live here about seven years back. She had great big black eyes, pretty cheeks an' a mouth that 'ud stampede anybody. Don't yu know now? She was about so high," holding out his hand in the darkness.

The door opened a trifle on a chain, and Hopalong peered eagerly forward.

"Ah, it is you, the brave Americano! You must go away quick or you will meet with harm. Manuel is awfully jealous and he will kill you! Go at once, please!"

Hopalong pulled at the half-hearted down upon his lip and laughed softly. Then he slid the guns back in their holsters and felt of his sombrero.

"Manuel wants to see me first, Star-eyes?"

"No! no!" she replied, stamping upon the floor vehemently. "You must go now —at once!"

"I'd shore look nice hittin' th' trail because Manuel Somebody wants to get hurt, wouldn't I? Don't yu remember how I used to shinny up this here wall an' skin th' cat gettin' through that hole up there

what yu said was a window? Ah, come on an' open th' door—I'd shore like to see yu again!" pleaded the irrepressible.

"No! no! Go away. Oh, won't you please go away!"

Hopalong sighed audibly and turned his horse. As he did so he heard the door open and a sigh reached his ears. He wheeled like a flash and found the door closed again on its chain. A laugh of delight came from behind it.

"Come out, please!—just for a minute," he begged, wishing that he was brave enough to smash the door to splinters and grab her.

"If I do, will you go away?" asked the girl. "Oh, what will Manuel say if he comes? And all those people, they'll tell him!"

"Hey, yu!" shouted Hopalong, brandishing his Colts at the protruding heads. "Git scarce! I'll shore plug th' last one in!" Then he laughed at the sudden vanishing.

The door slowly opened and Carmencita, fat and frowsy, wobbled out to him. Hopalong's feelings were interfering with his breathing as he surveyed her. "Oh, yu shore are mistaken, Mrs. Carmencita. I wants to see yore *daughter!*"

"Ah, you have forgotten the little Carmencita who used to look for you. Like all the men, you have forgotten," she cooed reproachfully. Then her fear predominated again and she cried, "Oh, if my husband should see me now!"

Hopalong mastered his astonishment and bowed. He had a desire to ride madly into the Rio Grande and collect his senses.

"Yu are right—this *is* too dangerous— I'll amble on some," he replied hastily. Under his breath he prayed that the outfit would never learn of this. He turned his horse and rode slowly up the street as the door closed.

Rounding the corner he heard a soft footfall, and swerving in his saddle, he turned and struck with all his might in the face of a man who leaped at him, at the same time grasping the uplifted wrist with his other hand. A curse and the tinkle of thin steel on the pavement accompanied the fall of his opponent. Bending down from his saddle he picked up the weapon, and the next minute the enraged assassin was staring into the unwavering and, to him, growing muzzle of a Colt's .45.

"Yu shore had a bum teacher. Don't yu know better'n to *push* it in? An' me a cow-puncher, too! I'm most grieved at yore conduct—it shows yu don't appreciate cow-wrastlers. This is safer," he remarked, throwing the stiletto through the air and into a door, where it rang out angrily and quivered. "I don't know as I wants to ventilate yu; we mostly poisons coyotes up my way," he added. Then a thought struck him. "Yu must be that dear Manuel I've been hearin' so much about?"

A snarl was the only reply and Hopalong grinned.

"Yu shore ain't got no call to go loco that way, none whatever. I don't want yore Carmencita. I only called to say hulloo," responded Hopalong, his sympathies being aroused for the wounded man before him from his vivid recollection of the woman who had opened the door.

"Yah!" snarled Manuel. "You wants to poison my little bird. You with your fair hair and your cursed swagger!"

The six-shooter tentatively expanded and then stopped six inches from the Mexican's nose. "Yu wants to ride easy, hombre. I ain't no angel, but I don't poison no woman; an' don't yu amble off with th' idea in yore head that she wants to be poisoned. Why, she near stuck a knife in me!" he lied.

The Mexican's face brightened somewhat, but it would take more than that to wipe out the insult of the blow. The horse became restless, and when Hopalong had effectively quieted it he spoke again.

"Did yu ever hear of Tamale José?"

"Yes."

"Well, I'm th' fellow that stopped him in th' 'dobe hut by th' arroyo. I'm tellin' yu this so yu won't do nothin' rash an' leave Carmencita a widow. Sabe?"

The hate on the Mexican's face redoubled, and he took a short step forward, but stopped when the muzzle of the Colt kissed his nose. He was the brother of Tamale José. As he backed away from the cool touch of the weapon he thought out swiftly his revenge. Some of his brother's old companions were at that moment drinking mescal in a saloon down the street, and they would be glad to see this Americano die. He glanced past his house at the saloon and Hopalong misconstrued his thoughts.

"Shore, go home. I'll just circulate around some for exercise. No hard feelings, only yu better throw it next time," he said as he backed away and rode off. Manuel went down the street and then ran into the saloon, where he caused an uproar.

Hopalong rode to the end of the plaza and tried to sing, but it was a dismal failure. Then he felt thirsty and wondered why he hadn't thought of it before. Turning his horse and seeing the saloon he rode up to it and in, lying flat on the animal's neck to avoid being swept off by the door frame. His entrance scared white some half a dozen loungers, who immediately sprang up in a decidedly hostile manner. Hopalong's Colts peeped over the ears of his horse and he backed into a corner near the bar.

"One, two, three — now, altogether, *breathe!* Yu acts like yu never saw a real puncher afore. All th' same," he remarked, nodding at several in the crowd, "I've seen yu afore. Yu are th' gents with th' hotfoot get-a-way that vamoosed when we got Tamale."

Curses were flung at him and only the humorous mood he was in saved trouble. One, bolder than the rest, spoke up: "The señor will not see any 'hotfoot get-a-way,' as he calls it, now! The señor was not wise to go so far away from his friends!"

Hopalong looked at the speaker, and a quizzical grin slowly spread over his face. "They'll shore feel glad when I tells them yu was askin' for 'em. But didn't yu see too much of 'em once, or was yu poundin' leather in the other direction? Yu don't want to worry none about me—*an' if yu don't get yore hands closter to yore neck they'll be h—l to pay!* There, that's more like home," he remarked, nodding assurance.

Reaching over he grasped a bottle and poured out a drink, his Colt slipping from his hand and dangling from his wrist by a thong. As the weapon started to fall several of the audience involuntarily moved as if to pick it up. Hopalong noticed this and paused with the glass half way to his lips. "Don't bother yoreselves none; I can git it again," he said, tossing off the liquor.

"Wow! Holy smoke!" he yelled. "This ain't drink! Sufferin' coyotes, nobody can accuse yu of sellin' liquor! Did yu make

this all by yoreself?" he asked incredulously of the proprietor, who didn't know
whether to run or to pray. Then he noticed that the crowd was spreading out,
and his Colts again became the center of
interest.

"Yu with th' lovely face, *sit down!*" he
ordered as the person addressed was gliding
toward the door. "I ain't a-goin' to let
yu pot me from th' street. Th' first man
who tries to git scarce will stop something
hot. An' yu *all* better sit down," he suggested, sweeping them with his guns. One
man, more obdurate than the rest, was slow
in complying, and Hopalong sent a bullet
through the top of his high sombrero, which
had a most gratifying effect.

"You'll regret this!" hissed a man in the
rear, and a murmur of assent arose. Some
one stirred slightly in searching for a weapon, and immediately a blazing Colt froze
him into a statue.

"Yu shore looks funny; eeny, meeny,
miny, mo," counted off the daring horseman; "move a bit an' off yu go," he finished. Then his face broke out in another
grin as he thought of more enjoyment.

"That there gent on th' left," he said,
pointing out with a gun the man he meant.
"Yu sing us a song. Sing a nice little
song."

As the object of his remarks remained
mute, he let his thumb ostentatiously slide
back with the hammer of the gun under it.
"Sing! Quick!" The man sang.

As Hopalong leaned forward to say something a stiletto flashed past his neck and
crashed into the bottle beside him. The
echo of the crash was merged into a report
as Hopalong fired from his waist. Then
he backed out into the street, his horse
carefully avoiding the outstretched form of
Manuel. Wheeling, he galloped across the
plaza and again faced the saloon. A flash
split the darkness and a bullet hummed
over his head and thudded into an adobe
wall at his back. Another shot and he
replied, aiming at the flash. From down
the street came the sound of a window
opening, and he promptly caused it to
close again. Several more windows opened
and hastily closed, and he rode slowly toward the far end of the plaza. As he
faced the saloon once more he heard a command to throw up his hands and saw the
glint of a gun, held by a man who wore the

insignia of sheriff. Hopalong complied,
but as his hands went up two spurts of
fire shot forth and the sheriff dropped his
weapon, reeled and sat down. Hopalong
rode over to him and, swinging down,
picked up the gun and looked the officer
over.

"Shoo, yu'll be all right soon—yore only
plugged in th' arms," he remarked as he
glanced up the street. Shadowy forms
were gliding from cover to cover, and he
immediately caused consternation among
them by his accuracy.

"Ain't it h—l?" he complained to the
wounded man. "I never starts out but
what somebody makes me shoot 'em. Came
down here to see a girl, an' finds she's married. Then when I moves on peaceable
like, her husband makes me hit him. Then
I wants a drink, an' he goes an' fans a knife
at me, an' me just teachin' him how! Then
yu has to come along an' make more trouble. Now look at them fools over there,"
he said, pointing at a dark shadow some
fifty paces off. "They're pattin' their
backs because I don't see 'em, an' if I hurts
them they'll git mad. Guess I'll make
'em dust along," he added, shooting into
the spot. A howl went up and two men
ran away at top speed.

The sheriff nodded his sympathy and
spoke. "I reckons you had better give up.
You can't get away. Every house, every
corner and shadow holds a man. You are
a brave man—but, as you say, unfortunate.
Better help me up and come with me—
they'll tear you to pieces."

"Shore I'll help yu up—I ain't got no
grudge against nobody. But my friends
know where I am, an' they'll come down
here an' raise a ruction if I don't show up.
So, if it's all the same to yu, I'll be ambling
right along," he said as he helped the sheriff
to his feet.

"Have you any objections to telling me
your name?" asked the sheriff as he looked
himself over.

"None whatever," answered Hopalong
heartily. "I'm Hopalong Cassidy of th'
Bar 20, Texas."

"You don't surprise me—I've heard of
you," replied the sheriff, wearily. "You
are the man who killed Tamale José, whom
I hunted for unceasingly. I found him
when you had left and I got the reward.
Come again some time and I'll divide with

you; two hundred and fifty dollars," he added craftily.

"I shore will, but I don't want no money," replied Hopalong as he turned away. "Adios, señor," he called back.

"Adios," replied the sheriff as he kicked a near-by door for assistance.

The cow-pony tied itself up in knots as it pounded down the street toward the trail, and, although he was fired on, he swung into the dusty trail with a song on his lips. Several hours later he stood dripping wet on the American side of the Rio Grande, and shouted advice to a score of Mexican cavalrymen on the opposite bank. Then he slowly picked his way toward El Paso for a game at Faro Dan's.

The sheriff sat in his easy chair one night some three weeks later, gravely engaged in rolling a cigarette. His arms were practically well, the wounds being in the fleshy parts. He was a philosopher and was disposed to take things easy, which accounted for his being in his official position for fifteen years. A gentleman at the core, he was well educated and had visited a goodly portion of the world. A book of Horace lay open on his knees and on the table at his side lay a shining new revolver, Hopalong having carried off his former weapon. He read aloud several lines and, in reaching for a light for his cigarette, noticed the new six-shooter. His mind leaped from Horace to Hopalong, and he smiled grimly at the latter's promise to call.

Glancing up, his eyes fell on a poster which conveyed the information in Spanish and in English that there was offered

FIVE HUNDRED DOLLARS ($500) REWARD
FOR HOPALONG CASSIDY,
of the ranch known as the Bar 20,
Texas, U. S. A.

and which gave a good description of that gentleman.

Sighing for the five hundred, he again took up his book and was lost in its pages when he heard a knock, rather low and timid. Wearily laying aside his reading, he strode to the door, expecting to hear a lengthy complaint from one of his townsmen. As he threw the door wide open, the light streamed out and lighted up a revolver, and behind it the beaming face of a cowboy, who grinned.

"Well, I'll be damned!" ejaculated the sheriff, starting back in amazement.

"Don't say that, sheriff, you've got lots of time to reform," replied a humorous voice. "How's th' wings?"

"Almost well; you were considerate," responded the sheriff.

"Let's go in—somebody might see me out here an' get into trouble," suggested the visitor, placing his foot on the sill.

"Certainly — pardon my discourtesy," said the sheriff. "You see, I wasn't expecting you to-night," he explained, thinking of the elaborate preparations that he would have gone to if he had thought the irrepressible would call.

"Well, I was down this way, an' seeing as how I had promised to drop in, I just natchurally dropped," replied Hopalong, as he took the chair proffered by his host.

After talking awhile on everything and nothing, the sheriff coughed and looked uneasily at his guest.

"Mr. Cassidy, I am sorry you called, for I like men of your energy and courage, and I very much dislike to arrest you," remarked the sheriff. "Of course you understand that you are under arrest," he added with anxiety.

"Who, me?" asked Hopalong with a rising inflection.

"Most assuredly," breathed the sheriff.

"Why, this is the first time I ever heard anything about it," replied the astonished cow-puncher. "I'm an American—don't that make any difference?"

"Not in this case, I'm afraid. You see, it's for manslaughter."

"Well, don't that beat th' devil, now?" said Hopalong. He felt sorry that a citizen of the glorious United States should be prey for troublesome sheriffs, but he was sure that his duty to Texas called upon him never to submit to arrest at the hands of a Greaser. Remembering the Alamo, and still behind his Colt, he reached over and took up the shining weapon from the table and snapped it open on his knee. After placing the cartridges in his pocket he tossed the gun over on the bed and, reaching inside his shirt, drew out another and threw it after the first.

"That's yore gun; I forgot to leave it," he said, apologetically. "Anyhow yu needs two," he added.

Then he glanced around the room, noticed the poster and walked over and read it. A full swift sweep of his gloved hand tore it from its fastenings and crammed it under his belt. The glimmer of anger in his eyes gave way as he realized that his head was worth a definite price, and he smiled at what the boys would say when he showed it to them. Planting his feet far apart and placing his arms akimbo, he faced his host in grim defiance.

"Got any more of these?" he inquired, placing his hand on the poster under his belt.

"Several," replied the sheriff.

"Trot 'em out," ordered Hopalong shortly.

The sheriff sighed, stretched and went over to a shelf from which he took a bundle of the articles in question. Turning slowly he looked at the puncher and handed them to him.

"I reckons they's all over this here town," remarked Hopalong.

"They are, and you may never see Texas again."

"So? Well, yu tell yore most particular friends that the job is worth five thousand, and that it will take so many to do it that when th' mazuma is divided up it won't buy a meal. There's only one man in this country to-night that can earn that money, an' that's me," said the puncher. "An' I don't need it," he added, smiling.

"But you are my prisoner—you are under arrest," enlightened the sheriff, rolling another cigarette. The sheriff spoke as if asking a question. Never before had five hundred dollars been so close at hand and yet so unobtainable. It was like having a check-book but no bank account.

"I'm shore sorry to treat yu mean," remarked Hopalong, "but I was paid a month in advance an' I'll have to go back an' earn it."

"You can—if you say that you will return," replied the sheriff, tentatively. The sheriff meant what he said, and for the moment had forgotten that he was powerless and was not the one to make terms.

Hopalong was amazed and for a time his ideas of Greasers staggered under the blow. Then he smiled sympathetically as he realized that he faced a white man.

"Never like to promise nothin'," he replied. "I might get plugged, or something might happen that wouldn't let me." Then his face lighted up as a thought came to him; "Say, I'll cut th' cards with yu to see if I comes back or not."

The sheriff leaned back and gazed at the cool youngster before him. A smile of satisfaction, partly at the self-reliance of his guest and partly at the novelty of his situation, spread over his face. He reached for a pack of Mexican cards and laughed. "God! You're a cool one—I'll do it. What do you call?"

"Red," answered Hopalong.

The sheriff slowly raised his hand and revealed the ace of hearts.

Hopalong leaned back and laughed, at the same time taking from his pocket the six extracted cartridges. Arising and going over to the bed, he slipped them in the chambers of the new gun and then placed the loaded weapon at the sheriff's elbow.

"Well, I reckon I'll amble, sheriff," he said as he opened the door. "If yu ever sifts up my way, drop in an' see me—th' boys 'll give yu a good time."

"Thanks; I will be glad to," replied the sheriff. "You'll take your pitcher to the well once too often, some day, my friend. This courtesy," glancing at the restored revolver, "might have cost you dearly."

"Shoo! I did that once an' th' feller tried to use it," replied the cowboy, as he backed through the door. "Some people are awfully careless," he added. "So long——"

"So long," replied the sheriff, wondering what sort of a man he had been entertaining.

The door closed softly, and soon after a joyous whoop floated in from the street. The sheriff toyed with the new gun and listened to the low caress of a distant guitar.

"Well, don't that beat hell?" he ejaculated.

11

The Advent of McAllister

CLARENCE EDWARD MULFORD

BAR 20 RANGE YARNS

V. THE ADVENT OF McALLISTER

BY CLARENCE EDWARD MULFORD

THE blazing sun shone pitilessly on an arid plain which was spotted with dust-gray clumps of mesquite and thorny chapparal. Basking in the burning sand and alkali lay several Gila monsters, which raised their heads and hissed with wide-open jaws as several faint, whip-like reports echoed flatly over the desolate plain, showing that even they had learned that danger was associated with such sounds.

Off to the north there became visible a cloud of dust and at intervals something swayed in it, something that rose and fell and then became hidden again. Out of that cloud came sharp, splitting sounds which were faintly responded to by another and larger cloud in its rear. As it came nearer and finally swept past, the Gilas, to their terror, saw a madly pounding horse and it carried a man. The latter turned in his saddle and raised a gun to his shoulder, and the thunder that issued from it caused the creeping audience to throw up their tails in sudden panic and bury themselves out of sight in the sand.

The horse was only a broncho, its sides covered with hideous yellow spots, and on its near flank was a peculiar scar, the brand. Foam flecked from its crimson jaws and found a resting place on its sides and on the hairy chaps of its rider. Sweat rolled and streamed from its heaving flanks and was greedily sucked up by the drought-cursed alkali. Close to the rider's knee a bloody furrow ran forward and one of the broncho's ears was torn and limp. The broncho was doing its best—it could run at that pace until it dropped dead. Every ounce of strength it possessed was put forth to bring those hind hoofs well in front of the forward ones and to send them pushing the sand behind in streaming clouds. The horse had done this same thing many times. —when would its master learn sense?

The man was typical in appearance with many of that broad land. Lithe, sinewy and bronzed by hard riding and hot suns, he sat in his Cheyenne saddle like a centaur, all his weight on the heavy, leather-guarded stirrups, his body rising in one magnificent straight line. A bleached moustache hid the thin lips, and a gray sombrero threw a heavy shadow across his eyes. Around his neck and over his open, blue flannel shirt lay loosely a knotted silk kerchief, and on his thighs a pair of open-flapped holsters swung uneasily with their ivory handled burdens. He turned abruptly, raised his gun to his shoulder and fired. One of his pursuers threw up his arms and slid from his horse, and a second later an agonized, quavering scream floated faintly past. The man laughed recklessly and patted his mount, which responded to the confident caress by lying flatter to the earth in a spurt of heart-breaking speed.

"I'll show 'em who they're trailin'. This is th' second time I've started for Muddy Wells, an' I'm goin' to git there, too, for all th' Cheyennes an' Sioux out of Hades!"

To the south another cloud of dust rapidly approached and the rider scanned it closely, for it was directly in his path. As he watched it he saw something wave and it was a sombrero! Shortly afterward a real cowboy yell reached his ears. He grinned and slid another cartridge in the greasy, smoking barrel of the Sharp's and fired again at the cloud in his rear. Some few minutes later a whooping, bunched crowd of madly riding cowboys thundered past him and he was recognized.

"Hullo, Frenchy!" yelled the nearest one. "Comin' back?"

"Come on, McAllister!" shouted another, "we'll give 'em blazes!" In response the straining broncho suddenly stiffened, bunched and slid on its haunches, wheeled and retraced its course.

The rear cloud suddenly scattered into many smaller ones and all swept off to the east. The rescuing band overtook them and, several hours later, when seated around a table in Tom Lee's saloon, Muddy Wells, a count was taken of them: two had escaped and the other twelve lay somewhere under the stolid sun.

"We was huntin' coyotes when we saw yu," said a smiling puncher who was known as Salvation Carroll chiefly because he wasn't.

"Yep! They've been stalkin' Tom's chickens," supplied Waffles, the champion poker player of the outfit. Tom Lee's chickens could whip anything of their kind for miles around and were reverenced accordingly.

"Sho! Is that so?" asked Frenchy with mild incredulity, such a state of affairs being deplorable.

"She shore is!" answered Tex Le Blanc, and then, as an afterthought, he added, "Where'd yu hit th' War-whoops?"

"'Bout four hours back. This here's th' second time I've headed for this place—last time they chased me to Las Cruces."

"That so?" asked Bigfoot Baker, a giant. "Ain't they *allus* interferin', now? Anyhow, they're better 'n coyotes."

"They was purty well heeled," suggested Tex, glancing at a dozen repeating Winchesters of late model that lay stacked in a corner. "Charley here said he thought they was from th' way yore cayuse looked, didn't yu, Charley?" Charley nodded and filled his pipe.

"'Pears like a feller can't amble around much nowadays without havin' to fight," grumbled Lefty Allen, who usually went out of his way hunting up trouble.

"We're goin' to th' Hills as soon as our cookie turns up," volunteered Tenspot Davis, looking inquiringly at Frenchy. "Heard any more news?"

"Nope. Same old story—lots of gold. Shucks, I've bit on so many of them rumors that they don't feaze me no more. One man who don't know nothin' about prospectin' goes an' stumbles over a fortune, an' those who know it from A to Izzard goes 'round pullin' in their belts."

"*We* don't pull in no belts—*we* knows just where to look, *don't* we, Tenspot?" remarked Tex, looking very wise.

"Ya-as we do," answered Tenspot, "if yu hasn't dreamed about it, we do."

"Yu wait; I wasn't dreamin', none whatever," assured Tex. "I *saw* it!"

"Ya-as, I saw it too, onct," replied Frenchy with sarcasm. "Went and lugged fifty pound of it all th' way to th' assay office—took me two days; an' that there four-eyed cuss looks at it an' snickers. Then he takes me by th' arm an' leads me to th' window. 'See that pile, my friend? That's all like yourn,' sez he. 'It's worth about one simoleon a ton, at th' coast. They use it for ballast.'"

"Aw! But this what *I* saw was *gold!*" exploded Tex.

"So was mine, for a while!" laughed Frenchy, nodding to the bartender for another round.

"Well, we're tired of punchin' cows! Ride sixteen hours a day, year in an' year out, an' what do we get? Fifty a month an' no chance to spend it, an' grub that 'd make a coyote sniffle! I'm for a vacation, an' if I goes broke, why, I'll punch again!" asserted Waffles, the foreman, thus revealing the real purpose of the trip.

"What 'd yore boss say?" asked Frenchy.

"Whoop! What didn't he say! Honest, I never thought he had it in him. It was fine. He cussed an hour frontways an' then trailed back on a dead gallop, with us a-laughin' fit to bust. *Then* he rustles for his gun, an' we rustles for town," answered Waffles, laughing at his remembrance of it.

As Frenchy was about to reply his sombrero was snatched from his head and disappeared. If he "got mad" he was to be regarded as not sufficiently well acquainted for banter and he was at once in hot water; if he took it good-naturedly he was one of the crowd in spirit; but in either case he didn't get his hat without begging or fighting for it. This was a recognized custom among the O-Bar-O outfit and was not intended as an insult.

Frenchy grabbed at the empty air and arose. Punching Lefty playfully in the ribs, he passed his hands behind that person's back. Not finding the lost head-gear he laughed and tripping Lefty up, fell with him and, reaching up on the table for his glass, poured the contents down Lefty's back and arose.

"Yu son-of-a-gun!" indignantly wailed that unfortunate. "Gee, it feels funny," he added, grinning, as he pulled the wet shirt away from his spine.

"Well, I've got to be amblin'," said Frenchy, totally ignoring the loss of his hat. "Goin' down to Buckskin," he offered and then asked, "When's yore cook comin'?"

"Day after to-morrow, if he don't get loaded," replied Tex.

"Who is he?"

"A one-eyed Greaser—Quiensabe Antonio."

"*I* used to know him. He's a h—l of a cook. Dished up the grub one season when I was punchin' for th' Tin-Cup, up in Montana," replied Frenchy.

"Oh, he kin cook *now*, all right," replied Waffles.

"That's about all he can cook. Useter wash his knives in th' coffee pot an' blow on th' tins. I chased him a mile one night for leavin' sand in th' skillet. Yu can have him — I don't envy yu none whatever."

"He don't sand no skillet when little Tenspot's around," assured that person, slapping his holster. "Does he, Lefty?"

"If he does yu oughter be lynched," consoled Lefty.

"Well, so long," remarked Frenchy, riding off to a small store where he bought a cheap sombrero.

Frenchy was a jack-of-all-trades, having been cow-puncher, prospector, proprietor of a "hotel" in Albuquerque, foreman of a ranch, sheriff and at one time had played angel to a venturesome but poor show troupe. Besides his versatility, he was well known as the man who took the stage through the Sioux country when no one else volunteered. He could shoot with the best, and his one pride was the brand of poker he handed out. Furthermore, he had never been known to take an unjust advantage over any man, and, on the contrary, had frequently voluntarily handicapped himself to make the event more interesting. But he must not be classed as being hampered with self-restraint.

His reasons for making this trip were two-fold: he wished to see Buck Peters, the foreman of the Bar 20 outfit, as he and Buck had punched cows together twenty years before and were firm friends; the other was that he wished to get square with Hopalong Cassidy, who had decisively cleaned him out the year before at poker. Hopalong played either in great good luck or the contrary, and I have, myself, out of curiosity, counted his consecutive winnings up to seventeen. Frenchy played an even, consistent game and usually left off richer than when he began, and this decisive defeat bothered him more than he would admit, even to himself.

Hopalong Cassidy, the younger by a score of years, was a product of the land; he had grown up there and he had been "toting" a gun ever since his arrival when a boy of seven. He ranked high as a gunfighter, his quickness and accuracy being among those things for which he was justly famed. He had wandered to the Bar 20, where he had worked his way from chore boy to an expert, full-fledged cowpuncher, as he had been taken in hand and trained by a master, or rather, by several of them. For some years all his money had been spent for cartridges and he had developed a passion for shooting, which, under the guiding hands of Buck Peters and the others, had made his ability in this line almost beyond belief. Naturally irrepressible and sunny, he had adopted the good points of his associates with a minimum of the bad, for the foreman's eye was quick to detect and his hand as quick to chastise; he was a combination of reckless nerve, humor, mischievousness, earnestness and nonchalance, and, as a result, he was continually getting into trouble, which he promptly got out of.

The ranch of the Bar 20 in what is now a well-known county of southwestern Texas, was made up of eight irrepressible cow-punchers, who were very well known throughout the cow country as an aggregation that never "took water." They enjoyed the reputation of being square, and that fact extended to them some privileges.

The round-up season was at hand and the Bar 20 was short of ropers, the rumors of fresh gold discoveries in the Black Hills having drawn all the more restless men north. The outfit also had a slight touch of the gold fever, and only their peculiar loyalty to the ranch and the assurance of the foreman that when the work was over he would accompany them, kept them from joining the rush of those who desired sudden and much wealth as the necessary preliminary of painting some cow-town in all the "bang up" style such an event would call for. Therefore, they had been given orders to secure the required assistance and they intended to do so, and were prepared to kidnap if necessary, for the glamour of wealth and the hilarity of the vacation made the hours falter in their speed.

As Frenchy leaned back in his chair in Cowan's saloon, Buckskin, early the next morning, planning to get revenge on Hopalong and then to recover his sombrero, he heard a medley of yells and whoops, and soon the door flew open before the strenuous and concentrated entry of a mass of twisting and kicking arms and legs, which magically found their respective owners and reverted to the established order of things. When the alkali dust had thinned he saw seven cow-punchers sitting on the prostrate form of another, who was earnestly engaged in trying to push Johnny Nelson's head out in the street with one foot as he voiced his lucid opinion of things in general and the seven in particular. After Red Connors had been stabbed in the back several times by the victim's energetic elbow, he ran out of the room, and presently returned with a pleased expression and a sombrero full of water, his finger plugging an old bullet hole in the crown.

"Is he enny better, Buck?" anxiously inquired the man with the reservoir.

"About a dollar's worth," replied the foreman. "Jest put a little right here," he drawled, as he pulled back the collar of the unfortunate's shirt.

"Ow! wow! WOW!" wailed the recipient, heaving and straining. The unengaged leg was suddenly wrested loose, and as it shot up and out Billy Williams, with his pessimism aroused to a blue-ribbon pitch, sat down forcibly in an adjacent part of the room, from where he lectured between gasps on the follies of mankind and the attributes of army mules.

Red tiptoed around the squirming bunch, looking for an opening, his pleased expression now having added a grin.

"Seems to be gittin' violent like," he soliloquized, as he aimed a stream at Hopalong's ear, which showed for a second as Pete Wilson strove for a half-nelson, and he managed to include Johnny and Pete in his effort.

Several minutes later, when the storm had subsided, the woeful crowd enthusiastically urged Hopalong to the bar, where he "bought."

"Of all th' ornery outfits I ever saw—" began the man at the table, grinning from ear to ear at the spectacle he had just witnessed.

Hearing the strange voice, Hopalong, who was always on the alert, wheeled with his hand going toward his thigh and then stretched it forth in greeting.

"Why, hullo, Frenchy! Glad to see yu, yu old son-of-a-gun! What's th' news from th' Hills?"

"Rather locoed, an' there's a locoed gang that's headin' that way. Goin' up?" he asked.

"Shore, after round-up. Seen any punchers trailin' around loose?"

"Ya-as," drawled Frenchy, delving into the possibilities suddenly opened to him, and determining to utilize to the fullest extent the opportunity that had come to him unsought. "There's nine over to Muddy Wells that yu might git if yu wants them bad enough. They've got a sombrero of mine," he added, deprecatingly.

"Nine! Twisted Jerusalem, Buck! Nine whole cow-punchers a-pinin' for work," he shouted, but then added thoughtfully, "Mebby they's engaged," it being one of the courtesies of the land not to take another man's help.

"Nope. They've stampeded for th' Hills an' left their boss *all* alone," replied Frenchy, well knowing that such desertion would not add any merits to the case of the distant outfit.

"Th' sons-of-guns," said Hopalong, "let's go an' get 'em," he suggested, turning to Buck, who nodded a smiling assent.

"Oh, what's th' hurry?" asked Frenchy, seeing his projected game slipping away into the uncertain future and happy in the thought that he would be avenged on the O-Bar-O outfit. "They'll be there till to-morrow noon — they's waitin' for their cookie, who's goin' with them."

"A cook! A cook! Oh, joy, a cook!" exulted Johnny, not for one instant doubting Buck's ability to capture the whole outfit, and seeing a whirl of excitement in the effort.

"Anybody we knows?" inquired Skinny Thompson.

"Shore. Tenspot Davis, Waffles, Salvation Carroll, Bigfoot Baker, Charley Lane, Lefty Allen, Kid Morris, Curley Tate an' Tex Le Blanc," responded Frenchy.

"Umm-m. Might as well rope a blizzard," grumbled Billy. "Might as well try to git th' Seventh Cavalry. We'll have a pious time corralling that bunch. Them's th' fellows that hit that bunch 'of inquiring Crow braves that time up in th' Bad Lands an' then said by-bye to th' Ninth."

"Aw, shut up! They's only two that's very much, an' Buck an' Hopalong can sing 'em to sleep," interposed Johnny, afraid that the expedition would fall through.

"How about Curley and Tex?" pugnaciously asked Billy.

"Huh, jest because they buffaloed yu over to Las Vegas, yu needn't think they's dangerous. Salvation an' Tenspot are th' only ones who can shoot," stoutly maintained Johnny.

"Here yu, get mum," ordered Buck to the pair. "When this outfit goes after anything it generally gets it. All in favor of kidnappin' that outfit signify th' same by kickin' Billy," whereupon Bill swore.

"Do yu want yore hat?" asked Buck, turning to Frenchy.

"I shore do," answered that individual.

"If yu helps us at th' round-up, we'll get it for yu. Fifty a month an' grub," offered the foreman.

"O. K.," replied Frenchy, anxious to even matters.

Buck looked at his watch. "Seven o'clock—we ought to get there by five if we relays at th' Barred-Horseshoe. Come on."

"How are we goin' to git them?" asked Billy.

"Yu leave that to me, son. Hopalong an' Frenchy 'll tend to that part of it. All yu has to do is to keep yore gun loose, in case any trouble busts, which I ain't a-figurin' on," replied Buck, making for his horse and swinging into the saddle, an example which was followed by the others, including Frenchy.

As they swung off Buck noticed the condition of Frenchy's mount and halted.

"Yu take that cayuse back an' get Cowan's," he ordered.

"That cayuse is good for Cheyenne—she eats work, an' besides, I wants my own," laughed Frenchy.

"Yu must had a reg'lar picnic, from th' looks of that crease," volunteered Hopalong, whose curiosity was mastering him.

"Shoo! I had a little argument with some feather dusters—th' O-Bar-O crowd cleaned them up."

"That so?" asked Buck.

"Yep! They sorter got into th' habit of chasin' me to Las Cruces an' forgot to stop."

"How many'd yu get?" asked Lanky Smith.

"Twelve. Two got away. I got two before th' crowd showed up—that makes fo'teen."

"Now th' cavalry 'll be huntin' yu," croaked Billy.

"Hunt nothin'! They was in war-paint —think I was a target?—think I was goin' to call off their shots for 'em?"

They relayed at the Barred-Horseshoe and went on their way at the same pace. Shortly after leaving the last-named ranch Buck turned to Frenchy and asked, "Any of that outfit think they can play poker?"

"Shore. Waffles."

"Does th' reverend Mr. Waffles think so very hard?"

"He shore does."

"Do th' rest of them mavericks think so too?"

"They'd bet their shirts on him."

At this juncture all were startled by a sudden eruption from Billy. "Haw! Haw! Haw!" he roared as the drift of Buck's intentions struck him. "Haw! Haw! Haw!"

"Here, yu long-winded coyote," yelled Red, banging him over the head with his quirt. "If yu don't 'Haw! Haw!' away from my ear, I'll make it a Wow! Wow! What d'yu mean? .Think I am a echo cliff? Yu slab-sided doodle-bug, yu!"

"G'way, yu crimson topknot, think my head's a hunk of quartz? Fer a plugged peso I'd strew yu all over th' scenery!" shouted Billy, feigning anger and rubbing his head.

"There ain't no scenery around here," interposed Lanky. "This here ·be-utiful prospect is a sublime conception of th' devil."

"Easy, boy! Them highfalutin' words 'll give yu a cramp some day. Yu talk like a newly made sergeant," remarked Skinny.

"He learned them words from that sky-pilot over at El Paso," volunteered Hopalong, winking at Red. "He used to amble down th' aisle afore th' lights was lit so's he could get a front seat. That was all hunky for a while, but every time he'd go out to irrigate, that female organ-wrastler would seem to call th' music off for his special benefit. So in a month he'd sneak in an' freeze to a chair by th' door, an' after a while he'd shy like blazes every time he got within eye range of th' church."

"Shore. But do yu know what made him get religion all of a sudden? He used to hang around on th' outside after th' joint let out an' trail along behind th' music-slinger lookin' like he didn't know what to do with his hands. Then when he got woozy one time she up an' told him that she had got a nice long letter from her hubby. Then Mr. Lanky hit th' trail for Santa Fé so hard that there wasn't hardly none of it left. I didn't see him for a whole month," supplied Red innocently.

"Yore shore funny, ain't yu?" sarcastically grunted Lanky. "Why, I can tell things on yu that 'd make yu stand treat for a year."

"I wouldn't sneak off to Santa Fé an' cheat yu out of them. Yu ought to be ashamed of yoreself."

"Yah!" snorted the aggrieved little man. "I had business over to Santa Fé!"

"Shore," indorsed Hopalong. "We've all had business over to Santa Fé. Why, about eight years ago I had business——"

"Choke up," interposed Red. "About eight years ago yu was washing pans for cookie an' askin' me for cartridges. Buck used to larrup yu about four times a day, eight years ago."

To their roars of laughter Hopalong dropped to the rear where, red-faced and quiet, he bent his thoughts on how to get square.

"We'll have a *pleasant* time corralling that gang," began Billy for the third time.

"For heaven's sake get off that trail!" replied Lanky. "Most of them knows Buck an' Hopalong, an' when they sees them with their holsters tied open they won't make no getaway. Of course they ain't none of them empty-guns, an' I never heard of them skedaddlin' from trouble, but they's square when the joke's on 'em. We ain't goin' to hold 'em up. De-plom-acy's th' game."

Billy looked dubious and said nothing. If he hadn't proven that he was as nervy as any man in the outfit they might have taken more stock in his grumbling.

"What's th' latest from Abilene way?" asked Buck of Frenchy.

"Nothin' much 'cept th' barb-wire ruction," replied the recruit.

"What's that?" asked Red, glancing apprehensively back at Hopalong.

"Why, th' settlers put up barb-wire fence so's th' cattle wouldn't get on their farms. That would a been all right, for there wasn't much of it. But some Brit-ishers who own a couple of big ranches out there got smart all of a sudden an' strung wire all along their lines. Punchers cross-in' th' country would run plumb into a fence an' would have to ride a day an' a half, mebby, afore they found th' corner. Well, naturally, when a man has been used to ridin' where he blame pleases an' as straight as he pleases, he ain't goin' to chase along a five-foot fence to 'Frisco when he wants to get to Waco. So th' punchers got to totin' wire-snips, an' when they runs up agin a fence they cuts down half a mile or so. Sometimes they'd tie their ropes to a strand an' pull off a couple of miles an' then go back after the rest. Th' ranch bosses sent out men to watch th' fences an' told 'em to shoot any festive puncher that monkeyed with th' hardware. Well, yu know what happens when a puncher gets shot at."

"When fences grow in Texas there'll be th' devil to pay," said Buck. He hated to think that some day the freedom of the range would be annulled, for he knew that it would be the first blow against the cow-boys' occupation. When a man's cattle couldn't spread out all over the land he wouldn't have to keep so many men. Farms would spring up and the sun of the free and easy cowboy would slowly set.

"I reckons th' cutters are classed th' same as rustlers," remarked Red with a gleam of temper.

"By th' owners, but not by th' punchers; an' it's th' punchers that count," replied Frenchy.

"Well, we'll give them a fight," interposed Hopalong, riding up. "When it gets so I can't go where I please I'll start on th' warpath. I won't buck th' cavalry, but I'll keep it busy huntin' for me an' I'll have time to 'tend to th' wire-fence men, too. Why, we'll be told we can't tote our guns!"

"They're sayin' that now," replied Frenchy. "Up in Topeka, Smith, who's now marshal, makes yu leave 'em with th' bartenders."

"I'd like to see any two-laigged cuss get my guns if I didn't want him to!" began Hopalong, indignant at the idea.

"Easy, son," cautioned Buck. "Yu would do what th' rest did because yu are a square man. I'm about as hard-headed a puncher as ever straddled leather an' I've had to use my guns purty considerable, but I reckons if any decent marshal asked me to cache them in a decent way, why, I'd do it. An' let me brand somethin' on yore mind—I've heard of Smith of Topeka, an' he's mighty nifty with his hands. He don't stand off an' tell yu to unload yore lead-ranch, but he ambles up close an' taps yu on yore shirt; if yu makes a gun-play he naturally knocks yu clean across th' room an' unloads yu afore yu gets yore senses back. He weighs about a hundred an' eighty an' he's shore got sand to burn."

"Yah! When I makes a gun play she plays! I'd look nice in Abilene or Paso or Albuquerque without my guns, wouldn't I? Just because I totes them in plain sight I've got to hand 'em over to some liquor-wrastler? I reckons not! Some hip-pocket skunk would plug me afore I could wink. I'd shore look nice loping around a keno layout without my guns, in th' same town with some cuss huntin' me, wouldn't I? A whole lot of good a marshal would a done Jimmy, an' didn't Harris get his from a cur in th' dark?" shouted Hopalong, angered by the prospect.

"We're talkin' about Topeka, where everybody has to hang up their guns," replied Buck. "An' there's th' law——"

"To blazes with th' law!" whooped Hopalong in Red's ear, as he unfastened the cinch of Red's saddle and at the same time stabbing that unfortunate's mount with his spurs, thereby causing a hasty separation of the two. When Red had picked himself up and things had quieted down again the subject was changed and several hours later they rode into Muddy Wells, a town with a little more excuse for its existence than Buckskin. The wells were in an arid valley west of Guadaloupe Pass, and were not only muddy but more or less alkaline.

As they neared the central group of buildings they heard a hilarious and assertive song which sprang from the door and windows of the main saloon. It was in jig time, rollicking and boisterous, but the words had evidently been improvised for the occasion, as they clashed immediately with those which sprang to the minds of the outfit, although they could not be clearly distinguished. As they approached nearer and finally dismounted, however, the words became recognizable, and the visitors were at once placed in harmony with the air of jovial recklessness by the roaring of the verses and the stamping of the time. Hopalong grinned and closed his holster flaps; no trouble would be likely to exist there.

Oh, we're red-hot cow-punchers playin' on our
   luck,
An' there ain't a proposition that we won't
   buck:
From sunrise to sunset we've ridden on th'
   range,
But now we're off for a howlin' change.

Chorus.

Laugh a little, sing a little, all th' day;
Play a little, drink a little—we can pay;
Ride a little, dig a little an' rich we'll grow.
Oh, we're that bunch from th' O-Bar-O!

Oh, there was a little tenderfoot an' he had a
   little gun,
An' th' gun an' him went a-trailin' up some fun.
They ambles up to Santa Fé to find a quiet
   game,
An' now they're planted with some more of th'
   same!

As Hopalong, followed by the others, pushed open the door and entered, he took up the chorus with all the power of Texan lungs and even Billy joined in. The sight that met their eyes was typical of the men and the mood and the place. Leaning along the walls, lounging on the table and straddling chairs with their forearms crossed on the backs were nine cowboys, ranging from old twenty to young fifty in years, and all were shouting the song and keeping time with their hands and feet. In the center of the room was a large man dancing a fair buck-and-wing to the time so uproariously set by his companions. Hatless, neck-kerchief loose, holsters flapping, chaps rippling out and close, spurs clinking and perspiration streaming from his tanned face, danced Bigfoot Baker as though his life depended on speed and noise. Bottles shook and the air was fogged with smoke and dust. Suddenly, his belt slipping and letting his chaps fall around his ankles, he tripped and sat down heavily. Gasping for breath, he held out his hand and received a huge plug of tobacco, for Bigfoot had won a contest.

Shouts of greeting were hurled at the newcomers and many questions were fired at them regarding "th' latest from th' Hills." Waffles made a rush for Hopalong, but fell over Bigfoot's feet and all three were piled up in a heap. All were beaming with good nature, for they were as so many schoolboys playing truant. Prosaic cowpunching was relegated to the rear and they looked eagerly forward to their several missions. Frenchy told of the barb-wire fence war and of the new regulations of "Smith of Topeka" regarding cow-punchers' guns, and from the caustic remarks explosively given it was plain to be seen what a wire fence could expect should one be met with, and there were many imaginary Smiths put *hors de combat*.

Kid Morris, after vainly trying to slip a blue-bottle fly inside of Hopalong's shirt, gave it up and slammed his hand on Hopalong's back instead, crying: "Well, I'll be dog-goned if here ain't Hopalong! How's th' missus an' th' deacon an' all th' folks to hum? I hears yu an' Frenchy's reg'lar poker fiends!"

"Oh, we plays onct in a while, but we don't want none of yore dust. Yu'll shore need it all afore th' Hills get through with yu," laughingly replied Hopalong.

"Oh, yore shore kind! But I was a sort of reckonin' that we needs some more. Perfesser P. D. Q. Waffles is our poker man an' he shore can clean out anything I ever saw. Mebby yu fellers feels reckless-like an' would like to make a pool," he cried, addressing the outfit of the Bar 20, "an' back yore boss of th' full house agin ourn?"

Red turned slowly around and took a full minute in which to size the Kid up. Then he snorted and turned his back again. The Kid stared at him in outraged dignity. "Well, what t'ell!" he softly murmured. Then he leaped forward and walloped Red on the back. "Hey, yore royal highness!" he shouted. "Yu-yu-yu—oh, hang it—*yu!* Yu slab-sided, ring-boned, saddle-galled shade of a coyote, do yu think I'm only meanderin' in th' misty vales of—of——"

Suggestions intruded from various sources. "Hades?" offered Hopalong. "Cheyenne?" murmured Johnny. "Misty mistiness of misty?" tentatively supplied Waffles.

Red turned around again. "Better come up an' have somethin'," he sympathetically invited, wiping away an imaginary tear.

"An' he's so young!" sobbed Frenchy.

"An' so fair!" wailed Tex.

"An' so ornery!" howled Lefty, throwing his arms around the discomfited youngster. Other arms went around him, and out of the sobbing mob could be heard earnest and heartfelt cussing, interspersed with imperative commands, which were gradually obeyed.

The Kid straightened up his wearing apparel. "Come on, yu locoed——"

"Angels?" queried Charley Lane, interrupting him. "Sweet things?" breathed Hopalong in hopeful expectancy.

"Oh, d—n it!" yelled the Kid as he ran out into the street to escape the persecution.

"Good Kid, all right," remarked Waffles. "He'll go around and lick some Greaser an' come back sweet as honey."

"Did somebody say poker?" asked Bigfoot, digressing from the Kid.

"Oh, yu fellows don't want no poker. Of course yu don't. Poker's mighty uncertain," replied Red.

"Yah!" exclaimed Tex Le Blanc, pushing forward. "I'll just bet yu to a stand-still that Waffles an' Salvation 'll round up all th' festive simoleons yu can get together! An' I'll throw in Frenchy's hat as an inducement."

"Well, if yore shore set on it make her a pool," replied Red, "an' th' winners divide with their outfit. Here's a starter," he added, tossing a buckskin bag in the table. "Come on, pile 'em up."

The crowd divided as the players seated themselves at the table, the O-Bar-O crowd grouping themselves behind their representatives; the Bar 20 behind theirs. A deck of cards was brought and the game was on.

Red, true to his nature, leaned back in a corner, where, hands on hips, he awaited any hostile demonstration on the part of the O-Bar-O; then, suddenly remembering, he looked half ashamed of his warlike position and became a peaceful citizen again. Buck leaned with his broad back against the bar, talking over his shoulder to the bartender, but watching Tenspot Davis, who was assiduously engaged in juggling a handful of Mexican dollars. Up by the door Bigfoot Baker, elated at winning the buck-and-wing contest, was endeavoring to learn a new step, while his late rival was drowning his defeat at Buck's elbow. Lefty Allen was softly singing a Mexican love song, humming when the words would not come. At the table could be heard low-spoken card terms and good-natured banter, interspersed with the clink of gold and silver and the soft pat-pat of the onlookers' feet unconsciously keeping time to Lefty's song. Notwithstanding the grim assertiveness of belts full of .44's and the peeping handles of long-barreled Colt's, set off with picturesque chaps, sombreros and tinkling spurs, the scene was one of peaceful content and good-fellowship.

"Ugh!" grunted Johnny, walking over to Red and informing that person that he, Red, was a worm-eaten prune, and that for half a wink he, Johnny, would prove it. Red grabbed him by the seat of his corduroys and the collar of his shirt and helped him outside, where they strolled about taking pot shots at whatever their fancy suggested.

Down the street in a cloud of dust rumbled the Las Cruces-El Paso stage, and the two punchers went up to meet it. Raw furrows showed in the woodwork, one mule was missing and the driver and guard wore fresh bandages. A tired tenderfoot leaped out with a sigh of relief and hunted for his baggage, which he found to be generously perforated. Swearing at the God-forsaken land where a man had to fight highwaymen and Indians inside of half a day, he grumblingly lugged his valise toward a forbidding-looking shack which was called a hotel.

The driver released his teams and then turned to Red. "Hullo, old hoss, how's th' gang?" he asked genially. "We've had a h—l of a time this yere trip," he went on without waiting for Red to reply. "Five miles out of Las Cruces we stood off a son-of-a-gun that wanted th' dude's wealth. Then just this side of the San Andre foothills we runs into a bunch of young bucks who turned us off this yere way an' gave us a runnin' fight purty near all th' way. I'm a whole lot farther from Paso now than I was when I started, an' seein' as I lost a jack I'll be some time gittin' there. Yu don't happen to sabe a jack I can borrow, do yu?"

"I don't know about no jack, but I'll rope yu a bronch," offered Red, winking at Johnny.

"I'll pull her myself before I'll put dynamite in th' traces," replied the driver. "Yu fellers might amble back a ways with me—them buddin' warriors 'll be layin' for me."

"We shore will," responded Johnny eagerly. "There's nine of us now an' there'll be nine more an' a cook to-morrow, mebby."

"Gosh, yu grows some," replied the guard. "Eighteen 'll be a plenty for them glory hunters."

"We won't be able to," contradicted Red, "for things are peculiar."

At this moment the conversation was interrupted by the tenderfoot, who sported a new and cheap sombrero and also a belt and holster complete.

"Will you gentlemen join me?" he asked, turning to Red and nodding at the saloon. "I am very dry and much averse to drinking alone."

"Why, shore," responded Red heartily, wishing to put the stranger at ease.

The game was running about even as they entered and Lefty Allen was still singing his love song, the rich tenor softening the harshness of the surroundings. Hopalong laughed joyously at a remark made by Waffles and the stranger glanced quickly at him. His merry, boyish face, underlined by a jaw showing great firmness and set off with an expression of aggressive self-reliance, impressed the stranger, and he remarked to Red, who lounged lazily near him, that he was surprised to see such a face on so young a man and he asked who the player was.

"Oh, his name's Hopalong Cassidy," answered Red. "He's th' cuss that raised that ruction down in Mexico last spring. Rode his cayuse in a saloon and played with the loungers and had to shoot one before he got out. When he did get out he had to fight a whole bunch of Greasers an' even potted their marshal, who had th' drop on him. Then he returned and visited the marshal about a month later, took his gun away from him and then cut the cards to see if he was a prisoner or not. He's a shore funny cuss."

The tenderfoot gasped his amazement. "Are you not fooling with me?" he asked.

"Tell him yu came after that five hundred dollars reward and see," answered Red good-naturedly.

"Holy smoke!" shouted Waffles as Hopalong won his sixth consecutive pot. "Did yu ever see such luck!" Frenchy grinned and some time later raked in his third. Salvation then staked his last cent against Hopalong's flush and dropped out.

Tenspot flipped to Waffles the money he had been juggling, and Lefty searched his clothes for wealth. Buck, still leaning against the bar, grinned and winked at Johnny, who was pouring hair-raising tales into the receptive ears of the stranger. Thereupon Johnny confided to his newly found acquaintance the facts about the game, nearly causing that person to explode with delight.

Waffles pushed back his chair, stood up and stretched. At the finish of a yawn he grinned at his late adversary. "I'm all in, yu old son-of-a-gun. Yu shore can play draw. I'm goin' to try yu again some time. I was beat fair and square an' I ain't got no kick comin', none whatever," he remarked, as he shook hands with Hopalong.

"'Oh, we're that gang from th' O-Bar-O,'" hummed the Kid as he sauntered in. One cheek was slightly swollen and his clothes shed dust at every step. "Who wins?" he inquired, not having heard Waffles.

"They did, d—n it!" exploded Bigfoot.

One of the Kid's peculiarities was revealed in the unreasoning and hasty conclusions he arrived at. From no desire to imply unfairness, but rather because of his bitterness against failure of any kind and his loyalty to Waffles, came his next words: "Mebby they skinned yu."

Like a flash Waffles sprang before him, his hand held up, palm out. "He don't mean nothin'—he's only a damn-fool kid!" he cried.

Buck smiled and wrested the Colt from Johnny's ever ready hand. "Here's another," he said. Red laughed softly and rolled Johnny on the floor. "Yu jackass," he said, "don't yu know better'n to make a gun-play when we needs them all?"

"What are we goin' to do?" asked Tex, glancing at the bulging pockets of Hopalong's chaps.

"We're goin' to punch cows again, that's what we're goin' to do," answered Bigfoot dismally.

"An' whose are we goin' to punch? We can't go back to the old man," grumbled Tex.

Salvation looked askance at Buck and then at the others. "Mebby," he began, "mebby we kin git a job on th' Bar 20. Then turning to Buck again he bluntly asked, "Are yu short of punchers?"

"Well, I might use some," answered the foreman, hesitating. "But I ain't got only one cook, an'——"

"We'll git yu th' cook, all O. K.," interrupted Charley Lane vehemently. "Hi, yu cook!" he shouted, "amble in here an' git a rustle on!"

There was no reply and, after waiting for a minute, he and Waffles went into the rear room, from which there immediately issued great chunks of profanity and noise. They returned looking pugnacious and disgusted, with a wildly fighting man who was more full of liquor than was the bottle which he belligerently waved.

"This here animated distillery what yu sees is our cook," said Waffles. "*We* eats his grub, nobody else. If he gits drunk that's *our* funeral; *but he won't get drunk!* If yu wants us to punch for yu say so an' we does; if yu don't, we don't."

"Well," replied Buck thoughtfully, "mebby I *can* use yu." Then with a burst of recklessness he added, "Yes, if I lose my job! But yu might sober that Greaser up if yu let him fall in th' horse-trough."

As the procession wended its way on its mission of wet charity, carrying the cook in any manner at all, Frenchy waved his long-lost sombrero at Buck, who stood in the door, and shouted, "Yu old son-of-a-gun, I'm proud to know yu!"

Buck smiled and snapped his watch shut. "Time to amble," he said.

12

Holding the Claim

CLARENCE EDWARD MULFORD

BAR 20 RANGE YARNS

VI.—HOLDING THE CLAIM

BY CLARENCE EDWARD MULFORD

PAINTING BY FRANK E. SCHOONOVER

H, we're that gang from th' O-Bar-O," hummed Waffles, sinking the branding-iron in the flank of a calf. The scene was one of great activity and hilarity. Several fires were burning near the huge corral and in them half a dozen irons were getting hot. Three calves were being held down for the brand of the "Bar 20" and two more were being dragged up on their sides by the ropes of the cowboys, the proud cow-ponies showing off their accomplishments at the expense of the calves' feelings. In the corral the dust arose in steady clouds as calf after calf was "cut out" by the ropers and dragged out to get "tagged." Angry cows fought valiantly for their terrorized offspring, but always to no avail, for the hated rope of some perspiring and dust-grimed rider sent them crashing to earth. Over the plain were herds of cattle and groups of madly riding cowboys, and two cook wagons were stalled a short distance from the corral. The round-up of the Bar 20 was taking place.

The outfit of this ranch was composed of eight cowboys, one of whom, Buck Peters, was foreman. All were well known throughout the cattle country as a prize-winning aggregation at any game. Having been short of help, they had paid a visit to Muddy Wells and cleaned up at poker the outfit of the "O-Bar-O," which had just started for the Black Hills in response to a rumor of fresh gold discoveries. This loss of capital had forced the would-be prospectors to secure work under the foreman of the Bar 20, and the two outfits were going to the Hills as soon as the round-up was over. Each outfit tried to outdo the other and each individual strove for a prize. The man who cut out and dragged to the fire the most calves in three days could leave at the expiration of that time, the rest to follow as soon as they could.

In this contest Hopalong Cassidy led his nearest rival, Red Connors, both of whom were Bar 20 men, by twenty cut-outs, and there remained but half an hour more in which to compete. As Red disappeared into the sea of tossing horns Hopalong dashed out with a whoop, dragging a calf at the end of his rope.

"Hi, yu trellis-built rack of bones, come along there! Whoop!" he yelled, turning the prisoner over to the squad by the fire. "Chalk up this here insignificant wart of cross-eyed perversity: an' how many?" he called as he galloped back to the corral.

"One ninety-eight," announced Buck, blowing the sand from the tally sheet. "That's shore goin' some," he remarked to himself.

When the calf sprang up it was filled with terror, rage and pain, and charged at Billy from the rear as that pessimistic soul was leaning over and poking his finger at a somber horned-toad. "Wow!" he yelled as his feet took huge steps up in the air, each one strictly on its own course. "Woof!" he grunted in the hot sand as he arose on his hands and knees and spat alkali.

"What's s'matter?" he asked dazedly of Johnny Nelson. *Ain't it funny!*" he yelled sarcastically as he beheld Johnny holding his sides with laughter. "*Ain't* it

125

funny!" he repeated belligerently. "Of course that four-laigged, knock-kneed, wobblin' son-of-a-Piute had to cut *me* out. They wasn't *nobody* in sight but Billy! Why didn't yu *say* he was comin'? Think I can see four ways to onct? Why *didn't*—"

At this point Red cantered up with a calf and, by a quick maneuver, drew the taut rope against the rear of Billy's knees, causing that unfortunate to sit down heavily. As he arose choking with broken-winded profanity Red dragged the animal to the fire, and Billy forgot his grievances in the press of labor.

"How many, Buck?" asked Red.

"One-eighty."

"How does she stand?"

"Yore eighteen to th' bad," replied the foreman.

"Th' son-of-a-gun!" marveled Red, riding off.

Another whoop interrupted them, and Billy quit watching out of the corner eye for pugnacious calves as he prepared for Hopalong.

"Hey, Buck, this here cuss was with a Barred-Horseshoe cow," he announced as he turned it over to the branding man. Buck made a tally in a separate column and released the animal. "Hullo, Red! Workin'?" asked Hopalong of his rival.

"Some, yu little cuss," answered Red with all the good nature in the world. Hopalong was his particular "side partner," and he could lose to him with the best of feelings.

"Yu looks so nice an' cool an' clean, I didn't know," responded Hopalong, eyeing a streak of sweat and dust which ran from Red's eyes to his chin and then on down his neck.

"What yu been doin'? Plowin' with yore nose?" returned Red, smiling blandly at his friend's appearance.

"Yah!" snorted Hopalong, wheeling toward the corral. "Come on, yu pie-eatin' dodle-bug; I'll beat yu to the gate!"

The two ponies sent showers of sand all over Billy, who eyed them in pugnacious disgust. "Of all th' locoed imps that ever made life miserable fer a man, them's th' worst! Is there any piece of fool nonsense they hain't harnessed me with?" he beseeched of Buck. "Is there anything they hain't done to me? They hides my liquor; they stuffs th' sweat band of my hat with

rope; they ties up my pants; they puts *water* in my *boots* an' *toads* in my *bunk*—ain't they *never* goin' to get sane?"

"Oh, they're only kids—they can't help it," offered Buck. "Didn't they hobble my cayuse when I was on him an' near bust my neck?"

Hopalong interrupted the conversation by bringing up another calf, and Buck, glancing at his watch, declared the contest at an end.

"Yu wins," he remarked to the newcomer. "An' now yu get scarce or Billy will shore straddle yore nerves. He said as how he was goin' to get square on yu to-night."

"I didn't, neither, Hoppy!" earnestly contradicted Billy, who had visions of a night spent in torment as a reprisal for such a threat. "Honest I didn't, did I, Johnny?" he asked appealingly.

"Yu shore did," lied Johnny, winking at Red, who had just ridden up.

"I don't know what yore talkin' about, but yu shore did," replied Red.

"If yu did," grinned Hopalong, "I'll shore make yu hard to find. Come on, fellows," he said; "grub's ready. Where's Frenchy?"

"Over chewin' th' rag with Waffles about his hat—he's lost it again," answered Red. "He needs a guardian fer that bonnet. Th' Kid an' Salvation has jammed it in th' corral fence an' Waffles has to stand fer it."

"Let's put it in th' grub wagon an' see him cuss cookie," suggested Hopalong.

"Shore," indorsed Johnny; "Cookie 'll feed him bum grub for a week to get square."

Hopalong and Johnny ambled over to the corral and after some trouble located the missing sombrero, which they carried to the grub wagon and hid in the flour barrel. Then they went over by the excited owner and dropped a few remarks about how strange the cook was acting and how he was watching Frenchy.

Frenchy jumped at the bait and tore over to the wagon, where he and the cook spent some time in mutual recrimination. Hopalong nosed around and finally dug up the hat, white as new-fallen snow.

"Here's a hat—found it in th' dough barrel," he announced, handing it over to Frenchy, who received it in open-mouthed stupefaction.

"Yu pie-makin' pirate! *Yu* didn't know where my lid was, *did* yu! Yu cross-eyed lump of hypocrisy!" yelled Frenchy, dusting off the flour with one full-armed swing on the cook's face, driving it into that unfortunate's nose and eyes and mouth. "Yu white-washed Chink, yu—rub yore face with water an' yu've got pancakes."

"Hey! What yu doin'!" yelled the cook, kicking the spot where he had last seen Frenchy. "Don't yu know better'n that!"

"Yu live close to yoreself or I'll throw yu so high th' sun'll duck," replied Frenchy, a smile illuminating his face.

"Hey, cookie," remarked Hopalong confidentially, "I know who put up this joke on yu. Yu ask Billy who hid th' hat," suggested the tease. "Here he comes now —see how queer he looks."

"Th' mournful Piute," ejaculated the cook. "I'll shore make him wish he'd kept on his own trail. I'll flavor his slush [coffee] with year-old dish-rags!"

At this juncture Billy ambled up, keeping his weather eye peeled for trouble. "Who's a dish-rag?" he queried. The cook mumbled something about crazy hens not knowing when to quit cackling and climbed up in his wagon. And that night Billy swore off drinking coffee.

When the dawn of the next day broke, Hopalong was riding toward the Black Hills, leaving Billy to untie himself as best he might.

The trip was uneventful and several days later he entered Red Dog, a rambling shanty town, one of those western mushrooms that sprang up in a night. He took up his stand at the Miner's Rest, and finally secured six claims at the cost of nine hundred hard-earned dollars, a fund subscribed by the outfits, as it was to be a partnership affair.

He rode out to a staked-off piece of hillside and surveyed his purchase, which consisted of a patch of ground, six holes, six piles of dirt and a log hut. The holes showed that the claims had been tried and found wanting.

He dumped his pack of tools and provisions, which he had bought on the way up, and lugged them into the cabin. After satisfying his curiosity he went outside and sat down for a smoke, figuring up in his mind how much gold he could carry on a horse. Then, as he realized that he could get a pack mule to carry the surplus, he became aware of a strange presence near at hand and looked up into the muzzle of a Sharp's rifle. He grasped the situation in a flash and calmly blew several heavy smoke rings around the frowning barrel.

"Well?" he asked slowly.

"Nice day, stranger," replied the man with the rifle, "but don't yu reckon yu've made a mistake?"

Hopalong glanced at the number burned on a near-by stake and blew another smoke ring. He was waiting for the gun to waver. "No, I reckons not," he answered. "Why?"

"Well, I'll jest tell yu since yu asks. This yere claim's mine an' I'm a reg'lar terror, I am. That's why; an' seein' as it is, yu better amble some."

Hopalong glanced down the street and saw an interested group watching him, which only added to his rage for being in such a position. Then he started to say something, faltered and stared with horror at a point several feet behind his opponent. The "terror" sprang to one side in response to Hopalong's expression, as if fearing that a snake or some such danger threatened him. As he alighted in his new position he fell forward and Hopalong slid a smoking Colt in its holster.

Several men left the distant group and ran toward the claim. Hopalong reached his arm inside the door and brought forth his Sharp's rifle, with which he covered their advance.

"Anything yu want?" he shouted savagely.

The men stopped and two of them started to sidle in front of two others, but Hopalong was not there for the purpose of permitting a move that would screen any gun play and he stopped the game with a warning shout. Then the two held up their hands and advanced.

"We wants to git Dan," called out one of them, nodding at the prostrate figure.

"Come ahead," replied Hopalong, substituting a Colt for the rifle.

They carried their badly wounded and insensible burden back to those whom they had left, and several curses were hurled at the cowboy, who only smiled grimly and entered the hut to place things ready for a siege, should one come. He had one hundred rounds of ammunition and provisions enough for two weeks, with the assurance of reinforcements long before that time would expire. He cut several rough loopholes and laid out his weapons for quick handling. He knew that he could stop any advance during the day and planned only for night attacks. How long he could do without sleep did not bother him, because he gave it no thought, as he was accustomed to short naps and could awaken at will or at the slightest sound.

As dusk merged into dark he crept forth and collected several handfuls of dry twigs, which he scattered around the hut, as the cracking of these would warn him of an approach. Then he went in and went to sleep.

He awoke at daylight after a good night's rest, and feasted on canned beans and peaches. Then he tossed the cans out of the door and shoved his hat out. Receiving no response he walked out and surveyed the town at his feet. A sheepish grin spread over his face as he realized that there was no danger. Several red-shirted men passed by him on their way to town, and one, a grizzled veteran of many gold camps, stopped and sauntered up to him.

"Mornin'," said Hopalong.

"Mornin'," replied the stranger. "I thought I'd drop in an' say that I saw that gun-play of yourn yesterday. Yu ain't got no reason to look fer a rush. This camp is half white men an' half bullies, an th' white men won't stand fer no play like that. Them fellers that jest passed are neighbors of yourn, an' they won't lay abed if yu needs them. But yu wants to look out fer th' joints in th' town. Guess this business is out of yore line," he finished as he sized Hopalong up.

"She shore is, but I'm here to stay. Got tired of punchin' an' reckoned I'd git rich." Here he smiled and glanced at the hole. "How're yu makin' out?" he asked.

"'Bout five dollars a day apiece, but that ain't nothin' when grub's so high. Got reckless th' other day an' had a egg at fifty cents."

Hopalong whistled and glanced at the empty cans at his feet. "Any marshal in this burg?"

"Yep. But he's one of th' gang. No good, an' drunk half th' time an' half drunk

th' rest. Better come down an' have something," invited the miner.

"I'd shore like to, but I can't let no gang get in that door," replied the puncher.

"Oh, that's all right; I'll call my pardner down to keep house till yu gits back. He can hold her all right. Hey, Jake!" he called to a man who was some hundred paces distant; "come down here an' keep house till we gits back, will yu?"

The man lumbered down to them and took possession as Hopalong and his newly found friend started for the town.

They entered the "Miner's Rest" and Hopalong fixed the room in his mind with one swift glance. Three men — and they looked like the crowd he had stopped the day before — were playing poker at a table near the window. Hopalong leaned with his back to the bar and talked, with the players always in sight.

Soon the door opened and a bewhiskered, heavy-set man tramped in and, walking up to Hopalong, looked him over.

"Huh," he sneered, "yu are th' gent with th' festive guns that plugged Dan, ain't yu?"

Hopalong looked him in the eyes and quietly replied: "An' who th' h—l are yu?"

The stranger's eyes blazed and his face wrinkled with rage as he aggressively shoved his jaw close to Hopalong's face.

"Yu runt, I'm a better man than yu even if yu do wear hair pants," referring to Hopalong's chaps. "Yu cow-wrastlers make me tired, an' I'm goin' to show yu that this town is too good for you. Yu can say it right now that yu are a ornery, game-leg——"

Hopalong, blind with rage, smashed his insulter squarely between the eyes with all the power of his sinewy body behind the blow, knocking him in a heap under the table. Then he quickly glanced at the card players and saw a hostile movement. His gun was out in a flash and he covered the trio as he walked up to them. Never in all his life had he felt such a desire to kill. His eyes were diamond points of accumulated fury, and those whom he faced quailed before him.

"Yu scum of th' earth! Draw, please, draw! Pull yore guns an' gimme my chance! Three to one, an' I'll lay my guns here," he said, placing them on the bar and removing his hands. "'Nearer My God to Thee' is purty appropriate fer yu just now! Yu seem to be a-scared of yore own guns. Git down on yore dirty knees an' say good an' loud that yu eats dirt! Shout out that yu are too currish to live with decent men," he said, even-toned and distinct, his voice vibrant with passion as he took up his Colts. "Get down!" he repeated, shoving the weapons forward and pulling back the hammers.

The trio glanced at each other, and all three dropped to their knees and repeated in venomous hatred the words Hopalong said for them.

"Now git! An' if I sees yu when I leaves I'll send yu after yore friend. I'll shoot on sight now. Git!" He escorted them to the door and kicked the last one out.

His miner friend still leaned against the bar and looked his approval.

"Well done, youngster! But yu wants to look out—that man," pointing to the now groping victim of Hopalong's blow, "is th' marshal of this town. He or his pals will get yu if yu don't watch th' corners."

Hopalong walked over to the marshal, jerked him to his feet and slammed him against the bar. Then he tore the cheap badge from its place and threw it on the floor. Reaching down, he drew the marshal's revolver from its holster and shoved it in its owner's hand.

"Yore th' marshal of this place an' it's too good for me, but yore goin' to pick up that tin lie," pointing at the badge, "an' yore goin' to do it right now. Then yore goin' to get kicked out of that door, an' if yu stops runnin' while I can see yu I'll fill yu so full of holes yu'll catch cold. Yore a sumptious marshal, yu are! Yore th' snortingest ki-yi that ever stuck its tail atween its laigs, yu are. Yu pop-eyed wall flower, yu wants to peep to yore-self or some papoose 'll slide yu over th' Divide so fast yu won't have time to grease yore pants. Pick up that license-tag an' let me see yu perculate so lively that yore back 'll look like a ten-cent piece in five seconds. Flit!"

The marshal, dazed and bewildered, stooped and fumbled for the badge. Then he stood up and glanced at the gun in his hand and at the eager man before him. He slid the weapon in his belt and drew his hand across his fast-closing eyes. Cursing streaks of profanity, he staggered to the door and landed in a heap in the street from the force of Hopalong's kick. Struggling to his feet, he ran unsteadily down the block and disappeared around a corner.

The bartender, cool and unperturbed, pushed out three glasses on his treat: "I've seen yu afore, up in Cheyenne—'member? How's yore friend Red?" he asked as he filled the glasses with the best the house afforded.

"Well, shore 'nuff! Glad to see yu, Jimmy! What yu doin' away off here?" asked Hopalong, beginning to feel at home.

"Oh, jest filterin' round like. I'm awful glad to see yu—this yere wart of a town needs siftin' out. It was only last week I was wishin' one of yore bunch 'ud show up—that ornament yu jest buffaloed shore raised th' devil in here, an' I wished I had somebody to prospect his anatomy for a lead mine. But he's got a tough gang circulating with him. Ever hear of Dutch Shannon or Blinky Neary? They's with him."

"Dutch Shannon? Nope," he replied.

"Bad eggs, an' not a-carin' how they gits square. Th' feller yu salted yesterday was a bosom friend of th' marshal's, an' he passed in his chips last night."

"So?"

"Yep. Bought a bottle of ready-made nerve an' went to his own funeral. Aristotle Smith was lookin' fer him up in Cheyenne last year. Aristotle said he'd give a century fer five minutes' palaver with him, but he shied th' town an' didn't come back. Yu know Aristotle, don't yu? He's th' geezer that made fame up to Poison Knob three years ago. He used to go to town ridin' astride a log on th' lumber flume. Made four miles in six minutes with th' promise of a ruction when he stopped. Once when he was loaded he tried to ride back th' same way he came, an' th' first thing he knowed he was three miles farther from his supper an' a-slippin' down that valley like he wanted to go somewhere. He swum out at Potter's Dam an' it took him a day to walk back. But he didn't make that play again, because he was frequently sober, an' when he wasn't he'd only stand off an' swear at th' slide."

"That's Aristotle, all hunk. He's th' chap that used to play checkers with Deacon Rawlins. They used empty an' loaded shells for men, an' when they got a king they'd lay one on its side. Sometimes they'd jar th' board an' they'd all be kings an' then they'd have a cussin' match," replied Hopalong, once more restored to good humor.

"Why," responded Jimmy, "he counted his wealth over twice by mistake an' shore raised a howl when he went to blow it—thought he'd been robbed, an' laid behind th' houses fer a week lookin' fer th' feller that done it."

"I've heard of that cuss—he shore was th' limit. What become of him?" asked the miner.

"He ambled up to Laramie an' stuck his head in th' window of that joint by th' plaza an' hollered 'Fire,' an' they did. He was shore a good feller, all th' same," answered the bartender.

Hopalong laughed and started for the door. Turning around he looked at his miner friend and asked: "Comin' along? I'm goin' back now."

"Nope. Reckon I'll hit th' tiger a whirl. I'll stop in when I passes."

"All right. So long," replied Hopalong, slipping out of the door and watching for trouble. There was no opposition shown him, and he arrived at his claim to find Jake in a heated argument with another of the gang.

"Here he comes now," he said as Hopalong walked up. "Tell him what yu said to me."

"I said yu made a mistake," said the other, turning to the cowboy in a half apologetic manner.

"An' what else?" insisted Jake.

"Why, ain't that all?" asked the claim-jumper's friend in feigned surprise, wishing that he had kept quiet.

"Well, I reckons it is if yu can't back up yore words," responded Jake in open contempt.

Hopalong grabbed the intruder by the collar of his shirt and hauled him off the claim. "Yu keep off this, understand? I just kicked yore marshal out in th' street, an' I'll pay yu th' next call. If yu rambles in range of my guns yu'll shore get in th' way of a slug. Yu an' yore gang wants to browse on th' far side of th' range or yu'll miss a sunrise some mornin'. Scoot!"

Hopalong turned to his companion and smiled. "What 'd he say?" he asked genially.

"Oh, he jest shot off his mouth a little. They's all no good. I've collided with lots of them all over this country. They can't face a good man an' keep their nerve. What 'd yu say to th' marshal?"

"I told him what he was an' threw him outen th' street," replied Hopalong. "In about two weeks we'll have a new marshal an' he'll shore be a dandy."

"Yes? Why don't yu take th' job yore-self? We're with yu."

"Better man comin'. Ever hear of Buck Peters or Red Connors of th' Bar 20, Texas?"

"Buck Peters? Seems to me I have. Did he punch fer th' Tin-Cup up in Montana, 'bout twenty years back?"

"Shore! Him and Frenchy McAllister punched all over that country an' they used to paint Cheyenne, too," replied Hopalong, eagerly.

"I knows him, then. I used to know Frenchy, too. Are they comin' up here?"

"Yes," responded Hopalong, struggling with another can while waiting for the fire to catch up. "Better have some grub with me—don't like to eat alone," invited the cowboy, the reaction of his late rage swinging him to the other extreme.

When their tobacco had got well started at the close of the meal and content had taken possession of them Hopalong laughed quietly and finally spoke:

"Did yu ever know Aristotle Smith when yu was up in Montana?"

"Did I! Well, me an' Aristotle prospected all through that country till he got so locoed I had to watch him fer fear he'd blow us both up. He greased th' fryin' pan with dynamite one night, an' we shore had to eat jerked meat an' canned stuff all th' rest of that trip. What made yu ask? Is he comin' up too?"

"No, I reckons not. Jimmy, th' bartender, said that he cashed in up at Laramie. Wasn't he th' cuss that built that boat out there on th' Arizona desert because he was scared that a flood might come? Th' sun shore warped that punt till it wasn't even good for a hencoop."

"Nope. That was Sister-Annie Tompkins. He was purty near as bad as Aristotle, though. He roped a puma up on th' Sacramentos, an' didn't punch no more fer

three weeks. Well, here comes my pardner an' I reckons I'll amble right along. If
yu needs any referee or a side pardner in
any ruction yu has only got to warble up
my way. So long."

The next ten days passed quietly and on
the afternoon of the eleventh Hopalong's
miner friend paid him a visit.

"Jake recommends yore peaches," he
laughed as he shook Hopalong's hand.
"He says yu boosted another of that crowd.
That bein' so I thought I would drop in an'
say that they're comin' after yu to-night,
shore. Just heard of it from yore friend
Jimmy. Yu can count on us when th'
rush comes. But why didn't yu say yu
was a pard of Buck Peters'? Me an' him
used to shoot up Laramie together. From
what yore friend James says, yu can handle
this gang by yore lonesome, but if yu needs
any encouragement yu make some sign an'
we'll help th' event along some. They's
eight of us that 'll be waitin' up to get th'
returns an' we're shore goin' to be in
range."

"Gee, it's nice to run across a friend of
Buck's! Ain't he a son-of-a-gun?" asked
Hopalong, delighted at the news. Then,
without waiting for a reply, he went on:
"Yore shore square, all right, an' I hates to
refuse yore offer, but I got eighteen friends
comin' up an' they ought to get here by to-
morrow. Yu tell Jimmy to head them
this way when they shows up an' I'll have
th' claim for them. There ain't no use of
yu fellers gettin' mixed up in this. Th'
bunch that's comin' can clean out any
gang this side of sunup, an' I expects they'll
shore be anxious to begin when they finds
me eatin' peaches an' wastin' my time
shootin' bums. Yu pass th' word along to
yore friends, an' tell them to lay low an' see
th' Arory Boerallis hit this town with its
tail up. Tell Jimmy to do it up good when
he speaks about me holdin' th' claim—I
likes to see Buck an' Red fight when they're
good an' mad."

The miner laughed and slapped Hopalong
on the shoulder. "Yore all right, youngster! Yore just like Buck was at yore age.
Say now, I reckons he wasn't a reg'lar
terror on wheels! Why, I've seen him do
more foolish things than any man I knows
of, an' I calculate that if Buck pals with
yu there ain't no water in yore sand. My
name's Tom Halloway," he suggested.

"An' mine's Hopalong Cassidy," was the
reply. "I've heard Buck speak of yu."

"Has yu? Well, don't it beat all how
little this world is? Somebody allus turnin'
up that knows somebody yu knows. I'll
just amble along, Mr. Cassidy, an' don't
yu be none bashful about callin' if yu
needs me. Any pal of Buck's is my friend.
Well, so long," said the visitor as he strode
off. Then he stopped and turned around.
"Hey, mister!" he called. "They are goin'
to roll a fire barrel down agin yu from behind," indicating by an outstretched arm
the point from where it would start. "If
it burns yu out I'm goin' to take a hand
from up there," pointing to a cluster of
rocks well to the rear of where the crowd
would work from, "an' I don't care whether
yu likes it or not," he added to himself.

Hopalong scratched his head and then
laughed. Taking up a pick and shovel, he
went out behind the cabin and dug a trench
parallel with and about twenty paces
away from the rear wall. Heaping the
excavated dirt up on the near side of the
cut, he stepped back and surveyed his
labor with open satisfaction. "Roll yore
fire barrel an' be d——," he muttered.
"Mebby she won't make a bully light for
pot shots, though," he added, grinning at
the execution he would do.

Taking up his tools, he went up to the
place from where the gang would roll the
barrel, and made half a dozen mounds of
twigs, being careful to make them very
flimsy. Then he covered them with earth
and packed them gently. The mounds
looked very tempting from the view-point
of a marksman in search of earthworks, and
appeared capable of stopping any rifle ball
that could be fired against them. Hopalong looked them over critically and
stepped back.

"I'd like to see th' look on th' face of
th' son-of-a-gun that uses them for cover—
won't he be surprised?" and he grinned
gleefully as he pictured his shots boring
through them. Then he placed in the
center of each a chip or a pebble or something that he thought would show up well
in the firelight.

Returning to the cabin, he banked it up
well with dirt and gravel, and tossed a few
shovelfuls up on the roof as a safety valve
to his exuberance. When he entered the
door he had another idea, and fell to work

scooping out a shallow cellar, deep enough
to shelter him when lying at full length.
Then he stuck his head out of the window
and grinned at the false covers with their
prominent bull's-eyes.

"When that prize-winnin' gang of ossified idiots runs up agin these fortifica-
tions they shore will be disgusted. I'll
bet four dollars an' seven cents they'll
think their medicine-man's no good. I
hopes that puff-eyed marshal will pick out
that hump with th' chip on it," and he
hugged himself in anticipation.

He then cut down a sapling and fastened
it to the roof and on it he tied his neck-
kerchief, which fluttered valiantly and with
defiance in the light breeze. "I shore hopes
they appreciates that," he remarked whimsically, as he went inside the hut and closed
the door.

The early part of the evening passed in
peace, and Hopalong, tired of watching in
vain, wished for action. Midnight came,
and it was not until half an hour before
dawn that he was attacked. Then a noise
sent him to a locphole, where he fired two
shots at skulking figures some distance off.
A fusillade of bullets replied; one of them
ripped through the door at a weak spot
and drilled a hole in a can of the everlast-
ing peaches. Hopalong set the can in the
frying pan and then flitted from loophole
to loophole, shooting quick and straight.
Several curses told him that he had not
missed, and he scooped up a finger of peach
juice. Shots thudded into the walls of his
fort in an unceasing stream, and, as it grew
lighter, several whizzed through the loopholes. He kept close to the earth and
waited for the rush, and when it came sent
it back minus two of its members.

As he reloaded his Colts a bullet passed
through his shirt sleeve and he promptly
nailed the marksman. He looked out of
a crack in the rear wall and saw the top of
an adjoining hill crowned with spectators,
all of whom were armed. Some time later
he repulsed another attack and heard a
faint cheer from his friends on the hill.
Then he saw a barrel, blazing from end to
end, roll out from the place he had so carefully covered with mounds. It gathered
speed and bounded over the rough ground,
flashed between two rocks and leaped into
the trench, where it crackled and roared in
vain.

"Now," said Hopalong, blazing at the
mounds as fast as he could load and fire
his Sharp's, "we'll just see what yu thinks
of yore nice little covers."

Yells of consternation and pain rang out
in a swelling chorus, and legs and arms
jerked and flopped, one man, in his astonishment at the shot that tore open his
cheek, sitting up in plain sight of that
marksman, who then killed him. Roars of
rage floated up from the main body of the
besiegers, and the discomfited remnant of
barrel-rollers broke for real cover, Hopalong picking off two in their flight.

Then he stopped another rush from the
front, made upon the supposition that he
was thinking only of the second detachment. A hearty cheer arose from Tom
Halloway and his friends, ensconced in
their rocky position, and it was taken up
by those on the hill, who danced and yelled
their delight at the battle, to them more
humorous than otherwise.

This recognition of his prowess from men
of the caliber of his audience made him feel
good, and he grinned: "Gee, I'll bet Hallo-
way an' his friend is shore itchin' to get in
this," he murmured, firing at a head that
was foolishly shown for an instant. "Got
yu!" he exclaimed, scooping up more peach
juice. "Wonder what Red 'll say when
Jimmy tells him—bet he'll plow dust like
a cyclone," and Hopalong laughed, picturing to himself the satiation of Red's
anger. "Old red-headed son-of-a-gun,"
murmured the cowboy affectionately, "he
shore can fight."

As he squinted over the sights of his
rifle his eye caught sight of a moving body
of men as they cantered over the flats about
two miles away. In his eagerness he forgot to shoot and carefully counted them.
"Nine," he grumbled. "Wonder what's th'
matter?"—fearing that they were not his
friends. Then a second body numbering
eight cantered into sight and followed the
first.

"Whoop! There's th' Red-head!" he
shouted, dancing in his joy. "Now," he
shouted at the peach can joyously, "yu
wait about thirty minutes an' yu'll shore
reckon Hades has busted loose!"

He grabbed up his Colts, which he kept
loaded for repelling rushes, and recklessly
emptied them into the bushes and between
the rocks and trees, searching every likely

place for a human target. Then he slipped his rifle in a loophole and waited for good shots, having worked off the dangerous pressure of his exuberance.

Soon he heard a yell from the direction of the "Miner's Rest," and fell to jamming cartridges into his revolvers so that he could sally out and join in the fray by the side of Red.

The thunder of madly pounding hoofs rolled up the trail, and soon a horse and rider shot around the corner and headed for the copse. Three more raced close behind, and then a bunch of six, followed by the rest, spread out and searched for trouble.

Red, a Colt in each hand and hatless, stood up in his stirrups and sent shot after shot into the fleeing mob, which he could not follow on account of the nature of the ground. Buck wheeled and dashed down the trail again with Red a close second, the others packed in a solid mass and after them. At the first level stretch the newcomers swept down and hit their enemies, going through them like a knife through cheese. Hopalong danced up and down with rage when he could not find his horse, and had to stand and yell, a spectator.

The fight drifted in among the buildings, where it became a series of isolated duels, and soon Hopalong saw panic-stricken horses carrying their riders out of the other side of the town. Then he went gunning for the man who had rustled his horse. He was unsuccessful and returned to his peaches.

Soon the riders came up, and when they saw Hopalong shove a peach into his powder-grimed mouth they yelled their delight. "Yu old maverick! Eatin' peaches like

yu was afraid we'd git some!" shouted Red indignantly, leaping down and running up to his pal as though to thrash him.

Hopalong grinned pleasantly and fired a peach against Red's eye. "I was savin' that one for yu, Reddie," he remarked, as he avoided Buck's playful kick. "Yu fellers git to work an' dig up some wealth —I'm hungry." Then he turned to Buck: "Yore th' marshal of this town, an' any son-of-a-gun what don't like it had better write. Oh, yes, here comes Tom Hallo-way—'member him?"

Buck turned and faced the miner and his hand went out with a jerk.

"Well, I'll be locoed if I didn't punch with yu on th' Tin-Cup!" he said.

"Yu shore did an' yu was purty devilish, but that there Cassidy of yourn beats anything I ever seen." ·

"He's a good kid," replied Buck, glancing to where Red and Hopalong were quarreling as to who had eaten the most pie in a contest held some years before.

Johnny, nosing around, came upon the perforated and partially scattered piles of earth and twigs, and vented his disgust of them by kicking them to pieces. "Hey! Hoppy! Oh, Hoppy!" he called, "what are these things?"

Hopalong jammed Red's hat over that person's eyes and replied: "Oh, them's some loaded dice I fixed for them."

"Yu son-of-a-gun!" sputtered Red, as he wrestled with his friend in the exuberance of his pride. "Yu son-of-a-gun! Yu shore ought to be ashamed to treat 'em that way!"

"Shore," replied Hopalong. "But I ain't!"

13

Cassidy at Cactus

CLARENCE EDWARD MULFORD

BAR 20 RANGE YARNS

VII.—CASSIDY AT CACTUS

BY CLARENCE EDWARD MULFORD

PAINTING BY N. C. WYETH

R. BUCK PETERS, fore-man of the cow-punch-ing outfit of the Bar 20, a ranch situated in what is now Pécos county, Texas, rode into Alka-line one bright Septem-ber morning and sought refreshment at the Emporium. Mr. Peters had just finished some business for his employer and felt the satisfaction that comes with the knowledge of work well done. He expected to remain in Alkaline for several days, where he was to be joined by two of his friends and punchers, Mr. Hopalong Cassidy and Mr. Red Con-nors, both of whom were at Cactus Springs, seventy miles to the east. Mr. Cassidy and his friend had just finished a nocturnal tour of Santa Fé and felt somewhat peevish and dull in consequence, not to mention the sadness occasioned by the expenditure of the greater part of their combined cap-ital on such foolishness as faro, roulette and wet-goods.

Mr. Peters and his friends had been members of a crowd that sought wealth at a point near the town of Raw Dog in the Black Hills, where the eighteen individuals representing the merged out-fits of the Bar 20 and the O-Bar-O had enthusiastically disfigured the earth in the fond expectation of uncovering vast stores of virgin gold. Their hopes were of an optimistic brand and had existed until the last canister of corn-meal flour had been emptied by Mr. Cassidy's burro, which waited not upon its master's pleas-ure nor upon the ethics of the case. When Mr. Cassidy had returned from exercising the animal and himself over two miles of rocky hillside in the vain endeavor to give it his opinion of burros, and sundry chas-tisements, he was requested, as owner of the beast, to give his counsel as to the best way of securing eighteen breakfasts. Re-membering that the animal was headed north when he last saw it, and that it was too old to eat, anyway, he suggested a plan that had worked successfully at other times for other ends, namely, poker. Mr. McAllister, an expert at the great Ameri·can game, volunteered his services in ac-cordance with the spirit of the occasion and, half an hour later, he and Mr. Cassidy drifted into Pell's poker parlors, which were located in the rear of a Chinese laun-dry, where they gathered unto themselves the wherewithal for the required break-fasts. An hour spent in the card room of the "Hurrah" convinced its proprietor that they had wasted their talents for the past six weeks in digging for gold. The proof of this permitted the departure of the outfits with their customary éclat.

At Santa Fé the various individuals had gone their respective ways, to reassemble at the ranch in the near future, and for several days they had been drifting south in groups of twos and threes and, like chaff upon a stream, had eddied into Alkaline, where Mr. Peters had found them arduously engaged in postponing the final journey. After he had gladdened their hearts and soothed their throats by making several pithy remarks to the bartender, with whom he established their credit, he cau-tioned them against letting any one harm them and, smiling at the humor of his warning, left abruptly.

Cactus Springs was burdened with a zealous and initiative organization known as vigilantes, whose duty it was to extend the courtesies of the land to cattle thieves and the like. This organization boasted of the name of Travennes' Terrors and of a muster roll of twenty. There was also a boast that no one had ever escaped them, which, if true, was in many cases unfortunate. Mr. Slim Travennes, with whom Mr. Cassidy had participated in an extemporaneous exchange of Colt's courtesies in Santa Fé the year before, was the head of the organization and was also chairman of the committee on arrivals, and the two gentlemen of the Bar 20 had not been in town an hour before he knew of it. Being anxious to show the strangers every attention and having a keen recollection of the brand of gun-play commanded by Mr. Cassidy, he planned a smoother method of procedure and one calculated to permit him to enjoy the pleasures of a good old age. Mr. Travennes knew that horse thieves were regarded as social enemies, that the necessary proof of their guilt was the finding of stolen animals in their possession, that death was the penalty, and that every man, whether directly concerned or not, regarded himself as judge, jury and executioner. He had several acquaintances who were bound to him by his knowledge of crimes they had committed and who could not refuse his slightest wish. Even if they had been free agents they were not above causing the death of an innocent man. Mr. Travennes, feeling very self-satisfied at his cleverness, arranged to have the proof placed where it would do the most harm and intended to take care of the rest himself.

Mr. Connors, feeling much refreshed and very hungry, arose at daylight the next morning and, dressing quickly, started off to feed and water the horses. After having several tilts with the landlord about the bucket, he took his departure toward the corral at the rear. Peering through the gate, he could hardly believe his eyes. He climbed over it and inspected the animals at close range. He found that the horses which he and his friend had ridden for the last two months were not to be seen, but in their places were two better animals, which concerned him greatly. Being fair and square himself, he could not understand the change and sought enlightenment of his more imaginative and suspicious friend.

"Hey, Hopalong!" he called (Mr. Connors was anything but formal), "come out here an' see what th' devil has happened!"

Mr. Cassidy stuck his auburn head out of the wounded shutter and complacently surveyed his companion. Then he saw the horses and looked hard.

"Quit yore foolin', yu old cuss," he remarked pleasantly, as he groped around behind him with his feet, searching for his boots. "Anybody would think yu was a little boy with yore fool jokes. Ain't yu ever goin' to grow up?"

"They've got our bronchs," replied Mr. Connors in an injured tone. "Honest, I ain't kiddin' yu," he added for the sake of peace.

"Who has?" came from the window, followed immediately by, "Yu've got my boots!"

"I ain't—they're under th' bunk," contradicted and explained Mr. Connors. Then, turning to the matter in his mind he replied, "I don't know who's got them. If I did do yu think I'd be holdin' hands with myself?"

"Nobody'd accuse yu of anything like that," came from the window, accompanied by an overdone snicker.

Mr. Connors flushed under his accumulated tan as he remembered the varied pleasures of Santa Fé, and he regarded the bronchos in anything but a pleasant state of mind.

Mr. Cassidy slid through the window and approached his friend, looking as serious as he could.

"Any tracks?" he inquired, as he glanced quickly over the ground to see for himself.

"Not after that wind we had last night. They might have growed there for all I can see," growled Mr. Connors.

"I reckon we better hold a pow-wow with th' foreman of this shack an' find out what he knows," suggested Mr. Cassidy. "This looks too good to be a swap."

Mr. Connors looked his disgust at the idea and then a light broke in upon him. "Mebby they was hard pushed an' wanted fresh cayuses," he said. "A whole lot of people get hard pushed in this country. Anyhow, we'll prospect th' boss."

They found the proprietor in his stocking feet, getting the breakfast, and Mr. Cassidy regarded the preparations with open approval. He counted the tin plates and found only three and, thinking that there would be more plates if there were others to feed, glanced into the landlord's room. Not finding signs of other guests on whom to lay the blame for the loss of his horse, he began to ask questions.

"Much trade?" he inquired solicitously.

"Yep," replied the landlord.

Mr. Cassidy looked at the three tins and wondered if there had ever been any more with which to supply this trade. "Been out this morning?" he pursued.

"Nope."

"Talks purty nigh as much as Buck," thought Mr. Cassidy, and then said aloud, "Anybody else here?"

"Nope."

Mr. Cassidy relapsed into a painful and disgusted silence and his friend tried his hand.

"Who owns a mosaic bronch, Chinee flag on th' near side, Skillet brand?" asked Mr. Connors.

"Quien sabe?"

"Gosh, he can nearly keep still in two lingoes," thought Mr. Cassidy.

"Who owns a bob-tailed pinto, saddle-galled, cast in th' near eye, Star Diamond brand, white stocking on th' off front prop, with a habit of scratching itself every other minute?" went on Mr. Connors.

"Slim Travennes," replied. the proprietor, flopping a flapjack.

Mr. Cassidy reflectively scratched the back of his hand and looked innocent, but his mind was working overtime.

"Who's Slim Travennes?" asked Mr. Connors, never having heard of that person, owing to the reticence of his friend.

"Captain of th' vigilantes."

"What does he look like on th' general run?" blandly inquired Mr. Cassidy, wishing to verify his suspicions. He thought of the trouble he had with Mr. Travennes up in Santa Fé and of the reputation that gentleman possessed. Then the fact that Mr. Travennes was the leader of the local vigilantes came to his assistance, and he was sure that the captain had a hand in the change. All these points existed in misty groups in his mind, but the next remark of the landlord caused them to rush together and reveal the plot.

"Good," said the landlord, flopping another flapjack, "and a warnin' to hoss thieves."

"Ahem," coughed Mr. Cassidy and then continued, "is he a tall, lanky, yaller-headed son-of-a-gun, with a big nose an' lots of ears?"

"Mebbyso," answered the host.

"Um, slopping over into bad Sioux," thought Mr. Cassidy, and then said aloud, "How long has he hung around this here layout?" at the same time passing a warning glance to his companion.

The landlord straightened ·up. "Look here, stranger, if yu hankers after his pedigree so all-fired hard yu had best pump him."

"I told yu this here feller wasn't a man what would give away all he knowed," lied Mr. Connors, turning to his friend and indicating the host. "He ain't got time for that. Anybody can see that he is a powerful busy man. An' then, he ain't 'no child."

Mr. Cassidy thought that the landlord could tell all he knew in about five minutes and then not break any speed records for conversation, but he looked properly awed and impressed. "Well, yu needn't'go an' get mad about it! I didn't know, did I?"

"Who's gettin' mad?" pugnaciously asked Mr. Connors. After his injured feelings had been soothed by Mr. Cassidy's sullen silence he again turned to the landlord.

"What did this Travennes look like when yu saw him last?" coaxed Mr. Connors.

"Th' same as he does now, as yu can see by lookin' out of th' window. That's him down th' street," enlightened the host, thawing to the pleasant Mr. Connors.

Mr. Cassidy adopted the suggestion and frowned. Mr. Travennes and two companions were walking toward the corral and Mr. Cassidy once again slid out of the window, his friend going by the door.

When Mr. Travennes looked over the corral fence he was much chagrined to see a man and a .45 Colt, both paying strict attention to his nose.

"Mornin', Duke," said the man with the gun. "Lose anything?"

Mr. Travennes looked back at his friends and saw Mr. Connors sitting on a rock holding two guns. Mr. Travennes' right and left wings were the targets and they pitted their frowns against Mr. Connors' smile.

"Not that I knows of," replied Mr. Travennes, shifting his feet uneasily.

"Find anything?" came from Mr. Cassidy as he sidled out of the gate.

"Nope," replied the captain of the Terrors, eying the Colt.

"Are yu in th' habit of payin' early mornin' calls to this here corral?" persisted Mr. Cassidy, playing with the gun.

"Ya-as. That's my business—I'm th' captain of th' vigilantes."

"That's too bad," sympathized Mr. Cassidy, moving forward a step.

Mr. Travennes looked put out and backed off. "What yu mean, sticking me up this away?" he asked indignantly.

"Yu needn't go an' get mad," responded Mr. Cassidy. "Just business. Yore cayuse an' another shore climbed this corral fence last night an' ate up our bronchs, an' I just nachurlly want to know about it."

Mr. Travennes looked his surprise and incredulity and craned his neck to see for himself. When he saw his horse peacefully scratching itself he swore and looked angrily up the street. Mr. Connors, behind the shack, was hidden to the view of those on the street, and when two men ran up at a signal from Mr. Travennes, intending to insert themselves in the misunderstanding, they were promptly lined up with the first two by the man on the rock.

"Sit down," invited Mr. Connors, pushing a chunk of air out of the way with his guns. The last two felt a desire to talk and to argue the case on its merits, but refrained, as the black holes in Mr. Connors' guns hinted at eruption. "Every time yu opens yore mouths yu gets closer to th' Great Divide," enlightened that person, and they were childlike in their belief.

Mr. Travennes acted as though he would like to scratch his thigh where his Colt chafed him, but postponed the event and listened to Mr. Cassidy, who was asking questions.

"Where's our cayuses, General?"

Mr. Travennes allowed that he didn't know. He was worried, for he feared that his captor didn't have a secure hold on the hammer of the ubiquitous Colt.

"Where's *my* cayuse?" persisted Mr. Cassidy.

"I don't know, but I wants to ask yu how yu got mine," replied Mr. Travennes.

"Yu tell me how mine got out an' I'll tell yu how yourn got in," proposed Mr. Cassidy.

Mr. Connors added another to his collection before the captain replied.

"Out in this country people get in trouble when they're found with other folks' cayuses," Mr. Travennes suggested.

Mr. Cassidy looked interested and replied: "Yu shore ought to borrow some experience, an' there's lots floating around. More than one man has smoked in a powder mill an' th' number of them planted who looked in th' muzzle of a empty gun is scandalous. If my remarks don't perculate right smart I'll explain."

Mr. Travennes looked down the street again, saw number six added to the line-up, and coughed up chunks of broken profanity, grieving his host by his lack of courtesy.

"Time," announced Mr. Cassidy, interrupting the round. "I wants them cayuses an' I wants 'em right now. Yu an' me will amble off an' get 'em. I won't bore yu with tellin' yu what 'll happen if yu gets skittish. Slope along an' don't be scared: I'm with yu," assured Mr. Cassidy as he looked over at Mr. Connors, whose ascetic soul pined for the flapjacks of which his olfactories caught intermittent whiffs.

"Well, Red, I reckons yu has got plenty of room out here for all yu may corral: anyhow, there ain't a whole lot more. My friend Slim an' I are shore going to have a devil of a time if we can't find them cussed bronchs. Whew, them flapjacks smell like a plain trail to payday. Just think of th' nice maple juice we used to get up to Cheyenne on them frosty mornings."

"Get out of here an' lemme alone! What do yu allus want to go an' make a feller unhappy for? Can't yu keep still about grub when yu knows I ain't had my morning's feed yet?" asked Mr. Connors, much aggrieved.

"Well, I'll be back directly an' I'll have them cayuses or a scalp. Yu tend to business an' watch th' herd. That shorthorn yearling at th' end of th' line"—pointing to a young man who looked capable of taking risks—"he looks like he might take a chance an' gamble with yu," remarked Mr. Cassidy, placing Mr. Travennes in front of him and pushing back his own sombrero. "Don't put too much maple juice on them flapjacks, Red," he warned as he poked his captive in the back of the neck as a hint to get going. Fortunately Mr. Connors' closing remarks are lost to history.

Observing that Mr. Travennes headed south on the quest, Mr. Cassidy reasoned that the missing bronchos ought to be somewhere in the north, and he postponed the southern trip until such time when they would have more leisure at their disposal. Mr. Travennes showed a strong inclination to shy at this arrangement, but quieted down under persuasion, and they started off toward where Mr. Cassidy firmly believed the North Pole, and the cayuses, to be.

"Yu has got quite a metropolis here," pleasantly remarked Mr. Cassidy as, under his direction, they made for a distant corral. "I can see four different types of architecture, two of 'em on one residence," he continued as they passed a wood and adobe hut. "No doubt the railroad will put a branch down here some day an' then yu can hire their old cars for yore public buildings. Then when yu gets a post-office yu will shore make Chicago hustle some to keep her end up. Let's assay that hollow for horsehide: it looks promisin'."

The hollow was investigated but showed nothing other than cacti and baked alkali. The corral came next and there, too, was emptiness. For an hour the search was unavailing, but at the end of that time Mr. Cassidy began to notice signs of nervousness on the part of his guest, which grew less as they proceeded. Then Mr. Cassidy retraced their steps to the place where the nervousness first developed and tried another way and once more returned to the starting point.

"Yu seems to hanker for this fool exercise," quoth Mr. Travennes with much sarcasm. "If yu reckons I'm fond of this locoed ramblin' yu shore needs enlightenment."

"Sometimes I do get these fits," confessed Mr. Cassidy, "an' when I do I'm dead sore on objections. Let's peep in that there hut," he suggested.

"Huh! yore ideas of cayuses are mighty peculiar. Why don't you look for 'em up on those cactuses or behind that mesquite? *I* wouldn't be a heap surprised if they was roostin' on th' roof. They are mighty knowing animals, cayuses. I once saw one that could figger like a schoolmarm," remarked Mr. Travennes, beginning sar-

castically and toning it down as he proceeded, out of respect for his companion's gun.

"Well, they might be in th' shack," replied Mr. Cassidy. "Cayuses know so much that it takes a month to unlearn them. I wouldn't like to bet they ain't in that hut, though."

Mr. Travennes snickered in a manner decidedly uncomplimentary and began to whistle, softly at first. The gentleman from the Bar 20 noticed that his companion was a musician; that when he came to a strong part he increased the tones until they bid to be heard at several hundred yards. When Mr. Travennes had reached a most passionate part in "Juanita" and was expanding his lungs to do it justice, he was rudely stopped by the insistent pressure of his guard's Colt's on the most ticklish part of his ear.

"I shore wish yu wouldn't strain yoreself thataway," said Mr. Cassidy, thinking that Mr. Travennes might be endeavoring to call assistance. "I went an' promised my mother on her death-bed that I wouldn't let nobody whistle out loud like that, an' th' opery is hereby stopped. Besides, somebody might hear them mournful tones an' think that something is th' matter, which it ain't."

Mr. Travennes substituted heartfelt cussing, all of which was heavily accented.

As they approached the hut Mr. Cassidy again tickled his prisoner and insisted that he be very quiet, as his cayuse was very sensitive to noise and it might be there. Mr. Cassidy still thought Mr. Travennes might have friends in the hut and wouldn't for the world disturb them, as he would present a splendid target as he approached the building and he knew it.

The open door revealed three men asleep on the earthen floor, two of whom were Mexicans. Mr. Cassidy then, for the first time, felt called upon to relieve his companion of the Colt's which so sorely itched that gentleman's thigh, and then disarmed the sleeping guards.

"One man an' a half," murmured Mr. Cassidy, it being in his creed that it took four "Greasers" to make one Texan.

In the far corner of the room were two bronchos, one of which tried in vain to kick Mr. Cassidy, not realizing that he was ten feet away. The noise awakened the sleepers, who sat up and then sprang to their feet, their hands instinctively streaking to their thighs for the weapons which peeped contentedly from the bosom of Mr. Cassidy's open shirt. One of the Mexicans made a lightning-like grab for the back of his neck, for the knife which lay along his spine, and was shot in the front of his neck for his trouble. The shot spoiled his aim, as the knife flashed past Mr. Cassidy's arm, wide by two feet, and thudded into the door frame, where it hummed angrily.

"Th' only man who could do that right was th' man who invented it, Mr. Bowie, of Texas," explained Mr. Cassidy to the other Mexican. Then he glanced at the broncho, which was squealing in rage and fear at the shot, which sounded like a cannon in the small room, and laughed.

"That's my cayuse all right, an' he wasn't up no cactus nor roosting on th' roof, neither. He's th' most affectionate beast I ever saw. It took me nigh onto six months afore I could ride him without fighting him to a standstill," said Mr. Cassidy to his guest. Then he turned to the horse and looked it over. "Come here, yu blankety-blank son of th' Old Boy! What d'yu mean, acting thataway? Yu ragged end of nothin' wobbling in space! Yu wall-eyed, ornery, locoed guide to Hades! Yu won't be so frisky when yu've made them seventy hot miles between here an' Alkaline in five hours," he promised, as he made his way toward the animal.

Mr. Travennes walked over to the opposite wall and took down a pouch of tobacco which hung from a peg. He did this in a manner suggesting ownership, and after he had deftly rolled a cigarette with one hand he put the pouch in his pocket and, lighting up, inhaled deeply and with much satisfaction. Mr. Cassidy turned around and glanced the group over, wondering if the tobacco had been left in the hut on a former call.

"Did yu find yore makings?" he asked, with a note of congratulation in his voice.

"Yep. Want one?" asked Mr. Travennes.

Mr. Cassidy ignored the offer and turned to the guard whom he had found asleep.

"Is that his tobacco?" he asked, and the guard, anxious to make everything run smoothly, told the truth and answered:

"Shore. He left it here last night." Whereupon Mr. Travennes swore and Mr. Cassidy smiled grimly.

"Then yu knows how yore cayuse got in an' how mine got out," said the latter. "I wish yu would explain," he added, fondling his Colt.

Mr. Travennes frowned and remained silent.

"I can tell yu, anyhow," continued Mr. Cassidy, still smiling, but his eyes and jaw belied the smile. "Yu took them cayuses out because yu wanted yourn to be found in their places. Yu remembered Santa Fé an' it rankled in yu. Not being man enough to notify me that yu'd shoot on sight an' being afraid my friends would get yu if yu plugged me on th' sly, yu tried to make out that me an' Red rustled yore cayuses. That meant a lynching, with me an' Red in th' places of honor. Yu never saw Red afore, but yu didn't care if he went with me. Yu don't deserve fair play, but I'm going to give it to yu because I don't want anybody to say that any of th' Bar 20 ever murdered a man, not even a skunk like yu. My friends have treated me too square for that. Yu can take this gun an' yu can do one of three things with it, which are: walk out in th' open a hundred paces an' then turn an' walk toward me—after yu face me yu can set it a-going whenever yu want to; th' second is, put it under yore hat an' I'll put mine an' th' others back by th' cayuses. Then we 'll toss up an' th' lucky man gets it to use as he wants. Th' third is, shoot yoreself."

Mr. Cassidy punctuated the close of his ultimatum by handing over the weapon, muzzle first, and, because the other might be an adept at "twirling" (spinning the weapon on the forefinger and discharging it by jerking the hand when the muzzle comes up), he kept its recipient covered during the operation. Then, placing his second Colt with the captured weapons, he threw them through the door and far out on the desert, being very careful not to lose the drop on his armed prisoner.

Mr. Travennes looked around and wiped the sweat from his forehead, and being an observant gentleman, took the proffered weapon and walked to the east, directly toward the sun, which at this time was halfway to the meridian. The glare of its straight rays and those reflected from the shining sand would, in a measure, bother Mr. Cassidy and interfere with the accuracy of his aim, and he was always thankful for small favors.

Mr. Travennes was the possessor of accurate knowledge regarding the lay of the land, and the thought came to him that there was a small but deep hole out toward the east and that it was about the required distance away. This had been dug by a man who had labored all day in the burning sun to make an oven, so that he could cook mesquite root in the manner he had seen the Apaches cook it. Mr. Travennes blessed hobbies, specific and general, stumbled thoughtlessly and disappeared from sight as the surprised Mr. Cassidy started forward to offer his assistance. Upon emphatic notification from the man in the hole that his help was not needed, Mr. Cassidy wheeled around and in great haste covered the distance separating him from the hut, whereupon Mr. Travennes swore in self-congratulation and regret. Mr. Cassidy's shots barked a cactus which leaned near Mr. Travennes' head, and flecked several clouds of alkali near that person's nose, causing him to sneeze, duck and grin.

"It's his own gun," grumbled Mr. Cassidy as a bullet passed through his sombrero, having in mind the fact that his opponent had a whole belt full of .41's. If it had been Mr. Cassidy's gun that had been handed over, he would have enjoyed the joke on Mr. Travennes, who would have had five cartridges between himself and the promised eternity, as he would have been unable to use the .41s in Mr. Cassidy's .45, while the latter would have gladly consented to the change, having as he did an extra .45. Never before had Mr. Cassidy looked with reproach upon his .45 caliber Colt, and he sighed as he used it to notify Mr. Travennes that arbitration was not to be considered, which that person indorsed: said indorsement passing so close to Mr. Cassidy's ear that he felt the breeze made by it.

"He's been practicin' since I plugged him up in Santa Fé," thought Mr. Cassidy, as he retired around the hut to formulate a plan of campaign.

Mr. Travennes sang "Hi-le, hi-lo," and other selections, principally others, and wondered how Mr. Cassidy could hoist him out. The slack of his belt informed him that he was in the middle of a fast and suggested starvation as the derrick that his honorable and disgusted adversary might employ.

Mr. Cassidy, while figuring out his method of procedure, absent-mindedly jabbed a finger in his eye, and the ensuing tears floated an idea to him. He had always had great respect for ricochet shots since his friend Skinny Thompson had proved their worth on the hides of Sioux. If he could disturb the sand and convey several grains of it to Mr. Travennes' eyes, the game would be much simplified. While planning for the proposed excavation, *a la* Colt, he noticed several stones lying near at hand, and a new and better scheme presented itself for his consideration.

Mr. Cassidy lined up his gloomy collection and tersely ordered them to turn their backs to him and to stay in that position, the suggestion being that if they looked around they wouldn't be able to dodge quickly enough. He then slipped bits of his lariat over their wrists and ankles, tying wrists to ankles and each man to his neighbor. That finished to his satisfaction, he dragged them into the hut, to save them from the burning rays of the sun. Having performed this act of kindness, he crept along the hot sand, taking advantage of every bit of cover afforded, and at last he reached a point within a hundred feet of the besieged. During the trip Mr. Travennes sang to his heart's content, some of the words being improvised for the occasion and were not calculated to increase Mr. Cassidy's respect for his own wisdom, if he should hear them. Mr. Cassidy heard, however, and several fragments so forcibly intruded on his peace of mind that he determined to put on the last verse himself and to suit himself.

Suddenly Mr. Travennes poked his head up and glanced at the hut. He was down again so quickly that there was no chance for a shot at him, and he believed that his enemy was still sojourning in the rear of the building, which caused him to fear that he was expected to live on nothing as long as he could and then give himself up. Just to show his defiance he stretched himself out on his back and sang with all his might, his sombrero over his face to keep the glare of the sun out of his eyes. He was interrupted, however, forgot to finish a verse as he had intended, and jumped to one side as a stone bounced off his leg. Looking up, he saw another missile curve into his patch of sky and swiftly bear down on him. He avoided it by a hair's breadth and wondered what had happened. Then what Mr. Travennes thought was a balloon, being unsophisticated in matters pertaining to aerial navigation, swooped down upon him and smote him on the shoulder and also bounced off. Mr. Travennes hastily laid music aside and took up elocution, as he dodged another stone, and wished that the mesquite-loving crank had put on a roof. In evading the projectile he let his sombrero appear on a level with the desert, and the hum of a bullet as it passed through his head-gear and into the opposite wall made him wish that there had been constructed a cellar, also.

"Hi-le, hi-lo" intruded upon his ear, as Mr. Cassidy got rid of the surplus of his heart's joy.

"Hibernate, blank yu!" derisively shouted the human catapult as he released a chunk of sandstone the size of a quail.

"Hey, yu!" indignantly yowled Mr. Travennes from his defective storm cellar. "Don't yu know any better'n to heave things thataway?"

"Hi-le, hi-lo," sang Mr. Cassidy, as another stone soared aloft in the direction of the complainant. Then he stood erect and awaited results with a Colt in his hand leveled at the rim of the hole. A hat waved and an excited voice bit off chunks of expostulation and asked for an armistice. Then two hands shot up, and Mr. Travennes, sore and disgusted and desperate, popped his head up and blinked at Mr. Cassidy's gun.

"Yu was fillin' th' hole up," remarked Mr. Travennes in an accusing tone, hiding the real reason for his evacuation. "In a little while I'd a been th' top of a pile instead of th' bottom of a hole," he announced, crawling out and rubbing his head.

"Yu remind me of a feller I used to know," remarked Mr. Travennes, as he led the way to the hut, trying not to limp. "Only he throwed dynamite. That was th' way he cleared off chaparral—blowed it off. He got so used to heaving away everything he lit that he spoiled three pipes in two days."

Mr. Cassidy laughed at the fiction, and then became grave as he pictured Mr. Connors sitting on the rock and facing down a line of men, any one of whom was capable of his destruction if given the interval of a second.

When they arrived at the hut Mr. Cassidy observed that the prisoners had moved considerably. There was a cleanly swept trail four yards long where they had dragged themselves, and they sat in the end nearer the guns. Mr. Cassidy smiled and fired close to the Mexican's ear, who lost in one frightened jump a little of what he had so laboriously gained.

"Yu'll wear out yore pants," said Mr. Cassidy, and then added grimly, "an' my patience."

Mr. Travennes smiled and thought of the man who had so ably seconded Mr. Cassidy's efforts and who was probably shot by this time. An unreasoning streak of sarcasm swept over him and he could not resist the opportunity to get in a stab at his captor.

"Mebby yore pard has wore out somebody's patience, too," said Mr. Travennes, suggestively and with venom.

His captor wheeled toward him, his face white with passion.

"I ain't shootin' dogs this here trip," said Mr. Cassidy, trembling with scorn and anger, "so yu can pull yourself together. I'll give yu another chance, but yu wants to hope almighty hard that Red is O. K. If he ain't, I'll blow yu so many ways at once that if yu sprouts yu'll make a good acre of weeds. If he *is* all right yu'd better vamose this range, for there won't be no hole for yu to crawl into next time. What friends yu have left will have to tote yu off an' plant yu," he finished with emphasis. He drove the horses outside and, after severing their bonds, lined up his prisoners.

"Yu," he began, indicating all but Mr. Travennes, "yu amble right smart toward Canada," pointing to the north. "Keep a-going till yu gets far enough away so a Colt won't find yu." Here he grinned with delight as he saw his Sharp's rifle in its sheath on his saddle and, drawing it forth, he put away his Colt and glanced at the trio, who were already industriously plodding northward. "Hey!" he shouted, and when they sullenly turned to see what new

"Mr. Cassidy . . . saw a crimson rider sweep down
upon him . . . heralded by a blazing .41."

Painting by N. C. Wyeth.

idea he had found, he gleefully waved his rifle at them and warned them farther: "This is a Sharp an' its good for half a mile, so don't stop none too soon."

Having sent them directly away from their friends so they could not have him "potted" on the way back, he mounted his broncho and indicated to Mr. Travennes that he, too, was to ride, watching that that person did not make use of the Winchester which Mr. Connors was foolish enough to carry around on his saddle. Winchesters were Mr. Cassidy's pet aversion and Mr. Connors' most prized possession, this difference of opinion having upon many occasions caused hasty words between them. Mr. Connors, being better with his Winchester than Mr. Cassidy was with his Sharp, had frequently proved that his choice was the wiser; but Mr. Cassidy was loyal to the Sharp and refused to be convinced. Now, however, the Winchester became pregnant with possibilities and, therefore, Mr. Travennes rode a few yards to the left and in advance, where the rifle was in plain sight, hanging as it did on the right of Mr. Connors' saddle, which Mr. Travennes graced so well.

The journey back to town was made in good time, and when they came to the buildings Mr. Cassidy dismounted and bade his companion do likewise, there being too many corners that a fleeing rider could take advantage of. Mr. Travennes felt of his bumps and did so, wishing hard things about his captor.

While Mr. Travennes had been entertained in the manner narrated, Mr. Connors had passed the time by relating stale jokes to the uproarious laughter of his extremely bored audience. The landlord, hearing the hilarity, had taken advantage of the opportunity offered to see a free show. Not being able to see what the occasion was for the mirth, he had pulled on his boots and made his way to the show with a flapjack in the skillet, which, in his haste, he had forgotten to put down. He felt sure that he would be entertained, and he was not disappointed. He rounded the corner and was enthusiastically welcomed by the hungry Mr. Connors, whose ubiquitous guns coaxed from the skillet its dyspeptic wad.

"Th' saints be praised!" ejaculated Mr. Connors as a matter of form, not having a very clear idea of just what saints were, but he knew what flapjacks were and greedily overcame the heroic resistance of the one provided by chance and his own guns. As he rolled his eyes in ecstatic content, the very man Mr. Cassidy had warned him against suddenly arose and in great haste disappeared around the corner of the corral, from which point of vantage he vented his displeasure at the treatment he had received by wasting six shots at the mortified Mr. Connors.

"Steady!" sang out that gentleman as the line-up wavered. "He's a precedent to hell for yu fellers! Don't yu get ambitious, none whatever." Then he wondered how long it would take the fugitive to secure a rifle and return to release the others by drilling him at long range, and also if Mr. Cassidy would drift up and weep over his remains.

His thoughts were interrupted by the vision of a red head that climbed into view over a rise a short distance off, and he grinned his delight as Mr. Cassidy loomed up, jaunty and triumphant. Mr. Cassidy was executing calisthenics with a Colt in the rear of Mr. Travennes' neck and was leading the horses.

Mr. Connors waved the skillet, and his friend grinned his congratulations at what the token signified.

"I see yu got some more," said Mr. Cassidy as he went down the line-up from the rear and collected nineteen revolvers of various makes and conditions, this number being explained by the fact that all but one of the prisoners wore two. Then he added the five that had kicked against his ribs ever since he had left the hut, and carefully threaded the end of his lariat through the trigger guards.

"Looks like we stuck up a government supply mule, Red," he remarked, as he fastened the whole collection to his saddle. "Fourteen Colt, six Stevens, three Remington an' one puzzle," he added, examining the "puzzle." "'Made in Germany,' it says, an' it shore looks like it. It's got little pins stickin' out of th' cylinder, like yu had to swat it with a hammer or a rock, or something. It's real dangerous—warranted to go off, but mostly by itself, I reckon. It looks more like a cactus than a six-shooter—gosh, it's a eight-shooter! I allus said them Dutchmen were bloody.

minded cusses—think of being able to shoot yoreself eight times before th' blamed thing stops!" Then, looking at the line-up for the owner of the weapon, he laughed at the woeful countenances displayed. "Did they sidle in by companies or squads?" he asked.

"By twos, mostly. Then they parade-rested an' got discharged from duty. I had eleven, but one got homesick, or disgusted, or something, an' deserted. It was that cussed flapjack," confessed and explained Mr. Connors.

"*What!*" said Mr. Cassidy in a loud voice. "Got away! Well, we'll have to make our get-away plumb sudden or we'll never go."

At this instant the escaped man again began his bombardment from the corner of the corral and Mr. Cassidy paused, indignant at the fusillade which tore up the dust at his feet. He looked reproachfully at Mr. Connors and then circled out on the plain until he caught a glimpse of a fleeing cow-puncher, whose back rapidly grew smaller in the fast-increasing distance.

"That's yore friend, Red," said Mr. Cassidy, as he returned from his reconnaissance. "He's th' same I spoke to yu about. Mebby he'll come back again," he added hopefully. "Anyhow, we've got to move. He'll collect reinforcements an' mebby they all won't shoot like him. Get up on yore Clarinda an' hold th' fort for me," he ordered, pushing the farther horse over to his friend. Mr. Connors proved that an agile man can mount a restless horse and not lose the drop, and backed off three hundred yards, deftly substituting his Winchester for the Colt. Then Mr. Cassidy likewise mounted with his attention riveted elsewhere and backed off to the side of his companion.

The bombardment commenced again from the corral, but this time Mr. Connors' rifle slid around in his lap and exploded twice. The bellicose gentleman of the corral yelled in pain and surprise and vanished.

"Purty good for a Winchester," said Mr. Cassidy in doubtful congratulation.

"That's why I got him," snapped Mr. Connors in brief reply, and then he laughed: "Is them th' vigilantes what never let a man get away?" he scornfully asked, backing down the street and patting his Winchester.

"Well, Red, they wasn't all there. They was only twelve all told," excused Mr. Cassidy. "An' then we was two," he explained, as he wished the collection of six-shooters was on Mr. Connors' horse so they wouldn't bark his shin.

"An' we still are," corrected Mr. Connors, as they wheeled and galloped for Alkaline.

As the sun sank low on the horizon Mr. Peters finished ordering provisions at the general store, the only one Alkaline boasted, and sauntered to the saloon where he had left his men. He found them a few dollars richer, as they had borrowed ten dollars from the bartender on their reputations as poker players, and had used the money to stake Mr. McAllister in a game against the local poker champion.

"Has Hopalong an' Red showed up yet?" asked Mr. Peters, frowning at the delay already caused.

"Nope," replied Mr. Johnny Nelson, the pet of the outfit.

At that minute the doorway was darkened and Mr. Cassidy and Mr. Connors entered and called for refreshments. Mr. Cassidy dropped a huge bundle of six-shooters on the floor, making caustic remarks regarding their utility.

"What's th' matter?" inquired Mr. Peters of Mr. Cassidy. "Yu looks mad an' anxious. An' where in h—l did yu corral them guns?"

Mr. Cassidy drank deep and then reported with much heat what had occurred at Cactus Springs, and added that he wanted to go back and wipe out the town, said desire being luridly endorsed by Mr. Connors.

"Why, shore," said Mr. Peters, "we'll *all* go. Such doings must be stopped instanter." Then he turned to the assembled outfits and asked for a vote, which was unanimous for war.

Shortly afterward eighteen angry cow-punchers rode to the east, two red-haired gentlemen well in front and urging speed. It was eight o'clock when they left Alkaline, and the cool of the night was so delightful that the feeling of ease which came upon them made them lax and they lost three hours in straying from the dim trail. At eight o'clock the next morning they came in sight of their destination and separated into two squads, Mr. Cassidy leading the northern division and Mr. Connors the one which circled to the south. The intention was to attack from two directions, thus taking the town from front and rear.

Cactus Springs lay gasping in the excessive heat and the vigilantes who had toed Mr. Connors' line the day before were lounging in the shade of the "Palace" saloon, telling what they would do if they ever faced the same man again. Half a dozen sympathizers offered gratuitous condolence and advice, and all were positive that they knew where Mr. Cassidy and Mr. Connors would go when they died.

The rolling thunder of madly pounding hoofs disturbed their post-mortem and they arose in a body to flee from half their number, who, guns in hands, charged down upon them through clouds of sickly white smoke. Travennes' Terrors were minus many weapons and they could not be expected to give a glorious account of themselves. Windows rattled and fell in and doors and walls gave off peculiar sounds as they grew full of holes. Above the riot rattled the incessant crack of Colt and Winchester, emphasized at close intervals by the assertive roar of .60 caliber buffalo guns. Off to the south came another rumble of hoofs and Mr. Connors, leading the second squad, arrived to participate in the payment of the debt.

Smoke spurted from windows and other points of vantage and hung wavering in the heated air. The shattering of woodwork told of .60 calibers finding their rest, and the whines that grew and diminished in the air sang the course of .45s.

While the fight raged hottest Mr. Nelson sprang from his horse and ran to the "Palace," where he collected and piled a heap of tinderlike wood, and soon the building burst out in flames, which, spreading, swept the town from end to end.

Mr. Cassidy fired slowly and seemed to be waiting for something. Mr. Connors laid aside his hot Winchester and devoted his attention to his Colts. A spurt of flame and smoke leaped from the window of a 'dobe hut and Mr. Connors sat down, firing as he went. A howl from the window informed him that he had made a hit, and Mr. Cassidy ran out and dragged him to the shelter of a near-by bowlder and asked how much he was hurt.

"Not much—in th' calf," grunted Mr. Connors. "He was a bad shot—must have been the cuss that got away yesterday," speculated the injured man as he slowly arose to his feet. Mr. Cassidy dissented from force of habit and returned to his station.

Mr. Travennes, who was sleeping late that morning, coughed and fought for air in his sleep, awakened in smoke, rubbed his eyes to make sure, and, scorning trousers and shirt, ran clad in his red woolen undergarments to the corral, where he mounted his scared horse and rode for the desert and safety.

Mr. Cassidy, swearing at the marksmanship of a man who fired at his head and perforated his sombrero, saw a crimson rider sweep down upon him, said rider being heralded by a blazing .41.

"Gosh!" ejaculated Mr. Cassidy, scarcely believing his eyes. "Oh, it's my friend Slim going to h—l," he remarked to himself in audible and relieved explanation. Mr. Cassidy's Colt cracked a protest and the rider rising high in his saddle, dove headlong to earth, where he rolled over several times and then lay still.

An hour later Mr. Connors glanced behind him at the smoke silhouetted on the horizon and pushed his way to where Mr. Cassidy rode in silence. Mr. Connors grinned at his friend of the red hair, who responded in the same manner.

"Did yu see Slim?" casually inquired Mr. Connors, looking off to the south.

Mr. Cassidy sat upright in his saddle and felt of his Colt. "Yes," he replied, "I saw him."

Mr. Connors thereupon galloped on in silence.

14

Roping a Rustler

CLARENCE EDWARD MULFORD

BAR 20 RANGE YARNS

VIII—ROPING A RUSTLER

BY CLARENCE EDWARD MULFORD

DRAWING BY FRANK E. SCHOONOVER

I

RUSTLERS ON THE RANGE

MR. BUCK PETERS rode into Buckskin one bright October morning and then out the other side of the town. Coming to himself with a start, he looked around shamefacedly and retraced his course. He was very much troubled for, as foreman of the Bar 20, he had many responsibilities, and when things ceased to go aright he was expected not only to find the cause of the evil but also the remedy. That was why he was paid seventy dollars a month and that was what he had been endeavoring to do. As yet, however, he had only accomplished what the meanest cook's assistant had done. He knew the cause of his present woes to be rustlers (cattle thieves) and that was all.

Riding down the wide, quiet street, he stopped and dismounted before the ever-open door of a ramshackle, one-story frame building. Tossing the reins over the flattened ears of his vicious pinto, he strode into the building and leaned easily against the bar, where he drummed with his fingers and sank into a reverie.

A shining bald pate, bowed over an open box, turned and revealed a florid face, set with two small, twinkling, blue eyes, as the proprietor, wiping his hands on his trousers, made his way to Buck's end of the bar.

"Mornin', Buck. How's things?"

The foreman, lost in his reverie, continued to stare out the door.

"Mornin'," repeated the man behind the bar. "How's things?"

"Oh!" ejaculated the foreman, smiling. "Purty cussed."

"Anything new?"

"Th' C 80 lost another herd last night."

His companion swore and placed a bottle at the foreman's elbow, but the latter shook his head. "Not this mornin'—I'll try one of them vile cigars, however."

"Them cigars are th' very best that—" began the proprietor, executing the order.

"Oh, hell!" exclaimed Buck with weary disgust. "Yu don't have to palaver none. I shore knows all that by heart."

"Them cigars——"

"Yas, yas; them cigars—I know all about them cigars. Yu gets them for twenty dollars a thousand an' hypnotizes us into payin' yu a hundred," replied the foreman, biting off the end of his weed. Then he stared moodily and frowned. "I wonder why it is?" he asked. "We punchers like good stuff an' we pays good prices with good money. What do we get? Why, cabbage leaves an' leather for our smokin', an' alcohol an' extract for our drink. Now, up in Kansas City we goes to a sumptious lay-out, pays less an' gets bang-up stuff. If yu smelled one of them K. C. cigars yu'd shore have to ask what it was, an' as for th' liquor, why, yu'd think St. Peter asked yu to have one with him. It's shore wrong somewhere."

"They have more trade in K. C.," suggested the proprietor.

"An' help, an' taxes, an' a license, an' rent, an' brass, cut-glass, mahogany an' French mirrors," countered the foreman.

The proprietor grinned out the window: "Here comes one of your men."

The newcomer stopped his horse in a cloud of dust, playfully kicked the animal in the ribs and entered, dusting the alkali from him with a huge sombrero. Then he straightened up and sniffed: "What's burnin'?" he asked, simulating alarm. Then he noticed the cigar between the teeth of his foreman and grinned: "Gee, but yore a brave man, Buck."

"Hullo, Hopalong," said the foreman. "Want a smoke?" waving his hand toward the box on the bar.

Mr. Hopalong Cassidy side-stepped and began to roll a cigarette: "Shore, but I'll burn my own—I know what it is."

"What was yu doin' to my cayuse afore yu come in?" asked Buck.

"Nothin'," replied the newcomer. "That was mine what I kicked in th' corrugations."

"How is it yore ridin' th' calico?" asked the foreman. "I thought yu was dead stuck on that piebald."

"That piebald's a goat: he's been livin' off my pants lately," responded Hopalong. "Every time I looks th' other way he ambles over an' takes a bite at me. Yu just wait till this rustler business is roped an' branded, an' yu'll see me eddicate that blessed scrap-heap into eatin' grass again. He swiped Billy's shirt th' other day—took it right off th' corral wall, where Billy'd left it to dry." Then, seeing Buck raise his eyebrows, he explained: "Shore, he washed it again. That makes three times since last fall."

The proprietor laughed and pushed out the ever-ready bottle, but Hopalong shoved it aside and told the reason: "Ever since I was up to K. C. I've been spoiled. I'm drinkin' water an' slush (coffee)."

"For Gawd's sake, has any more of yu fellers been up to K. C.?" queried the proprietor in alarm.

"Shore; Red an' Billy was up there, too," responded Hopalong. "Red's got a few remarks to shout to yu about yore pain-killer. Yu better send for some decent stuff afore he comes to town," he warned.

Buck swung away from the bar and looked at his dead cigar. Then he turned to Hopalong: "What did yu find?" he asked.

"Same old story: nice wide trail up to th' Staked Plain—then nothin'."

"It shore beats me," soliloquized the foreman. "It shore beats me."

"Think it was Tamale José's old gang?" asked Hopalong.

"If it was they took the wrong trail home—that ain't th' way to Mexico."

Hopalong tossed aside his half-smoked cigarette: "Well, come on home; what's th' use stewin' over it? It'll come out all O.K. in th' wash." Then he laughed: "There won't be no piebald waitin' for it."

Evading Buck's playful blow he led the way to the door and soon they were a cloud of dust on the plain. The proprietor, despairing of customers under the circumstances, absent-mindedly wiped off the bar and sought his chair for a nap.

The Bar 20 contained about five hundred square miles of land. It was an irregular ellipse in shape, about thirty miles in length and seventeen in width. The eastern boundary was sharply defined by the Pecos River; the others, where the encroaching desert turned back the cattle. Surrounding it were three other ranches of about the same size, and others lay in the adjacent territory wherever grazing land was to be found. The immediate ranches were the Three-Triangle, the C 80 and the Double-Arrow; the others, the O-Bar-O, the Barred-Horseshoe and the Cross-Bar-X.

For several weeks cattle had been disappearing from the ranges and the losses had long since passed the magnitude of those suffered nine years before, when Tamale José and his men had crossed the Rio Grande and repeatedly levied heavy toll on the sleek herds of the Pecos Valley. Tamale José had raided once too often, paced the outfit of the Bar 20 into Mexico and died as he had lived—hard. His band had been wiped out of organized existence and the survivors were content to sit in pulque saloons and sip mescal as they dilated on the prowess of their former leader. Prosperity and plenty had followed on the ranches and the losses of nine years before had been forgotten until the fall round-ups clearly showed that rustlers were again at work.

Despite the ingenuity of the ranch owners and the unceasing vigilance and night rides of the cow punchers, the losses steadily increased until there was promised a shortage which would permit no drive to the western terminals of the railroad that year. For two weeks the banks of the Rio Grande had been patrolled and sharp-eyed men searched daily for trails leading southward, for it was not strange to think that the old raiders were again at work, notwithstanding the fact that they had paid dearly for their former depredations. The patrols failed to discover anything out of the ordinary and the searchers found no trails. Then it was that the owners and foremen of the four central ranches met in Cowan's saloon at Buckskin and sat closeted together for all of one hot afternoon.

The conference resulted in riders being dispatched from all the ranches represented, and one of the couriers, Mr. Red Connors, rode north, his destination being far-away Montana. All the ranches within a radius of a hundred miles received letters and blanks and one week later the Pecos Valley Cattle-Thief Elimination Association was organized and working, with Buck as Chief Ranger.

One of the outcomes of Buck's appointment was a sudden and marked immigration into the affected territory. Mr. Connors returned from Montana with Mr. Frenchy McAllister, the foreman of the Tin-Cup, who was accompanied by six of his best and most trusted men. Mr. McAllister and party were followed by Mr. You-bet Somes, foreman of the 2-X-2 of Arizona, and five of his punchers; and later on the same day Mr. Pie Willis, accompanied by Mr. Billy Jordan and his two brothers, arrived from the Panhandle. The O-Bar-O, situated close to the town of Muddy Wells, increased its payroll by the addition of nine men, each of whom bore the written recommendation of the foreman of the Bar 20. The C 80, Double-Arrow and the Three-Triangle also received heavy reinforcements and even Carter, owner of the Barred-Horseshoe, far removed from the zone of the depredations, increased his outfits by half their regular strength. Buck believed that if a thing was worth doing at all that it was worth doing very well, and his acquaintances were numerous and loyal. The collection of individuals that responded to the call were noteworthy examples of "gun-play" and their aggregate value was at par with twice their number in cavalry.

Each ranch had one large ranch-house and numerous line-houses were scattered along the boundaries. These latter, while intended as camps for the out-riders, had been erected in the days, none too remote, when Apaches, Arrapahoes, Sioux and even Cheyennes raided southward, and they had been constructed with the idea of defense paramount. Upon more than one occasion a solitary line-rider had retreated within their adobe walls and had successfully resisted all the cunning and ferocity of a score of paint-bedaubed warriors and, when his outfit had rescued him, emerged none the worse for his ordeal.

On the Bar 20, Buck placed these houses in condition to withstand siege. Twin barrels of water stood in opposite corners, provisions were stored on the hanging shelves and the bunks once again reveled in untidiness. Spare rifles, in patterns ranging from long range Sharps and buffalo guns to repeating carbines, leaned against the walls, and unbroken boxes of cartridges were piled above the bunks. Instead of the lonesome out-rider, he placed four men to each house, two of whom were to remain at home and hold the house while their companions rode side by side on their multi-mile beat. There were six of these houses and, instead of returning each night to the same line-house, the outriders kept on and made the circuit, thus keeping every one well informed and breaking the monotony. These measures were expected to cause the rustling operations to cease at once, but the effect was to shift the losses to the Double-Arrow, the line-houses of which boasted only one puncher each.

It was in line-house Number Three, most remote of all, that Johnny Redmond fought his last fight and was found face down in the half-ruined house with a hole in the back of his head, which proved that one man was incapable of watching all the loopholes in four walls at once. There must have been some casualties on the other side, for Johnny was reputed to be very painstaking in his "gun-play," and the empty shells which lay scattered on the floor did not stand for as many ciphers, of that his foreman was positive. He was buried the day he was found and the news of his death ran quickly from ranch to ranch and made more than one careless puncher arise and pace the floor in anger. More men came to the Double-Arrow and its sentries were doubled. The depredations continued, however, and one night a week later Frank Swift reeled into the ranch-house and fell exhausted across the supper table. Rolling hoof-beats echoed flatly and died away on the plain, but the men who pursued them returned empty handed. The wounds of the unfortunate were roughly dressed and in his delirium he recounted the fight. His companion was found literally shot to pieces twenty paces from the door. One wall was found blown in and this episode, when coupled with the use of dynamite, was more than could be tolerated.

When Buck had been informed of this he called to him Hopalong Cassidy, daredevil and gun expert; Red Connors, a twin of the first named in warlike attributes, and Frenchy McAllister, who was a veteran of many ranches and battles. The next day the three men rode north and the contingents of the ranches represented in the Association were divided into two squads, one of which was to remain at home and guard the ranches; the other, to sleep fully dressed and armed and never to stray far from their ranch-houses and horses. These latter would be called upon to ride swiftly and far when the word came.

II

MR. TRENDLEY ASSUMES ADDED IMPORTANCE

That the rustlers were working under a well-organized system was evident. That they were directed by a master of the game was ceaselessly beaten into the consciousness of the Association by the diversity, dash and success of their raids. No one, save the three men whom they had destroyed, had ever seen them. But, like Tamale José, they had raided once too often.

Mr. Trendley, more familiarly known to men as "Slippery," was the possessor of a biased conscience, if any at all. Tall, gaunt and weather-beaten and with coal-black eyes set deep beneath hairless eyebrows, he was sinister and forbidding. In his forty-five years of existence he had crowded a century of experience. Unsavory rumors about him existed in all parts of the great West. From Canada to Mexico and from Sacramento to Westport his name stood for brigandage. His operations had been conducted with such consummate cleverness that in all the accusations there was lacking proof. Only once had he erred, and then in the spirit of pure deviltry and in the days of youthful folly, and his mistake was a written note. He was even thought by some to have been concerned in the Mountain Meadow Massacre; others thought him to have been the leader of the band of outlaws that had plundered along the Santa Fé Trail in the late '60's. In Montana and Wyoming he was held responsible for the outrages of the band that had descended from the Hole-in-the-Wall territory and for over a hundred miles carried murder and theft that shamed as being weak the most assiduous efforts of zealous Cheyennes. It was in this last raid where he had made the mistake, and it was in this raid that Frenchy McAllister had lost his wife.

When the three mounted and came to him for final instructions, Buck forced himself to be almost repellent in order to be capable of coherent speech. Hopalong glanced sharply at him and then understood; Red was all attention and eagerness and remarked nothing but the words.

"Have yu ever heard of Slippery Trendley?" harshly inquired the foreman.

They nodded, and on the faces of the younger men a glint of hatred showed itself. Frenchy wore his poker countenance.

Buck continued: "Th' reason I asked yu was because I don't want yu to think yore goin' on no picnic. I ain't shore it's him, but I've had some hopeful information. Besides, he is th' only man I knows of who's capable of th' plays that have been made. It's hardly necessary for me to tell yu to sleep with one eye open and never to get away from yore guns. Now I'm goin' to tell yu th' hardest part: yu are goin' to search th' Staked Plain from one end to th' other, an' that's what no white man's ever done to my knowledge.

"Now listen to this an' don't forget it: Twenty miles north from Last Stand Rock is a spring; ten miles south of that bend in Hell Arroyo is another. If yu gets lost within two days from th' time yu enters th' Plain, put yore left hand on a cactus some time between sun-up an' noon, move around until yu are over its shadow an' then ride straight ahead—that's south. If yu goes loco beyond Last Stand Rock, follow th' shadows made before noon—

that's th' quickest way to th' Pecos. Yu all knows what to do in a sand-storm, so I won't bore yu with that. Repeat all I've told yu," he ordered, and they complied.

"I'm tellin' yu this," continued the foreman, indicating the two auxiliaries, "because yu might get separated from Frenchy. Now I suggests that yu look around near th' Devil's Rocks: I've heard that there are several water holes among them, an' besides, they might be turned into fair corrals. Mind yu, I know what I've said sounds damned idiotic for anybody that has had as much experience with th' Staked Plain as I have, but I've had every other place searched for miles around. Th' men of all th' ranches have been scoutin' an' th' Plain is th' only place left. Them rustlers has got to be found if we have to dig to hell for them. They've taken th' pot so many times that they reckons they owns it, an' we've got to at least make a bluff at drawin' cards. Mebby they're at th' bottom of th' Pecos," here he smiled faintly, "but wherever they are, we've *got* to find them. I want to holler 'Keno.'

"If yu finds where they hangs out, come away instanter," here his face hardened and his eyes narrowed, "for it 'll take more than yu three to deal with them th' way I'm a-hankerin' for. Come right back to th' Double-Arrow, send me word by one of their punchers an' get all th' rest yu can afore I gets there. It'll take me a day to get th' men together an' to reach yu. I'm goin' to use smoke signals to call th' other ranches, so there won't be no time lost. Carry all th' water yu can pack when yu leaves th' Double-Arrow an' don't depend none on cactus juice. Yu better take a pack horse to carry it an' yore grub—yu can shoot it if yu have to hit th' trail real hard."

The three riders felt of their accouterments, said "So long," and cantered off for the pack horse and extra ammunition. Then they rode toward the Double-Arrow, stopping at Cowan's long enough to spend some money, and reached their destination at nightfall. Early the next morning they passed the last line-house and, with the profane well-wishes of its occupants ringing in their ears, passed on to one of nature's worst blunders—the Staked Plain.

III

HOPALONG'S DECISION

Shortly after noon, Hopalong, who had ridden with his head bowed low in meditation, looked up and slapped his thigh. Then he looked at Red and grinned.

"Look ahere, Red," he began, "there ain't no rustlers with their headquarters on this God-forsaken sand-heap, an' there never was. They have to have water an' lots of it, too, an' th' nearest of any account is th' Pecos, or some of them streams over in th' Panhandle. Th' Panhandle is th' best place. There are lots of streams an' lakes over there an' they're right in a good grass country. Why, an' army could hide over there an' never be found unless it was hunted for blamed good. Then, again, it's close to th' railroad. Up north a ways is th' south branch of th' Santa Fé trail an' it's far enough away not to bother anybody in th' middle Panhandle. Then there's Fort Worth purty near, an' other trails. Didn't Buck say he had all th' rest of th' country searched? He meant th' Pecos Valley an' th' Davis Mountains country. All th' rustlers would have to do if they were in th' Panhandle would be to cross th' Canadian an' th' Cimarron an' hit th' trail for th' railroad. Good fords, good grass an' water all th' way, cattle fat when they are delivered an' plenty of room. Th' more I thinks about it th' more I cottons to th' Panhandle."

"Well, it shore does sound good," replied Red reflectively. "Do yu mean th' Cunningham Lake region or farther north?"

"Just th' other side of this blasted desert: anywhere where there's water," responded Hopalong enthusiastically. "I've been doin' some hot reckonin' for th' last two hours an' this is th' way it looks to me: they drives th' cows up on this skillet for a ways, then turns east an' hits th' trail for home an' water. They can get around th' cañon near Thatcher's Lake by a swing to th' north. I tell yu that's th' only way out'n this. Who could tell where they turned with th' wind raisin' th' devil with th' trail? Didn't we follow a trail for a ways, an' then what? Why, there wasn't none to follow. We can ride north till we walk behind ourselves an' never get a peek at them. I am in favor of headin' for th' Sulphur Spring Creek district. We can spend a couple of weeks, if we has to, an' prospect that whole region without havin' to cut our water down to a smell an' a taste an' live on jerked beef. If we investigates that country we'll find something else than sand-storms, poisoned water holes an' blisters."

"Ain't th' Panhandle full of nesters (farmers)?" inquired Red doubtfully.

"Along th' Canadian an' th' edges, yas; in th' middle, no," explained Hopalong. "They hang close together on account of th' War-whoops an' they like th' trails purty well because of there allus bein' somebody passin'."

"Buck ought to send some of th' Panhandle boys up there," suggested Red. "There's Pie Willis an' th' Jordans—they knows th' Panhandle like yu knows poker."

Frenchy had paid no apparent attention to the conversation up to this point, but now he declared himself. "Yu heard what Buck said, didn't you?" he asked. "We were told to search th' Staked Plain from one end to th' other an' I'm goin' to do it if I can hold out long enough. I ain't goin' to palaver with yu because what yu say can't be denied as far as wisdom is concerned. Yu may have hit it plumb center, but I knows what I was ordered to do, an' yu can't get me to go over there if yu shouts all night. When Buck says anything, she goes. He wants to know where th' cards are stacked an' why he can't holler 'Keno,' an' I'm goin' to find out if I can. Yu can go to Patagonia if yu wants to, but yu go alone as far as I am concerned."

"Well, it's better if yu don't go with us," replied Hopalong, taking it for granted that Red would accompany him. "Yu can prospect this end of th' game an' we'll be takin' care of th' other. It's two chances now where we only had one afore."

"Yu go east an' I'll hunt around as ordered," responded Frenchy.

"East nothin'," replied Hopalong. "Yu don't get me to wallow in hot alkali an' lose time ridin' in ankle-deep sand when I can hit th' south trail, skirt th' White Sand Hills an' be in God's country again. I ain't goin' to wrastle with no cañon this here trip, none whatever. I'm goin' to travel in style, get to Big Spring by ridin' two miles to where I could only make one on this stove. Then I'll head north along

Sulphur Spring Creek an' have water an' grass all th' way, barrin' a few stretches. While yu are bein' fricasseed I'll be streakin' through cottonwood groves an' ridin' in th' creek."

"Yu'll have to go alone, then," said Red resolutely. "Frenchy ain't a-goin' to die of lonesomeness on this desert if I knows what I'm about, an' I reckon I do, some. Me an' him 'll follow out what Buck said, hunt around for a while an' then Frenchy can go back to th' ranch to tell Buck what's up an' I'll take th' trail yu are ascared of an' meet yu at th' east end of Cunningham Lake three days from now."

"Yu better come with me," coaxed Hopalong, not liking what his friend had said about being afraid of the trail past the cañon and wishing to have some one with whom to talk on his trip. "I'm goin' to have a nice long swim to-morrow night," he added, trying bribery.

"An' I'm goin' to try to keep from hittin' my blisters," responded Red. "I don't want to go swimmin' in no creek full of moccasins—I'd rather sleep with rattlers or copperheads, Every time I sees a cottonmouth I feels like I had just sit down on one."

"I'll flip a coin to see whether yu comes or not," proposed Hopalong.

"If yu wants to gamble so bad I'll flip yu to see who draws our pay next month, but not for what yu said," responded Red, choking down the desire to try his luck.

Hopalong grinned and turned toward the south. "If I sees Buck afore yu do, I'll tell him yu an' Frenchy are growin' watermelons up near Last Stand Rock an' are waitin' for rain. Well, so long," he said.

"Yu tell Buck we're obeyin' orders!" shouted Red, sorry that he was not going with his bunkie.

An hour later they searched the Devil's Rocks, but found no rustlers. Filling their canteens at a tiny spring and allowing their mounts to drink the remainder of the water, they turned toward Hell Arroyo, which they reached at nightfall. Here, also, their search availed them nothing and they paused in indecision. Then Frenchy turned toward his companion and advised him to ride toward the Lake in the night, when it was comparatively cool.

Red considered and then decided that the advice was good. He rolled a ciga-

"He swung his rifle out over a forked limb and let it settle
in the crotch."

Drawing by Frank E. Schoonover.

rette, wheeled and faced the east and spurred forward. "So long," he called.

"So long," replied Frenchy, who turned toward the south and departed for the ranch.

The foreman of the Bar 20 was cleaning his rifle when he heard the hoof-beats of a galloping horse, and he ran around the corner of the house to meet the newcomer, whom he thought to be a courier from the Double-Arrow. Frenchy dismounted and explained why he returned alone.

Buck listened to the report and then, noting the fire which gleamed in his friend's eyes, nodded his approval to the course. "I reckon it's Trendley, Frenchy—I've heard a few things since you left. An' yu can bet that if Hopalong an' Red have gone for him he'll be found. I expect action any time now, so we'll light th' signal fire." Then he hesitated: "Yu light it—yu've been waiting a long time for this."

The balls of smoke which rolled upward were replied to by other balls at different points on the plain and the Bar 20 prepared to feed the numbers of hungry punchers who would arrive within the next twenty-four hours.

Two hours had not passed when eleven men rode up from the Three-Triangle, followed eight hours later by ten from the O-Bar-O. The outfits of the Star-Circle and the Barred-Horseshoe, eighteen in all, came next and had scarcely dismounted when those of the C 80 and the Double-Arrow, fretting at the delay, rode up. With the sixteen from the Bar 20 the force numbered seventy-five resolute and pugnacious cow punchers, all aching to wipe out the indignities suffered.

IV

A PROBLEM SOLVED

Hopalong worried his way out of the desert on a straight line, thus cutting in half the distance he had traveled when going into it. He camped that night on the sand, and early the next morning took up his journey. It was noon when he began to notice familiar sights and an hour later he passed within a mile of line-house Number Three, Double-Arrow. Half an hour later he espied a cow puncher riding

like mad. Thinking that an investigation would not be out of place, he rode after the rider and overtook him, when that person paused and retraced his course.

"Hullo, Hopalong," shouted the puncher as he came near enough to recognize his pursuer. "Thought yu was farmin' up on th' Staked Plain."

"Hullo, Pie," replied Hopalong, recognizing Pie Willis. "What was yu chasin' so hard?"

"Coyote—damn 'em, but can't they go some? They're gettin' so thick we'll shore have to try strychnine an' thin 'em out."

"I thought anybody that had been raised in th' Panhandle would know better 'n to chase greased lightnin'," rebuked Hopalong. "Yu has got about as much show catchin' one of them as a tenderfoot has of bustin' an outlawed cayuse."

"Shore; I know it," responded Pie, grinning. "But it's fun seein' them hunt th' horizon. What are yu doin' down here an' where are yore pardners?"

Thereupon, Hopalong enlightened his inquisitive companion as to what had occurred and as to his reasons for riding south. Pie immediately became enthusiastic and announced his intention of accompanying Hopalong on his quest, which intention struck that gentleman as highly proper and wise. Then Pie hastily turned and played at chasing coyotes in the direction of the line-house, where he announced that his absence would be accounted for by the fact that he and Hopalong were going on a journey of investigation into the Panhandle. Billy Jordan, who shared with Pie the accommodations of the house, objected and showed very clearly why he was eminently better qualified to take up the proposed labors than his companion. The suggestions were fast getting tangled up with the remarks, when Pie, grabbing a chunk of jerked beef, leaped into his saddle and absolutely refused to heed the calls of his former companion and return. He rode to where Hopalong was awaiting him as if he was afraid he wasn't going to live long enough to get there. Confiding to his companion that Billy was a "locoed sage hen," he led the way along to the base of the White Sand Hills and asked many questions. Then they turned toward the east and galloped hard.

It had been Hopalong's intention to carry out what he had told Red and to go to Big Spring first, and thence north along Sulphur Spring Creek, but to this his guide strongly dissented. There was a short-cut, or several of them for that matter, was Pie's contention, and any one of them would save a day's hard riding. Hopalong made no objection to allowing his companion to lead the way over any trail he saw fit, for he knew that Pie had been born and brought up in the Panhandle, the Cunningham Lake district having been his back yard, as it were. So they followed the short-cut having the most water and grass and pounded out a lively tattoo as they raced over the stretches of sand which seemed to slide beneath them.

"What do yu know about this here business?" inquired Pie as they raced past a chaparral and on to the edge of a grassy plain.

"Nothin' more 'n yu do, only Buck said he thought Slippery Trendley is at th' bottom of it."

"What!" ejaculated Pie in surprise; "him!"

"Yore on. An' between yu an' me an' th' devil, I wouldn't be a heap surprised if Deacon Rankin is with him, neither."

Pie whistled: "Are him an' th' Deacon pals?"

"Shore," replied Hopalong, buttoning up his vest and rolling a cigarette. "Didn't they allus hang out together? One watched that th' other didn't get plugged from behind. It was a sort of yu-scratch-my-back-an'-I'll-scratch-yourn arrangement."

"Well, if they still hangs out together I know where to hunt for our cows," responded Pie. "Th' Deacon used to range along th' head-waters of th' Colorado—it ain't far from Cunningham Lake. Thunderation!" he shouted, "I knows th' very ground they're on—I can take yu to th' very shack!" Then to himself he muttered: "An' that doodlebug Billy Jordan thinkin' he knowed more about th' Panhandle than me!"

Hopalong showed his elation in an appropriate manner and his companion drank deeply from the proffered flask. Thereupon they treated their mounts to liberal doses of strap-oil and covered the ground with great speed.

They camped early, for Hopalong was almost worn out from the exertions of the past few days and the loss of sleep he had sustained. Pie, too excited to sleep, and having had unbroken rest for a long period, volunteered to keep guard, and his companion eagerly consented.

Early the next morning they broke camp and the evening of the same day found them fording Sulphur Spring Creek, and their quarry lay only an hour beyond, according to Pie. Then they forded one of the streams which form the head-waters of the Colorado, and two hours later they dismounted in a cottonwood grove. Picketing their horses, they carefully made their way through the timber, which was heavily grown with brush, and, after half an hour's maneuvering, came within sight of the further edge. Dropping on all fours, they crawled to the last line of brush and looked out over an extensive bottom. At their feet lay a small river, and in a clearing on the farther side was a rough camp, consisting of about a dozen lean-to shacks and log cabins in the main collection, and a few scattered cabins along the edge. A huge fire was blazing before the main collection of huts and to the rear of these was an indistinct black mass, which they knew to be the corral.

At a rude table before the fire more than a score of men were eating supper and others could be heard moving about and talking at different points in the background. While the two scouts were learning the lay of the land, they saw Mr. Trendley and Deacon Rankin walk out of the cabin most distant from the fire, and the latter limped. Then they saw two men lying on rude cots and they wore bandages. Evidently Johnny Redmond had scored in his fight.

The odor of burning cowhide came from the corral, accompanied by the squeals of cattle, and informed them that brands were being blotted out. Hopalong longed to charge down and do some blotting out of another kind, but a heavy hand was placed on his shoulder and he silently wormed his way after Pie as that person led the way back to the horses. Mounting, they picked their way out of the grove and rode over the plain at a walk. When far enough away to insure that the noise made by their horses would not reach the ears of those in the camp, they cantered toward the ford they had taken on the way up.

After emerging from the waters of the last forded stream, Pie raised his hand and pointed off toward the northwest, telling his companion to take that course to reach Cunningham Lake. He himself would ride south, taking, for the saving of time, a yet shorter trail to the Double-Arrow, from where he would ride to Buck. He and the others would meet Hopalong and Red at the split rock they had noticed on their way up.

Hopalong shook hands with his guide and watched him disappear into the night. He imagined he could still catch whiffs of burning cowhide and again the picture of the camp came to his mind. Glancing again at the point where Pie had disappeared, he stuffed his sombrero under a strap on his saddle and slowly rode toward the lake. A coyote slunk past him on a time-destroying lope, and an owl hooted at the foolishness of men. He camped at the base of a cottonwood and at daylight took up his journey after a scanty breakfast from his saddle-bags.

Shortly before noon he came in sight of the lake and looked for his friend. He had just ridden around a clump of cottonwoods when he was hit on the back with something large and soft. Turning in his saddle, with his Colt ready, he saw Red sitting on a stump, a huge grin extending over his features. He replaced the weapon, said something about fools and dismounted, kicking aside the bundle of grass his friend had thrown.

"Yore shore easy," remarked Red, tossing aside his cold cigarette. "Suppose I was Trendley, where would yu be now?"

"Diggin' a hole to put yu in," pleasantly replied Hopalong. "If I didn't know he wasn't around this part of the country I wouldn't a rode as I did."

The man on the stump laughed and rolled a fresh cigarette. Lighting it, he inquired where Mr. Trendley was, intimating by his words that the rustler had not been found.

"About thirty miles to the southeast," responded the other. "He's figurin' up how much dust he'll have when he gets our cows on th' market. Deacon Rankin is with him, too."

"Th' devil!" exclaimed Red in profound astonishment.

"Yore right," replied his companion. Then he explained all the arrangements and told of the camp.

Red was for riding to the rendezvous at once, but his friend thought otherwise and proposed a swim, which met with approval. After enjoying themselves in the lake they dressed and rode along the trail Hopalong had made in coming for his companion, it being the intention of the former to learn more thoroughly the lay of the land immediately surrounding the camp. Red was pleased with this, and while they rode he narrated all that had taken place since the separation on the Plain, adding that he had found the trail made by the rustlers after they had quitted the desert, and that he had followed it for the last two hours of his journey. It was well beaten and an eighth of a mile wide.

At dark they came within sight of the grove and picketed their horses at the place used by Pie and Hopalong. Then they moved forward and the same sight greeted their eyes that had been seen the night before. Keeping well within the edge of the grove and looking carefully for sentries, they went entirely around the camp and picked out several places which would be of strategic value later on. They noticed that the cabin used by Slippery Trendley was a hundred paces from the main collection of huts and that the woods came to within a tenth part of that distance of its door. It was heavily built, had no windows and faced the wrong direction.

Moving on, they discovered the storehouse of the enemy, another tempting place. It was just possible, if a siege became necessary, for several of the attacking force to slip up to it and either destroy it by fire or take it and hold it against all comers. This suggested a look at the enemy's water supply, which was the river. A hundred paces separated it from the nearest cabin and any rustler who could cross that zone under the fire of the besiegers would be welcome to his drink.

It was very evident that the rustlers had no thought of defense, thinking, perhaps, that they were immune from attack with such a well-covered trail between them and their foes. Hopalong mentally accused them of harboring suicidal inclinations and returned with his companion to the horses. They mounted and sat quietly for a while and then rode slowly away, and at dawn reached the split rock, where they awaited the arrival of their friends, one sleeping while the other kept guard. Then they drew a rough map of the camp, using the sand for paper, and laid out the plan of attack.

As the evening of the next day came on they saw Pie, followed by many punchers, ride over a rise a mile to the south, and they rode out to meet him.

When the force arrived at the camp of the two scouts they were shown the plan prepared for them. Buck made a few changes in the disposition of the men and then each member was shown where he was to go and was told why. Weapons were put in a high state of efficiency, canteens were refilled and haversacks were somewhat depleted. Then the newcomers turned in and slept while Hopalong and Red kept guard.

V

THE CALL

At three o'clock the next morning a long line of men slowly filed into the cottonwood grove, being silently swallowed up by the darkness. Dismounting, they left their horses in the care of three of their number and disappeared into the brush. Ten minutes later forty of the force were distributed along the edge of the grove fringing on the bank of the river and twenty more minutes gave ample time for a detachment of twenty to cross the stream and find concealment in the edge of the woods which ran from the river to where the corral made an effective barrier on the south. Eight crept down on the western side of the camp and worked their way close to Mr. Trendley's cabin door, and the seven who followed this detachment continued and took up their positions at the rear of the corral, where, it was hoped, some of the rustlers would endeavor to escape into the woods by working their way through the cattle in the corral and then scaling the stockade wall. These seven were from the Three-Triangle and the Double-Arrow and they were positive that any such attempt would not be a success from the view-point of the rustlers.

Two of those who awaited the pleasure of Mr. Trendley crept forward and a rope

swished through the air and settled over a stump which lay most convenient on the other side of the cabin door. Then the slack moved toward the woods, raised from the ground as it grew taut, and, with the stump for its axis, swung toward the door, where it rubbed gently against the rough logs. It was made of braided horsehair, was half an inch in diameter and was stretched eight inches above the ground.

As it touched the door, Lanky Smith, the Bar 20 rope expert, Hopalong and Red stepped out of the shelter of the woods and took up their positions behind the cabin, Lanky behind the northeast corner where he would be permitted to swing his right arm. In his gloved right hand he held the carefully arranged coils of a fifty-foot lariat, and should the chief of the rustlers escape tripping he would have to avoid the cast of the best roper in the southwest. The two others took the northwest corner and one of them leaned slightly forward and gently twitched the tripping rope. The man at the other end felt the signal and whispered to a companion, who quietly disappeared in the direction of the river and shortly afterward the mournful cry of a whip-poor-will dirged out on the early morning air. It had hardly died away when the quiet was broken by one terrific crash of rifles, and the two camp guards asleep at the fire awoke in another world.

Mr. Trendley, sleeping unusually well for the unjust, leaped from his bed to the middle of the floor and alighted on his feet and wide awake. Fearing that a plot was being consummated to deprive him of his leadership, he grasped the Winchester which leaned at the head of his bed and, tearing open the door, crashed headlong to the earth. As he touched the ground, two shadows sped out from the shelter of the cabin wall and pounced upon him. Men who can rope, throw and tie a wild steer in thirty seconds flat, do not waste time in trussing operations, and before a minute had elapsed he was being carried into the woods, bound and helpless. Lanky sighed, threw the rope over one shoulder and departed after his friends.

When Mr. Trendley came to his senses he found himself bound to a tree in the grove near the horses. A man sat on a stump not far from him, three others were seated around a small fire some distance to the north and four others, one of whom carried a rope, made their way into the brush. He strained at his bonds, decided that the effort was useless and watched the man on the stump, who struck a match and lit a pipe. The prisoner watched the light flicker up and go out and there was left in his mind a picture that he could never forget. The face which had been so cruelly, so grotesquely revealed was that of Frenchy McAllister, and across his knee lay a heavy caliber Winchester. A curse escaped from the lips of the outlaw; the man on the stump spat at a firefly and smiled.

From the south came the crack of rifles, incessant and sharp. The reports rolled from one end of the clearing to the other and seemed to sweep in waves from the center of the line to the ends. Faintly in the infrequent lulls in the firing came an occasional report from the rear of the corral, where some desperate rustler paid for his venture.

Buck went along the line and spoke to the riflemen, and after some time had passed and the light had become stronger, he collected the men into groups of five and six. Taking one group and watching it closely, it could be seen that there was a world of meaning in this maneuver. One man started firing at a particular window in an opposite hut and then laid aside his empty gun and waited. When the muzzle of his enemy's gun came into sight and lowered until it had nearly gained its sight level, the rifles of the remainder of the group crashed out in a volley and usually one of the bullets, at least, found its intended billet. This volley firing became universal among the besiegers and the effect was marked.

Two men sprinted from the edge of the woods near Mr. Trendley's cabin and gained the shelter of the storehouse, which soon broke out in flames. The burning brands fell over the main collection of huts, where there was much confusion and swearing. The early hour at which the attack had been delivered at first led the besieged to believe that it was an Indian affair, but this impression was soon corrected by the volley firing, which turned hope into despair. It was no great matter to fight Indians; that they had done many times

and found more or less enjoyment in it; but there was a vast difference between brave and puncher and the chances of their salvation became very small. They surmised that it was the work of the cow men on whom they had preyed, and that vengeful punchers lay hidden behind that death-fringe of green willow and hazel.

Red, assisted by his inseparable companion, Hopalong, laboriously climbed up among the branches of a black walnut and hooked one leg over a convenient limb. Then he lowered his rope and drew up the Winchester which his accommodating friend fastened to it. Settling himself in a comfortable position and sheltering his body somewhat by the tree, he shaded his eyes by a hand and peered into the windows of the distant cabins.

"How is she, Red?" anxiously inquired the man on the ground.

"Bully; want to come up?"

"Nope. I'm goin' to catch yu when yu lets go," replied Hopalong with a grin.

"Which same I ain't goin' to," responded the man in the tree.

He swung his rifle out over a forked limb and let it settle in the crotch. Then he slewed his head around until he gained the bead he wished. Five minutes passed before he caught sight of his man and then he fired. Jerking out the empty shell he smiled and called out to his friend: "One."

Hopalong grinned and went off to tell Buck to put all the men in trees.

Suddenly an explosion shook the woods. The storehouse had blown up. A sky-full of burning timber fell on the cabins and soon three were half consumed, their occupants dropping as they gained the open air. One hundred paces makes fine pot-shooting, as Deacon Rankin discovered when evacuation was the choice necessary to avoid cremation. He never moved after he touched the ground and Red called out, "Two," not knowing that his companion had departed.

Eleven o'clock found a wearied and hopeless garrison and shortly before noon a soiled white shirt was flung from a window in the nearest cabin. Buck ran along the line and ordered the firing to cease and caused to be raised an answering flag of truce. A full minute passed and then the door slowly opened and a leg protruded, more slowly followed by the rest of the man, and Cheyenne Charley strode out to the bank of the river and sat down. His example was followed by several others and then an unexpected event occurred. Those in the cabins who preferred to die fighting, angered at this desertion, opened fire on their former comrades, who barely escaped by rolling down the slightly inclined bank into the river. Red fired again and laughed to himself. Then the fugitives swam down the river and landed under the guns of the last squad. They were taken to the rear and, after being bound, were placed under a guard. There were seven in the party and they looked worn out.

When the huts were burning the fiercest, the uproar in the corral arose to such a pitch as to drown all other sounds. There were left within its walls a few hundred cattle whose brands had not yet been blotted out, and these, maddened to frenzy by the shooting and the flames, tore from one end of the inclosure to the other, crashing against the alternate walls with a noise which could be heard far out on the plain. Scores were trampled to death in each charge and finally the uproar subsided in sheer want of cattle left with energy enough to continue. When the corral was investigated the next day there were found the bodies of four rustlers, but recognition was impossible.

Several of the defenders were housed in cabins having windows in the rear walls, which the occupants considered fortunate. This opinion was revised, however, after several had endeavored to escape by these openings. The first thing which occurred when a man put his head out was the hum of a bullet, and in two cases the experimenters lost all need of escape.

The volley firing had the desired effect and at dusk there remained only one cabin from which came opposition. Such a fire was concentrated on it that before an hour had passed the door fell in and the firing ceased.

There was a rush from the side and the Barred-Horseshoe men who swarmed through the cabins emerged without firing a shot. The organization that had stirred up the Pecos Valley ranches had ceased to exist.

VI

THE SHOWDOWN

A fire burned briskly in front of Mr. Trendley's cabin that night and several punchers sat around it occupied in various ways. Two men leaned against the wall and sang softly of the joys of the trail and the range. One of them, Lefty Allen of the O-Bar-O, sang in his sweet tenor, and other men gradually strolled up and seated themselves on the ground, where the fitful gleam of responsive pipes and cigarettes showed like fireflies. The songs followed one after another, first a lover's plea in soft Spanish and then a rollicking tale of the cow towns and men. Supper had long since been enjoyed and all felt that life was indeed well worth living.

A shadow loomed against the cabin wall and a procession slowly made its way toward the open door. The leader, Hopalong, disappeared within and was followed by Mr. Trendley, bound and hobbled and tied to Red, the rear being brought up by Frenchy, whose rifle lolled easily in the crotch of his elbow. The singing went on uninterrupted and the hum of voices between the selections remained unchanged. Buck left the crowd around the fire and went into the cabin, where his voice was heard assenting to something. Hopalong emerged and took a seat at the fire, sending two punchers to take his place. He was joined by Frenchy and Red, the former very quiet.

In the center of a distant group were seven men who were not armed. Their belts, half full of cartridges, supported empty holsters. They sat and talked to the men around them, swapping notes and experiences, and in several instances found former friends and acquaintances. These men were not bound and were apparently members of Buck's force. Then one of them broke down, but quickly regained his nerve and proposed a game of cards. A fire was started and several games were immediately in progress. These seven men were to die at daybreak.

As the night grew older man after man rolled himself in his blanket and lay down where he sat, sinking off to sleep with a swiftness that bespoke tired muscles and weariness. All through the night, however, there were twelve men on guard, of whom three were in the cabin.

At daybreak a shot from one of the guards awakened every man within hearing and soon they romped and scampered down to the river's edge to indulge in the luxury of a morning plunge. After an hour's horseplay they trooped back to the cabin and soon had breakfast out of the way.

Waffles, foreman of the O-Bar-O, and You-bet Somes strolled over to the seven unfortunates who had just completed a choking breakfast and nodded a hearty "Good morning." Then others came up, and finally all moved off toward the river. Crossing it, they disappeared into the grove and all sounds of their advance grew into silence.

Mr. Trendley, escorted outside for the air, saw the procession as it became lost to sight in the brush. He sneered and asked for a smoke, which was granted. Then his guards were changed and the men began to straggle back from the grove.

Mr. Trendley, with his back to the cabin, scowled defiantly at the crowd that hemmed him in. The coolest, most damnable murderer in the West was not now going to beg for mercy. When he had taken up crime as a means of livelihood he had decided that if the price to be paid for his course was death, he would pay like a man. He glanced at the cottonwood grove, wherein were many ghastly secrets, and smiled. His hairless eyebrows looked like livid scars and his lips quivered in scorn and anger.

As he sneered at Buck there was a movement in the crowd before him and a pathway opened for Frenchy, who stepped forward slowly and deliberately, as if on his way to some bar for a drink. There was something different about the man who had searched the Staked Plain with Hopalong and Red; he was not the same puncher who had arrived from Montana three weeks before. There was lacking a certain air of carelessness and he chilled his friends, who looked upon him as if they had never really known him. He walked up to Mr. Trendley and gazed deep into the evil eyes.

Twenty years before, Frenchy McAllister had changed his identity from a happy-go-lucky, devil-may-care cow puncher and become a machine. The grief which had torn his soul was not of the kind which seeks its outlet in tears and wailing: it had turned and struck inward and now his deliberate

ferocity was icy and devilish. Only a glint in his eyes told of exultation and his words were sharp and incisive; one could well imagine one heard the click of his teeth as they bit off the consonants: every letter was clear-cut, every syllable startling in its clearness.

"Twenty years and two months ago to-day," he began, "you arrived at the ranch-house of the Double-Y, up near the Montana-Wyoming line. Everything was quiet, except, perhaps, a woman's voice, singing. You entered, and before you left you pinned a note to that woman's dress. I found it, and it is due."

The air of carelessness disappeared from the members of the crowd and the silence became oppressive. Most of those present knew parts of Frenchy's story and all were in hearty accord with anything he might do. He reached within his vest and brought forth a deerskin bag. Opening it, he drew out a package of oiled silk and from that he took a paper. Carefully replacing the silk and the bag, he slowly unfolded the sheet in his hand and handed it to Buck, whose face hardened. Two decades had passed since the foreman of the Bar 20 had seen that precious sheet, but the scene of its finding would never fade from his memory. He stood as if carved from stone, with a look on his face that made the crowd shift uneasily and glance at Trendley.

Frenchy turned to the rustler and regarded him evilly. "You are the hellish brute that wrote that note," pointing to the paper in the hand of his friend. Then, turning again to the foreman, he spoke: "Buck, read that paper."

The foreman cleared his throat and read distinctly:

"McAllister: Your wife is too damn good to live.   Trendley."

There was a shuffling sound, but Buck and Frenchy, silently backed up by Hopalong and Red, intervened, and the crowd fell back, where it surged in indecision.

"Gentlemen," said Frenchy, "I want you to vote on whether any man here has more right to do with Slippery Trendley as he sees fit than myself. Any one who thinks so, or that he should be treated like the *others*, step forward. Majority rules." There was no advance and he spoke again: "Is there any one here who objects to this man dying?"

Hopalong and Red awkwardly bumped their knuckles against their guns and there was no response.

The prisoner was bound with cowhide to the wall of the cabin and four men sat near and facing him. The noonday meal was eaten in silence and the punchers rode off to see about rounding up the cattle which grazed over the plain as far as eye could see. Supper time came and passed and busy men rode away in all directions. Others came and relieved the guards and at midnight another squad took up the vigil.

Day broke and the thunder of hoofs, as the punchers rounded up the cattle in herds of about five thousand each, became very noticeable. One herd swept past toward the south, guarded and guided by fifteen men. Two hours later and another followed, taking a slightly different trail so as to avoid the close-cropped grass left by the first. At irregular intervals during the day other herds swept by, until six had passed and denuded the plain of cattle.

Buck, perspiring and dusty, accompanied by Hopalong and Red, rode up to where the guards smoked and joked. Frenchy came out of the cabin and smiled at his friends. Swinging in his left hand was a newly filled Colt .45, which was recognized by his friends as the one found in the cabin, and it bore a rough "T" gouged in the butt.

Buck looked around and cleared his throat: "We've got th' cows on th' home trail, Frenchy," he suggested.

"Yas?" inquired Frenchy. "Are there many?"

"Six drives of about five thousand to the drive."

"All th' boys gone?" asked the man with the newly filled Colt.

"Yas," replied Buck, waving his hand at the guards, ordering them to follow their friends. "It's a good deal for us; we've done right smart this hand. An' it's a good thing we've got so many punchers: thirty thousand's a big contract. I hope almighty hard that we don't have no stampedes on this here drive. Thirty thousand locoed cattle would just about wipe up this here territory. If th' last herds go wild they'll pick up th' others, an' then there 'll be th' devil to pay."

Frenchy smiled again and shot a glance at where Mr. Trendley was bound to the cabin wall.

Buck looked steadily southward for some time and then flecked a foam-sud from the flank of his horse. "We are goin' south along th' Creek until we gets to Big Spring, where we'll turn right smart to th' west. We won't be able to make more 'n twelve miles a day, though I'm goin' to drive them hard. How's yore grub?"

"Grub to burn."

"Got yore rope?" asked the foreman of the Bar 20, speaking as if the question had no especial meaning.

Frenchy smiled: "Yes."

Hopalong absent-mindedly jabbed his spurs into his mount, with the result that when the storm had subsided the spell was broken and he said "So long" and rode south, followed by Buck and Red. As they swept out of sight behind a grove Red turned in his saddle and waved his hat. He could see a tall, broad-shouldered man standing with his feet spread far apart, swinging a Colt .45, and Hopalong swore at everything under the sun. Dust arose in streaming clouds far to the south and they spurred forward to overtake the outfits.

Buck Peters, riding over the starlit plain, in his desire to reach the first herd, was so completely lost in reverie that he failed to hear the muffled hoof-beats of a horse which steadily gained upon him, and when Frenchy McAllister placed a friendly hand on his shoulder he started as if from a deep sleep.

The two looked at each other and their hands met. The question which sprang into Buck's eyes found a silent answer in those of his friend. They rode on side by side through the clear night, and together drifted back to the days of the Double-Y.

After an hour had passed, the foreman of the Bar 20 turned to his companion and then hesitated:

"Did—did—was he a cur?"

Frenchy looked off toward the south and, after an interval, replied: "Yas." Then, as an afterthought, he added, "Yu see, he never reckoned it would be that way."

Buck nodded, although he did not fully understand, and the subject was forever closed.

15

Arizona Nights

STEWART EDWARD WHITE

ARIZONA NIGHTS

BY

STEWART EDWARD WHITE

AUTHOR OF "THE BLAZED TRAIL," "THE RAWHIDE," "THE FOREST," ETC.

I

UNCLE JIM'S YARN: THE INDIAN STORY

ILLUSTRATED BY CHARLES M. RUSSELL

THE ring around the sun had thickened all day long, and the turquoise blue of the Arizona sky had filmed. Storms in the dry countries are infrequent, but heavy; and this surely meant storm. We had ridden since sun-up over broad mesas, down and out of deep cañons, along the base of the mountains in the wildest parts of the territory. The cattle were winding leisurely toward the high country; the jack rabbits had disappeared; the quail lacked; we did not see a single antelope in the open.

"It's a case of hole up," the Cattleman ventured his opinion. "I have a ranch over in the Double R. Charley and Windy Bill hold it down. We'll tackle it. What do you think?"

The four cow-boys agreed. We dropped into a low, broad watercourse, ascended it to big cottonwoods and flowing water, followed it into box cañons between rim-rock carved fantastically and painted like a Moorish facade, until at last in a widening below a rounded hill, we came upon an adobe house, a fruit tree, and a round corral. This was the Double R.

Charley and Windy Bill welcomed us with soda biscuits. We turned our horses out, spread our beds on the floor, filled our pipes, and squatted on our heels. Various dogs of various breeds investigated us. It was very pleasant, and we did not mind the ring around the sun.

"Somebody else coming," announced the Cattleman finally.

"Uncle Jim," said Charley after a glance.

A hawk-faced old man, with a long, white beard and long, white hair rode out from the cottonwoods. He had on a battered, broad hat abnormally high of crown, carried across his saddle a heavy "eight square" rifle, and was followed by a half-dozen lolloping hounds.

The largest and fiercest of the latter, catching sight of our group, launched himself with lightning rapidity at the biggest of the ranch dogs, promptly nailed that canine by the back of the neck, shook him violently a score of times, flung him aside, and pounced on the next. During the ensuing few moments that hound was the busiest thing in the West. He satisfactorily whipped four dogs, pursued two cats up a tree, upset the Dutch oven and the rest of the soda biscuits, stampeded the horses and raised a cloud of dust adequate to represent the smoke of battle. We others were too paralyzed to move. Uncle Jim sat placidly on his white horse, his thin knees bent to the ox-bow stirrups, smoking.

In ten seconds the trouble was over, principally because there was no more trouble to make. The hound returned leisurely, licking from his chops the hair of his victims. Uncle Jim shook his head.

"Trailer," said he sadly, "is a ·little severe."

We agreed heartily, and turned in to welcome Uncle Jim with a fresh batch of soda biscuits.

The old man was one of the typical "long hairs." He had come to the Galiuro Mountains in sixty-nine, and since sixty-nine he had remained in the Galiuro Mountains spite of man or the devil. At present he possessed some hundreds of cattle which he was reputed to water, in a dry season, from an ordinary dish-pan. In times past he had prospected. That evening, the severe Trailer having dropped to slumber, he held forth on big game hunting and dogs, quartz claims and Apaches.

"Did you ever have any very close calls?" I asked.

He ruminated a few moments, refilled his pipe with some awful tobacco, and told the following experience.

In the time of Geronimo I was living just about where I do now; and that was just about in line with the raiding. You see, Geronimo, and Ju,* and old Loco used to pile out of the reservation at Camp Apache, raid south to the line, slip over into Mexico when the soldiers got too promiscuous, and raid there until they got ready to come back. Then there was always a big medicine talk. Says Geronimo:

"I am tired of the war-path. I will come back from Mexico with all my warriors, if you will escort me with soldiers and protect my people."

"All right," says the General, being only too glad to get him back at all.

So, then, in ten minutes there wouldn't be a buck in camp, but next morning they shows up again, each with about fifty head of horses.

"Where'd you get those horses?" asks the General suspicious.

"Had 'em pastured in the hills," answers Geronimo.

"I can't take all those horses with me; I believe they're stolen!" says the General.

"My people cannot go without their horses," says Geronimo.

So, across the line they goes, and back to the reservation. In about a week there's fifty-two frantic Greasers wanting to know where's their horses? The army is nothing but an importer of stolen stock, and knows it, and can't help it.

Well, as I says, I'm between Camp Apache and the Mexican line, so that every raiding party goes right on past me. The point is that I'm a thousand feet or so above the valley, and the renegades is in such a devil of a hurry about that time that they never stops to climb up and collect me. Often I've watched them trailing down the valley in a cloud of dust. Then, in a day or two, a squad of soldiers would come up and camp at

*Pronounced "Who."

my spring for a while. They used to send soldiers to guard every water-hole in the country so the renegades couldn't get water. After a while, from not being bothered none, I got to thinking I wasn't worth while with them.

Me and Johnny Hooper were pecking away at the Ole Virginia mine then. We'd got down about sixty feet, all timbered, and was thinking of cross-cutting. One day Johnny went to town, and that same day I got in a hurry and left my gun at camp.

I worked all the morning down at the bottom of the shaft, and when I see by the sun it was getting along towards noon, I put in three good shots, tamped 'em down, lit the fuses, and started to climb out.

It ain't noways pleasant to light a fuse in a shaft, and then have to climb out a fifty-foot ladder, with it burning behind you. I never did get used to it. You keep thinking, "now, suppose there's a flaw in that fuse, or something, and she goes off in six seconds instead of two minutes? where'll you be then?" It would give you a good boost towards your home on high, anyway.

So I climbed fast, and stuck my head out the top without looking — and then I froze solid enough. There, about fifty feet away, climbing up the hill on mighty tired hosses, was a dozen of the ugliest Chiricahuas you ever don't want to meet, and in addition a Mexican renegade named Maria, who was worse than any of 'em. I see at once their hosses was tired out, and they had a notion of camping at my water-hole, not knowing nothing about the Ole Virginia mine.

For two bits I'd have let go all holts and dropped backwards, trusting to my thick head for easy lighting. Then I heard a little fizz and sputter from below. At that my hair riz right up so I could feel the breeze blow under my hat. For about six seconds I stood there like an imbecile, grinning amiably. Then one of the Chiricahuas made a sort of grunt, and I sabed that they'd seen the original exhibit your Uncle Jim was making of himself.

Then that fuse gave another sputter, and one of the Apaches said "un dah." That means "white man." It was harder to turn my head than if I'd had a stiff-neck; but I managed to do it, and I see that my ore dump wasn't more than ten foot away. I mighty near overjumped it; and the next I knew I was on one side of it and those

Apaches on the other. Probably I flew; leastways I don't seem to remember jumping.

That didn't seem to do me much good. The renegades were grinning and laughing to think how easy a thing they had; and I couldn't rightly think up any arguments against that notion — at least from their standpoint. They were chattering away to each other in Mexican for the benefit of Maria. Oh, they had me all distributed, down to my suspender-buttons! And me squatting behind that ore dump about as formidable as a brush rabbit!

Then, all at once, one of my shots went off down in the shaft.

"Boom!" say she, plenty big; and a slather of rocks and stones come out of the mouth and began to dump down promiscuous on the scenery. I got one little one in the shoulder-blade, and found time to wish my ore dump had a roof. But those renegades caught it square in the thick of trouble. One got knocked out entirely for a minute, by a nice piece of country rock in the head

"Otra vez!" yells I, which means 'again.'

"Boom!" goes the Ole Virginia prompt as an answer.

I put in my time dodging, but when I gets a chance to look, the Apaches has all got to cover, and is looking scared.

"Otra vez!" yells I again.

"Boom!" says the Ole Virginia.

This was the biggest shot of the lot, and she surely cut loose. I ought to have been half-way up the hill watching things from a safe distance, but I wasn't. Lucky for me the shaft was a little on the drift, so she didn't quite shoot my way. But she distributed about a ton over those renegades. They sort of half got to their feet, uncertain.

"Otra vez!" yells I once more, as bold as if I could keep her shooting all day.

It was just a cold, raw blazer; and if it didn't go through I could see me as an Apache parlor ornament. But it did. Those Chiricahuas give one yell and skipped. It was surely a funny sight, after they got aboard their war ponies, to see them trying to dig out on horses too tired to trot.

I didn't stop to get all the laughs though. In fact, I give one jump off that ledge, and I lit a-running. A quarter-hoss couldn't have beat me to that shack. There I grabbed old Meat-in-the-pot and made a climb for the tall country, aiming to wait around until dark, and then to pull out for Benson. Johnny Hooper wasn't expected till next day, which was lucky. From where I lay I could see the Apaches camped out beyond my draw, and I didn't doubt they'd visited the place. Along about sunset they all left their camp, and went into the draw, so there, I thinks, I sees a good chance to make a start before dark. I dropped down from the mesa, skirted the butte, and angled down across the country. After I'd gone a half mile from the cliffs, I ran across Johnny Hooper's fresh trail headed towards camp!

My heart jumped right up into my mouth at that. Here was poor old Johnny, a day too early, with a pack-mule of grub, walking innocent as a yearling, right into the hands of those hostiles. The trail looked pretty fresh, and Benson's a good long day with a pack animal, so I thought perhaps I might catch him before he runs into trouble. So I ran back on the trail as fast as I could make it. The sun was down by now, and it was getting dusk.

I didn't overtake him, and when I got to the top of the cañon I crawled along very cautious and took a look. Of course, I expected to see everything up in smoke, but I nearly got up and yelled when I see everything all right, and old Sukey, the pack-mule, and Johnny's hoss hitched up as peaceful as babies to the corral.

"*That's* all right!" thinks I, "they're back in their camp, and haven't discovered Johnny yet. I'll snail him out of there."

So I ran down the hill and into the shack. Johnny sat in his chair — what there was of him. He must have got in about two hours before sundown, for they'd had lots of time to put in on him. That's the reason they'd stayed so long up the draw. Poor old Johnny! I was glad it was night, and he was dead. Apaches are the worst Injins there is for tortures. They cut off the bottoms of old man Wilkins's feet, and stood him on an ant-hill ——

In a minute or so, though, my wits gets to work.

"Why ain't the shack burned?" I asks myself, "and why is the hoss and the mule tied all so peaceful to the corral?"

It didn't take long for a man who knows Injins to answer *those* conundrums. The whole thing was a trap — for me — and I'd walked into it, chuckle-headed as a prairie-dog!

With that I makes a run outside — by now it was dark — and listens. Sure enough, I hears hosses. So I makes a rapid sneak back over the trail.

Everything seemed all right till I got up to the rim-rock. Then I heard more hosses — ahead of me. And when I looked back, I could see some Injuns already at the shack, and starting to build a fire outside.

In a tight fix, a man is pretty apt to get scared till all hope is gone. Then he is pretty apt to get cool and calm. That was my case. I couldn't go ahead — there was those hosses coming along the trail. I couldn't go back — there was those Injuns building the fire. So I skirmished around till I got a bright star right over the trail ahead, and I trained old Meat-in-the-pot to bear on that star, and I made up my mind that when the star was darkened I'd turn loose. So I lay there a while listening. By and by the star was blotted out, and I cut loose, and old Meat-in-the-pot missed fire — she never did it before nor since — I think that cartridge ——

Well, I don't know where the Injins came from, but it seemed as if the hammer had hardly clicked before three or four of them had piled on me. I put up the best fight I could, for I wasn't figuring to be caught alive, and this miss-fire deal had fooled me all along the line. They surely had a lively time. I expected every minute to feel a knife in my back, but when I didn't get it, then I knew they wanted to bring me in alive, and that made me fight harder. First and last we rolled and plunged all the way from the rim-rock down to the cañon-bed. Then one of the Injins sung out :

"Maria !"

And I thought of that renegade Mexican, and what I'd heard about him, and that made me fight harder yet.

But after we'd fought down to the cañon-bed, and had lost most of our skin, a half-dozen more fell on me, and in less than no time they had me tied. Then they picked me up and carried me over to where they'd built a big fire by the corral.

Uncle Jim stopped with an air of finality, and began lazily to refill his pipe. From the open, mud fireplace he picked a coal. Outside the rain, faithful to the prophecy of the wide-ringed sun, beat fitfully against the roof.

"That was the closest call I ever had," said he at last.

"But, Uncle Jim," we cried in a confused chorus, "how did you get away ? What did the Indians do to you ? Who rescued you ?"

Uncle Jim chuckled.

"The first man I saw sitting at that fire," said he, "was Lieutenant Price of the United States Army, and by him was Tom Horn.

"'What's this ?' he asks, and Horn talks to the Injins in Apache.

"'They say they've caught Maria,' translates Horn back again.

"'Maria nothing !' says Lieutenant Price. 'This is Jim Fox. I know him.'

"So they turned me loose. It seems the troops had driven off the rengades an hour before."

"And the Indians who caught you, Uncle Jim ? You said they were Indians."

"Were Tonto Basin Apaches," explained the old man — "government scouts under Tom Horn."

ARIZONA NIGHTS

BY

STEWART EDWARD WHITE

AUTHOR OF "THE BLAZED TRAIL," "THE RAWHIDE," "THE FOREST," ETC.

II

WINDY BILL'S YARN: THE EMIGRANT STORY

ILLUSTRATED BY CHARLES M. RUSSELL

AFTER the rain that had held us holed up at the Double R over one day, we discussed what we should do next.

"The flats will be too boggy for riding, and anyway the cattle will be in the high country," the Cattleman summed up the situation. "We'd bog down the chuck-wagon if we tried to get back to the J. H. But now after the rain the weather ought to be beautiful. What shall we do?"

"Was you ever in the Jackson country?" asked Uncle Jim. "It's the wildest part of Arizona. It's a big country and rough, and no one lives there, and there's lots of deer and mountain lions and bear. Here's my dogs. We might have a hunt."

"Good!" said we.

We skirmished around and found a condemned army pack saddle with aparejos, and a saw-buck saddle with kyacks. On these we managed to condense our grub and utensils. There were plenty of horses, so our bedding we bound flat about their naked barrels by means of the squaw-hitch. Then we started.

That day furnished us with a demonstration of what Arizona horses can do. Our way led first through a cañon-bed filled with rounded boulders and rocks, slippery and unstable. Big cottonwoods and oaks grew so thick as partially to conceal the cliffs on either side of us. The rim-rock was mysterious with caves; beautiful with hanging gardens of tree ferns and grasses growing thick in long transverse crevices; wonderful in color and shape. We passed the little cañons fenced off by the rustlers as corrals into which to shunt from the herds their choice of beeves.

"Many a man has come from Texas and established a herd with no other asset than a couple of horses and a branding-iron," said the Cattleman.

Then we worked up gradually to a divide, whence we could see a range of wild and rugged mountains on our right. They rose by slopes and ledges, steep and rough, and at last ended in the thousand foot cliffs of the buttes, running sheer and unbroken for many miles. During all the rest of our trip they were to be our companions, the only constant factors in the tumult of lesser peaks, precipitous cañons, and twisted systems in which we were constantly involved.

The sky was sun-and-shadow after the rain. Each and every Arizonian predicted clearing.

"Why, it almost never rains in Arizona," said Jed Parker. "And when it does it quits before it begins."

Nevertheless, about noon a thick cloud gathered about the tops of the Galiuros above us. Almost immediately it was dissipated by the wind, but when the peaks again showed, we stared with astonishment to see that they were white with snow. It was as though a magician had passed a sheet before them the brief instant necessary to work his great transformation. Shortly the sky thickened, and it began to rain.

Travel had been precarious before; but now its difficulties were infinitely increased. The clay substructure to the rubble turned slippery and adhesive. On the sides of the mountains it was almost impossible to keep a footing. We speedily became wet, our hands puffed and purple, our boots sodden with the water that had trickled from our clothing into them.

"Over the next ridge," Uncle Jim promised us, "is an old shack that I fixed up seven year ago. We can all make out to get in it."

Over the next ridge, therefore, we slipped and slid, thanking the god of luck for each ten feet gained. It was growing cold. The cliffs and palisades near at hand showed dimly behind the falling rain ; beyond them waved and eddied the storm mists through which the mountains revealed and concealed proportions exaggerated into unearthly grandeur. Deep in the clefts of the box cañons the streams were filling. The roar of their rapids echoed from innumerable precipices. A soft swish of water usurped the world of sound.

Nothing more uncomfortable or more magnificent could be imagined. We rode shivering. Each said to himself, "I can stand this — right now — at the present moment. Very well ; I will do so, and I will refuse to look forward even five minutes to what I may have to stand," which is the true philosophy of tough times and the only effective way to endure discomfort.

By luck we reached the bottom of that cañon without a fall. It was wide, well grown with oak trees, and belly deep in rich horse feed — an ideal place to camp were it not for the fact that a thin sheet of water a quarter of an inch deep was flowing over the entire surface of the ground. We spurred on desperately, thinking of a warm fire and a chance to steam.

The roof of the shack had fallen in, and the floor was six inches deep in adobe mud. We did not dismount — that would have wet our saddles — but sat on our horses taking in the details. Finally Uncle Jim came to the front with a suggestion.

"I know of a cave," said he, "close under a butte. It's a big cave, but it has such a steep floor that I don't know as we could stay in it ; and it's back the other side of that ridge."

"I don't know how the ridge is to get back over — it was slippery enough coming this way — and the cave may shoot us out into space, but I'd like to *look* at a dry place anyway," replied the Cattleman.

We all felt the same about it, so back over the ridge we went. About half way down

the other side Uncle Jim turned sharp to the right, and as the "hog back" dropped behind us, we found ourselves out on the steep side of a mountain, the perpendicular cliff over us to the right, the river roaring savagely far down below our left, and sheets of water glazing the footing we could find among the boulders and debris. Hardly could the ponies keep from slipping sideways on the slope, so as we proceeded farther and farther from the solidity of the ridge behind us, we experienced the illusion of venturing out on a tight rope over abysses of space. Even the feeling of danger was only an illusion, however, composite of the falling rain, the deepening twilight, and the night that had already enveloped the plunge of the cañon below.

Finally Uncle Jim stopped just within the drip from the cliffs.

"Here she is," said he.

We descended eagerly. A deer bounded away from the base of the buttes. The cave ran steep, in the manner of an inclined tunnel, far up into the dimness. We had to dig our toes in and scramble to make way up it at all, but we found it dry, and after a little search discovered a foot-ledge of earth sufficiently broad for a seat.

"That's all right," quoth Jed Parker. "Now for sleeping places."

We scattered. Uncle Jim and Charley promptly annexed the slight overhang of the cliff whence the deer had jumped. It was dry at the moment, but we uttered pessimistic predictions if the wind should change. Tom Rich and Jim Lester had a little tent, and insisted on descending to the cañon bed.

"Got to cook there, anyways," said they, and departed with the two pack mules and their bed horse.

That left the Cattleman, Windy Bill, Jed Parker, and me. In a moment Windy Bill came up to us whispering and mysterious.

"Get your cavallos and follow me," said he.

We did so. He led us two hundred yards to another cave, twenty feet high, fifteen feet in diameter, level as a floor.

"How's that?" he cried in triumph. "Found her just now while I was rustling nigger-heads for a fire."

We unpacked our beds with chuckles of joy, and spread them carefully within the shelter of the cave. Except for the very edges, which did not much matter, our blankets and "so-guns," protected by the canvas "tarp," were reasonably dry. Every once in a while a spasm of conscience would seize one or the other of us.

"It seems sort of mean on the other fellows," ruminated Jed Parker.

"They had their first choice," cried we all.

"Uncle Jim's an old man," the Cattleman pointed out.

But Windy Bill had thought of that. "I told him of this yere cave first. But he allowed he was plumb satisfied."

We finished laying out our blankets. The result looked good to us. We all burst out laughing.

"Well, I'm sorry for those fellows," cried the Cattleman.

We hobbled our horses and descended to the gleam of the fire, like guilty conspirators. There we ate hastily of meat, bread and coffee, merely for the sake of sustenance. It certainly amounted to little in the way of pleasure. The water from the direct rain, the shivering trees, and our hat brims accumulated in our plates faster than we could bail it out. The dishes were thrust under a canvas. Rich and Lester decided to remain with their tent, and so we saw them no more until morning.

We broke off back-loads of mesquite and toiled up the hill, tasting thickly the high altitude in the severe labor. At the big cave we dumped down our burdens, transported our fuel piecemeal to the vicinity of the narrow ledge, built a good fire, sat in a row, and lit our pipes. In a few moments the blaze was burning high, and our bodies had ceased shivering. Fantastically the firelight revealed the knobs and crevices, the ledges and the arching walls. Their shadows leaped, following the flames, receding and advancing like playful beasts. Far above us was a single tiny opening through which the smoke was sucked as through a chimney. The glow ruddied the men's features. Outside was thick darkness, and the swish and rush and roar of rising waters. Listening, Windy Bill was reminded of a story. We leaned back comfortably against the sloping walls of the cave, thrust our feet toward the blaze, smoked, and hearkened to the tale of Windy Bill.

There's a tur'ble lot of water running loose here, but I've seen the time and place where even what is in that drip would be worth a gold mine. That was in the emigrant days. They used to come over south of here, through what they called Emigrant Pass, on their way to Californy. I was a kid then, about eighteen year old and what I did n't know about Injins and Agency cattle was n't a patch of alkali. I had a kid outfit of h'ar bridle, lots of silver and such, and I used to ride over and be the handsome boy before such outfits as happened along.

They were queer people, most of 'em from Missoury and such-like southern seaports, and they were tur'ble sick of travel by the time they come in sight of Emigrant Pass. Up to Santa Fé they mostly hiked along any old way, but once there they herded up together in bunches of twenty wagons or so, 'count of our old friends Geronimo and Loco. A good many of 'em had horned cattle to their wagons, and they crawled along about two miles an hour, hotter 'n h—— with the blower on, nothin' to look at but a mountain a week away, chuck full of alkali, plenty of sage brush and rattlesnakes — but mighty little water.

Why, you boys know that country down there. Between the Chiricahui Mountains and Emigrant Pass it's maybe a three or four days journey for these yere bull-skinners.

Mostly they filled up their bellies and their kegs hopin' to last through, but they sure found it drier than cork legs, and generally long before they hit the Springs their tongues was hangin' out a foot. You see, for all their plumb nerve in comin' so far, the most of them did n't know sic 'em. They were plumb innocent in regard to savin' their water, and Injins, and such; and the long-haired buckskin fakes they picked up at Santa Fé for guides was n't much better.

That was where Texas Pete made his killin'.

Texas Pete was a tough citizen from the Lone Star. He was about as broad as he was long, and wore all sorts of big whiskers and big eyebrows. His heart was very bad. You never could tell where Texas Pete was goin' to jump next. He was a sidewinder and a diamond-back and a little black rattlesnake all rolled into one. I believe that Texas Pete person cared about as little for killin' a man as for takin' a drink — and he surely drank without an effort. Peaceable citizens just spoke soft and minded their own business; onpeaceable citizens Texas Pete used to plant out in the sage-brush.

Now this Texas Pete happened to discover a water-hole right out in the plumb middle of the desert. He promptly annexed said water-hole, digs her out, timbers her up, and lays for emigrants. He charged two bits a head — man or beast — and nobody got a mouthful till he paid up in hard coin. Think of the wads he raked in ! I used to figure it up, just for the joy of envyin' him, I reckon. An average twenty wagon outfit, first and last, would bring him in somewheres about fifty dollars — and besides he had forty-rod at four bits a glass. And outfits at that time were thicker 'n splatter.

We used all to go down sometimes to watch them come in. When they see that little canvas shack and that well, they begun to cheer up and move fast._ And when they see that sign, "Water, to bits a head," their eyes stuck out like two raw oysters.

Then come the kicks. What a howl they did raise, surely. But it did n't do no manner of good. Texas Pete did n't do nothin' but sit there and smoke, with a kind of sulky gleam in one corner of his eye. He did n't even take the trouble to answer, but his Winchester lay across his lap. There was n't no humor in the situation for him.

"How much is your water for humans?" asks one emigrant.

"Can't you read that sign?" Texas Pete asks him.

"But you don't mean two bits a head for *humans!*" yells the man. "Why you can get whisky for that !"

"You can read the sign, can't you?" insists Texas Pete.

"I can read it all right?" says the man, tryin' a new deal, "but they tell me not to believe more 'n half I read."

But that don't go ; and Mr. Emigrant shells out with the rest.

I did n't blame them for raisin' their howl: Why, at that time the regular waterholes was chargin' five cents a head from the government freighters, and the motto was always "Hold up Uncle Sam," at that. Once in a while some outfit would get mad and go chargin' off dry ; but it was a long, long way to the Springs, and mighty hot and dusty. Texas Pete and his one lonesome water-hole surely did a big business.

Late one afternoon me and Gentleman Tim was joggin' along above Texas Pete's place. It was a tur'ble hot day — you had to prime yourself to spit — and we was just gettin' back from drivin' some beef up to the troops at Fort Huachuca. We was due to cross the Emigrant Trail — she 's wore in tur'ble deep — you can see the ruts to-day.

When we topped the rise we see a little old outfit just makin' out to drag along.

It was one little schooner all by herself, drug along by two poor old cavallos that could n't have pulled my hat off. Their tongues was out, and every once in a while they 'd stick in a chuck-hole. Then a man would get down and put his shoulder to the wheel, and everybody 'd take a heave, and up they 'd come, all a-trembling and weak.

Tim and I rode down just to take a look at the curiosity.

A thin-lookin' man was drivin', all humped up.

"Hullo, stranger," says I, "ain't you 'fraid of Injins ?"

"Yes," says he.

"Then why are you travelin' through an Injin country all alone ?"

"Could n't keep up," says he. ''Can I get water here ?''

"I reckon," I answers.

He drove up to the water trough there at Texas Pete's ; me and Gentleman Tim followin' along because our trail led that way. But he had n't more 'n stopped before Texas Pete was out.

"Cost you four bits to water them hosses," says he.

The man looked up kind of bewildered.

"I 'm sorry," says he, "I ain't got no four bits. I got my roll lifted off 'n me."

"No water, then," growls Texas Pete back at him.

The man looked about him helpless.

"How far is it to the next water?" he asks me.

"Twenty mile," I tells him.

"My God !" he says, to himself-like.

Then he shrugged his shoulders very tired.

"All right. It 's gettin' the cool of the evenin' ; we 'll make it." He turns into the inside of that old schooner. "Gi' me the cup, Sue."

A white-faced woman who looked mighty good to us alkalis opened the flaps and gave out a tin cup, which the man pointed out to fill.

"How many of you is they ?" asks Texas Pete.

"Three," replies the man, wondering.

"Well, six bits, then," says Texas Pete, "cash down."

At that the man straightens up a little.

"I ain't askin' for no water for my stock," says he, ''but my wife and baby has been out in this sun all day without a drop of water. Our cask slipped a hoop and bust just this side of Dos Cabezos. The poor kid is plumb dry."

"Two bits a head," says Texas Pete.

At that the woman comes out, a little bit of a baby in her arms. The kid had fuzzy yellow hair, and its face was now flushed red and shiny.

"Surely you won't refuse a sick child a drink of water, sir," says she.

But Texas Pete had some sort of a special grouch; I guess he was just beginning to get his snowshoes off after a fight with his own forty-rod.

"What the h—— are you-all doin' on the trail without no money at all?" he growls, "and how do you expect to get along? Such plumb tenderfeet drive me weary."

"Well," says the man, still reasonable, "I ain't got no money, but I'll give you six bits' worth of flour or trade or an'thin' I got."

"I don't run no truck store," snaps Texas Pete, and turns square on his heel and goes back to his chair.

"Got six bits about you?" whispers Gentleman Tim to me.

"Not a red," I answers.

Gentleman Tim turns to Texas Pete.

"Let 'em have a drink, Pete. I'll pay you next time I come down."

"Cash down," growls Pete.

"You're the meanest man I ever see," observes Tim. "I wouldn't speak to you if I met you in h—— carryin' of a lump of ice in your hand."

"You're the softest *I* ever see," sneers Pete. "Don't they have any genooine Texans down your way?"

"Not enough to make it disagreeable," says Tim.

"That lets you out," growls Pete, gettin' hostile and handlin' of his rifle.

Which the man had been standin' there bewildered, the cup hangin' from his finger. At last, looking pretty desperate, he stooped down to dip up a little of the wet from an overflow puddle lyin' at his feet. At the same time the hosses, left sort of to themselves, and bein' drier than a covered bridge, drug forward and stuck their noses in the trough.

Gentleman Tim and me was sittin' there on our hosses, a little to one side. We saw Texas Pete jump up from his chair, take a quick aim, and cut loose with his rifle. It was plumb unexpected to us. We hadn't

thought of any shootin', and our six-shooters was tied in, 'count of the jumpy country we'd been drivin' the steers over. But Gentleman Tim, who had unslung his rope, aimin' to help the hosses out of the chuck hole, snatched her off the horn, and with one of the prettiest twenty-foot flip throws I ever see done he snaked old Texas Pete right out of his wicky-up, gun and all. The old renegade did his best to twist around for a shot at us; but it was no go; and I never enjoyed hog-tying a critter more in my life than I enjoyed hog-tying Texas Pete. Then we turned to see what damage had been done.

We were some relieved to find the family all right, but Texas Pete had bored one of them poor old crow-bait hosses plumb through the head.

"It's lucky for you you don't get the old man," says Gentleman Tim very quiet and polite.

Which Gentleman Tim was an Irishman, and I'd been on the range long enough with him to know that when he got quiet and polite it was time to dodge behind something.

"I hope, sir," says he to the stranger, "that you will give your wife and baby a satisfying drink. As for your hoss, pray do not be under any apprehension. Our friend, Mr. Texas Pete, here, has kindly consented to make good any deficiencies from his own corral."

Tim could talk high, wide, and handsome when he set out to.

The man started to say something; but I managed to herd him to one side.

"Let him alone," I whispers. "When he talks that way, he's mad; and when he's mad, it's better to leave nature to supply the lightnin' rods."

He seemed to sabe all right, so we built us a little fire and started some grub, while Gentleman Tim walked up and down very grand and fierce.

By and by he seemed to make up his mind. He went over and untied Texas Pete.

"Stand up, you hound," says he. "Now listen to me. If you make a break to get away, or if you refuse to do just as I tell you, I won't shoot you, but I'll march you up country and see that Geronimo gets you."

He sorted out a shovel and pick, made Texas Pete carry them right along the trail a quarter, and started him to diggin' a hole.

Texas Pete started in hard enough, Tim sittin' over him on his hoss, his six-shooter loose, and his rope free. The man and I

"OVER THE NEXT RIDGE, THEREFORE, WE SLIPPED AND SLID, THANKING
THE GOD OF LUCK FOR EACH TEN FEET GAINED"

"HE SNAKED OLD TEXAS PETE RIGHT OUT OF HIS WICKY-UP, GUN AND ALL"

stood by, not darin' to say a word. After a
minute or so Texas Pete began to work
slower and slower. By and by he stopped.
"Look here," says he, "is this here thing
my grave?"
"I am goin' to see that you give the gentleman's hoss decent interment," says Gentleman Tim very polite.
"Bury a hoss!" growls Texas Pete.
But he didn't say any more. Tim
cocked his six-shooter.
"Perhaps you'd better quit panting and
sweat a little," says he.
Texas Pete worked hard for a while, for
Tim's quietness was beginning to scare him
up the worst way. By and by he had got
down maybe four or five feet, and Tim got off
his hoss.
"I think that will do," says he. "You
may come out. Billy, my son, cover him.
Now, Mr. Texas Pete," he says cold as steel,
"there is the grave. We will place the hoss
in it. Then I intend to shoot you and put
you in with the hoss, and write you an epi-
taph that will be a comfort to such travelers
of the Trail as are honest, and a warnin' to
such as are not. I'd as soon kill you now as
an hour from now, so you may make a break
for it if you feel like it."
He stooped over to look in the hole. I
thought he looked an extra long time, but
when he raised his head his face had changed
complete.
"March!" says he very brisk.
We all went back to the shack. From
the corral Tim took Texas Pete's best team
and hitched her to the old schooner.
"There," says he to the man. "Now
you'd better hit the trail. Take that whisky keg there for water. Good-by."
We sat there without sayin' a word for
some time after the schooner had pulled out.
Then Tim says very abrupt :
"I've changed my mind."
He got up.
"Come on, Billy," says he to me. "We'll
just leave our friend tied up. I'll be

back to-morrow to turn you loose. In the
meantime it won't hurt you a bit to be a
little uncomfortable, and hungry — and
thirsty."
We rode off just about sundown, leavin'
Texas Pete lashed tight.
Now all this knocked me h——west and
crooked, and I said so, but I couldn't get a
word out of Gentleman Tim. All the answer I could get was just little laughs.
We drawed into the ranch near midnight, but next mornin' Tim had a long talk
with the boss, and the result was that the
whole outfit was instructed to arm up with a
pick or a shovel apiece, and to get set for
Texas Pete's. We got there a little after
noon, turned the old boy out — without fire-
arms — and then began to dig at a place Tim
told us to, near that grave of Texas Pete's. In
three hours we had the finest water-hole developed you ever want to see. Then the
boss stuck up a sign that said :

PUBLIC WATER-HOLE. WATER FREE.

"Now you old skin," says he to Texas
Pete, "charge all you want to on your own
property. But if I ever hear of your layin'
claim to this other hole, I'll sure make you
hard to catch."
Then we rode off home.
You see, when Gentleman Tim inspected
that grave, he noted indications of water ;
and it struck him that runnin' the old renegade out of business was a neater way of gettin' even than merely killin' him.

Somebody threw a fresh mesquite on the
fire. The flames leaped up again, showing
a thin trickle of water running down the
other side of the cave. The steady down-
pour again made itself prominent through
the re-established silence.
"What did Texas Pete do after that?"
asked the Cattleman.
"Texas Pete?" chuckled Windy Bill.
"Well, he put in a heap of his spare time lettin' Tim alone."

ARIZONA NIGHTS

BY

STEWART EDWARD WHITE

AUTHOR OF "THE BLAZED TRAIL," "THE RAWHIDE," "THE FOREST," ETC.

III

THE CATTLEMAN'S YARN: THE REMITTANCE MAN STORY

ILLUSTRATED BY N. C. WYETH

FTER Windy Bill had finished his story, we began to think it time to turn in. Uncle Jim and Charley slid and slipped down the chute-like passage leading from the cave and disappeared in the direction of the overhang beneath which they had spread their bed. After a moment we tore off long bundles of the nigger-head blades, lit the resinous ends at our fire, and with these torches started to make our way along the base of the cliff to the other cave.

Once without the influence of the fire our impromptu links cast an adequate light. The sheets of rain became suddenly visible as they entered the circle of illumination. By careful scrutiny of the footing I gained the entrance to our cave without mishap. I looked back. Here and there irregularly gleamed and spluttered my companions' torches. Across each slanted the rain. All else was of inky blackness except where, between them and me, a faint red reflection shone on the wet rocks. Then I turned inside.

Now to judge from the crumbling powder of the footing, that cave had been dry since Noah. In fact, its roof was nearly a thousand feet thick. But since we had spread our blankets, the persistent waters had soaked down and through. The thousand foot roof had sprung aleak. Three separate and distinct streams of water ran as from spigots. I lowered my torch. The canvas tarpaulin shone with wet, and in its exact center glimmered a pool of water three inches deep and at least two feet in diameter.

"Well, I'll be — " I began. Then I remembered those three wending their way along a wet and disagreeable trail, happy and peaceful in anticipation of warm blankets and a level floor. I chuckled and sat on my heels out of the drip.

First came Jed Parker, his head bent to protect the fire in his pipe. He gained the very center of the cave before he looked up. Then he cast one glance at each bed, and one at me. His grave, hawk-like features relaxed. A faint grin appeared under his long mustache. Without a word he squatted down beside me.

Next the Cattleman. He looked about him with a comical expression of dismay, and burst into a hearty laugh.

"I believe I said I was sorry for those other fellows," he remarked.

Windy Bill was the last. He stooped his head to enter, straightened his lank figure, and took in the situation without expression.

"Well, this is handy," said he, "I was gettin' tur'ble dry, and was thinkin' I would have to climb way down to the creek in all this rain."

He stooped to the pool in the center of the tarpaulin, and drank.

But now our torches began to run low. A small dry bush grew near the entrance. We ignited it, and while it blazed we hastily sorted a blanket apiece and tumbled the rest out of the drip.

Our return without torches along the base of that butte was something to remember.

"AN ALMIGHTY EXCITING RACE"

The night was so thick you could feel the darkness pressing on you : the mountain dropped abruptly to the left, was strewn with boulders and blocks of stone. Collisions and stumbles were frequent. Once I stepped off a little ledge five or six feet high — nothing worse than a barked shin. And all the while the rain, pelting us unmercifully, searched out what poor little remnants of dryness we had been able to retain.

At last we opened out the gleam of fire in our cave, and a minute later were engaged in struggling desperately up the slant that brought us to our ledge and the slope on which our fire burned.

"My Lord !" panted Windy Bill, "a man had ought to have hooks on his eyebrows to climb up here !"

We renewed the fire — and blessed the back-loads of mesquite we had packed up earlier in the evening. Our blankets we wrapped around our shoulders, our feet we hung over the ledge toward the blaze, our backs we leaned against the hollow slant of the cave's wall. We were not uncomfortable. The beat of the rain sprang up in the stillness, growing louder and louder, like horsemen passing on a hard road. Gradually we dozed off.

For a time everything was pleasant. Dreams came, fused with realities ; the firelight faded from consciousness or returned fantastic to our half-awakening ; a delicious numbness overspread our tired bodies. The shadows leaped, became solid, monstrous. We fell asleep.

After a time the fact obtruded itself dimly through our stupor, that the constant pressure of the hard rock had impeded our circulation. We stirred uneasily, shifting to a better position. That was the beginning of awakening. The new position did not suit. A slight shivering seized us, which the drawing closer of the blanket failed to end. Finally I threw aside my hat and looked out. Jed Parker, a vivid patchwork comforter wrapped about his shoulders, stood upright and silent by the fire. I kept still, fearing to awaken the others. In a short time I became aware that the others were doing identically the same thing. We laughed, threw off our blankets, stretched, and fed the fire.

A thick acrid smoke filled the air. The Cattleman, rising, left a trail of incandescent footprints. We investigated hastily, and discovered that the supposed earth on the slant of the cave was nothing more than bat guano, tons of it. The fire, eating its way beneath, had rendered untenable its immediate vicinity. We felt as though we were living over a volcano. How soon our ledge, of the same material, might be attacked, we had no means of knowing. Overcome with drowsiness we again disposed our blankets, resolved to get as many naps as possible before even these constrained quarters were taken from us.

This happened sooner and in a different manner than we had expected. Windy Bill brought us to consciousness by a wild yell. Consciousness reported us a strange hurried sound like the long roll on a drum. Investigation showed us that this cave, too, had sprung aleak, not with any premonitory drip, but all at once, as though some one had turned on a faucet. In ten seconds a very competent streamlet six inches wide had eroded a course down through the guano, past the fire and to the outer slope. And by the irony of fate that one — and only one — leak in all the roof expanse of a big cave was directly over one end of our tiny ledge. The Cattleman laughed.

"Reminds me of the old farmer and his kind friend," said he. "Kind friend hunts up the old farmer in the village.

"'John,' says he, 'I've sad news for you. Your barn has burned up.'

"'My Lord !' says the farmer.

"'But that ain't the worst. Your cow was burned, too.'

"'My Lord !' says the farmer.

"'But that ain't the worst. Your horses were burned.'

"'My Lord !' says the farmer.

"'But that ain't the worst. The barn set fire to the house, and it was burned — total loss.'

"'My Lord !' groans the farmer.

"'But that ain't the worst. Your wife and child were killed, too.'

"At that the farmer began to roar with laughter.

"'Good Heavens, man !' cries his friend astonished, 'what in the world do you find to laugh at in that ?'

"'Don't you see ?' answers the farmer. 'Why, it's so darn *complete !*'

"Well," finished the Cattleman, "that's what strikes me about our case ; it's so darn complete !"

"What time is it ?" asked Windy Bill.

"Midnight," I announced.

"Lord! Six hours to day!" groaned Windy Bill. "How'd you like to be doin' a nice quiet job at gardenin' in the East where you could belly up to the bar reg'lar every evenin', and drink a pussy cafe and smoke tailor-made cigareets?"

"You wouldn't like it a bit," put in the Cattleman with decision; whereupon in proof he told us the following story.

Windy has mentioned Gentleman Tim, and that reminded me of the first time I ever saw him. He was an Irishman all right, but he had been educated in England, and except for his accent he was more an Englishman than anything else. A freight outfit brought him into Tucson from Santa Fé and dumped him down on the plaza where at once every idler in town gathered to quiz him.

Certainly he was one of the greenest specimens I ever saw in this country. He had on a pair of balloon pants and a Norfolk jacket, and was surrounded by a half-dozen baby trunks. His face was red-cheeked and aggressively clean, and his eye limpid as a child's. Most of those present thought that indicated childishness; but I could see that it was only utter unselfconsciousness.

It seemed that he was out for big game, and intended to go after silver-tips somewhere in these very mountains. Of course he was offered plenty of advice, and would probably have made engagements much to be regretted had I not taken a strong fancy to him.

"My friend," said I, drawing him aside, "I don't want to be inquisitive, but what might you do when you're home?"

"I'm a younger son," said he.

I was green myself in those days, and knew nothing of primogeniture.

"That is a very interesting piece of family history," said I, "but it does not answer my question."

He smiled.

"Well now, I hadn't thought of that," said he, "but in a manner of speaking, it does. I do nothing."

"Well," said I, unabashed, "if you saw me trying to be a younger son and likely to forget myself and do something without meaning to, wouldn't you be apt to warn me?"

"Well, 'pon honor, you're a queer chap. What do you mean?"

"I mean that if you hire any of those men to guide you in the mountains, you'll be outrageously cheated, and will be lucky if you're not gobbled by Apaches."

"Do you do any guiding yourself, now?" he asked most innocent of manner.

But I fired up.

"You damn ungrateful pup," I said, "go to the devil in your own way;" and turned square on my heel.

But the young man was at my elbow, his hand on my shoulder.

"Oh, I say now, I'm sorry. I didn't rightly understand. Do wait one moment until I dispose of these boxes of mine, and then I want the honor of your further acquaintance."

He got some Greasers to take his trunks over to the hotel, then linked his arm in mine most engagingly.

"Now, my dear chap," said he, "let's go somewhere for a B & S, and find out about each other."

We were both young and expansive. We exchanged views, names, and confidences, and before noon had arranged to hunt together, I to collect the outfit.

The upshot of the matter was that the Honorable Timothy Clare and I had a most excellent month's excursion, shot several good bear, and returned to Tucson the best of friends.

At Tucson was Schiefflein and his stories of a big strike down in the Apache country. Nothing would do but that we should both go to see for ourselves. We joined the second expedition; crept in the gullies, tied bushes about ourselves when monumenting corners, and so helped establish the town of Tombstone. We made nothing, nor attempted to. Neither of us knew anything of mining, but we were both thirsty for adventure, and took a schoolboy delight in playing the game of life or death with the Chiricahuas.

In fact I never saw anybody take to the wild life as eagerly as the Honorable Timothy Clare. He wanted to attempt everything. With him it was no sooner see than try, and he had such an abundance of enthusiasm that he generally succeeded. The balloon pants soon went. In a month his outfit was irreproachable. He used to study us by the hour, taking in every detail of our equipment, from the smallest to the most important. Then he asked questions. For all his desire to be one of the country, he was never ashamed to acknowledge his ignorance

"Now, don't you chaps think it silly to wear such high heels to your boots?" he would ask. "It seems to me a very useless sort of vanity."

"No vanity about it, Tim," I explained. "In the first place, it keeps your foot from slipping through the stirrup. In the second place, it is good to grip on the ground when you are roping afoot."

"By Jove, that's true!" he cried.

So he'd get him a pair of boots. For a while it was enough to wear and own all these things. He seemed to delight in his six-shooter and his rope just as ornaments to himself and horse. But he soon got over that. Then he had to learn to use them.

For the time being, pistol practise, for instance, would absorb all his thoughts. He'd bang away at intervals all day, and figure out new theories all night.

"That bally scheme won't work," he would complain. "I believe if I extended my thumb along the cylinder, it would help that side jump."

He was always easing the trigger-pull, filing the sights. In time he got to be a fairly accurate and very quick shot.

The same way with roping and hog-tying and all the rest.

"What's the use?" I used to ask him. "If you were going to be a buckeroo, you couldn't go into harder training."

"I like it," was always his answer.

He had only one real vice that I could see. He would gamble. Stud poker was his favorite; and I never saw a Britisher yet who could play poker. I used to head him off when I could, and he was always grateful, but the passion was strong.

After we got back from founding Tombstone, I was busted and had to go to work.

"I've got plenty," said Tim, "and it's all yours."

"I know, old fellow," I told him, "but your money wouldn't do for me."

Buck Johnson was just seeing his chance then, and was preparing to take some breeding cattle over into the Soda Springs Valley. Everybody laughed at him — said it was right in the line of the Chiricahua raids, which was true. But Buck had been in there with Agency steers, and thought he knew. So he collected a trail crew, brought some Oregon cattle across, and built his home ranch of three foot adobe walls with portholes. I joined the trail crew; and somehow or another the Honorable Timothy got permission to go along on his own hook.

The trail was a long one. We had thirst and heat and stampedes and some Indian scares. But in the queer atmospheric conditions that prevailed that summer, I never saw the desert more wonderful. It was like waking to the glory of God to sit up at dawn and see the colors change on the dry ranges.

At the home ranch, again, Tim managed to get permission to stay on. He kept his own remuda of horses, took care of them, hunted, and took part in all the cow work. We lost some cattle from Indians, of course, but it was too near the Reservation for them to do more than pick up a few stray head on their way through. The troops were always after them full jump, and so they never had time to round up the beef. But of course we had to look out or we'd lose our hair, and many a cowboy has won out to the home ranch in an almighty exciting race. This was nuts for the Honorable Timothy Clare, much better than hunting silver-tips, and he enjoyed it no limit.

Things went along that way for some time, until one evening as I was turning out the horses, a buckboard drew in, and from it descended Tony Riggs and a dapper little fellow dressed all in black and with a plug hat.

"Which I accounts for said hat reachin' the ranch, because it's Friday and the boys not in town," Tony whispered to me.

As I happened to be the only man in sight, the stranger addressed me.

"I am looking," said he in a peculiar sing-song manner I have since learned to be English, "for the Honorable Timothy Clare. Is he here?"

"Oh, you're looking for him, are you?" said I. "And who might you be?"

You see, I liked Tim, and I didn't intend to deliver him over into trouble.

The man picked a pair of eye-glasses off his stomach where they dangled at the end of a chain, perched them on his nose, and stared me over. I must have looked uncompromising, for after a few seconds he abruptly wrinkled his nose so that the glasses fell promptly to his stomach again, felt in his waistcoat pocket, and produced a card. I took it, and read:

JEFFERIES CASE, *Barrister.*

"A lawyer!" said I suspiciously.

"My dear man," he rejoined with a slight impatience, "I am not here to do your young friend a harm. In fact, my firm have been his family solicitors for generations."

"Very well," I agreed, and led the way to the one-room adobe that Tim and I occupied.

If I had expected an enthusiastic greeting for the boyhood friend from the old home, I would have been disappointed. Tim was sitting with his back to the door reading an old magazine. When we entered, he glanced over his shoulder.

"Ah, Case," said he, and went on reading. After a moment he said without looking up, "Sit down."

The little man took it calmly, deposited himself in a chair and his bag between his feet, and looked about him daintily at our rough quarters. I made a move to go, whereupon Tim laid down his magazine, yawned, stretched his arms over his head, and sighed.

"Don't go, Harry," he begged. "Well, Case," he addressed the barrister, "what is it this time? Must be something devilish important to bring you — how many thousand miles is it — into such a country as this."

"It is important, Mr. Clare," stated the lawyer in his dry sing-song tones; "but my journey might have been avoided had you paid some attention to my letters."

"Letters!" repeated Tim opening his eyes. "My dear chap, I've had no letters."

"Addressed as usual to your New York bankers."

Tim laughed softly. "Where they are, with my last two quarters' allowance. I especially instructed them to send me no mail. One spends no money in this country." He paused, pulling his mustache. "I'm truly sorry you had to come so far," he continued, "and if your business is, as I suspect, the old one of inducing me to return to my dear uncle's arms, I assure you the mission will prove quite fruitless. Uncle Hillary and I could never live in the same county, let alone the same house."

"And yet your uncle, the Viscount Mar, was very fond of you," ventured Case. "Your allowances —— "

"Oh, I grant you his generosity in *money* affairs —— "

"He has continued that generosity in the terms of his will, and those terms I am here to communicate to you."

"Uncle Hillary is dead!" cried Tim.

"He passed away the sixteenth of last June."

A slight pause ensued.

"I am ready to hear you," said Tim soberly at last.

The barrister stooped and began to fumble with his bag.

"No, not that!" cried Tim with some impatience. "Tell me in your own words."

The lawyer sat back, and pressed his finger points together over his stomach.

"The late Viscount," said he, "has been graciously pleased to leave you in fee simple his entire estate of Staghurst, together with its buildings, rentals, and privileges. This, besides the residential rights, amounts to some ten thousand pounds sterling per annum."

"A little less than fifty thousand dollars a year, Harry," Tim shot over his shoulder at me.

"There is one condition," put in the lawyer.

"Oh, there is!" exclaimed Tim, his crest falling. "Well, knowing my Uncle Hillary —— "

"The condition is not extravagant," the lawyer hastily interposed. "It merely entails continued residence in England, and a minimum of nine months on the estate. This provision is absolute, and the estate reverts on its discontinuance, but may I be permitted to observe that the majority of men, myself among the number, are content to spend the most of their lives, not merely in the confines of a kingdom, but between the four walls of a room, for much less than ten thousand pounds a year. Also that England is not without its attractions for an Englishman, and that Staghurst is a country place of many possibilities."

The Honorable Timothy had recovered from his first surprise.

"And if the condition is not complied with?" he enquired.

"Then the estate reverts to the heirs at law; and you receive an annuity of one hundred pounds, payable quarterly."

"May I ask further the reason for this extraordinary condition?"

"My distinguished client never informed me," replied the lawyer, "but" — and a twinkle appeared in his eye — "as an occasional disbursor of funds — Monte Carlo — "

Tim burst out laughing.

"Oh, but I recognize Uncle Hillary there!" he cried. "Well, Mr. Case, I am sure Mr. Johnson, the owner of this ranch, can put you up, and to-morrow we'll start back."

He returned after a few minutes to find me sitting smoking a moody pipe. I liked Tim, and I was sorry to have him go. Then, too, I was ruffled in the senseless manner of youth, by the sudden altitude to which his changed fortunes had lifted him. He stood in the middle of the room, surveying me, then came across and laid his arm on my shoulder.

"Well," I growled, without looking up, "you're a very rich man now, Mr. Clare."

At that he jerked me bodily out of my seat and stood me up in the center of the room, the Irish blazing out of his eyes.

"Here, none of that!" he snapped. "You —— little fool! Don't you 'Mr. Clare' me!"

So in five minutes we were talking it over. Tim was very much excited at the prospect. He knew Staghurst well, and told me all about the big stone house, and the avenue through the trees, and the hedge-row roads, and the lawn with its peacocks, and the round green hills, and the laborers' cottages.

"It's home," said he, "and I didn't realize before how much I wanted to see it. And I'll be a man of weight there, Harry, and it'll be mighty good."

We made all sorts of plans as to how I was going to visit him just as soon as I could get together the money for the passage. He had the delicacy not to offer to let me have it; and that clinched my trust and love of him.

The next day he drove away with Tony and the dapper little lawyer. I am not ashamed to say that I watched the buckboard until it disappeared in the mirage.

I was with Buck Johnson all that summer and the following winter as well. We had our first round-up, found the natural increase much in excess of the loss by Indians, and extended our holdings up over the Rock Creek country. We witnessed the start of many Indian campaigns, participated in a few little brushes with the Chiricahuas, saw the beginning of the cattle-rustling. A man had not much opportunity to think of anything but what he had right on hand, but I found time for a few speculations on Tim. I wondered how he looked now, and what he was doing, and how in blazes he managed to get away with fifty thousand a year.

And then one Sunday in June, while I was lying on my bunk, Tim pushed open the door and walked in. I was young, but I'd seen a lot, and I knew the expression of his face. So I laid low and said nothing.

In a minute the door opened again, and Buck Johnson himself came in.

"How do," said he, "I saw you ride up."

"How do you do," replied Tim.

"I know all about you," said Buck, without any preliminaries, "your man, Case, has wrote me. I don't know your reasons, and I don't want to know — it's none of my business — and I ain't goin' to tell you just what kind of a —— fool I think you are — that's none of my business, either. But I want you to understand without question how you stand on the ranch."

"Quite good, sir," said Tim very quietly.

"When you were out here before, I was glad to have you here as a sort of guest. Then you were what I've heerd called a gentleman of leisure. Now you're nothin' but a remittance man. Your money's nothin' to me, but the principle of the thing is. The country is plumb pestered with remittance men, doin' nothin', and I don't aim to run no home for incompetents. I had a son of a duke drivin' wagon for me; and he couldn't drive nails in a snow-bank. So don't you herd up with the idea that you can come on this ranch and loaf."

"I don't want to loaf," put in Tim, "I want a job."

"I'm willin' to give you a job," replied Buck, "but it's jest an ordinary cow-puncher's job at forty a month. And if you don't fill your saddle, it goes to some one else."

"That is satisfactory," agreed Tim.

"All right," finished Buck, "so that's understood. Your friend Case wanted me to give you a lot of advice. A man generally has about as much use for advice as a cow has for four hind legs."

He went out.

"For God's sake, what's up?" I cried, leaping from my bunk.

"Hullo, Harry," said he, as though he had seen me the day before, "I've come back."

"How come back?" I asked. "I thought you couldn't leave the estate. Have they broken the will?"

"No," said he.

"Is the money lost?"

"No."

"Then what?"

"The long and short of it is, that I couldn't afford that estate and that money."

"What do you mean?"

"I've given it up."

"Given it up! What for?"

"To come back here."

I took this all in slowly.

"WE JOINED THE SECOND EXPEDITION"

"Tim Clare," said I at last, "do you mean to say that you have given up an English estate and fifty thousand dollars a year to be a remittance man at five hundred and a cowpuncher on as much more?"

"Exactly," said he.

"Tim," I adjured him solemnly, "you are a —— fool!"

"Maybe," he agreed.

"Why did you do it?" I begged.

He walked to the door and looked out across the desert to where the mountains hovered like soap-bubbles on the horizon. For a long time he looked; then whirled on me.

"Harry," said he in a low voice, "do you remember the camp we made on the shoulder of the mountain that night we were caught out? And do you remember how the dawn came up on the big snow peaks across the way — and all the cañon below us filled with whirling mists — and the steel stars leaving us one by one? Where could I find room for that in English paddocks? And do you recall the day we trailed across the Yuma deserts, and the sun beat into our skulls, and the dry, brittle hills looked like papier maché, and the gray sage-brush ran off into the rise of the hills; and then came sunset and the hard dry mountains grew filmy like gauze veils of many colors, and melted and glowed and faded to slate blue, and the stars came out? The English hills are rounded and green and curried, and the sky is near, and the stars only a few miles up. And do you recollect that dark night when old Loco and his warriors were camped at the base of Cochise's Stronghold, and we crept down through the velvet dark wondering when we would be discovered, our mouths sticky with excitement, and the little winds blowing?"

He walked up and down a half-dozen times, his breast heaving.

"It's all very well for the man who is brought up to it, and who has seen nothing else. Case can exist in four walls; he has been brought up to it and knows nothing different. But a man like me ——

"They wanted me to canter between hedge-rows — I who have ridden the desert where the sky over me and the plain under me were bigger than the Islander's universe! They wanted me to oversee little farms — I who have watched the sun rising over half a world! Talk of your ten thou' a year and what they'll buy! You know, Harry, how it feels when a steer takes the slack of your rope and your pony sits back! Where in England can I buy that? You know the rising and the falling of days, and the boundless spaces where your heart grows big, and the thirst of the desert and the hunger of the trail, and a sun that shines and fills the sky, and a wind that blows fresh from the wide places! Where in parcelled, snug, green, tight little England could I buy that with ten thou' — aye, or an hundred times ten thou'? No, no, Harry, that fortune would cost me too dear. I have seen and done and been too much. I've come back to the Big Country, where the pay is poor and the work is hard and the comfort small; but where a man and his soul meet their Maker face to face."

The Cattleman had finished his yarn. For a time no one spoke. Outside, the volume of rain was subsiding. Windy Bill reported a few stars shining through rifts in the showers. The chill that precedes the dawn brought us as close to the fire as the smouldering guano would permit.

"I don't know whether he was right or wrong," mused the Cattleman after a while. "A man can do a heap with that much money. And yet an old 'alkali' is never happy anywhere else. However," he concluded emphatically, "one thing I do know: rain, cold, hunger, discomfort, curses, kicks, and violent deaths included, there isn't one of you grumblers who would hold that gardening job you spoke of three days!"

"AT THE SAME TIME HAHN PULLED HIS GUN AND SHOT
HIM THROUGH THE MIDDLE"

ARIZONA NIGHTS

BY

STEWART EDWARD WHITE

AUTHOR OF ''THE BLAZED TRAIL,'' ''THE RAWHIDE,'' ''THE FOREST,'' ETC

THE RANCH FOREMAN'S YARN: THE CATTLE RUSTLER STORY

ILLUSTRATED BY N. C. WYETH

DAWN broke, so we descended through wet grasses to the cañon. There, after some difficulty, we managed to start a fire, and so ate breakfast, the rain still pouring down on us. About nine o'clock, with miraculous suddenness, the torrent stopped. It began to turn cold. The Cattleman and I decided to climb to the top of the butte after meat, which we entirely lacked.

It was rather a stiff ascent, but once above the sheer cliffs we found ourselves on a rolling meadow table-land, a half-mile broad by, perhaps, a mile and a half in length. Grass grew high; here and there were small, live oaks planted park-like; slight and rounded ravines accommodated brooklets. As we walked back, the edges blended in the edges of the mesa across the cañon. The deep gorges, which had heretofore seemed the most prominent elements of the scenery, were lost. We stood, apparently, in the middle of a wide and undulating plain, diversified by little ridges, and running with a free sweep to the very foot of the snowy Galiuros. It seemed as though we should be able to ride horseback in almost any given direction. Yet we knew that ten minutes walk would take us to the brink of most stupendous chasms — so deep that the water flowing in them hardly seemed to move; so rugged that only with the greatest difficulty could a horseman make his way through the country at all; and yet so ancient that the bottoms supported forests, rich grasses, and rounded, gentle knolls. It was a most astonishing set of double impressions.

"I SAW HIS HORSE JUMP BACK, DODGIN' A RATTLESNAKE OR SOMETHIN'"

We succeeded in killing a nice, fat, white-tail buck, and so returned to camp happy. The rain held off. We dug ditches, organized shelters, cooked a warm meal. For the next day we planned a bear hunt afoot, far up a manzanita cañon where Uncle Jim knew of some "holing up" caves.

But when we awoke in the morning we threw aside our coverings with some difficulty to look on a ground covered with snow; trees laden almost to the breaking point with snow; and the air filled with it.

"No bear to-day," said the Cattleman.

"No," agreed Uncle Jim dryly. "No b'ar. And what's more, unless yo're aimin' to stop here somewhat of a spell, we'll have to make out to-day."

We cooked with freezing fingers, ate while dodging avalanches from the trees, and packed reluctantly. The ropes were frozen, the hobbles stiff, everything either crackling or wet. Finally the task was finished. We took a last warming of the fingers, and climbed on.

The country was wonderfully beautiful with the white not yet shaken from the trees and rock ledges. Also it was wonderfully slippery. The snow was soft enough to ball under the horses' hoofs, so that most of the time the poor animals skated and stumbled along on stilts. Thus we made our way back over ground which, naked of these difficulties, we had considered bad enough. Imagine riding along a slant of rock shelving off to a bad tumble, so steep that your pony has to do more or less expert ankle work to keep from slipping off sideways. During the passage of that rock you are apt to sit very light. Now cover it with several inches of snow, stick a snowball on each hoof of your mount, and try again. When you have ridden it — or its duplicate — a few score of times, select a steep mountain side, cover it with round rocks the size of your head, and over that spread a concealing blanket of the same sticky snow. You may vary these to the limits of your imagination.

Once across the divide, we ran into a new sort of trouble. You may remember that on our journey over we had been forced to travel for some distance in a narrow stream-bed. During our passage we had scrambled up some rather steep and rough slopes; and hopped up some fairly high ledges. Now we found the heretofore dry bed flowing a good eight inches deep. The steep slopes had become cascades: the ledges, waterfalls.

When we came to them, we had to "shoot the rapids" as best we could, only to land with a *plunk* in an indeterminately deep pool at the bottom. Some of the pack horses went down, sousing again our unfortunate bedding, but by the grace of fortune not a saddle pony lost his feet.

After a time the gorge widened. We came out into the box cañon with its trees. Here the water spread and shoaled to a depth of only two or three inches. We splashed along gaily enough, for with the exception of an occasional quicksand or boggy spot, our troubles were over.

Jed Parker and I happened to ride side by side, bringing up the rear and seeing to it that the pack animals did not stray nor linger. As we passed the first of the rustlers' corrals, he called my attention to them.

"Go take a look," said he. "We only got those fellows out of here a few years ago."

I rode over. At this point the rim-rock broke to admit the ingress of a ravine into the main cañon. Riding a short distance up the ravine I could see that it ended abruptly in a perpendicular cliff. As the sides also were precipitous, it became necessary only to build a fence across the entrance into the main cañon to become possessed of a corral completely closed in. Remembering the absolute invisibility of these sunken cañons until the rider is almost directly over them; and also the extreme roughness and remoteness of the district, I could see that the spot was admirably adapted to concealment.

"There's quite a yarn about the gang that held this hole," said Jed Parker to me when I had ridden back to him. "I'll tell you about it sometime."

We climbed the hill, descended on the Double R, built a fire in the stove, dried out, and were happy. After a square meal — and a dry one — I reminded Jed Parker of his promise, and so, sitting cross-legged on his "so-gun" in the middle of the floor, he told us the following yarn:

There's a good deal of romance been written about the "bad man," and there's about the same amount of nonsense. The bad man is just a plain murderer, neither more nor less. He never does get into a real, good, plain, stand-up gun fight if he can possibly help it. His killin's are done from behind a door, or when he's got his man dead to rights. There's Sam Cook. You've all heard of him. He had nerve, of course, and when he was backed into a corner he made good; and he was sure sudden death with a gun. But when he went out for a man deliberate, he didn't take no special chances. For a while he was marshal at Willets. Pretty soon it was noted that there was a heap of cases of resisting arrest, where Sam as marshal had to shoot, and that those cases almost always happened to be his personal enemies. Of course, that might be all right, but it looked suspicious. Then one day he killed poor old Max Schmidt out behind his own saloon. Called him out and shot him in the stomach. Said Max resisted arrest on a warrant for keepin' open out of hours! That was a sweet warrant to take out in Willets, anyway! Mrs. Schmidt always claimed that she saw that deal played, and that while they were talkin' perfectly peaceable, Cook let drive from the hip at about two yards range. Anyway, we decided we needed another marshal. Nothin' else was ever done, for the Vigilantes hadn't been formed, and your individual and decent citizen doesn't care to be marked by a bad man of that stripe. Leastways, unless he wants to go in for bad-man methods and do a little ambusheein' on his own account.

The point is, that these yere bad men are a low-down, miserable proposition, and plain, cold-blood murderers, willin' to wait for a sure thing, and without no compunctions whatever. The bad man takes you unawares, when your sleepin', or talkin', or drinkin', or lookin' to see what for a day its goin' to be, anyway. He don't give you no show, and sooner or later he's goin' to get you in the safest and easiest way for himself. There ain't no romance about that.

And, until you've seen a few men called out of their shacks for a·friendly conversation, and shot when they happen to look away; or asked for a drink of water and killed when they stoop to the spring; or potted from behind as they go into a room, it's pretty hard to believe that any man can be so plumb lackin' in fair play or pity or just natural humanity.

As you boys know, I come in from Texas to Buck Johnson's about ten year back. I had a pretty good remuda of ponies that I knew, and I hated to let them go at prices they were offerin' then, so I made up my mind to ride across and bring them in with me. It wasn't so awful far, and I figured that I'd like to take in what New Mexico looked like anyway.

About down by Albuquerque I tracked up with another outfit headed my way. There was five of them, three men, and a woman, and a yearlin' baby. They had a dozen hosses, and that was about all I could see. There was only two packed, and no wagon. I suppose the whole outfit — pots, pans, and kettles — was worth five dollars. It was just supper when I run across them, and it didn't take more'n one look to discover that flour, coffee, sugar, and salt was all they carried. A yearlin' carcass, half-skinned, lay near, and the fry-pan was full of meat.

"Howdy, strangers," says I, ridin' up.

They nodded a little, but didn't say nothin'. My hosses fell to grazin', and I eased myself around in my saddle and made a cigareet. The men was tall, lank fellows, with kind of sullen faces, and sly, shifty eyes; the woman was dirty and generally mussed up. I knowed that sort all right. Texas was gettin' too many fences for them.

"Havin' supper?" says I cheerful.

One of 'em grunted "yes" at me; and, after a while, the biggest asked me very grudgin' if I wouldn't light and eat. I told them "no," that I was travelin' in the cool of the evenin'.

"You seem to have more meat than you need, though," says I. "I could use a little of that."

"Help yourself," says they. "It's a maverick we come across."

I took a steak and noted that the hide had been mighty well cut to ribbons around the flanks, and that the head was gone.

"Well," says I to the carcass, "no one's goin' to be able to swear whether you're a maverick or not, but I bet you knew the feel of a brandin' iron all right."

I gave them a thank-you, and climbed on again. My hosses acted some surprised at bein' gathered up again, but I couldn't help that.

"It looks like a plumb imposition, cavallos," says I to them, "after an all-day, but you sure don't want to join that outfit any more than I do the angels, and if we camp here we're likely to do both."

I didn't see them any more after that until I'd hit the Lazy Y, and had started in running cattle in the Soda Springs Valley. Larry Eagen and I rode together those days, and that's how I got to know him pretty well. One day, over in the Elm Flat, we ran smack on this Texas outfit again, headed north. This time I was on my own range, and I knew where I stood, so I could show a little more curiosity in the case.

"Well, you got this far," says I.

"Yes," says they.

"Where you headed?"

"Over towards the hills."

"What to do?"

"Make a ranch, raise some truck; perhaps buy a few cows."

They went on.

"Truck farmin'," says I to Larry "is ine prospects in this country."

He sat on his horse lookin' after them.

"I'm sorry for them," says he. "It must be almighty hard scratchin'."

Well, we rode the range for upwards of two year. In that time we saw our Texas friends — name of Hahn — two or three times in Willets, and heard of them off and on. They bought an old brand of Steve McWilliams for seventy-five dollars, carryin' six or eight head of cows. After that, from time to time, we heard of them buyin' more — two or three head from one man, and two or three from another. They branded them all with that McWilliams iron — T O — so, pretty soon, we began to see the cattle on the range.

Now, a good cattleman knows cattle just as well as you know people, and he can tell them about as far off. Horned critters look alike to you, but even in a country supportin' a good many thousand head, a man used to the business can recognize most every individual as far as he can see him. Some is better than others at it. I suppose you really have to be brought up to it. So we boys at the Lazy Y noted all the cattle with the new T O, and could estimate pretty close that the Hahn outfit might own, maybe, thirty-five head all told.

That was all very well, and nobody had any kick comin'. Then, one day in the spring, we came across our first "sleeper."

What's a sleeper? A sleeper is a calf that has been ear-marked, but not branded. Every owner has a certain brand, as you know, and then he crops and slits the ears in a certain way, too. In that manner he don't have to look at the brand, except to corroborate the ears; and, as the critter generally sticks his ears up inquirin'-like to any one ridin' up, its easy to know the brand without lookin' at it merely from the ear-marks. Once in a great while, when a man comes across an unbranded calf, and it ain't handy to build a fire, he just ear-marks it and let's

the brandin' go till later. But it isn't done often; and our outfit had strict orders never to make sleepers.

Well, one day in the spring, as I say, Larry and me was ridin', when we came across a Lazy Y cow and calf. The little fellow was ear-marked all right, so we rode on, and never would have discovered nothin' if a bush rabbit hadn't jumped and scared the calf right across in front of our hosses. Then we couldn't help but see that there wasn't no brand.

Of course we roped him and put the iron on him. I took the chance to look at his ears and saw that the marking had been done quite recent, so when we got in that night I reported to Buck Johnson that one of the punchers was gettin' lazy and sleeperin'. Naturally he went after the man who had done it; but every puncher swore up and down and back and across that he'd branded every calf he'd had a rope on that spring. We put it down that some one was lyin', and let it go at that.

And then, about a week later, one of the other boys reported a triangle H sleeper. The triangle H was the Goodrich brand, so we didn't have nothin' to do with that. Some of them might be sleeperin' for all we knew. Three other cases of the same kind we happened across that same spring.

So far, so good. Sleepers runnin' in such numbers was a little astonishin', but nothin' suspicious. Cattle did well that summer, and when we come to round up in the fall, we cut out maybe a dozen of those T O cattle that had strayed out of that Hahn country. Of the dozen there was five grown cows, and seven yearlin'.

"My Lord, Jed," says Buck to me. "They's a heap of these youngsters comin' over our way."

But still as a young critter is more apt to stray than an old one that's got his range established, we didn't lay no great store by that neither. The Hahns took their bunch, and that's all there was to it.

Next spring though we found a few more sleepers, and one day we came on a cow that had gone dead lame. That was usual, too, but Buck, who was with me, had somethin' on his mind. Finally he turned back and roped her and threw her.

"Look here, Jed," says he, "what do you make of this?"

I could see where the hind legs below the hocks had been burned.

"Looks like somebody had roped her by the hind feet," says I.

"Might be," says he, "but her bein' lame that way makes it look more like hobbles."

So we didn't say nothin' more about that neither, until just by luck we came on another lame cow. We threw her, too.

"Well, what do you think of this one?" Buck Johnson asks me.

"The feet is pretty well tore up," says I, "and down to the quick; but I've see them tore up just as bad on the rocks when they come down out of the mountains."

You sabe what that meant, don't you? You see, a rustler will take a cow and hobble her, or lame her so she can't follow, and then he'll take her calf a long ways off and brand it with his iron. Of course, if we was to see a calf of one brand followin' of a cow with another, it would be just too easy to guess what had happened.

We rode on mighty thoughtful. There couldn't be much doubt that cattle rustlers was at work. The sleepers they had ear-marked, hopin' that no one would discover the lack of a brand. Then, after the calf was weaned, and quit followin' of his mother, the rustler would brand it with his own iron, and change its ear-mark to match. It made a nice, easy way of gettin' together a bunch of cattle cheap.

But it was pretty hard to guess off-hand who the rustlers might be. There were a lot of renegades down toward the Mexican line who made a raid once in a while, and a few oilers livin' near had water-holes in the foot-hills, and any amount of little cattle holders, like this T O outfit, and any of them wouldn't shy very hard at a little sleeperin' on the side. Buck Johnson told us all to watch out, and passed the word quiet among the big owners to try and see whose cattle seemed to have too many calves for the number of cows.

The Texas outfit I'm tellin' you about had settled up above in this Double R cañon where I showed you those natural corrals this morning. They'd built them a 'dobe, and cleared some land, and planted a few trees, and made an irrigated patch for alfalfa. Nobody never rode over his way very much, cause the country was most too rough for cattle, and our ranges lay farther to the southward. Now, however, we began to extend our ridin' a little. I was down towards Dos Cabezos to look over the cattle there, and they used to send Larry up into the Double R country. One evenin' he took me to one side.

"Look here, Jed," says he, "I know you pretty well, and I'm not ashamed to say that I'm all new at this cattle business — in fact, I haven't been at it more'n a year. What should be the proportion of cows to calves anyhow?"

"There ought to be about twice as many cows as there're calves," I tells him.

"Then, with only about fifty head of grown cows there ought not to be an equal number of yearlin's?"

"I should say not," says I. "What are you drivin' at?"

"Nothin' yet," says he.

A few days later he tackled me again.

"Jed," says he, "I'm not good, like you fellows are, at knowin' one cow from another, but there's a calf down there branded T O that I'd pretty near swear I saw with an X Y cow last month. I wish you could come down with me."

We got that fixed easy enough, and for the next month rammed around through this broken country, lookin' for evidence. I saw enough to satisfy me to a moral certainty, but nothin' for a sheriff; and, of course, we couldn't go shoot up a peaceful rancher on mere suspicion. Finally, one day, we run on a four-months' calf all by himself, with the T O iron onto him — a mighty healthy lookin' calf, too.

"Wonder where *his* mother is!" says I.

"Maybe it's a 'dogie,'" says Larry Eagen — we calls calves whose mothers have died "dogies."

"No," says I, "I don't hardly think so. A dogie is always under size and poor, and he's layin' around water-holes, and he always has a big, sway belly onto him. No, this is no dogie; and if it's an honest calf, there sure ought to be a T O cow around somewhere."

So we separated to have a good look. Larry rode up on the edge of a little rimrock. In a minute I saw his horse jump back, dodgin' a rattlesnake or somethin', and then fall back out of sight. I jumped my hoss up there tur'ble quick, and looked over, expectin' to see nothin' but mangled remains. It was only about fifteen foot down, but I couldn't see bottom 'count of some brush.

"Are you all right?" I yells.

"Yes, yes!" cries Larry, "but for the love of God get down here as quick as you can."

I hopped off my hoss, and scrambled down somehow.

"Hurt ?" says I as soon as I lit.

"Not a bit — look here."

There was a dead cow with the Lazy Y on her flank.

"And a bullet-hole in her forehead," adds Larry. "And, look here, that T O calf was bald-faced, and so was this cow."

"Reckon we found our sleepers," says I.

So, there we was. Larry had to lead his cavallo down the barranca to the main cañon. I followed along on the rim, waitin' until a place gave me a chance to get down, too, or Larry a chance to get up. We were talkin' back and forth when, all at once, Larry shouted again.

"Big game this time," he yells. "Here's a cave and a mountain lion squallin' in it."

I slid down to him at once, and we drew our six-shooters and went up to the cave openin', right under the rim-rock. There, sure enough, were fresh lion tracks, and we could hear a little faint cryin' like a woman.

"First chance," claims Larry, and dropped to his hands and knees at the entrance.

"Well, d—— me !" he cries, and crawls in at once, payin' no attention to me tellin' him to be more cautious. In a minute he backed out, carryin' a three-year-old girl.

"We seem to be in for adventures to-day," says he. "Now, where do you suppose that came from, and how did it get here ?"

"Well," says I, "I've followed lion tracks where they've carried yearlin's across their backs like a fox does a goose. They're tur'ble strong."

"But where did she come from ?" he wonders.

"As for that," says I, "don't you remember now that T O outfit had a yearlin' kid when it came into the country ?"

"That's right," says he. "It's only a mile down the cañon. I'll take it home. They must be most distracted about it."

So I scratched up to the top where my pony was waitin'. It was a tur'ble hard climb, and I most had to have hooks on my eyebrows to get up at all. It's easier to slide down than to climb back. I dropped my gun out of my holster, and she went way to the bottom, but I wouldn't have gone back for six guns. Larry picked it up for me.

So we went along, me on the rim-rock and around the barrancas, and Larry in the bottom carryin' of the kid.

By and by we came to the ranch house, so I stopped to wait. The minute Larry hove in sight everybody was out to once, and in two winks the woman had that baby. They didn't see me at all, but I could hear, plain enough, what they said. Larry told how he had found her in the cave, and all about the lion tracks, and the woman cried and held the kid close to her, and kissed him about forty times. Then when she'd wore the edge off a little, she took the kid inside to feed it or somethin'.

"Well," says Larry, still laughin', "I must hit the trail."

"You say you found her up the Double R ?" asks Hahn. "Was it that cave near the three cottonwoods ?"

"Yes," says Larry.

"Where'd you get into the cañon ?"

"Oh, my hoss slipped off into the barranca just above."

"The barranca just above," repeats Hahn lookin' straight at him.

Larry took one step back.

"You ought to be almighty glad I got into the cañon at all." says he.

Hahn stepped up, holdin' out his hand.

"That's right," says he. "You done us a good turn there."

Larry took his hand. At the same time Hahn pulled his gun and shot him through the middle.

It was all so sudden and unexpected that I stood there paralyzed. Larry fell forward the way a m an mostly will when he's hit in the stomach, but somehow he jerked loose a gun and got it off twice. He didn't hit nothin', and I reckon he was dead before he hit the ground. And there he had my gun, and I was about as useless as a pocket in a shirt !

No, sir, you can talk as much as you please, but the killer is a low-down ornery scrub, and he do n't hesitate at no treachery or ingratitude to keep his carcass safe.

Jed Parker cea sed talking. The dusk had fallen in the little room, and dimly could be seen the recumbe nt figures lying at ease on their blankets. The ranch foreman was sitting bolt upright, cross-legged. A faint glow from his pipe barely distinguished his features.

"What became of the rustlers ? ' I asked him.

"Well, sir, that is the queer part. Hahn himself, who had done the killin', skipped out. We got out warrants, of course, but they never got served. He was a sort of half outlaw from that time, and was killed finally in the train hold-up of '97. But the others we tried for rustling. We didn't have much of a case, as the law went then, and they'd have gone free if the woman hadn't turned evidence against them. The killing was too much for her. And as the precedent held good in a lot of other rustlin' cases, Larry's death was really the beginnin' of law and order in the cattle business."

We smoked. The last light suddenly showed red against the grimy window Windy Bill arose and looked out the door.

"Boys," said he returning, "she's cleared off. We can get back to the ranch tomorrow."

ARIZONA NIGHTS

BY

STEWART EDWARD WHITE

AUTHOR OF "THE BLAZED TRAIL," "THE RAWHIDE," "THE FOREST," ETC.

CYCLONE BILL'S YARN: THE MINING CAMP STORY

ILLUSTRATED BY N. C. WYETH

IT was dark night. We had been cutting the herd all the afternoon, but the task was only just begun. The stray-herd bellowed frantically from one of the big corrals ; the cow-and-calf-herd from a second ; the main-herd from a third. Already the remuda, driven in from the open plains, scattered about the thousand acres of pasture. Away from conveniences of fence and corral, men would have had to patrol all night. Now, however, every one was gathered about the camp-fire.

Probably forty cowboys were in the group, representing all types, from old John, who had been in the business forty years and had punched from the Rio Grande to the Pacific, to the Kid who would have given his chance of salvation if he could have been taken for ten years older than he was. At the moment Jed Parker was holding forth to his friend Johnny Stone in reference to another old crony who had that evening joined the round-up.

"Johnny," inquired Jed with elaborate gravity and entirely ignoring the presence of the subject of conversation, "what is that thing just beyond the fire, and where did it come from ? "

Johnny Stone squinted to make sure.

"That ? " he replied. "Oh, this evenin' the dogs see something run down a hole, and they dug it out, and that's what they got."

The new-comer grinned.

"The trouble with you fellows," he proffered, "is that you're so plumb alkalied you don't know the real thing when you see it."

"That's right," supplemented Windy Bill dryly. "*He* come from New York."

"No !" cried Jed. "You don't say so ? Did he come in one box or in two ? "

Under cover of the laugh, the new-comer made a raid on the dutch ovens and pails. Having filled his plate, he squatted on his heels and fell to his belated meal. He was a tall, slab-sided individual, with a lean, leathery face, a sweeping white mustache, and a grave and sardonic eye. His leather chaps were plain and worn, and his hat had been fashioned by time and wear into much individuality. I was not surprised to hear him nicknamed Cyclone Bill.

"Just ask him how he got that game foot," suggested Johnny Stone to me in an undertone, so, of course, I did not.

Later some one told me that the lameness resulted from his refusal of an urgent invitation to return across a river. Mr. Cyclone Bill happened not to be riding his own horse at the time.

The Cattleman dropped down beside me a moment later.

"I wish," said he in a low voice, "we could get that fellow talking. He is a queer one. Pretty well educated apparently. Claims to be writing a book of memoirs. Sometimes he will open up in good shape, and sometimes he will not. It does no good to ask him direct, and he is as shy as an old crow when you try to lead him up to a subject. We must just lie low and trust to Providence."

A man was playing on the mouth organ. He played excellently well, with all sorts of variations and frills. We smoked in silence. The deep rumble of the cattle filled the air with its diapason. Always the shrill coyotes raved out in the mesquite. Cyclone Bill had finished his meal, and had gone to sit by Jed Parker, his old friend. They talked together low-voiced. The evening grew, and the eastern sky silvered over the mountains in anticipation of the moon.

Cyclone Bill suddenly threw back his head and laughed.

"Reminds me of the time I went to Colorado!" he cried.

"He's off!" whispered the Cattleman.

A dead silence fell on the circle. Everybody shifted position the better to listen to the story of Cyclone Bill.

About ten year ago I got plumb sick of punchin' cows around my part of the country. She hadn't rained since Noah, and I'd forgot what water outside a pail or a trough looked like. So I scouted around inside of me to see what part of the world I'd jump to, and as I seemed to know as little of Colorado and minin' as anything else I made up the pint of bean soup I called my brains to go there. So I catches me a buyer at Benson and turns over my poor little bunch of cattle and prepared to fly. The last day I hauled up about twenty good buckets of water and threw her up against the cabin. My buyer was settin' his hoss waitin' for me to get a ready. He didn't say nothin' until we'd got down about ten mile or so.

"Mr. Hicks," says he, hesitatin' like, "I find it a good rule in this country not to overlook other folks's plays; but I'd take it mighty kind if you'd explain those actions of yours with the pails of water."

"Mr. Jones," says I, "it's very simple. I built that shack five year ago, and it's never rained since. I just wanted to settle in my mind whether or not that d—— roof leaked."

So I quit Arizona, and in about a week I see my reflection in the winders of a little place called Cyanide in the Colorado mountains.

Fellows, she was a bird. They wasn't a pony in sight, nor a squar' foot of land that wasn't either street or straight up. It made me plumb lonesome for a country where you could see a long ways even if you didn't see much. And this early in the evenin' they wasn't hardly anybody in the streets at all.

I took a look at them dark, gloomy old mountains, and a sniff at a breeze that would have frozen the whiskers of hope, and I made a dive for the nearest lit winder. They was a sign over it that just said:

THIS IS A SALOON

I was glad they labeled her. I'd never have known it. They had a fifteen-year old kid tendin' bar, no games goin', and not a soul in the place.

"Sorry to disturb your repose, bub," says I, "but see if you can sort out any rye among them collections of sarsapariller of your's."

I took a drink, and then another to keep it company — I was beginnin' to sympathize with anythin' lonesome. Then I kind of sauntered out to the back room where the hurdy-gurdy ought to be. Sure enough there was a girl settin' on the pianner stool, another in a chair, and a nice shiny Jew drummer danglin' his feet from a table. They looked up when they see me come in, and went right on talkin'.

"Hello, girls!" says I.

At that they stopped talkin' complete.

"How's tricks?" says I.

"Who's your woolly friend?" the shiny Jew asks of the girls.

I looked at him a minute, but I see he'd been raised a pet, and then, too, I was so hungry for sassiety I was willin' to pass a bet or two.

"Don't you *admire* these cow gents?" snickers one of the girls.

"Play somethin', sister," says I to the one at the pianner.

She just grinned at me.

"Interdooce me," says the drummer in a kind of a way that made them all laugh a heap.

"Give us a tune," I begs, tryin' to be jolly, too.

"She don't know any pieces," says the Jew.

"Don't you?" I asks pretty sharp.

"No," says she.

"Well, I do," says I.

I walked up to her, jerked out my guns, and reached around both sides of her to the pianner. I run the muzzles up and down the keyboard two or three times, and then shot out half a dozen keys.

"That's the piece I know," says I.

But the other girl and the Jew drummer had punched the breeze.

The girl at the pianner just grinned, and pointed to the winder where they was some ragged glass hangin'. She was dead game.

"Say, Susie," says I, "you're all right, but your friends is tur'ble. I may be rough, and I ain't never been curried below the knees, but I'm better to tie to than them sons of guns."

"I believe it," says she.

So we had a drink at the bar, and started out to investigate the wonders of Cyanide.

"'LOOK HERE!' HE YELLS. 'LISTEN TO WHAT I'M TELLIN' YE!'"

Say, that night *was* a wonder. Susie faded after about three drinks, but I didn't seem to mind that. I hooked up to another saloon kept by a thin Dutchman. A fat Dutchman is stupid, but a thin one is all right.

In ten minutes I had more friends in Cyanide than they is fiddlers in h——. I begun to conclude Cyanide wasn't so lonesome. About four o'clock in comes a little Irishman about four foot high, with more upper lip than a muley cow, and enough red hair to make an artificial aurorer borealis. He had big red hands with freckles pasted onto them, and stiff red hairs standin' up separate and lonesome like signal stations. Also his legs were bowed.

He gets a drink at the bar, and stands back and yells;

"God bless the Irish and let the Dutch rustle !"

Now this was none of my town, so I just stepped back of the end of the bar quick where I wouldn't stop no lead. The shootin' didn't begin.

"Probably Dutchy didn't take no note of what the locoed little dogie *did* say," thinks I to myself.

The Irishman bellied up to the bar again, and pounded on it with his fist.

"Look here !" he yells. "Listen to what I'm tellin' ye ! God bless the Irish and let the Dutch rustle ! Do ye hear me ?"

"Sure, I hear ye," says Dutchy, and goes on swabbin' his bar with a towel.

At that my soul just grew sick. I asked the man next to me why Dutchy didn't kill the little fellow.

"Kill him !" says this man. "What for ?"

"For insultin' of him, of course."

"Oh, he's drunk," says the man, as if that explained anythin'.

That settled it with me. I left that place, and went home, and it wasn't more than four o'clock neither. No, I don't call four o'clock late. It may be a little late for night before last, but it's just the shank of the evenin' for to-night.

Well, it took me six weeks and two days to go broke. I didn't know sic 'em about minin' ; and before long I *knew* that I didn't know sic 'em. Most all day I poked around them mountains — not like ourn — too much timber to be comfortable. At night I got to droppin' in at Dutchy's. He had a couple of quiet games goin' and they was one

fellow among that lot of grubbin' prairie dogs that had heerd tell that cows had horns. He was the wisest of the bunch on the cattle business. So I stowed away my consolation, and made out to forget comparing Colorado with God's country.

About three times a week this Irishman I told you of — name O'Toole — comes bulgin' in. When he was sober he talked minin' high, wide, and handsome. When he was drunk he pounded both fists on the bar and yelled for action, tryin' to get Dutchy on the peck.

"God bless the Irish and let the Dutch rustle !" he yells about six times. "Say, do you hear ?"

"Sure," says Dutchy, calm as a milk cow, "sure, I hears ye !"

I was plumb sorry for O'Toole. I'd like to have given him a run ; but, of course, I couldn't take it up without makin' myself out a friend of this Dutchy party, and I couldn't stand for that. But I did tackle Dutchy about it one night when they wasn't nobody else there.

"Dutchy," says I, "what makes you let that bow-legged cross between a bull-dog and a flamin' red sunset tromp on you so ? It looks to me like you're plumb spiritless."

Dutchy stopped wipin' glasses for a minute.

"Just you hold on," says he. "I ain't ready yet. Bimeby I make him sick ; also those others who laugh with him."

He had a little gray flicker in his eye ; and I thinks to myself that maybe they'd get Dutchy on the peck yet.

As I said, I went broke in just six weeks and two days. And I was broke a plenty. No hold-outs anywhere. It was a heap long ways to cows ; and I'd be t-totally chawed up and spit out if I was goin' to join these minin terrapins defacin' the bosom of nature. It sure looked to me like hard work.

While I was figurin' what next, Dutchy came in. Which I was tur'ble surprised at that, but I said good mornin' and would he rest his poor feet.

"You like to make some money ?" he asks.

"That depends," says I, "on how easy it is."

"It is easy," says he. "I want you to buy hosses for me."

"Hosses ! Sure !" I yells, jumpin' up. "You bet you ! Why, hosses is where I live ! What hosses do you want ?"

"All hosses," says he, calm as a faro dealer.

"What?" says I. "Elucidate, my bucko. I don't take no such blanket order. Spread your cards."

"I mean just that," says he. "I want you to buy all the hosses in this camp, and in the mountains. Every one."

"Whew!" I whistles. "That's a large order. But I'm your meat."

"Come with me, then," says he. I hadn't but just got up, but I went with him to his little old poison factory. Of course, I hadn't had no breakfast; but he staked me to a Kentucky breakfast. What's a Kentucky breakfast? Why, a Kentucky breakfast is a three-pound steak, a bottle of whisky, and a setter dog. What's the dog for? Why, to eat the steak, of course.

We come to an agreement. I was to get two-fifty a head commission. So I started out. There wasn't many hosses in that country; and what there was the owners hadn't much use for unless it was to work a whim. I picked up about a hundred head quick enough, and reported to Dutchy.

"How about burros and mules?" I asks Dutchy.

"They goes," says he. "Mules same as hosses; burros four bits a head to you."

At the end of a week I had a remuda of probably two hundred animals. We kept them over the hills in some "parks" as these sots calls meadows in that country. I rode into town and told Dutchy.

"Got them all?" he asks.

"All but a cross-eyed buckskin that's mean, and the bay mare that Noah bred to."

"Get them," says he.

"The bandits want too much," I explains.

"Get them anyway," says he.

I went away and got them. It was scand'lous; such prices.

When I hit Cyanide again I ran into scenes of wild excitement. The whole passel of them was on that one street of their'n, talkin' sixteen ounces to the pound. In the middle was Dutchy, drunk as a soldier — just plain foolish drunk.

"Good Lord!" thinks I to myself, "he ain't celebratin' gettin' that bunch of buzzards, is he?"

But I found he wasn't that bad. When he caught sight of me, he fell on me drivellin.'

"Look there!" he weeps, showin' me a letter.

I was the last to come in; so I kept that letter — here she is. I'll read her.

DEAR DUTCHY:— I suppose you thought I'd flew the coop, but I haven't and this is to prove it. Pack up your outfit and hit the trail. I've made the biggest free gold strike you ever see. I'm sending you specimens. There's tons just like it, tons and tons. I got all the claims I can hold myself; but there's heaps more. I've writ to Johnny and Ed at Denver to come on. Don't give this away. Make tracks. Come in to Buck Cañon in the Whetstones and oblige

Yours truly,

HENRY SMITH.

Somebody showed me a handful of white rock with yeller streaks in it. His eyes was bulgin' until you could have hung your hat on them. That O'Toole party was walkin' around, wettin' his lips with his tongue and swearin' soft.

"God bless the Irish and let the Dutch rustle!" says he. "And the fool had to get drunk and give it away!"

The excitement was just started, but it didn't last long. The crowd got the same notion at the same time, and it just melted. Me and Dutchy was left alone.

I went home. Pretty soon a fellow named Jimmy Tack come around a little out of breath.

"Say, you know that buckskin you bought off'n me?" says he, "I want to buy him back."

"Oh, you do," says I.

"Yes," says he. "I got to leave town for a couple of days, and I got to have somethin' to pack."

"Wait and I'll see," says I.

Outside the door I met another fellow.

"Look here," he stops me with. "How about that bay mare I sold you? Can you call that sale off? I got to leave town for a day or two and —— "

"Wait," says I. "I'll see."

By the gate was another hurryin' up.

"Oh, yes," says I when he opens his mouth. "I know all your troubles. You have to leave town for a couple of days, and you want back that buzzard you sold me. Well, wait."

After that I had to quit the main street and dodge back of the hog ranch. They was all headed my way. I was as popular as a snake in a prohibition town.

I hit Dutchy's by the back door.

"Do you want to sell hosses?" I asks. "Every one in town wants to buy."

Dutchy looked hurt.

"I wanted to keep them for the valley market," says he, "but — How much did you give Jimmy Tack for his buckskin?"

"THEY GOT TO FIGHTIN' ON WHICH SHOULD GET THE FIRST HOSS; SO
I BENT MY GUN ON THEM AND MADE THEM DRAW LOTS"

"Twenty," says I.

"Well, let him have it for eighty," says Dutchy; "and the others in proportion."

I lay back and breathed hard.

"Sell them all, but the one best hoss," says he — "no, the *two* best."

".Holy smoke!" says I gettin' my breath. "If you mean that, Dutchy, you lend me another gun and give me a drink."

He done so; and I went back home to where the whole camp of Cyanide was waitin'.

I got up and made them a speech and told them I'd sell them hosses all right, and to come back. Then I got an Injin boy to help, and we rustled over the remuda and held them in a blind cañon. Then I called up these miners one at a time, and made bargains with them. Roar! Well, you could hear them at Denver, they tell me, and the weather reports said, "Thunder in the mountains." But it was cash on delivery, and they all paid up. They had see that white quartz with the gold stickin' into it, and that's the same as a dose of loco to miner gents.

Why didn't I take a hoss and start first? I did think of it — for about one second. I wouldn't stay in that country then for a million dollars a minute. I was plumb sick and loathin' it, and just waitin' to make high jumps back to Arizona. So I wasn't aimin' to join this stampede, and didn't have no vivid emotions.

They got to fightin' on which should get the first hoss; so I bent my gun on them and made them draw lots. They roared some more, but done so; and as fast as each one handed over his dust or dinero he made a rush for his cabin, piled on his saddle and pack, and pulled his freight in a cloud of dust. It was sure a grand stampede and I enjoyed it to the limit.

So by sundown I was alone with the Injin. Those two hundred head brought in about twenty thousand dollars. It was heavy, but I could carry it. I was about alone in the landscape; and there were the two best hosses I had saved out for Dutchy. I was sure some tempted. But I had enough to get home on anyway; and I never yet drank behind the bar, even if I might hold up the saloon from the floor. So I grieved some inside that I was so tur'ble conscientious, shouldered the sacks, and went down to find Dutchy.

I met him headed his way, and carryin' of a sheet of paper.

"Here's your dinero," says I, dumpin' the four big sacks on the ground.

He stooped over and hefted them. Then he passed one over to me.

"What's that for?" I asks.

"For you," says he.

"My commission ain't that much." I objects.

"You've earned it," says he, "and you might have skipped with the whole wad."

"How did you know I wouldn't?" I asks.

"Well," says he, and I noted that jag of his had flew. "You see, I was behind that rock up there, and I had you covered."

I saw; and I began to feel better about bein' so tur'ble conscientious.

We walked a little ways without sayin' nothin'.

"But ain't you goin' to join the game?" I asks.

"Guess not," says he, jinglin' of his gold. "I'm satisfied."

"But if you don't get a wiggle on you, you are sure goin' to get left on those gold claims," says I.

"There ain't no gold claims," says he.

"But Henry Smith — " I cries.

"There ain't no Henry Smith," says he.

I let that soak in about six inches.

"But there's a Buck Cañon," I pleads. "Please say there's a Buck Cañon."

"Oh, yes, there's a Buck Cañon," he allows. "Nice limestone formation — make good hard water."

"Well you're a marvel," says I.

We walked on together down to Dutchy's saloon. We stopped outside.

"Now," says he, "I'm goin' to take one of those hosses and go somewheres else. Maybe you'd better do likewise on the other."

"You bet I will," says I.

He turned around and tacked up the paper he was carryin'. It was a sign. It read:

THE DUTCH HAS RUSTLED

"Nice sentiment," says I. "It will be appreciated when the crowd comes back from that little *pasear* into Buck Cañon. But why not tack her up where the trail hits the camp? Why on this particular door?"

"Well," said Dutchy, squintin' at the sign sideways, "you see I sold this place day before yesterday — to Mike O'Toole."

16

The General's Bluff

OWEN WISTER

THE GENERAL'S BLUFF.

BY OWEN WISTER.

THE troops this day had gone into winter quarters, and sat down to kill the idle time with pleasure until spring. After two hundred and forty days it is a good thing to sit down. The season had been spent in trailing, and sometimes catching, small bands of Indians. These had taken the habit of relieving settlers of their cattle and the tops of their heads. The weather-beaten troops had scouted over some two thousand aimless, veering miles, for the savages were fleet and mostly invisible, and knew the desert well. So, while the year turned, and the heat came, held sway, and went, the ragged troopers on the frontier were led an endless chase by the hostiles, who took them back and forth over flats of lime and ridges of slate, occasionally picking off a packer or a couple of privates, until now the sun was setting at 4.28 and it froze at any time of day. Therefore the rest of the packers and privates were glad to march into Boisé Barracks this morning by eleven, and see a stove.

They rolled for a moment on their bunks to get the feel of a bunk again after two hundred and forty days; they ate their dinner at a table; those who owned any further baggage than that which partially covered their nakedness unpacked it, perhaps nailed up a photograph or two, and found it grateful to sit and do nothing under a roof and listen to the grated snow whip the windows of the gray sandstone quarters. Such comfort, and the prospect of more ahead, of weeks of nothing but post duty and staying in the same place, obliterated Dry Camp, Cow Creek Lake, the blizzard on Meacham's Hill, the horse-killing in the John Day Valley, Saw-Tooth stampede, and all the recent evils of the past; the quarters hummed with cheerfulness. The nearest railroad was some four hundred miles to the southwest, slowly constructing, to meet the next nearest, which was some nine hundred to the southeast; but Boisé City was only three-quarters of a mile away, the largest town in the Territory, the capital, not a temperance town, a winter resort; and several hundred people lived in it, men and women, few of whom ever died in their beds. The coming days and nights were a luxury to think of.

"Blamed if there ain't a real tree!" exclaimed Private Jones.

"Thet eer ain't no tree, ye plum; thet's the flag-pole 'n' th' Merrickin flag," observed a civilian. His name was Jack Long, and he was pack-master.

Sergeant Keyser, listening, smiled. During the winter of '64–65 he had been in command of the first battalion of his regiment, but, on a theory of education, had enlisted after the war. This being known held the men more shy of him than was his desire.

Jones continued to pick his banjo, while a boyish trooper with tough black hair sat near him, and kept time with his heels. "It's a cottonwood-tree I was speakin' of," observed Jones. There was one, a little shivering white stalk. It stood above the flat where the barracks were, on a bench twenty or thirty feet higher, on which were built the officers' quarters. The air was getting dim with the fine hard snow that slanted through it. The thermometer was ten above out there. At the mere sight and thought Mr. Long produced a flat bottle, warm from proximity to his flesh. Jones swallowed some drink, and looked at the little tree. "Snakes! but it feels good," said he, "to get something inside yu' and be inside yerself. What's the tax at Mike's dance-house now?"

"Dance 'n' drinks fer two fer one dollar," responded Mr. Long, accurately. He was sixty, but that made no difference.

"You and me 'll take that in, Jock," said Jones to his friend, the black-haired boy. "Sigh no more, ladies," he continued, singing. "The blamed banjo won't accompany that," he remarked, and looked out again at the tree. "There's a chap riding into the post now. Shabby-lookin'. Maybe he's got stuff to sell."

Jack Long looked up on the bench at a rusty figure moving slowly through the storm. "Th' ole man?" he said.

"He ain't specially old," Jones answered. "They're apt to be older, them peddlers."

"Peddlers! Oh, ye-es." A seizure of very remarkable coughing took Jack Long by the throat; but he really had a cough, and on the fit's leaving him, swallowed a drink, and offered his bottle in a manner so cold and usual that Jones forgot to note anything but the excellence of the whiskey. Mr. Long winked at Sergeant Keyser; he thought it a good plan not to inform his young friends, not just yet at any rate, that their peddler was General Crook. It would be pleasant to hear what else they might have to say.

The General had reached Boisé City that morning by the stage, quietly and unknown, as was his way. He had come to hunt Indians in the district of the Owyhee. Jack Long had discovered this, but only a few had been told the news, for the General wished to ask questions and receive answers, and to find out about all things; and he had noticed that this is not easy when too many people know who you are. He had called upon a friend or two in Boisé, walked about unnoticed, learned a number of facts, and now, true to his habit, entered the post wearing no uniform, none being necessary under the circumstances, and unattended by a single orderly. Jones and the black-haired Cumnor hoped he was a peddler, and innocently sat looking out of the window at him riding along the bench in front of the quarters, and occasionally slouching his wide dark hat-brim against the stinging of the hard flakes. Jack Long, old and much experienced with the army, had scouted with Crook before, and knew him and his ways well. He also looked out of the window, standing behind Jones and Cumnor, with a huge hairy hand on a shoulder of each, and a huge wink again at Keyser.

"Blamed if he 'ain't stopped in front of the commanding officer's," said Jones.

"Lor'!" said Mr. Long, "there's jest nothin' them peddlers won't do."

"They ain't likely to buy anything off him in there," said Cumnor.

"Mwell, ef he's purvided with any kind o' Injun cur'os'tees, the missis she'll fly right on to 'em. Sh' 'ain't been merried out yere only haff'n year, 'n' when she spies feathers 'n' bead truck 'n' buckskin fer sale sh' hollers like a son of a gun. Enthoosiastic, ye know."

"He 'ain't got much of a pack," Jones commented, and at that moment "stables" sounded, and the men ran out to form and march to their grooming. Jack Long stood at the door and watched them file through the snow.

Very few enlisted men of the small

command that had come in this morning from its campaign had ever seen General Crook. Jones, though not new to the frontier, had not been long in the army. He and Cumnor had enlisted in a happy-go-lucky manner together at Grant, in Arizona, when the General was elsewhere. Discipline was galling to his vagrant spirit, and after each pay-day he had generally slept off the effects in the guard-house, going there for other offences between-whiles; but he was not of the stuff that deserts ; also, he was excellent tempered, and his captain liked him for the way in which he could shoot Indians. Jack Long liked him too, and getting always a harmless pleasure from the mistakes of his friends, sincerely trusted there might be more about the peddler. He was startled at hearing his name spoken in his ear.

" *Nah!* Johnny, how you get on?"

" Hello, Sarah! Kla-how-ya, six?" said Long, greeting in Chinook the squaw interpreter who had approached him so noiselessly. " Hy-as kloshe o-coke sun " (It is a beautiful day).

The interpreter laughed — she had a broad, sweet, coarse face and laughed easily — and said in English, " You hear about E-egante?"

Long had heard nothing recently of this Pah-Ute chieftain.

" He heap bad," continued Sarah, laughing broadly. " Come round ranch up here—"

" Anybody killed?" Long interrupted.

" No. All run away quick. Meester Dailey, he old man, he run all same young one. His old woman she run all same man. Get horse. Run away quick. Hu-hu!" and Sarah's rich mockery sounded again. No tragedy had happened this time, and the squaw narrated her story greatly to the relish of Mr. Long. This veteran of trails and mines had seen too much of life's bleakness not to cherish whatever of mirth his days might bring.

" Didn't burn the house?" he said.

" Not burn. Just make heap mess. Cut up feather bed hy-as ten-as [very small] and eat big dinner, hu-hu! Sugar, onions, meat, eat all. Then they find litt' cats walkin' round there."

" Lor'!" said Mr. Long, deeply interested, " they didn't eat *them?*"

" No. Not eat litt' cats. Put 'em two —man-cat and woman-cat—in molasses; put 'em in feather bed ; all same bird. Then they hunt for whiskey, break every-

thing, hunt all over, ha-lo whiskey !" Sarah shook her head. " Meester Dailey he good man. Hy-iu temperance. Drink water. They find his medicine; drink all up; make awful sick."

" I guess 'twar th' ole man's liniment," muttered Jack Long.

" Yas, milinut. They can't walk. Stay there long time, then Meester Dailey come back with friends. They think Injuns all gone; make noise, and E-egante he hear him come, and he not very sick. Run away. Some more run. But two Injuns heap sick; can't run. Meester Dailey he come round corner; see awful mess everywhere; see two litt' cats sittin' in door all same bird, sing very loud. Then he see two Injuns on ground. They dead now."

" Mwell," said Long, " none of eer 'll do. We'll hev to ketch E-egante."

" A—h!" drawled Sarah the squaw, in musical derision. " Maybe no catch him. All same jack-rabbit."

" Jest ye wait, Sarah ; Gray Fox hez come."

" Gen'l Crook!" said the squaw. " He come! Hó! He heap savvy." She stopped, and laughed again, like a pleased child. " Maybe no catch E-egante," she added, rolling her pretty brown eyes at Jack Long.

" You know E-egante?" he demanded.

" Yas, one time. Long time now. I litt' girl then." But Sarah remembered that long time, when she slept in a tent and had not been captured and put to school. And she remembered the tall young boys whom she used to watch shoot arrows, and the tallest, who shot most truly—at least he certainly did now in her imagination. He had never spoken to her or looked at her. He was a boy of fourteen and she a girl of eight. Now she was twenty-five. Also she was tame and domesticated, with a white husband who was not bad to her, and children for each year of wedlock, who would grow up to speak English better than she could, and her own tongue not at all. And E-egante was not tame, and still lived in a tent. Sarah regarded white people as her friends, but she was proud of being an Indian, and she liked to think that her race could outwit the soldier now and then. She laughed again when she thought of old Mrs. Dailey running from E-egante.

" What's up with ye, Sarah?" said Jack Long, for the squaw's laughter had come suddenly on a spell of silence.

"Hé!" said she. "All same jack-rabbit. No catch him." She stood shaking her head at Long and showing her white regular teeth. Then abruptly she went away to her tent without any word, not because she was in ill humor or had thought of something, but because she was an Indian and had thought of nothing, and had no more to say. She met the men returning from the stables; admired Jones and smiled at him, upon which he murmured "Oh fie!" as he passed her. The troop broke ranks and dispersed, to lounge and gossip until mess-call. Cumnor and Jones were putting a little snow down each other's necks with friendly profanity, when Jones saw the peddler standing close and watching them. A high collar of some ragged fur was turned up round his neck, disguising the character of the ancient army overcoat to which it was attached, and spots and long stains extended down the legs of his corduroys to the charred holes at the bottom, where the owner had scorched them warming his heels and calves at many camp-fires.

"Hello, uncle," said Jones. "What yu' got in your pack?" He and Cumnor left their gambols and eagerly approached, while Mr. Jack Long, seeing the interview, came up also to hear it. "'Ain't yu' got something to sell?" continued Jones. "Yu' haven't gone and dumped yer whole outfit at the commanding officer's, have yu' now?"

"I'm afraid I have." The low voice shook ever so little, and if Jones had looked, he would have seen a twinkle come and go in the gray-blue eyes.

"We've been out eight months, yu' know, fairly steady," pursued Jones, "and haven't seen nothing; and we'd buy most anything that ain't too d—— bad," he concluded, plaintively.

Mr. Long in the background was whining to himself with joy, and he now urgently beckoned Keyser to come and hear this.

"If you've got some cheap poker chips," suggested Cumnor.

"And say, uncle," said Jones, raising his voice, for the peddler was moving away, "decks, and tobacco better than what they keep at the commissary. Me and my friend 'll take some off your hands. And if you're comin' with new stock to-morrow, uncle" (Jones was now shouting after him), "why, we're single

men, and yu' might fetch along a couple of squaws!"

"Holy smoke!" screeched Mr. Long, dancing on one leg; "tell him not to forgit a parson while he's about it."

"What's up with you, yu' ape?" inquired Specimen Jones. He looked at the departing peddler and saw Sergeant Keyser meet him and salute with stern soldierly respect. Then the peddler shook hands with the sergeant, seemed to speak pleasantly, and again Keyser saluted as he passed on. "What's that for?" Jones asked, uneasily. "Who is that obo?"

But Mr. Long was talking to himself in a highly moralizing strain. "It ain't every young enlisted man," he was saying, "ez hez th' privilege of explainin' his wants at headquarters."

"Jones," said Sergeant Keyser, arriving, "I've a compliment for you. General Crook said you were a fine-looking man."

"General?—What's that?—Where did yu' see—What? Him?" The disgusting truth flashed clear on Jones. Uttering a single disconcerted syllable of rage, he wheeled and went by himself into the barracks, and lay down solitary on his bunk and read a newspaper until mess-call without taking in a word of it. "If they go to put me in the mill fer that," he said, sulkily, to many friends who brought him their congratulations, "I'm going to give 'em what I think about wearin' disguises."

"What do you think, Specimen?" said one.

"Give it to us now, Specimen," said another.

"Against the law, ain't it, Specimen?"

"Begosh!" said Jack Long, "ef thet's so, don't lose no time warnin' the General, Specimen. Th' ole man 'd hate to be arrested."

And Specimen Jones told them all to shut their heads.

But no thought was more distant from General Crook's busy mind than putting poor Jones in the guard-house. The trooper's willingness, after eight months hunting Indians, to buy almost anything brought a smile to his lips, and a certain sympathy in his heart. He knew what those eight months had been like; how monotonous, how well endured, how often dangerous, how invariably plucky, how scant of even the necessities of life, how barren of glory, and unrewarded by public recognition. The American "statesman " does not care about our army until it becomes necessary for his immediate personal protection. General Crook knew all this well; and realizing that these soldiers, who had come into winter quarters this morning at eleven, had earned a holiday, he was sorry to feel obliged to start them out again to-morrow morning at two; for this was what he had decided upon.

He had received orders to drive on the reservation the various small bands of Indians that were roving through the country of the Snake and its tributaries, a danger to the miners in the Bannock Basin, and to the various ranches in west Idaho and east Oregon. As usual, he had been given an insufficient force to accomplish this, and, as always, he had been instructed by the "statesmen" to do it without violence—that is to say, he must never shoot the poor Indian until after the poor Indian has shot him; he must make him do something he did not want to, pleasantly, by the fascination of argument, in the way a "statesman" would achieve it. The force at the General's disposal was the garrison at Boisé Barracks—one troop of cavalry and one company of infantry. The latter was not adapted to the matter in hand—rapid marching and surprises; all it could be used for was as a re-enforcement, and, moreover, somebody must be left at Boisé Barracks. The cavalry had had its full dose of scouting and skirmishing and long exposed marches, the horses were poor, and nobody had any trousers to speak of. Also, the troop was greatly depleted; it numbered forty men. Forty had deserted, and three—a sergeant and two privates—had cooked and eaten a vegetable they had been glad to dig up one day, and had spent the ensuing forty-five minutes in attempting to make their ankles beat the backs of their heads; after that the captain had read over them a sentence beginning, " Man that is born of a woman hath but a short time to live, and is full of misery "; and after that the camp was referred to as Wild Carrot Camp, because the sergeant had said the vegetable was wild carrot, whereas it had really been wild parsnip, which is quite another thing.

General Crook shook his head over what he saw. The men were ill-provided, the commissary and the quartermaster department were ill-provided; but it would have to do; the " statesmen " said our army was an extravagance. The Indians must be impressed and intimidated by the unlimited resources which the General had—not. Having come to this conclusion, he went up to the post commander's, and at supper astonished that officer by casual remarks which revealed a knowledge of the surrounding country, the small streams, the best camps for pasture, spots to avoid on account of bad water, what mules had sore backs, and many other things that the post commander would have liked dearly to ask the General where and when he had learned, only he did not dare. He did not even venture to ask him what he was going to do. Neither did Captain Glynn, who had been asked to meet the General. The General soon told them, however. " It may be a little cold," he concluded.

" To-morrow, sir?" This from Captain Glynn. He had come in with the forty that morning. He had been enjoying his supper very much.

" I think so," said the General. " This E-egante is likely to make trouble if he is not checked." Then, understanding the thoughts of Captain Glynn, he added, with an invisible smile, " *You* need no preparations. You're in marching order. It's not as if your men had been here a long time and had to get ready for a start."

" Oh no," said Glynn, "it isn't like that." He was silent. " I think, if you'll excuse me, General," he said next, " I'll see my sergeant and give some orders."

" Certainly. And, Captain Glynn, I took the liberty of giving a few directions myself. We'll take an A tent, you know, for you and me. I see Keyser is sergeant in F troop. Glad we have a non-commissioned officer so competent. Haven't seen him since '64, at Winchester. Why, it's cleared off, I declare !"

It had, and the General looked out of the open door as Captain Glynn, departing, was pulling at his cigar. " How beautiful the planets are !" exclaimed Crook. " Look at Jupiter —there, just to the left of that little cottonwood-tree. Haven't you often noticed how much finer the stars shine in this atmosphere than in the East? Oh, captain! I forgot to speak of extra horseshoes. I want some brought along."

" I'll attend to it, General."

" They shouldn't be too large. These California fourteen - and - a - half horses have smallish hoofs."

"I'll see the blacksmith myself, General."

"Thank you. Good-night. And just order fresh stuffing put into the aparejos. I noticed three that had got lumpy." And the General shut the door and went to wipe out the immaculate barrels of his shot-gun; for besides Indians there were grouse among the hills where he expected to go.

Captain Glynn, arriving at his own door, stuck his glowing cigar against the thermometer hanging outside: twenty-three below zero. "Oh Lord!" said the captain, briefly. He went in and told his striker to get Sergeant Keyser. Then he sat down and waited. "'Look at Jupiter!'" he muttered, angrily. "What an awful old man!"

It was rather awful. The captain had not supposed Generals in the first two hours of their arrival at a post to be in the habit of finding out more about your aparejos than you knew yourself. But old the General was not. At the present day many captains are older than Crook was then.

Down at the barracks there was the same curiosity about what the "Old Man" was going to do as existed at the post commander's during the early part of supper. It pleased the cavalry to tell the infantry that the Old Man proposed to take the infantry to the Columbia River next week; and the infantry replied to the cavalry that they were quite right as to the river and the week, and it was hard luck the General needed only mounted troops on this trip. Others had heard he had come to superintend the building of a line of telegraph to Klamath, which would be a good winter's job for somebody; but nobody supposed that anything would happen yet awhile.

And then a man came in and told them the General had sent his boots to the saddler to have nails hammered in the soles.

"That eer means business," said Jack Long, "'n' I guess I'll nail up mee own cowhides."

"Jock," said Specimen Jones to Cumnor, "you and me 'ain't got any soles to ourn because they're contract boots, yu' see. I'll nail up yer feet if yu' say so. It's liable to be slippery."

Cumnor did not take in the situation at once. "What's your hurry?" he inquired of Jack Long. Therefore it was explained to him that when General Crook ordered his boots fixed you might expect to be on the road shortly. Cumnor swore some resigned unemphatic oaths, fondly supposing that "shortly" meant some time or other; but hearing in the next five minutes the definite fact that F troop would get up at two, he made use of profound and thorough language, and compared the soldier with the slave.

"Why yu' talk almost like a man, Jock," said Specimen Jones. "Blamed if yu' don't sound pretty near growed up."

Cumnor invited Jones to mind his business.

"Yer mustache has come since Arizona," continued Jones, admiringly, "and yer blue eye is bad-lookin'—worse than when we shot at yer heels and yu' danced fer us."

"I thought they were going to give us a rest," mumbled the youth, flushing. "I thought we'd be let stay here a spell."

"I thought so too, Jock. A little monotony would be fine variety. But a man must take his medicine, yu' know, and not squeal." Jones had lowered his voice, and now spoke without satire to the boy whom he had in a curious manner taken under his protection.

"Look at what they give us for a blanket to sleep in," said Cumnor. "A fellow can see to read the newspaper through it."

"Look at my coat, Cumnor." It was Sergeant Keyser showing the article furnished the soldier by the government. "You can spit through that." He had overheard their talk, and stepped up to show that all were in the same box. At his presence reticence fell upon the privates, and Cumnor hauled his black felt hat down tight in embarrassment, which strain split it open half-way round his head. It was another sample of regulation clothing, and they laughed at it.

"We all know the way it is," said Keyser, "and I've seen it a big sight worse. Cumnor, I've a cap I guess will keep your scalp warm till we get back."

And so at two in the morning F troop left the bunks it had expected to sleep in for some undisturbed weeks, and by four o'clock had eaten its well-known breakfast of bacon and bad coffee, and was following the "awful old man" down the north bank of the Boisé, leaving the silent dead wooden town of shanties on the other side half a mile behind in the darkness. The mountains south stood distant, ignoble, plain-featured heights, looming a clean-cut black beneath the piercing stars and the slice of hard sharp-edged moon, and the surrounding plains of sage and dry-cracking weed slanted up and down to nowhere and nothing with desolate perpetuity. The snowfall was light and dry as sand, and the bare ground jutted through it at every sudden lump or knoll. The column moved through the dead polar silence, scarcely breaking it. Now and then a hoof rang on a stone, here and there a bridle or a sabre clinked lightly; but it was too cold and early for talking, and the only steady sound was the flat canlike tankle of the square bell that hung on the neck of the long-eared leader of the pack-train. They passed the Dailey ranch, and saw the kittens and the liniment bottle, but could get no information as to what way E-egante had gone. The General did not care for that, however; he had devised his own route for the present, after a talk with the Indian guides. At the second dismounting during march he had word sent back to the pack-train not to fall behind, and the bell was to be taken off if the rest of the mules would follow without the sound of its shallow music. No wind moved the weeds or shook the stiff grass, and the rising sun glittered pink on the patched and motley-shirted men as they blew on their red hands or beat them against their legs. Some were lucky enough to have woollen or fur gloves, but many had only the white cotton affairs furnished by the government. Sarah the squaw laughed at them: the interpreter was warm as she rode in her bright green shawl. While the dismounted troopers stretched their limbs during the halt, she remained on her pony talking to one and another.

"Gray Fox heap savvy," said she to Mr. Long. "He heap get up in the mornin'."

"Thet's what he does, Sarah."

"Yas. No give soldier hy-as Sunday" (a holiday).

"No, no," assented Mr. Long. "Gray Fox go téh-téh" (trot).

"Maybe he catch E-egante, maybe put him in skookum-house [prison]?" suggested Sarah.

"Oh no! Lor'! E-egante good Injun. White Father he feed him. Give him heap clothes," said Mr. Long.

"A—h!" drawled Sarah, dubiously, and rode by herself.

"You'll need watchin'," muttered Jack Long.

The trumpet sounded, the troopers swung into their saddles, and the line of march was taken up as before, Crook at the head of the column, his ragged fur collar turned up, his corduroys stuffed inside a wrinkled pair of boots, the shotgun balanced across his saddle, and nothing to reveal that he was any one in particular, unless you saw his face. As the morning grew bright, and empty silent Idaho glistened under the clear blue, the General talked a little to Captain Glynn.

"E-egante will have crossed Snake River, I think," said he. "I shall try to do that to-day; but we must be easy on those horses of yours. We ought to be able to find these Indians in three days."

"If I were a lusty young chief," said Glynn, "I should think it pretty tough to be put on a reservation for dipping a couple of kittens in the molasses."

"So should I, captain. But next time he might dip Mrs. Dailey. And I'm not sure he didn't have a hand in more serious work. Didn't you run across his tracks anywhere this summer?"

"No, sir. He was over on the Des Chutes."

"Did you hear what he was doing?"

"Having rows about fish and game with those Warm Spring Indians on the west side of the Des Chutes."

"They're always poaching on each other. There's bad blood between E-egante and Uma-Pine."

"Uma-Pine's friendly, sir, isn't he?"

"Well, that's a question," said Crook. "But there's no question about this E-egante and his Pah-Utes. We've got to catch him. I'm sorry for him. He doesn't see why he shouldn't hunt anywhere as his fathers did. I shouldn't see that either."

"How strong is this band reported, sir?"

"I've heard nothing I can set reliance upon," said Crook, instinctively lévelling his shot-gun at a big bird that rose; then he replaced the piece across his saddle and was silent. Now Captain Glynn had heard there were three hundred Indians with E-egante, which was a larger number than he had been in the habit of attacking with forty men. But he felt discreet about volunteering any information to the General after last night's exhibition of what the General knew. Crook partly answered what was in Glynn's mind.

"This is the only available force I have," said he. "We must do what we can with it. You've found out by this time, captain, that rapidity in following Indians up often works well. They have made up their minds—that is, if I know them—that we're going to loaf inside Boisé Barracks until the hard weather lets up."

Captain Glynn had thought so too, but he did not mention this, and the General continued. "I find that most people entertained this notion," he said, "and I'm glad they did, for it will help my first operations very materially."

The captain agreed that there was nothing like a false impression for assisting the efficacy of military movements, and presently the General asked him to command a halt. It was high noon, and the sun gleamed on the brass trumpet as the long note blew. Again the musical strain sounded on the cold bright stillness, and the double line of twenty legs swung in a simultaneous arc over the horses' backs as the men dismounted.

"We'll noon here," said the General; and while the cook broke the ice on Boisé River to fill his kettles, Crook went back to the mules to see how the sore backs were standing the march. "How d'ye do, Jack Long?" said he. "Your stock is travelling pretty well, I see. They're loaded with thirty days' rations, but I trust we're not going to need it all."

"Mwell, General, I don't specially kyeer meself 'bout eatin' the hull outfit." Mr. Long showed his respect for the General by never swearing in his presence.

"I see you haven't forgotten how to pack," Crook said to him. "Can we make Snake River to-day, Jack?"

"That 'll be forty miles, General. The days are pretty short."

"What are you feeding to the animals?" Crook inquired.

"Why, General, *you* know jest 's well 's me," said Jack, grinning.

"I suppose I do if you say so, Jack. Ten pounds first ten days, five pounds next ten, and you're out of grain for the next ten. Is that the way still?"

"Thet's the way, General, on these yere thirty-day affairs."

Through all this small-talk Crook had been inspecting the mules and the horses on picket-line, and silently forming his conclusion. He now returned to Captain Glynn and shared his mess-box.

They made Snake River. Crook knew better than Long what the animals could do. And next day they crossed, again by starlight, turned for a little way up the Owyhee, decided that E-egante had not gone that road, trailed up the bluffs and ledges from the Snake Valley on to the barren height of land, and made for the Malheur River, finding the eight hoofs of two deer lying in a melted place where a fire had been. Mr. Dailey had insisted that at least fifty Indians had drunk his liniment and trifled with his cats. Indeed, at times during his talk with General Crook the old gentleman had been sure there were a hundred. If this were their trail which the command had now struck, there may possibly have been eight. It was quite evident that the chief had not taken any three hundred warriors upon that visit, if he had that number anywhere. So the column went up the Malheur main stream through the sagebrush and the gray weather (it was still cold, but no sun any more these last two days), and coming to the North Fork, turned up towards a spur of the mountains and Castle Rock. The water ran smooth black between its edging of ice, thick, white, and crusted like slabs of cocoanut candy, and there in the hollow of a bend they came suddenly upon what they sought.

Stems of smoke, faint and blue, spindled up from a blurred acre of willow thicket, dense, tall as two men, a netted brown and yellow mesh of twigs and stiff wintry rods. Out from the level of their close, nature-woven tops rose at distances the straight slight blue smoke-lines, marking each the position of some invisible lodge. The whole acre was a bottom ploughed at some former time by a wash-out, and the troops looked down on it from the edge of the higher ground, silent in the quiet gray afternoon, the empty sage-brush territory stretching a short way to fluted hills that were white below and blackened with pines above.

The General, taking a rough chance as he often did, sent ground scouts forward and ordered a charge instantly, to catch the savages unready; and the stiff rods snapped and tangled between the beating hoofs. The horses plunged at the elastic edges of this excellent fortress, sometimes half lifted as a bent willow levered up against their bellies, and the forward-tilting men fended their faces from the whipping twigs. They could not wedge a man's length into that pliant labyrinth, and the General called them out. They rallied among the sage-brush above, Crook's cheeks and many others painted with purple lines of blood, hardened already and cracking like enamel. The baffled troopers glared at the thicket. Not a sign nor a sound came from in there. The willows, with the gentle tints of winter veiling their misty twigs, looked serene and even innocent, fitted to harbor birds —not birds of prey—and the quiet smoke threaded upwards through the air. Of course the liniment-drinkers must have heard the noise.

"What do you suppose they're doing?" inquired Glynn.

"Looking at us," said Crook.

"I wish we could return the compliment," said the captain.

Crook pointed. Had any wind been blowing, what the General saw would have been less worth watching. Two willow branches shook, making a vanishing ripple on the smooth surface of the tree-tops. The pack-train was just coming in sight over the rise, and Crook immediately sent an orderly with some message. More willow branches shivered an instant and were still; then, while the General and the captain sat on their horses and watched, the thicket gave up its secret to them; for, as little light gusts coming abreast over a lake travel and touch the water, so in different spots the level maze of twigs was stirred; and if the eye fastened upon any one of these it could have been seen to come out from the centre towards the edge, successive twigs moving, as the tops of long grass tremble and mark the progress of a snake. During a short while this increased greatly, the whole thicket moving with innumerable tracks. Then everything ceased, with the blue wands of smoke rising always into the quiet afternoon.

"Can you see 'em?" said Glynn.

"Not a bit. Did you happen to hear any one give an estimate of this band?"

Glynn mentioned his tale of the three hundred.

It was not new to the General, but he remarked now that it must be pretty nearly correct; and his eye turned a moment upon his forty troopers waiting there, grim and humorous; for they knew that the thicket was looking at them, and it amused their American minds to wonder what the Old Man was going to do about it.

"It's his bet, and he holds poor cards," murmured Specimen Jones; and the neighbors grinned.

And here the Old Man continued the play that he had begun when he sent the orderly to the pack-train. That part of the command had halted in consequence, disposed itself in an easy-going way, half in, half out of sight on the ridge, and men and mules looked entirely careless. Glynn wondered; but no one ever asked the General questions, in spite of his amiable voice and countenance. He now sent for Sarah the squaw.

"You tell E-egante," he said, "that I am not going to fight with his people unless his people make me. I am not going to do them any harm, and I wish to be their friend. The White Father has sent me. Ask E-egante if he has heard of Gray Fox. Tell him Gray Fox wishes E-egante and all his people to be ready to go with him to-morrow at nine o'clock."

And Sarah, standing on the frozen bank, pulled her green shawl closer, and shouted her message faithfully to the willows. Nothing moved or showed, and Crook, riding up to the squaw, held his hand up as a further sign to the flag of peace that had been raised already. "Say that I am Gray Fox," said he.

On that there was a moving in the bushes further along, and going opposite that place with the squaw, Crook and Glynn saw a narrow entrance across which some few branches reached that were now spread aside for three figures to stand there.

"E-egante!" said Sarah, eagerly. "See him big man!" she added to Crook, pointing. A tall and splendid buck, gleaming with colors, and rich with fringe and buckskin, watched them. He seemed to look at Sarah, too. She, being ordered, repeated what she had said; but the chief did not answer.

"He is counting our strength," said Glynn.

"He's done that some time ago," said Crook. "Tell E-egante," he continued to the squaw, "that I will not send for more soldiers than he sees here. I do not wish anything but peace unless he wishes otherwise."

Sarah's musical voice sounded again from the bank, and E-egante watched her intently till she was finished. This time he replied at some length. He and his people had not done any harm. He had

THE CHARGE.

heard of Gray Fox often. All his people knew Gray Fox was a good man and would not make trouble. There were some flies that stung a man sitting in his house, when he had not hurt them. Gray Fox would not hurt any one till their hand was raised against him first. E-egante and his people had wondered why the horses made so much noise just now. He and his people would come to-morrow with Gray Fox.

And then he went inside the thicket again, and the willows looked as innocent as ever. Crook and the captain rode away.

"My speech was just a little weak coming on top of a charge of cavalry," the General admitted. "And that fellow put his finger right on the place. I'll give you my notion, captain. If I had said we had more soldiers behind the hill, like as not this squaw of ours would have told him I lied; she's an uncertain quantity, I find. But I told him the exact truth—that I had no more—and he won't believe it, and that's what I want."

So Glynn understood. The pack-train had been halted in a purposely exposed position, which would look to the Indians as if another force was certainly behind it, and every move was now made to give an impression that the forty were only the advance of a large command. Crook pitched his A tent close to the red men's village, and the troops went into camp regardlessly near. The horses were turn-ed out to graze ostentatiously unprotected, so that the people in the thicket should have every chance to notice how secure the white men felt. The mules pastured comfortably over the shallow snow that crushed as they wandered among the sage-brush, and the square bell hung once more from the neck of the leader and tankled upon the hill. The shelter-tents littered the flat above the wash-out, and besides the cook fire others were built irregularly far down the Malheur North Fork, shedding an extended glimmer of deceit. It might have been the camp of many hundred. A little blaze shone comfortably on the canvas of Crook's tent, and Sergeant Keyser, being in charge of camp, had adopted the troop cook fire for his camp guard after the cooks had fin-ished their work. The willow thicket below grew black and mysterious, and quiet fell on the white camp. By eight the troopers had gone to bed. Night

had come pretty cold, and a little occa-sional breeze, that passed like a chill hand laid a moment on the face, and went down into the willows. Now and again the water running through the ice would lap and gurgle at some air-hole. Sergeant Keyser sat by his fire and listened to the lonely bell sounding from the dark. He wished the men would feel more at home with him. With Jack Long, satirical, old, and experienced, they were perfectly familiar, because he was a civilian; but to Keyser, because he had been in com-mand of a battalion, they held the atti-tude of school-boys to a master—the in-stinctive feeling of all privates towards all officers. Jones and Cumnor were members of his camp guard. Being just now off post, they stood at the fire, but away from him.

"How do you boys like this compared with barracks?" the sergeant said, con-versationally.

"It's all right," said Jones.

"Did you think it was all right that first morning? I didn't enjoy it much myself. Sit down and get warm, won't you?"

The men came and stood awkwardly. "I 'ain't never found any excitement in getting up early," said Jones, and was silent. A burning log shifted, and the bell sounded in a new place as the leader pastured along. Jones kicked the log into better position. "But this affair's gettin' inter-esting," he added.

"Don't you smoke?" Keyser inquired of Cumnor, and tossed him his tobacco-pouch. Presently they were seated, and the conversation going better. Arizona was compared with Idaho. Everybody had gone to bed.

"Arizona's the most outrageous outrage in the United States," declared Jones.

"Why did you stay there six years, then?" said Cumnor.

"Guess I'd been there yet but for you comin' along and us both enlistin' that crazy way. Idaho's better. Only," said Jones, thoughtfully, "coming to an ice-box from a hundred thousand in the shade, it's a wonder a man don't just split like a glass chimbly."

The willows crackled, and all laid hands on their pistols.

"How! how!" said a strange propitia-ting voice.

It was a man on a horse, and directly they recognized E-egante himself. They would have raised an alarm, but he was alone, and plainly not running away. Nor had he weapons. He rode into the firelight, and "How! how!" he repeated anxiously. He looked and nodded at the three, who remained seated.

"Good-evening," said the sergeant.

"Christmas is coming," said Jones, amicably.

"How! how!" said E-egante. It was all the English he had. He sat on his horse, looking at the men, the camp, the cook fire, the A tent, and beyond into the surrounding silence. He started when the bell suddenly jangled near by. The wandering mule had only shifted in towards the camp and shaken its head; but the Indian's nerves were evidently on the sharpest strain.

"Sit down!" said Keyser, making signs, and at these E-egante started suspiciously.

"Warm here!" Jones called to him, and Cumnor showed his pipe.

The chief edged a thought closer. His intent brilliant eyes seemed almost to listen as well as look, and though he sat his horse with heedless grace and security, there was never a figure more ready for vanishing upon the instant. He came a little nearer still, alert and pretty as an inquisitive buck antelope, watching not the three soldiers only, but everything else at once. He eyed their signs to dismount, looked at their faces, considered, and with the greatest slowness got off and came stalking to the fire. He was a fine tall man, and they smiled and nodded at him, admiring his clean blankets and the magnificence of his buckskin shirt and leggings.

"He's a jim-dandy," said Cumnor.

"You bet the girls think so," said Jones. "He gets his pick. For you're a fighter too, ain't yu'?" he added, to E-egante.

"How! how!" said that personage, looking at them with grave affability from the other side of the fire. Reassured presently, he accepted the sergeant's pipe; but even while he smoked and responded to their gestures, the alertness never left his eye, and his tall body gave no sense of being relaxed. And so they all looked at each other across the waning embers, while the old pack-mule moved about at the edge of camp, crushing the crusted snow and pasturing along. After a time E-egante gave a nod, handed the pipe back, and went into his thicket as he

had come. His visit had told him nothing; perhaps he had never supposed it would, and came from curiosity. One person had watched this interview. Sarah the squaw sat out in the night, afraid for her ancient hero; but she was content to look upon his beauty, and go to sleep after he had taken himself from her sight. The soldiers went to bed, and Keyser lay wondering for a while before he took his nap between his surveillances. The little breeze still passed at times, the running water and the ice made sounds together, and he could hear the wandering bell, now distant on the hill, irregularly punctuating the flight of the dark hours.

By nine next day there was the thicket sure enough, and the forty waiting for the three hundred to come out of it. Then it became ten o'clock, but that was the only difference, unless perhaps Sarah the squaw grew more restless. The troopers stood ready to be told what to do, joking together in low voices now and then; Crook sat watching Glynn smoke; and through these stationary people walked Sarah, looking wistfully at the thicket, and then at the faces of the adopted race she served. She hardly knew what was in her own mind. Then it became eleven, and Crook was tired of it, and made the capping move in his bluff. He gave the orders himself.

"Sergeant."

Keyser saluted.

"You will detail eight men to go with you into the Indian camp. The men are to carry pistols under their overcoats, and no other arms. You will tell the Indians to come out. Repeat what I said to them last night. Make it short. I'll give them ten minutes. If they don't come by then a shot will be fired out here. At that signal you will remain in there, and blaze away at the Indians."

So Keyser picked his men.

The thirty-one remaining troopers stopped joking, and watched the squad of nine and the interpreter file down the bank to visit the three hundred. The dingy overcoats and the bright green shawl passed into the thicket, and the General looked at his watch. Along the bend of the stream clear noises tinkled from the water and the ice.

"What are they up to?" whispered a teamster to Jack Long. Long's face was stern, but the teamster's was chalky and tight drawn. "Say," he repeated, insistently, "what are we going to do?"

"We're to wait," Long whispered back, "till nothin' happens, and then th' Ole Man'll fire a gun and signal them boys to shoot in there."

"Oh, it's to be waitin'?" said the teamster. He fastened his eyes on the thicket, and his lips grew bloodless. The running river sounded more plainly. "Let's start the fun, then," burst out the teamster, desperately, with an oath. He whipped out his pistol, and Jack Long had just time to seize him and stop a false signal.

"Why, you must be skeered," said Long. "I've a mind to beat yer skull in."

"Waitin's so awful," whimpered the man. "I wisht I was along with them in there."

Jack gave him back his revolver. "There," said he; "ye're not skeered, I see. Waitin' ain't nice."

The eight troopers with Keyser were not having anything like so distasteful a time. "Jock," said Specimen Jones to Cumnor as they followed the sergeant into the willows and began to come among the lodges and striped savages, "you and me has saw Injuns before, Jock."

"And we'll do it again," said Cumnor. Keyser looked at his watch: Four minutes gone. "Jones," said he, "you patrol this path to the right so you can cover that gang there. There must be four or five lodges down that way. Cumnor, see that dugout with side-thatch and roofing of tule? You attend to that family. It's a big one—all brothers." Thus the sergeant disposed his men quietly and quick through the labyrinth till they became invisible to each other; and all the while flights of Indians passed, half seen, among the tangle, fleeting visions of yellow and red through the quiet-colored twigs. Others squatted stoically, doing nothing. A few had guns, but most used arrows, and had these stacked beside them where they squatted. Keyser singled out a somewhat central figure—Fur Cap was his name—as his starting-point if the signal should sound. It must sound now in a second or two. He would not look at his watch lest it should hamper him. Fur Cap sat by a pile of arrows, with a gun across his knees besides. Keyser calculated that by standing close to him as he was, his boot would catch the Indian under the chin just right, and save one cartridge. Not a red man spoke, but Sarah the squaw dutifully speechified in a central place where paths met near Keyser and Fur Cap. Her voice was persuasive and warning. Some of the savages moved up and felt Keyser's overcoat. They fingered the hard bulge of the pistol underneath, and passed on, laughing, to the next soldier's coat, while Sarah did not cease to harangue. The tall stately man of last night appeared. His full dark eye met Sarah's, and the woman's voice faltered and her breathing grew troubled as she gazed at him. Once more Keyser looked at his watch: Seven minutes. E-egante noticed Sarah's emotion, and his face showed that her face pleased him. He spoke in a deep voice to Fur Cap, stretching a fringed arm out towards the hill with a royal gesture, at which Fur Cap rose.

"He will come, he will come!" said the squaw, running to Keyser. "They all come now. Do not shoot."

"Let them show outside, then," thundered Keyser, "or it's too late. If that gun goes before I can tell my men—" He broke off and rushed to the entrance. There were skirmishers deploying from three points, and Crook was raising his hand slowly. There was a pistol in it. "General! General!" Keyser shouted, waving both hands, "No!" Behind him came E-egante, with Sarah, talking in low tones, and Fur Cap came too. The General saw, and did not give the signal. The sight of the skirmishers hastened E-egante's mind. He spoke in a loud voice, and at once his warriors began to emerge from the willows obediently. Crook's bluff was succeeding. The Indians in waiting after nine were attempting a little bluff of their own; but the unprecedented visit of nine men appeared to them so dauntless that all notion of resistance left them. They were sure Gray Fox had a large army. And they came, and kept coming, and the place became full of them. The troopers had all they could do to form an escort and keep up the delusion, but by degrees order began, and the column was forming. Riding along the edge of the willows came E-egante, gay in his blankets, and saying, "How! how!" to Keyser, the only man at all near him. The pony ambled, and sidled, paused, trotted a little, and Key-

"HE HESITATED TO KILL THE WOMAN."

ser was beginning to wonder, when all at once a woman in a green shawl sprang from the thicket, leapt behind the chief, and the pony flashed by and away, round the curve. Keyser had lifted his carbine, but forbore; for he hesitated to kill the woman. Once more the two appeared, diminutive and scurrying, the green shawl bright against the hill-side they climbed. Sarah had been willing to take her chances of death with her hero, and now she vanished with him among his mountains, returning to her kind, and leaving her wedded white man and half-breeds forever.

"I don't feel so mad as I ought," said Specimen Jones.

Crook laughed to Glynn about it.

"We've got a big balance of 'em," he said, "if we can get 'em all to Boisé. They'll probably roast me in the East." And they did. Hearing how forty took three hundred, but let one escape (and a few more on the march home), the super-annuated cattle of the War Department sat sipping their drink at the club in Washington, and explained to each other how they would have done it.

And so the General's bluff partly failed. E-egante kept his freedom, "all along o' thet yere pizen squaw," as Mr. Long judiciously remarked. It was not until many years after that the chief's desti-ny overtook him; and concerning that, things both curious and sad could be told.

17

Destiny at Drybone

OWEN WISTER

DESTINY AT DRYBONE.

BY OWEN WISTER.

I.

CHILDREN have many special endowments, and of these the chiefest is to ask questions that their elders must skirmish to evade. Married people and aunts and uncles commonly discover this, but mere instinct does not guide one to it. A maiden of twenty-three will not necessarily divine it. Now except in one unhappy hour of stress and surprise, Miss Jessamine Buckner had been more than equal to life thus far. But never yet had she been shut up a whole day in one room with a boy of nine. Had this experience been hers, perhaps she would not have written Mr. McLean the friendly and singular letter in which she hoped he was well, and said that she was very well, and how was dear little Billy? She was glad Mr. McLean had staid away. That was just like his honorable nature, and what she expected of him. And she was perfectly happy at Separ, and "yours sincerely and always, 'Neighbor.'" Postscript. Talking of Billy Lusk—if Lin was busy with gathering the cattle, why not send Billy down to stop quietly with her? She would make him a bed in the ticket-office, and there she would be to see after him all the time. She knew Lin did not like his adopted child to be too much in cow-camp with the men. She would adopt him, too, for just as long as convenient to Lin—until the school opened on Bear Creek, if Lin so wished. Jessamine wrote a quantity concerning how much better care any woman can take of a boy of Billy's age than any man knows. The stage-coach brought the answer to this remarkably soon—young Billy with a trunk and a letter of twelve pages in pencil and ink—the only writing of this length ever done by Mr. McLean.

"I can write a lot quicker than Lin," said Billy upon arriving. "He was fussing at that away late by the fire in camp, an' waked me up crawling in our bed. An' then he had to finish it next night when we went over to the cabin for my clothes."

"You don't say!" said Jessamine. And Billy suffered her to kiss him again.

When not otherwise occupied, Jessamine took the letter out of its locked box, and read it, or looked at it. Thus the first days had gone finely at Separ, the weather being beautiful and Billy much out-of-doors. But sometimes the weather changes in Wyoming; and now it was that Miss Jessamine learned the talents of childhood.

Soon after breakfast this stormy morning Billy observed the twelve pages being taken out of their box, and spoke from his sudden brain. "Honey Wiggin says Lin's losing his grip about girls," he remarked. "He says you couldn't 'a' downed him onced. You'd 'a' had to marry him. Honey says Lin 'ain't worked it like he done in old times."

"Now I shouldn't wonder if he was right," said Jessamine, buoyantly. "And that being the case, I'm going to set to work at your things till it clears, and then we'll go for our ride."

"Yes," said Billy. "When does a man get too old to marry?"

"I'm only a girl, and I don't know."

"Yes. Honey said he wouldn't 'a' thought Lin was that old. But I guess he must be thirty."

"Old!" exclaimed Jessamine. And she looked at a photograph upon her table.

"But Lin 'ain't been married very much," pursued Billy. "Mother's the only one they speak of. You don't have to stay married always, do you?"

"It's better to," said Jessamine.

"Ah, I don't think so," said Billy, with disparagement. "You ought to see mother and father. I wish you would leave Lin marry you, though," said the boy, coming to her with an impulse of affection. "Why won't you if he don't mind?"

She continued to parry him; but this was not a very smooth start for eight in the morning. Moments of lull there were, when the telegraph called her to the front room, and Billy's young mind shifted to inquiries about the cipher alphabet. And she gained at least an hour teaching him to read various words by the sound. At dinner, too, he was refreshingly silent. But such silences are unsafe, and the weather was still bad. Four o'clock found them much where they had been at eight.

"Please tell me why you won't leave Lin marry you." He was at the window, kicking the wall.

"That's nine times since dinner," she replied, with tireless good-humor. "Now if you ask me twelve—"

"You'll tell?" said the boy, swiftly.

She broke into a laugh. "No. I'll go riding and you'll stay at home. When I was little and would ask things beyond me, they only gave me three times."

"I've got two more, anyway. Ha-ha!"

"Better save 'em up, though."

"What did they do to you? Ah, I don't want to go a-riding. It's nasty all over." He stared out at the day against which Separ's doors had been tight closed since morning. Eight hours of furious wind had raised the dust like a sea. "I wish the old train would come," observed Billy, continuing to kick the wall. "I wish I was going somewheres." Smoky, level, and hot, the south wind leapt into Separ across five hundred unbroken miles. The plain was blanketed in a tawny eclipse. Each minute the near buildings became invisible in a turbulent herd of clouds. Above this travelling blur of the soil the top of the water-tank alone rose bulging into the clear sun. The sand spirals would lick like flames along the bulk of the lofty tub, and soar skyward. It was not shipping season.

LIN McLEAN.

The freight-cars stood idle in a long line. No cattle huddled in the corrals. No strangers moved in town. No cow-ponies dozed in front of the saloon. Their riders were distant in ranch and camp. Human noise was extinct in Separ. Beneath the thunder of the sultry blasts the place lay dead in its flapping shroud of dust. "Why won't you tell me?" droned Billy. For some time he had been returning, like a mosquito brushed away.

"That's ten times," said Jessamine, promptly.

"Oh, goodness! Pretty soon I'll not be glad I came. I'm about twiced as less glad now."

"Well," said Jessamine, "there's a man coming to-day to mend the government telegraph line between Drybone and McKinney. Maybe he would take you back as far as Box Elder, if you want to go very much. Shall I ask him?"

Billy was disappointed at this cordial seconding of his mood. He did not make a direct rejoinder. "I guess I'll go outside now," said he, with a threat in his tone.

She continued mending his stockings. Finished ones lay rolled at one side of her chair, and upon the other were more waiting her attention.

"And I'm going to turn back handsprings on top of all the freight-cars," he stated, more loudly.

She indulged again in merriment, laughing sweetly at him, and without restraint.

"And I'm sick of what you all keep a-saying to me!" he shouted. "Just as if I was a baby."

"Why, Billy, who ever said you were a baby?"

"All of you do. Honey, and Lin, and you now, and everybody. What makes you say 'that's nine times, Billy, oh, Billy, that's ten times,' if you don't mean I'm a baby? And you laugh me off, just like they do, and just like I was a regular baby. You won't tell me—"

"Billy, listen. Did nobody ever ask you something you did not want to tell them?"

"That's not a bit the same, because—because—because I treat 'em square, and because it's not their business. But every time I ask anybody 'most anything, they say I'm not old enough to understand; and I'll be ten soon. And it is my business when it's about the kind of a mother

I'm a-going to have. Suppose I quit acting square, an' told 'em, when they bothered me, they weren't young enough to understand! Wish I had. Guess I will, too, and watch 'em step around." For a moment his mind dwelt upon this, and he whistled a revengeful strain.

"Goodness, Billy!" said Jessamine, at the sight of the next stocking. "The whole heel is scorched off."

He eyed the ruin with indifference. "Ah, that was last month, when I and Lin shot the bear in the swamp-willows. He made me dry off my legs. Chuck it away."

"And spoil the pair? No, indeed!"

"Mother always chucked 'em, an' father'd buy new ones, till I skipped from home. Lin kind o' mends 'em."

"Does he?" said Jessamine, softly. And she looked at the photograph.

"Yes. What made you write him for to let me come and bring my stockin's and things?"

"Don't you see, Billy, there is so little work at this station that I'd be looking out of the window all day just the pitiful way you do?"

"Oh!" Billy pondered. "And so I said to Lin," he continued, "why didn't he send down his own clothes, too, an' let you fix 'em all? And Honey Wiggin laughed right in his coffee-cup so it all sploshed out. And the cook he asked me if mother used to mend Lin's clothes. But I guess she chucked 'em, like she always did father's and mine. I was with father, you know, when mother was married to Lin that time." He paused again, while his thoughts and fears struggled. "But Lin says I needn't ever go back," he went on, reasoning and confiding to her. "Lin don't like mother any more, I guess." His pondering grew still deeper, and he looked at Jessamine for some while. Then his face wakened with a new theory. "Don't Lin like you any more?" he inquired.

"Oh," cried Jessamine, crimsoning, "yes! Why, he sent you to me!"

"Well, he got hot in camp when I said that about sending his clothes to you. He quit supper pretty soon, and went away off a-walking. And that's another time they said I was too young. But Lin don't come to see you any more."

"Why, I hope he loves me," murmured Jessamine. "Always."

"Well, I hope so too," said Billy, earnestly. "For I like you. When I seen him show you our cabin on Box Elder, and the room he had fixed for you, I was glad you were coming to be my mother. Mother used to be awful. I wouldn't 'a' minded her licking me if she'd done other things. Ah, pshaw! I wasn't going to stand that." Billy now came close to Jessamine. "I do wish you would come and live with me and Lin," said he. "Lin's awful nice."

"Don't I know it?" said Jessamine, tenderly.

"'Cause I heard you say you were going to marry him," went on Billy. "And I seen him kiss you and you let him that time we went away when you found out about mother. And you're not mad, and he's not, and nothing happens at all, all the same! Won't you tell me, please?"

Jessamine's eyes were glistening, and she took him in her lap. She was not going to tell him that he was too young this time. But whatever things she had shaped to say to the boy were never said.

Through the noise of the gale came the steadier sound of the train, and the girl rose quickly to preside over her ticket-office and duties behind the railing in the front room of the station. The boy ran to the window to watch the great event of Separ's day. The locomotive loomed out from the yellow clots of drift, paused at the water-tank, and then with steam and humming came slowly on by the platform. Slowly its long dust-choked train emerged trundling behind it, and ponderously halted. There was no one to go. No one came to buy a ticket of Jessamine. The conductor looked in on business, but she had no telegraphic orders for him. The express agent jumped off and looked in for pleasure. He received his daily smile and nod of friendly discouragement. Then the light bundle of mail was flung inside the door. Separ had no mail to go out. As she was picking up the letters, young Billy passed her like a shadow, and fled out. Two passengers had descended from the train, a man and a large woman. His clothes were loose and careless upon him. He held valises, and stood uncertainly looking about him in the storm. Her firm heavy body was closely dressed. In her hat was a large handsome feather. Along between the several cars brakemen leaned out, watched her, and grinned

to each other. But her big, hard-shining blue eyes were fixed curiously upon the station where Jessamine was.

"It's all night we may be here, is it?" she said to the man, harshly.

"How am I to help that?" he retorted.

"I'll help it. If this hotel's the sty it used to be, I'll walk to Tommy's. I've not saw him since I left Bear Creek."

She stalked into the hotel, while the man went slowly to the station. He entered, and found Jessamine behind her railing, sorting the slim mail.

"Good-evening," he said. "Excuse me. There was to be a wagon sent here."

"For the telegraph-mender? Yes, sir. It came Tuesday. You're to find the pole-wagon at Drybone."

This news was good, and all that he wished to know. He could drive out and escape a night at the Hotel Brunswick. But he lingered, because Jessamine spoke so pleasantly to him. He had heard of her also.

"Governor Barker has not been around here?" he said.

"Not yet, sir. We understand he is expected through on a hunting-trip."

"I suppose there is room for two and a trunk in that wagon?"

"I reckon so, sir." Jessamine glanced at the man, and he took himself out. Most men took themselves out if Jessamine so willed; and it was mostly achieved thus, in amity.

On the platform the man found his wife again.

"Then I needn't to walk to Tommy's," she said. "And we'll eat as we travel. But you'll wait till I'm through with her." She made a gesture toward the station.

"Why—why—what do you want with her? Don't you know who she is?"

"It was me told you who she was, James Lusk. You'll wait till I've been and asked her after Lin McLean's health, and till I've saw how the likes of her talks to the likes of me."

He made a feeble protest that this would do no one any good.

"Sew yourself up, James Lusk. If it has been your idea I come with yus clear from Laramie to watch yus plant telegraph poles in the sage-brush, why you're off. I 'ain't heard much o' Lin since the day he learned it was you and not him that was my husband. And I've come back in this country to have a look at my old friends—and" (she laughed loudly and nodded at the station) "my old friends' new friends!"

Thus ordered, the husband wandered away to find his wagon and the horse.

Jessamine, in the office, had finished her station duties and returned to her needle. She sat contemplating the scorched sock of Billy's, and heard a heavy step at the threshold. She turned, and there was the large woman with the feather quietly surveying her. The words which the stranger spoke then were usual enough for a beginning. But there was something of threat in the strong animal countenance, something of laughter ready to break out. Much beauty of its kind had evidently been in the face, and now, as substitute for what was gone, was the brag look of assertion that it was still all there. Many stranded travellers knocked at Jessamine's door, and now, as always, she offered the hospitalities of her neat abode, the only room in Separ fit for a woman. As she spoke, and the guest surveyed and listened, the door blew shut with a crash.

Outside in a shed, Billy had placed the wagon between himself and his father.

"How you have grown!" the man was saying; and he smiled. "Come, shake hands. I did not think to see you here."

"Dare you to touch me!" Billy screamed. "No, I'll never come with you. Lin says I needn't to."

The man passed his hand across his forehead, and leaned against the wheel. "Lord! Lord!" he muttered.

His son warily slid out of the shed and left him leaning there.

II.

Lin McLean, bachelor, sat out in front of his cabin, looking at a small bright pistol that lay in his hand. He held it tenderly, cherishing it, and did not cease slowly to polish it. Revery filled his eyes, and in his whole face was sadness unmasked, because only the animals were there to perceive his true feelings. Sunlight and waving shadows moved together upon the green of his pasture, cattle and horses loitered in the opens by the stream. Down Box Elder's course, its valley and golden-chimneyed bluffs widened away into the level and the blue of the greater valley. Upstream, the branches and shining quiet leaves entered the mountains where the rock chimneys narrowed to a gateway, a citadel of shafts and turrets, crimson and gold above the filmy emerald of the trees. Through there the road went up from the cottonwoods into the cool quaking-asps and pines, and so across the range and away to Separ. Along the ridge-pole of the new stable, two hundred yards downstream, sat McLean's turkeys, and cocks and hens walked in front of him here by his cabin and fenced garden. Slow smoke rose from the cabin's chimney into the air, in which were no sounds but the running water and the afternoon chirp of birds. Amid this framework of a home the cow-puncher sat, lonely, inattentive, polishing the treasured weapon as if it were not already long clean. His target stood some twenty steps in front of him— a small cottonwood-tree, its trunk chipped and honeycombed with bullets which he had fired into it each day for memory's sake. Presently he lifted the pistol and looked at its name—the word "Neighbor" engraved upon it.

"I wonder," said he aloud, "if she keeps the rust off mine?" Then he lifted it slowly to his lips and kissed the word "Neighbor."

The clank of wheels sounded on the road, and he put the pistol quickly down. Dreaminess vanished from his face. He looked around alertly, but no one had seen him. The clanking was still among the trees a little distance up Box Elder. It approached deliberately, while he watched for the vehicle to emerge upon the open where his cabin stood; and then they came, a man and a woman. At sight of her Mr. McLean half rose, but sat down again. Neither of them had noticed him, sitting as they were in silence and the drowsiness of a long drive. The man was weak-faced, with good looks sallowed by dissipation, and a vanquished glance of the eye. As the woman had stood on the platform at Separ, so she sat now, upright, bold, and massive. The brag of past beauty was a habit settled upon her stolid features. Both sat inattentive to each other and to everything around them. The wheels turned slowly and with a dry dead noise, the reins bellied loosely to the shafts, the horse's head hung low. So they drew close. Then the man saw McLean, and color came into his face and went away.

"Good-evening," said he, clearing his

throat. "We heard you was in cow-camp."

The cow-puncher noted how he tried to smile, and a freakish change crossed his own countenance. He nodded slightly, and stretched his legs out as he sat.

"You look natural," said the woman, familiarly.

"Seem to be fixed nice here," continued the man. "Hadn't heard of it. Well, we'll be going along. Glad to have seen you."

"Your wheel wants greasing," said McLean, briefly, his eye upon the man.

"Can't stop. I expect she'll last to Drybone. Good-evening."

"Stay to supper," said McLean, always seated on his chair.

"Can't stop, thank you. I expect we can last to Drybone." He twitched the reins.

McLean levelled a pistol at a chicken, and knocked off its head. "Better stay to supper," he suggested, very distinctly.

"It's business, I tell you. I've got to catch Governor Barker before he—"

The pistol cracked and a second chicken shuffled in the dust. "Better stay to supper," drawled McLean.

The man looked up at his wife.

"So yus need me!" she broke out. "'Ain't got heart enough in yer played-out body to stand up to a man. We'll eat here. Get down."

The husband stepped to the ground. "I didn't suppose you'd want—"

"Ho! want? What's Lin, or you, or anything to me? Help me out."

Both men came forward. She descended, leaning heavily upon each, her blue staring eyes fixed upon the cow-puncher.

"No, yus ain't changed," she said. "Same in your looks and same in your actions. Was you expecting you could scare me, you Lin McLean?"

"I just wanted chickens for supper," said he.

Mrs. Lusk gave a hard high laugh. "I'll eat 'em. It's not I that cares. As for—" She stopped. Her eye had fallen upon the pistol and the name "Neighbor." "As for you," she continued to Mr. Lusk, "don't you be standing dumb same as the horse."

"Better take him to the stable, Lusk," said McLean.

He picked the chickens up, showed the woman to the best chair in his room, and went into his kitchen to cook supper for three. He gave his guests no further attention, nor did either of them come in where he was, nor did the husband rejoin the wife. He walked slowly up and down in the air, and she sat by herself in the room. Lin's steps as he made ready round the stove and table, and Lusk's slow tread out in the setting sunlight, were the only sounds about the cabin. When the host looked into the door of the next room to announce that his meal was served, the woman sat in·her chair no longer, but stood with her back to him by a shelf. She gave a slight start at his summons, and replaced something. He saw that she had been examining "Neighbor," and his face hardened suddenly to fierceness as he looked at her; but he repeated quietly that she had better come in. Thus did the three sit down to their meal. Occasionally a word about handing some dish fell from one or other of them, but nothing more, until Lusk took out his watch and mentioned the hour.

"Yu've not ate especially hearty," said Lin, resting his arms upon the table.

"I'm going," asserted Lusk. "Governor Barker may start out. I've got my interests to look after."

"Why, sure," said Lin. "I can't hope you'll waste all your time on just me."

Lusk rose and looked at his wife. "It'll be ten now before we get to Drybone," said he. And he went down to the stable.

The woman sat still, pressing the crumbs of her bread. "I know you seen me," she said, without looking at him.

"Saw you when?"

"I knowed it. And I seen how you looked at me." She sat twisting and pressing the crumb. Sometimes it was round, sometimes it was a cube, now and then she flattened it to a disc. Mr. McLean seemed to have nothing that he wished to reply.

"If you claim that pistol is yourn," she said next, "I'll tell you I know better. If you ask me whose should it be if not yourn, I would not have to guess the name. She has talked to me, and me to her."

She was still looking away from him at the bread-crumb, or she could have seen that McLean's hand was trembling as he watched her, leaning on his arms.

"Oh yes, she was willing to talk to me!" The woman uttered another sudden laugh. "I knowed about her—all. Things get heard of in this world. Did not all about you and me come to her knowledge in its own good time, and it done and gone how many years? My! my! my!" Her voice grew slow and absent. She stopped for a moment, and then more rapidly resumed: "It had travelled around about you and her like it always will travel. It was known how you had asked her, and how she had told you she would have you, and then told you she would not when she learned about you and me. Folks that knowed yus and folks that never seen yus in their lives had to have their word about her facing you down you had another wife, though she knowed the truth about me being married to Lusk and him livin' the day you married me, and ten and twenty marriages could not have tied you and me up, no matter how honest you swore to no hind'rance. Folks said it was plain she did not want yus. It give me a queer feelin' to see that girl. It give me a wish to tell her to her face that she did not love yus and did not know love. Wait, wait, Lin! Yu' never hit me yet."

"No," said the cow-puncher. "Nor now. I'm not Lusk."

"Yu' looked so—so bad, Lin. I never seen yu' look so bad in old days. Wait, now, and I must tell it. I wished to laugh in her face and say, 'What do you know about love?' So I walked in. Lin, she does love yus!"

"Yes," breathed McLean.

"She was sittin' back in her room at Separ. Not the ticket-office, but—"

"I know," the cow-puncher said. His eyes were burning.

"It's snug, the way she has it. 'Good-afternoon,' I says. 'Is this Miss Jessamine Buckner?'"

At his sweetheart's name the glow in Lin's eyes seemed to quiver to a flash.

"And she spoke pleasant to me—pleasant and gay like. But a woman can tell sorrow in a woman's eyes. And she asked me would I rest in her room there, and what was my name. 'They tell me you claim to know it better than I do,' I says. 'They tell me you say it is Mrs. McLean.' She put her hand on her breast, and she keeps lookin' at me without never speaking. 'Maybe I am not so welcome now,' I says. 'One minute,' says she. 'Let me get used to it.' And she sat down.

"Lin, she is a square-lookin' girl. I'll say that for her.

"I never thought to sit down onced myself; I don't know why, but I kep'

a-standing, and I took in that room of hers. She had flowers and things around there, and I seen your picture standing on the table, and I seen your six-shooter right by it—and, oh, Lin, hadn't I knowed your face before ever she did, and that gun you used to let me shoot on Bear Creek? It took me that sudden! Why, it rushed over me so I spoke right out different from what I'd meant and what I had ready fixed up to say.

"'Why did you do it?' I says to her, while she was a-sitting. 'How could you act so, and you a woman?' She just sat, and her sad eyes made me madder at the idea of her. 'You have had real sorrow,' says I, 'if they report correct. You have knowed your share of death, and misery, and hard work, and all. Great God! ain't there things enough that come to yus uncalled-for and natural, but you must run around huntin' up more that was leavin' yus alone and givin' yus a chance? I knowed him onced. I knowed your Lin McLean. And when that was over, I knowed for the first time how men can be different.' I'm started, Lin, I'm started. Leave me go on, and when I'm through I'll quit. 'Some of 'em, anyway,' I says to her, 'has hearts and self-respect, and ain't hogs clean through.'

"'I know,' she says, thoughtful like.

"And at her whispering that way I gets madder.

"'You know!' I says then. 'What is it that you know? Do you know that you have hurt a good man's heart? For onced I hurt it myself, though different. And hurts in them kind of hearts stays. Some hearts is that luscious and pasty you can stab 'em and it closes up so yu'd never suspicion the place; but Lin McLean! Nor yet don't yus believe his is the kind that breaks—if any kind does that. You may sit till the gray hairs, and you may wall up your womanhood, but if a man has got manhood like him, he will never sit till the gray hairs. Grief over losin' the best will not stop him from searchin' for a second best after a while. He wants a home, and he has got a right to one,' says I to Miss Jessamine. 'You have not walled up Lin McLean,' I says to her. Wait, Lin, wait. Yus needn't to tell me that's a lie. I know a man thinks he's walled up for a while."

"She could have told you it was a lie," said the cow-puncher.

"She did not. 'Let him get a home,'

says she. 'I want him to be happy.'
'That flash in your eyes talks different,'
says I. 'Sure enough yus wants him to
be happy. Sure enough. But not happy along with Miss Second Best.'

"Lin, she looked at me that piercin'!

"And I goes on, for I was wound away
up. 'And he will be happy, too,' I says.
'Miss Second Best will have a talk with
him about your picture and little "Neighbor," which he'll not send back to yus,
because the hurt in his heart is there. And
he will keep 'em out of sight somewheres
after his talk with Miss Second Best.'
Lin, Lin, I laughed at them words of
mine, but I was that wound up I was
strange to myself. And she watchin' me
that way! And I says to her: 'Miss
Second Best will not be the crazy thing
to think I am any wife of his standing in
her way. He will tell her about me. He
will tell how onced he thought he was
solid married to me till Lusk came back;
and she will drop me out of sight along
with the rest that went nameless. They
was not oncomprehensible to you, was
they? You had learned something by
livin', I guess! And Lin—your Lin, not
mine, nor never mine in heart for a day
so deep as he's yourn right now—he has
been gay—gay as any I've knowed. Why,
look at that face of his! Could a boy
with a face like that help bein' gay? But
that don't touch what's the true Lin deep
down. Nor will his deep-down love for
you hinder him like it will hinder you.
Don't you know men and us is different
when it comes to passion? We're all one
thing then; but they ain't simple. They
keep along with lots of other things. I
can't make yus know, and I guess it takes
a woman like I have been to learn their
nature. But you did know he loved you,
and you sent him away, and you'll be
homeless in yer house when he has done
the right thing by himself and found another girl.'

"Lin, all the while I was talkin' all I
knowed to her without knowin' what I'd
be sayin' next, for it come that unexpected, she was lookin' at me with them steady
eyes. And all she says when I quit was,
'If I saw him I would tell him to find a
home.'"

"Didn't she tell yu' she'd made me
promise to keep away from seeing her?"
asked the cow-puncher.

Mrs. Lusk laughed. "Oh, you innocent!" said she.

"She said if I came she would leave
Separ," muttered McLean, brooding.

Again the large woman laughed out,
but more harshly.

"I have kept my promise," Lin continued.

"Keep it some more. Sit here rotting
in your chair till she goes away. Maybe
she's gone."

"What's that?" said Lin. But still
she only laughed harshly. "I could be
there by to-morrow night," he murmured. Then his face softened. "She would
never do such a thing!" he said to himself.

He had forgotten the woman at the
table. While she had told him matters
that concerned him he had listened eagerly. Now she was of no more interest
than she had been before her story was
begun. She looked at his eyes as he sat
thinking and dwelling upon his sweetheart. She looked at him, and a longing
welled up into her face. A certain youth
and heavy beauty relighted the features.

"You are the same, same Lin every-
ways," she said. "A woman is too many
for you still, Lin!" she whispered.

At her summons he looked up from his
revery.

"Lin, I would not have treated you
so."

The caress that filled her voice was
plain. His look met hers as he sat quite
still, his arms on the table. Then he took
his turn at laughing.

"You!" he said. "At least I've had
plenty of education in you."

"Lin, Lin, don't talk that brutal to me
to-day. If yus knowed how near I come
shooting myself with 'Neighbor.' That
would have been funny! I knowed yus
wanted to tear that pistol out of my hand
because it was hern. But yus never did
such things to me, fer there's a gentleman
in you somewheres, Lin. And yus didn't
never hit me, not even when you come to
know me well. And when I seen you
so unexpected again to-night, and you
just the same old Lin, scaring Lusk with
shooting them chickens, so comic and
splendid, I could 'a' just killed Lusk sittin' in the wagon. Say, Lin, what made
yus do that, anyway?"

"I can't hardly say," said the cow-
puncher. "Only noticing him so turruble anxious not to stop—well, a man acts
without thinking."

"You always did, Lin. You was always a comical genius. Lin, them were good times."

"Which times?"'

"You know. You can't tell me you have forgot."

"I have not forgot much. What's the sense in this?"

"Yus never loved me!" she exclaimed. "Shucks!"

"Lin, Lin, is it all over? You know yus loved me on Bear Creek. Say you did. Only say it was once that way." And as he sat, she came and put her arms round his neck. For a moment he did not move, letting himself be held; and then she kissed him. The plates crashed as he beat and struck her down upon the table. He was on his feet, cursing himself. As he went out of the door, she lay where she had fallen beneath his fist, looking after him and smiling.

McLean walked down Box Elder Creek through the trees towards the stable, where Lusk had gone to put the horse in the wagon. Once he leaned his hand against a big cottonwood, and stood still with half-closed eyes. Then he continued on his way. "Lusk!" he called presently, and in a few steps more, "Lusk!" Then, as he came slowly out of the trees to meet the husband, he began, with quiet evenness, "Your wife wants to know—" But he stopped. No husband was there. Wagon and horse were not there. The door was shut. The bewildered cowpuncher looked up the stream where the road went, and he looked down. Out of the sky where daylight and stars were faintly shining together sounded the long cries of the night-hawks as they sped and swooped to their hunting in the dusk. From among the trees by the stream floated a cooler air, and distant and close by sounded the plashing water. About the meadow where Lin stood, his horses fed, quietly crunching. He went to the door, looked in, and shut it again. He walked to his shed and stood contemplating his own wagon alone there. Then he lifted away a piece of trailing vine from the gate of the corral, while the turkeys moved their heads and watched him from the roof. A rope was hanging from the corral, and seeing it, he dropped the vine. He opened the corral gate, and walked quickly back into the middle of the field, where the horses saw him and his rope, and scattered. But he ran and herded them, whirling the rope, and so

drove them into the corral, and flung his noose over two. He dragged two saddles — men's saddles — from the stable, and next he was again at his cabin door with the horses saddled. She was sitting quite still by the table where she had sat during the meal, nor did she speak or move when she saw him look in at the door.

"Lusk has gone," said he. "I don't know what he expected you would do. Or I would do. But we will catch him before he gets to Drybone."

She looked at him with her dumb stare. "Gone?" she said.

"Get up and ride," said McLean. "You are going to Drybone."

"Drybone," she echoed. Her voice was toneless and dull.

He made no more explanations to her, but went quickly about the cabin. Soon he had set it in order, the dishes on their shelves, the table clean, the fire in the stove arranged; and all these movements she followed with a sort of blank mechanical patience. He made a small bundle for his own journey, tied it behind his saddle, brought her horse beside a stump. When at his sharp order she came out, he locked his cabin and hung the key by a window, where travellers could find it and be at home.

She stood looking where her husband had slunk off. Then she laughed. "It's about his size," she murmured.

Her old lover helped her in silence to mount into the man's saddle—this they had often done together in former years —and so they took their way down the silent road. They had not many miles to go, and after the first two lay behind them, when the horses were limbered and had been put to a canter, they made time quickly. They had soon passed out of the trees and pastures of Box Elder and among the vast low stretches of the greater valley. Not even by day was the river's course often discernible through the ridges and cheating sameness of this wilderness; and beneath this half-darkness of stars and a quarter-moon the sage spread shapeless to the looming mountains, or to nothing.

"I will ask you one thing," said Lin, after ten miles.

The woman made no sign of attention as she rode beside him.

"Did I understand that she — Miss Buckner, I mean—mentioned she might be going away from Separ?"

"How do I know what you understood?"

"I thought you said—"

"Don't you bother me, Lin McLean." Her laugh rang out, loud and forlorn— one brief burst that startled the horses and that must have sounded far across the sage-brush. "You men are rich," she said.

They rode on, side by side, and saying nothing after that. The Drybone road was a broad trail, a worn strip of bareness going onward over the endless shelvings of the plain, visible even in this light; and presently, moving upon its grayness on a hill in front of them, they made out the wagon. They hastened and overtook it.

"Put your carbine down," said McLean to Lusk. "It's not robbers. It's your wife I'm bringing you." He spoke very quietly.

The husband addressed no word to the cow-puncher. "Get in, then," he said to his wife.

"Town's not far now," said Lin. "Maybe you would prefer riding the balance of the way?"

"I'd—" But the note of pity that she felt in McLean's question overcame her, and her utterance choked. She nodded her head, and the three continued slowly climbing the hill together.

From the narrows of the steep, sandy, weather-beaten banks that the road slanted upward through for a while, they came out again upon the immensity of the table-land. Here, abruptly, like an ambush, was the whole unsuspected river close below to their right, as if it had emerged from the earth. With a circling sweep from somewhere out in the gloom it cut in close to the lofty mesa beneath tall clean-graded descents of sand, smooth as a railroad embankment. As they paused on the level to breathe their horses, the wet gulp of its eddies rose to them through the stillness. Upstream they could make out the light of the Drybone bridge, but not the bridge itself; and two lights on the further bank showed where stood the hog-ranch opposite Drybone. They went on over the table-land, and reached the next herald of the town, Drybone's chief historian, the graveyard. Beneath its slanting head-boards and wind-shifted sand lay many more people than lived in Drybone. They passed by the fence of this shelterless acre on the hill and shoutings and high music began to reach them.

At the foot of the hill they saw the sparse lights and shapes of the town where ended the gray stripe of road. The many sounds, feet, voices, and music, grew clearer, unravelling from their muffled confusion, and the fiddling became a tune that could be known.

"There's a dance to-night," said the wife to the husband. "Hurry."

He drove as he had been driving. Perhaps he had not heard her.

"I'm telling you to hurry," she repeated. "My new dress is in that wagon. There'll be folks to welcome me here that's older friends than you."

She put her horse to a gallop down the broad road toward the music and the older friends. The husband spoke to his horse, cleared his throat and spoke louder, cleared his throat again, and this time his sullen voice carried, and the animal started. So Lusk went ahead of Lin McLean, following his wife with the new dress at as good a pace as he might. If he did not want her company, perhaps to be alone with the cow-puncher was still less to his mind.

"It ain't only her he's stopped caring for," mused Lin, as he rode slowly along. "He don't care for himself any more."

III.

To-day, Drybone has altogether returned to the dust. Even in that day its hour could have been heard beginning to sound, but its inhabitants were rather deaf. Gamblers, saloon-keepers, murderers, outlaws, male and female, all were so busy with their cards, their lovers, and their bottles as to make the place seem young and vigorous; but it was second childhood which had set in.

Drybone had known a wholesome adventurous youth, where manly lives and deaths were plenty. It had been an army post. It had seen horse and foot, and heard the trumpet. Brave wives had kept house for their captains upon its bluffs. Winter and summer they had made the best of it. When the War Department ordered the captains to catch Indians, the wives bade them God-speed. When the Interior Department ordered the captains to let the Indians go again, still they made the best of it. You must not waste Indians. Indians were a source of revenue to so many people in Washington and elsewhere. But the process of catching Indians armed with weapons sold them by friends of the Interior Department, was not entirely harmless. Therefore there came to be graves in the Drybone graveyard. The pale weather-washed head-boards told all about it: "Sacred to the memory of Private So-and-So, killed on the Dry Cheyenne, May 6, 1875." Or it would be, "Mrs. So-and-So, found scalped on Sage Creek." But even the financiers at Washington could not wholly preserve the Indian in Drybone's neighborhood. As the cattle by ten thousands came treading with the next step of civilization into this huge domain, the soldiers were taken away. Some of them went west to fight more Indians in Idaho, Oregon, or Arizona. The battles of the others being done, they went east in better coffins to sleep where their mothers or their comrades wanted them. Though wind and rain wrought changes upon the hill, the ready-made graves and boxes which these soldiers left behind proved heirlooms as serviceable in their way as were the tenements that the living had bequeathed to Drybone. Into these empty barracks came to dwell and to do business every joy that made the cow-puncher's holiday, and every hunted person who was baffling the sheriff. For the sheriff must stop outside the line of Drybone, as shall presently be made clear. The captain's quarters were a saloon now; professional cards were going in the adjutant's office night and day; and the commissary building made a good dance-hall and hotel. Instead of guard-mounting, you would see a horse-race on the parade-ground, and there was no provost-sergeant to gather up the broken bottles and old boots. Heaps of these choked the rusty fountain. In the tufts of yellow ragged grass that dotted the place plentifully were lodged many aces and queens and ten-spots, which the Drybone wind had blown wide from the doors out of which they had been thrown when a new pack was called for inside. Among the grass tufts would lie visitors who had applied for beds too late at the dance-hall, frankly sleeping their whiskey off in the morning air.

Above on the hill, the graveyard quietly chronicled this new epoch of Drybone. So-and-So was seldom killed very far out of town, and of course scalping had disappeared. "Sacred to the memory of Four-Ace Johnston, accidently shot, Sep. 4, 1885." Perhaps one is still there unal-

tered: "Sacred to the memory of Mrs. Ryan's babe. Aged two months." This unique corpse had succeeded in dying with its boots off.

But a succession of graves was not always needed to read the changing tale of the place, and how people died there; one grave would often be enough. The soldiers, of course, had kept treeless Drybone supplied with wood. But in these latter days wood was very scarce. None grew nearer than twenty or thirty miles—none, that is, to make boards of a sufficient width for epitaphs. And twenty miles was naturally far to go to hew a board for a man of whom you knew perhaps nothing but what he said his name was, and to whom you owed nothing, perhaps, but a trifling poker debt. Hence it came to pass that head-boards grew into a sort of directory. They were light to lift from one place to another. A single coat of white paint would wipe out the first tenant's name sufficiently to paint over it the next comer's. By this thrifty habit the original boards belonging to the soldiers could go round, keeping pace with the new civilian population; and though at first sight you might be puzzled by the layers of names still visible beneath the white paint, you could be sure that the clearest and blackest was the one to which the present tenant had answered.

So there on the hill lay the graveyard, steadily writing Drybone's history; and making that history lay the town at the bottom—one thin line of houses framing three sides of the old parade-ground. In these slowly rotting shells people rioted, believing the golden age was here, the age when everybody should have money and nobody should be arrested. For Drybone soil, you see, was still government soil, not yet handed over to Wyoming; and only government could arrest there, and only for government crimes. But government had gone, and seldom worried Drybone. The spot was a postage-stamp of sanctuary pasted in the middle of Wyoming's big map, a paradise for the Four-Ace Johnstons. Only, you must not steal a horse. That was really wicked, and brought you instantly to the notice of Drybone's one official—the coroner. For they did keep a coroner—Judge Slaghammer. He was perfectly illegal, and lived next door in Albany County. But that county paid him fees and mileage to keep tally of

Drybone's casualties. His wife owned the dance-hall, and between their industries they made out a living. And all the citizens made out a living. The happy cow-punchers on ranches far and near still earned and instantly spent the high wages still paid them. With their bodies full of youth and their pockets full of gold, they rode into town by twenties, by fifties, and out again next morning, penniless always and happy. And then the Four-Ace Johnstons would sit card-playing with each other till the innocents should come to town again.

To-night the innocents had certainly come to town, and Drybone was furnishing to them all its joys. Their many horses stood tied at every post and corner—patient, experienced cow-ponies, well knowing it was an all-night affair. The talk and laughter of the riders was in the saloons; they leaned joking over the bars, they sat behind their cards at the tables, they strolled to the post-trader's to buy presents for their easy sweethearts, their boots were keeping audible time with the fiddle at Mrs. Slaghammer's. From the multitude and vigor of the sounds there, the dance was being done regularly. "Regularly" meant that upon the conclusion of each set the gentleman led his lady to the bar and invited her to choose; and it was also regular that the lady should choose. Beer and whiskey were the alternatives.

Lin McLean's horse took him across the square without guiding from the cow-puncher, who sat absently with his hands folded upon the horn of his saddle. This horse, too, was patient and experienced, and could not know what remote thoughts filled his master's mind. He looked around to see why his master did not get off lightly, as he had done during so many gallant years, and hasten in to the conviviality. But the lonely cow-puncher sat mechanically identifying the horses of acquaintances.

"Toothpick Kid is here," said he, "and Limber Jim, and the Doughie. You'd think he'd stay away after the trouble he— I expect that pinto is Jerky Bill's."

"Go home!" said a hearty voice.

McLean eagerly turned. For the moment his face lighted from its sombreness. "I'd forgot you'd be here," said he. And he sprang to the ground. "It's fine to see you."

"Go home!" repeated the Governor of Wyoming, shaking his ancient friend's hand. "You in Drybone to-night, and claim you're reformed? Fie!"

"Yu' seem to be on hand yourself," said the cow-puncher, bracing to be jocular, if he could.

"Me! I've gone fishing. Don't you read the papers? If we poor Governors can't lock up the State House and take a whirl now and then—"

"Doc," interrupted Lin, "it's plumb fine to see yu'!" Again he shook hands.

"Why, yes! we've met here before, you and I." His Excellency the Hon. Amory W. Barker, M. D., stood laughing, familiar and genial, his sound white teeth shining. But behind his round spectacles he scrutinized McLean. For in this second hand-shaking was a fervor that seemed a grasp, a reaching out, for comfort. Barker had passed through Separ. Though an older acquaintance than Billy, he had asked Jessamine fewer and different questions. But he knew what he knew. "Well, Drybone's the same old Drybone," said he. "Sweet-scented hole of iniquity! Let's see how you walk nowadays."

Lin took a few steps.

"Pooh! I said you'd never get over it." And his Excellency beamed with professional pride. In his doctor days Barker had set the boy McLean's leg; and before it was properly knit the boy had escaped from the hospital to revel loose in Drybone on such another night as this. Soon he had been carried back, with the fracture split open again.

"It shows, does it?" said Lin. "Well, it don't usually. Not except when I'm —when I'm—"

"Down?" suggested his Excellency.

"Yes, Doc. Down," the cow-puncher confessed.

Barker looked into his friend's clear hazel eyes. Beneath their dauntless sparkle was something that touched the Governor's good heart. "I've got some whiskey along on the trip — Eastern whiskey," said he. "Come over to my room awhile."

"I used to sleep all night onced," said McLean, as they went. "Then I come to know different. But I'd never have believed just mere thoughts could make yu'—make yu' feel like the steam was only half on.—I eat, yu' know!" he stated suddenly. "And I expect one or two in camp lately have not found my muscle lacking. Feel me, Doc."

Barker dutifully obeyed, and praised the excellent sinews.

Across from the dance-hall the whining of the fiddle came, high and gay; feet blurred the talk of voices, and voices rose above the trampling of feet. Here and there some lurking form stumbled through the dark among the rubbish; and, clearest sound of all, the light crack of billiard-balls reached dry and far into the night. Barker contemplated the stars and calm splendid dimness of the plain. "'Though every prospect pleases, and only man is vile,'" he quoted. "But don't tell the Republican party I said so."

"It's awful true, though, Doc. I'm vile myself. Yu' don't know. Why, I didn't know!"

And then they sat down to confidences and whiskey; for so long as the world goes round a man must talk to a man sometimes, and both must drink over it. The cow-puncher unburdened himself to the Governor; and the Governor filled up his friend's glass with the Eastern whiskey, and nodded his spectacles, and listened, and advised, and said he should have done the same, and like the good Governor that he was, never remembered he was Governor at all with political friends here who had begged a word or two. He became just Dr. Barker again, the young hospital surgeon (the hospital that now stood a ruin), and Lin was again his patient — Lin, the sunburnt free lance of nineteen, reckless, engaging, disobedient, his leg broken and his heart light, with no Jessamine or conscience to rob his salt of its savor. While he now told his troubles, the quadrilles fiddled away careless as ever, and the crack of the billiard-balls sounded as of old.

"Nobody has told you about this, I expect," said the lover. He brought forth the little pistol, "Neighbor." He did not hand it across to Barker, but walked over to Barker's chair, and stood holding it for the doctor to see. When Barker reached for it to see better, since it was half hidden in the cow-puncher's big hand, Lin yielded it to him, but still stood and soon drew it back. "I take it around," he said, "and when one of those stories comes along, like there's plenty of, that she wants to get rid of me, I just kind o' take a look at 'Neighbor' when I'm off where it's handy, and it

busts the story right out of my mind. I have to tell you what a fool I am."

"The whiskey's your side," said Barker. "Go on."

"But, Doc, my courage has quit me. They see what I'm thinking about just like I was a tenderfoot trying his first bluff. I can't stick it out no more, and I'm going to see her, come what will. I've got to. I'm going to ride right up to her window and shoot off 'Neighbor,' and if she don't come out I'll know—"

A knocking came at the Governor's room, and Judge Slaghammer entered. "Not been to our dance, Governor?" said he.

The Governor thought that perhaps he was tired, that perhaps this evening he must forego the pleasure.

"It may be wiser. In your position it may be advisable," said the coroner. "They're getting on rollers over there. We do not like trouble in Drybone, but trouble comes to us—as everywhere."

"Shooting," suggested his Excellency, recalling his hospital practice.

"Well, Governor, you know how it is. Our boys are as big-hearted as any in this big-hearted Western country. You know, Governor. Those generous, warm-blooded spirits are ever ready for anything."

"Especially after Mrs. Slaghammer's whiskey," remarked the Governor.

The coroner shot a shrewd eye at Wyoming's chief executive. It was not politically harmonious to be reminded that but for his wife's liquor a number of fine young men, with nothing save youth untrained and health the matter with them, would to-day be riding their horses instead of sleeping on the hill. But the coroner wanted support in the next campaign. "Boys will be boys," said he. "They 'ain't pulled any guns to-night. But I come away, though. Some of 'em's making up pretty free to Mrs. Lusk. It ain't suitable for me to see too much. Lusk says he's after you," he mentioned incidentally to Lin. "He's fillin' up, and says he's after you." McLean nodded placidly, and with scant politeness. He wished this visitor would go. But Judge Slaghammer had noticed the whiskey. He filled himself a glass. "Governor, it has my compliments," said he. "Ambrosier. Honey-doo."

"Mrs. Slaghammer seems to have a large gathering," said Barker.

"Good boys, good boys!" The judge

blew importantly, and waved his arm. "Bull - whackers, cow - punchers, mule-skinners, tin horns. All spending generous. Governor, once more! Ambrosier. Honey-doo." He settled himself deep in a chair, and closed his eyes.

McLean rose abruptly. "Good-night," said he. "I'm going to Separ."

"Separ!" exclaimed Slaghammer, rousing slightly. "Oh, stay with us, stay with us." He closed his eyes again, but sustained his smile of office.

"You know how well I wish you," said Barker to Lin. "I'll just see you start."

Forthwith the friends left the coroner quiet beside his glass, and walked toward the horses through Drybone's gaping quadrangle. The dead ruins loomed among the lights of the card-halls, and always the keen jockey cadences of the fiddle sang across the night. But a calling and confusion were set up, and the tune broke off.

"Just like old times!" said his Excellency. "Where's the dump pile?" It was where it should be, close by, and the two stepped behind it to be screened from wandering bullets. "A man don't forget his habits," declared the Governor. "Makes me feel young again."

"Makes me feel old," said McLean. "Hark!"

"Sounds like my name," said Barker. They listened. "Oh yes. Of course. That's it. They're shouting for the doctor. But we'll just spare them a minute or so to finish their excitement."

"I didn't hear any shooting," said McLean. "It's something, though."

As they waited, no shots came; but still the fiddle was silent, and the murmur of many voices grew in the dance-hall, while single voices wandered outside, calling the doctor's name.

"I'm the Governor on a fishing-trip," said he. "But it's to be done, I suppose."

They left their dump hill and proceeded over to the dance. The musician sat high and solitary upon two starch-boxes, fiddle on knee, staring and waiting. Half the floor was bare; on the other half the revellers were densely clotted. At the crowd's outer rim the young horsemen, flushed and swaying, retained their gaudy dance partners strongly by the waist, to be ready when the music should resume. "What is it?" they asked. "Who is it?"

And they looked in across heads and shoulders, inattentive to the caresses which the partners gave them.

Mrs. Lusk was who it was, and she had taken poison here in their midst, after many dances and drinks.

"Here's Doc!" cried an older one.

"Here's Doc!" chorussed the young blood that had come into this country since his day. And the throng caught up the words. "Here's Doc! here's Doc!"

In a moment McLean and Barker were sundered from each other in this flood. Barker, sucked in toward the centre, but often eddied back by those who meant to help him, heard the mixed explanations pass his ear unfinished—versions, contradictions, a score of facts. It had been wolf-poison. It had been rat-poison. It had been something in a bottle. There was little steering in this clamorous sea; but Barker reached his patient, where she sat in her new dress, hailing him with wild inebriate gayety.

"I must get her to her room, friends," said he.

"He must get her to her room," went the word. "Leave Doc get her to her room." And they tangled in their eagerness around him and his patient.

"Give us 'Buffalo Girls!'" shouted Mrs. Lusk. "'Buffalo Girls,' you fiddler!"

"We'll come back," said Barker to her.

"'Buffalo Girls,' I tell yus. Ho! there's no sense in looking at that bottle, Doc. Take yer dance while there's time!" She was holding the chair.

"Help him!" said the crowd. "Help Doc."

They took her from her chair, and she fought, a big pink mass of ribbons, fluttering and wrenching itself among them.

"She has six ounces of laudanum in her," Barker told them, at the top of his voice. "It won't wait all night."

"I'm a whirlwind!" said Mrs. Lusk. "That's my game! And you done your share," she cried to the fiddler. "Here's my regards, old man! 'Buffalo Girls' once more!"

She flung out her hand, and from it fell notes and coins, rolling and ringing around the starch-boxes. Some dragged her on, while some fiercely forbade the musician to touch the money, because it was hers, and she would want it when she came to. Thus they gathered it up for her. But now she had sunk down,

asking in a new voice where was Lin
McLean. And when one grinning intimate reminded her that Lusk had gone
to shoot him, she laughed out richly, and
the crowd joined in her mirth. But even
in the midst of the joke she asked again
in the same voice where was Lin McLean.
He came beside her among more jokes.
He had kept himself near, and now at
sight of him she reached out and held
him. "Tell them to leave me go to sleep,
Lin," said she.

Barker saw a chance. "Persuade her
to come along," said he to McLean.
"Minutes are counting now."

"Oh, I'll come," she said, with a laugh,
overhearing him, and holding still to Lin.

The rest of the old friends nudged each
other. "Back seats for us," they said.
"But we've had our turn in front ones."
Then, thinking they would be useful in
encouraging her to walk, they clustered
again, rendering Barker and McLean once
more wellnigh helpless. Clumsily the escort made its slow way across the quadrangle, cautioning itself about stones and
holes. Thus, presently, she was brought
into the room. The escort set her down,
crowding the little place as thick as it
would hold; the rest gathered thick at
the door, and all of them had no thought
of departing. The notion to stay was plain
on their faces.

Barker surveyed them. "Give the doctor a show now, boys," said he. "You've
done it all so far. Don't crowd my elbows. I'll want you," he whispered to
McLean.

At the argument of fair play, obedience
swept over them like a veering of wind.
"Don't crowd his elbows," they began to
say at once, and told each other to come
away. "We'll sure give the Doc room.
You don't want to be shovin' your auger
in, Chalkeye. You want to get yourself
pretty near absent." The room thinned
of them forthwith. "Fix her up good,
Doc," they said, over their shoulders.
They shuffled across the threshold and
porch with roundabout schemes to tread
quietly. When one or other stumbled
on the steps and fell, he was jerked to his
feet. "You want to tame yourself," was
the word. Then suddenly Chalkeye and
Toothpick Kid came precipitately back.
"Her cash," they said. And leaving the
notes and coins, they hastened to catch
their comrades on the way back to the
dance.

"I want you," repeated Barker to Mc-
Lean.

"Him!" cried Mrs. Lusk, flashing alert
again. "Jessamine wants him about now,
I guess. Don't keep him from his girl!"
And she laughed her hard, rich laugh,
looking from one to the other. "Not the
two of yus can't save me," she stated, defiantly. But even in these last words a
sort of thickness sounded.

"Walk her up and down," said Barker.
"Keep her moving. I'll look what I can
find. Keep her moving brisk." At once
he was out of the door; and before his
running steps had died away, the fiddle
had taken up its tune across the quadrangle.

"'Buffalo Girls!'" exclaimed the woman. "Old times! Old times!"

"Come," said McLean. "Walk." And
he took her.

Her head was full of the music. Forgetting all but that, she went with him
easily, and the two made their first turns
around the room. Whenever he brought
her near the entrance, she leaned away
from him toward the open door, where
the old fiddle tune was coming in from
the dark. But presently she noticed that
she was being led, and her face turned
sullen.

"Walk," said McLean.

"Do you think so?" said she, laughing. But she found that she must go
with him. Thus they took a few more
turns.

"You're hurting me," she said next.
Then a look of drowsy cunning filled her
eyes, and she fixed them upon McLean's
dogged face. "He's gone, Lin," she murmured, raising her hand where Barker
had disappeared.

She knew McLean had heard her, and
she held back on the quickened pace that
he had set.

"Leave me down. You hurt," she
pleaded, hanging on him.

The cow-puncher put forth more
strength.

"Just the floor," she pleaded again.
"Just one minute on the floor. He'll
think you could not keep me lifted."

Still McLean made no answer, but
steadily led her round and round, as he
had undertaken.

"He's playing out!" she exclaimed.
"You'll be played out soon!" She laughed herself half awake. The man drew a
breath, and she laughed more to feel his

hand and arm strain to surmount her increasing resistance. "Jessamine!" she whispered to him. "Jessamine! Doc'll never suspicion you, Lin."

"Talk sense," said he.

"It's sense I'm talking. Leave me go to sleep. Ah, ah, I'm going! I'll go; you can't—"

"Walk! walk!" he repeated. He looked at the door. An ache was numbing his arms.

"Oh, yes, walk! What can you and all your muscle— Ah, walk me to glory then, craziness! I'm going; I'll go. I'm quitting this outfit for keeps. Lin, you're awful handsome to-night! I'll bet—I'll bet she has never seen you look so. Let me — let me watch yus. Anyway, she knows I came first!"

He grasped her savagely. "First! You and twenty of yu' don't— God! what do I talk to her for?"

"Because—because—I'm going; I'll go. He slung me off—but he had to sling— You can't—stop—"

Her head was rolling, while the lips smiled. Her words came through deeper and deeper veils, fearless, defiant, a challenge inarticulate, a continuous mutter. Again he looked at the door as he struggled to move with her dragging weight. The drops rolled on his forehead and neck, his shirt was wet, his hands slipped upon her ribbons. Suddenly the drugged body folded and sank with him, pulling him to his knees. While he took breath so, the mutter went on, and through the door came the jigging fiddle. A fire of desperation lighted in his eyes. "'Buffalo Girls!'" he shouted hoarsely in her ear, and got once more on his feet with her. Still shouting at her to wake, he struck a tottering sort of step, and so, with the bending load in his grip, strove feebly to dance the laudanum away.

Feet stumbled across the porch, and Lusk was in the room. "So I've got you!" he said. He had no weapon, but made a dive under the bed and came up with a carbine. The two men locked, wrenching impotently, and fell together. The carbine's loud shot rang in the room, but did no harm; and McLean lay sick and panting upon Lusk as Barker rushed in.

"Thank God!" said he, and flung Lusk's pistol down. The man, deranged and encouraged by drink, had come across the doctor, delayed him, threatened him with his pistol, and when he had torn it away, had left him suddenly and vanished. But Barker had feared, and come after him here. He glanced at the woman slumbering motionless beside the two men. The husband's brief courage had gone, and he lay beneath McLean, who himself could not rise. Barker pulled them apart.

"Lin, boy, you're not hurt?" he asked, affectionately, and lifted the cow-puncher.

McLean sat passive, with dazed eyes, letting himself be supported.

"You're not hurt?" repeated Barker.

"No," answered the cow-puncher, slowly. "I guess not." He looked about the room and at the door. "I got interrupted," he said.

"You'll be all right soon," said Barker.

"Nobody cares for me!" cried Lusk, suddenly, and took to querulous weeping.

"Get up," ordered Barker, sternly.

"Don't accuse me, Governor," screamed Lusk. "I'm innocent." And he rose.

Barker looked at the woman and then at the husband. "I'll not say there was much chance for her," he said. "But any she had is gone through you. She'll die."

"Nobody cares for me!" repeated the man. "He has learned my boy to scorn me." He ran out aimlessly, and away into the night, leaving peace in the room.

"Stay sitting," said Barker to McLean, and went to Mrs. Lusk.

But the cow-puncher, seeing him begin to lift her toward the bed without help, tried to rise. His strength was not sufficiently come back, and he sank as he had been. "I guess I don't amount to much," said he. "I feel like I was nothing."

"Well, I'm something," said Barker, coming back to his friend, out of breath. "And I know what she weighs." He stared admiringly through his spectacles at the seated man.

The cow-puncher's eyes slowly travelled over his body, and then sought Barker's face. "Doc," said he, "ain't I young to have my nerve quit me this way?"

His Excellency broke into his broad smile.

"I know I've racketed some, but ain't it rather early?" pursued McLean, wistfully.

"You six-foot infant!" said Barker. "Look at your hand."

Lin stared at it—the fingers quivering and bloody, and the skin grooved raw between them. That was the buckle of her belt, which in the struggle had worked round and been held by him unknowingly. Both his wrists and his shirt were ribbed with the pink of her sashes. He looked over at the bed where lay the woman heavily breathing. It was a something, a sound, not like the breath of life; and Barker saw the cow-puncher shudder.

"She is strong," he said. "Her system will fight to the end. Two hours yet, maybe. Queer world!" he moralized. "People half killing themselves to keep one in it who wanted to go—and one that nobody wanted to stay!"

McLean did not hear. He was musing, his eyes fixed absently in front of him. "I would not want," he said, "I'd not wish for even my enemy to have a thing like what I've had to do to-night."

Barker touched him on the arm. "If there had been another man I could trust—"

"Trust!" broke in the cow-puncher. "Why, Doc, it is the best turn yu' ever done me. I know I am a man now—if my nerve ain't gone."

"I've known you were a man since I knew you!" said the hearty Governor. And he helped the still unsteady six-foot to a chair. "As for your nerve, I'll bring you some whiskey now. And after"— he glanced at the bed—"and to-morrow you'll go try if Miss Jessamine won't put the nerve—"

"Yes, Doc, I'll go there, I know. But don't yu'—don't let's while she's— I'm goin' to be glad about this, Doc, after a while, but—"

At the sight of a new-comer in the door he stopped in what his soul was stammering to say. "What do you want, Judge?" he inquired, coldly.

"I understand," began Slaghammer to Barker—"I am informed—"

"Speak quieter, Judge," said the cow-puncher.

"I understand," repeated Slaghammer, more official than ever, "that there was a case for the coroner."

"You'll be notified," put in McLean again. "Meanwhile you'll talk quiet in this room."

Slaghammer turned, and saw the breathing mass on the bed.

"You are a little early, Judge," said Barker, "but—"

"But your ten dollars are safe," said McLean.

The coroner shot one of his shrewd glances at the cow-puncher, and sat down with an amiable countenance. His fee was, indeed, ten dollars; and he was desirous of a second term.

"Under the apprehension that it had already occurred—the misapprehension—I took steps to impanel a jury," said he, addressing both Barker and McLean. "They are—ah—waiting outside. Responsible men, Governor, and have sat before. Drybone has few responsible men to-night, but I procured these at a little game where they were—ah—losing. You may go back, gentlemen," said he, going to the door. "I will summon you in proper time." He looked in the room again. "Is the husband not intending—"

"That's enough, Judge," said McLean. "There's too many here without adding him."

"Judge," spoke a voice at the door, "ain't she ready yet?"

"She is still passing away," observed Slaghammer, piously.

"Because I was thinking," said the man—"I was just— You see us jury is dry and dead broke. Doggonedest cards I've held this year, and—Judge, would there be anything out of the way in me touching my fee in advance, if it's a sure thing?"

"I see none, my friend," said Slaghammer, benevolently, "since it must be." He shook his head and nodded it by turns. Then, with full-blown importance, he sat again, and wrote a paper, his coroner's certificate. Next door in Albany County these vouchers brought their face value of five dollars to the holder; but on Drybone's neutral soil the saloons would always pay four for them, and it was rare that any juryman could withstand the temptation of four immediate dollars. This one gratefully received his paper, and, cherishing it like a bird in the hand, he with his colleagues bore it where they might wait for duty and slake their thirst.

In the silent room sat Lin McLean, his body coming to life more readily than his shaken spirit. Barker, seeing that the cow-puncher meant to watch until the end, brought the whiskey to him. Slaghammer drew documents from his pocket to fill the time, but was soon in slumber over them. In all precincts of the quadrangle Drybone was keeping it up late. The fiddle, the occasional shouts, and the crack of the billiard-balls travelled clear and far through the vast darkness outside. Presently steps unsteadily drew near, and round the corner of the door a voice, plaintive and diffident, said, "Judge, ain't she 'most pretty near ready?"

"Wake up, Judge!" said Barker. "Your jury has gone dry again."

The man appeared round the door—a handsome, dishevelled fellow—with hat in hand, balancing himself with respectful anxiety. There was a second voucher made out, and the messenger strayed back happy to his friends. Barker and McLean sat wakeful, and Slaghammer fell at once to napping. From time to time he was roused by new messengers, each arriving more unsteady than the last, until every juryman had got his fee and no more messengers came. The coroner slept undisturbed in his chair. McLean and Barker sat. On the bed the mass, with its pink ribbons, breathed and breathed, while moths flew round the lamp, tapping and falling with light sounds. So did the heart of the darkness wear itself away, and through the stone-cold air the dawn began to filter and expand.

Barker rose, bent over the bed, and then stood. Seeing him, McLean stood also.

"Judge," said Barker, quietly, "you may call them now." And with careful steps the Judge got himself out of the room to summon his jury.

For a short while the cow-puncher stood looking down upon the woman. She lay lumped in her gaudiness, the ribbons stained by the laudanum; but into the stolid, bold features death had called up the faint-colored ghost of youth, and McLean remembered all his Bear Creek days. "Hindsight is a turrible clear way o' seein' things," said he. "I think I'll take a walk."

"Go," said Barker. "The jury only need me, and I'll join you."

But the jury needed no witness. Their long waiting and the advance pay had been too much for these responsible men. Like brothers they had shared each others' vouchers until responsibility had melted from their brains and the whiskey was finished. Then, no longer entertained, and growing weary of Drybone, they had remembered nothing but their distant beds. Each had mounted his pony, holding trustingly to the saddle, and thus, unguided, the experienced ponies had taken them right. Across the wide sage-brush and up and down the river they were now asleep or riding, dispersed irrevocably. But the coroner was here. He duly received Barker's testimony, brought his verdict in, and signed it, and even while he was issuing to himself his own proper voucher for ten dollars came Chalkeye and Toothpick Kid on their ponies, galloping, eager in their hopes and good wishes for Mrs. Lusk. Life ran strong in them both. The night had gone well with them. Here was the new day going to be fine. It must be well with everybody.

"You don't say!" they exclaimed, taken aback. "Too bad."

They sat still in their saddles, and upon their reckless, kindly faces thought paused for a moment. "Her gone!" they murmured. "Hard to get used to the idea. What's anybody doing about the coffin?"

"Mr. Lusk," answered Slaghammer, "doubtless—"

"Lusk! He'll not know anything this forenoon. He's out there in the grass. She didn't think nothing of him. Tell Bill—not Dollar Bill, Jerky Bill, yu' know; he's over the bridge—to fix up a hearse, and we'll be back." The two drove their spurs in with vigorous heels, and instantly were gone rushing up the road to the graveyard.

The fiddle had lately ceased, and no dancers staid any longer in the hall. Eastward the rose and gold began to flow down upon the plain over the tops of the distant hills. Of the revellers, many had never gone to bed, and many now were already risen from their excesses to revive in the cool glory of the morning. Some were drinking to stay their hunger until breakfast; some splashed and sported in the river, calling and joking; and across the river some were holding horse-races upon the level beyond the hog-ranch. Drybone air rang with them. Their lusty, wandering shouts broke out in gusts of hilarity. Their pistols, aimed at cans or prairie-dogs or anything, cracked as they galloped at large. Their speeding, clear-cut forms would shine upon the bluffs, and descending, merge in the dust their horses had raised. Yet all this was nothing in the vastness of the growing day. Beyond their voices the rim of the sun moved above the violet hills, and Drybone, amid the quiet, long, new fields of radiance, stood august and strange.

Down along the tall, bare slant from the graveyard the two horsemen were riding back. They could be seen across the river, and the horse-racers grew curious. As more and more watched, the crowd began to speak. It was a calf the two were bringing. It was too small for a calf. It was dead. It was a coyote they had roped. See it swing! See it fall on the road!

"It's a coffin, boys!" said one, shrewd at guessing.

At that the event of last night drifted across their memories, and they wheeled and spurred their ponies. Their crowding hoofs on the bridge brought the swimmers from the water below, and dressing, they climbed quickly to the plain and followed the gathering. By the door already were Jerky Bill and Limber Jim and the Doughie, and always more dashing up with their ponies, halting with a sharp scatter of gravel to hear and comment. Barker was gone, but the important coroner told his news. And it amazed each comer, and set him speaking and remembering past things with the others.

"Dead!" each one began.

"Her, does he say?"

"Why, pshaw!"

"Why, Frenchy said Doc had her cured!"

"Jack Saunders claimed she had rode to Box Elder with Lin McLean."

"Dead? Why, pshaw!"

"Seems Doc couldn't swim her out."

"Couldn't swim her out?"

"That's it. Doc couldn't swim her out."

"Well—there's one less of us."

"Sure! She was one of the boys."

"She grub-staked me when I went broke in '84."

"She gave me fifty dollars onced at Lander, to buy a saddle."

"I run agin her when she was a biscuit-shooter."

"Sidney, Nebraska. I run agin her there, too."

"I knowed her at Laramie."

"Where's Lin? He knowed her all the way from Bear Creek to Cheyenne."

They laughed loudly at this.

"That's a lonesome coffin," said the Doughie. "That the best you could do?"

"You'd say so!" said Toothpick Kid.

"Choices are getting scarce up there," said Chalkeye. "We looked the lot over."

They were arriving from their search among the old dug-up graves on the hill. Now they descended from their ponies, with the box roped and rattling between them. "Where's your hearse, Jerky?" asked Chalkeye.

"Have her round in a minute," said the cowboy, and galloped away with three or four others to help.

"Turrible lonesome coffin, all the same," repeated the Doughie. And they surveyed the box that had once held some soldier.

"She did like fixin's," said Limber Jim.

"Fixin's!" said Toothpick Kid. "That's easy."

While some six of them with Chalkeye bore the light, half-rotted coffin into the room, many followed Toothpick Kid to the post-trader's store. Breaking in here, they found men sleeping on the counters. These had been able to find no other beds in Drybone, and lay as they had stretched themselves on entering. They sprawled in heavy slumber, some with not even their hats taken off, and some with their boots against the rough hair of the next one. They were quickly pushed together, few waking, and so there was space for spreading cloth and chintz. Stuffs were unrolled and flung aside, till many folds and colors draped the motionless sleepers, and at length a choice was made. Unmeasured yards of this drab chintz were ripped off, money treble its worth was thumped upon the counter, and they returned, bearing it like a streamer to the coffin. While the noise of their hammers filled the room, the hearse came tottering to the door, pulled and pushed by twenty men. It was an ambulance left behind by the soldiers, and of the old-fashioned shape, concave in body, its top blown away in winds of long ago; and as they revolved, its wheels dished in and out, like hoops about to fall. While some made a harness from ropes, and throwing the saddles off two ponies backed them to the vehicle, the body was put in the coffin, now covered by the chintz. But the laudanum upon the front of her dress revolted those who remembered their holidays with her, and turning the woman upon her face, they looked their last upon her flashing colored ribbons, and nailed the lid down. So they carried her out, but the concave body of the hearse was too short for the coffin; the end reached out, and it might have fallen. But Limber Jim, taking the reins, sat upon the other end, waiting and smoking. For all Drybone was making ready to follow in some way. They had sought the husband, the chief mourner. He, however, still lay in the grass of the quadrangle, and despising him as she had done, they left him to wake when he should choose. Those men who could sit in their saddles rode escort, the old friends nearest, and four held the heads of the frightened cow-ponies who were to draw the hearse. They had never known harness before, and they plunged with the men who held them. Behind the hearse the women followed in a large ranch-wagon, this moment arrived in town. Two mares drew this, and their foals gambolled around them. The great flat-topped dray for hauling poles came last, with its four government mules. The cowboys had caught sight of it and captured it. Rushing to the post-trader's, they carried the sleeping men from the counter and laid them on the dray. Then, searching Drybone outside and in for any more incapable of following, they brought them, and the dray was piled.

Limber Jim called for another drink, and, with his cigar between his teeth, cracked his long bull-whacker whip. The ponies, terrified, sprang away, scattering the men that held them, and the swaying hearse leaped past the husband, over the stones and the many playing-cards in the grass. Masterfully steered, it came safe to an open level, while the throng cheered the unmoved driver on his coffin, his cigar between his teeth.

"Stay with it, Jim!" they shouted. "You're a king!"

A steep ditch lay across the flat where he was veering, abrupt and nearly hidden; but his eye caught the danger in time, and swinging from it leftward so that two wheels of the leaning coach were in the air, he faced the open again, safe, as the rescue swooped down upon him. The horsemen came at the ditch, a body of daring, a sultry blast of youth. Wheeling at the brink, they turned, whirling their long ropes. The skilful nooses flew, and the ponies, caught by the neck and foot, were dragged back to the quad-

rangle and held in line. So the pageant started; the wild ponies quivering but subdued by the tightened ropes, and the coffin steady in the ambulance beneath the driver. The escort, in their fringed leather and broad hats, moved slowly beside and behind it, many of them swaying, their faces full of health, and the sun, and the strong drink. The women followed, whispering a little; and behind them the slow dray jolted, with its heap of men waking from the depths of their whiskey, and asking what this was. So they went up the hill. When the riders reached the tilted gate of the graveyard, they sprang off and scattered among the hillocks, stumbling and eager. They nodded to Barker and McLean, quietly waiting there, and began choosing among the open, weather-drifted graves from which the soldiers had been taken. Their figures went up and down the uneven ridges, calling and comparing.

"Here," said the Doughie, "here's a good hole."

"Here's a deep one," said another.

"We've struck a well here," said some more. "Put her in here."

The sand hills became clamorous with voices until they arrived at a choice, when some one with a spade quickly squared the rain-washed opening. With lariats looping the coffin round they brought it, and were about to lower it, when Chalkeye, too near the edge, fell in, and one end of the box rested upon him. He could not rise by himself, and they pulled the ropes helplessly above.

McLean spoke to Barker. "I'd like to stop this," said he, "but a man might as well—"

"Might as well stop a cloud-burst," said Barker.

"Yes, Doc. But it feels—it feels like I was looking at ten dozen Lin McLeans." And seeing them still helpless with Chalkeye, he joined them and lifted the cowboy out.

"I think," said Slaghammer, stepping forward, "this should proceed no further without some— Perhaps some friend would recite 'Now I lay me'?"

"They don't use that on funerals," said the Doughie.

"Will some gentleman give the Lord's Prayer?" inquired the coroner.

Foreheads were knotted; trial mutterings ran among them; but some one remembered a prayer-book in one of the rooms in Drybone, and the notion was hailed. Four mounted, and raced to bring it. They went down the hill in a flowing knot, shirts ballooning and elbows flapping, and so returned. But the book was beyond them. "Take it you; you take it," each one said. False beginnings were made, big thumbs pushed the leaves back and forth, until impatience conquered them. They left the book and lowered the coffin, helped again by McLean. The weight sank slowly, decently, steadily, down between the banks. The sound that it struck the bottom with was a slight sound, the grating of the load upon the solid sand; and a little sand strewed from the edge and fell on the box at the same moment. The rattle came up from below, compact and brief, a single jar, quietly smiting through the crowd, smiting it to silence. One removed his hat, and then another, and then all. They stood eying each his neighbor, and shifting their eyes, looked away at the great valley. Then they filled in the grave, brought a head-board from a grave near by, and wrote the name and date upon it by scratching with a stone.

"She was sure one of us," said Chalkeye. "Let's give her the Lament."

And they followed his lead:

"Once in the saddle I used to go dashing,
Once in the saddle I used to go gay;
First took to drinking, and then to card-playing;
Got shot in the body, and now here I lay.

"Beat the drum slowly,
Play the fife lowly,
Sound the dead march as you bear me along.
Take me to Boot Hill, and throw the sod over me—
I'm but a poor cowboy, I know I done wrong."

When the song was ended, they left the graveyard quietly, and went down the hill. The morning was grown warm. Their work waited them across many sunny miles of range and plain. Soon their voices and themselves had emptied away into the splendid vastness and silence, and they were gone—ready with all their might to live or to die, to be animals or heroes, as the hours might bring them opportunity. In Drybone's deserted quadrangle the sun shone down upon Lusk still sleeping, and the wind shook the aces and kings in the grass.

IV.

Over at Separ, Jessamine Buckner had no more stockings of Billy's to mend, and much time for thinking and a change of mind. The day after that strange visit when she had been told that she had hurt a good man's heart without reason, she took up her work; and while her hands despatched it her thoughts already accused her. Could she have seen that visitor now, she would have thanked her. She looked at the photograph on her table. "Why did he go away so quickly?" she sighed. But when young Billy returned to his questions she was buoyant again, and more than a match for him. He reached the forbidden twelfth time of asking why Lin McLean did not come back and marry her. Nor did she punish him as she had threatened. She looked at him confidentially, and he drew near, full of hope.

"Billy, I'll tell you just why it is," said she. "Lin thinks I'm not a real girl."

"A—ah," drawled Billy, backing from her with suspicion.

"Indeed that's what it is, Billy. If he knew I was a real girl—"

"A—ah," went the boy, entirely angry. "Anybody can tell you're a girl." And he marched out, mystified, and nursing a sense of wrong. Nor did his dignity allow him to reopen the subject.

To-day, two miles out in the sage-brush by himself, he was shooting jack-rabbits, but began suddenly to run in toward Separ. A horseman had passed him, and he had loudly called; but the rider rode on, intent upon the little distant station. Man and horse were soon far ahead of the boy, and the man came into town galloping.

No need to fire the little pistol by her window, as he had once thought to do! She was outside before he could leap to the ground. And as he held her, she could only laugh, and cry, and say "Forgive me! Oh, why have you been so long?" She took him back to the room where his picture was, and made him sit, and sat herself close. "What is it?" she asked him. For through the love she read something else in his serious face. So then he told her how nothing was wrong; and as she listened to all that he had to tell, she too grew serious, and held very close to him. "Dear, dear neighbor!" she said.

As they sat so, happy with deepening happiness, but not gay yet, young Billy burst open the door. "There!" he cried. "I knowed Lin knowed you were a girl!"

18

The Evolution of the Cow-Puncher

OWEN WISTER

THE EVOLUTION OF THE COW-PUNCHER.

BY OWEN WISTER.

TWO men sat opposite me once, despising each other so heartily that I am unlikely to forget them. They had never met before—if they can be said to have met this time—and they were both unknown to me. It happened in a train by which we journeyed together from Leamington to London. The cause of their mutual disesteem was appearance; neither liked the other's outward man, and told him so silently for three hours; that is all they ever knew of each other. This object-lesson afterward gained greatly by my learning the name and estate of one of these gentlemen. He was a peer. He had good rugs, a good umbrella, several newspapers—but read only the pink one,--and a leather and silver thing which I took to be a travelling - bag beside him. He opened it between Banbury and Oxford, and I saw, not handkerchiefs and ivory, but cut - glass bottles with stoppers. I noticed further the strong sumptuous monogram engraved here and there. The peer leisurely took brandy, and was not aware of our presence. But the point of him is that he garnished those miles of railroad with incomparably greater comfort than we did who had no rugs, no cut glass, no sandwich-box, no monogram. He had understood life's upholstery and trappings for several hundred years, getting the best to be had in each generation of his noble descent.

The enemy that he had made, as a dog makes an enemy of a cat by the mere preliminary of being a dog, sat in the other corner. He wore a shiny silk hat, smooth new lean black trousers, with high boots stiff and swelling to stove-pipe symmetry beneath, and a tie devoid of interest. I did not ascertain if the pistol was in his hip pocket, but at stated intervals he spit out of his window. By his hawk nose and eye and the lank strength of his chin he was a male who could take care of himself, and had done so.   One could be sure he had wrested success from this world somehow, somewhere; and here he was, in a first-class carriage, on a first-class train, come for a first-class time, with a mind as complacently shut against being taught by foreign travel as any American patriot of to-day can attain or recommend, or any Englishman can reveal in his ten-day book about our continent and people.   Charles Dickens and Mark Twain have immortalized their own blindness almost equally; and the sad truth is that enlightenment is mostly a stay-at-home creature, who crosses neither ocean nor frontier.   This stranger was of course going to have a bad time, and feel relieved to get home and tell of the absence of baggage-checks and of the effete despot who had not set up the drinks.   Once he addressed the despot, who was serenely smoking.

"I'll trouble you for a light," said he; and in his drawl I heard plainly his poor opinion of feudalism.

His lordship returned the drawl—not audibly, but with his eye, which he ran slowly up and down the stranger.   His was the Piccadilly drawl; the other made use of the trans-Missouri variety; and both these are at bottom one and the same —the Anglo-Saxon's note of eternal contempt for whatever lies outside the beat of his personal experience.   So I took an observation of these two Anglo-Saxons drawling at each other across the prejudice of a hundred years, and I thought it might come to a row.   For the American was, on the quiet face of him, a "bad man," and so, to any save the provincial eye, was the nobleman.   Fine feathers had deceived trans-Missouri, whose list of "bad men" was limited to specimens of the cut of his own jib, who know nothing of cut-glass bottles.   But John gave Jonathan the light he asked, and for the remainder of our journey ceased to know that such a person existed.

Though we three never met again, my object-lesson did not end when we parted at Paddington.   Before many seasons were sped the fortunes of the nobleman took a turn for the scandalous.   He left cut glass behind him and went to Texas. I wish I could veraciously tell that he saw the stranger there—the traveller between whose bird-of-freedom nostrils and the wind his luxurious nobility had passed

so offensively.   But I do know that his second and more general skirmish with democracy left both sides amicable.   In fact, the nobleman won the Western heart forthwith.   Took it by surprise: democracy had read in the papers so often about the despot and his effeteness.   This despot vaulted into the saddle and stuck to the remarkably ingenious ponies that had been chosen with care to disconcert him.   When they showed him pistols, he was found to be already acquainted with that weapon.   He quickly learned how to rope a steer.   The card habit ran in his noble blood as it did in the cowboy's.   He could sleep on the ground and rough it with the best of them, and with the best of them he could drink and help make a town clamorous.   Deep in him lay virtues and vices coarse and elemental as theirs.   Doubtless the windows of St. James Street sometimes opened in his memory, and he looked into them and desired to speak with those whom he saw inside.   And the whiskey was not like the old stuff in the cut-glass bottles; but he never said so; and in time he died, widely esteemed.   Texas found no count against him save his pronunciation of such words as bath and fancy—a misfortune laid to the accident of his birth; and you will hear to-day in that flannel-shirted democracy only good concerning this aristocrat born and bred.

Now, besides several morals which no pious person will find difficult to draw from the decline and fall of this aristocrat, there is something more germane to my democratic contemplation: after all, when driven to flock with Texas, he was a bird of that wild feather.   That is the object-lesson; that is the gist of the matter.   Directly the English nobleman smelt Texas, the slumbering untamed Saxon awoke in him, and mindful of the tournament, mindful of the hunting-field, galloped howling after wild cattle, a born horseman, a perfect athlete, and spite of the peerage and gules and argent, fundamentally kin with the drifting vagabonds who swore and galloped by his side.   The man's outcome typifies the way of his race from the beginning.   Hundreds like him have gone to Australia, Canada, India, and have done likewise, and in our own continent you may see the thing plainer than anywhere else.   No rood of modern ground is more debased and mongrel with its hordes of encroaching alien ver-min, that turn our cities to Babels and our citizenship to a hybrid farce, who degrade our commonwealth from a nation into something half pawn-shop, half broker's office. But to survive in the clean cattle country requires spirit of adventure, courage, and self-sufficiency; you will not find many Poles or Huns or Russian Jews in that district; it stands as yet untainted by the benevolence of Baron Hirsch. Even in the cattle country the respectable Swedes settle chiefly to farming, and are seldom horsemen. The community of which the aristocrat appropriately made one speaks English. The Frenchman to-day is seen at his best inside a house; he can paint and he can play comedy, but he seldom climbs a new mountain. The Italian has forgotten Columbus, and sells fruit. Among the Spaniards and the Portuguese no Cortez or Magellan is found to-day. Except in Prussia, the Teuton is too often a tame, slippered animal, with his pedantic mind swaddled in a dressing-gown. But the Anglo-Saxon is still forever homesick for out-of-doors.

Throughout his career it has been his love to push further into the wilderness, and his fate thereby to serve larger causes than his own. In following his native bent he furthers unwittingly a design outside himself; he cuts the way for the common law and self-government, and new creeds, polities, and nations arise in his wake; in his own immense commonwealth this planless rover is obliterated. Roving took him (the Viking portion of him) from his Norse crags across to Albion. From that hearth of Albion the footprints of his sons lead to the corners of the earth; beside that hearth how inveterate remains his flavor! At Hastings he tasted defeat, but was not vanquished; to the Invincible Armada he proved a grievous surprise; one way or another he came through Waterloo—possibly because he is inveterately dull at perceiving himself beaten; when not otherwise busy at Balaklava or by the Alma, he was getting up horse-races, ready for sport or killing, and all with that silver and cut-glass finish which so offends our whistling, vacant-minded democracy. Greatest triumph and glory of all, because spiritual, his shoulders bore the Reformation when its own originators had tottered. Away from the hearth the cut-glass stage will not generally have been attained by him, and in

Maine or Kentucky you can recognize at sight the chip of the old rough block. But if you meet him upon his island, in the shape of a peer, and find him particular to dress for dinner seven days of the week, do not on that account imagine that his white tie has throttled the man in him. That is a whistling Fourth-of-July misconception. It's no symptom of patriotism to be unable to see a man through cut glass, and if it comes to an appraisement of the stranger and the peer, I should say, put each in the other's place, and let us see if the stranger could play the peer as completely as the nobleman played the cowboy. Sir Francis Drake was such a one; and Raleigh, the fine essence of Anglo-Saxon, with his fashionable gallant cloak, his adventure upon new seas, and his immediate appreciation of tobacco. The rover may return with looted treasure or incidentally stolen corners of territory to clap in his strong-box (this Angle is no angel), but it is not the dollars that played first fiddle with him, else our Hebrew friends would pioneer the whole of us. Adventure, to be out-of-doors, to find some new place far away from the postman, to enjoy independence of spirit or mind or body (according to his high or low standards)—this is the cardinal surviving fittest instinct that makes the Saxon through the centuries conqueror, invader, navigator, buccaneer, explorer, colonist, tiger-shooter; lifts him a pilgrim among the immortals at Plymouth Rock, dangles him a pirate from the gallows on the docks of Bristol. At all times when historic conditions or private stress have burst his domestic crust and let him fly out naturally, there he is, on Darien's peak, or through Magellan, or across the Missouri, or up the Columbia, a Hawkins, a Boone, a Grey, or a nameless vagrant, the same Saxon, ploughing the seas and carving the forests in every shape of man, from preacher to thief, and in each shape changelessly untamed. And as he has ruled the waves with his ship from that Viking time until yesterday at Samoa, when approaching death could extract no sound from him save American cheers and music, so upon land has the horse been his foster-brother, his ally, his playfellow, from the tournament at Camelot to the round-up at Abilene. The blood and the sweat of his jousting, and all the dirt and stains, have faded in the long sunlight of

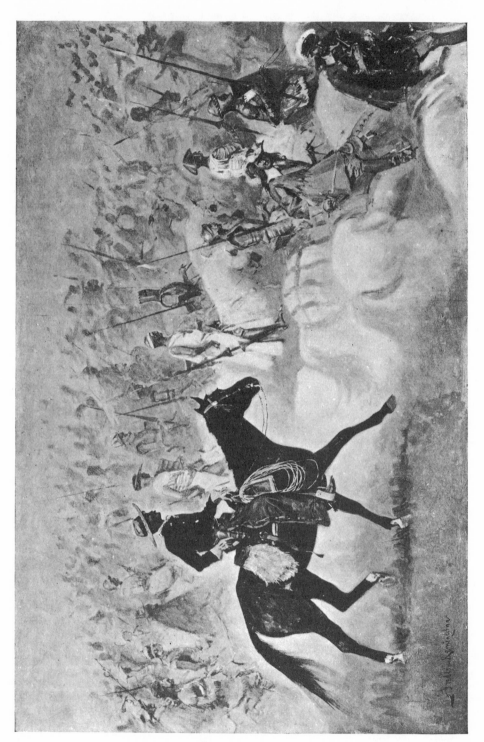

THE LAST CAVALIER.

tradition, and in the chronicles of romance we hear none of his curses or obscenity; the clash of his armor rings mellow and heroic down the ages into our modern ears. But his direct lineal offspring among our Western mountains has had no poet to connect him with the eternal, no distance to lend him enchantment; though he has fought single-handed with savages, and through skill and daring prevailed, though he has made his nightly bed in a thousand miles of snow and loneliness, he has not, and never will have, the "consecration of memory." No doubt Sir Launcelot bore himself with a grace and breeding of which our unpolished fellow of the cattle trail has only the latent possibility; but in personal daring and in skill as to the horse, the knight and the cowboy are nothing but the same Saxon of different environments, the nobleman in London and the nobleman in Texas; and no hoof in Sir Thomas Mallory shakes the crumbling plains with quadruped sound more valiant than the galloping that has echoed from the Rio Grande to the Big Horn Mountains. But we have no Sir Thomas Mallory! Since Hawthorne, Longfellow, and Cooper were taken from us, our flippant and impoverished imagination has ceased to be national, and the rider among Indians and cattle, the frontiersman, the American who replaces Miles Standish and the Pathfinder, is now beneath the notice of polite writers.

From the tournament to the round-up! Deprive the Saxon of his horse, and put him to forest-clearing or in a counting-house for a couple of generations, and you may pass him by without ever seeing that his legs are designed for the gripping of saddles. Our first hundred years afforded his horsemanship but little opportunity. Though his out-of-door spirit, most at home when at large, sported free in the elbow-room granted by the surrender of Cornwallis, it was on foot and with an axe that he chiefly enjoyed himself. He moved his log cabin slowly inward from the Atlantic, slowly over the wooded knolls of Cumberland and Allegheny, down and across the valley beyond, until the infrequent news of him ceased, and his kinsfolk who had staid by the sea, and were merchanting themselves upwards to the level of family portraits and the cut-glass finish, forgot that the prodigal in the backwoods belonged to them, and was part

of their United States, bone of their bone. And thus did our wide country become as a man whose East hand knoweth not what his West hand doeth.

Mr. Herndon, in telling of Lincoln's early days in Illinois, gives us a complete picture of the roving Saxon upon our continent in 1830. "The boys.... were a terror to the entire region—seemingly a necessary product of frontier civilization. They were friendly and good-natured.... They would do almost anything for sport or fun, love or necessity. Though rude and rough, though life's forces ran over the edge of their bowl, foaming and sparkling in pure deviltry for deviltry's sake, ... yet place before them a poor man who needed their aid, ... a defenceless woman, ... they melted into sympathy and charity at once. They gave all they had, and willingly toiled or played cards for more.... A stranger's introduction was likely to be the most unpleasant part of his acquaintance.... They were in the habit of 'cleaning out' New Salem." Friendly and good-natured, and in the habit of cleaning out New Salem! Quite so. There you have him. Here is the American variety of the Saxon set down for you as accurately as if Audubon himself had done it. A colored plate of Robin Hood and the Sheriff of Nottingham should go on the opposite page. Nothing but the horse is left out of the description, and that is because the Saxon and his horse seldom met during the rail-splitting era of our growth. But the man of 1830 would give away all that he had and play cards for more. Decidedly nothing was missing except the horse—and the horse was waiting in another part of our large map until the man should arrive and jump on his back again.

A few words about this horse — the horse of the plains. Whether or no his forefathers looked on when Montezuma fell, they certainly hailed from Spain. And whether it was missionaries or thieves who carried them northward from Mexico, until the Sioux heard of the new animal, certain it also is that this pony ran wild for a century or two, either alone or with various red-skinned owners; and as he gathered the sundry experiences of war and peace, of being stolen, and of being abandoned in the snow at inconvenient distances from home, of being ridden by two women and a baby at once, and of being eaten by a bear, his wide range of contretemps brought him a wit sharper

A SIGN POST (?) EXCITING

than the street Arab's, and an attitude towards life more blasé than in the united capitals of Europe. I have frequently caught him watching me with an eye of such sardonic depreciation that I felt it quite vain to attempt any hiding from him of my incompetence; and as for surprising him, a locomotive cannot do it, for I have tried this. He relishes putting a man in absurd positions, and will wait many days in patience to compass this uncharitable thing; and when he cannot bring a man to derision, he contents himself with a steer or a buffalo, helping the man to rope and throw these animals with an ingenuity surpassing any circus, to my thinking. A number of delighted passengers on the Kansas Pacific Railway passed by a Mexican vaquero, who had been sent out from Kansas City to rope a buffalo as an advertisement for the stock-yards. The train stopped to take a look at the solitary horseman fast to a buffalo in the midst of the plains. José, who had his bull safely roped, shouted to ask if they had water on the train. "We'll bring you some," said they. "Oh, I come get," said he; and jumping off, he left his accomplished pony in sole charge of the buffalo. Whenever the huge beast struggled for freedom, the clever pony stiffened his legs and leaned back as in a tug of war, by jumps and dodges so anticipating each move of the enemy that escape was entirely hopeless. The boy got his drink, and his employer sent out a car for the buffalo, which was taken in triumph into Kansas City behind the passenger train. The Mexican narrated the exploit to his employer thus: "Oh, Shirley, when the train start they all give three greata big cheers for me, and then they give three mucha bigger cheers for the little gray hoss!"

Ah, progress is truly a wonder! and admirable beyond all doubt it is to behold the rapid new square miles of brick, and the stream rich with the contributions of an increased population, and tall factories that have stopped dividends just for the present, and long empty railroads in the hands of the receiver; but I prefer that unenlightened day when we had plenty of money and cheered for the little gray hoss. Such was the animal that awaited the coming of the rail-splitter. The meeting was a long way off in 1830. Not the Mexican war, not the gold on the Pacific

in '49 (though this, except for the horse, revealed the whole Saxon at his best and worst, and for a brief and beautiful moment waked once more the American muse), not any national event until the war of the rebellion was over and we had a railroad from coast to coast, brought the man and his horse together. It was in the late sixties that this happened in Texas. The adventurous sons of Kentucky and Tennessee, forever following the native bent to roam, and having no longer a war to give them the life they preferred, came into a new country full of grass and cattle. Here they found Mexicans by the hundred, all on horses and at large over the flat of the world. This sight must have stirred memories in the rail-splitter's blood, for he joined the sport upon the instant. I do not think he rode with bolder skill than the Mexican's, but he brought other and grittier qualities to bear upon that wild life, and also the Saxon contempt for the foreigner. Soon he had taken what was good from this small, deceitful alien, including his name, Vaquero, which he translated into Cowboy. He took his saddle, his bridle, his spurs, his rope, his methods of branding and herding—indeed, most of his customs and accoutrements—and with them he went rioting over the hills. His play-ground was two thousand miles long and a thousand wide. The hoofs of his horse were tough as iron, and the pony waged the joyous battle of self-preservation as stoutly as did his rider. When the man lay rolled in his blankets sleeping, warm and unconcerned beneath a driving storm of snow, the beast pawed through to the sage-brush and subsisted; so that it came to be said of such an animal, "A meal a day is enough for a man who gets to ride that horse."

The cow-puncher's play-ground in those first glorious days of his prosperity included battle and murder and sudden death as every-day matters. From 1865 to 1878 in Texas he fought his way with knife and gun, and any hour of the twenty-four might see him flattened behind the rocks among the whiz of bullets and the flight of arrows, or dragged bloody and folded together from some adobe hovel. Seventy-five dollars a month and absolute health and strength were his wages; and when the news of all this excellence drifted from Texas eastward, they came in shoals—Saxon boys

WHAT AN UNBRANDED COW HAS COST.

of picked courage (none but plucky ones could survive) from South and North, from town and country. Every sort and degree of home tradition came with them from their far birthplaces. Some had known the evening hymn at one time, others could remember no parent or teacher earlier than the street; some spoke with the gentle accent of Virginia, others in the dialect of baked beans and codfish; here and there was the baccalaureate, already beginning to forget his Greek alphabet, but still able to repeat the two notable words with which Xenophon always marches upon the next stage of his journey. Hither to the cattle country they flocked from forty kinds of home, each bringing a deadly weapon.

What motlier tribe, what heap of cards shuffled from more various unmatched packs, could be found? Yet this tribe did not remain motley, but soon grew into a unit. To begin with, the old spirit burned alike in all, the unextinguished fire of adventure and independence. And then, the same stress of shifting for self, the same vigorous and peculiar habits of life, were forced upon each one: watching for Indians, guarding huge herds at night, chasing cattle, wild as deer, over rocks and counties, sleeping in the dust and waking in the snow, cooking in the open, swimming the swollen rivers. Such gymnasium for mind and body develops a like pattern in the unlike. Thus, late in the nineteenth century, was the race once again subjected to battles and darkness, rain and shine, to the fierceness and generosity of the desert. Destiny tried her latest experiment upon the Saxon, and plucking him from the library, the haystack, and the gutter, set him upon his horse; then it was that, face to face with the eternal simplicity of death, his modern guise fell away and showed once again the mediæval man. It was no new type, no product of the frontier, but just the original kernel of the nut with the shell broken.

This bottom bond of race unified the divers young men, who came riding from various points of the compass, speaking university and gutter English simultaneously; and as the knights of Camelot prized their armor and were particular about their swords, so these dusty successors had an extreme pride of equipment, and put aside their jeans and New York suits for the tribal dress. Though each

particle of gearing for man and horse was evoked from daily necessity, gold and silver instantly stepped in to play their customary ornamental part, as with all primitive races. The cow-puncher's legs must be fended from the thorny miles of the Rio Grande, the thousand mongrel shrubs that lace their bristles together stiff over the country—the mesquite, the shin-oak, the cat's-claw, the Spanish-dagger; widespreading, from six inches to ten feet high, every vegetable vicious with an embroidery of teeth and nails; a continent of peevish thicket called *chaparral*, as we indiscriminately call a dog with too many sorts of grandfathers a cur. Into this saw-mill dives the wild steer through paths and passages known to himself, and after him the pursuing man must also dive at a rate that would tear his flesh to ribbons if the blades and points could get hold of him. But he cases his leg against the hostile *chaparral* from thigh to ankle in chaps—leathern breeches, next door to armor: his daily bread is scarcely more needful to him. Soon his barbaric pleasure in finery sews tough leather fringe along their sides, and the leather flap of the pocket becomes stamped with a heavy rose. Sagging in a slant upon his hips leans his leather belt of cartridges buckled with jaunty arrogance, and though he uses his pistol with murderous skill, it is pretty, with ivory or mother-of-pearl for a handle. His arm must be loose to swing his looped rope free and drop its noose over the neck of the animal that bounds in front of his rushing pony. Therefore he rides in a loose flannel shirt that will not cramp him as he whirls the coils; but the handkerchief knotted at his throat, though it is there to prevent sunburn, will in time of prosperity be chosen for its color and soft texture, a scarf to draw the eye of woman. His heavy splendid saddle is, in its shape and luxury of straps and leather thongs, the completest instrument for night and day travel, and the freighting along with you of board and lodging, that any nomad has so far devised. With its trappings and stamped leather, its horn and high cantle, we are well acquainted. It must stand the strain of eight hundred sudden pounds of live beef tearing at it for freedom; it must be the anchor that shall not drag during the furious rages of such a typhoon. For the cattle of the wilderness have often run wild for three, four, and five years, through rocks and forests, never seeing the face of man from the day when as little calves they were branded. And some were never branded at all. They have grown up in company with the deer, and like the deer they fly at the approach of the horseman. Then, if he has ridden out to gather these waifs from their remote untenanted pastures and bring them in to be counted and driven to sale, he must abandon himself to the headlong pursuit. The open easy plain with its harmless footing lies behind, the steep valley narrows up to an entering wedge among the rocks, and into these untoward regions rush the beeves. The shale and detritus of shelving land-slides, the slippery knobs in the beds of brooks, the uncertain edges of the jumping-off place, all lie in the road of the day's necessity, and where the steer goes, goes the cow-puncher too — balancing, swaying, doubling upon his shrewd pony. The noose uncoiling flies swinging through the air and closes round the throat—or perhaps only the hind leg—of the quarry. In the shock of stopping short or of leaning to circle, the rider's stirrups must be long, and his seat a forked pliant poise on the horse's back; no grip of the knee will answer in these contortions; his leg must have its straight length, a lever of muscle and sinew to yield or close vise-like on the pony's ribs; and when the steer feels that he is taken and the rope tightens from the saddle horn, then must the gearing be solid, else, like a fisherman floundering with snapped rod and tangled line, the cow-puncher will have misfortunes to repair and nothing to repair them with. Such a thing as this has happened in New Mexico: The steer, pursued and frantic at feeling the throttle of the flung rope, ran blindly over a cliff, one end of the line fast to him, the other to the rider's saddle horn, and no time to think once, much less twice, about anything in this or the next world. The pony braced his legs at the edge, but his gait swept him onward, as with the fast skater whose skate has stuck upon a frozen chip. The horse fell over the mountain, and with him his rider; but the sixty-foot rope was new, and it hooked over a stump. Steer and horse swung like scales gently above the man, who lay at the bottom, hurt nearly to death, but not enough to dull his appreciation of the unusual arrangement.

It is well, then, to wear leathern armor and sit in a stout saddle if you would thrive among the thorns and rocks; and without any such casualty as falling over a mountain, the day's common events call for uncommon strength of gear. Not otherwise can the steer be hooked and landed safely, and not otherwise is the man to hoist resisting beeves up a hill somewhat as safes are conducted to the sixth story, nor could the rider plunge galloping from the sixth story to the ground, or swerve and heavily lean to keep from flying into space, were his stirrup leathers not laced, and every other crucial spot of strain independent of so weak a thing as a buckle. To go up where you have come down is another and easier process for man and straps and everything except the horse. His breath and legs are not immortal. And in order that each day the man may be hardily borne over rough and smooth he must own several mounts—a "string"; sometimes six and more, either his own property, or allotted to him by the foreman of the outfit for which he rides. The unused animals run in a herd—the *ramuda;* and to get a fresh mount from the ramuda means not seldom the ceremony of catching your hare. The ponies walk sedately together in the pasture, good as gold, and eying you without concern until they perceive that you are come with an object. They then put forth against you all the circus knowledge you have bestowed upon them so painfully. They comprehend ropes and loops and the law of gravity; they have observed the errors of steers in similar cases, and the unattractive result of running inside any enclosure, such as a corral, they strategize to keep at large, and altogether chasing a steer is tortoise play to the game they can set up for you. They relish the sight of you whirling impotent among them, rejoice in the smoking pace and the doublings they perpetrate; and with one eye attentive to you and your poised rope, and the other dexterously commanding the universe, they will intertangle as in cross-tag, pushing between your design and its victim, mingling confusedly like a driven mist, and all this with nostrils leaning level to the wind and bellies close to the speeding ground. But when the desired one is at last taken and your successful rope is on his neck, you would not dream he had ever wished for anything else. He stands, submitting absent-mindedly to bit and blanket, mild as any unconscious lamb, while placidity descends once more upon the herd; again they pasture good as gold, and butter would not melt in the mouth of one of these conscientious creatures. I have known a number of dogs, one crow, and two monkeys, but these combined have seemed to me less fertile in expedient than the cow-pony, the sardonic cayuse. The bit his master gave him, and the bridle and spurs, have the same origin from necessity and the same history as to ornament. If stopping and starting and turning must be like flashes of light, the apparatus is accordingly severe; and as for the spurs, those wheels with long spikes cease to seem grotesque when you learn that with shorter and sharper rowels they would catch in the corded meshes of the girth, and bring the rider to ruin. Silver and gold, when he could pay for them, went into the make and decoration of this smaller machinery; and his hat would cost him fifteen dollars, and he wore fringed gloves. His boots often cost twenty-five dollars in his brief hour of opulence. Come to town for his holiday, he wore his careful finery, and from his wide hat-brim to his jingling heels made something of a figure—as self-conscious and deliberate a show as any painted buck in council or bull-elk among his aspiring cows; and out of town in the mountains, as wild and lean and dangerous as buck or bull knows how to be.

As with his get-up, so it went with his vocabulary; for any manner of life with a rule and flavor of its own strong enough to put a new kind of dress on a man's body will put new speech in his mouth, and an idiom derived from the exigencies of his days and nights was soon spoken by the cow-puncher. Like all creators, he not only built, but borrowed his own wherever he found it. *Chaps*, from *chapparajos*, is only one of many transfers from the Mexican, one out of (I should suppose) several hundred; and in *lover-wolf* is a singular instance of half-baked translation. *Lobo*, pronounced *lovo*, being the Spanish for wolf, and the coyote being a sort of wolf, the dialect of the southern border has slid into this name for a wolf that is larger, and a worse enemy to steers than the small coward coyote. Lover-wolf is a word anchored to its district. In the

Northwest, though the same animal roams there as dangerously, his Texas name would be as unknown as the Northwest's word for Indian, *siwash*, from *sauvage*, would be along the Rio Grande. Thus at the top and bottom of our map do French and Spanish trickle across the frontier, and with English melt into two separate amalgams which are wholly distinct, and which remain near the spot where they were moulded; while other compounds, having the same Northern and Southern starting-point, drift far and wide, and become established in the cow-puncher's dialect over his whole country. No better French specimen can be instanced than *cache*, verb and noun, from the verb *cacher*, to conceal. In our Eastern life words such as these are of no pertinent avail; and as it is only universal pertinence which can lift a fragment of dialect into the dictionary's good society, most of them must pass with the transient generation that spoke them. Certain ones there are deserving to survive; *cinch*, for instance, from *cincha*, the Mexican girth. From its narrow office under the horse's belly it has come to perform in metaphor a hundred services. In cinching somebody or something you may mean that you hold four aces, or the key of a political crisis; and when a man is very much indeed upper-dog, then he is said to have an air-tight cinch; and this phrase is to me so pleasantly eloquent that I am withheld from using it in polite gatherings only by that prudery which we carry as a burden along with the benefits of academic training. Besides the foreign importations, such as *arroyo* and *riata*, that stand unchanged, and those others which under the action of our own speech have sloughed their native shape and come out something new, like quirt—once *cuerta*, Mexican for rawhide—is the third large class of words which the cowboy has taken from our sober old dictionary stock and made over for himself. Pie-biter refers not to those hailing from our pie belt, but to a cow-pony who secretly forages in a camp kitchen to indulge his acquired tastes. Western whiskey, besides being known as tonsil varnish and a hundred different things, goes as benzine, not unjustly. The same knack of imagery that upon our Eastern slope gave visitors from the country the brief, sure name of hayseed, calls their Western equivalents junipers.

THERE WAS NO FLORA MCIVOR.

Hay grows scant upon the Rocky Mountains, but those seclusions are filled with evergreens. No one has accounted to me for *hobo*. A hobo is a wandering unemployed person, a stealer of rides on freight-trains, a diner at the back door, eternally seeking honest work, and when brought face to face with it eternally retreating. The hobo is he against whom we have all sinned by earning our living. Perhaps some cowboy saw an Italian playing a pipe to the accompaniment of the harp, and made the generalization: oboe may have given us hobo. Hobo-ken has been suggested by an ingenious friend; but the word seems of purely Western origin, and I heard it in the West several years before it became used in the East. The cow-puncher's talent for making a useful verb out of anything shows his individuality. Any young strong race will always lay firm hands on language and squeeze juice from it; and you instantly comprehend the man who tells you of his acquaintances, whom you know to be drunk at the moment, that they are *helling* around town. Unsleeping need for quick thinking and doing gave these nomads the pith of utterance. They say, for instance, that they intend *camping on a man's trail*, meaning, concisely, "So-and-so has injured us, and we are going to follow him day and night until we are quits." Thus do these ordinary words and phrases, freshened to novelty by the cow-puncher's wits, show his unpremeditated art of brevity, varying in aptness, but in imagination constant; and with one last example of his fancy I shall leave his craft of word-making.

It is to be noted in all peoples that for whatever particular thing in life is of frequent and familiar practice among them they will devise many gradations of epithet. *To go* is in the cattle country a common act, and a man may go for different reasons, in several manners, at various speeds. For example:

"Do I understand you went up the tree with the bear just behind you?"

"The bear was not in front of me."

Here the cowboy made ordinary words suffice for showing the way he went, but his goings can be of many sorts besides in front of and behind something, and his rich choice of synonyms embodies a latent chapter of life and habits. To the several phases of going known to the pioneer as vamose, skip, light out, dust, and

git, the cowboy adds, burn the earth, hit, hit the breeze, pull your freight, jog, amble, move, pack, rattle your hocks, brindle, and more, very likely, if I knew or could recall them; I think that the observer who caught the shifting flicker of a race or a pursuit, and said brindle first, had a mind of liveliness and art.

It may be that some of these words I have named as home-bred natives of our wilderness are really of long standing and archaic repute, and that the scholar can point to them in the sonnets of Shakespeare, but I, at least, first learned them west of the Missouri.

With a speech and dress of his own, then, the cow-puncher drove his herds to Abilene or Westport Landing in the Texas times, and the easy abundant dollars came, and left him for spurs and bridles of barbaric decoration. Let it be remembered that the Mexican was the original cowboy, and that the American improved on him. Those were the days in which he was long in advance of settlers, and when he literally fought his right of way. Along the waste hundreds of miles that he had to journey, three sorts of inveterate enemies infested the road—the thief (the cattle-thief, I mean), who was as daring as himself; the supplanted Mexican, who hated the new encroaching Northern race; and the Indian, whose hand was against all races but his own immediate tribe, and who flayed the feet of his captives, and made them walk so through the mountain passes to the fires in which he slowly burned them. Among these perils the cow-puncher took wild pleasure in existing. No soldier of fortune ever adventured with bolder carelessness, no fiercer blood ever stained a border. If his raids, his triumphs, and his reverses have inspired no minstrel to sing of him who rode by the Pecos River and the hills of San Andreas, it is not so much the Rob Roy as the Walter Scott who is lacking. And the Flora McIvor! Alas! the stability of the clan, the blessing of the home background, was not there. These wild men sprang from the loins of no similar father, and begot no sons to continue their hardihood. War they made in plenty, but not love; for the woman they saw was not the woman a man can take into his heart. That their fighting Saxon ancestors awoke in them for a moment and made them figures for poetry and romance is due to the strange accidents of a young country, where, while cities flourish by the coast and in the direct paths of trade, the herd-trading interior remains mediæval in its simplicity and violence. And yet this transient generation deserves more chronicling than it will ever have. Deeds in plenty were done that are all and more than imagination should require. One high noon upon the plains by the Rio Grande the long irons lay hot in the fire. The young cattle were being branded, and the gathered herd covered the plain. Two owners claimed one animal. They talked at first quietly round the fire, then the dispute quickened. One roped the animal, throwing it to the ground to burn his mark upon it. A third came, saying the steer was his. The friends of each drew close to hear, and a claimant thrust his red-hot iron against the hide of the animal tied on the ground. Another seized it from him, and as they fell struggling, their adherents flung themselves upon their horses, and massing into clans, volleyed with their guns across the fire. In a few minutes fourteen riders lay dead on the plain, and the tied animal over which they had quarrelled bawled and bleated in the silence. Here is skirmishing enough for a ballad. And there was a certain tireless man in northern New Mexico whose war upon cattle-thieves made his life so shining a mark that he had in bank five thousand dollars to go to the man who killed the man who killed him. A neighborhood where one looks so far beyond his own assassination as to provide a competence for his avenger is discouraging to family life, but a promising field for literature.

Such existence soon makes a strange man of any one, and the early cow-punchers rapidly grew unlike all people but each other and the wild superstitious ancestors whose blood was in their veins. Their hair became long, and their glance rested with serene penetration upon the stranger; they laughed seldom, and their spirit was in the permanent attitude of war. Grim lean men of few topics, and not many words concerning these; comprehending no middle between the poles of brutality and tenderness; indifferent to death, but disconcerted by a good woman; some with violent Old Testament religion, some avowing none, and all of them uneasy about corpses and the dark. These

hermited horsemen would dismount in camp at nightfall and lie looking at the stars, or else squat about the fire conversing with crude sombreness of brands and horses and cows, speaking of *humans* when they referred to men.

To-day they are still to be found in New Mexico, their last domain. The extreme barrenness of those mountains has held tamer people at a distance. That next stage of Western progress—that unparalleled compound of new hotels, electric lights, and invincible ignorance which has given us the Populist—has been retarded, and the civilization of Colorado and silver does not yet redeem New Mexico. But in these shrunk days the cow-puncher no longer can earn money to spend on ornament; he dresses poorly and wears his chaps very wide and ungainly. But he still has three mounts, with seven horses to each mount, and his life is in the saddle among vast solitudes. In the North he was a later comer, and never quite so formidable a person. By the time he had ridden up into Wyoming and Montana the Indian was mostly gone, the locomotive upon the scene, and going West far less an exploration than in the Texas days. Into these new pastures drifted youths from town and country whose grit would scarcely have lasted them to Abilene, and who were not the grim long-haired type, but a sort of glorified farm hand. They too wore their pistols, and rode gallantly, and out of them nature and simplicity did undoubtedly forge manlier, cleaner men than what our streets breed of no worse material. They galloped by the side of the older hands, and caught something of the swing and tradition of the first years. They developed heartiness and honesty in virtue and in vice alike. Their evil deeds were not of the sneaking kind, but had always the saving grace of courage. Their code had no place for the man who steals a pocket-book or stabs in the back.

And what has become of them? Where is this latest outcropping of the Saxon gone? Except where he lingers in the mountains of New Mexico he has been dispersed, as the elk, as the buffalo, as all wild animals must inevitably be dispersed. Three things swept him away—the exhausting of the virgin pastures, the coming of the wire fence, and Mr. Armour of Chicago, who set the price of beef to suit himself. But all this may be summed up

THE FALL OF THE COWBOY.

in the word Progress. When the bankrupt cow-puncher felt Progress dispersing him, he seized whatever plank floated nearest him in the wreck. He went to town for a job; he got a position on the railroad; he set up a saloon; he married, and fenced in a little farm ; and he turned "rustler," and stole the cattle from the men for whom he had once worked. In these capacities will you find him to-day. The ex-cowboy who set himself to some new way of wage-earning is all over the West, and his old courage and frankness still stick to him, but his peculiar independence is of necessity dimmed. The only man who has retained that wholly is the outlaw, the horse and cattle thief, on whose grim face hostility to Progress forever sits. He has had a checkered career. He has been often hanged, often shot; he is generally "wanted" in several widely scattered districts. I know one who used to play the banjo to me on Powder River as he swung his long boots over the side of his bunk. I have never listened to any man's talk with more interest and diversion. Once he has been to Paris on the proceeds of a lengthy well - conducted theft; once he has been in prison for

murder. He has the bluest eye, the longest nose, and the coldest face I ever saw. This stripe of gentleman still lives and thrives through the cattle country, occasionally goes out into the waste of land in the most delicate way, and presently cows and steers are missed. But he has driven them many miles to avoid live-stock inspectors, and it may be that if you know him by sight and happen to be in a town where cattle are bought, such as Kansas City, you will meet him at the best hotel there, full of geniality and affluence.

Such is the story of the cow-puncher, the American descendant of Saxon ancestors, who for thirty years flourished upon our part of the earth, and, because he was not compatible with Progress, is now departed, never to return. But because Progress has just now given us the Populist and silver in exchange for him, is no ground for lament. He has never made a good citizen, but only a good soldier, from his tournament days down. And if our nation in its growth have no worse distemper than the Populist to weather through, there is hope for us, even though present signs disincline us to make much noise upon the Fourth of July.

19

The Shyness of Shorty

REX E. BEACH

THE SHYNESS OF SHORTY

BY

REX E. BEACH

ILLUSTRATED BY J. N. MARCHAND

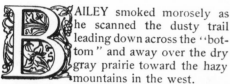

BAILEY smoked morosely as he scanned the dusty trail leading down across the "bottom" and away over the dry gray prairie toward the hazy mountains in the west.

From his back-tilted chair on the veranda, the road was visible for miles, as well as the river trail from the south, sneaking up through the cottonwoods and leprous sycamores.

He called gruffly into the silence of the house, and his speech held the surliness of his attitude.

"Hot Joy! Bar X outfit comin'. Git supper."

A Chinaman appeared in the door and gazed at the six-mule team descending the distant gully to the ford.

"Jesse one man, hey? All light," and slid quietly back to the kitchen.

Whatever might be said, or, rather, whatever might be suspected, of Bailey's roadhouse — for people did not run to wordy conjecture in this country — it was known that it boasted a good cook, and this atoned for a catalogue of shortcomings. So it waxed popular among the hands of the big cattle ranges near-by. Those given to idle talk held that Bailey acted strangely at times, and rumor painted occasional black doings at the hacienda, squatting vulture-like above the ford, but it was nobody's business, and he kept a good cook.

Bailey did not recall the face that greeted him from above the three span as they swung in front of his corral, but the brand on their flanks was the Bar X, so he nodded with as near an approach to hospitality as he permitted.

It was a large face, strong-featured and rugged, balanced on wide square shoulders, yet some oddness of posture held the gaze of the other till the stranger clambered over the wheel to the ground. Then Bailey removed his brier and heaved tempestuously in the throes of great and silent mirth.

It was a dwarf. The head of a Titan, the body of a whisky barrel, rolling ludicrously on the tiny limbs of a bug, presented so startling a sight that even Hot Joy, appearing around the corner, cackled shrilly. His laughter rose to a shriek of dismay, however, as the little man made at him with the rush and roar of a cannon ball. In Bailey's amazed eyes he seemed to bounce galvanically, landing on Joy's back with such vicious suddenness that the breath fled from him in a squawk of terror; then, seizing his cue, he kicked and belabored the prostrate Celestial in feverish silence. He desisted and rolled across the porch to Bailey. Staring truculently up at the landlord, he spoke for the first time.

"Was I right in supposin' that something amused you?"

Bailey gasped incredulously, for the voice rumbled heavily an octave below his own bass. Either the look of the stocky catapult, as he launched himself at the fleeing servant, or the invidious servility of the innkeeper, sobered the landlord, and he answered gravely:

"No, sir; I reckon you're mistaken. I ain't observed anything frivolous yet."

"Glad of it," said the little man. "I don't like a feller to hog a joke all by himself. Some of the Bar X boys took to absorbin' humor out of my shape when I first went to work, but they're sort of educated out of it now. I got an eye from one and a finger off of another; the last one donated a ear."

Bailey readily conceived this man as a bad antagonist, for the heavy corded neck had split buttons from the blue shirt, and he glimpsed a chest hairy, and round as a drum, while the brown arms showed knotty and hardened.

"Let's liquor," he said, and led the way into the big, low room, serving as bar, dining and living room. From the rear came vicious clatterings and slammings of pots, mingled with Oriental lamentations, indicating an aching body rather than a chastened spirit.

"Don't see you often," he continued, with a touch of implied curiosity, which grew as his guest, with lingering fondness, up-ended a glass brimful of the raw, fiery spirits.

"No, the old man don't lemme get away much. He knows that dwellin' close to the ground, as I do, I pine for spiritual elevation," with a melting glance at the bottles behind the bar doing much to explain the size of his first drink.

"Like it, do ye?" questioned Bailey, indicating the shelf.

"Well, not exactly! Booze is like air—I need it. It makes a new man out of me—and usually ends by gettin' both me and the new one laid off."

"Didn't hear nothing of the weddin' over at Los Huecos, did ye?"

"No! Whose weddin'?"

"Ross Turney, the new sheriff."

"Ye don't say! Him that's been elected on purpose to round up the Tremper gang, hey? Who's his antagonist?"

"Old man Miller's gal. He's celebratin' his election by gettin' spliced. I been expectin' of 'em across this way to-night, but I guess they took the Black Butte trail. You heard what he said, didn't ye? Claims that inside of ninety days he'll rid the county of the Trempers and give the reward to his wife for a bridal present. Five thousand dollars on 'em, you know." Bailey grinned evilly and continued: "Say! Marsh Tremper'll ride up to his house some night and make him eat his own gun in front of his bride, see if he don't. Then there'll be cause for an inquest and an election." He spoke with what struck the teamster as unnecessary heat.

"Dunno," said the other; "Turney's a brash young feller, I hear, but he's game. 'Tain't any of my business, though, and I don't want none of his contrac'. I'm violently addicted to peace and quiet, I am. Guess I'll unhitch," and he toddled out into the gathering dusk to his mules, while the landlord peered uneasily down the darkening trail.

As the saddened Joy lit candles in the front room there came the rattle of wheels without, and a buckboard stopped in the bar of light from the door. Bailey's anxiety was replaced by a mask of listless surprise as the voice of Ross Turney called to him.

"Hello there, Bailey! Are we in time for supper? If not, I'll start an insurrection with that Boxer of yours. He's got to turn out the snortingest supper of the season to-night. It isn't every day your shack is honored by a bride. Mr. Bailey, this is my wife, since ten o'clock A.M." He introduced a blushing happy girl, evidently in the grasp of many emotions. "We'll stay all night, I guess."

"Sure," said Bailey. "I'll show ye a room," and he led them up beneath the low roof where an unusual cleanliness betrayed the industry of Joy.

The two men returned and drank to the bride, Turney with the reckless lightness that distinguished him, Bailey sullen and watchful.

"Got another outfit here, haven't you?" questioned the bridegroom. "Who is it?"

Before answer could be made, from the kitchen arose a tortured howl and the smashing of dishes, mingled with stormy rumblings. The door burst inward, and an agonized Joy fled, flapping out into the night, while behind him rolled the caricature from Bar X.

"I just stopped for a drink of water," boomed the dwarf, then paused at the twitching face of the sheriff.

He swelled ominously, like a great pigeon, purple and congested with rage. Strutting to the new comer, he glared insolently up into his smiling face.

"What are ye laughin' at, ye shavetail?" His hands were clenched, till his arms showed tense and rigid, and the cords in his neck were thickly swollen.

"Lemme in on it, I'm strong on humor. What in —— ails ye?" he yelled, in a fury, as the tall young man gazed fixedly, and the glasses rattled at the bellow from barreled-up lungs.

"I'm not laughing at you," said the sheriff.

"Oh, ain't ye?" mocked the man of peace. "Well, take care that ye don't, ye big wart, or I'll trample them new clothes and browse around on some of your features. I'll take ye apart till ye look like cut feed. Guess ye don't know who I am, do ye! I'm——"

"Who is this man, Ross?" came the anxious voice of the bride, descending the stairs.

The little man spun like a dancer, and, spying the girl, blushed to the color of a prickly pear, then stammered painfully, while the sweat stood out under the labor of his discomfort:

"Just 'Shorty,' Miss," he finally quavered. "Plain 'Shorty' of the Bar X—er —a miserable, crawlin' worm for disturbin' of you." He rolled his eyes helplessly at Bailey, while he sopped with his crumpled sombrero at the glistening perspiration.

"Why didn't ye tell me?" he whispered ferociously at the host, and the volume of his query carried to Joy, hiding out in the night.

"Mr. Shorty," said the sheriff gravely; "let me introduce my wife, Mrs. Turney."

The bride smiled sweetly at the tremulous little man, who broke and fled to a high bench in the darkest corner, where he dangled his short legs in a silent ecstasy of bashfulness.

"I reckon I'll have to rope that Chink, then blindfold and back him into the kitchen, if we git any supper," said Bailey, disappearing.

Later the Chinaman stole in to set the table, but he worked with hectic and fitful energy, a fearful eye always upon the dim bulk in the corner, and at a fancied move he shook with an ague of apprehension. Backing and sidling, he finally announced the meal, prepared to stampede madly at notice.

During the supper Shorty ate ravenously of whatever lay to his hand, but asked no favors. The agony of his shyness paralyzed his huge vocal muscles till speech became a labor quite impossible.

To a pleasant remark of the bride he responded, but no sound issued, then breathing heavily into his larynx, the reply roared upon them like a burst of thunder, seriously threatening the gravity of the meal. He retired abruptly into moist and self-conscious silence, fearful of feasting his eyes on this disturbing loveliness.

As soon as compatible with decency, he slipped back to his bunk in the shed behind, and lay staring into the darkness, picturing the amazing occurrences of the evening. At the memory of her level glances he fell a-tremble and sighed ecstatically, prickling with a new, strange emotion. He lay till far into the night, wakeful and absorbed. He was able to grasp the fact but dimly that all this dazzling perfection was for one man. Were it not manifestly impossible he supposed other men in other lands knew other ladies as beautiful, and it furthermore grew upon him blackly, in the thick gloom, that in all this world of womanly sweetness and beauty, no modicum of it was for the misshapen dwarf of the Bar X outfit. All his life he had fought furiously to uphold the empty shell of his dignity in the eyes of his comrades, yet always morbidly conscious of the difference in his body. Whisky had been his solace, his sweetheart. It changed him, raised and beatified him into the likeness of other men, and now, as he pondered, he was aware of a consuming thirst engendered by the heat of his earlier emotions. Undoubtedly it must be quenched.

He rose and stole quietly out into the big front room. Perhaps the years of free life in the open had bred a suspicion of walls, perhaps he felt his conduct would not brook discovery, perhaps habit, prompted him to take the two heavy Colts from their holsters and thrust them inside his trousers band.

He slipped across the room, silent and cavern-like, its blackness broken by the window squares of starry sky, till he felt the paucity of glassware behind the bar.

"Here's to Her." It burned delightfully.

"Here's to the groom." It tingled more alluringly.

"I'll drink what I can, and get back to the bunk before it works," he thought, and the darkness veiled the measure of his potations.

He started at a noise on the stairway. His senses, not yet dulled, detected a stealthy tread. Not the careless step of a man unafraid, but the cautious rustle and halt of a marauder. Every nerve bristled to keenest alertness as the faint occasional sounds approached, passed the open end of the bar where he crouched, leading on to the window. Then a match flared and the darkness rushed out as a candle wick sputtered.

J·N·MARCHAND·

"'What are ye laughin' at, ye shavetail?'"

Shorty stretched on tiptoe, brought his eye to the level of the bar, and gazed upon the horrent head of Bailey. He sighed thankfully, but watched with interest his strange behavior.

Bailey moved the light across the window from left to right three times, paused, then wigwagged some code out into the night.

"He's signaling," mused Shorty. "Hope he gets through quick. I'm getting full." The fumes of the liquor were beating at his senses, and he knew that soon he would move with difficulty.

The man, however, showed no intention of leaving, for, his signals completed, he blew out the light, first listening for any sound from above, then his figure loomed black and immobile against the dim starlight of the window.

"Oh, Lord! I got to set down," and the watcher squatted upon the floor, bracing against the wall. His dulling perceptions were sufficiently acute to detect shuffling footsteps on the porch and the cautious unbarring of the door.

"Gettin late for visitors," he thought, as he entered a blissful doze. "When they're abed, I'll turn-in."

It seemed much later that a shot startled him. To his dizzy hearing came the sound of curses overhead, the stamp and shift of feet, the crashing fall of struggling men, and, what brought him unsteadily to his legs, the agonized scream of a woman. It echoed through the house, chilling him, and dwindled to an aching moan.

Something was wrong, he knew that, but it was hard to tell just what. He must think. What hard work it was to think, too ; he'd never noticed before what a laborious process it was. Probably that sheriff had got into trouble ; he was a fresh guy, anyhow ; and he'd laughed when he first saw Shorty. That settled it. He could get out of it himself. Evidently it was nothing serious, for there was no more disturbance above, only confused murmurings. Then a light showed in the stairs, and again the shuffling of feet came, as four strange men descended. They were lighted by the sardonic Bailey, and they dragged a sixth between them, bound and helpless. It was the sheriff.

Now, what had he been doing to get into such a fix ?

The prisoner stood against the wall, white and defiant. He strained at his bonds silently, while his captors watched his futile struggles. There was something terrible and menacing in the quietness with which they gloated — a suggestion of some horror to come. At last he desisted, and burst forth.

"You've got me all right. You did this, Bailey, you —— traitor."

"He's never been a traitor, as far as we know," sneered one of the four. "In fact, I might say he's been strictly on the square with us."

"I didn't think you made war on women, either, Marsh Tremper, but it seems you're everything from a dog-thief down. Why couldn't you fight me alone, in the daylight, like a man ? "

"You don't wait till a rattler's coiled before you stamp his head off," said the former speaker. "It's either you or us, and I reckon it's you."

So these were the Tremper boys, eh ? The worst desperadoes in the Southwest ; and Bailey was their ally. The watcher eyed them, mildly curious, and it seemed

to him that they were as bad a quartette as rumor had painted — bad, even, for this country of bad men. The sheriff was a fool for getting mixed up with such people. Shorty knew enough to mind *his* own business, anyway, if others didn't. He was a peaceful man, and didn't intend to get mixed up with outlaws. His mellow meditations were interrupted by the hoarse speech of the sheriff, who had broken down into his rage again, and struggled madly while words ran from him.

"Let me go ! —— you, let me free. I want to fight the coward that struck my wife. You've killed her. Who was it ? Let me get at him."

Shorty stiffened as though a douche of ice-water had struck him. "Killed her. Struck his wife !" My God ! Not that sweet creature of his dreams who had talked and smiled at him without noting his deformity ——

An awful anger rose in him and he moved out into the light.

"Han' sup ! "

Whatever of weakness may have dragged at his legs, none sounded in the great bellowing command that flooded the room. At the compelling volume of the sound every man whirled and eight empty hands shot skyward. Their startled eyes beheld a man's squat body waving uncertainly on the limbs of an insect while in each hand shone a blue-black Colt that waved and circled in maddening, erratic orbits.

At the command, Marsh Tremper's mind had leaped to the fact that behind him was one man ; one against five, and he took a gambler's chance.

As he whirled, he drew and fired. None but the dwarf of Bar X could have lived, for he was the deadliest hip shot in the territory. His bullet crashed into the wall a hand's breadth over Shorty's "cow-lick." It was a clean heart shot ; the practiced whirl and flip of the finished gun fighter ; but the roar of his explosion was echoed by another and the elder Tremper spun unsteadily against the table with a broken shoulder.

"Too high," moaned the big voice. "—— the liquor."

He swayed drunkenly, but at the slightest shift of his quarry, the aimless wanderings of a black muzzle stopped on the spot and the body behind the guns was congested with deadly menace.

" ' Han' sup ! ' "

"'Cut these strings, girlie, . . . Quick! He's blushing again.'"

"Face the wall," he cried. "Quick! Keep 'em up, higher!" They suddenly obeyed; their wounded leader reaching with his uninjured member.

To the complacent Shorty, it seemed that things were working nicely, though he was disturbingly conscious of his alcoholic lack of balance, and tortured by the fear that he might suddenly lose the iron grasp of his faculties.

Then, for the second time that night, from the stairs came the voice that threw him into the dreadful confusion of his modesty.

"O Ross!" it cried, "I've brought your gun," and there on the steps, dishevelled, pallid and quivering, was the bride, and grasped in one trembling hand was her husband's weapon.

"Ah — h!" sighed Shorty, seraphically, as the vision beat in upon his misty conceptions. "*She ain't hurt!*"

In his mind there was no room for desperadoes contemporaneously with Her. Then he became conscious of the lady's raiment, and his brown cheeks flamed brick-red, while he dropped his eyes. In his shrinking, groveling modesty, he made for his dark corner.

One of those at bay, familiar with this strange abashment, seized the moment, but at his motion the sheriff screamed: "Look out!"

The quick danger in the cry brought back with a surge the men against the wall and Shorty swung instantly, firing at the outstretched hand of Bailey as it reached for Tremper's weapon.

The landlord straightened, gazing affrightedly at his finger tips.

"Too low!" and Shorty's voice held aching tears. "I'll never touch another drop; it's plumb ruined my aim."

"Cut these strings, girlie," said the sheriff, as the little man's gaze again wavered, threatening to leave his prisoners. "Quick. He's blushing again."

When they were manacled, Shorty stood in moist exudation, trembling and speechless, under the incoherent thanks of the bride and the silent admiration of her handsome husband. She fluttered about him in a tremor of anxiety, lest he be wounded, caressing him here and there with solicitous pats till he felt his shamed and happy spirit would surely burst from its misshapen prison.

"You've made a good thing to-night," said Turney, clapping him heartily on his massive back. "You get the five thousand all right. We were going to Mexico City on that for a bridal trip when I rounded up the gang, but I'll see you get every cent of it, old man. If it wasn't for you, I'd have been a heap farther south than that by now."

The open camaraderie and good fellowship that rang in the man's voice affected Shorty strangely, accustomed as he was to the veiled contempt or open compassion of his fellows. Here was one who recognized him as a man, an equal.

He spread his lips, but the big voice squeaked dismally, then, inflating deeply, he spoke so that the prisoners chained in the corral outside heard him plainly.

"I'd rather she took it anyhow," blushing violently.

"No, no," they cried. "It's yours."

"Well, then, half of it" — and for once Shorty betrayed the strength of Gibraltar, even in the face of the lady, and so it stood.

As the dawn spread over the dusty prairie, tipping the westward mountains with silver caps, and sucking the mist out of the cottonwood bottoms, he bade them adieu.

"No, I got to get back to the Bar X, or the old man'll swear I been drinking again, and I don't want to dissipate no wrong impressions around." He winked gravely. Then, as the sheriff and his surly prisoners drove off, he called:

"Mr. Turney, take good care of them Trempers. I think a heap of 'em, for, outside of your wife, they're the only ones in this outfit that didn't laugh at me."

20

Billy's Tenderfoot

STEWART EDWARD WHITE

BILLY'S TENDERFOOT.

By Stewart Edward White,

Author of "The Westerner," "The Blazed Trail," etc.

DURING one spring of the early seventies Billy Knapp ran a species of road house or hotel at the crossing of the Deadwood and Big Horn trails through Custer Valley. Travelers changing from one route to the other frequently stopped there overnight. He sold accommodations for man and beast; the former comprising plenty of whiskey, the latter, plenty of hay. That was the best any one could say of it. The hotel was of logs, two-storied, with partitions of sheeting to insure a certain privacy of sight if not of sound; had three beds and a number of bunks; and boasted of a woman cook—one of the first in the Hills. Billy did not run it long. He was too restless.

The *personnel* of the establishment consisted of Billy and the woman already mentioned, and an ancient Pistol of the name of Charley. The latter wore many firearms, and had a good deal to say, but had never, as Billy expressed it, "made good." This, in the West, could not have been for lack of opportunity. His functions were those of general factotum.

One evening Billy sat chair-tilted against the logs of the hotel, waiting for the stage. By and by it drew in. Charley hobbled out, carrying buckets of water for the horses. The driver flung the reins from him with the lordly insolence of his class, descended slowly, and swaggered to the bar-room for his drink. Billy followed to serve it.

"Luck!" said the driver, and crooked his elbow.

"Anything new?" queried Billy.

"Nope."

"Held up?"

"Nope."

That exhausted the situation. The two men puffed silently for a moment at their pipes. In an instant the driver turned to go.

"I got you a tenderfoot," he remarked casually. "I reckon he's outside."

"Guess I ambles forth and sees what fer a tenderfoot it is," replied Billy, hastening from behind the bar.

The tenderfoot was seated on a small trunk just outside the door. As he held his hat in his hands, Billy could see his dome-like bald head. Beneath the dome was a little pink and white face, and below that were narrow sloping shoulders, a flat chest, and bandy legs. He wore a light check suit, and a flannel shirt whose collar was much too large for him. Billy took this all in while passing. As the driver climbed to the seat, the hotel-keeper commented.

"Say, Hen," said he, "would you stuff it, or put it under a glass case?"

"I'd serve it *a lay Tooloose*," replied the driver briefly, and brought his long lash 8-shaped across the four startled backs of his horses.

Billy turned to a reinspection of his guest, and met a deprecating smile.

"Can I get a shake-down here for to-night?" he inquired in a high, piping voice.

"You kin," replied Billy shortly, and began to howl for Charley.

That patriarch appeared around the corner, as did likewise the cook, a black-eyed, red-cheeked creature, afterwards counted by Billy as one of his eight matrimonial ventures.

"Snake this stranger's war-bag into th' shack," commanded Billy. "And Nell, jest nat'rally rustle a few grub."

The stranger picked up a small hand-satchel and followed Charley into the building. When, a little later, he reappeared for supper, he carried the hand-bag with him and placed it under the bench which flanked the table. Afterwards he deposited it next his hand while enjoying a pipe outside. Naturally all this did not escape Billy.

"Stranger," said he, "yo' seems mighty wedded to that thar satchel."

"Yes, sir," piped the stranger. Billy snorted at the title. "I has some personal belongings which is valuable to me." He opened the bag and produced a cheap portrait of rather a cheap-looking woman. "My mother that was," said he.

Billy snorted again and went inside. He hated sentiment of all kinds. The two men sat opposite each other and ate supper, which was served by the red-cheeked girl. The stranger kept his eyes on his plate while she was in the room. He perched on the edge of the bench with his feet tucked under him and resting on their toes. When she approached, the muscles of his shoulders and upper arms grew rigid with embarrassment, causing strange, awkward movements of the hands. He answered in monosyllables.

Billy ate expansively and earnestly. Towards the close of the meal Charley slipped into place beside him. Charley was out of humor, and found the meat cold.

"—— —— yore soul! Nell," he cried, "this yere ain't fitten fer a *hog* to eat!"

The girl did not mind, nor did Billy. It was the country's mode of speech. The stranger dropped his knife.

"I don't wonder yo' don't like it, then!" said he, with a funny little flare of anger.

"Meanin' what?" shouted Charley threateningly.

"You shore mustn't speak to a lady that way," replied the stranger firmly, in his little piping voice.

Billy caught the point, and exploded in a mighty guffaw.

"Bully fer you!" he cried, slapping his knee, "struck pyrites (he pronounced it 'pie rights') fer shore that trip, Charley."

The girl, too, laughed, but quietly. She was a little touched, though just this winter she had left Bismarck because the place would have no more of her.

In the face of Billy's approval the old man fell silent.

About midnight the four inmates of the frontier hotel were awakened by a tremendous racket outside. The stranger arose, fully clothed, from his bunk, and peered through the narrow open window. A dozen horses were standing grouped, in charge of a single mounted man, indistinguishable in the dark. Out of the open door a broad band of light streamed from the saloon, whence came the noise of voices and of boots tramping about.

"It is Black Hank," said Billy, at his elbow. "Black Hank and his outfit. He hitches to this yere snubbin' post occasional."

Black Hank in the Hills would have translated to Jesse James farther south.

The stranger turned suddenly energetic.

"Don't you make no fight?" he asked.

"Fight!" said Billy, wondering. "Fight? Co'se not. Hank ain't plunderin' *me* none. He jest ambles along and helps himself, and leaves th' dust fer it every shot. I jest lays low and lets him operate. I never has no *dealin's* with him, understand. He jest nat'rally waltzes in an' plants his grub hooks on what he needs. *I* doesn't know anything about it. *I'm* dead asleep."

He bestowed a shadowy wink upon the stranger.

Below, the outlaws moved here and there.

"Billy!" shouted a commanding voice. "Billy Knapp!"

The hotel keeper looked perplexed.

"Now what's he tollin' *me* for?" he asked of the man by his side.

"Billy!" shouted the voice again, "come down here, you siwash. I want to palaver with you."

"All right, Hank," replied Billy.

He went to his "room" and buckled on a heavy belt, then descended the steep stairs.

The barroom was lighted, and filled with men. Some of them were eating and drinking; others were strapping provisions into portable form. Against the corner of the bar a tall figure of a man leaned, smoking—a man lithe, active, and muscular, with a keen, dark face and black eyebrows which met over his nose. Billy walked directly to this man.

"What is it?" he inquired shortly. "This yere ain't in th' agreement."

"I know that," replied the stranger.

"Then leave yore dust, and vamoose."

"My dust is there," said Black Hank, placing his hand on a buckskin bag at his side, "and you're paid, Billy Knapp. I want to ask you a question. Standing Rock has sent fifty thousand dollars to Buck Tail. The messenger went through here to-day. Have you seen him?"

"Nary messenger," replied Billy, in relief. "Stage goes empty."

Charley had crept down the stairs and into the room.

"What 'n blazes you doin' yere, you rani-kaboo ijit?" asked Billy truculently.

"That thar stage ain't what you calls *empty*," observed Charley, unmoved.

A light broke on Billy's mind. He remembered the valise which the stranger had so carefully guarded, and though his common sense told him that an inoffensive non-combatant, such as his guest, would hardly be

" *A voice at his shoulder startled him.*"

chosen as express messenger, still the bare possibility remained.

"Yo're right," he assented carelessly, "thar *is* one tenderfoot, who knows as much of ridin' express as a pig does of war."

"I notices he's almighty particular 'bout that thar carpet bag of his'n," insisted Charley.

The man against the counter had lost nothing of the scene. Billy's denial, his hesitation, his half-truth, all looked suspicious to him. With one swift round sweep of the arm he had Billy covered. Billy's arms shot over his head without the necessity of a command.

The men ceased their occupations and gathered about. Scenes of this sort were too common to elicit comment or arouse excitement. They knew perfectly the *laissez-faire* relations which obtained between the two Westerners.

"Now," said Black Hank angrily, in a low tone, "I want to know why you tried that monkey game."

Billy, wary and unafraid, replied that he had tried no game, that he had forgotten the tenderfoot for a moment, and that he did not believe the latter would prove to be the sought-for express messenger.

One of the men, at a signal from his leader, relieved Billy's belt of considerable weight. Then the latter was permitted to sit on a cracker-box. Two more mounted the little stairs. In a moment they returned to report that the upper story contained no human beings, strange or otherwise, except the girl, but that there remained a small trunk. Under further orders they dragged the trunk down into the barroom. It was broken open and found to contain clothes, of the plainsman's cut, material, and state of wear, a neatly folded Mexican saddle, showing use, and a rawhide quirt.

"Tenderfoot!" said Black Hank contemptuously.

The outlaws had already scattered outside to look for the trail. In this they were unsuccessful, reporting, indeed, that not the faintest sign indicated escape in any direction.

Billy knew his man. The tightening of Black Hank's close-knit brows meant but one thing. One does not gain chieftainship of any kind in the West without propping this ascendancy with acts of ruthless decision. Billy leaped from his cracker-box with the suddenness of the puma, seized Black Hank firmly about the waist, whirled him into a sort of shield, and began an earnest struggle

Black Hank.

for the instant possession of the outlaw's drawn revolver. It was a gallant attempt, but unsuccessful. In a moment Billy was pinioned to the floor, and Black Hank was rubbing his abraded forearm. After that the only question was, whether it should be rope or bullet.

Now, when Billy had gone downstairs, the stranger had wasted no more time at the window. He had in his possession fifty thousand dollars in greenbacks which he was to deliver as soon as possible to the Buck Tail agency in Wyoming. The necessary change of stage lines had forced him to stay over night at Billy Knapp's hotel.

The messenger seized his bag and softly ran along through the canvas-partitioned rooms wherein Billy slept to a narrow window which he had already noticed gave out almost directly into the pine woods. The window was of oiled paper, and its catch baffled him. He knew it should slide back, but it refused to slide for him. He did not dare to break the paper because of the crackling noise. A voice at his shoulder startled him.

"I'll show you," whispered the red-cheeked girl.

She was wrapped loosely in a blanket, her hair falling about her shoulders, and her bare feet showing beneath her coverings. The little man suffered at once an agony of embarrassment in which the thought of his errand was lost. It was recalled to him by the girl.

"There you are!" she whispered, showing him the open window.

"Thank you," he stammered painfully, "I assure you—I wish——"

The girl laughed under her breath.

"That's all right," she said heartily, "I owe you that for calling old whiskers off his bronc," and she kissed him.

The messenger, trembling with self-consciousness, climbed hastily through the window, ran the broad loop of the satchel up his arm, and, instead of dropping to the ground, as the girl had expected, swung himself lightly into the branches of a rather large scrub oak that grew near. She listened to the rustle of the leaves for a moment as he neared the trunk, and then, unable longer to restrain her curiosity in regard to the doings below, turned to the stairway.

As she did so, two men mounted. They examined the rooms of the upper story hastily but carefully, paying scant attention to her, and departed swearing. In a few moments they returned for the stranger's trunk. Nell followed as far as the stairway. There she heard and saw things, and fled in bitter dismay to the back of the house when Billy Knapp was overpowered.

At the window she knelt, clasping her hands and placing her head between her bare arms. Women in the West, at least women like Nell, do not weep. But she came near it. Suddenly she raised her head. A voice next her ear had addressed her.

She looked here and there and around, but could discover nothing.

"Here, outside," came the low, guarded voice. "In the tree."

Then she saw that the little stranger had not stirred from his first sighting-place.

"Beg your pardon, ma'am, for startling you or for addressing you at all, which I shouldn't, but——"

"Oh, never mind that!" cried the girl impatiently, shaking back her hair. So deprecating and timid were the tones, that almost without an effort of the imagination she could picture the little man's blushes and his half-sidling method of delivery. At this supreme moment, his littleness and lack of self-assertion jarred on her mood. "What you doin' there? Thought you'd vamoosed."

"It was safest here," explained the stranger. "I left no trail."

She nodded comprehension of the common sense of this.

"But, ma'am, I took the liberty of speakin' to you because you seems to be in trouble. Of course I aint got no right to *ask*, an' if you don't care to tell me——"

"They're goin' to kill Billy!" broke in Nell with a sob.

"What for?"

"I don't jest rightly make out. They're after some one, and they thinks Billy's *cache*in' him. I reckon it's you. Billy ain't *cache*in' nothin'; but they thinks he is."

"Its me they's after, all right enough. Now you knows where I am, why don't you tell them an' save Billy?"

The girl started, but her keen Western mind saw the difficulty at once.

"They thinks Billy perfects you, jest the same."

"Do you love him?" asked the stranger.

"God knows I'm pretty tough," confessed Nell, sobbing, "but I jest do that!" and she dropped her head again.

The invisible stranger in the gloom fell silent, considering.

"I'm a purty rank proposition myself," said he at last, as if to himself, "and I got a job on hand which same I oughta put through without givin' attention on anythin' else. As a usual play, folks don't care for me, and I don't care much for folks. Women especial. They drives me plumb tired. I reckon I don't stack up very high on the blue chips when it comes to cashin' in with that sex, anyhow; but in general they gives me as much notice as they lavishes on a doodle bug. I ain't carin', you understand, nary bit; but onct in a dog's age I kind of hankers for a decent look from one of them. I ain't never had no women folks of my own—never. Sometimes I thinks it would be some scrumptious to know a little gal's waitin' for me somewheres. They ain't none. They never will be. I ain't built that way. You treated me white to-night. You're the first woman that ever kissed me of her own accord."

The girl heard a faint scramble, then the soft *pat* of some one landing on his feet. Peering from the window, she made out a faint shadowy form stealing around the corner of the hotel. She put her hand to her heart and listened. Her understanding of the stranger's motives was vague, but she had caught his confession that her kiss had meant much to him, and even in her anxiety she felt an inclination to laugh. She had bestowed that caress as she would have kissed the cold end of a dog's nose.

The men below stairs, after some discussion, had decided on bullet. This was out of consideration for Billy's standing as a frontiersman. Besides, he had stolen no horses. In order not to delay matters, the

poisoned pup. Ain't everyone kin corral a man and git fifty thousand dollars without turnin' a hair."

Black Hank distributed three men to do the business. There were no heroics. The execution of this man was necessary to him, not because he was particularly angry over the escape of the messenger—he expected

"" *'Nds up !' he commanded sharply.*"

execution was fixed for the present time and place. Billy stood with his back to the logs of his own hotel, his hands and feet bound, but his eyes uncovered. He had never lost his nerve. In the short respite which preparation demanded, he told his opponents what he thought of them.

"Proud ?" he concluded a long soliloquy as if to the reflector of the lamp, "Proud?" he repeated meditatively, "This yere Hank's jest that proud he's all swelled up like a

to capture that individual in due time,—but in order to preserve his authority over his men. He was in the act of moving back to give the shooters room, when he heard the door open and shut.

He turned. Before the door stood a small consumptive-looking man in a light check suit. The tenderfoot carried two short-barreled Colt's revolvers, one of which he presented directly at Black Hank.

"'Nds up !" he commanded sharply.

Hank was directly covered, so he obeyed. The new-comer's eye had a strangely restless quality. Of the other dozen inmates of the room, eleven were firmly convinced that the weapon and eye not directed at their leader were personally concerned with themselves. The twelfth thought he saw his chance. To the bewildered onlookers there seemed to be a flash and a bang, instantaneous; then things were as before. One of the stranger's weapons still pointed at Black Hank's breast; the second at each one of the others. Only, the twelfth man, he who had seen his chance, had collapsed forward to the floor. No one could assure himself positively that he had discerned the slightest motion on the part of the stranger.

" ' I'm layin' for the man that sticks his head outen that door.' "

"Now," said the latter sharply, "one at a time, gentlemen. Drop your gun !" this last to Black Hank. "Muzzle down. Drop it ! Correct."

One of the men in the back of the room stirred slightly on the ball of his foot.

"Steady there !" said the stranger. The man stiffened.

"Next gent," went on the little man, subtly indicating another. The latter obeyed without hesitation. "Next ! Now you. Now you in the corner."

One after another the pistols clashed to the floor. Not for an instant could a single inmate of the apartment, armed or unarmed, flatter himself that his slightest motion was overlooked. They were like tigers on the crouch, ready to spring the moment the man's guard lowered. It did not lower. The huddled figure on the floor reminded them of what might happen. They obeyed.

"Step back !" commanded the stranger next. In a moment he had them standing in a row against the wall, rigid, upright, their hands over their heads. Then for the first time the stranger moved from his position by the door.

"Call her," he said to Billy—"the girl."

Billy raised his voice. "Nell ! O, Nell !"

In a moment she appeared in the doorway at the foot of the stairs, without hesitation or fear. She had slipped on a dress. When she perceived the state of affairs, she brightened almost mischievously.

"Would you just as soon, ma'am, if it ain't troublin' you too much, just sort of naturally untie Billy ?" requested the stranger.

She did so. The hotelkeeper stretched his arms.

"Now pick up them guns, please."

The two set about it.

"Where's that infernal old reprobate ?" howled Billy suddenly, looking about for Charley.

The patriarch had quietly slipped away.

"You can drop them arms," advised the stranger, lowering the muzzles of his weapons. The leader started to say something.

"You shut up !" said Billy, selecting his own revolvers from the heap.

The stranger suddenly picked up one of the Colt's single-action revolvers which lay on the floor, and, holding the trigger back against the guard, exploded the six charges by hitting the hammer smartly with the palm of his hand. In the thrusting motion of this discharge he evidently had design, for the first six wine-glasses on Billy's bar were shivered. It was wonderful work, rattling fire, quicker than a self-cocker even. He selected another weapon. From a pile of tomato cans he took one and tossed it into the air. Before it had fallen he had perforated it twice, and as it rolled along the floor he helped its progression by four more bullets which left streams of tomato juice where they had hit. The room was full of smoke. The group watched, fascinated.

Then the men against the wall grew rigid. Out of the film of smoke long, vivid streams flashed towards them, right and left, like the alternating steam of a locomotive's pistons. *Smash, smash! smash, smash!* hit the bullets with regular thud. With the twelfth discharge the din ceased. Midway between the heads of each pair of men against the wall was a round hole. No one was touched.

A silence fell. The smoke lightened and blew slowly through the window and open door. The horses, long since deserted by their guardian in favor of the excitement within, whinnied. The stranger dropped the smoking Colts', and quietly reproduced his own short-barreled arms from his side pockets. Billy broke the spell at last.

"That's *shootin'!*" he observed with a sigh.

"The fifty thousand is outside," said the stranger. "Do you want 'em?"

There was no reply.

"I aims to pull out on one of these here broncs of yours," said he. "Billy, he's all right. He doesn't know nothin' about me."

He collected the six-shooters from the floor.

"I just takes these with me for a spell," he remarked. "You finds them, if you looks hard enough, along on th' trail—likewise your broncs."

He backed towards the door.

"I'm layin' for the man that sticks his head outen that door," he warned.

"Stranger," called Black Hank, as he neared the door.

The little man paused.

"Might I ask your name?"

"My name is Alfred," replied the latter.

Black Hank looked chagrined.

"I've heard tell of you," he remarked.

The stranger's eye ran over the room and encountered that of the girl. He shrank into himself and blushed.

"Good-night," he said hastily, and disappeared. A moment later the beat of hoofs became audible as he led the bunch of horses away.

For an instant no one spoke. Then Billy: "By God, Hank, I means to stand pat with you; but you let that kid alone, or I plugs you!" Billy was the only man armed.

"Kid, huh!" grunted Hank. "Alfred a kid! I've heard tell of him."

"What've you heard?" inquired the girl.

"He's the plumb best scout on the southern trail, and the best pistol shot in the West," replied Black Hank.

The year following, Billy Knapp, Alfred, and another man named Jim Buckley, took across to the Hills the only wagon train that dared set out that summer.

21

The Admirable Outlaw

M'CREADY SYKES

THE ADMIRABLE OUTLAW

By M'Cready Sykes

ILLUSTRATIONS BY N. C. WYETH

Y English friend thought it was a hold-up. So no doubt did the passengers jolting drowsily in the stage-coach. Two men rode quickly up to the open windows; the stage stopped, and they glanced inside. They were well browned and carried excellent Winchester rifles.

"He ain't there. Thank ye, gentlemen; an' you, Miss"—this last to the school ma'am, who was the least surprised of any.

"I don't suppose you've seen no foot-passenger up the road—nor on the bench, perhaps? Wa'al, that's about all."

My Englishman and I had been riding some two hundred yards behind the stage. It was a slow, lumpy road down the canyon. Farther up, on the bench, we had fallen in converse with Luther, the stage-driver. There the road was wide, and we could ride alongside; Luther spun for us many painful yarns, involving much of battle, murder and sudden death, of catamounts and rattle-snakes, of vast lakes and mighty deserts. Luther was on the whole the most varied and picturesque liar I have ever known, and he delighted the heart of my English globe-trotting friend. We promised ourselves a pleasant evening in Luther's company when we should reach North Star, and we had relinquished our place along the stage regretfully, and only when the road had become too narrow.

Morley had been drifting at leisurely pace around the world, and I had fallen in with him at Portland, fresh from two weeks on the Pacific. Then with vast delight he had come inland with me and had knocked about the mining camps in the mountains back of North Star. We were coming back to town, and our horses had overtaken the stage. Morley was grieving that we had only seven miles to go.

"A week in the mining camps," he had complained, "and no adventures; just fancy! But when I'm home I'll appropriate some of Luther's. Still, I rather hoped for an adventure of our own; that's the worst of the 'disappearing frontier.'"

So he rather welcomed the browned strangers with their rifles, and we all fell into conversation when we drew up by the coach.

"Prisoner broke jail—that's all; he come this way." Frank Simers, the big sheriff, felt a certain shame at confessing the escape, and his deputy coughed apologetically.

"An' the slickest cuss in this country," added the sheriff. "A low, dog-goned bank robber. Started a shootin' on the sidewalk an' sicked the cashier onto his pal, and then ran inside and cleaned out eight hundred dollars in gold, an' carried it away, too. 'Twan't much to get caught for, but they want him in Wyoming when we get through with him. Broke away this afternoon, an' Tom Husack here seen him headin' for the bench. Wa'al, so'long. We'll have him by nightfall."

Luther released the brake, took up his reins, and cried "Giddap!" Then he reflected, and holding back his four horses, said that it reminded him of a man that once tried to shoot him in Nevada—"a one-eyed man, so he shot on the bias, ye might say."

But Morley had quickly lost his liking for adventures at second hand. "Can't we help you in the search?" he said to the sheriff.

There is no hunt that stirs the blood of your Briton as does the noble sport of hunting Man. Morley had mourned at not killing a tiger; he was keen on this new scent.

"Sure, sure," said the sheriff, not displeased at the evident enthusiasm of his ally. "We can drive him in quick, all goin' together. He's afoot."

The stage lumbered down the canyon, and the four of us turned back toward the summit. Clearly there would be no connection with the Overland for us that night.

Simers explained that being mounted, and thus lifted above the sky-line, we were so far forth at a disadvantage, and would be seen by the robber long before we could see him. "He'll crouch along the sage-brush, an' work up into the pines, an' make shift to do his travelling by night. So the more of this bench we can cover by nightfall, the better chanct we'll have. Once he gets out o' the sage-brush an' into the sheep-grass, we can see him if he lies flat agin a stone."

So we thrashed over the bench all that afternoon, till we were choking with the universal smell of the dusty sage-brush; we started up jack-rabbits innumerable, and saw the gophers scudding to their holes. We came upon a sheep-herder, working his band of sheep down from the mountains, but could find no clue. At twilight we were together again.

"But I say," cried Morley, suddenly inspired, as we were sitting around on the grass for a brief pause, "we've no idea what the fellow looks like, you know. Haven't you a photograph, or something?"

Sheriff Frank uncoiled himself. "Now don't you worry about that, pardner. Ef you see a man wanderin' about here on the bench, unattached like, and not havin' no tag, nor no hoss, why, it's *him*. But it might be as I *hev* got a photograph, now— jest in case I had to do any mailin'. Look in Tom's coat over on that there pile, in the inside pocket. Ye can take it along. I'll be back in a minute."

While the sheriff was gone to replenish the supply of water, we found the coat and the photograph, and examined the picture minutely. It was not a bad face—on the contrary, it struck me as decidedly a good one, with a pleasing expression of frank good-nature, and almost a masterful look about the mouth and eyes.

The man in the picture had a pleasantly recalcitrant tuft of hair, that stood up defiantly in the middle of his forehead. We had finished our examination, and Morley had put the picture in his own pocket for future reference, when the sheriff rejoined us. "Now, my lord, you just keep the picter, an' you'll know your man when you see him."

Behind his back, Sheriff Frank had already begun to speak of Morley as "the Jook." To his face, he compromised on "my lord."

"We'll get him, boys—never fear. But I won't hear the last of this from Governor Yandee. My, but Yandee'll give it to me strong. If the feller wa'n't really gone, I'd think now 'twas a joke of the Governor's. He's always playin' them practical jokes o' his."

Frank's deputy nodded assent, intimating that Governor Yandee was "almost *too* ondignified for a governor of the state"; but Frank's commission ran in the name of the Chief Executive, and he upheld him.

"No, Tom, he ain't ondignified, Tom; he's jest high-spirited. But I'll never hear the end of this."

Morley said that he had in his pocket letters of introduction to Governor Yandee, and that he was anticipating with much delight meeting so pleasant an acquaintance.

"Yes sirree, a fine, whole-souled feller is Bob Yandee," cried the sheriff, "and when you see him ye just give him Frank Simers' regards—assumin' that we've catched this cuss of a bank-robber. Nice feller, Bob."

But that the outlaw would not be captured never seemed to enter the sanguine imagination of the sheriff. And this was not altogether groundless optimism, for the news of the escape would travel fast, and it is not easy to slip unobserved through a country where every new arrival or passer-by excites interest and comment, and affords discussion for a whole evening in half a dozen camps.

We hobbled our horses and turned them loose in the short, dry grass. Simers and Deputy Tom had brought a trifle of provisions, anticipating that the search might after all last over the day. The stars swung about, looming large in the rarefied air even of thirty-five hundred feet of altitude; and far down the canyon the desolate howling of the coyotes was all that broke the stillness.

Morley enjoyed it hugely, and was more communicative than his wont about his own wanderings. The sheriff and Tom Husack, born with the *Wanderlust* that is the Westerner's birthright, had much to tell of many men in many lands, and quickly established with the Englishman the *camaraderie* of them that wander about the earth. The deputy was soon plain Tom for us all; in another half hour we were all calling the sheriff Frank, and assuredly the Englishman would have gotten back to first principles and his first name had his new friends happened to know it. He took his friendly cross-examination like a little man, giving good-naturedly the details of his ancestry, his father's occupations and avocations, and his grandfather's, his religious and political views and the motives that had impelled him to travel around the world. He recognized

Drawn by N. C. Wyeth.

My English friend thought it was a hold-up.

clearly that his questioners were inspired by no idle curiosity, but welcomed him as a friend and took a friend's interest in his affairs. The problem of the future of Canada, and of the Anglo-American alliance, being happily solved, we fell asleep one by one to the howling of the distant coyotes and the occasional scrambling of the hobbled horses as they searched about for fresher bits of grass.

At dawn we separated pursuant to our plan of overnight, Morley and I keeping not too far from the canyon, from whose billowing sides we could command the trail along the stream. The sides of the canyon died away, and after an hour's riding we found ourselves on fairly level ground. The horses picked their way easily through the chapparal; we rode, silently for the most part, in and out among the great pines when the creek led us in their direction. Our man-hunt was becoming very mild.

Morley, riding a little in the lead, stopped suddenly, dismounted and crouched down, rifle in hand. I followed, and obeying his silent signal, we walked softly through the bushes to the edge of the stream. My Englishman pointed to his quarry.

Standing in the shallow stream, stark naked in the morning sun, a man was performing his matutinal ablutions. It was about eight o'clock, and the water was evidently very cold, for the bather instinctively expanded his chest under the inspiring sting of the water which he was splashing upon it. In a moment he turned and faced us. It was the original of our photograph. Morley gave a soft whistle that bespoke an amplitude of inward delight.

For my part, I distinctly wished that we had the sheriff and his deputy with us. Desperadoes are not ordinarily captured while bathing *en plein air*. Besides, I was nervously conscious, as indeed our photograph had forewarned us, that our man was not exactly the ordinary desperado. Perhaps we might prevail by strategy, and keep in with the man till we could set the duly constituted authorities in motion. It was while I was thinking all this, and a great deal more, that Morley's voice rang cheerfully out:

"Oh, I say: hands up, there."

I had read that phrase, many times, and often heard it quoted. Somehow it failed to strike me at the time as incongruous; yet

of course to compel a man standing in the water without a stitch of clothing to throw up his hands seems in a way superfluous. Certain it is that the man instantly threw up his hands, and held them up, as high as they would go.

"Now, my good fellow, I'm going through your clothes," was Morley's next comment, and keeping his rifle pretty steadily pointed at the captive he stepped a few yards along the bank to where the man's clothes lay. The prisoner made a step toward the bank, but Morley turned sharply upon him, keeping him covered with his rifle. "I'd stand still if I were you, and hands up, you know."

The warning was effective, and the Englishman went carefully through the pockets of the man's clothes, extracting five or six silver dollars, a box of tobacco, a pipe, two knives, and to his great joy, a long and gruesome six-shooter, of the kind that Mr. Colt, or his successors in business, make with such beautiful precision. Morley slipped the gun in his own pocket, and rejoined me.

"Confound it," he whispered, "do you know, they never told us the fellow's name. How can you arrest a man without naming him? Stupid of us never to have asked the sheriff for his name."

I weakly suggested something about our needing a warrant. Morley was almost scornful. "Why, he's an escaped prisoner. One doesn't need a warrant. One can take him wherever one finds him. We'll give him an *alias*."

He pointed his rifle at the captive and said, very slowly and distinctly: "You there, *alias* John Doe, I arrest you in the name of the King—no, I mean in the name of President Roosevelt, or the name of the Governor of this State, and I call on you to lay down your arms and submit."

Our captive gave a wild yell, and shook his fist at the tranquil Briton—"You—arrest me—in the name of—the President —and the Governor of the State—why, you —you—well of all"—but words became inadequate, and the man shook his fist impotently.

"Now, my man, we won't have any of that. Come on shore here and put on some of your clothes for decency's sake. You don't need much. When you've done that, you march along in front of us, and if you cut or run, I'll put a bullet through you as sure as I live. You can make any statement you want, but

Drawn by N. C. Wyeth.

Arranged the line of march so that there should be no possibility of escape.

you don't have to, and I warn you that anything you say can be used against you. I think there's something of that sort in Magna Charta, or the Bill of Rights, and I understand it's in all your constitutions here; so you see I'm looking after your rights. Here are your clothes. Wait a bit, let me take another look at them."

Morley attacked the coat this time, and drew forth a couple of newspaper clippings, a pencil and a paper folded like a legal document. The latter was endorsed "Memorandum on the requisition of the Governor of Wyoming for the extradition of George Selvey, *alias* Peter Dowling, accused of bank robbery."

Morley handed me the paper with a look of triumph. "I wasn't worrying about the fellow's name, but this may come in if we should meet anyone and the man should attempt to escape.

"So you've been collecting the documents of your case, Selvey," he said, turning again to the prisoner. "Well, Selvey, *alias* Dowling, get some clothes on, and we'll go along."

I confess that I was not entirely satisfied with the situation. It was all very well to go through the form of arresting our man, but conveying him to the jail at North Star was a very different matter. If he were to resist, I certainly had no relish for using our rifles, and after all, these were our only points of superiority. It is one thing for two men to overpower a third; it is a very different thing for them to carry him against his will ten miles through the mountains.

On the other hand, from his point of view, why should he resist? We were armed, and he was not; and perhaps he would never guess that we had no mind for subduing him with bullets. Certainly Morley had given no indication of any qualms of that sort. The Englishman was apparently too intent on bagging his game to look on the taking other than as the capture of a cold-blooded criminal who should at no cost be allowed to escape.

In the meantime the prisoner was putting on his clothes. When he was fully dressed, it seemed to me that it was with great difficulty that he was keeping himself under control; once or twice he began speaking angrily but checked himself by an evident effort of will; plainly he was a good actor. He was apparently trying to throw us off our guard. I think we both felt relieved that his Colt was safely in Morley's pocket.

This apparently studied repression of rage at his captors had mostly come about while he was dressing. When he was through he said to Morley very quietly and in a tone that was almost friendly:

"There seems to be some mistake here. You spoke to me a few minutes ago as Selvey. I am not Selvey, and as you don't seem to know who I am, I don't know what more I can say than that you have made an absurd mistake and that the sooner you leave the better. George Selvey is safe in jail at North Star, and if you want him you had better go there."

"That's the very worst thing you could have said," observed Morley judicially. "Twenty-four hours ago you were in jail, Selvey, and in another six hours you'll be there again. By the way, we happen to have your photograph here; I was going to get you to sign it as a souvenir, but I won't ask you to make evidence against yourself."

Morley drew from his pocket the picture the sheriff had given us, and displayed it to our captive with great triumph.

The outlaw was evidently disconcerted at this unwelcome evidence.

"Yes," he said, a little sullenly, "that's my photograph. Where you got it beats me, though I don't know as I much care. But you've got no right to take me. I'll just trouble you for the things you've been taking out of my clothes, and then I'll go my way and you'll go yours."

"You're quite right, Selvey," returned our amateur sheriff imperturbably, "and your way happens to be ours. You forget that you're under arrest. But I say, now, if you'll be decent about it, and go quietly along, and—if you'll tell us how you broke the jail and where you've been, why we'll make it decent and easy for you, and you can ride my horse part of the way. It doesn't really make any difference though, you know, whether you do or not, because we've got the guns, and the horses, and you can't get away, you know. And don't talk unless you want to, but anything you say can be used against you, as I told you before."

The fugitive, impressed by the double threatening of Morley's serious face and of his impassive rifle, laughed rather goodnaturedly, and stepped obediently in front. The sheriff had told us that the bank robber was no ordinary thief, but a smooth and polished villain who would, we inferred, if it were possible, deceive the very elect. So it was with some misgiving that I observed that the man was adopting a distinctly conciliatory tone. Morley observed this too, and arranged the line of march so that there should be no possibility of escape. We bound the prisoner's arms behind him, not without a slight scuffle, and ordered him to march fifteen paces in front. I had indulged in much wonderment as to whether our captive would submit when it came to the pinch, or would put Morley's shooting abilities to the test. But the preliminary struggle over the tying of his hands dissipated all these doubts; and in fact a single look at the Englishman's stern face, and his quick movement for his rifle at a threatening gesture of the robber's, was quite convincing. Morley would have used his rifle without compunction, doubtless shooting promptly upon any attempt at escape, and our captive evidently realized this. My mental inquiries as to what we were going to do with our prisoner were, it appeared, purely academic. Morley was solving the problem with such prompt and masterful efficiency that I felt ashamed of having doubted our own power. It was all in the day's work for Morley, and with the glorious doggedness of his people he would himself have been shot to death rather than let the outlaw escape. Morley consciously represented for the moment the police force of the commonwealth; he had not seriously sought the painful post; but he was a guest of the community, and had been suddenly called into his host's service; not for the world would he have violated the laws of hospitality, nor the obligations of a courteous guest. The prisoner realized the situation, after the little affair with his hands, and made no further effort to escape.

In fact, once reconciled to the inevitable, the escaped robber took his capture good-naturedly, and regaled us much on our journey to North Star. After a time Morley let him walk alongside instead of marching in front; but he was careful not to let his good nature run away with him, and the man's hands remained bound. In this fashion we made leisurely progress across the bench and down along the foothills. In the distant plain we caught for a moment the band of heavy smoke that marked the railway that connects North Star with the main line. We should have been speeding by there the night before on our way to catch the Overland; but the day's delay had not been unwelcome, and it was something to remember all one's life to have captured a bandit, charming a companion as the bandit might be. It happens not infrequently that swindlers lavish upon their chosen craft a wealth of ingenuity that if applied to an honest calling would earn them a comfortable living; and Selvey, for all that he was a bank robber, and a mean one at that, displayed such a lively and good-natured interest in the country whose hospitality he had abused, such a familiarity with all the outlying regions, such a knowledge of conditions, that it seemed pathetic that he should not have turned his inquiring and assimilative mind to better uses. Morley tried to lead him gently into his own field, hoping to pick up some good yarns of crime; I think the honest Englishman was led by conflicting impulses; one, a host's polite solicitude to turn the conversation to subjects in which his guest was thoroughly at home; the other, an overweening care lest a prisoner should be entrapped into making a confession. I believe Morley would have had fears for the continued existence of the republic if a captive in the custody of the law had been led by the sanctity of hospitality, imprisonment though the hospitality might be, into giving evidence against himself.

But our man rattled on, spinning many tales of violence in days gone by, but none of his own. He told us of the long conflict between the sheepmen and the cattlemen, of Tom Horn in Wyoming, his various murders, and of how he had been led to confess; of Diamond Field Jack, his conviction and sentence to death, how the Governor had pardoned him and the storm that the pardon raised, and how afterward Jack had drifted to Nevada, married there, struck it rich in a mine and was now a mighty nabob. He told us of Hangman's Gulch, through which we had come the day before, and of the great days of '63, when the lights of the mining camps were blazing in the Basin all night long, and of how Jenny Lind had sung in the little wooden shack they call the opera house in Placer City in the days of forty years ago when Placer City had been a great and thriving metropolis.

It seemed a pity to have to give our charming friend over to the clutches of the law. Personally, I should not have grieved altogether at an escape; but Morley was of the British sternness all compact; he was not displeased that our prisoner should fare as easily and comfortably as might be, nor that we should all join in friendly converse by the way; but after all, Morley was really, as I have said before, for the time the Police Force of the Commonwealth, and he would guard his captive though the heavens should fall. He kept his rifle across his saddle, and never let Selvey come within interfering distance. There would be no jail delivery that day.

We came into North Star about half an hour before noon, striking out of the sage-brush and on the road just before. The jail lies on the outskirts of the town, or what indeed had once been its outskirts, but was now rapidly being absorbed in the town's encroachment upon the sage-brush waste. In the streets of North Star, Morley again arranged his calvacade in order, and we entered in state. The bank robber really lent a dignity to the procession, as he walked in advance, his arms pinioned behind his back. There were but few in the streets; we were away from the business quarter. But as we approached the jail, the news of our coming seemed to spread, and a casual throng, mostly of women and children, followed along the sidewalk.

Before we turned in at the driveway at the county buildings, Morley ordered the party in close formation, putting the prisoner between our horses. In this fashion we halted before the jail steps.

"We'll turn him over, and then go to the hotel and have a bit of a wash and brush - up. Then we can hunt up the Governor this afternoon, and I'll give him my letters. I hope he won't be too hard on the sheriff for letting this fellow escape."

We did not have to wait long. Officials came piling out of the jail and from the Court House across the square. Ancient clerks appeared, attendants, stenographers, turnkeys, and finally Sheriff Frank himself.

"Well, well, boys, I got back afore ye. We got our man at nine o'clock this mornin'. We fired and signalled, but you was too fur off."

"What's that? Oh, I say now," cried Morley, turning inquiringly, amazement depicted on his face. "Are there *two* of them? We've got your man—got him by your photograph, and a pleasant enough prisoner he's been, and that's a fact."

The Englishman pulled his horse aside, and disclosed to the astonished throng of officials our charming prisoner, dusty with his long walk, his clothes torn by the chapparal and sage-brush, his hands ignominiously bound behind him.

"Mr. Sheriff," said Morley, slowly and impressively, "in the name of President Roosevelt and the United States Constitution, I deliver into your hands George Selvey, *alias* Peter Dowling, and—and—" Morley hesitated a moment, till a phrase of judicial import came to his relief—"and may the Lord have mercy on his soul. God save the United States!"

There had been a murmur of surprise in the crowd at the apparition of the prisoner —then a titter from an aged clerk with a pen behind his ear; the titter had spread and become a vague ripple of wonderment; some of the officials had fled back into the jail; men jabbed their neighbors; the crowd fell a little away from the centre, and we all turned inquiringly to the sheriff. Morley's face was stern with the pride of duty well performed; the Police Force of the Commonwealth was again in the hands of its legitimate custodian, and the Englishman turned to the sheriff for his discharge. The sheriff's face was a fiery·red, but I fancied I saw a twinkle in his eye.

"Boys," he said, "ye meant well; ye meant well. Ye must have got my coat instead of Tom's. Now boys, get out o' North Star jest as fast as ye know how—as fast as ye know how, boys. You've got the Governor of the State. I told him he'd get into trouble with that way o' his, goin' off by himself in the mountains; but he will do it. There's somebody that'll never hear the end o' this; but whether its him or me, I ain't quite clear."

And that was why Mr. Robert Morley never presented his letters of introduction to the Governor. But we found the Over·land an excellent train.

22

Finger-That-Kills Wins His Squaw

C.M. RUSSELL

"The next thing he knows three Injuns comes yelpin' down on him, quirtin' their ponies at every jump."

Drawing by C. M. Russell.

FINGER-THAT-KILLS WINS HIS SQUAW

BY C. M. RUSSELL

ILLUSTRATIONS BY THE AUTHOR

HAT story that Dad Lane tells the other n i g h t 'bout his compadre getting killed off sure shows the Injun up," says "Squaw" Owens, "Injuns is born bushwhackers; they believe in killin' off their enemy 'n' ain't particular how it's done, but prefer gettin' him from cover, 'n' I notice some of their white brothers play the same way. You watch these old gun-fighters 'n' you'll see most of 'em likes a shade the start in a draw; there's many a man that's fell under the smoke of a forty-five—down from a sneak—that ain't lookin when he got it.

"I've had plenty experience amongst Injuns, 'n' all the affection I got for 'em wouldn't make no love story, but with all their tricks 'n' treachery I call them a game people. It's their religion to die without a whimper; in olden times when a prisoner's took, there's no favors asked or given. He's up agin it—it's a sure case of cash in —skinned alive, cooked over a slow fire or some such pleasant trail to the huntin' ground, 'n' all Mister Prisoner does is to take his medicine without whinin'. If he makes any talk it's to tell ye you're a green hand at the business; of course he don't cuss none—he don't know how. That art belongs to civilized folks, but an Injun's got a string of names to call ye that'll do till something better comes along. They sure talk scandalous about you 'n' your relations.

"Talkin' about an Injun's nerve reminds me of an old buck I run onto on the Blackfoot Reserve a few years ago. I'm ridin' for the Flyin' O; this outfit's fillin' a beef contract, 'n' throwin' steers into the Agency near where we're holdin' the beef on Two Medicine, close herdin'.

"There's an old Injun comes visitin' our camp, 'n' after he feeds once you can bet on him showin' up 'bout noon every day. If there's a place where an Injun makes a hand, it's helpin' a neighbor hide grub, 'n' they ain't particular about quality—it's quantity they want. Uncle Sam's Injuns average about one good meal a week; nobody's got to graze this way long till a tin plate loaded with beans looks like a Christmas dinner.

"This old buck takes a great likin' to me 'n' the chuck wagon, 'n' as I can talk some Blackfoot, we get right sociable. I get this talk from a 'Live Dictionary' the year before, when I wintered up on Old Man's River; that is, I marry a B'ood woman. When I say marry, I traded her pa two ponies 'n' a Winchester 'n' in accordance with all Injun's law, we're necked all right. Of course I furnish grub 'n' material to her relations for a tea dance to make the weddin' fashionable.

"But our married life ain't joyful—I sure kick on that cookin', for there ain't enough Injun in me to like it.

"Thinkin' to civilize her a little I buy her a white woman's rig at McLeod, 'n' when she slips this on, I'm damned if you can tell which way she's travelin'.

"We ain't been married a week till I've learned enough of the talk to call her all the names known to Blackfeet, 'n' by spring we can pull off nearly as good a quarrel as civilized folks in harness. When grass comes we separate; there's no divorce needed as we're both willin', so we split the blankets; she pulls for camp 'n' I drift south.

"But this old buck I started to tell ye about—Finger-That-Kills is his name—is all Injun from his moccasins up. If it ain't for his calico shirt 'n' leggin's 'n' clout bein' made of blanket instead of skin, he's dressed like he'd be a hundred years ago.

"The first day he shows up I notice he's shy three fingers on his right hand, leavin' nothin' but his thumb 'n' trigger finger. Now he don't look to me like he's ever railroaded or worked in a saw mill, 'n' of course I'm curious to know who worked him over. So one day I'm layin' in the shade of my hoss on herd, when old Finger-That-Kills rides up on his little pinto whittledig for a visit. It's then I ask him how he gets trimmed up. He don't say nothin' for a long time but goes to gazin' off on the prairie like he's lookin' for some-thin'. Now folks that don't know Injuns 'ud think he don't hear me, but I heap savvy he's reachin' back in his history for the yarn I want.

"The only book he's got is these old prairies, but it's open to him 'n' he knows every leaf in her; I tell you, fellers, she sure holds good yarns for them that can read her.

"Finally he shakes out his black stone pipe, 'n' layin' her down, opens up on his yarn.

"'My cousin, it's a long way behind me,' says he, drawin' his crippled hand slow from his left out in front of him back over his shoulder, which means in signs 'very long.'

"'Forty times I've seen the snow come 'n' go since I took my first war trail. I was then young 'n' my heart was strong.'

"Now I can't give it to you as flowery as this Injun does, 'cause these people are sure pretty with talk, but as I interpret it he's 'bout nineteen—the age the Reds begin lookin' for a mate—when he starts ridin' 'round on a painted pony 'n' puttin' in his time lookin' pretty. When a bunch of young squaws is down gettin' water, he accidently rides through the creek, givin' them a chance to admire him. He's ablaze with paint 'n' feathers—to hear him tell it he's rigged out so it hurts your eyes to look at him, 'n' it ain't hard to imagine, 'cause I've seen young bucks stripped to the clout 'n' moccasins, painted till they're sure gaudy.

"Well, he finally sees the one he's lookin' for; she's as pretty as a painted wagon 'n' loves him right back. Now some folks think Injuns don't have love scrapes, but don't ever believe it. There's many a squaw that leaves camp with a rawhide under her blanket, 'n' next day she's found hangin' in a cottonwood—all because she can't get the buck she wants, 'n' the bucks are just as locoed in their way.

"Well, as I said before, Finger-That-Kills is sure warped on this squaw; they're both willin', but he ain't got the price; he's shy on ponies as her old dad's holdin' her for fifteen 'n' he's only got five, so it's a case of steal hosses or lose the girl.

"It's spring 'n' time for the Sun dance, so when that's pulled off he takes a hand 'n' goes through all right. Shortly after there's a war party starts for the Crow country, 'n' he's among 'em; there's fifteen, all afoot 'n' travelin' light—stealin' parties generally goes this way. Each man's packin' his bundle of moccasins, dried meat, a rawhide rope 'n' weepons—mostly bows, as guns is scarce them days; the ones they've got is flintlocks that go off whenever they feel like it.

"They travel many sleeps with nothin' happenin' except runnin' low on meat but that's nothin'—no Injun's supposed to get hungry on a war trip. Finally they run clean out of pemmican, 'n' they're gettin gan't 'n' wolfy. There's plenty of game, but they can't hunt, bein' afoot, 'n' its pretty ticklish work disturbin' buffalo in the enemy's country. There's no tellin' what butte holds a Red sentinel wrapped to the eyes in his robe. You can't see him but he's there—still as a sleepin' snake. He don't need no bring-'em-close glasses; nature's give him a couple of beady blinkers that ain't wore none by readin', 'n' what they overlook ain't worth huntin' up.

"He sees the herd way yonder in the open; maybe there's a couple of bulls locked horns to one side, or one gougin' out a waller. The herd may be trailin' in to water, leavin' long strings of dust. These maneuvers don't excite him none, but let 'em start runnin', millin' or churnin' 'n' he's sure interested, for there ain't but one animal that'll cause these brown grass eaters to act up that away—and it walks on hind legs 'n' ain't haired over.

"This lookout heap savvys, 'n' you can bet he ain't slow at signalin'. He's got several ways of telegraphin', accordin' to time 'n' weather. If the sun's right it's a lookin' glass; if it's too windy for smoke, a blanket or robe, 'n' at night a fire, 'n' it's surprisin' how quick he'll change that quiet peaceful scene. Before you know it the country's swarmin' with painted, feathered hair-hunters, 'n' hell's poppin'. Of course the Blackfeet know all this 'n' they're mighty cautious.

"They're nearin' the Crow country, travelin' nights mostly. One mornin' just breakin' day Finger-That-Kills is sneakin' along ahead of his party—kind of advance scout; he's sure hungry, his belt's cinched to its last hole 'n' he can't think of nothin' but eatin', when of a sudden he stumbles right onto a big bull. This old buffalo's got three wolves around him; he's ham-strung 'n' down behind, but whirlin' 'round 'n' makin' a good stand-off with his horns. When Mister Injun walks up, these wolves go slinkin' off, makin' faces at him; they don't like bein' busted in on at meal times.

"With a couple of arrows Finger-That-Kills finishes the bull, but before touchin' the meat, holdin' up his hands, he thanks the sun, who's just peepin' over the sky-line. You may not know it, but all Injuns is great people to give thanks to their God.

"Then he cuts in 'n' gets the liver; Redskins are sure fond of this—raw 'n' warm. He's so busy fillin' up that he gets careless; there's a flock of sage hens comes sailin' over that disturbs his meal 'n' the next thing he knows three Injuns comes yelpin' down on him, quirtin' their ponies at every jump.

"Now there's a bunch of cottonwoods not far from where he's sittin' that looks mighty handy, so he hits the breeze, not runnin' straight, but sidewindin', duckin', 'n' dodgin' like a grouse hen tollin' ye from her nest.

"He's a hard mark, but he ain't made three of these curves till a trade ball goes plowin' up under his scalp 'n' he turns over on his face as dead as he'll ever be for a minute. When he comes to, the stran-gers are down off their ponies, jokin' 'n' laughin'. Of course Finger-That-Kills don't see the humor; he's playin' dead for all there's in it. They're Gros Ventres—he knows this by the few words he savvys of their gutteral tongue. He feels the hand of his enemy twisted in his scalp lock,

"Droppin' the hair he reaches for the jeweled hand."

'n' it ain't no guess with him that he'll be losing some hair shortly. He is layin' face down, his right hand's stretched out along the ground, his left doubled under him. Bein' a dandy 'n' a leader of fashion, he wears jewelry regardless, 'n' his hands are loaded to the knuckles with brass trade rings.

"The Gros Ventre's eye for finery is caught by this glitter, 'n' droppin' the hair, he reaches for the jeweled hand, first tryin' to slip the rings, but they're tight, so takin' his knife he begins hackin' the fingers off.

"Now's when Finger-That-Kills comes in with that Injun nerve I'm tellin' you about. He lays there not movin' a muscle, 'n' all the comfort he gets is gnawin' a branch of sage brush his head's layin' in while this operation is goin' on.

"The Gros Ventre's sawin' away on his middle finger when Mister Blackfoot hears the welcome yelpin' of his party comin' up on the back trail.

"The minute these Big Bellies see they're outnumbered, they crawl their ponies 'n' bust the breeze; havin' hosses the best of it, they make a clean get-away. Finger-That-Kills is glad he's livin' 'n' got his hair, but he's sure sore 'bout losin' those rings.

"This little trouble don't stop the Blackfeet. They reach the Crows all right 'n' come back with two hundred stolen ponies.

"Of course Finger-That-Kills gets his squaw all right, but this don't end his love scrapes, for an Injun with one wife is a tolerable poor husband. These people set no limit to matrimony 'n' count wealth by squaws 'n' hosses.

"'How does it feel,' says I, 'when that Gros Ventre's trimmin' you?'

"'The Big Belly's lazy; his knife's dull —very dull. The dog-eater's foolish like a squaw when he leaves me this,' says he, smilin' 'n' holdin' up his lone finger. 'For this one has killed two Big Bellies for every one of his dead brothers, 'n' their scalps have long dried in the lodge of the Finger-That-Kills.'"

23

Longrope's Last Guard

C.M. RUSSELL

"Pullin' my gun I empty her in the air."

Drawing by C. M. Russell.

LONGROPE'S LAST GUARD

A FATAL STAMPEDE

BY C. M. RUSSELL

DRAWING BY THE AUTHOR

"W HOEVER told you that cattle stampede without cause was talkin' like a shorthorn," says Rawhide. "You can bet all you got that whenever cattle run, there's a reason for it.

"There's plenty of causes for a stampede; sometimes its a green hand or a careless cowpuncher scratchin' a match to light a cigarette. Maybe it's somethin' on the wind, or a tired night-hoss spraddles out 'n' shakes himself, 'n' the poppin' of the saddle leather causes 'em to jump the bed-ground. Scare a herd on the start, 'n' you're liable to have hell with them all the way. I've seen bunches well trail-broke that you couldn't fog off the bed-ground with a slicker and six-shooter; others that had had a scare, you'd have to ride a hundred yards away to spit. Some men's too careful with their herds, 'n' go tiptoein' around like a mother with a sick kid. I've had some experience, 'n' claim this won't do. I've seen herds start in broad daylight, with no cause that anybody knows of. The smell of blood will start 'em goin'; this generally comes off in the mornin' when they're quittin' the bed-ground. Now, in every herd you'll find steers that's regular old rounders. They won't go to bed like decent folks, but put in the night perusin' 'round, disturbin' the peace.

"If there's any bulls in the bunch there's liable to be fightin'. I've often watched an old bull walkin' 'round through the herd talkin' fight, hangin' up his bluff, with a bunch of these rounders at his heels.

They're sure backin' him up—boostin' 'n' ribbin' up trouble, 'n' if there's a fight pulled off you should hear these trouble builders takin' sides; every one of 'em with his tongue out 'n' tail kincked, buckin' 'n' bellerin' like his money's all up. These night ramblers that won't go to bed at decent hours, after raisin' hell all night are willin' to bed down 'n' are sleepin' like drunks when decent cattle are walkin' off the bed-ground.

"Now you know when a cow-brute quits his bed he bows his neck, gaps 'n' stretches all same 's a human after a night's rest. Maybe he accidentally tromps on one of these rounder's tails that's layin' along the ground. This hurts plenty 'n' Mister Night Rambler ain't slow about wakin' up; he raises like he's overslept 'n's afeared he'll miss the coach, leavin' the tossel of his tail under the other feller's hoof. He goes off ringin' his stub 'n' scatterin' blood on his rump 'n' quarters. Now the minute the other cattle winds the blood the ball opens. Every hoof's at his heels, barkin' 'n' bellerin'. Them that's close enough are hornin' him in the flank like they're stuck to finish him off. They're all plum hog-wild, 'n' if you want any beef left in your herd you'd better cut him out, 'cause an hour of this will take off more taller than they'll put on in a month.

"Cattle like open country to sleep in; I sure hate to hold a herd near any brakes or deep 'royos, 'cause no matter how gentle a herd is, let a coyote or any other animal loom up of a sudden close to 'em 'n' they don't stop to take no second look, but are gone like a flash in a pan. Old bulls comin' up without talkin' sometimes jump a herd this way, 'n' it pays a cow-puncher to sing when he's comin' up out of a 'royo close to a bed-ground.

"Some folks 'll tell you that cowboys sing their cows to sleep, but that's a mistake, judgin' from my experience, 'n' I've had some. The songs 'n' voices I've heard 'round cattle ain't soothin'. A cowpuncher sings to keep himself company; it ain't that he's got any motherly love for these longhorns he's put to bed 'n's ridin' herd on; he's amusin' himself 'n' nobody else. These ditties 're generally shy on melody 'n' strong for noise. Put a man alone in the dark, 'n' if his conscience is clear 'n' he ain't hidin' he'll sing 'n' don't need to be a born vocalist. Of course singin's a good thing around a herd, 'n' all punchers know it. In the darkness it lets the cows know where you're at.

"If you ever woke up in the night 'n' found somebody—you didn't know who or what—loomin' up over you, it would startle you, but if this somebody's singin' or whistlin' it wouldn't scare you none. It's the same with Mister Steer; that snaky, noiseless glidin' up on him 's what startles the animal.

"All herds has some of these lonesomes that won't lay down with the other cattle, but beds down alone maybe twenty-five or thirty yards from the edge of the herd. He's got his own reason for this; it might be he's short an eye. This bein' the case you can bet all you got he's layin' with the good blinker next to the herd. He don't figure on lettin' none of his playful brothers reef his ribs from a sneak. One-eyed hosses 's the same. Day or night you'll find him on the outside with his good eye watchin' the bunch. Like Mister Steer, the confidence he's got in his brothers 's mighty frail.

"But these lonesome cattle I started to tell about is the ones that a puncher's most liable to run onto in the dark, layin' out that way from the herd. If you come onto him singin' it don't startle Mister Steer; he raises easy, holdin' his ground till you pass; then he lays down in the same place. He's got the ground warm 'n' hates to quit her. Cows, the same as humans, likes warm beds. Many's the time in cool weather I've seen some evil-minded, lowdown steer stand 'round actin' like he ain't goin' to bed, but all the time he's got his eye on some poor under-sized brother layin' nearby, all innocent. As soon as he thinks this ground 's warm, Mister Lowdown walks over, horns him out 'n' jumps his claim. This lowdown trick is sometimes practiced by punchers when they get a gentle herd. It don't hurt a cowpuncher's conscience none to sleep in a bed he stole from a steer.

"If you ride sneakin' 'n' noiseless onto one of these lonesome fellers, he gets to his feet with dew-claws 'n' hoofs rattlin', 'n's runnin' before he's half up, hittin' the bunch like a canned dog, 'n' quicker than you can bat an eye, the whole herd's gone. Cows are slow animals, but scare 'em 'n' they're fast enough; a thousand 'll get to their feet as quick as one. It's sure a puzzler to cowmen to know how a herd 'll all scare at once, 'n' every animal 'll get to his feet at the same time. I've seen herds do what cowpunchers would call jump—that is, raise 'n' not run. I've been lookin' across a herd in bright moonlight—a thousand head or more, all down, when with no known cause there's a short, quick rumble, 'n' every hoof's standin'.

"I've read of stampedes that were sure dangerous 'n' scary, where a herd would run through a camp upsettin' wagons 'n' trompin' sleepin' punchers to death. When day broke they'd be fifty or a hundred miles from where they started, leavin' a trail strewed with blood, dead cowpunchers 'n' hosses, that looks like the work of a Kansas cyclone. This is all right in books, but the feller that writes it's romancin' 'n' don't savvy the cow. Most stampedes is noisy but harmless to anybody but the cattle. A herd in a bad storm might drift thirty miles in a night, but the worst run I ever see we ain't four miles from the bed-ground when day broke.

"This was down in Kansas; we're trailin' beef 'n' have got about seventeen hundred head. Barrin' a few dry ones, the herd's straight steers, mostly Spanish longhorns from down on the Cimarron. We're about fifty miles south of Dodge. Our herd 's well broke 'n' lookin' fine, 'n' the cowpunchers's all good natured, thinkin' of the good time comin' in Dodge.

"That evenin' when we're ropin' our hosses for night-guard the trail-boss, Old Spanish we call him—he ain't no real Spaniard, but has rode some in old Mexico 'n' talks some Spanish—says to me;

"'Them cattle ought to hold well; they ain't been off water four hours 'n' we grazed 'em plum onto the bed-ground. Every hoof of 'em's got a paunch full of grass 'n' water, 'n' that's what makes cattle lay good.'

"Me 'n' a feller we call Longrope, 's on first guard. He's a center-fire or single-cinch man from California; packs a sixty-foot rawhide riata, 'n' when he takes her down 'n' runs out about half of her into loop she looks big, but when it reaches the animal, comes pretty near fittin' hoof or horn. I never went much on these long-rope boys, but this man comes as near puttin' his loop where he wants to as any I ever see. You know Texas men ain't got much love for a single rig, 'n' many's the argument me 'n' Longrope's had on this subject. He claims a center-fire is the only saddle, but I 'low they'll do all right on a shad-bellied Western hoss, but for Spanish pot-gutted ponies they're no good. You're ridin' up on his withers all the time.

"When we reach the bed-ground most of the cattle's already down, lookin' comfortable. They're bedded in open country 'n' things look good for an easy night. It's been mighty hot all day, but there's a little breeze now, makin' it right pleasant, but down west I notice some nasty lookin' clouds hangin' 'round the new moon that's got one horn hooked over the skyline, 'n' it ain't long till there ain't a star in sight. There's a little lightnin' so far off that you can just hear her rumble, but she's walkin' up on us slow, 'n' I'm hopin' she'll go 'round. The cattle's all layin' quiet 'n' nice, so when me 'n' Longrope meet we stop to talk awhile.

"'They're layin' quiet,' says I.

"'Too damn quiet,' says he. 'I like cows to lay still all right, but I want some of the natural noises that goes with a herd this size. I want to hear 'em blowin' off, 'n' the creakin' of their joints, showin' they're easin' themselves in their beds. Listen, 'n' if you hear anything I'll eat that rimfire saddle of yours—grass-rope 'n' all.'

"I didn't notice till then, but when I straightened my ears it's quiet as a grave. If it ain't for the lightnin' showin' the herd once in awhile, I couldn't 'a' believed that seventeen hundred longhorns lay within forty feet of where I'm sittin' on my hoss. It's gettin' darker every minute, 'n' if it

wasn't for Longrope's slicker I couldn't 'a' made him out though he's so close I could have touched him with my hand. Finally it darkens up so I can't see him at all. It's black as a nigger's pocket; you couldn't find your nose with both hands.

"I remember askin' Longrope the time.

"'I guess I'll have to get help to find the timepiece,' says he, but gets her after feelin' over himself, 'n' holdin' her under his cigarette takes a long draw, lightin' up her face.

"'Half-past nine,' says he.

"'Half an hour more,' I says. 'Are you goin' to wake up the next guard or did you leave it to the hoss-wrangler?'

"'There won't be but one guard to-night,' he answers, ''n' we'll ride it. You might as well hunt for a hoss thief in heaven as look for that camp. Well I guess I'll mosey 'round,' 'n' with that he quits me.

"The lightnin's playin' every little while. It ain't makin' much noise, but lights up enough to show you where you're at. There ain't no use ridin'; by the flashes I can see every hoof's down. For a second it 'll be like broad day, then darker than the dungeons of hell, 'n' I notice the little fireballs on my hoss's ears; when I spit there's a streak in the air like scratchin' a wet match. These little fireballs is all I can see of my hoss, 'n' they tell me he's listenin' all ways; his ears are never still.

"I tell you there's something mighty ghostly about sittin' up on a hoss you can't see, with them two little blue sparks out in front of you wigglin' and movin' like a pair of spook eyes, 'n' it shows me the old night hoss is usin' his list'ners pretty plenty. I got my ears cocked too, hearin' nothin' but Longrope singin'; he's easy three hundred yards across the herd from me, but I can hear every word:

"'Sam Bass was born in Injiana,
    It was his native home;
    'Twas at the age of seventeen
    Young Sam began to roam.

"'He first went out to Texas,
    A cowboy for to be;
    A better hearted feller
    You'd seldom ever see.'

"It's so plain it sounds like he's singin' in my ear: I can even hear the click-clack of his spur-chains agin his stirrups when he moves 'round, 'n' the cricket in his bit —he's usin' one of them hollow conchoed half-breeds—she comes to me plain on the stillness. Once there's a steer layin' on the edge of the herd starts sniffin'. He's takin' long draws of the air like he's nosin' for somethin'. I don't like this, it's a bad sign; it shows he's layin' for trouble, 'n' all he needs is some little excuse.

"Now every steer when he beds down holds his breath for a few seconds, 'n' then blows off; that noise is all right 'n' shows he's settlin' himself for comfort. But when he curls his nose 'n' makes them long draws it's a sign he's sniffin' for something 'n' if anything crosses his wind that he don't like, there's liable to be trouble. I've seen dry trail herds mighty thirsty, layin' good, till a breeze springs off the water, maybe ten miles away; start sniffin', 'n' the minute they get the wind you could comb Texas 'n' wouldn't have enough punchers to turn 'em till they had wet their feet 'n' filled their paunches.

"I get tired sittin' there starin' at nothin' so start ridin' 'round. Now it's sure dark when animals can't see, but I can tell by the way my hoss moves he's feelin' his way, but I don't blame him none; it's like lookin' in a black pot. Sky 'n' ground's the same 'n' I ain't gone twenty-five yards till I hear cattle gettin' up 'round me; I'm in the herd 'n' its lucky I'm singin' 'n' they don't scare. Pullin' to the left I work cautious 'n' easy till I'm clear of the bunch. Ridin's useless so I flop my weight over on one stirrup 'n' go on singin'.

"The lightnin's quit now 'n' she's darker than ever; the breeze has died down 'n' it's hotter than the hubs of hell. Above my voice I can hear Longrope. He's singin' 'The Texas Ranger'; now the 'Ranger' 's a long song 'n' there's few punchers that knows it all, but Longrope's sprung a lot of new verses on me 'n' I'm interested. Seems like he's on about the twenty-fifth verse, 'n' there's danger of him chokin' down, when there's a whisperin' in the grass behind me; it's a breeze sneakin' up. It flaps the tail of my slicker 'n' goes by; in another second she hits the herd. The ground shakes 'n' they're all runnin'. My hoss takes the scare with 'em 'n's bustin' a hole in the darkness when he throws both front-feet in a badger hole, goin' to his knees, plowin' his nose in the dirt. But he's a good night-hoss 'n's hard to keep down. The minute he gets his feet under him right he raises, runnin' like a scared wolf. Hearin' the roar behind him he don't care to mix with them locoed long-horns. I got my head turned over my shoulder listenin', tryin' to make out which way they're goin' when there's a flash of lightnin' busts a hole in the sky—it's one of these kind that puts the fear of God in a man—thunder 'n' all together. My hoss whirls 'n' stops in his tracks, spraddlin' out squattin' like he's hit, 'n' I can feel his heart beatin' agin' my leg, while mine's poundin' my ribs like it 'll bust through. We're both plenty scared.

"This flash lights up the whole country, givin' me a glimpse of the herd runnin' a little to my left. Big drops of rain are poundin' my hat. The storm has broke now for sure, with the lightnin' bombardin' us at every jump. Once a flash shows me Longrope, ghostly in his wet slicker. He's so close that I could hit him with my quirt, 'n' I hollers to him:

"'This is hell.'

"'Yes,' he yells back above the roar, 'I wonder what damned fool kicked the lid off.'

"I can tell by the noise that they're runnin' straight; there ain't no clickin of horns. It's a kind of hummin' noise like a buzz saw, only a ten thousand times louder. There's no use in tryin' to turn 'em in this darkness, so I'm ridin' wide—just herdin' by ear 'n follerin' the noise. Pretty soon my ears tell me they're crowdin' 'n' comin' together; with the clickin' 'n' whettin' of thousands of horns, the next flash shows 'em all millin', with heads jammed together 'n' horns locked; some's rared up ridin' others, the whole herd squirmin' like a bristled snake. In the same light I see Longrope, 'n' from the blink I get of him he's among 'em or too close for safety, 'n' in the dark I thought I saw a gun flash three times with no report, but with the noise these longhorns are makin' now I doubt if I could 'a' heard a six-gun bark if I pulled the trigger myself, 'n' the next thing I know me 'n' my hoss goes over a bank, lightin' safe. I guess it ain't over four feet but it seems like fifty in the darkness, 'n' if it hadn't been for my chin-string I'd 'a' went from under my hat.

Again the light shows me we're in a 'royo with the cattle comin' over the edge, wigglin' 'n' weavin' like army worms.

"It's a case of all night's hard ridin'. Sometimes they'll mill 'n' quiet down, then start trottin' 'n' break into a run. Not until daybreak do they stop, 'n' maybe you think old day ain't welcome. My hoss is sure leg-weary, 'n' I ain't so rollicky myself. When she gets light enough I go to lookin' for Longrope, with nary a sign of him; 'n' the herd—you wouldn't know they were the same cattle—smeared with mud 'n' ga'nt as greyhounds; some of 'em with their tongues out, still lollin' from their night's run, but sizin' up the bunch I guess I got 'em all. I'm kind of worried about Longrope. Its a cinch that wher-e'er he is he's afoot, 'n' chances is he's layin' on the prairie with a broken leg.

"The cattle spreads out 'n' begin feedin'. There ain't much danger of losin' 'em now its broad daylight, so I ride up on a raise to take a look at the back trail. While I'm up there viewin' the country my eyes run onto somethin' about half a mile back in a draw. I can't make it out, but get curious, so spurrin' my tired hoss into a lope I take the back trail. 'Tain't no trouble to foller in the mud; it's plain as plowed ground. I ain't rode three hundred yards till the country raises a little 'n' shows me this thing's a hoss, 'n' by the white streak on his flank, I heap savvy it's Peon—that's the hoss Longrope's ridin'. When I get close he whinners pitiful like; he's lookin' for sympathy, 'n' I notice when he turns to face me, his right foreleg's broke. He's sure a sorry sight with that fancy, full-stamped center-fire saddle hangin' under his belly in the mud. While I'm lookin' him over, my hoss cocks his ears to the right, snortin' low. This scares me—I'm afeared to look. Somethin' tells me I won't see Longrope, only part of him —that part that stays here on earth when the man's gone. Bracin' up I foller my hoss's ears, 'n' there in the holler of the 'royo is a patch of yaller; it's part of a slicker. I spur up to get a better look over the bank, 'n' there tromped in the mud is all there is left of Longrope. Pullin' my gun I empty her in the air. This brings the boys that are follerin' the trail from the bed-ground. Nobody'd had to tell 'em we'd had hell, so they come in full

force, every man but the cook 'n' hoss wrangler.

"We all get off our hosses, long faced 'n' sorry. He's layin' face up with his slicker skirts pulled up under his head 'n' shoulders, showin' he's been dragged. It's the saddest sight I ever see—the drizzlin' rain, the wet hosses 'n' long-faced, quiet punchers.

"Nobody feels like talkin'. It don't matter how rough men are—I've knowed 'em that never spoke without cussin', that claimed to fear neither God, man nor devil, but let death visit camp 'n' it puts 'em thinkin'. They generally take their hat off to this old boy that comes everywhere 'n' any time. He's always ready to pilot you—willin' or not—over the long, dark trail that folks don't care to travel. He's never welcome, but you've got to respect him.

"'It's tough—damned tough,' says Spanish, raisin' poor Longrope's head 'n' wipin' the mud from his face with his neck handkerchief, tender, like he's afeared he'll hurt him. We find his hat tromped in the mud not fur from where he's layin'. His scabbard's empty 'n' we never do locate his gun.

"That afternoon when we're countin' out the herd to see if we're short any, we find a steer with a broken shoulder 'n' another with a hole plum through his nose. Both of these is gun wounds; this accounts for them flashes I see in the night. It looks like when Longrope gets mixed in the mill he tries to gun his way out, but the cattle crowd him to the bank 'n' he goes over. The chances are he was dragged from his hoss in a tangle of horns.

"Some's for takin' him to Dodge 'n' gettin' a box made for him, but Old Spanish says: 'Boys, Longrope is a prairie man, 'n' if she was a little rough at times, she's been a good foster mother. She cared for him while he's awake, let her nurse him in his sleep.' So we wrapped him in his blankets, 'n' put him to bed.

"It's been twenty years or more since we tucked him in with the end-gate of the bed-wagon for a headstone, which the cattle have long since rubbed down, leavin' the spot unmarked. It sounds lonesome, but he ain't alone, 'cause these old prairies has cradled many of his kind in their long sleep.

24

A Knot and a Slash

HENRY WALLACE PHILLIPS

A KNOT AND A SLASH

"RED SAUNDERS" PRESIDES AT A "LYNCHING BEE"

BY

HENRY WALLACE PHILLIPS

AUTHOR OF "RED SAUNDERS: HIS ADVENTURES WEST AND EAST"

ILLUSTRATED BY A. B. FROST

NE thing's certain, you can't run a sheep ranch, nor no other kind of ranch, without hired men. They're the most important thing, next to the sheep. I may have stated, absent-mindedly, that the Big Bend was organized on scientific principles : none of your gol-darned-heads-or-tails—who's-it—what-makes-the-ante-shy, about it. Napoleon Buonaparte in person, in his most complex minute, couldn't have got at this end of it better than I did. It looked a little roundabout, but that's the way with your Morgan strain of idees. Here's how I secured the first man ; he didn't look like good material to the careless eye.

Burton and me had just turned the top of that queer hill, that overlooks the Southwest road into the bad-lands, when I see a parcel of riders coming out. Somehow, they jarred me.

"Easy," says I, and grabs Burton's bridle.

"What the devil now?" he groans. "Injuns? Road-agents?"

"Nope," says I, getting out my field glass. I had guessed it : there was the bunch, riding close and looking ugly, with the white-faced man in the middle. If you should ask me how I knew that for a lynching, when all I could make out with my eyes was that they weren't cattle, I give it up. Seems like something passed from them to me that wasn't sight. And also if you ask why, when through the glass I got a better view of the poor devil about to be strung, I felt kind towards him, you have me speechless again. I couldn't make out his face, but there was something——

"See here, Burton," says I. "There's your peaceful prairie hanging, in its early stage."

"What!" says he, sick and hot at the same time. "How can you speak of the death of a human being so heartlessly? Let me go!"

"Hold!" says I. "You haven't heard me through. Perhaps you can be more use than to run away and hide your eyes. I ain't got a word to say against quick law. I've seen her work, and she works to a point. She beats having the lawyers sieving all the justice out of it. All the same, they've been too careless around here—that, and a small bad boy's desire to get their names up. I know one case where they hung a perfectly innocent man, for fun, and to brag about it."

He looked at me steady. I had suspected him of being no coward, when it comes to cases.

"Now," I says, "I don't know what that is down there. Perhaps it's all right; then you and me has got to stand by. If not—well, by the sacred photograph of Mary Ann, here's one roping that won't be an undiluted pleasure. Now listen. I'm something of a high private, when it comes to war, but no man is much more than one man, if the other side's blood is bad. Give 'em to me cold, and I can throw a crimp into 'em, for I don't care a hoot at any stage of the game and they do. But when they're warm —why, a hole between the eyes will stop me just as quick as though I wasn't Chantay Seeche Red. Are you with me? You never took longer chances in your life."

He wet his lips, and didn't speak very loud nor steady, but he says : "You lead."

"Well, hooray, Boston!" says I. "Beans is good food. Now don't take it too serious till you have to. Perhaps there ain't more'n a laugh in it. But—it's like smooth ice. How deep she is, you know when she cracks, or don't. Be as easy as you can when we get up to 'em. Nothing gained by bulling the ring. We must be prepared to look pleasant and act very different. Turn your back and see that your toy pistol is working."

Well, poor Burton! Wisht you seen him fumble his gun.

"I can't *see* the thing," says he, kind of sniffling. "I'd give something to be a man."

"You'll do for an imitation," I says. "Remember, I was born with red hair ; comes trouble, this hair of mine sheds a red light over the landscape ; I get happy-crazy ; it's summer, and I can smell the flowers ; there's music a long ways off—why, I could sing this minute, but there's no use in making matters worse. Honest, trouble makes me just drunk enough to be limber and—talk too much. Come on."

We single-footed it down the hillside. The party stopped and drawed together, four men quietly making a rank in front. That crowd had walked barefoot.

We come to twenty yards of 'em in silence ; then a tall lad swung out towards us.

"How Kola!" says I, wavin' my hand pleasant.

"How do you do!" says he, as if it wouldn't break his heart, no matter what the answer was.

"Why, nicely, thank you to hell," says I. "What's doin'? Horse race?"

"Probably," says he ; then kind of yawning: "We're not expectin' company this morning."

"Well," I answered, "it's the unexpected always happens, except the exceptions. You talk like a man that's got something on his mind."

Don't think I'd lost my wits and was pickin' a row to no advantage. I'll admit the gent riled me some, but the point I had in view was what old Judge Hinky used to call "shifting the issue." I wanted to make one stab at just one man—not the whole party—on grounds that the rest of the crowd, who was plainly all good two-handed punchers, would see was perfectly fair. And I intended to land that stab so's they'd see I was no trifler. It was my bad luck that not a soul in the crowd knew me—even by reputation, or my hair would have made it easy for me. So I put a little ginger in the tone of my voice.

"My friend," says the tall lad, "I wouldn't advise you to get gay with us. I would advise you to move right on—or I'll move you."

He played to me, you see. If he'd said, "*We*'ll move you," I'd had to chaw with him some more. Now I had him. Right under the harmless bundle of old clothes dangling from the saddle horn, was the gun

I'd borrowed from Ike—Mary Ann's twin sister, full of cartridges loaded by Ike himself—no miss-fire government issue. The next second that gun had its cold, hard eye upon Long Jim in front of me.

Whilst my hands seemed carelessly crossed on the horn, my right was really closed on the gun.

"I like to see a man back his advice," says I. "It's your move. Don't any other gentleman get restless with his hands, or I'll make our Christian brother into a

"through the glass I got a better view of the poor devil about to be strung"

"We called to him to halt, and he stopped, kind of grinned at us and says: 'Hello!'"

collection of holes. Now, you ill-mannered brute," I says, "I don't care what your business is: it's my business to see that you give me civil answers to civil questions."

He shrunk some. He was too durned important, anyhow, that feller.

"Quick!" says I. "Lord of the Mormon hosts! Do you think I'm going to yappee with you all day. Nice morning, ain't it? Say 'yes.'"

"Yes," says he.

"I thought so," says I. "It's a raw deal when a man that's sat a horse as long as me can't say howdy on the open, without havin' a pup like you bark at him."

"Why," says he, feelin' distressed, "I didn't mean to make no bad play at you."

He jerked his thumb over his shoulder toward the prisoner, who sat like a white stone. "That's it. Misplaced horse. Got him with the goods."

"Oh!" says I. "Well, 'twouldn't have done no harm to mention that first place. I wasn't noticing you particular, till you got too much alive for any man of my size to stand." I dropped my gun. "Excuse haste and a bad pen," says I; "but why don't I draw cards? Both parents were light complected and I've voted several times. How is it, boys?"

"Sure!" says they. "Take a stack, brick-top."

"Gentlemen," I says; "one word more and I am done. The question as to whether my hair is any particular color or not, is discussed in private, by familiar friends only—savvy the burro, how he kickee with hees hin' leg?"

They laughed. "All right, Colonel!" says they. "Come with us!"

I had that crowd. You see, they was all under twenty-five, and if there's anything a young man likes—a good, hearty boy— it's to see a brisk play pushed home. I'd called 'em down so their spinal columns shortened, and gagging about my hair, and the style I put on in general, caught their eye. And their own laughing and easiness wasn't so durned abandoned, as Charley Halleck used to say. There was a streak of not liking the job, and everything a little "put on," evident to the practised vision.

I'd gained two points. Made myself pretty solid with the boys, for one, and give 'em something besides hanging their fellow man to think of for another: distracted their attention, which you got to do with children.

"I speak for my friend," says I, pointing to Burton.

"We hear you talk, Colonel," says the joker. "He's with us." So we trotted on toward the cotton-woods.

The line of work was marked out for me. I put on a grim look and sized the prisoner up from time to time as though he was nothing but an obstruction to my sight, although the face of the poor devil bit my heart. He glanced neither way, mouth set, face green-white, the slow sweat glassy all over him. Not a bad man, by a mile, I knew. It don't take me a week to size a man up, and I've seen 'em in so many

conditions, red and pale, sick, dead, and well, that outside symptoms don't count for much.

I noticed another thing, that I expected. Out of the corner of my eye, I see them boys nudgin' each other and talkin' about me. And the more I rode along so quiet, the more scart of me they got.

I tell you how I'd test a brave man. I'd line the competitors up, and then spring a fright behind them. Last man to cross the mark is the bravest man—still, he might only be the poorest runner. With fellers like me, it ain't courage at all. It's lunacy. I ain't in my right mind when a sharp turn comes. Why, I've gone cold a year after, thinking of things I laughed my way through when they happened. But I'm not quarreling with fate—I thank the good Lord I'm built as I am, and don't feel scornful of a man that keeps his sense and acts scart and reasonable.

In one way, poor old Burton, lugging himself into the game by the scruff of his pants, showed more real man than I did. Yet, he couldn't accomplish anything; so there you are, if you know where that is.

I said nothing until we slid off beneath the first tree. Then I walked up to the three leaders and says, whilst the rest gathered around and listened:

"Has this critter been tried?"

"Why, no!" says one man. "We caught him on the horse."

"Yes, yes, yes," says I, raising my voice. "That's all right. But lend me your ears till I bray a thought or two. I'm that kind of a man that wouldn't string the meanest mistake the devil ever made when the Lord wasn't looking, without givin' him a trial."

"You give me a lot of trial this morning," says Long Jim.

I wasn't bringing up any argument; I was pulling them along with a mother's kind, but firm hand, so I says to him: "Ah! I wasn't talking about *gentlemen;* I'd shoot a gentleman if he did or didn't look cross-eyed at me, just as I happened to feel. I'm talking about a man that's suspected of dirty work."

Now, when a man that's held you stiff at the end of a gun, calls you a gentleman, you don't get very mad—just please remember my audience, when I tell you what I talked. Boys is boys, at any age; otherwise there wouldn't be no Knights Templars with tin swords nor a good many other

"that crowd of fierce lync'ers as lookin' industriously upon the ground"

things. I spoke grand, but they had it chalked down in their little books I was ready and willing to act grander. Had I struck any one or all of 'em, on the range, thinking of nothing special, and Fourth-o'-July'd to 'em like that, they would have give me the hee-hee of ridicule. Howsomever, they was at present engaged in tryin' to hang a man; a job one-half of which they didn't like, and would dispose of the balance cheap, for cash. And I'd run over their little attempt to be pompous like a 'Gul engine. Position is everything, you bet your neck.

So up speaks Mr. Long Jim, that I've called a gentleman, loud and clear.

"You're *right*," says he, and bangs his fist into his other hand. "You're dead right, old horse," says he; "and we'll try this son-of-a-gun now and here."

"Sure!" says everybody, which didn't surprise me so much. I told you I was used to handling sheep.

After a little talk with his friends, Long Jim comes up and says: "Will you preside, Colonel?"

"I have a friend here who is a lawyer," I suggested, waving my hand toward Burton.

The speaker rubbed his chin.

"I guess this isn't a case for a lawyer," he says. "The gentleman might give us a point or two, but we'd prefer you took charge. You see," he says to Burton and me earnestly; "there's been a heap of skulduggery around here lately—horse-stealin', maimin' cattle, and the like—till we're dead sick of it. This bucco made the most barefaced try you ever heard of—'twas like stealin' the whiskers right off your face—and us fellers in my neighborhood, old man and all, have saw fit to copper the deal from the soda-card. We ain't for doin' this man; we're for breaking up the play—'taint a case of law; it's a case of livin'—so if you'll oblige, Colonel?"

"All right, sir; I'll do the best I can. Who accuses this man?"

"I," says a straightforward-looking young man of about twenty odd.

"Step up, please, and tell us."

"Why, it's like this," he says. "I'm ranchin' lone-hand down on Badger. There's the wife and two kiddies, and a job for a circus-man to make both ends meet—piecin' out a few cattle and a dozen of hogs with a garden patch. All I got between me and a show-down is my team. Well, this feller comes along, played out, and asks for a drink of water. My wife's laid up—too darn much hard work for any woman—and I've got Jerry saddled by the fence, to ride for the doctor. Other horse is snake bit and weavin' in the stable with a leg like a barrel. I goes in to get the water, and when I comes out there's this sucker dustin' off with the horse. Then I run over to C-bar-nine and routs the boys out. We took out after him, corrallin' him in a draw near the Grindstones. That's about all."

"Make any fight?" I asked.

"Naw!" says the man, disgusted. "I was wanting to put my hands on him, but he comes in like a sick cow—seemed foolish."

"How foolish?"

"Oh, just stared at us. We called to him to halt, and he stopped, kind of grinned at us and says: 'Hello!' I'd a 'hello'd' him if the boys hadn't stopped me."

"Prisoner," I says; "this looks bad. I don't know where you come from, but you must have intelligence enough to see that this man's wife's life might have depended on that horse. You know we're straggled so out here that a horse means something more than so much a head. Why did you do this? Your actions don't seem to hang together."

The poor cuss changed face for the first time. He swallered hard and turned to his accuser. "Hope your lady didn't come to no harm?" says he.

"Why, no, thankee; she didn't," says the other lad. "'Bliged to you for inquirin'."

There was a stir in the rest of the crowd. The prisoner had done good work for himself without knowing it. That question of his proved what I thought—he was no bad man. Something peculiar in the case. Swinging an eye on the crowd, I saw I could act. I went forward and laid my hand on his shoulder, speaking kind and easy.

"Here," says I, "you've done a fool trick, and riled the boys considerable. You'd been mad, too, if somebody'd made you ride all day. But now you tell us just what happened. If it was intended to be comical, we'll kick your pants into one long ache, and let it go at that; if it was anything else, spit it out."

He stood there, fumblin' with his hands, runnin' the back of one over his forehead once in a while, tryin' to talk, but unable. You could see it stick in his throat.

"Take time," says I ; "there's lots of it both sides of us."

Then he braced.

"Boys," says he, "I got a wife an' two little roosters too. I feel sorry for the trouble I made that gentleman. I got split like this. Come to this town with seven hundred dollars, to make a start. Five hundred of that's my money, and two hundred m' wife saved up—and she was that proud and trustin' in me !" He stopped for a full minute, workin' his teeth together. "Well, I ain't much. I took to boozin' and tryin' to put the faro games out of business. Well, I went shy—quick. The five hundred was all right," he says, kind of defiant. "Man's got a right to do what he pleases with his own money; but . . . but . . . well, the girl worked hard for that little old two hundred. God Almighty ! I was drunk ! You don't s'pose I'd do such a thing sober ?" turning to us, savage. "That ain't no excuse, howsomever," he goes on, droppin' his crop. "Comes to the point when there's nothin' left, and then I get a letter." He begun taking things out of his pockets, dropping 'em from his big tremblin' hands. "It's somewheres here—ain't that it ? My eyes is no good."

He hands me a letter, addressed to Martin Hazel, in a woman's writing. "Well, that druv me crazy. So help me God, sir, I ain't pleadin' for no mercy—I'll take my medicine—but I didn't know no more what I was doin' when I jumped your horse, than nothin'. I only wanted to get away from everybody. I was crazy. You read 'em that letter," says he, taking hold of me. "See if it wouldn't drive any man crazy."

Now, there's no good repeatin' the letter. It wasn't written for an audience, and the spellin' was accordin' to the lady's own views, but it was all about how happy they was going to be, when Martin had things fixed up, and how funny the little boy was, and just like his pa, and, oh, couldn't he fix it so's they'd be with him soon, for her heart was near broke with waiting.

There was sand in my eyes before I'd read long, and that crowd of fierce lynchers was lookin' industriously upon the ground. One man chawed away on his baccy, like there'd be an earthquake if he stopped, and another lad, with a match in his mouth, scratched a cigarette on his leg, shieldin' it careful with his hands, and your Uncle Willy tried to fill a straight face on a four-card draw, and to talk in a tone of voice I wasn't ashamed of hearing.

During the last part of the letter, the prisoner stood thoughtful, with the back of his hand to his mouth ; you'd never known he was settin' his teeth into it, if it wasn't for the blood dropping from his thumb.

"The prisoner will retire," says I, with the remnants of my self-respect, "while the court passes sentence. Go sit down under the tree yonder." He shambled off. Soon's he was out of hearin' the feller that lost the horse jumps up into the air with an oath like a streak of lightning. "Here's a fine play we come near makin' by bein' so sudden," says he. "I wouldn't have that man's death on my soul for the whole territory— think of that poor woman ! And he's paid the freight. Colonel, I want to thank you for drawin' things down." So he come up and shook me by the hand, and up files the rest and does the same thing.

"Now, friends," says I, "hold on. Court hasn't passed sentence yet. I pass that this crowd put up to the tune of what it can spare to buy"—consulting the letter—"to buy Peggy a ticket West, kids included, exceptin' only the gentleman that lost the horse."

"Why, we ain't broke altogether on Badger !" says he. "You ain't goin' to bar me, boys ?"

"Not on your life, if that's the way you feel," says I. I don't know what amount that crowd could spare, but I'll bet high on one thing. If you'd strong-armed the gang, you wouldn't start a bank with the proceeds after the collection was taken. There wasn't a nickel in the outfit. "I'm glad I didn't bring any more with me," says Burton, strapping himself.

Of course, I was appointed to break the news to the prisoner. He busted then ; put his head on his arm and cried like a baby. But he braced quick and stepped up to the lads. "There ain't nothing I can say except thank you," says he. "I want to get each man's name so's I can pay him back. Now, if anybody here knows of a job of work I can get—well, you know what it would mean to me. Sporty life is done for me, friends ; I'll work hard for any man that'll take me."

"I got you," I says. "Come along with me and I'll explain."

Then we said by-by to the boys. I played the grand with 'em still, and I'll just tell you why, me and you bein' such old friends. Although it may sound queer, coming from my mouth, yet it was because I thought I might give them boys the proper steer, sometime. You can't talk Sunday-school to young fellers like that! They don't pay no attention to what a gent in black clothes and a choker tells 'em ; but suppose Chantay Seeche Red—rippin', roarin' Red Saunders, that fears the face of no man, nor the hoof of no jackass—lays his hand on a boy's shoulder, and says, "Son, I wouldn't twist it just like that." Is he goin' to get listened to? I reckon yes. So I played straight for their young imaginations, and I had 'em cinched to the last hole. And after the last one had pulled my flipper, and hoped he'd meet me soon again, me and Burton and the new hired man took out after sheep. "But," says Burton, still sort of dazed, "God only knows what we'll meet before we find them. Even sheep aren't so peaceful in this country."

He was right, too. However, when I start for sheep, I get 'em. You can see by the deep-laid plan I set to catch help for the ranch, how there's nothing for fortune to do but lay down and holler when I make up my mind.

25

How The Law Came to
Jenkins Creek

CHARLES WARREN

HOW THE LAW CAME TO JENKINS CREEK.

By Charles Warren,
Author of "The Governor's Rehearsal," and Other Stories.

INTRODUCING SANDY WILCOX, THE WASHORE COUNTY SHERIFF.

THE smoke had drifted out through the doorway and was floating dimly across the narrow street and up into the dark spruces on the mountain side opposite. The big, brown, wet blotch on the floor had been hastily covered with sawdust. The broken chair had been thrown behind the counter, and the barkeeper was picking up broken bits of glass, and mournfully inspecting a shattered window through which one of the bullets had flown wide.

A look at the three cattlemen, intent on their game of "frog," and the circle of five miners around the rickety poker table, busily re-piling their scattered chips on the frayed and dirty green cover, would have given no one any reason to suppose that only two minutes before a dead man had been carried out of the saloon, while his murderer had walked out unmolested and unaccompanied by any officer of the law.

Yet that was exactly what had happened at twenty minutes past eleven on Sunday morning in the most popular of the numerous saloons of the town of Buckhorn, a place euphoniously named "The Gus and Jim's."

Buckhorn, on Jenkins Creek, had the distinction of being the most unsafe town in all Washore County. A distinction it certainly was, for the rest of the county would have received extremely high marks in any competitive examination for lawlessness.

Buckhorn's character was largely due to the fact that it was not only at the hub of half a dozen rich, gold-bearing gulches diverging toward the north, but also at the apex of one of Montana's most fertile cattle valleys stretching southward. The consequent presence of both cattle punchers and placer miners in one small town of restricted area was not likely to conduce to a state of extreme peace or amicability ; and, in fact, the result had been an amount of pistol practice that had left few of the buildings in Buckhorn unscarred by bullets, had qualified every citizen as an expert, and had greatly overstocked the little graveyard.

Therefore, when Reddy Flagg, rich in his week's clean-up from the riffles, had met Joe Staley, just paid off on his return from Merriman's round-up, had won his whole pot from him, and in return for some slight provocation or other had shot him through the heart (after having one bullet pierce his own left arm and another whisk off the tip of his ear), the conflict created hardly more than a ripple of interest. It had disturbed the various games going on only because of the imminent danger of an upset of tables in the lively wrestling match ensuing before either of the combatants had been able to reach his gun ; and the circle of poker players had interrupted their play just long enough to see that the fight was a fair one, in which neither party was taking an underhand advantage of the other. They had also, for a moment, secured advantageous positions out of the range of the weapons. Then, while the lumpy body of the less skilful Staley was being carried out by three of the loafers around the saloon, they had quietly resumed their game.

It was with surprise, therefore, that they saw one of their number push his chair back from the table, throw down his hand, and rise with the words, "Boys, this business has got to stop."

Two of the players looked ugly, apparently finding in the speaker's words an insinuation of trickery in the game.

"I've thought so for a long time, and now I'm certain of it," the speaker continued, standing with his back against the bar, as if he was making an address. "There's altogether too many promiscuous deceases about this town fer the good of the community.

Now, I'm not a-goin' to preach, but I'm talkin' God's truth when I say there's too many dead men about this here town to make it attractive to settlers. I'm no more pertic'lar than the next man, but I've got my fill," continued the speaker, "an' I'm goin' to do my best from now on to put a stop to it."

A mocking laugh came from one of his auditors. Wilcox flushed, but affected to disregard it, and continued:

"This sort of thing is played out in a modern, up-to-date community. We're 'way behind the times. You're tryin' up here in this year 1895 games ez are dead an' rotten in every other minin' region in the West. I've been about everywhere in the last twenty years, an' I know what I'm talkin' about."

"Ef you're goin' to make a speech, Sandy, you'd better take a drink. You must be dry after all this yawp," interrupted Alf Nolen, owner of the Lone Hand claim.

"I'm in dead earnest, Alf; you can't josh me out of this. An' ef you fellows would take hold we could pull this town out of its bloody sink. Why, what is it that keeps Eastern capital from comin' in here and buyin' up your minin' claims an' my own and makin' us all rich men? Nothin' but our rotten reputation for bein' the most careless set of scoundrels with a gun that ever fingered triggers!"

"We don't want the Eastern money sharks in here," growled one of the miners.

"You don't, don't you? Well, you want their money pretty badly, even ef you don't want them. And you won't get either ez long ez that sort of thing goes on," he added, pointing with one foot to the heap of wettening sawdust.

"No, sir; I tell you, boys, we've got to make a break, an' we've got to have a little law an' order up on this blamed creek, an' the sooner it comes the better I'll like it."

"Well," interjected Bill Cooper, cattleman, "hain't we got a justice down at Hawkton? Hain't we got a constable up here, an' hain't there such things as sheriff an' coroners round in Washore County?"

"There are. I grant you that," answered Wilcox. "There are. An' a more disgustin' lot of fawn-hearted, water-livered, quaking-kneed, scared, double-dealin' office grabbers I never want to see. Why didn't some one of them have the sand to yank Reddy Flagg just now into custody? What has he done but just committed a plain, solid, cold murder? You know jest as well ez I do

there won't be a thing done to him; an' old twaddlin' Livermore will hold a coroner's inquest an' report 'unavoidable accident,' jest ez he's done on every killin' for the last six years. No, boys, I tell you, it's got to stop."

"Oh, cinch your talk," came from another of the cattlemen, as he looked up from his game of frog. "You're too loose with your tongue, Kid."

Kid, or Sandy, Wilcox suddenly stood up straight, and his hand went instinctively to his hip. Then he controlled himself and retorted: "An' when the time comes that we have a sheriff who'll have sand enough to jug a man, the jail will be filled up fer the whole first six months with cow-punchers."

The poker crowd gave a yell of derisive laughter, and the three cattlemen looked as if they were about to make a rush for them, but, taking account of their superiority in numbers, apparently thought better of it.

Then one of them replied: "Well, Kid, if it's got to stop, so long as you say so, I suppose it'll have to—but, why don't you stop it?"

Wilcox was silent a moment, then he said: "That's jest what I'm goin' to do." A totally unplanned idea had developed like a flash in his brain, and he paused in order to grasp its full significance—and also that its announcement might fall with due weight upon his companions. "I mean it. This ain't any fairy dream. I'm goin' to stop it, fer—I'm goin' to run for sheriff myself in this county, next election."

Sandy Wilcox could pride himself on having given the town of Buckhorn two genuine surprises in one day.

"The h—l you are!" shouted Bill Cooper.

"Hear the Kid talk!" said Alf Nolen. The crowd rose from the tables and surrounded the slight, youthful figure of Wilcox, who could not conceal a momentary look of pride at the sensation he had created. And as each man filed up and took his own brand of liquor, exclamations began to fly round: "That's the stuff, Sandy, my boy." "Go it, Kid." "We'll help you out."

Before Monday night the miners on lonely claims up the gulches thirty miles away, and settlers on solitary, fenced ranches forty miles down the Great Buffalo Basin, had heard the news that Sandy Wilcox, of Buckhorn, was going to run for sheriff, and that if he should be elected, a revolution in the order of things might be expected in Washore County.

After the first glow of excitement had been dulled, the crowd was talking it over down in David Stoner's general store.

"I don't say ez how the Kid ain't right," remarked Scammell; Scammell was a stage-driver of experiences on many routes, and had probably lived through as many "hold-ups" as any man of his age. "It does seem ez ef p'raps ye couldn't set on the coat-tails of Progress and holler 'whoa' much longer. It's the natur' of things to sort 'er git up and git. The rest of Montanna is gittin' kind 'er peaceful like, an' I s'pose we've got to come into line too. But Buckhorn has been a lovely place fer a gent with a sportin' natur' who likes excitement. It's been a lovely place while it's lasted," he repeated with a sigh.

"It's the railroads that's done it. It's them ez is the cuss of the West," observed "Hen" Dranger, another stageman, who in the cattle season acted as an expert yearling brander on the round-ups; "it's the railroads that's doin' it, and changin' the West from what it was. Montanna used to be ez nice and lively a place ez anybody could want. Now it's gittin' too blamed quiet fer a decent, self-respectin' man to live in. Why, back in the '70's, up Helena way — them was the times—when there was ez many ez six stages coming into Helena every day, everybody feeling good, all the drinks ye wanted, passengers tossing out the color. Now look at it!"

"There'll never be another Montanna anywhere in the world like the old Montanna was," Scammell rejoined.

"You men are soft," said big Jim Warster, who had the reputation of being the most loud-mouthed as well as the most dangerous of all the mining population of Buckhorn; "I'd like to see the man or the men that could put the law on any one in this town jest fer killin' a man in a good fair and square up and down fight. Kid Wilcox can't, nor any other dozen men like him."

"That's right," added Bill Cooper, "the law's all right ez it is on this creek; and if we need a change we can change it ourselves. We don't need a little loud-mouthed rooster gittin' up and kickin' because he can't stand the sight of a little blood."

"Ye know ye'd not care to sit there and say that ef the Kid was here," observed Friend, the assayer. "He's small, but he's pretty chipper himself with his gun. Do you remember Bill Stimson?"

Cooper ignored the question. He did remember Bill Stimson. In fact, all the town remembered him. That was the only time the Kid had been known to shoot. It was about a year after he had located his claim. His shooting had been rapid, accurate, decisive, and effective. From that day on no one had seriously worried the Kid.

Cooper saw the force of the illustration and continued his remarks with a more subdued air. "Well, anyway, this fuss only amounts to this. Jim Staley was the po'rest shot, an' he got a hole through him, an' the whole thing was ez pretty an' open a game ez I've ever laid my eyes on."

"That's so," put in one of the deceased Staley's own comrades. "This here town and what happens here is all right, an' if Kid Wilcox can't stand it, he'd better clear out of the valley an' settle back East—in—in—in Boston."

"Wilcox 'd better look out how he tries to jump the sheriff's claim. There ain't much lean gravel in Sheriff Barnes. He's good pay-dirt every time, an' we'll look out for him. He's a nice, good-natured man, ez knows when to jump in an' when to look on at the game," growled another miner.

"You'd have been lookin' through the gratings, I guess, long ago, ef he hadn't been so good-natured," remarked Friend to the last speaker.

"There ain't no use talkin', boys," said Scammell, looking worried at the effect of the last speech upon the person to whom it was addressed. "The Kid's some right— not that he don't go too far; but he's some right. The reputation that this here Creek has got ain't none too good. Buckhorn oughter be the county seat, an' you know that, Jim Warster, ez well ez I do. Hawkton ain't no call to be the county seat, ef Buckhorn was the place it oughter be."

At this point the conversation had become so heated, and signs seemed so to point to the imminence of the use of guns as arguments, that Stoner, the proprietor, announced that his store was now to be closed for the night, and that any gentleman who wanted to continue the discussion had better do so outside in the street.

Thus began a political campaign such as Washore County had never witnessed before. At first Sheriff Barnes treated the whole matter as a joke; in fact, most of the citizens of the county did the same. But those who were best acquainted with Mr. Alexander Wilcox knew that his two nicknames in Buckhorn were not without significance.

"Kid" had been applied to him ever since

his arrival six years before, when, in his restless search for the evasive big, single nugget that was to make his fortune, he had come over from Idaho and located the "Dolly" claim on the Creek. His youthful appearance and slightly built body had been then and still were deceptive. But a grasp of his hand disclosed muscles like strands of steel rope. The nattiness of his figure was emphasized by his manner of dress. For, unlike all the other inhabitants of the valley, Kid Wilcox was extremely careful in his attire. He alone of all the miners or cattlemen wore regularly every Saturday night and Sunday a starched white shirt. Whether he possessed more than one of these articles was not known ; but this shirt was always scrupulously clean, being starched for him, free of charge, by Molly Laverick, the general laundress for the more opulent citizens of Buckhorn, who expressed herself to him as being glad to have "some civilized work to do once in a while." He also occasionally wore the only long-tailed black cutaway coat in the region. These garments had at first been the subject of many gibes ; but the miners grew weary of such jesting when they found that it produced not the slightest effect upon the Kid.

He furthermore had that thin upper lip, that very light yellowish hair, and those blue eyes of the dull gray kind which men versed in a strenuous life learn from experience to associate with dangerous possibilities. The dwellers in Montana well knew that it was not the sinister, black-haired villain of the story books who was to be feared. It was the man with the gray-blue eye and the thin lip who, if pushed, was pretty sure to have no hesitation in "shooting to kill."

His nickname of "Sandy" was recognized as something more than a mere by-product of Alexander. Several acts of peculiar courage had given it a fitness of its own.

Wilcox's plan of campaign was very simple and very effective. It was to obtain a personal interview, if possible, with every voter in the county. Washore County, though having at times a large floating population, had not a very long list of regular voters.

So, wearing, apparently with a view to the dignity of his candidacy, his white shirt and a new black felt hat, he went on his tour of canvass. Up the gulches he rode, stopping at every claim where a heap of fresh dirt showed that tailings were still being piled up, conversing with the owner or worker, and earnestly arguing his position. Whether it were rock road, log road, wagon trail, mule trail, or simply a rocky scramble up the sides of the gulch, it made no difference to him and to his quick, hard, tough-footed Indian pony. Sometimes he would leave his pony outside and crawl into the bowels of the mountain, along the low tunnels, ice-cold as if the snow had pierced down through from the white peak on top ; and, meeting the quartz miners, he would point out the advantages to them of peace and order in the county. Up Corpse Gulch, where the hydraulic miners were roughly tearing the face of the landscape to pieces with their brutal, irresistible, glistening, round white stream, he preached the benefit of the introduction of capital in the valley. But his argument was not confined to the material and financial side of the question. In his rude way he gave them a new idea of the unlawfulness and wrong in the system of indiscriminate killing that had made the valley notorious.

During the last two weeks of the campaign he turned his pony southward to where trails through the soft buffalo-grass turf gave more grateful footing. He rode down the wide, fertile basin, scantily black-specked with cattle, and rimmed in by gently sloping brown mountains, on whose sides the dark shadows shifted with the passing of the clouds above. At every ranch he stopped and plead his own cause. Often he found only a woman with a lot of children at home. On such occasions he took especial pains to make his argument plain ; for women were scarce in that part of Montana, and their influence was powerful and well distributed over all the men-folk of the ranch.

But in the midst of all of his pleas for a *régime* of law and order, he retained his grip on his hearers by always insisting that he had no intention of trying to change the Valley into an "Eastern" settlement. His contempt for the East was as great as theirs.

"No, boys," he used to say, "the county ain't goin' to be any place fer sucklin' babes or young innocents, even ef I get in. But what I'm drivin' for is this. I'm goin' to see to it, ef I'm elected, that Washore County, and Jenkins Creek in particular, shall be a place where a peaceable straight man who keeps his mouth shut, the drinks out er him, and his hand off his hip pocket, can live if he wants to, without bein' forced to practise target-shootin' every spare moment. And ef there are any loud-mouthed bullies who try to worry a good, quiet citizen, why, they'll find that Kid Wilcox will be red-hot on their trail. On the other hand, ef there are any low-down card sharps or stage stoppers who think they'll be at liberty to carry on their little games just because they're quiet, they'll find themselves mistook also. And furthermore, I don't deny

barren claim, that the idea of him as sheriff of the county was almost inconceivable.

At once the whole Creek was split into two factions, the Kid's supporters and his

"'I'M GOIN' TO STOP IT . . . FER . . . I'M GOIN' TO RUN FOR SHERIFF MYSELF.'"

that there's some occasions when the use of a gun is not only pleasant, but also judicious an' necessary. No one need be afraid that I'll shut down on anything like that. No, boys, the thing I'm opposed to is this here promiscuousness and letting loose on any man who happens to be round, jest because he differs from your opinion. That's the kind of thing that's goin' to stop ef I get in."

It was not until the last two weeks of the campaign that the supporters of Sheriff Barnes awakened to the necessity of the most active work if they expected to re-elect their candidate.

Notwithstanding their efforts, however, the Kid was elected, though his majority was not large. To say that his fellow-townsmen of Buckhorn were astonished at this result would be inadequate. They had become so accustomed to the sight of the Kid working along steadily at his rather

opponents. His opponents, headed by Bill Cooper, Jim Warster, and Alf Nolen, maintained that "no such fancy Reform rackets as the Kid's should be sprung on this here creek."

The other side was equally insistent that the new sheriff "be given a fair show." If he wanted to enforce the letter of the law in Washore County, "why, give him a chance—a little time to see what he can do and see how it works."

As soon as Wilcox was sworn into office he initiated his revolution by removing every deputy sheriff in the county and replacing them with the most nervy, calm, steadfast, iron-willed men that he had met with in the long rides of his campaign up and down and across the valley. The next thing he did was to call in person on the local constables in each township and inform them, to their consternation, that whoever allowed any breach of the law to go unheeded without making an arrest, should be arrested himself on the ground of being a party accessory to the crime. Such instructions and warning startled the constables out of a long career of careless inactivity. The third thing he did was to have posted all over the county copies of the statutes of Montana relating to criminal assault, robbery, manslaughter, and murder.

Having made this radical start, Alexander Wilcox waited to see what would happen when he was called upon to put his theories into practice. He did not doubt that something would happen, and that, too, very soon, for there was ill-concealed discontent and rage among a large portion of the inhabitants of Jenkins Creek Valley.

He was sitting on the steps of the "Palace" Hotel of Buckhorn three nights after his assumption of his new office, when he saw fat Gus Heinneman trundling as rapidly as possible up the road.

"Sandy, Mr. Sheriff, you petter come ofer to mein saloon. Chim Vaister's got his gun out and svears he'll kill any man who comes in, and I know not vat to do, nor does nopoddy else know vat to do."

Wilcox nodded to himself, then sauntered slowly after the excited German. He found a crowd of miners outside "The Gus and Jim's" looking perplexed and uneasy, while from inside came a sound of breaking bottles and the crash of thrown chairs.

"Jim Warster's cut loose," said Friend to Wilcox, "and swears he'll shoot the first man who goes in there. He's had two shots already at Reddy Flagg, but Reddy'd been careless and left his gun over to his room, so he jumped out the window and has gone over to get it. There'll be lots of trouble when he gets back."

Just then Wilcox heard a yell down the street and saw the outraged Flagg tearing up with a pistol in his hand.

He did not hesitate. "Arrest that man," he shouted to Henselt, one of his new deputy sheriffs whom he happened to see in the crowd, and he pointed to Flagg. "I'll attend to Warster's case myself." With that he started for the door.

"For God's sake, Kid, look out," cried several men; "he'll shoot." Wilcox answered not a word, but walked calmly up to the door of the saloon and kicked it open. As it fell back, Warster, inside, now insanely drunk, gave a wild howl and raised his pistol. Wilcox walked straight ahead without a movement of the muscles of his face.

"Put down that there gun," he said sharply, but calmly. "Put down that gun, you drunken brute!"

Warster glared at him, as if paralyzed by his inability to understand his opponent's tactics. The room was small, so that a few steps brought Wilcox within four feet of the big miner.

"Put it down," he reiterated. The weapon was hesitatingly, uncertainly lowered in response. In a flash Wilcox made a dart for it, seized it out of Warster's hand, and before Warster could grab him, brought it down with a hideous crack on the miner's skull. Warster fell like a lump of lead. The crowd outside had pressed in and there was awe-struck silence at the feat they had just witnessed.

"Take that out," said Wilcox, contemptuously kicking the inert body. "No, don't carry it out, drag him out—drag him out down the street and throw him in the sluice." He pointed to a sluiceway which ran along some claims behind the houses on the other side of the street. "Let him lie there an' cool off; an' to-morrow, when the water's got in him and the drink out of him, he'll perceive, p'rhaps, that this kind of thing is all out of date nowadays on Jenkins Creek."

He stopped, and then suddenly a loud cheer rose from the crowd: "Good for the new sheriff!" And even Reddy Flagg, who after a struggle had been disarmed and was now in Henselt's hands, gave a grin of appreciation.

"The Kid," he said, "has got more nerve than any twenty men in the county. Wasn't that as pretty a piece of work as you ever saw? I didn't believe in his ideas before, but ef that's the way he's going to carry them out, d—— it, I guess I'll support him!"

"This is only the beginning of the trouble, but it's the beginning of the end, God willin'," muttered the sheriff as he resumed his seat on the piazza of the hotel.

His prophecy was perfectly accurate in both particulars, for the next evening, after a hard day's work on his claim, when he strolled into Dave Stoner's store there was a hush of alarmed expectancy as Bill Cooper, Jim Warster, and four other turbulent spirits came up to him. Their attitudes and looks were menacing. Warster had a large swelling on his forehead, and his clothes were tumbled and bedraggled.

"Alexander Wilcox," he said after a very evident effort to control himself, "this valley's too small to hold both you and me."

"A LOUD CHEER ROSE FROM THE CROWD: 'GOOD FOR THE NEW SHERIFF!'"

"I guess you're right, Jim," answered the sheriff, chewing reflectively on a toothpick.

"After this, Wilcox, I give you fair warning, ef one of us is missing, it won't be me ef I kin help it."

"Jim," said the sheriff, after a pause as if he were digesting the last remark, " I s'pose you mean that for a threat. Did you happen to know that for that threat I could have you bound over to keep the peace or jugged ?"

"Bring on your d—— law and let's see any man jug me," shouted Warster, losing his temper.

"No," Wilcox answered; "I merely thought you'd like to know that you're breakin' the law. I'm not goin' to jug you, though it's my duty to do so, but I guess I can protect myself. It's to protect the safety of other men that I'm goin' to have the law observed in this county."

"You daren't arrest me," Warster sneered.

Wilcox flushed and bit his lip.

"Well, p'raps not ; though I guess you'll have hard work makin' the boys believe it, I'm afraid—how is it, boys ?" He turned to the breathless crowd around. There were murmurs of approval. "But I'll tell you one thing, Jim Warster," he continued, "I don't propose to have you shoot me down in the dark, or when I'm off my guard, or whenever seems best to you. If there's goin' to be any shootin' I'm goin' to have a fair show at it myself—and I'll tell you the little game I've got fixed up fer me and you. It's a good, open game, and, by God, you'll come into it or I'll have you run out of the county fer a gutless bully."

"What's yer game?" growled Warster.

"Well, I figured it out like this," continued Wilcox slowly and reflectively. "Jim, you're spoilin' fer a shot at me. An' I don't deny as how 'twould give me considerable pleasure to put a hole in you. I guess anyhow there'd be a kind er aching void in both er us onless we got satisfied on this point. I ain't going to have nothing unfair 'bout this deal. It's goin' to be a good straight shuffle. The odds on the game's goin' to be even an' everything out in the open. An' it's goin' to be jest about this way. To-morrow morning at eleven o'clock, when the sun is well up over the mountains and shining across the street, you an' me we'll start, one at each end of this town. You can take this side of the street an' I'll take the other. We'll both walk down to where the cross-road crosses the street, an' goes down to the creek. Then when we reach the end of the plank walk at the cross-road, fire straight at each other; and ef anything happens to either of us, that squares our account fer good and all. That's my plan. Ef I'm killed—well, that settles everything; but ef I'm not killed, it 'll mean that I'm goin' to have order up in this valley ef I have to kill every d——d one of you to get it."

Warster stared at the sheriff in blank amazement. No one else said a word. All were startled into silence at the originality of the plan. Dueling was an unheard-of thing in the creek; and this particular form of dueling had a unique, cold-blooded horror.

Warster attempted several times to speak and then choked down the words. Finally he said, "I'll do it."

"Remember," said the sheriff coldly, "ef either you or I fire before we reach the edge of the plank walk, that will be murder; an' one of us will be hung for it, ez sure ez there is a God in heaven."

Men talked in low voices the rest of that evening in Buckhorn, and an air of unaccustomed, strained solemnity seemed to

"'JIM ... WALKED ALONG LOOKIN' FIERCE, AN' HOT, AN' UGLY, WITH ... HIS HAND ON THE TRIGGER ALL THE TIME.'"

hang over the town. The more they thought of it the less they liked it, but the greater became their admiration for the little sheriff.

The next morning, by half-past ten, when the sun shone clear over the tops of the mountain and down into the little town, the one long street of Buckhorn was filled with miners and cattlemen. Again the news had flown far and wide up the gulches and down the valley, and there was no work done that day by any one; all had but one idea—to witness the sheriff's brand-new plan for promoting order in Washore County.

Meanwhile the calmest and most absolutely unconcerned man in the Creek was Alexander Wilcox himself. He was sitting up at his cabin, smoking a pipe and looking down at the gravel piles fringing his claim below. He was dressed with great precision, in his stiff white shirt, his cutaway coat, and a pair of new trousers bought for the special purpose of dignifying the day of his installation into office. As a finishing touch, carefully stuck in his buttonhole was a late autumn flower. Big Jim Warster in his cabin, on the other hand, was giving little thought to dress. He knew that the sheriff

was a good shot, but he knew himself to be a better one. In fact he was called the greatest expert with a revolver in the valley. He also knew that, if there was any advantage in position, his side of the street, being most in the shadow, was the better. Notwithstanding these considerations, Warster was not easy in his mind. This newly invented game of the sheriff's was a little too unusual for him.

It had been arranged that the two men should meet at "The Gus and Jim's," that they should then repair each to his own end of the street, and begin to walk down towards each other. Warster was the first on hand at the saloon, and he grew nervous as he awaited the sheriff's arrival. Finally Wilcox sauntered in, looking cool and undisturbed, though somewhat whiter than ordinarily.

"A fine morning, boys," he remarked. Then the two walked out, and amid great silence they turned their backs on each other and walked towards their respective starting points.

The story of the sheriff's new game and how it was played has been often told in Buckhorn, but never better than it was re-

"'THE SHERIFF .. WAS A-STROLLIN' ALONG AS SLOW AND CARELESS LIKE EZ EF HE WAS GOIN' TO GET HIS MAIL.'"

lated that very night by Nat Scammel to Hen Dranger, who had been obliged to miss the event of the day owing to his duties as stage-driver at Hawkton.

"Ye never saw anything like it, and ye never will if ye live to be a thousand and three years old, Hen," he narrated. "There we was, thick ez fleas, all lined up and down the street, only keepin' pretty well clear er the cross-road where the shots was likely to fly. Well, sir, them two, big Jim and the little sheriff, they got down to their ends of the streets plaguey quick, and then they jest a-started to walk for each other. Jim, he was in a kind er hurry and walked along lookin' fierce, an' hot, an' ugly, with his gun in his belt an' his hand on the trigger all the time. When we looked at him I tell ye the stomach fell right out of us. We said good-by to the sheriff, fer Jim always was a nasty shot.

"Well, Hen, we looked up the street t'other way, and I swear ef it hadn't been so darned serious we'd 'a' laughed right out. As it was, ye could hear a pine needle drop; there warn't a word nor a snicker. But darn my socks, ye'd oughter seen the sheriff. There was that blamed little cuss a-strollin' down the plank walk, with his natty tail coat, and his lavender pants, and a darned little sprig of flower stuck in his buttonhole. There he was a-strollin' along as slow and careless like ez ef he was goin' to get his mail, and, ye'd never believed it, he was whistlin' a tune; yes, sir, jest a-walkin' and whistlin', the darned little cuss; and he didn't have no gun out, though of course we knew he had it somewhere where he could reach it handy an' get it out lively when he'd strike the end of the plank walk.

"Well, sir, he jest a-walked on like that, ez ef he was a-goin' to a Sunday-school picnic. Then we looked back at Jim. Well, Jim was tearin' along in jest the same ugly way, an' we all see as how he'd get to the plank walk end first, an' would have a chance to get his gun in rest for a sure aim. Well, sir, that made us pretty scared for the little sheriff, because ye know what Jim was with a gun; but pretty soon the sheriff hove plainly in sight of Jim, an' then we saw Jim look kind er surprised. His fingers sort er went up and down on the trigger, an' he looked pretty white—dangerous white. But ez he watched the sheriff

strollin' along, so natty and calm-like, it seemed ez ef big Jim got nervous. Then he didn't seem to hurry so much, an' sort er wabbled ez ef he didn't know but what he'd better go slow too. The Kid kept gettin' nearer an' nearer, not lookin' across an' down the street at Jim at all, but jest whistlin' softly with his gun still hid.

"Well, Hen, that sight must have unnerved old Jim, for—ye won't believe it when I tell ye—when the little sheriff was about eight feet away from the edge of the cross-road Jim Warster he gave one big yell, threw up his hands, an' before we could tell what was happenin' he dove into the door of Slade's butcher shop, right by where he'd got to, an' didn't come out. So when the Kid got to the plank walk an' pulled out his gun to fire, he looked across an' there wasn't any one to fire at.

"Well, sir, ye never saw anybody seem so surprised in all your life. No, sir; he was jest amazed—I know it, because all he did was to stand there and laugh softly in a kind er silly way.

"Then he put his gun back into his pocket an' said, 'Well, boys, the fight's over an' ye'd better get back to work. But before ye'd go ye'll all have a drink on me. I think,' says he, 'the law is going to work first rate in this county.'

"Well, ye oughter have heard the boys cheer him. The Kid can own Buckhorn now, there's no use talking.

"And Warster? Well, Jim ain't never turned up to-day, and what's more he never will. He jest dove into that shop an' out the back door an' down the creek an' down the valley, an' ye'll never see Jim Warster at this creek again, never, I tell ye.

"What was the matter? Jest lost his nerve. Caved in teetotally. Jim always was a bully, an' when the time came to be a real man he hadn't the stuff in him to stand up an' shoot with that nervy little cuss comin' along so clipper an' cool an' careless-like on the other side of the street."

Scammell was right in his two predictions. From that day Mr. James Warster was neither heard of nor seen in all that region. And from that day Mr. Alexander Wilcox, sheriff of Washore County, owned the town of Buckhorn and its inhabitants. And that was the way in which law came to Jenkins Creek.

26

Twenty Minutes for Refreshments

OWEN WISTER

TWENTY MINUTES FOR REFRESHMENTS

BY OWEN WISTER

UPON turning over again my diary of that excursion to the Pacific, I find that I set out from Atlantic waters on the 30th day of a backward and forlorn April, which had come and done nothing toward making its share of spring, but had gone, missing its chance, leaving the trees as bare as it had received them from the winds of March. It was not bleak weather alone, but care, that I sought to escape by a change of sky; and I hoped for some fellow-traveller who might begin to interest my thoughts at once. No such person met me in the several Pullmans I inhabited from that afternoon until the forenoon of the following Friday. Through that long distance, though I had slanted southwestward across a multitude of States and vegetations, and the Mississippi lay eleven hundred miles to my rear, the single event is my purchasing some cat's-eyes of the news-agent at Sierra Blanca. Save this, my diary contains only neat additions of daily expenses, and moral reflections of a delicate and restrained melancholy. They were Pecos cat's-eyes, he told me, obtained in the rocky cañons of that stream, and destined to be worth little until fashion turned from foreign jewels to become aware of these fine native stones. And I, glad to possess the jewels of my country, chose two bracelets and a necklace of them, paying but twenty dollars for fifteen or sixteen cat's-eyes, and resolved to give them a setting worthy of their beauty. The diary continues with moral reflections upon the servility of our taste before anything European, and the hand-writing is most clear. It abruptly becomes hurried, and at length wellnigh illegible. It is best, I think, that you should have this portion as it comes, unpolished, unamended, unarranged—hot, so to speak, from my immediate pencil, instead of cold from my subsequent pen. I shall disguise certain names, but that is all.

Friday forenoon, May 5.—I don't have to gaze at my cat's-eyes to kill time any more. I'm not the only passenger any more. There's a lady. She got in at El Paso. She has taken the drawing-room, but sits outside reading newspaper cuttings and writing letters. She is sixty, I should say, and has a cap and one gray curl. This comes down over her left ear as far as a purple ribbon which suspends a medallion at her throat. She came in wearing a sage-green duster of pongee silk, pretty nice, only the buttons are as big as those largest mint drops. "You porter," she said, "brush this." He put down her many things and received it. Her dress was sage-green and pretty nice too. "You porter," said she, "open every window. Why, they are, I declare! What's the thermometer in this car?" "Ninety-five, ma'am. Folks mostly travelling—" "That will do, porter. Now you go make me a pitcher of lemonade right quick." She went into the state-room and shut the door. When she came out she was dressed in what appeared to be chintz bed-room curtains. They hang and flow loosely about her, and are covered with a pattern of pink peonies. She has slippers—Turkish—that stare up in the air, pretty handsome and comfortable. But I never before saw any one travel with fly-paper. It must be hard to pack. But it's quite an idea in this train. Fully a dozen flies have stuck to it already; and she reads her clippings, and writes away, and sips another glass of lemonade, all with the most extreme appearance of leisure, not to say sloth. I can't imagine how she manages to produce this atmosphere of indolence when in reality she is steadily occupied. Possibly the way she sits. But I think it's partly the bed-room curtains.

These notes were interrupted by the entrance of the new conductor. "If you folks have chartered a private car, just say so," he shouted instantly at the sight of us. He stood still at the extreme end and removed his hat, which was acknowledged by the lady. "Travel is surely very light, Gadsden," she assented, and went on with her writing. But he remained standing still, and shouting like an orator: "Sprinkle the floor of this car, Julius, and let the pore passengers get a breath of cool. My lands!" He fanned himself sweepingly with his hat. He seemed but little larger than a red squirrel, and precisely that color. Sorrel hair, sorrel eyebrows, sorrel freckles, light sorrel mustache, thin aggressive nose, receding chin, and black, attentive, prominent eyes. He approached, and I gave him my ticket, which is as long as a neck-tie. "Why, you ain't middle-aged!" he shouted, and a singular croak sounded behind me. But the lady was writing. "I have been growing younger since I left home," I replied. "That's it, that's it," he sang; "a man's always as old as he feels, and a woman—is ever young," he finished. "I see you are true to the old teachings and the old-time chivalry, Gadsden," said the lady, continuously busy. "Yes, ma'am. Jacob served seven years for Leah and seven more for Rachel." "Such men are raised to-day in every worthy Louisiana home, Gadsden, be it ever so humble." "Yes, ma'am. Give a fresh sprinkle to the floor, Julius, soon as it goes to get dry. Excuse me, but do you shave yourself, sir?" I told him that I did, but without excusing him. "You will see that I have a reason for asking," he consequently pursued, and took out of his coat tails a round tin box handsomely labelled "Nat. Fly Paper Co.," so that I supposed it was thus, of course, that the lady came by her fly-paper. But this was pure coincidence, and the conductor explained: "That company's me and a man at Shreveport, but he dissatisfies me right frequently. You know what heaven a good razor is for a man, and what you feel about a bad one. Vaseline and ground shells," he said, opening the box, "and I'm not saying anything except it will last your lifetime and never hardens. Rub the size of a pea on the fine side of your strop, spread it to an inch with your thumb. May I beg a favor on so short a meeting? Join me in the gentlemen's lavatory with your razor-strop in five minutes. I have to attend to a corpse in the baggage-car, and will return at once." "Anybody's corpse I know, Gadsden?" said the lady. "No, ma'am. Just a corpse."

When I joined him, for I was now willing to do anything, he was apologetic again. "'Tis a short acquaintance," he said, "but may I also beg your razor? Quick as I get out of the National Fly

I am going to register my new label. First there will be Uncle Sam embracing the world, signifying this mixture is universal, then my name, then the word *Stropine*, which is a novelty and carries copyright, and I shall win comfort and doubtless luxury. The post barber at Fort Bayard took a dozen off me at sight to retail to the niggers of the Twenty-fourth, and as he did not happen to have the requisite cash on his person I charged him two roosters and fifty cents, and both of us done well. He's after more Stropine, and I got Pullman prices for my roosters, the buffet-car being out of chicken à la Marengo. There is your razor, sir, and I appreciate your courtesy." It was beautifully sharpened, and I bought a box of the Stropine and asked him who the lady was. "Mrs. Porcher Brewton!" he exclaimed. "Have you never met her socially? Why she—why she is the most intellectual lady in Bee Bayou." "Indeed!" I said. "Why she visits New Orleans, and Charleston, and all the principal centres of refinement, and is welcomed in Washington. She converses freely with our statesmen, and is considered a queen of learning. Why she writes po'try, sir, and is strong-minded. But a man wouldn't want to pick her up for a fool, all the samey." "I shouldn't; I don't," said I. "Don't you do it, sir. She's run her plantation all alone since the Colonel was killed in sixty-two. She taught me Sunday-school when I was a lad, and she used to catch me at her pecan-trees 'most every time in Bee Bayou."

He went forward, and I went back with the Stropine in my pocket. The lady was sipping the last of the lemonade and looking haughtily over the top of her glass into (I suppose) the world of her thoughts. Her eyes met mine, however. "Has Gadsden — yes, I perceive he has been telling about me," she said, in her languid, formidable voice. She set her glass down and reclined among the folds of the bed-room curtains, considering me. "Gadsden has always been lavish," she mused, caressingly. "He seems destined to succeed in life," I hazarded. "O — h n — o!" she sighed, with decision. "He will fail." As she said no more, and as I began to resent the manner in which she surveyed me, I remarked, "You seem rather sure of his failure." "I am old enough to be his mother, and yours," said Mrs. Porcher Brewton among her curtains. "He is a noble-hearted fellow, and would have been a high-souled Southern gentleman if born to that station. But what should a conductor earning $103 50 a month be dispersing his attention on silly patents for? Many's the time I've told him what I think; but Gadsden will always be flighty." No further observations occurring to me, I took up my necklace and bracelets from the seat and put them in my pocket. "Will you permit a meddlesome old woman to inquire what made you buy those cat's-eyes?" said Mrs. Brewton. "Why—" I dubiously began. "Never mind," she cried, archly. "If you were thinking of some one in your Northern home, they will be prized because the thought, at any rate, was beautiful and genuine. 'Where'er I roam, whatever realms to see, my heart, untravelled, fondly turns to thee.' Now don't you be embarrassed by an old woman!" I desired to inform her that I disliked her, but one can never do those things; and, anxious to learn what was the matter with the cat's-eyes, I spoke amiably and politely to her. "Twenty dollars!" she murmured. "And he told you they came from the Pecos!" She gave that single melodious croak I had heard once before. Then she sat up with her back as straight as if she was twenty. "My dear young fellow, never do you buy trash in these trains. Here you are with your coat full of—what's Gadsden's absurd razor concoction?—strut—strup—bother! And Chinese paste buttons. Last summer, on the Northern Pacific, the man offered your cat's-eyes to me as native gems found exclusively in Dakota. But I just sat and mentioned to him that I was on my way home from a holiday in China, and he went right out of the car. The last day I was in Canton I bought a box of those cat's-eyes at eight cents a dozen." After this we spoke a little on other subjects, and now she's busy writing again. She's on business in California, but will read a paper at Los Angeles at the annual meeting of the Golden Daughters of the West. The meal station is coming, but we have agreed to—

Later, Friday afternoon.—I have been interrupted again. Gadsden entered, removed his hat, and shouted: "Sharon. Twenty minutes for dinner." I was call-

ing the porter to order a buffet lunch in the car, when there tramped in upon us three large men of such appearance that a flash of thankfulness went through me at having so little ready money and only a silver watch. Mrs. Brewton looked at them and said, "Well, gentlemen?" and they took off their embroidered Mexican hats. "We've got a baby show here," said one of them, slowly, looking at me, "and we'd be kind of obliged if you'd hold the box." "There's lunch put up in a basket for you to take along," said the next, "and a bottle of wine—champagne. So losing your dinner won't lose you nothing." "We're looking for somebody raised East and without local prejudice," said the third. "So we come to the Pullman." I now saw that so far from purposing to rob us they were in a great and honest distress of mind. "But I am no judge of a baby," said I; "not being mar—" "You don't have to be," broke in the first, more slowly and earnestly. "It's a fair and secret ballot we're striving for. The votes is wrote out and ready, and all we're shy of is a stranger without family ties or business interests to hold the box and do the counting." His deep tones ceased, and he wiped heavy drops from his forehead with his shirt sleeve. "We'd be kind of awful obliged to you," he urged. "The town would be liable to make it two bottles," said the second. The third brought his fist down on the back of a seat and said, "I'll make it that now." "But, gentlemen," said I, "five, six, and seven years ago I was not a stranger in Sharon. If my friend Dean Drake was still here—" "But he ain't. Now you might as well help folks, and eat later. This town will trust you. And if you quit us—" Once more he wiped the heavy drops away, while in a voice full of appeal his friend finished his thought: "If we lose you, we'll likely have to wait till this train comes in tomorrow for a man satisfactory to this town. And the show is costing us a heap." A light hand tapped my arm, and here was Mrs. Brewton saying: "For shame! Show your enterprise." "I'll hold this yere train," shouted Gadsden, "if necessary." Mrs. Brewton rose alertly, and they all hurried me out. "My slippers will stay right on when I'm down the steps," said Mrs. Brewton, and Gadsden helped her descend into the blazing dust and sun of Sharon. "Gracious!"

said she, "what a place! But I make it a point to see everything as I go." Nothing had changed. There, as of old, lay the flat litter of the town—sheds, stores, and dwellings, a shapeless congregation in the desert, gaping wide everywhere to the glassy, quivering immensity; and there, above the roofs, turned the slatted wind-wheels. But close to the tracks, opposite the hotel, was an edifice, a sort of tent of bunting, from which brass music issued, while about a hundred pink and blue sun-bonnets moved and mixed near the entrance. Little black Mexicans, like charred toys, lounged and lay staring among the ungraded dunes of sand. "Gracious!" said Mrs. Brewton again. Her eye lost nothing; and as she made for the tent the chintz peonies flowed around her, and her step was surprisingly light. We passed through the sun-bonnets and entered where the music played. "The precious blessed darlings!" she exclaimed, clasping her hands. "This will do for the Golden Daughters," she rapidly added, "yes, this will distinctly do." And she hastened away from me into the throng.

I had no time to look at much this first general minute. I could see there were booths, each containing a separate baby. I passed a whole section of naked babies, and one baby farther along had on golden wings and a crown, and was bawling frightfully. Their names were over the booths, and I noticed Lucille, Erskine Wales, Banquo Lick Nolin, Cuba, Manilla, Ellabelle, Bosco Grady, James J. Corbett Nash, and Aqua Marine. There was a great sign at the end, painted "Mrs. Eden's Manna in the Wilderness," and another sign, labelled "Shot-gun Smith's twins." In the midst of these first few impressions I found myself seated behind a bare table raised three feet or so, with two boxes on it, and a quantity of blank paper and pencils, while one of the men was explaining me the rules and facts. I can't remember them all now, because I couldn't understand them all then, and Mrs. Brewton was distant among the sun-bonnets, talking to a gathering crowd and feeling in the mouths of babies that were being snatched out of the booths and brought to her. The man was instructing me steadily all the while, and it occurred to me to nod silently and coldly now and then, as if I was doing this sort of thing every day. But I insisted that some one

should help me count, and they gave me Gadsden.

Now these facts I do remember very clearly, and shall never forget them. The babies came from two towns—Sharon, and Rincon its neighbor. Alone, neither had enough for a good show, though in both it was every family's pride to have a baby every year. The babies were in three classes: Six months and under, one prize offered; eighteen months, two prizes; three years, two prizes. A three-fourths vote of all cast was necessary to a choice. No one entitled to vote unless of immediate family of a competing baby. No one entitled to cast more than one vote. There were rules of entry and fees, but I forget them, except that no one could have two exhibits in the same class. When I read this I asked, how about twins? "Well, we didn't kind of foresee that," muttered my instructor, painfully. "What would be your idea?" "Look here, you sir," interposed Mrs. Brewton, "he came in to count votes." I was very glad to have her back. "That's right, ma'am," admitted the man; "he needn't to say a thing. We've only got one twins entered," he pursued, "which we're glad of. Shot-gun—" "Where is this Mr. Smith?" interrupted Mrs. Brewton. "Uptown drinking, ma'am." "And who may Mr. Smith be?" "Most popular citizen of Rincon, ma'am. We had to accept his twins because—well, he come down here himself, and most of Rincon come with him, and as we aimed to have everything pass off pleasant-like—" "I quite comprehend," said Mrs. Brewton. "And I should consider twins within the rule; or any number born at one time. But little Aqua Marine is the finest single child in that six months class. I told her mother she ought to take that splurgy ring off the poor little thing's thumb. It's most unsafe. But I should vote for that child myself." "Thank you for your valuable endorsement," said a spruce, slim young man. "But the public is not allowed to vote here," he added. He was standing on the floor and resting his elbows on the table. Mrs. Brewton stared down at him. "Are you the father of the child?" she inquired. "Oh no! I am the agent. I—" "Aqua Marine's agent?" said Mrs. Brewton, sharply. "Ha, ha!" went the young man. "Ha, ha! Well, that's good too. She's part of our exhibit. I'm in charge of the manna-feds, don't you know?" "I don't know," said Mrs. Brewton. "Why, Mrs. Eden's Manna in the Wilderness! Nourishes, strengthens, and makes no unhealthy fat. Take a circular, and welcome. I'm travelling for the manna. I organized this show. I've conducted twenty-eight similar shows in two years. We hold them in every State and Territory. Second of last March I gave Denver — you heard of it, probably?" "I did not," said Mrs. Brewton. "Well! Ha, ha! I thought every person up to date had heard of Denver's Olympic Offspring Olio." "Is it up to date to loll your elbows on the table when you're speaking to a lady?" inquired Mrs. Brewton. He jumped, and then grew scarlet with rage. "I didn't expect to learn manners in New Mexico," said he. "I doubt if you will," said Mrs. Brewton, and turned her back on him. He was white now; but better instincts, or else business, prevailed in his injured bosom. "Well," said he, "I had no bad intentions. I was going to say you'd have seen ten thousand people and five hundred babies at Denver. And our manna-feds won out to beat the band. Three first medals, and all exclusively manna-fed. We took the costume prize also. Of course here in Sharon I've simplified. No special medal for weight, beauty, costume, or decorated perambulator. Well, I must go back to our exhibit. Glad to have you give us a call up there and see the medals we're offering, and our fifteen manna-feds, and take a package away with you." He was gone.

The voters had been now voting in my two boxes for some time, and I found myself hoping the manna would not win, whoever did; but it seemed this agent was a very capable person. To begin with, every family entering a baby drew a package of the manna free, and one package contained a diamond ring. Then, he had managed to have the finest babies of all classes in his own exhibit. This was incontestable, Mrs. Brewton admitted after returning from a general inspection; and it seemed to us extraordinary. "That's easy, ma'am," said Gadsden; "he came around here a month ago. Don't you see?" I did not see, but Mrs. Brewton saw at once. He had made a quiet selection of babies beforehand, and then introduced the manna into those homes. And everybody in the room was remark-

ing that his show was very superior, taken as a whole—they all added, "taken as a whole"; I heard them as they came up to vote for the 3-year and the 18-month classes. The 6-month was to wait till last, because the third box had been accidentally smashed by Mr. Smith. Gadsden caught several trying to vote twice. "No, you don't!" he would shout. "I know faces. I'm not a conductor for nothing." And the victim would fall back amid jeers from the sun-bonnets. Once the passengers sent over to know when the train was going. "Tell them to step over here and they'll not feel so lonesome!" shouted Gadsden; and I think a good many came. The band was playing "White Wings," with quite a number singing it, when Gadsden noticed the voting had ceased, and announced this ballot closed. The music paused for him, and we could suddenly hear how many babies were in distress; but for a moment only; as we began our counting, "White Wings" resumed, and the sun-bonnets outsang their progeny. There was something quite singular in the way they had voted. Here are some of the 3-year-old tickets: "First choice, Ulysses Grant Blum; 2d choice, Lewis Hendricks." "First choice, James Redfield; 2d, Lewis Hendricks." "First, Elk Chester; 2d, Lewis Hendricks." "Can it be?" said the excited Gadsden. "Finish these quick. I'll open the 18-monthers." But he swung round to me at once. "See there!" he cried. "Read that! and that!" He plunged among more, and I read: "First choice, Lawrence Nepton Ford, Jr.; 2d, Iona Judd." "First choice, Mary Louise Kenton; 2d, Iona Judd." "Hurry up!" said Gadsden; "that's it!" And as we counted, Mrs. Brewton looked over my shoulder and uttered her melodious croak, for which I saw no reason. "That young whipper-snapper will go far," she observed; nor did I understand this. But when they stopped the band for me to announce the returns, one fact did dawn on me even while I was reading: "Three-year-olds: Whole number of votes cast, 300; necessary to a choice, 225. Second prize, Lewis Hendricks, receiving 300. First prize, largest number of votes cast, 11, for Salvisa van Meter. No award. Eighteen-month class: Whole number of votes cast, 300; necessary to a choice, 225. Second prize, Iona Judd, receiving 300. Lillian Brown gets 15 for 1st prize.

None awarded." There was a very feeble applause, and then silence for a second, and then the sun-bonnets rushed together, rushed away to others, rushed back; and talk swept like hail through the place. Yes, that is what they had done. They had all voted for Lewis Hendricks and Iona Judd for second prize, and every family had voted the first prize to its own baby. The Browns and van Meters happened to be the largest families present. "He'll go far! he'll go far!" repeated Mrs. Brewton. Sport glittered in her eye. She gathered her curtains, and was among the sun-bonnets in a moment. Then it fully dawned on me. The agent for Mrs. Eden's Manna in the Wilderness was indeed a shrewd strategist, and knew his people to the roots of the grass. They had never seen a baby show. They were innocent. He came among them. He gave away packages of manna and a diamond ring. He offered the prizes. But he proposed to win some. Therefore he made that rule about only the immediate families voting. He foresaw what they would do; and now they had done it. Whatever happened, two prizes went to his manna-feds. "They don't see through it in the least, which is just as well," said Mrs. Brewton, returning. "And it's little matter that only second prizes go to the best babies. But what's to be done now?" I had no idea, but it was not necessary that I should.

"You folks of Rincon and Sharon," spoke a deep voice. It was the first man in the Pullman, and drops were rolling from his forehead, and his eyes were the eyes of a beleaguered ox. "You fathers and mothers," he said, and took another breath. They grew quiet. "I'm a father myself, as is well known." They applauded this. "Salvisa is mine, and she got my vote. The father that will not support his own child· is not—does not—is worse than if they were orphans." He breathed again, while they loudly applauded. "But, folks, I've got to get home to Rincon. I've got to. And I'll give up Salvisa if I'm met fair." "Yes, yes, you'll be met," said voices of men. "Well, here's my proposition: Mrs. Eden's manna has took two, and I'm satisfied it should. We voted, and will stay voted." "Yes! yes!" "Well, now, here's Sharon and Rincon, two of the finest towns in this section, and I say Sharon and Rincon has equal rights to

get something out of this, and drop private feelings, and everybody back their town. And I say let this lady and gentleman, who will act elegant and on the square, take a view and nominate the finest Rincon 3-year-old and the finest Sharon 18-month they can cut out of the herd. And I say let's vote unanimous on their pick, and let each town hold a first prize and go home in friendship, feeling it has been treated right."

Universal cheers endorsed him, and he got down panting. The band played "Union Forever," and I accompanied Mrs. Brewton to the booths. "You'll remember!" shouted the orator urgently after us; "one apiece." We nodded. "Don't get mixed," he appealingly insisted. We shook our heads, and out of the booths rushed two women, and simultaneously dashed their infants in our faces. "You'll never pass Cuba by!" entreated one. "This is Bosco Grady," said the other. Cuba wore an immense garment made of the American flag, but her mother whirled her out of it in a second. "See them dimples; see them knees!" she said. "See them feet! Only feel of her toes!" "Look at his arms!" screamed the mother of Bosco. "Doubled his weight in four months." "Did he indeed, ma'am?" said Cuba's mother; "well he hadn't much to double." "Didn't he, then? Didn't he indeed?" "No at you; he didn't indeed and indeed! I guess Cuba is known to Sharon. I guess Sharon 'll not let Cuba be slighted." "Well, and I guess Rincon 'll see that Bosco Grady gets his rights." "Ladies," said Mrs. Brewton, towering but poetical with her curl, "I am a mother myself, and raised five noble boys and two sweet peerless girls." This stopped them immediately; they stared at her and her chintz peonies as she put the curl gently away from her medallion and proceeded: "But never did I think of myself in those dark weary days of the long ago. I thought of my country and the Lost Cause." They stared at her, fascinated. "Yes, m'm," whispered they, quite humbly. "Now," said Mrs. Brewton, "what is more sacred than an American mother's love? Therefore let her not shame it with anger and strife. All little boys and girls are precious gems to me and to you. What is a cold, lifeless medal compared to one of them? Though I would that all could get the prize! But they can't, you know." "No, m'm." Many mothers, with their children in their arms, were now dumbly watching Mrs. Brewton, who held them with a honeyed, convincing smile. "If I choose only one in this beautiful and encouraging harvest, it is because I have no other choice. Thank you so much for letting me see that little hero and that lovely angel," she added, with a yet sweeter glance to the mothers of Bosco and Cuba. And I wish them all luck when their turn comes. I've no say about the 6-month class, you know. And now a little room, please."

The mothers fell back. But my head swam slightly. The 6-month class, to be sure! The orator had forgotten all about it. In the general joy over his wise and fair proposition, nobody had thought of it. But they would pretty soon. Cuba and Bosco were likely to remind them. Then we should still be face to face with a state of things that— I cast a glance behind at those two mothers of Sharon and Rincon following us, and I asked Mrs. Brewton to look at them. "Don't think about it now," said she; "it will only mix you. I always like to take a thing when it comes, and not before." We now reached the 18-month class. They were the naked ones. The 6-month had staid nicely in people's arms; these were crawling hastily everywhere, like crabs upset in the market, and they screamed fiercely when taken upon the lap. The mother of Thomas Jefferson Brayin Lucas showed us a framed letter from the statesman for whom her child was called. The letter reeked with gratitude, and said that offspring was man's proudest privilege; that a souvenir sixteen-to-one spoon would have been cheerfully sent, but 428 babies had been named after Mr. Brayin since January. It congratulated the swelling army of the People's Cause. But there was nothing eminent about little Thomas except the letter; and we selected Reese Moran, a vigorous Sharon baby, who, when they attempted to set him down and pacify him, stiffened his legs, dashed his candy to the floor, and burst into lamentation. We were soon on our way to the 3-year class, for Mrs. Brewton was rapid and thorough. As we went by the Manna Exhibit, the agent among his packages and babies invited us in. He was loudly declaring that he would vote for Bosco if he could. But when he examined Cuba, he became sure that Den

ver had nothing finer than that. Mrs. Brewton took no notice of him, but bade me admire Aqua Marine as far surpassing any other 6-month child. I proclaimed her splendid (she was a wide-eyed, contented thing, with a head shaped like a croquet mallet), and the agent smiled modestly and told the mother that as for his babies two prizes was luck enough for them; they didn't want the earth. "If that thing happened to be brass," said Mrs. Brewton, bending over the ring that Aqua was still sucking; and again remonstrating with the mother for this imprudence, she passed on. The three-year-olds were, many of them, in costume, with extraordinary arrangements of hair; and here was the child with gold wings and a crown I had seen on arriving. Her name was Verbena M., and she personated Faith. She had colored slippers, and was drinking tea from her mother's cup. Another child, named Broderick McGowan, represented Columbus, and joyfully shouted "Ki-yi!" every half-minute. One child was attired as a prominent admiral; another as a prominent general; and one stood in a boat and was Washington. As Mrs. Brewton examined them and dealt with the mothers, the names struck me afresh—not so much the boys; Ulysses Grant and James J. Corbett explained themselves; but I read the names of five adjacent girls — Lula, Ocilla, Nila, Cusseta, and Maylene. And I asked Mrs. Brewton how they got them. "From romances," she told me, "in papers that we of the upper classes never see." In choosing for his hair, his full set of front teeth well cared for, and his general beauty, Horace Boyd, of Rincon, I think both of us were also influenced by his good sensible name, and his good clean sensible clothes. With both our selections, once they were settled, were Sharon and Rincon satisfied. We were turning back to the table to announce our choice when a sudden clamor arose behind us, and we saw confusion in the manna department. Women were running and shrieking, and I hastened after Mrs. Brewton to see what was the matter. Aqua Marine had swallowed the ring on her thumb. "It was gold! it was pure gold!" wailed the mother, clutching Mrs. Brewton. "It cost a whole dollar in El Paso." "She must have white of egg instantly," said Mrs. Brewton, handing me her purse.

"Run to the hotel—" "Save your money," said the agent, springing forward with some eggs in a bowl. "Lord! you don't catch us without all the appliances handy. We'd run behind the trade in no time. There, now, there," he added comfortingly to the mother. "Will you make her swallow it? Better let me— better let me. And here's the emetic. Lord! why, we had three swallowed rings at the Denver Olio, and I got 'em all safe back within ten minutes after time of swallowing." "You go away," said Mrs. Brewton to me, "and tell them our nominations." The mothers sympathetically surrounded poor little Aqua, saying to each other: "She's a beautiful child!" "Sure indeed she is!" "But the manna-feds has had their turn." "Sure indeed they've been recognized," and so forth, while I was glad to retire to the voting table. The music paused for me, and as the crowd cheered my small speech, some one said, "And now what are you going to do about me?" It was Bosco Grady back again, and close behind him Cuba. They had escaped from Mrs. Brewton's eye and had got me alone. But I pretended in the noise and cheering not to see these mothers. I noticed a woman hurrying out of the tent, and hoped Aqua was not in further trouble— she was still surrounded, I could see. Then the orator made some silence, thanked us in the names of Sharon and Rincon, and proposed our candidates be voted on by acclamation. This was done. Rincon voted for Sharon and Reese Moran in a solid roar, and Sharon voted for Rincon and Horace Boyd in a roar equally solid. So now each had a prize, and the whole place was applauding happily, and the band was beginning again, when the mothers with Cuba and Bosco jumped up beside me on the platform, and the sight of them produced immediate silence.

"There's a good many here has a right to feel satisfied," said Mrs. Grady, looking about, "and they're welcome to their feelings. But if this meeting thinks it is through with its business, I can tell it that it ain't—not if it acts honorable, it ain't. Does those that have had their chance and those that can take home their prizes expect us 6-month mothers come here for nothing? Do they expect I brought my Bosco from Rincon to be insulted, and him the pride of the town?" "Cuba is known to Sharon," spoke the other lady. "I'll say no more." "Jumping Jeans!" murmured the orator to himself. "I can't hold this train much longer," said Gadsden. "She's due at Lordsburg now." "You'll have made it up by Tucson, Gadsden," spoke Mrs. Brewton, quietly, across the whole assembly from the manna department. "As for towns," continued Mrs. Grady, "that think anything of a baby that's only got three teeth—" "Ha! ha!" laughed Cuba's mother, shrilly. "Teeth! Well, we're not proud of bald babies in Sharon." Bosco was certainly bald. All the men were looking wretched, and all the women were growing more and more like eagles. Moreover, they were separating into two bands and taking their husbands with them—Sharon and Rincon drawing to opposite parts of the tent—and what was coming I cannot say; for we all had to think of something else. A third woman bringing a man mounted the platform. It was she I had seen hurry out. "My name's Shot-gun Smith," said the man, very carefully, "and I'm told you've reached my case." He was extremely good-looking, with a blue eye and a blond mustache, not above thirty, and was trying hard to be sober, holding himself with dignity. "Are you the judge?" said he to me. "Well—" I began. "N-not guilty, your honor," said he. At this his wife looked anxious. "S-self-defence," he slowly continued; "told you once already." "Why, Rolfe!" exclaimed his wife, touching his elbow. "Don't you cry, little woman," said he. "This'll come out all right. Where're the witnesses?" "Why, Rolfe! *Rolfe!*" She shook him as you shake a sleepy child. "Now see here," said he, and wagged a finger at her affectionately, "you promised me you'd not cry if I let you come." "Rolfe dear, it's not that to-day; it's the twins." "It's your twins, Shot-gun, this time," said many men's voices. "We acquitted you all right last month." "Justifiable homicide," said Gadsden. "Don't you remember?" "Twins?" said Shot-gun, drowsily. "Oh, yes, mine. Why—" He opened on us his blue eyes that looked about as innocent as Aqua Marine's, and he grew more awake. Then he blushed deeply, face and forehead. "I was not coming to this kind of thing," he explained. "But she wanted the twins to get something." He put his hand on her shoulder and straightened himself. "I done a heap of prospecting before I struck this claim," said he, patting her shoulder. "We got married last March a year. It's our first—first—first"— he turned to me with a confiding smile—"it's our first dividend, judge." "Rolfe! I never! You come right down." "And now let's go get a prize," he declared, with his confiding pleasantness. "I remember now! I remember! They claimed twins was barred. And I kicked down the bars. Take me to those twins. They're not named yet, judge. After they get the prize we'll name them fine names, as good as any they got anywhere—Europe, Asia, Africa—anywhere. My gracious! I wish they was boys. Come on, judge! You and me 'll go give 'em a prize, and then we'll drink to 'em." He lugged me suddenly and affectionately, and we half fell down the steps. But Gadsden as suddenly caught him and righted him, and we proceeded to the twins. Mrs. Smith looked at me helplessly, saying: "I'm that sorry, sir! I had no idea he was going to be that gamesome." "Not at all," I said; "not at all!" Under many circumstances I should have delighted in Shotgun's society. He seemed so utterly sure that, now he had explained himself, everybody would rejoice to give the remaining medal to his little girls! But Bosco and Cuba had not been idle. Shot-gun did not notice the spread of whispers, nor feel the divided and jealous currents in the air as he sat and, in expanding good-will, talked himself almost sober. To entice him out there was no way. Several of his friends had tried it. But beneath his innocence there seemed to lurk something wary, and I grew apprehensive about holding the box this last time. But Gadsden relieved me as our count began. "Shot-gun is a splendid man," said he, "and he has trailed more train-robbers than any deputy in New Mexico. But he has seen too many friends to-day, and is not quite himself. So when he fell down that time I just took this off him." He opened the drawer, and there lay a sixshooter. "It was touch and go," said Gadsden; "but he's thinking that hard about his twins he's not missed it yet. 'Twould have been the act of an enemy to leave that on him to-day.—Well, d'you say!" he broke off. "Well, well, well!" It was the tickets we took out of the box that set him exclaiming. I began to read them, and saw that the agent was no mere politician, but a statesman. His Aqua Marine had a solid vote. I remembered his extreme praise of both Bosco and Cuba. This had set Rincon and Sharon bitterly against each other. I remembered his modesty about Aqua Marine. Of course. Each town, unable to bear the idea of the other's beating it, had voted for the manna-fed, who had 299 votes. Shot-gun and his wife had voted for their twins. I looked towards the manna department, and could see that Aqua Marine was placid once more, and Mrs. Brewton was dancing the ring before her eyes. I hope I announced the returns in a firm voice. "What!" said Shot-gun Smith; and at that sound Mrs. Brewton stopped dancing the ring. He strode to our table. "There's the winner," said Gadsden, quickly pointing to the Manna Exhibit. "What!" shouted Smith again; "and they quit me for that hammer-headed son-of-a-gun?" He whirled around. The men stood ready, and the women fled shrieking and cowering to their infants in the booths. "Gentlemen! Gentlemen!" cried Gadsden, "don't hurt him! Look here!" And from the drawer he displayed Shot-gun's weapon. They understood in a second, and calmly watched the enraged and disappointed Shot-gun. But he was a man. He saw how he had frightened the women, and he stood in the middle of the floor with eyes that did not at all resemble Aqua Marine's at present. "I'm all right now, boys," he said. "I hope I've harmed no one. Ladies, will you try and forget about me making such a break? It got ahead of me, I guess; for I had promised the little woman—" He stopped himself; and then his eye fell upon the manna department. "I guess I don't like one thing much now. I'm not after prizes. I'd not accept one from a goldbug-combine-trust that comes sneaking around stuffing wholesale concoctions into our children's systems. My twins are not manna-fed. My twins are raised as nature intended. Perhaps if they were swelled out with trash that acts like baking-powder, they would have a medal too—for I notice he has made you vote his way pretty often this afternoon." I saw the agent at the end of the room look very queer. "That's so!" said several. "I think I'll clear out his boxes," said Shot-gun, with rising joy. "I feel like I've got to do something before I go home. Come on, judge!" He swooped towards the manna with a yell, and the men swooped with him, and Gadsden and I were swooped with them. Again the women shrieked. But Mrs. Brewton stood out before the boxes with her curl and her chintz.

"Mr. Smith," said she, "you are not going to do anything like that. You are going to behave yourself like the gentleman you are, and not like the wild beast that's inside you." Never in his life before, probably, had Shot-gun been addressed in such a manner, and he too became hypnotized, fixing his blue eyes upon the strange lady. "I do not believe in patent foods for children," said Mrs. Brewton. "We agree on that, Mr. Smith, and I am a grandmother, and I attend to what my grandchildren eat. But this highly adroit young man has done you no harm. If he has the prizes, whose doing is that, please? And who paid for them? Will you tell me, please? Ah, you are all silent!" And she croaked melodiously. "Now let him and his manna go along. But I have enjoyed meeting you all, and I shall not forget you soon. And, Mr. Smith, I want you to remember me. Will you, please?" She walked to Mrs. Smith and the twins, and Shot-gun followed her, entirely hypnotized. She beckoned to me. "Your judge and I," she said, "consider not only your beautiful twins worthy of a prize, but also the mother and father who can so proudly claim them." She put her hand in my pocket. "These cat's-eyes," she said, "you will wear, and think of me and the judge who presents them." She placed a bracelet on each twin, and the necklace upon Mrs. Smith's neck. "Give him Gadsden's stuff," she whispered to me. "Do you shave yourself, sir?" said I, taking out the Stropine. "Vaseline and ground shells, and will last your life. Rub the size of a pea on your strop and spread it to an inch." I placed the box in Shot-gun's motionless hand. "And now, Gadsden, we'll take the train," said Mrs. Brewton. "Here's your lunch! Here's your wine!" said the orator, forcing a basket upon me. "I don't know what we'd have done without you and your mother." A flash of indignation crossed Mrs. Brewton's face, but changed to a smile. "You've forgot to name my girls!" exclaimed Shot-gun, suddenly finding his voice. "Suppose you try

that," said Mrs. Brewton to me, a trifle viciously. "Thank you," I said to Smith. "Thank you. I—" "Something handsome," he urged. "How would Cynthia do for one?" I suggested. "Shucks, no! I've known two Cynthias. You don't want that?" he asked Mrs. Smith; and she did not at all. "Something extra, something fine, something not stale," said he. I looked about the room. There was no time for thought, but my eye fell once more upon Cuba. This reminded me of Spain, and the Spanish; and my brain leaped. "I have them!" I cried. "'Armada' and 'Loyola.'" "That's what they're named!" said Shot-gun, "write it for us." And I did. Once more the band played, and we left them, all calling, "Good-by, ma'am. Good-by, judge," happy as possible. The train was soon going sixty miles an hour through the desert. We had passed Lordsburg, San Simon, and were nearly at Benson before Mrs. Brewton and Gadsden (whom she made sit down with us) and I finished the lunch and champagne. "I wonder how long he'll remember me?" mused Mrs. Brewton at Tucson, where we were on time. "That woman is not worth one of his boots."

Saturday afternoon, May 6. — Near Los Angeles. I have been writing all day, to be sure and get everything in, and now Sharon is twenty-four hours ago, and here there are roses, gardens, and many nice houses at the way-stations. Oh, George Washington, father of your country what a brindled litter have you sired!

But here the moral reflections begin again, and I copy no more diary. Mrs. Brewton liked my names for the twins. "They'll pronounce it Loyóla," she said, "and that sounds right lovely." Later she sent me her paper for the Golden Daughters. It is full of poetry and sentiment and all the things I have missed. She wrote that if she had been sure the agent had helped Aqua Marine to swallow the ring, she would have let them smash his boxes. And I think she was a little in love with Shot-gun Smith. But what a pity we shall soon have no more Mrs. Brewtons! The causes that produced her — slavery, isolation, literary tendencies, adversity, game blood—that combination is broken forever. I shall speak to Mr. Howells about her. She ought to be recorded.

27

Grandmother Stark

OWEN WISTER

GRANDMOTHER STARK.

BY OWEN WISTER.

EXCEPT for its chairs and bed, the cabin was stripped almost bare. Amid its emptiness of dismantled shelves and walls and floor, only the tiny ancestress still hung in her place, last token of the home that had been. This miniature tacked against the despoiled boards, and its descendant, the angry girl with her hand on an open box-lid, made a sort of couple in the loneliness: she on the wall sweet and serene, she by the box sweet and stormy. The picture was her final treasure waiting to be packed for the journey. In whatever room she had called her own since childhood, there it had also lived and looked at her, not quite familiar, not quite smiling, but in its prim colonial hues delicate as some pressed flower. Its pale oval, of color blue and rose and flaxen, in a battered, pretty gold frame, unquellably pervaded any surroundings with a something like last year's lavender. Till yesterday a Crow Indian war-bonnet had hung next it, a sumptuous cascade of feathers; on the other side a bow with arrows had dangled; opposite had been a Navajo blanket, staring in zigzags of barbarity; over the door had spread the antlers of a black-tail deer; a bear-skin stretched beneath it. Thus had the whole cozy log cabin been upholstered, lavish with trophies of the frontier; and yet it was in front of the miniature that the visitors used to stop.

Shining quietly now in the cabin's blankness this summer day, the heirloom was presiding until the end. Molly Wood did not bear the family name; but as her eyes fell on her ancestress of Bennington, 1777, there flashed a spark of steel in them, alone here in the room she was leaving forever. She was not going to teach school any more on Bear Creek, Wyoming; she was going home to Bennington, Vermont. She stood among her possessions. Antlers and blanket and all were being packed away, and her books—Robert Browning, Jane Austen, and others; works that none but herself on Bear Creek had found much sincere joy in, not even her most constant guest. After a long ride one day with the cow-puncher from Virginia, she had pressed *Pride and Prejudice* and *Emma* upon him. He had removed the masterpieces carefully to Sunk Creek Ranch, where he was now foreman, and scrupulously returned them upon a later visit.

"How do you like them?" she had then inquired; and he had smiled slowly at her. "You haven't read them!" she exclaimed.

"No, ma'am."

"Are you going to tell me there has been no time?"

"No, ma'am."

Then Molly had scolded her cow-puncher, and to this he had listened with pleasure undisguised, as indeed he listened to every word that she said.

"Why, it has come too late," he had told her when the scolding was over. "If I was one of your little scholars hyeh in Bear Creek school-house, yu' could learn me, I reckon. But I'm a mighty ignorant, growed-up man."

"So much the worse for you!" said Molly.

"No. I am pretty glad I am a man. Else I could not have learned the thing you have taught me."

But she shut her lips and looked away. On the desk was a letter written from Vermont. "If you don't tell me at once when you decide," had said the arch writer, "never hope to speak to me again. Mary Wood, seriously, I am suspicious. Why do you never mention him nowadays? How exciting to have you bring a live cowboy to Bennington! We should all come to dinner. Though of course I understand now that many of them have excellent manners. But would he wear his pistol at table?" So the letter ran on. It recounted the latest home gossip and jokes. In answering it Molly Wood had taken no notice of its childish tone here and there.

"Hyeh's some of them cactus blossoms yu' wanted," said the Virginian. His voice recalled the girl with almost a start. "This ride is the last I'll get for quite a while; I've branding and a heap o' things to see to oveh in our country. But I've brought a good hawse I've gentled for yu', and Taylor 'll keep him till I need him."

"Thank you so much! but I wish—"

"I reckon yu' can't stop me lendin'

Taylor a hawse. And you cert'nly 'll get sick school-teachin' if yu' don't keep outdoors some."

Once more she received the man's flowers; once more she rode with him long and long, as three winters and summers had seen them riding whenever he could come. Betweenwhiles it would be two months sometimes and more, for Sunk Creek was far across the mountains, and his work often lay from there even further, to Butte Creek and Drybone. This day the thick bushes along the stream were pink with wild roses again, and again the meadow-larks, invisible in the grass, sent up unexpectedly across the empty miles of air their ambushed song. Then he had bidden her good-by until next time. "And there will be a next time," he said at parting.

"There always is!" answered she, lightly.

"There always will be. Don't yu' know that?"

She did not reply.

"I have discouraged spells," he pursued, "but I down them. For I've told yu' you were going to love me. You are goin' to learn back the thing you have taught me. I'm not askin' anything now; I don't want you to speak a word to me. But I'm never goin' to quit till 'next time' is no more, and it's 'all the time' for you and me."

With that he had ridden away, not even touching her hand. Long after he had gone she was still in her chair, her eyes lingering upon his flowers, those yellow cups of the prickly-pear. At length she had risen impatiently, caught up the flowers, gone with them to the open window—and then, after all, set them with pains in water.

But to-day Bear Creek was over. She was going home now. By the week's end she would be started. By the time the mail brought him her good-by letter she would be gone. She had acted. A new schoolmarm was engaged to succeed her for the new term, and her mother in Bennington was even now counting the days until her wandering girl should be there to lay head once more upon her bosom.

To Bear Creek, the neighborly, the friendly, the not comprehending, this move had come unlooked-for, and had brought regret. Only one hard word had been spoken to Molly, and that by her next-door neighbor and kindest

friend. In Mrs. Taylor's house the girl had daily come and gone as a daughter, and that lady reached the subject thus:

"When I took Taylor," said she, sitting by as Robert Browning and Jane Austen were going into their box, "I married for love."

"Do you wish it had been money?" said Molly, stooping to her industries.

"You know both of us better than that, child."

"I know I've seen people at home who couldn't possibly have had any other reason. They seemed satisfied too."

"Maybe the poor ignorant things were!"

"And so I have never been sure how I might choose."

"Yes, you are sure, deary. Don't you think I know you? And when it comes over Taylor once in a while, and he tells me I'm the best thing in his life, and I tell him he ain't merely the best but the only thing in mine—him and the children—why, we just agree we'd do it all over the same way if we had the chance."

Molly continued to be industrious.

"And that's why," said Mrs. Taylor, "I want every girl that's anything to me to know her luck when it comes. For I was that near telling Taylor I wouldn't!"

"If ever my luck comes," said Molly, with her back to her friend, "I shall say 'I will' at once."

"Then you'll say it at Bennington next week."

Molly wheeled round.

"Why, you surely will. Do you expect he's going to stay here, and you in Bennington?" And the campaigner sat back in her chair.

"He? Goodness! Who is he?"

"Child, child, you're talking cross to-day because you're at outs with yourself. You've been at outs ever since you took this idea of leaving the school and us and everything this needless way. You have not treated him right. And why, I can't make out to save me. What have you found out in one week you hadn't learned in three years? If he was not good enough for you, I— But, oh, it's a prime one you're losing, Molly! When a man like that stays faithful to a girl 'spite all the chances he gets, her luck is come."

"Oh, my luck! People have different notions of luck."

"Notions!"

"He has been very kind."

"Kind! Bother! I thought you were waking up."

"And I should like to show him some return. I am afraid he would scarcely enjoy Bennington society."

"There! And so you actually have let the roughness hide the diamond."

Molly broke into high dudgeon. What she said is not important.

While it was going on and after it was done Mrs. Taylor surveyed the room, and then she spoke the hard word—"I expect you will find better grammar in Vermont, deary."

She did not wait for Molly to find speech. The good dame stalked out and across to her own cabin, and left the girl flashing independence in solitude among her boxes. It was in vain she fell to work upon them. Presently something had to be done over again, and when it was, the box held several chattels less than before the readjustment. She played a sort of desperate dominoes to fit these objects in the space, but here were a paper-weight, a portfolio, with two wretched volumes that no chink would harbor; and letting them fall all at once, she straightened herself, still stormy with revolt, eyes and cheeks still hot from the sting of long-parried truth. Then it was that in this pause from her forlorn home-breaking her glance rested defiant and intimate upon the quiet little miniature, appealed to it for support across the hundred years between them. So the flaxen girl on the wall and she among the boxes stood a moment face to face in seeming communion, and then the descendant turned again to her work. But after a desultory touch here and there she drew a long breath and walked to the open door. What use was in finishing to-day, when she had nearly a week? This first spurt of toil had swept the cabin bare of all indwelling charm, and its look was chill. Across the lane his horse, the one he had "gentled" for her, was grazing idly. She walked there and caught him, and led him to her gate. Mrs. Taylor saw her go in, and soon come out in riding-dress; and she watched the girl throw the saddle on with quick ease—the ease he had taught her. Mrs. Taylor also saw the sharp cut she gave the horse, and laughed grimly to herself in her window as horse and rider galloped into the beautiful sunny loneliness.

To the punished animal this switching was new, and at its third repetition he turned his head in surprise, but was no more heeded than were the bluffs and flowers where he was taking his own undirected choice of way. He carried her over ground she knew by heart—Corncliff Mesa, Crowheart Butte, Westfall's Crossing, Upper Cañon; open land and woodland, pines and sage-brush, all silent and grave and lustrous in the sunshine. Once and again a ranchman greeted her, and wondered if she had forgotten who he was; once she passed some cow-punchers with a small herd of steers, and they stared after her too. Bear Creek narrowed, its mountain-sides drew near, its little falls began to rush white in mid-day shadow, and the horse suddenly pricked his ears. Unguided, he was taking this advantage to go home. Though he had made but little way—a mere beginning yet—on this trail over to Sunk Creek, here was already a Sunk Creek friend whinnying good-day to him, so he whinnied back and quickened his pace, and Molly started to life. She saw the black horse she knew also, saddled, with reins dragging on the trail as the rider had dropped them to dismount. A cold spring bubbled out beyond the next rock, and she knew her lover's horse was waiting for him while he drank. She pulled at the reins, but loosed them, for to turn and escape now was ridiculous; and riding boldly round the rock, she came upon him by the spring. One of his arms hung up to its elbow in the pool, the other was crooked beside his head, but the face was sunk downward against the shelving rock, so that she saw only his black tangled hair. As her horse snorted and tossed his head she looked swiftly at the other horse, as if to question him. Seeing now the sweat matted on his coat, and noting the white rim of his eye, she sprang and ran to the motionless figure. A patch of blood at his shoulder behind stained the soft flannel shirt, spreading down beneath his belt, and the man's whole strong body lay slack, and pitifully helpless.

She touched the hand beside his head, but it seemed neither warm nor cold to her; she felt for the pulse, as nearly as she could remember the doctors did, but could not tell whether she imagined or not that it was still; twice with painful care her fingers sought and waited for the beat, and her face seemed like one of listening. She leaned down and lifted his other arm and hand from the water, and as their ice-coldness reached her senses clearly she saw the patch near the shoulder she had moved grow wet with new blood, and at that sight she grasped at the stones upon which she herself now sank. She held tight by two rocks, sitting straight beside him, staring, and murmuring aloud, "I must not faint; I will not faint"; and the standing horses looked at her, pricking their ears.

In this cup-round spread of the ravine the sun shone warmly down, the tall red cliff was warm, the pines were a warm film and filter of green; outside the shade across Bear Creek rose the steep, soft, open yellow hill, warm and high to the blue, and Bear Creek tumbled upon its sun-sparkling stones. The two horses on the margin trail still looked at the spring and trees, where sat the neat flaxen girl so rigid by the slack prone body in its flannel shirt and leathern chaps. Suddenly her face livened. "But the blood ran!" she exclaimed, as if to the horses, her companions in this. She moved to him, and put her hand in through his shirt against his heart.

Next moment she had sprung up and was at his saddle, searching, then swiftly went on to her own and got her small flask and was back beside him. Here was the cold water he had sought, and she put it against his forehead and drenched the wounded shoulder with it. Three times she tried to move him, so he might lie more easy, but his dead weight was too much, and desisting, she sat close and raised his head to let it rest against her. Thus she saw the blood that was running from in front of the shoulder also; but she said no more about fainting. She tore strips from her dress and soaked them, keeping them cold and wet upon both openings of his wound, and she drew her pocket-knife out and cut his shirt away from the place. As she continually rinsed and cleaned it, she watched his eyelashes, long and soft and thick, but they did not stir. Again she tried the flask, but failed from being still too gentle, and her searching eyes fell upon ashes near the pool. Still undispersed by the weather lay the small charred ends of a fire he and she had made once here together, and ridden home after coffee and fried trout. She built another fire now, and when the flames were going

well, filled her flask-cup from the spring and set it to heat, meanwhile returning to nurse his head and wound, which her cold water had stopped bleeding. Then she poured her brandy in the steaming cup, and, made rough by her desperate helplessness, forced some between his lips and teeth.

Instantly, almost, she felt the tremble of life creeping back, and as his dark eyes opened upon her she sat still and mute. But the gaze seemed luminous with an unnoting calm, and she wondered if perhaps he could not recognize her; she watched this internal clearness of his vision, scarcely daring to breathe, until presently he began to speak, with the same profound and clear impersonality sounding in his slowly uttered words.

"I thought they had found me. I expected they were going to kill me." He stopped, and she gave him more of the hot drink, which he took, still lying and looking at her as if the present did not reach his senses. "I knew hands were touching me. I reckon I was not dead. I knew about them soon as they began, only I could not interfere." He waited again. "It is mighty strange where I have been. No. Mighty natural." Then he went back into his revery, and lay with his eyes still full open upon her where she sat motionless.

She began to feel a greater awe in this living presence than when it had been his body with an ice-cold hand; and she quietly spoke his name, venturing scarcely more than a whisper.

At this, some nearer thing wakened in his look. "But it was you all along," he resumed. "It is you now. You must not stay—" Weakness overcame him, and his eyes closed. She sat ministering to him, and when he roused again, he began anxiously at once: "You must not stay. They would get you too."

She glanced at him with a sort of fierceness, then reached for his pistol, in which was nothing but blackened empty cartridges. She threw these out and drew six from his belt, loaded the weapon, and snapped shut its hinge.

"Please take it, ma'am," he said, more anxious and more himself. "I ain't worth tryin' to keep. Look at me."

"Are you giving up?" she inquired, trying to put scorn in her tone. Then she seated herself.

"Where is the sense in both of us—"

"You had better save your strength," she interrupted.

He tried to sit up.

"Lie down!" she ordered.

He sank obediently, and began to smile. When she saw that, she smiled too, and unexpectedly took his hand. "Listen, friend," said she. "Nobody shall get you, and nobody shall get me. Now take some more brandy."

"It must be noon," said the cow-puncher, when she had drawn her hand away from him. "I remember it was dark when—when—when I can remember. I reckon they were scared to follow me in so close to settlers. Else they would have been here."

"You must rest," she observed.

She broke the soft ends of some evergreen, and putting them beneath his head, went to the horses, loosened the cinches, took off the bridles, led them to drink, and picketed them to feed. Further still, to leave nothing undone she could herself manage, she took the horses' saddles off to refold the blankets when the time should come, and meanwhile brought them for him. But he put them away from him. He was sitting up against a rock, stronger evidently, and asking for cold water. His head was fire-hot, and the paleness beneath his swarthy skin had changed to a deepening flush.

"Only five miles!" she said to him, bathing his head.

"Yes. I must hold it steady," he answered, waving his hand at the cliff.

She told him to try and keep it steady until they got home.

"Yes," he repeated. "Only five miles. But it's fightin' to turn around." Half aware that he was becoming light-headed, he looked from the rock to her and from her to the rock with dilating eyes.

"We can hold it together," she said. "You must get on your horse." She took his handkerchief from round his neck, knotting it with her own, and to make more bandage she ran to the roll of clothes behind his saddle and tore in half a clean shirt. A handkerchief fell from it, which she seized also, and opening, saw her own initials by the hem. Then she remembered: she saw again their first meeting, the swollen river, the overset stage, the unknown horseman who carried her to the bank on his saddle and went away unthanked—her whole first adventure on that first day of her coming to this new country—and now she knew how her long-forgotten handkerchief had gone that day. She refolded it gently and put it back in his bundle, for there was enough bandage without it. She said not a word to him, and he placed a wrong meaning upon the look she gave him as she returned to bind his shoulder.

"It don't hurt so much," he assured her (though pain was clearing his head for the moment, and he had been able to hold the cliff from turning). "Yu' must not squander your pity."

"Do not squander your strength," said she.

"Oh, I could put up a pretty good fight now!" But he tottered in showing her how strong he was, and she told him that, after all, he was a child still.

"Yes," he slowly said, looking after her as she went to bring his horse, "the same child that wanted to touch the moon, I guess." And during the slow climb down into the saddle from a rock to which she helped him he said, "You have got to be the man all through this mess."

She saw his teeth clinched and his drooping muscles compelled by will; and as he rode and she walked to lend him support, leading her horse by a backward-stretched left hand, she counted off the distance to him continually—the increasing gain, the lessening road, the landmarks nearing and dropping behind: here was the tree with the wasp-nest gone; now the burned cabin was passed; now the cottonwoods at the ford were in sight. He was silent, and held to the saddle-horn, leaning more and more against his two hands clasped over it; and just after they had made the crossing he fell, without a sound, slipping to the grass, and his descent broken by her. But it started the blood a little, and she dared not leave him to seek help. She gave him the last of the flask and all the water he craved.

Revived, he managed to smile. "Yu' see, I ain't worth keeping."

"It's only a mile," said she. So she found a log, a fallen trunk, and he crawled to that, and from there crawled to his saddle, and she marched on with him, talking, bidding him note the steps accomplished. For the next half-mile they went thus, the silent man clinched on the horse, and by his side the girl walking and cheering him forward, when suddenly he began to speak:

"I will say good-by to you now, ma'am."

She did not understand at first.

"He is getting away," pursued the Virginian. "I must ask you to excuse me, ma'am." He would have turned his horse, but she caught the bridle.

"You must take me home," said she. "I am afraid of the Indians."

"Why, you — why, they've all gone. There he goes. Ma'am—that hawse—"

"No," said she, holding firmly his rein and quickening her step. "A gentleman does not invite a lady to go out riding and leave her."

His eyes lost their purpose. "I'll cert'nly take you home. That sorrel has gone in there by the wallow, and Judge Henry will understand." With his eyes watching imaginary objects, he rode and rambled, and it was now the girl who was silent, except to keep his mind from its half-fixed idea of the sorrel. As he grew more fluent she hastened still more, listening to head off that notion of return, skilfully inventing questions to engage him, so that when she brought him to her gate she held him in a manner subjected, answering faithfully the shrewd unrealities she devised, whatever makeshifts she could summon to her mind; and next she had got him inside her dwelling and set him down docile, but now completely wandering; and then — no help was at hand even here. She had made sure of aid from next door, and there she hastened, to find the Taylors' cabin locked and silent; and this meant parents and children were gone to drive; nor might she be luckier at her next nearest neighbors', should she travel the intervening mile to fetch them. With a mind jostled once more into uncertainty, she returned to her room, and saw a change in him already. Illness had stridden upon him; his face was not as she had left it, and the whole body, the splendid supple horseman, showed sickness in every line and limb, its spurs and pistol and bold leather chaps a mockery of trappings. She looked at him, and decision came back to her, clear and steady. She supported him over to her bed and laid him on it. His head sank flat, and his loose nerveless arms staid as she left them. Then among her packing-boxes and beneath the little miniature, blue and flaxen and gold upon its lonely wall, she undressed him. He was cold, and she covered him to the face, and ar-

ranged the pillow, and got from its box her scarlet and black Navajo blanket and spread it over him. There was no more she could do, and she sat down by him to wait. Among the many and many things that came into her mind was a word he said to her lightly a long while ago. "Cow-punchers do not live long enough to get old," he had told her. And now she looked at the head upon the pillow, grave and strong, but still the head of luxurious unworn youth.

At the distant jingle of the wagon in the lane she was out, and had met her returning neighbors midway. They heard her with amazement, and came in haste to the bedside; then Taylor departed to spread news of the Indians and bring the doctor, twenty-five miles away. The two women friends stood alone again, as they had stood in the morning when anger had been between them.

"Kiss me, deary," said Mrs. Taylor. "Now I will look after him—and you'll need some looking after yourself."

But on returning from her cabin with what store she possessed of lint and stimulants, she encountered a rebel, independent as ever. Molly would hear no talk about saving her strength, would not be in any room but this one until the doctor should arrive; then perhaps it would be time to think about resting. So together the dame and the girl rinsed the man's wound and wrapped him in clean things, and did all the little that they knew—which was, in truth, the very thing needed. Then they sat watching him toss and mutter. It was no longer upon Indians or the sorrel horse that his talk seemed to run, or anything recent, apparently, always excepting his work. This flowingly merged with whatever scene he was inventing or living again, and he wandered unendingly in that incompatible world we dream in. In the medley of occasion and names, often thickly spoken, but rising at times to grotesque coherence, the listeners now and then could piece out the reference from their own knowledge. "Monte," for example, was his pet horse, continually addressed, and Molly heard her own name, but invariably as "Miss Wood"; nothing less respectful came out, and frequently he answered some one as "ma'am." At these fragments of revelation Mrs. Taylor abstained from speech, but eyed Molly Wood with caustic reproach. As the night wore on, short lulls of silence intervened, and the watchers were deceived into hope the fever was abating. And when the Virginian sat quietly up in bed, essayed to move his bandage, and looked steadily at Mrs. Taylor, she rose quickly and went to him with a question as to how he was doing.

"Rise on your laigs, you polecat," said he, "and tell them you're a liar."

The good dame gasped, then bade him lie down, and he obeyed her with that strange double understanding of the delirious; for even while submitting he muttered "liar," "polecat," and then "Trampas."

At that name light flashed on Mrs. Taylor, and she turned to Molly; and there was the girl struggling with a fit of mirth at his speech, but the laughter was fast becoming a painful seizure. Mrs. Taylor walked Molly up and down, speaking immediately to arrest her attention.

"You might as well know it," she said. "He would blame me for speaking of it, but where's the harm all this while after? And you would never hear it from his mouth. Molly, child, they say Trampas would kill him if he dared, and that's on account of you."

"I never saw Trampas," said Molly, attentive.

"No, deary. But before a lot of men —Taylor has told me about it—Trampas spoke disrespectfully of you, and before them all he made Trampas say he was a liar. That is what he did when you were almost a stranger among us, and he had not started seeing so much of you. I expect Trampas is the only enemy he ever had in this country. But he would never let you know about that."

"No," whispered Molly, "I did not know."

"You had better go to bed, child. You look about ready for the doctor yourself."

"Then I will wait for him," said Molly.

So the two nurses continued to sit until darkness at the windows weakened into gray, and the lamp was no more needed. Their patient was rambling again. Yet, into whatever scenes he went, there in some guise did the throb of his pain evidently follow him, and he lay hitching his great shoulder as if to rid it of the cumbrance. They waited for the doctor, not daring much more than to turn pillows and give what other ease they could; and then, instead of the doctor, came a messenger, about noon, to say he was gone

on a visit some thirty miles beyond, where Taylor had followed to bring him here as soon as might be. At this Molly consented to rest and to watch, turn about; and once she was over in her friend's house lying down, they tried to keep her there. But the revolutionist could not be put down, and when, as a last pretext, Mrs. Taylor urged the proprieties and conventions, the pale girl from Vermont laughed sweetly in her face and returned to sit by the sick man. With the approach of the second night his fever seemed to rise and master him more completely than they had yet seen it, and presently it so raged that the women called in stronger arms to hold him down. There were times when he broke out in the language of the round-up, and Mrs. Taylor renewed her protests. "Why," said Molly, "don't you suppose I knew they could swear?" So the dame, in deepening astonishment and affection, gave up these shifts at decorum. Nor did the delirium run into the intimate, coarse matters that she dreaded. The cow-puncher had lived like his kind, but his natural daily thoughts were clean, and came from the untamed but unstained mind of a man. And towards morning, as Mrs. Taylor sat taking her turn, suddenly he asked had he been sick long, and looked at her with a quieted eye. The wandering seemed to drop from him at a stroke, leaving him altogether himself. He lay very feeble, and inquired once or twice of his state and how he came here; nor was anything left in his memory of even coming to the spring where he had been found.

When the doctor arrived, he pronounced it would be long—or very short. He praised their clean water treatment; the wound was fortunately well up on the shoulder, and gave so far no bad signs; there were not any bad signs; and the blood and strength of the patient had been as few men's were; each hour was now an hour nearer certainty, and meanwhile — meanwhile the doctor would remain as long as he could. He had many inquiries to satisfy. Dusty fellows would ride up, listen to him, and reply, as they rode away, "Don't yu' let him die, doc." And Judge Henry sent over from Sunk Creek to answer for any attendance or medicine that might help his foreman. The country was moved with concern and interest; and in Molly's ears its words of good feeling seemed to unite and sum up

a burden: "Don't yu' let him die, doc."
The Indians who had done this were now
in military custody. They had come un-
permitted from a southern reservation,
hunting, next thieving, and as the slumbering spirit roused in one or two of the
young and ambitious, they had ventured
this in the secret mountains, and perhaps
had killed a trapper found there. Editors
immediately reared a tall war out of it;
but from five Indians in a guard-house
waiting punishment not even an editor
can supply war for more than two edi-
tions, and if the recent alarm was still a
matter of talk anywhere, it was not here
in the sick-room. Whichever way the
case should turn, it was through Molly
alone (the doctor told her) that the
wounded man had got this chance—this
good chance, he repeated. And he told
her she had done not a woman's part, but
a man's part, and now had no more to do;
no more till the patient got well, and
could thank her in his own way, said the
doctor, smiling, and supposing things that
were not so — misled perhaps by Mrs.
Taylor.

"I'm afraid I'll be gone by the time he
is well," said Molly, coldly; and the discreet physician said ah, and that she
would find Bennington quite a change
from Bear Creek.

But Mrs. Taylor spoke otherwise, and
at that the girl said: "I shall stay as long
as I am needed. I will nurse him. I
want to nurse him. I will do everything
for him that I can!" she exclaimed, with
force.

"And that won't be anything, deary,"
said Mrs. Taylor, harshly. "A year of
nursing don't equal a day of sweetheart."

The girl went walking—she was of no
more service in the room at present—but
she turned without going far, and Mrs.
Taylor spied her come to lean over the
pasture fence and watch the two horses—
that one the Virginian had "gentled" for
her, and his own Monte. During this
suspense came a new call for the doctor,
neighbors profiting by his visit to Bear
Creek; and in his going away to them,
even under promise of quick return, Mrs.
Taylor suspected a favorable sign. He
kept his word as punctually as had been
possible, arriving after some six hours
with a confident face, and spending now
upon the patient a care not needed, save
to reassure the bystanders. He spoke his
opinion that all was even better than he

could have hoped it would be so soon.
Here was now the beginning of the fifth
day; the wound's look was wholesome,
no further delirium had come, and the
fever had abated a degree while he was
absent. He believed the serious danger-
line lay behind, and (short of the unfore-
seen) the man's deep untainted strength
would reassert its control. He had much
blood to make, and must be cared for
during weeks — three, four, five — there
was no saying how long yet. These next
few days it must be utter quiet for him;
he must not talk nor hear anything likely to disturb him; and then the time for
cheerfulness and gradual company would
come—sooner than later, the doctor hoped.
So he departed, and sent next day some
bottles, with further cautions regarding
the wound and dirt, and to say he should
be calling the day after to-morrow.

Upon that occasion he found two pa-
tients. Molly Wood lay in bed at Mrs.
Taylor's, filled with apology and indignation. With little to do, and deprived of
the strong stimulant of anxiety and action, her strength had quite suddenly left
her, so that she had spoken only in a sort
of whisper. But upon waking from a
long sleep, after Mrs. Taylor had taken
her firmly, almost severely, in hand, her
natural voice had returned, and now the
chief treatment the doctor gave her was
a sort of scolding, which it pleased Mrs.
Taylor to hear. The doctor even dropped
a phrase concerning the arrogance of
strong nerves in slender bodies, and of
undertaking several people's work when
several people were at hand to do it for
themselves, and this pleased Mrs. Taylor
remarkably. As for the wounded man,
he was behaving himself properly. Perhaps in another week he could be moved
to a more cheerful room. Just now, with
cleanliness and pure air, any barn would
do.

"We are real lucky to have such a
sensible doctor in the country," Mrs.
Taylor observed, after the physician had
gone.

"No doubt," said Molly. "He said
my room was a barn."

"That's what you've made it, deary.
But sick men don't notice much."

Nevertheless, one may believe, without
going widely astray, that illness, so far
from veiling, more often quickens the
perceptions—at any rate those of the naturally keen. On a later day—and the

interval was brief—while Molly was on her second drive to take the air with Mrs. Taylor, that lady informed her that the sick man had noticed. "And I could not tell him things liable to disturb him," said she, "and so I—well, I expect I just didn't exactly tell him the facts. I said yes, you were packing up for a little visit to your folks. They had not seen you for quite a while, I said. And he looked at those boxes kind of silent like."

"There's no need to move him," said Molly. "It is simpler to move them—the boxes. I could take out some of my things, you know. Just while he has to be kept there. I mean—you see, if the doctor says the room should be cheerful—"

"Yes, deary."

"I will ask the doctor next time," said Molly, "if he believes I am—competent—to spread a rug upon a floor." Molly's references to the leech were usually acid these days. And this he totally failed to observe, telling her when he came, why, to be sure! the very thing! And if she could play cards or read aloud, or afford any other light distractions, provided they did not lead the patient to talk and tire himself, that she would be most useful. Accordingly she took over the cribbage-board, and came with unexpected hesitation face to face again with the swarthy man she had saved and tended. He was not so swarthy now, but neat, with chin clean, and hair and mustache trimmed and smooth, and he sat propped among pillows watching for her.

"You are better," she said, speaking first, and with uncertain voice.

"Yes, ma'am. They have given me awdehs not to talk," said the Southerner, smiling.

"Oh yes. Please do not talk — not to-day."

"No, ma'am. Only this"—he looked at her, and saw her seem to shrink—"thank you for what you have done," he said, simply.

She took tenderly the hand he stretched to her; and upon these terms they set to work at cribbage. She won, and won again, and the third time laid down her cards and reproached him with playing in order to lose.

"No," he said, and his eye wandered to the boxes. "But my thoughts get away from me. I'll be strong enough to hold them on the cyards next time, I reckon."

Then they played a little more, and she put away the board for this first time.

"You are going now?" he asked.

"When I have made this room look a little less forlorn. They haven't wanted to meddle with my things, I suppose." And Molly stooped once again among the chattels destined for Vermont. Out they came; again the bear-skin was spread on the floor, various possessions and ornaments went back into their ancient niches, the shelves grew comfortable with books, and, last, some flowers were stood on the table.

"More like old times," said the Virginian, but sadly.

"It's too bad," said Molly, "you had to be brought into such a looking place."

"And your folks waiting for you," said he.

"Oh, I'll pay my visit later," said Molly, putting the rug a trifle straighter.

"May I ask one thing?" pleaded the Virginian, and at the gentleness of his voice her face grew rosy, and she fixed her eyes on him with a sort of dread.

"Anything that I can answer," said she.

"Oh yes. Did I tell yu' to quit me, and did you load up my gun and stay? Was that a real business? I have been mixed up in my haid."

"That was real," said Molly. "What else was there to do?"

"Just nothing—for such as you!" he exclaimed. "My haid has been mighty crazy; and that little grandmother of yours yondeh, she—but I can't just quite catch a-hold of these things"—he passed a hand over his forehead—"so many—or else one right along—well, it's all foolishness!" he concluded, with something almost savage in his tone. And after she had gone from the cabin he lay very still, looking at the miniature on the wall.

He was in another sort of mood the next time, cribbage not interesting him in the least. "Your folks will be wondering about you," said he.

"I don't think they will mind which month I go to them," said Molly. "Especially when they know the reason."

"Don't let me keep you, ma'am," said he. Molly stared at him; but he pursued, with the same edge lurking in his slow words: "Though I'll never forget. How could I forget any of all you have done —and been? If there had been none of this, why, I had enough to remember!

But please don't stay, ma'am. We'll say I had a claim when yu' found me pretty well dead, but I'm gettin' well, yu' see— right smart, too!"

"I can't understand, indeed I can't," said Molly, "why you're talking so!"

"Oh, a sick man is funny. And, yu' know, I'm grateful to you."

"Please say no more about that, or I shall go this afternoon. I don't want to go. I am not ready. I think I had better read something now."

"Why, yes. That's cert'nly a good notion. Why, this is the best show you'll ever get to give me education. Won't yu' please try that *Emma* book now, ma'am? Listening to you will be different." This was said with softness and humility.

Uncertain — as his gravity often left her—precisely what he meant by what he said, Molly proceeded with *Emma*; slackly at first, but soon with the enthusiasm that Miss Austen invariably gave her. She held the volume and read away at it, commenting briefly, and then, finishing a chapter of the sprightly classic, found her pupil slumbering peacefully. There was no uncertainty about that.

"You couldn't be doing a healthier thing for him, deary," said Mrs. Taylor. "If it gets to make him wakeful, try something harder." This was the lady's scarcely sympathetic view.

But it turned out to be not obscurity in which Miss Austen sinned.

When Molly next appeared at the Virginian's threshold, he said, plaintively, "I reckon I am a dunce, ma'am." And he sued for pardon. "When I waked up," he said, "I was ashamed of myself for a plumb half-hour." Nor could she doubt this day that he meant what he said. His mood was again serene and gentle, and without referring to his singular words that had distressed her, he made her feel his contrition, even in his silence. "I am right glad you have come," he said. And as he saw her going to the bookshelf, he continued, with diffidence: "As regyards that *Emma* book, ma'am, yu' see—yu' see, the doings and sayings of folks like them are above me. But I think" (he spoke most diffidently), "if yu' could read me something that was *about* something, I—I'd be liable to keep awake." And he smiled with a certain shyness.

"Something *about* something!" queried Molly, at a loss.

"Why, yes. I saw a fine play one time. The British king was fighting, and there was his son the prince. He cert'nly must have been a jim-dandy boy if that is all true. Only he would go around town with a mighty triflin' gang. They sported and they held up citizens. And his father hated his travelling with trash like them. It was right natural — the boy and the old man! But the boy showed himself a man too. He killed a big fighter on the other side who was another jim-dandy— and he was sorry for having it to do." The Virginian warmed to his recital. "I wish I could see that play again. There was a fat man kept everybody laughing. He was awful natural too; except yu' don't commonly meet 'em so fat. But the prince — that play was bed-rock, ma'am! Have you got something like that?"

"Yes, I think so," she replied. "I believe I see what you would appreciate."

She took her Browning, her idol, her imagined affinity. For the pale decadence of New England had somewhat watered her good old Revolutionary blood too, and she was inclined to think under glass and to live underdone—when there were no Indians to shoot! She would have joyed to venture "Paracelsus" on him, and some lengthy rhymed discourses; and she fondly turned leaves and leaves of her pet doggerel analytics. "Pippa Passes" and others she had to skip, from discreet motives—things he would have doubtless staid awake at; but she chose a poem at length. This was better than *Emma*, he pronounced. And short. The horse was a good horse. He thought a man whose horse must not play out on him would watch the ground he was galloping over for holes, and not be likely to see what color the rims of his animal's eye-sockets were. You could not see them if you sat as you ought to for such a hard ride. Of the next piece that she read him he thought still better. "And it is short," said he. "But the last part drops."

Molly instantly exacted particulars.

"The soldier should not have told the general he was killed," stated the cowpuncher.

"What should he have told him, I'd like to know?" said Molly.

"Why, just nothing. If the soldier could ride out of the battle all shot up, and tell his general about their takin' the town—that was being gritty, yu' see. But that truck at the finish—will yu' please say it again, ma'am?"

So Molly read:

"'You're wounded!' 'Nay,' the soldier's pride
    Touched to the quick, he said:
'I'm killed, sire!' And, his chief beside,
    Smiling the boy fell dead."

"'Nay, I'm killed, sire,'" drawled the Virginian, amiably; for (symptom of convalescence) his freakish irony was revived in him. "Now a man who was man enough to act like he did, yu' see, would fall dead without mentioning it."

None of Molly's sweet girl friends had ever thus challenged Mr. Browning. They had been wont to cluster over him with a joyous awe that deepened proportionally with their misunderstanding. Molly paused to consider this novelty of view about the soldier. "He was a Frenchman, you know," she said, under inspiration.

"A Frenchman," murmured the grave cow-puncher. "I never knowed a Frenchman, but I reckon they might perform that class of foolishness."

"But why was it foolish?" she cried.

"His soldier's pride—don't you see?"

"No, ma'am."

Molly now burst into a luxury of discussion. She leaned toward her cowpuncher with bright eyes searching his; with elbow on knee and hand propping chin, her lap became a slant, and from it Browning the poet slid and toppled, and lay unrescued. For the slow cow-puncher unfolded his notions of masculine courage and modesty (though he did not deal in such high-sounding names), and Molly forgot everything to listen to him, as he forgot himself and his inveterate shyness and grew talkative to her. "I would never have supposed that!" she would exclaim as she heard him; or, presently again, "I never had such an idea!" And her mind opened with delight to these new things which came from the man's mind so simple and direct. To Browning they did come back, but the Virginian, though interested, conceived a dislike for him. "He is a smarty," said he, once or twice.

"Now here is something," said Molly. "I have never known what to think."

"Oh, heavens!" murmured the sick man, smiling. "Is it short?"

"Very short. Now please attend." And she read him twelve lines about a lover who rowed to a beach in the dusk,

crossed a field, tapped at a pane, and was admitted.

"That is the best yet," said the Virginian. "There's only one thing yu' can think about that."

"But wait," said the girl, swiftly. "Here is how they parted:

"Round the cape of a sudden came the sea,
    And the sun looked over the mountain's rim—
    And straight was a path of gold for him,
And the need of a world of men for me."

"That is very, very true," murmured the Virginian, dropping his eyes from the girl's intent ones.

"Had they quarrelled?" she inquired.

"Oh no, ma'am!"

"But—"

"I reckon he loved her very much, ma'am."

"Then you're sure they hadn't quarrelled?"

"Dead sure, ma'am. He would come back afteh he had played some more of the game."

"The game?"

"Life, ma'am. Whatever he was a-doin' in the world of men. That's a bedrock piece, ma'am!"

"Well, I don't see why you think it's so much better than some of the others."

"I could sca'cely explain," answered the man. "But that writer does know something."

"I am glad they hadn't quarrelled," said Molly, thoughtfully. And she began to like having her opinions refuted.

His bandages, becoming a little irksome, had to be shifted, and this turned their discourse from literature to Wyoming; and Molly inquired, had he ever been shot before? No, he told her. "I have been lucky in having few fusses," said he. "I hate them. If a man has to be killed—"

"You never—" broke in Molly.

"No. I have never had to kill a man —unless I got one of those Indians, and I wasn't waitin' to see! But I came mighty near doing for a white man that day. He had been hurting a hawse."

"Hurting?" said Molly.

"Injuring. I will not tell yu' about that, ma'am. It would hurt you to hear such things. But hawses—don't they depend on us? Ain't they somethin' like children? I did not lay up the man very bad. He was able to travel 'most right away. Why, ma'am, you'd have wanted to kill him yourself!"

So the Virginian talked, nor knew

what he was doing to the girl. Nor was she aware of what she was receiving from him as he unwittingly spoke himself out to her in these Browning meetings they held each day. But Mrs. Taylor grew pleased. The kindly dame would sometimes cross the road to see if she were needed, and steal away again after a peep at the window. There, inside, among the restored home treasures, sat the two: the rosy alert girl, sweet as she talked or read to him; and he, the grave, half-weak giant among his wraps, watching her.

Of her delayed home visit he never again spoke, either to her or to Mrs. Taylor; and Molly veered aside from any trend of talk she foresaw was leading in that subject's direction. But in those hours when no visitors came, and he was by himself in the quiet, he would lie often sombrely contemplating the girl's room, her little dainty knickknacks, her home photographs, all the delicate manifestations of what she came from and what she was. Strength was flowing back into him each day, and Judge Henry's latest messenger had brought him clothes and mail from Sunk Creek and many inquiries of kindness, and returned taking the news of the cow-puncher's improvement, and how soon he would be permitted the fresh air. Hence Molly found him waiting in a flannel shirt of highly becoming shade, and with a silk handkerchief knotted round his throat; and he told her it was good to feel respectable again. In his lap lay one of the letters brought over by the messenger; and though she was midway in a book that engaged his full attention—*David Copperfield*—his silence and absent look this morning stopped her, and she accused him of not attending.

"No," he admitted; "I am thinking of something else."

She looked at him with that apprehension which he knew.

"It had to come," said he. "And today I see my thoughts straighter than I've been up to managing since—since my haid got clear. And now I must say these thoughts—if I can, if I can!" He stopped. His dark eyes were intent upon her; one hand was gripping the arm of his chair.

"You promised—" trembled Molly.

"I promised you should love me," he sternly interrupted. "Promised that to myself. I have broken that word."

She shut *David Copperfield* mechanically, and grew white.

"Your letter has come to me hyeh, ma'am," he continued, gentle again.

"My—" She had forgotten it.

"The letter you wrote to tell me goodby. You wrote it a little while ago—not a month yet, but it's away and away long gone for me."

"I have never let you know—" began Molly.

"The doctor," he interrupted once more, but very gently now. "He gave awdehs I must be kept quiet. I reckon yu' thought tellin' me might—"

"Forgive me!" cried the girl. "Indeed I ought to have told you sooner! Indeed I had no excuse!"

"Why, ma'am, why should yu' tell me if yu' preferred not? You had written. And you speak" (he lifted the letter) "of never being able to repay kindness; but you have turned the tables. I can never repay you by anything! by anything! So I had figured I would just jog back to Sunk Creek and let you get away, if you did not want to say that kind of good-by. For I saw the boxes, ma'am. Mrs. Taylor is too nice a woman to know the trick of lyin', and she could not deceive me. I have knowed yu' were going away for good ever since I saw those boxes. But now hyeh comes your letter, and it seems no way but I must speak. I have thought a deal, lyin' in this room. And—to-day—I can say what I have thought. I could not make you happy, ma'am." He stopped, but she did not answer.

"Once, I thought love must surely be enough," he continued. "And I thought if I could make you love me, you could learn me to be less—less—more your kind. And I think I could give you a pretty good sort of love. But that don't help the little mean pesky things of day by day that make roughness or smoothness for folks tied together so awful close. Mrs. Taylor hyeh—she don't know anything better than Taylor does. She don't want anything he can't give her. Her friends will do for him and his for her. And when I dreamed of you in my home——" he closed his eyes and drew a long breath. At last he looked at her again. "This is no country for a lady, ma'am. Will yu' forget and forgive the bothering I have done?"

"Oh!" cried Molly. "Oh!" And she

put her hands to her eyes. She had risen, and stood with her face covered.

"I surely had to tell you this all out, didn't I?" said the cow-puncher in his sick-chair.

"Oh!" said Molly again.

"I have put it clear how it is?" he pursued. "I ought to have seen from the start I was not the sort to keep you happy."

"But," said Molly—"but I—you ought —please try to keep me happy!" And sinking by his chair, she hid her face on his knees.

Speechless, he bent down and folded her round, putting his hands on the hair that had been always his delight. Presently he whispered,

"You have beat me; how can I fight this?"

She answered nothing. So they remained long, the flaxen head nesting in the great arms, and the black head laid against it, while over the silent room presided the little Grandmother Stark in her frame, rosy, blue, and flaxen, not quite familiar, not quite smiling.

28

The Patronage of High Bear

OWEN WISTER

THE PATRONAGE OF HIGH BEAR.

By Owen Wister.

(With illustrations by E. L. Williams.)

ALWAYS remember this: That an Indian, even if he be a warrior, and a grandfather, and a chief, and have slain many white men with his own red hand, nevertheless remains until death as innocent as the nursery. His child-mind is extremely like yours in the days when you could be amazed by a jumping-jack. That is the moral of this story. I have put it first, because I didn't want you to skip it. Knowledge of it may some day save you from something like the dreadful mistake made by Horace Pericles Byram, whom his friends generally called Horacles. He thought because the head of High Bear was like the snow, and his eye like the eagle's, and his song was of battles long ago, that therefore the old chief must be grown up. He thought such a thing. Scipio Le Moyne knew better. Now listen to the consequences.

Scipio Le Moyne, with his broken leg still in plaster, sat in charge of the agency store, speaking disparagement to the Virginian about Horacles. A Bar-Circle-Zee three-year-old had done Scipio's leg this mischief at the forks of Stinking Water; and Judge Henry always sent his cow-punchers to the nearest surgical aid, which in this case was at the hospital on the reservation. The healthy Scipio had been soon out of bed, anxious to employ his body again, but allowed to exercise only his eminently wiry mind. How athletic his brains were was easily perceived by the Indian agent. The convalescent would hobble over to the store after breakfast, and hail the assistant clerk at once. "Morning, Horacles," he would begin. "How's uncle?" Now this uncle was a United States Senator. "Oh, when are you going to give us a new joke?" the worried Horacles would retort. "Just as soon as you give us a new uncle, Horacles. Or any other relation to make us feel proud we know you." By dinner-time an audience would be round Scipio where he sat with his leg on a chair, and Horacles over

his ledger would be furiously muttering that some day they would all see.

But small talk was not the whole of Scipio's brains. He advised the agent prudently about a sale of beeves, and he introduced a simple contrivance for luring customers to the store—cheese and crackers every day, and deviled ham on payday. It was merely a free lunch counter, but it put up the daily receipts. Therefore the agent thought highly of Scipio, and said to him, one morning, "I am going to St. Paul. I shall be back before they let you and your leg run loose. I'd sooner leave you than Horacles in charge here. You understand Indians. Will you do it, and take two dollars a day?" "Do it for nothing," answered Scipio, "Horacles'll be pay enough." "No, he won't," insisted the agent. "And see here; he can't help it." "Enough said," said Scipio; "I'll strive to pity him. None of us were consulted about being born. And I'll keep remembering that we were both raised at Gallipo-*lice*, Ohio,

and that he inherited a bigger outrage for a name than I did. That's what comes from having a French ancestor. Only—" and Scipio's bleached blue eye grew cold—"he used to eat my lunch at school." "Didn't you whale him?" asked the agent. "Every time," said Scipio; "till he told his uncle. Uncle was mayor of Gallipo*lice* then. So I didn't want to get expelled, and I locked up my lunch after that." "Uncle's pretty good to him," muttered the agent. "Got him this position. Well, nobody will expel you here. Look after things." And he departed to St. Paul, trusting the whole conduct of his business to the competent Scipio. And now he was about to return.

But now a thing of utter dismay had fallen, so to speak, from the stars. A horrid, ruinous thing; the first news which the agent would hear. It made Scipio sick. Vainly the Virginian reasoned with him. The Virginian had come to see if he was enough recovered to be driven home to Sunk Creek ranch. In body he was; but his pride, his deep pride, had suffered a hurt beyond the reach of consolation. Sage words were of no help, unless they could tell him how to retrieve himself in his own esteem. It was nothing that the agent would not blame him. For under

his long, wary nose a treachery had been done to the agency store, and by Horacles! Therefore Scipio sat mourning the evil day that had come to him, and speaking disparagement about the assistant clerk.

"And top of all his other meanness," finished Scipio, "he's got false teeth."

The Virginian pondered. "I reckon," he said, "'twould be hasty to call false teeth meanness. Maybe the day'll come when they'll be helping you and me chew our tenderloin."

"That's different. We'll be old. Y'u can feel compassion for age. But Horacles!"

"Twenty-five is certainly young to commence eatin' by machinery," asserted the Virginian.

"And he's proud of 'em," whined Scipio. "*Proud.* Sticks 'em out at y'u on the end of his tongue."

"A man should be more modest," said the Virginian, very gravely.

"Thinks it's funny," pursued Scipio.

"Saw him do it as a wind-up to his conjuring entertainment at the officers' club. The K. O.'s wife said it gave her the creeps. And she don't look like a sensitive lady."

"Well," dissented the Virginian, "if I weighed three hundred pounds, I'd be mighty sensitive."

Thus these cow-punchers discussed a grave matter. And all the while their keen minds were seriously busy beneath. It is a native way we have, misunderstood by many English-speaking people. Somehow I like it. "No," Scipio resumed; "he's mean. Horacles is plumb mean. I've knowed it since school. He ain't got strength. He ain't got beauty. He ain't got riches. He ain't got brains. He's just got sense enough for parlor-conjuring tricks. But he's got an uncle in the Senate. That's where he has beat us." The disconsolate Scipio had taken a pull at his cigar between each sentence.

It is time for you to hear about Hor-

acles and his uncle.   Curious things are done upon Indian reservations.   Our management of them may be likened to putting the Lord's Prayer and the Ten Commandments into a bag and crushing them to powder. Let our statesmen at Washington get their hands on an Indian reservation, and not even honor among thieves remains. As to this one, it having been long settled by the sacredest compacts and guarantees of which our statesmen are capable, that there should be but two stores upon it, and that the post-trader should have one and the agent the other, and that never a third competitor should lessen the trade of these two, the uncle got a notion one day, as he was meditating how to serve his country and increase his income.   There was a railroad at the big end of his notion, but its entering wedge was only a little, new store down in that corner of the reservation, much needed by Indian families, for whom it was a hardship to have to travel so far for supplies as they did at present.   So the uncle in Washington had promised somebody something; and the somebody had promised something else to somebody; and the Indian Department was moved; and a word was mentioned at the White House; and presently there was no doubt at all but that the poor Indians needed a third store.

"Can you suggest anybody to run it?" had been asked of the uncle by the proper person.

"I have a nephew," said the uncle.   "I placed him at the agency some time ago.   He writes me that he has learned the business."

All this was a secret beautifully kept, of course.   When the agent had left for St. Paul, everyone believed the judicious rumor in the air that the new building down in the corner of the reservation had something to do with the Quartermaster's Department, and they thought no more about it—everyone, that is, except the agent himself.   He considered it odd that the post quartermaster had heard nothing of this sort. Then, Horacles was receiving more letters from his uncle than uncles often write.   Further-

more, Horacles had taken a week's holiday—hunting, he said. But the agent happened to find that he had been to the railroad about freight.   So when the agent spoke of going to St. Paul, he went there, it is true, and much farther. He went to Washington as fast as he could travel. For he had begun to suspect the uncle. Now Horacles at once perceived that this was a comfortable time for him to hurry his new store into readiness, and be safely established behind its rival counter before his old employer should return. It is much pleasanter to talk about what you are going to do after you have done it. Accordingly, the complacent little Horacles had perfected his arrangements to his heart's content, and made them known this morning to all the world. It was a bombshell to Scipio. You can understand how he felt; his rage,

for the twentieth time. "You can't help his having an uncle."

"But he put me in charge. He handed me the reins. And here's a big smash."

"When a stage is held up," said the Virginian, "the driver ain't responsible."

But Scipio would not be comforted. "I received the business in good shape," said he, "and I'll give it back in bad."

At this point Horacles entered. He was a small person, with red eyelids and a fluffy moustache. He wore his frontier hat tilted to make him look like the daredevil that he was not. He smiled the smile of revenge and triumph at Scipio; and Scipio

his sorrow, his mortification. He did not know that the absent friend who was paying him two dollars a day to protect his interests, was returning from Washington with a full knowledge of the uncle, and also with a disgusted but resigned spirit.

"What can I do? What *can* I?" he demanded of the Virginian, as he limped up and down the empty store. The new one was to open upon the morrow. Horacles was over there now; and the fickle Indians were all on his side, for they had been told that things would be much cheaper. In this respect the red man does not greatly differ from the white.

"Let it alone," answered the Virginian,

smiled back at him sweetly, and much more dangerously. Many Indians had followed Horacles into the store.

"Are you boys coming to see me?" said he, to the two cow-punchers.

"See you what?" said Scipio.

"Open up to-morrow. Fine line of fresh Eastern goods, and, hee-hee! free lunch. Mr. Le Moyne, I want to thank you publicly for that idea."

"Thank me publicly? Well, you're welcome to it. Guess I'll hardly be over to-morrow, though. With such a competitor as you, I expect I'll have to stay here and hustle." Scipio was quite friendly.

"Well, I should smile, you'll hustle!" exclaimed the complacent Horacles, happily. "Big capital is back of me. And I'm going to make it pay big interest. My uncle—say, boys! do come see me to-morrow. It's all business, this, you know. There's no hard feelings between us?"

"Oh, no," cried Scipio. "Not a feeling." And he clapped Horacles between his little round shoulders. He cocked his head and looked down along his lengthy jocular nose at Horacles for a moment. Then his eye shone like the edge of a knife upon the company, who laughed at him because he was laughing so contagiously at them. The solemnity of the Indian is a myth. He will often join your mirth without understanding it, just like a child. That is what High Bear did now in the agency store. High Bear, the ancient war-chief, showed all his white teeth at young Scipio, whom he fancied so much that he had offered him his fourteenth daughter to wed as soon as his leg should be well. But Scipio had sorrowfully explained to the father that he was already married, which, I fear, was not true.

"Hey!" said High Bear now to Scipio. "New store. Pretty good. Heap cheap."

"Yes, High Bear. Heap cheap. You savvy why?" Scipio was now impressively nodding at the white-haired Indian in his bright-green blanket and the long, fringed, yellow, soft buckskins. Behind the store-counter the happy Horacles was unconsciously practising conjuring tricks from sheer elation.

"No," said High Bear. "Me no savvy why."

"Heap cheap," repeated Scipio, "because," (and here he leaned close to High Bear, dropped to a whisper, and stretched a long, pointing arm at Horacles), "because his uncle medicine-man. He big medicine-man himself.

High Bear looked at Horacles. "Ah, nah," he grunted. "He no medicine-man. He fall off horse. He no catch him. My little girl catch him. Ah, nah!" and High Bear laughed profusely at what he took for "Sippo's" joke. "Sippo" is what the Indians called Le Moyne. Of course they had their Indian name for him, also; but I can't tell you that one here.

But Sippo grew entirely mysterious now. "He big medicine-man," he said again, bearing heavy on each word, and drilling his bleached blue eyes into the brown eye of the savage. "See him now!" he exclaimed suddenly, pointing.

Horacles was gaily treating a pack of cards in the true conjuring spirit. He fluttered it open in the air and fluttered it shut again, pulling it out and pushing it in, as you do to a concertina or a Chinese lantern or an opera-hat. Of course it was very remarkable, and High Bear watched it hard; but High Bear laughed. "He pretty good," he declared. "All same tin horn monte-man. I see one Miles City."

"Maybe monte-man medicine-man, too," suggested Scipio.

"Ah, nah!" said High Bear.

The younger Indians, squaws and bucks, were enjoying Horacles very much. He was explaining how cheap everything would be to-morrow forevermore; and they were laughing and joking. They admired his pack of cards, too. And they chaffed their friend Sippo. "Why you not sell cheap like him?" they asked. "We stay then. We buy everything you." "Heap shirts," one would specify; and another, "Heap tobacco. Heap cartridge. You not sell cheap. We go. Ah!'' And they laughed like pleased children. Scipio, solemn as possible, explained how much he would like to sell cheap, but he was not a medicine-man like Horacles.

''You medicine-man?'' they asked the assistant clerk.

''Yes,'' said Horacles, pleased. ''I big medicine-man.''

''Ah, nah!'' said the crowd, hugely diverted.

Soon they began to go home to their tepees, scattering wide across the sagebrush on their ponies. High Bear was one of the last. He had been standing quite still for a long time. He had not joined in the general talk and laughter. Horacles had gone to an inner room. The Virginian was reading a newspaper. High Bear looked at his friend Sippo. Sippo was bent down, deeply engaged with his leg. The cards lay distant, alone on the counter near the door. High Bear went quickly to them, touched them, lifted them, set them down, and looked around. Sippo was carefully pulling on his boot again. High Bear laughed a little, grunted a little, and went out where his horse was tied. As he was throwing his soft buckskin leg over the saddle, there was Scipio's head poking out of the door, and nodding strangely at him.

''Good-night, High Bear. He big medicine-man.''

High Bear gave a slash to his pony, and galloped away into the dusk.

Scipio watched him till he was nearly gone, and then turned back into the store. His countenance wore a very particular look—the expression of a cat who is going to purr in a minute.

''What trouble are you studying?'' gently drawled the Virginian.

''Me?'' whined Scipio, innocently; ''why I was never knowed to harm a fly. Why Horacles,'' said he, completely purring, to the assistant clerk who now joined them, ''I expect you have me beat. I do for a fact.''

The flattered Horacles could only nod and show his bright, false teeth.

''Y'u have a right to smile,'' continued Scipio. ''Y'u have for a fact.''

''Well, I guess I have. I guess I played it pretty slick. Of course, my uncle had something to do with it.''

''You'd oughtn't to quite leave him out,'' said the Virginian.

''Oh, no; certainly. But there's everything in being on the spot. Now I've been on the spot. And I'll get my reward. You saw them just now; you see how it is; the whole reservation is going to trade with me. This store'll not do ten cents' worth of business in a week.''

''Yes, Horacles, I see how it is. But supposing—just supposing—I cut our prices to meet yours?''

''Hee—hee! D'you think I didn't anticipate that?''

''Of *course* you did, Horacles. And you tell me, 'cut if you want to,' and I tell you, 'no, for you have me beat.' Ain't that it?'' And Scipio tapped his pocket.

''That's it. I've double, treble, longer money than you. Not you, of course, Mr. Le Moyne. It's not you I'm

making war on. I do hope there's no hard
feelings——''

"Why no, °Horacles, why no! How
can y'u entertain such an awful idea?
Don't I feel happy whenever an honest man
betters himself in this world?'' And
Scipio shook him by the hand and smiled
like an angel at him—a fallen angel. He
also looked down him along his nose.
"Guess I'll have to change my mind, Horacles,'' he continued. "Guess I'll have
to attend your opening to-morrow. Big
sight to see all them Indians shoppin' like
Christmas! I'll come. This store might
just as well close to-morrow, anyway.''

"Why, just as well!'' exclaimed Horacles, beaming. "Give us a call and bring
all your friends.'' And he went away
happily to supper.

Scipio gazed out of the window after
him. "He ain't got the faintest notion,''
said he, meditatively, "what a grease-spot
he is on the face of these nice, clean
hills.''

"I don't reckon you'll cut prices on
him?'' the Virginian inquired.

"Daren't. Not on my own responsibility.'' Scipio gave a sigh of sadness.
This symptom revealed a mind in joy as
plainly as his previous jocularity had be-
tokened a mind in distress.

"What trouble are you studÿing?'' repeated the Virginian, grinning.

Scipio touched him with a confidential
finger. "You watch,'' he said. "That's
all you've to do.''

The Virginian managed to look decently

indifferent for a while, and resorted to his
paper. Then he got an idea, and it was
too much for him. "You're going to buy
him out yourself!'' he declared, and regretted his haste immediately.

"I'm beyond y'u! I'm beyond y'u for
once!'' screeched Scipio, beating his
crutch on the floor.

"Oh, come to grub,'' said the Virginian.

But next morning it was still on his
mind. The delighted Scipio perceived
this instantly, and mentioned it skilfully
all the way as they drove across the reservation to the new store. "I never liked
being alone in trouble,'' he remarked.
"I never did.''
And presently,
"If I knew
where to look
for advice.''
And again, "'A
friend in need
is a friend in-
deed.'''

"I'll throw
you out,'' said
the Virginian,
"and break your
laig fresh.''

"Didn't I tell
you at Medora,''
said Scipio,
"that there was
two of us phil-
osophers in
Montana? And

did you outline your play to me that time? You watch.''

Horacles stood behind his counter. His moustache was combed, his broad hat tilted rakishly askew. He smiled and spoke, and handled and displayed his abundance; the bright calicoes, the shining knives, the bridles, the fishing-tackle, the gum-drops, all his plenty and its cheapness. Squaws and bucks, young and old, thronged his establishment. Their green and yellow blankets, and their feathers and paint, and their soft footfalls went everywhere. They whispered, and laughed, and stared, and priced and liberally bought. High Bear held a dozen fresh eggs in a beautiful crock. With the other hand the old chief was eating the free lunch. The voices were all rather subdued until Scipio's cheery greeting.

"My goodness, Horacles! You ain't going to send 'em home without an entertainment? Where's your vanishing handkerchief? Where's your interstate commerce dollar? Get 'em quick, Horacles. I tell you," he said to the Indians, "he big medicine-man. Make come. Make go. You no see. Nobody see. Make jackrabbit in hat——"

"I couldn't this morning," simpered Horacles. "Needs preparation, you know."

And he winked at Scipio.

Scipio struggled upon the counter, and stood up to finish his speech. "No jackrabbit to-day," said he. ("Ah, nah!" laughed the Indians. "No catch um.") "Yes. Catch um any time. Catch anything. Make anything. Make all this store"—Scipio waved his arms eloquently about—"that's how make heap cheap. See that!" He stopped dramatically, and clasped his hands together. Horacles flirted a handkerchief in the air, caught it, wiggled his fingers, shut his hand, opened it; no handkerchief there. "His hand swallow it, all same mouth!" shouted Scipio. "Now other hand spit it out. You see. He big medicine-man." But Horacles varied the trick. He opened both hands empty, clutched space, and drew two silver dollars from it. Then he threw them back into space, made a playful dive at High Bear's eggs and brought handkerchief and dollars out of them suddenly. "Huh!" went High Bear, and backed a little from the counter. He looked into the crock a moment, but after that his eyes watched Horacles and never left him again. Scipio saw that eye, and his own narrowed to a slit.

"Big medicine-man!" he called, loudly,

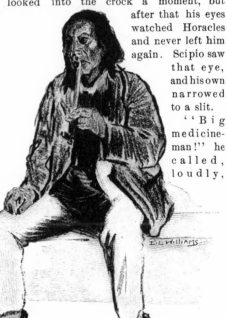

again, with gestures. "Hand all same mouth. Foot all same hand." Here Horacles removed a dollar from the hair of High Bear's fourteenth daughter, threw it into one boot and brought it out of the other. The Indians were packing together like jam, and Scipio, high on the counter, made gestures at them without ceasing. "Hand all same mouth. Foot all same head. Take off head, throw it out of window. Take out teeth. See, see him, see big medicine-man!" shrieked Scipio.

A long, red tongue came slowly, horribly, from Horacles' jaws, and upon the end of it glittered his front teeth. There was a crash on the floor, and one long, terrific yell. High Bear, with his blanket over his face, went flying through the door, leaving his eggs and crock a creeping mess of atoms. The tribe followed him like flapping birds. In two minutes or so the horses were gone, and in a little while the plain could be seen empty for miles.

"Horacles," said Scipio, still on the counter, "y'u thanked me in public for the free lunch idea, and I'd figured to thank you in public for this little notion —*but they didn't give me time!*"

When the agent returned he found business unchanged, except for Horacles. The Indians never came back to that new store. They made a mile circuit to pass it in safety. So when Horacles realized what he had done, he closed the store and went away—possibly to tell his uncle about Scipio.

Of course this story has another moral, which is: The American citizen is frequently superior to the American statesman.

29

The Winning of the Bisquit-Shooter

OWEN WISTER

THE WINNING OF THE BISCUIT-SHOOTER.

BY OWEN WISTER.

ONE day in February my friend Mrs. Taylor had an unusual experience. She received a letter. This was so marked an event that when I stopped the next noon to take a meal on my way to the Goose-egg ranch, she displayed the letter at once, and made me read it through, which took me a long time. It was signed, "Ever your affectionate friend, Katie Peck."

"Well," I said, "how long will she stay?"

"Just as long as she wants! Me and Katie hasn't met since we was girls in Dubuque, for I left when I married Mr. Taylor, and come here to Bear Creek; and it 'ain't been like Dubuque much, though if I had it to do over again, I'd do just the same. Well, it 'll be like old times. Katie 'll be twenty-four now. Poor thing! she 'ain't ever got married, and I expect she didn't have a good chance, for there was a big family of them children, and old Peck used to act real scandalous, getting drunk so folks didn't visit there evenings scarcely at all. And you see how she writes, how she quit home and got a position at Sidney, and now she's got poor health with feeding them travellers day and night."

Miss Peck's letter apprised us that at Sidney, on the Union Pacific Railway, she had performed the duties of what is commonly termed a biscuit-shooter. That is to say, when the trains halted for a twenty-minute meal, it was her function to stand behind the chair of the transcontinental public and recite the bill of fare with a velocity that telescoped each item, subsequently bringing the various refreshments that the dazed passengers had been able to rescue from this wreck of words.

In due time Miss Peck appeared on Bear Creek, and it was swiftly noised abroad among the cow-punchers that a new girl had come into the country. The young blood in the district circulated freely round the Taylors' residence, and the new-comer was pronounced better company than the school-marm, Miss Wood, a native of Bennington, Vermont. This prim, competent lady was to my Eastern eyes fairer than the biscuit-shooter from Dubuque; and I forbore to remind Lin McLean and a number of other impulsive bachelors how high their several enthusiasms for the school-

marm had run in the near past, and how some of these had ceased with a sudden chill. The broken health of Miss Peck mended rapidly under the attention of twenty cow-punchers. They put their bridles, saddles, horses, and themselves at her disposal, and laid presents of rattle-snake skins and elk teeth at her feet. By June she had bloomed into brutal comeliness. She had a broad face, a thick waist, black eyes, white teeth, a big mouth, and her cheeks were a lusty, overbearing red.

One sunset during the round-up we had worked from Salt Creek to Bear Creek, and the Taylor ranch was again within visiting distance, after an interval of gathering and branding far across the country. There was a Virginian in the round-up whom I had known at Judge Henny's ranch on Sunk Creek. He was gravely regarding Mr. McLean, and after a prolonged silence spoke. "Lin," said he, "I reckon you ain't right smart in health."

"Me? How do yu' figure that out?"

"You cert'nly feed hearty, but you ain't all right. You don't work spry cuttin' out the calves, and your conversation is mighty scanty."

"Feller gets tired ropin' all day," Lin explained. "Keepin' still's a good change."

"Yes," the Virginian said; "when the stock keeps dodgin' a man's rope and him all the time a-foggin' after 'em, he's liable to go plumb absent-minded."

"It ain't many dodges my rope," boasted Lin.

"Why, they say as how that Dubuque stock over at Taylor's is mighty aggravatin' that way."

Lin sat up angrily, but reclined again. "The school-marm 'ain't absented your mind any turrible lot lately," said he; and the company laughed a loud, merciless laugh.

The Virginian struck a match thoughtfully on the seat of his overalls.

"Probably," continued Lin, "a feller's mind can stay right with him after a girl's been and promised she'd sure be his sister."

"Some girls in this hyeh county," remarked the Southerner, "will end up the sister of most every male inhabitant."

"And the men they do marry 'll have a heap o' brothers-in-law," said Lin.

" It 'll be plumb confusin'," the Virginian commented, gently. "Lin, I reckon you'll get related to 'Rapaho Dick by that pro-cess."

Lin was silent.

"He's makin' hard runnin' for yu' right now. He's an excitin' fighter in conversation. I heard him recountin' his wars up at the Taylors'."

"What were yu' doin' there yerself?" Lin demanded.

"Visitin' Miss Wood," replied the Virginian, with entire self-possession. "'Rapaho Dick was talkin', and your girl certainly appeared mighty inter-ested in his statements."

"Why," I inquired, "is all that talk bogus?"

"So he's been entertainin' you too?" the Virginian said, giving me a glance of slight pity. "Well, 'Rapaho Dick has seen a heap o' Injuns in Buffalo Bill's show. He's been a darin' man."

Mr. M'Lean, lying on the ground, applied an epithet to his rival, at which the pleasant Virginian began to praise the rival's appearance. Lin listened to this with his eye jocularly cocked on the Southerner, and at length he remarked as to the rival that he would "fix his white liver fer him." With this complacent threat he rose and stalked to the margin of the creek, watching the first relief ride round and round the great recumbent herd.

"I reckon Lin means business," said the Southerner.

"Not he," I ventured to assert, and we went to bed; for most of us would go on second or third relief, and all would begin the next day by four in the morning.

"I guess I'll be goin' up to the Taylors' fer a spell," said Lin to me next afternoon, and I went with him, wondering a little. With the cow-puncher, love had been usually a transient disturbance. I had witnessed a series of flighty romances where he had come, seen, often conquered, and moved on. This afternoon he discoursed upon the beautiful wisdom of economy, and how few achieved it. He had some money saved; that is, he had a credit on the books of the store over at Drybone. Also, his friend Shorty owed him some fifty dollars. "After the round-up," said he, "I'll get my time, and all in all I'll be able to rustle up near five hundred dollars. I've got a claim on Butte Creek next Balaam's ranch, and

it 'll make me a homestead as soon as the land's surveyed. I'd be sorry fer myself if I couldn't stand off that harmless-eyed calf 'Rapaho Dick, when it come to competin' fer a woman. I'd take in Cheyenne on our weddin' trip."

"*Marry* her!" I sang out. "Marry *her!*"

Lin's eye met mine and fell. "Well, I might 'a' knowed yu'd act like that," he muttered, and dropped behind some hundred yards.

My candor had not been happy. Total silence would be the best antidote. He had seen the girl about four times. Once will do, it's said, and mine were cold, cautious, Eastern standards about friendship, and lending, and matrimony. Miss Peck might make a good helpmeet in spite of her horticultural appearance. A deserted home in Dubuque, a career in a railroad eating-house, a somewhat vague past, and a present lacking context—this was nothing to him, and ought to be nothing if he really loved the girl. But it seemed to me that this gay-hearted, manly vagrant deserved something better than the biscuit-shooter, and that if he waited till his colthood was over and then took the right woman to wed, she would bring out the good that was scattered through him in disorderly plenty. These Eastern notions I resigned with a sigh. The passion of a cow-puncher is ardent, and Lin would merely laugh.

Presently I was aware he had ridden up. "Miss Wood don't get tired boardin' with the Taylors," he said, still about ten yards in the rear.

"It's the nearest she could be to the school-house," I answered.

"She's a sure fine lady."

"Yes; she's a rare sort to see in this country."

"And she's got education beyond most that comes into this country, 'ain't she?" Lin had now restored himself beside me, and regarded me with humor. "I expect our tastes—mine and yourn—as to women don't agree."

"Are you imagining—"

"Oh no! oh no! You'll get spliced East when yu' get around to it, and don't yu' forget I'm comin'. That school-marm now, she ain't takin' any of the boys fer keeps. Tell yu'," said Lin, leaning over and touching my arm confidentially, "with all her stand-off manners and Vermont language, she's an all-the-same woman, you bet! She likes that Virginia feller danglin' around her, him that no-body ever seen dangle before. And he's plumb quit spreein' with the boys in town. I expect most every time she sees him she renoos her promise to be his sister. It ain't the least bit use neither, his comin' back at her."

"Not the slightest," said I. "I wish it was. But there's a native of Benning-ton, Vermont."

"Where?"

"There. She writes him letters all the time."

"Shoo! that ain't it. I seen the hand-writin' on the letters she gets back, and it's female writin'. Tell yu', Miss Wood knows the life the boys lead in this coun-try, and she ain't the kind that makes al-lowances. Strange kind, to my thinkin'. I'm glad I wasn't raised good enough to appreciate the Miss Woods of this world except at long range. What made yu' say that to me?"

"Say what?"

"Yu' know what I mean. Yu' don't figure I'd ought to get married."

"It's none of my business."

"It is if I ask yu'. But I know. Onced in a while you tell me I'm flighty. Well, I am. Hoop-ya! Oiee! Oiee!"

"You're a miserable fool, Lin," said I, diverted.

"Ain't I, just? And don't that prove I'd ought to quit and get responsible? You know yu'd like to visit me in my nice cabin all fixed up, with a dear little wife takin' care of me when I come home nights. But you're an Eastern man, anyway."

"You're right there. And Eastern men don't marry on a capital of five hundred dollars unless they're contract-ing for a girl that has the rest."

"Heaps starts in this country with nuthin' but their pluck and a horse. Just now she's got a fool idea about me. Claims I showed the white feather."

"I'm glad of it. She'll never marry you thinking that."

"She don't think it! Shoo! She knows a man when she sees one. She's puttin' that all on, playin' me and that white-livered Dick. He got her a bear-skin and I didn't. Now I'll tell yu' how I come to let that bear go. I found where she had her cubs caché right at the foot of a big rock in the range over Ten Sleep. Well, sir, I put back the leaves and stuff on top of them little things near as I could the

way I found 'em, and I told her about it, and she said she'd sure like a bear-hide. So I went back. The she-bear was off, and I got up inside the rock, and I waited a turrible long while till the sun travelled clean around the cañon. She come, though, a big cinnamon, and I raised my gun, but laid it down to see what she'd do. She scrapes around and snuffs, and the cubs starts whinin', and she whines back, makin' a noise like regular talk. Next she sits up awful big, and picks up a cub and holds it to her close with both her hands. Tell yu' a man don't expect a sight like that! There that cinnamon sat, nursin' and playin' with them little cubs, and rollin' them over onced in a while fer a change, and talkin' to 'em so yu' could 'most figure what she was sayin'. I'd as soon shot my mother. I watched 'em quite a while, and then come away quiet, you bet, fer I wasn't aimin' to be noticed any by Mrs. Bear. She said I was afraid, and I felt plumb foolish tellin' her why I didn't shoot. But she'll take me, you'll see. 'Rapaho Dick can please a woman—him and his blue eyes—but he don't know how to make a woman want him any more'n he knows about killin' Injuns."

"Did you hear about the Crows?" said I.

"About young bucks goin' on the war-trail? Shoo! the papers put up that talk —them little local papers that's published in towns around military posts. They're aimin' to scare Uncle Sam into keepin' the troops out here to make trade. If 'Rapaho Dick believed any Crows— Oh, mother!" The cow-puncher broke off speech, and swore in delight at the thought which had inspired him.

Two were before us at the Taylors' ranch. I joined Miss Wood and the Virginian, while Lin went to hamper 'Rapaho Dick at the other end of the room.

"How are yu', Miss Peck? How are yu', Dick?" said he. "Hear the news? Crow Injuns on the war-trail."

"Oh dear!" said the biscuit-shooter.

"You needn't to be afraid, Miss Peck," said Dick. "There's lots of white men here."

"Mostly with red livers," said Lin, "though some has not."

"I hadn't heard this report," said Dick.

"Guess it's like most news we get in

this country," Lin remarked—"two weeks stale and a lie when it was fresh."

"Oh, Dick!" called Taylor, outside, "your horse is getting away on you."

Dick rose, and ruefully sped after the runaway.

"I must cook supper now," said Katie, shortly.

"I'll stir for yu'," said Lin; and they departed to the adjacent kitchen.

"We were speaking of cowboy life," said Miss Wood to me. "What is your opinion of it?"

"Naturally a high one, since there are two big cowboys in the house."

"No; but you surely consider it rough and brutalizing."

"Well, I'm afraid I don't mind what you would probably call brutalizing. I believe if twin brothers separated and one staid in the streets and the other took his chances in the cattle country, that five years would see the cowboy morally the superior."

"That's correct, ma'am," said the Virginian; "that's right so."

A loud voice came from the kitchen. "You Lin, if you try any of yer foolin' with me, I'll h'ist yus over the j'ist!"

"All cowboys—" I attempted to resume.

"Quit, now, Lin McLean!" shouted the voice, "or I'll put yer through that window, *and it shut.*"

"Well, Miss Peck, I'm gettin' 'most tired of this treatment. Ever since yu' come I've been doin' my best. Yu've had my horses to ride, and I've put my coat on yu' when it was cold. I've sat talkin' and ready to do anything yu' said. And yu' just cough in my face. And now I'm goin' to quit and cough back."

"Would you enjoy walkin' out before supper, ma'am?" inquired the Virginian. "It's right close in this hyeh cabin."

"Oh, I think it's so pleasant!" said Miss Wood, sweetly.

"You was speakin' of gatherin' some flowers over yondeh."

"Was I? So I did." But she sat comfortably in the chair.

"I reckon there ain't goin' to be much time, ma'am."

"Then let's go." Miss Wood rose. "And you'll come and help," said she to me.

"I must look after my horse," said I, and went out to the corrals.

Day was going slowly as I took my pony to the water. The long castle of red sandstone, two miles away to see, ten to walk, lifted its nature-hewn turrets and flat forms in the setting sun, mellowing from hardness into tender saffron light and purple shade. Where I walked the odor of thousands of wild roses hung over the margin where the thickets grew. High in the upper air magpies were sailing across the silent blue. I found Mrs. Taylor looking for eggs, and accompanied her. Near supper-time various groups converged at the door—Taylor with 'Rapaho Dick, who was declaring all this Indian talk to be very foolish; Mrs. Taylor with me carrying the eggs; Miss Wood with the Virginian bearing flowers.

"It's all very fine," she was saying, "this making and spending everything. But how long will that last?"

"Till we can't spend anything, I reckon."

"And you work hard for months, and one week in town takes all your wages!"

"Yes, ma'am, when it ain't one day."

"Dear me, how dreadful! I suppose you're twenty-eight?"

"Twenty-five, ma'am."

"Indeed! You seem older."

"I reckon I'm pretty healthy."

"Oh yes!" laughed the school-marm; "and excuse my being personal. But you'll not always be twenty-five. Think what it would be to have nothing laid by when you were tired of this life and beginning to get old."

"Why, we don't live long enough to get old, ma'am," said the cow-puncher, looking down at her in surprise.

Miss Wood gave him a startled glance, compressed her lips, and murmuring something about arranging the table, took the flowers from him and went into the house.

Lin came hurrying out and seized the Southerner's arm. "You too," he said to me. "Just you fellers take the note from me. I'm goin' to fix 'Rapaho Dick. Back me up," he added to the Virginian. "I've helped you before now." He confided to me a remarkable conversation. "I told her my plans fer provin' up my claim, and about the money I'd saved. 'Well,' I says to her, after a lot o' back talk she give me, 'I've asked yu' twiced, and I'm goin' to let yu' have one more chance to get me, and that's right now. If yu' don't take me this evenin', Kate Peck, it's closed,' I says. 'You don't say!' says she. 'Why, ain't

Dick the better man? He's got a ranch started he can take me to.' 'If you're marryin' a log cabin,' says I, 'Dick's a sure good wooden piece of furniture to put in it.' 'Prove it,' she says. 'Shoo!' I says, 'if that's all.' 'I ain't sayin' that's all,' she says, and she called me Mr. Bear-hunter. And she laffed and hit me a clip with the broiler, so I expect things is likely comin' my way. If I can't kill bears, I'll show her how Dick kills Injuns, you bet."

At supper, after a little talk of the round-up and the probable price of steers in the coming fall, Lin observed that some of the cattle-men would lose stock if the Crows got down as far as this on their raid.

"I reckon they scarcely will," said the Virginian, and Mrs. Taylor suppressed a giggle. "Ain't it hawses and not cattle they're repawted as drivin' off?" continued the Southerner.

"Reported?" snapped 'Rapaho Dick. "Who made any such ridiculous report as that?"

"Feller come into the round-up this afternoon," said Lin. "But he was scared, and told a heap of facts that wouldn't square."

"Of course they wouldn't," said Dick, looking at a glass where his curly hair was reflected, and altering the position of one lock in consequence. "There's men in this country lose their heads directly you say Indian to 'em;" and he laughed in pity for these men. "What did he say?" he added.

"Oh, there's nuthin' in it," said Lin. "Have yu' been to the opera since we went in Cheyenne, Mr. Taylor?"

"What did the fool say at the round-up, anyway?" inquired 'Rapaho Dick of the Virginian.

"I didn't get around to listen to his triflin' trash. Lin, did yu' ever see that opera *Cyarmen*?"

"The one where the girl goes after the bull-fighter, and her feller stabs her? You bet! I'd hev gone too. He wasn't any good, and she was half on to him at the tavern."

"I reckon she wanted to be plumb sure, and took him to them mount'ins, where her experiment wouldn't be interrupted any."

"Talking of mountains," said 'Rapaho Dick, "the range back of here used to be very favorable for Indians."

"You bet it was before the Rosebud disaster. I wonder if she got tired of the bull-fighter too?"

"I reckon not. I expect him and her got married."

"Well, let 'em come off their reservation. There's plenty of good Sharps and Winchesters to point the road home to the red sons of guns."

Here the conversation forked upon widely diverging topics. 'Rapaho Dick thrilled the ladies with a lecture upon how to kill Indians, and the other gentlemen, pleased that he should do this, discussed the lyric drama and alfalfa-grass, recently introduced into the Territory.

"Mr. Taylor," said Lin, after the table was cleared, "the ladies might feel better if you fixed your fire-arms. It's wastin' time, of course, except oilin' 'em onced in a while is good."

"I'll do it, Lin. I've been taught there ain't smoke without fire."

"There ain't mostly. But Injun excitements—"

"I'd just like to know, once for all," interrupted 'Rapaho Dick, "what that man said. I can tell you quick enough if there's anything in it."

"You'd cert'nly better tell him, then, Lin," said the Virginian, who had relapsed into his customary silence, and was looking gravely at Miss Wood as often as he supposed no one would see him.

"Well, it don't amount to much. He claimed the cabin twenty-five miles north of Ten Sleep had been burned—"

"Ten Sleep? That's right near my ranch!"

"Yes, Dick, it sure is. House had been burned, and man missin'."

"See that, now? Do you suppose I'd have not heard of that? If any such occurrence had took place, it would have been me that would have told the round-up, and we'd have got the murdering devils inside of a day. Why, Ten Sleep ain't fifty miles from my place."

"No, Dick, it sure ain't."

"What further talk did that chap make?"

"Not much. Said warnin' reports had come from Montana, but could not tell what they were or who sent 'em. Well, I must be gettin' back, I expect."

I was stopping for the night, because I liked the notion of a roof after so many sleeps under the sky.

"I wish you'd stay too," said Mrs. Taylor to 'Rapaho Dick.

"Me!" he said, surprised.

Lin took him aside. "Don't you go," he whispered. "The ladies 'll feel easier to have another man besides Taylor in the house."

"In that case I'm always ready to oblige. Taylor is not used to the idea of being attacked, I guess. All you want to do is stay covered and pump lead into 'em. Pump it into the sons of guns, and they'll run. My cabin's pretty far to go so late, anyway. There's plenty of weapons here, ain't there?"

"Lots," said Lin; and simultaneously he and the Virginian laid a hand on their saddle horns, swung up, and soon all sound of the galloping hoofs had ceased.

Taylor cleaned his weapons, carefully loaded them, and we went to bed. Sleep must have surprised me, as it always did in that blessed country, for when the expected signal came, I sprang from the sheets with a start as genuine as 'Rapaho Dick's.

"Did you hear that?" said he, in the middle of the room.

Immediately it came again, a long wild yell. A door flew open, and Dick sprang hip high in the air. It was Mrs. Taylor in her night-gown. She said, rather feebly, "Oh, we shall all be murdered in our beds!" and began to laugh. She was a poor actress; but Dick was already beyond criticising shades of expression.

"My gun!" he said, hoarsely; and holding it in one hand, ran round the cabin from window to window, jerking at the buttons of his overalls. I suppose he imagined that he was dressing himself. Taylor now appeared, very solemn, holding a lantern.

"Put that thing out!" screeched Dick, and once again leaped into the air as a shot was fired near the house. I fell on the feather bolster, ramming my head deep into it.

"Get up, you Eastern dude!" Dick said, "and be of some use, if you know how."

He dragged me to my feet, and seeing the lantern still burning in Taylor's shaking grip, made a dash at it, and it fell in fragments to the floor, together with his rifle, which immediately exploded, splintering a log in the wall just behind my leg. This was a God-sent

mercy to the rest of us, for we did not know it had been cocked.

"Pick it up quick, and keep it away from him," whispered Taylor, "or he'll kill us all."

Dick was putting boards against a window.

"Well, I declare!" said Miss Peck, standing at the kitchen door, in contempt undisguised.

"Shoot 'em! shoot 'em!" said the lunatic, as a volley of shots cracked outside, and yell upon yell was raised amid the rush of horses. Miss Wood did not appear, but I thought I heard her mocking treble laugh coming from somewhere. Also the two Taylor babies were squalling.

"Back from the window! Bar the door!"

The din was now as loud inside as it was out. We all became very efficient in helping Dick pile furniture, when the door was burst open and three chairs went spinning. The Indian-fighter flew into a corner, while Mr. Taylor boldly fired a shot into the sky.

"That settles one!" he roared, and fired again. "That downs another. B' gosh, they're runnin'! Out, and at 'em!"

We emerged with our Winchesters, and his helpmeet in her night-gown and the biscuit-shooter each seized a broom, and so in a body we went three times round the yard, firing plenteously until the yell grew distant.

"Stop, friends," said Taylor, gasping. "I'll be gol-darned if I'll have Lin McLean make any more of a fool of me to-night."

"You!" said his wife. "Look at that!"

We had come into the kitchen. The table was covered with tin plates, and they were rattling up and down like castanets. Under the table a voice ceaselessly howled, "Let the sons of guns come here, and I'll do for them; let the red devils show themselves, and I'll tear 'em open." After a decent while we persuaded Dick out, and the ladies explained matters to him.

When the round-up was over I watched the happy Lin bear off his biscuit-shooter to the nearest justice of the peace. She got astride the horse he brought for her, and they rode away across the sunny sage brush.

The Virginian gazed after them a long time. "Some folks, anyway, get what they want in this hyeh world," he said.

30

The Wedding of Beaver Eyes

EMERSON HOUGH

THE WEDDING OF BEAVER EYES

By Emerson Hough

THE tribes had gathered and fought the white men, killing their long-haired leader. Days before the battle the trailers had told the general he would find the Indians, and find more of them than he wanted; yet the etiquette of their calling kept them with the column before the battle. After the battle had begun they could not get away; therefore they remained and became heroes. The trailers had seen much of killing in their time. They talked of it now. It was a Valhalla journey for these men. Their bloody and dirty faces were stolid, but lit by a certain fire. Pride of conflict, joy of heart, had taken hold of them all. They sang, contending with each other in deeds of unconcern. The blue-eyed man, knowing that all was over, at last pushed out quite in front of the willows and knelt in the grass, uncovered. Here he cut cleanly out of his saddle a big Indian who rode back and forth across the front of the thicket. Again loading, though now struck by the fire of the Indians, who wheeled and charged back again, he killed yet another Indian, close up to him, one who rode a yellow dun horse. Then Walking Dog shot him down, his head rolling back where he fell, as did those of the Indians dragged away. Then Billy shot Walking Dog. Then the others of the trailers, whites, breeds and reds, came up to the edge of the thicket, and they and the charging Indians shot at each other for a while. Two things brought an end to it; the supply of trailers ran out, and at just about that time the charging Indians, attracted by a great outcry a mile farther back up the valley, swept off and away to join in better paying business with the main village, which now had many officers and rank and file to strip.

Smilingly, Billy hitched around his cartridge belt and filled the loops in front, let down the hammer of his gun and stepped out of the willows to find a drink of water. As he passed by the blue-eyed man, who lay with his face turned up and his yellow hair trailing off into the yellow grass, Billy for a moment lost his smile. Stooping over the fallen body of Walking Dog he thoughtfully cut off an ear and put it in his pocket.

II.

After the fight, and after the arrival of the supporting column, the new commander called together the trailers, the three who were left from the fight at the willows, a few more who had not been in the fight, and a few more new ones, Snakes and Rees, just as good as the old ones. To these the commander explained that the ———— Regiment would now need recruiting, pretty much to the extent of a new set of officers and men, and incidentally a new supply of horses and mules. The ———— Regiment was always needing recruiting. This time it was to be recruited at Fort Lincoln. The trailers were to proceed to that post, in no hurry, but with such speed as would bring them there in the course of the next few weeks.

Two young Ree scouts, good men, but very homesick, had asked permission to go home to see their people, this meaning that they were to leave the direct route by a few hundred miles, no very great distance on the plains. It fell out that Billy went along with the Rees to their village. He took with him a few horses which he had incidentally stolen somewhere; one of them a black runner, a very good buffalo horse.

Billy and the two Rees rode along together over the blistering plains, a few hundred miles, day by day, not talking much, because they saw all there was to see, and each knew that the others saw it all, so there was no need to talk. Billy did not speak their language, nor they his; not that this would have prevented their conversation had they cared to talk. Billy did not know where their village was, and he did not ask, because he knew that the Rees knew, and that they would go to it in due time. His arm pained him somewhat, where a bullet had cut it across, but this was only incidental. Nobody referred to it, though when it was necessary that meat should be killed, the Rees would leave Billy and go out and do that themselves. Billy endured the pain of the

383

arm as part of what he got for the five dollars a day and all the horses he could steal.

Billy was a half-breed, a tall and sinewy,
good-looking and good-natured half-breed,
who had been scouting with the army ever
since he was sixteen years of age. As he
rode with the silent Rees for the fifth day,
the white half of Billy began to be bored
with the monotony. The red half of him was
non-committal. Both halves of him were very

for a few crumbs, and feeling there something tobaccoish, he absent-mindedly drew
it out and took a bite at it. This substance,
being the ear of Walking Dog, afforded no
real satisfaction. Billy was first disgusted,
and then amused. Thoughtfully restoring
the curio to his pocket, he rode on; but ever
and anon, for the next dozen miles, he smiled
cheerfully, as one who was blessed with happy
meditations.

" DOWN THE SLOPE AT FULL SPEED."

hungry. The Rees would not stop to hunt
that day, but made signs that on that night
they would sleep in their village. This meant
that they would get plenty to eat then,
which was easier than to go out and kill
and cook plenty now. Billy demurred not,
but chewed tobacco. By noon his tobacco
was nearly gone. Reaching into his pocket

Presently the two Rees pulled up their
horses and dismounted. They untied bundles from the backs of their saddles, and
brought forth new moccasins and leggins.
From little bags at their necks they produced pigments, and shortly appeared in solemn dignity, nobly barred with the grim colors of war. Billy did not paint, but he lent a

couple of scalp tufts to Crane Caller, and told him to lie all he liked about them. Then they rode to the crest of the hill beyond which lay the village of the Rees, and thence all set heels to their horses and went down the slope at full speed, driving in their loose horses, firing their guns, and yelling in great style, as have the triumphant warriors of all times, from Rome, Gaul and India down.

III.

Not lacking in hospitality were the Plains people. The two Ree scouts soon disappeared in the lodges of their families, leaving Billy sitting alone on his horse in the middle of the village, for the moment abandoned by the sweep of welcoming ones. For him the situation seemed not much changed, both halves of him still being very hungry, though the red half was non-committal and the white half slightly amused; yet, it being etiquette to wait, he waited, hungry but confident. Presently an oldish squaw came, and without saying a word to him took his horse by the bridle and led him some distance through the village. "I'll just follow you, old girl," said Billy to himself; and, so doing, the procession at length halted in front of a very large and fine lodge, a sort of brown stone front habitation, relatively speaking. The woman signed for him to enter, and he did so, stranger as he was and ignorant of the local tongue. Sioux, Crow, Cree, Piegan, French and English Billy could speak, but he did not know Arickaree. He knew chiefly that he was hungry, so he stooped down and entered the lodge.

It was dark inside the dwelling, no fire being lighted at that hour, but as Billy's eyes became accustomed to the gloom he made out, near the door (the post of little honor) the figure of an old woman, and in the back of the lodge (the post of greatest honor), a large and dignified Indian, evidently master of the house and a man of some consequence. Billy, being versed in the etiquette of good society, made care not to disturb the ashes of the fire, neither did he pass in front of the tripod at the rear of the lodge, where hung the sacred bundles, the "medicine" of the family. The chief doubled his fist and struck it upon the robe beside him; whereby Billy knew that he was invited to take a seat, which he did, remaining there, very hungry but very polite. Presently the chief put his two forefingers together parallel in front of him. Billy knew by this that the chief

meant to say that they two were to be friends. "Good," said Billy, in equal silence, extending his hand in front of him, palm down. None the less he was very hungry.

The chief sat gravely silent, showing very becoming dignity for what seemed to Billy a very long time. Then he had a sudden afflux of Indian conversation, on Indian lines of thought. "Me, you see me, here," he said, mutely and in signs, "Very poor, awfully poor, in fact a deadbroke Indian" (raising his forefinger and scraping it with the other forefinger; as who should find a bone with no meat on it; he was that poor.) "I am about the poorest Indian ever was." "You old liar," thought Billy, "I wonder what you want."

"The Sioux came down on us not long ago, while we were out hunting," said the chief (drawing his hand across his throat to say "Sioux").

"Uh-huh," said Billy.

"They took all my horses." (Two fingers a-straddle of another finger, the sign for "horse;" otherwise, the "clothes-pinned animal," which is "horse," as plain as the nose on your face).

"Uh-huh," said Billy.

"No, not one horse have I left with which to run the buffalo." (Crooked finger on each side of head for "buffalo").

"Uh-huh," said Billy.

"Therefore I am ashamed. My heart is small, it is weak, it is poor. When I go out to hunt I get no meat, because I have no good horse to run the buffalo. I am ashamed before my people."

Grave silence on the part of Billy. After a diplomatic pause the chief resumed, still, of course, in signs.

"My friend and brother, my great warrior, is it possible that you happen to have such a thing about you as a good running horse?"

"Brother and friend," said Billy, in signs, "Horse, me, my horse, outside, see? Black horse, the black one, you comprehend? Yes, he's a good runner, a fine buffalo horse. That black horse, me, you, I make a present of this horse to you. (You old fraud, you. But I'll steal him again, anyway, when I go away, so we'll let it go at that.)" This last was in English and to himself, and as he said it, Billy smiled most amiably.

Instantly the demeanor of the chief changed. His solemnity vanished. He grasped Billy by the hand. Best of all, he gave orders in a loud tone of voice to the old woman sitting near the door, and to Billy's great delight the squaw began to make a fire. In due course she set before him a large pan of meat, corn and beans, after the fashion of the Rees, who trucked a bit as well as butchered. Thereupon Billy ate his four or five lost meals in one, and, finally, bringing his finger up level with his lips, signified that he was full up to that altitude.

him back to the lodge where he had first been received. "Sit down here in this house," signed the chief. "Here you shall sleep. This shall be your home." But first," he added hospitably, "we really must have just a bit to eat, you know, you being my guest." Nor could Billy evade this. As they sat at table dining, which is to say, as they sat on the edge of the

"THEN BILLY SHOT WALKING DOG."

Meantime much calling and shouting and joymaking was going on in the village outside. Billy was tired and sleepy, and now wished very much to roll over on the robes and go to sleep, but his host gave him no opportunity to do so. He was haled hospitably forth and taken visiting. At every house where they paused they were offered dishes of meat and corn and beans, and as gentlemen they must eat. Billy wished heartily that he had his hunger back. But everywhere he accepted his rôle as returning brave, and acted as became a hero. As evening came, and after Billy had finished his twentieth meal for the afternoon, his host at last conveyed

robe bed, about the fire, holding on their knees the wooden and horn vessels, they became conscious of the arrival of visitors at the door. The skin flap of the door was pulled aside, and there was intruded the head of an Indian girl; a very sleek, black head, with cheek bones nicely reddened with paint. The owner of the sleek head and round face came in silently, save for the tinkle of her glass beads and brass cylinders and bits of copper wire, and seated herself ungreeted and ungreeting upon the robes at the side of the fire, at a point between Billy and the lady of the house. The full dress, or woman's tunic which she wore, made of the skin of the mountain sheep, was white as snow, and covered with scores of elk teeth, which rattled. Her jewels of copper and glass shone as bravely in the firelight as ever flashed the gems of high dame of any land at dinner of state. Nor was ever heard of any maiden smoother and sleeker, nor of eyes any brighter. There was no introduction at this dinner party. Of course, Billy recognized the introduction of the roof, but at the first opportunity he faced about to his host and asked him, in the silent language of signs, what was the name of the girl in the elk-tooth gown.

"I didn't quite understand you—her name, you know?" said he, querying with his undecided fingers shaken loosely in the air.

"Beaver Eyes," said the chief; and Billy at that moment swore that Beaver Eyes was the one maid in all the world for him.

IV.

Billy might have been considered fortunate. He had stepped at once into the best society of the city. He had been approved as a man and applauded as a hero. He had been invited and fêted by the best families, and treated with every mark of the most distinguished social consideration. The making of a hero sometimes overleaps the slow circles of evolution. Billy was utterly happy. The Ree corn and beans palled upon him, it is true; yet had he not seen Beaver Eyes? Had he not urged his suit? Had he not promised many things? Had he not touched her hand?

For two weeks the feasting continued in the village, and both Billy and the young Ree scouts had forgotten about the orders to report at the recruiting post. Each day the crier went abroad, calling out to all persons to assemble at the lodge of this or that person anxious to entertain the returning braves. One day the herald invited by those presents all members of good society to be and appear at the residence of Wolf Dog, the headman. Naturally, Billy could not fail to attend this function, and after dining he participated in the dance.

The red half of Billy was now rapidly getting the ascendency. Nude to the waist and hopping like a brave, he joined the circle of dancers as one to the manner born. In the dark circle of spectators which surrounded the dancing men were eyes that saw more than they seemed to see. Color, light, music, beauty—all the inspiration of the grand ball was there. Last and most potent factor in his exaltation, Billy saw, as he trod the repeated measure of the dance, a sleek, black head, half hid in a far corner, and a shoulder over which hung the white fabric of an elk-tooth decorated gown. Never in any village did Billy dance as he was dancing now. Yet dignity must be preserved. No glance into that corner for many a long moment. None, until that one which discovered the sleek head and white tunic to be gone! "I shall seek her in the conservatory," thought Billy; or thoughts in Plains language equivalent to that.

But though he sought her beneath the silent stars, he found her not, and trod disconsolate the moonlit street. Afar came the sound of galloping, and thither Billy turned his feet with the rapid curiosity of the scout. He, the stranger within the gates, was the first to receive the messenger and to discover that he was a friend; not a messenger from the King, but a messenger from the K. O., asking why in the name of all saints dwelling west of the Missouri River, Billy had not come into post with the other scouts. The red faded out of Billy's heart. He became white again, and subject to the call of duty. Telling the rider to wait, he hurried off to find Crane Caller and order him to prepare to march far from the sound of this revelry by night.

Billy himself could never explain how it was that he went the wrong way to find the lodge of Crane Caller. He was born and raised in an Indian village, and had lived many years among the tribes. The dark cones of these monotonous abodes had each an architecture to his eye, and the heraldry of the shields before the doors was obvious to him. Sometimes, when he was feeling more Indian than white man, he would explain this blunder by saying that it was his "dream" that led him apparently wrong, but actually to his own best interests. What Billy did was to go to the lodge where he supposed Crane Caller lived, and to look in at the door. Seeing in the foreground an old woman who was in the act of invoking her patron saints, Billy delicately withdrew, and passed around to the rear of the lodge, to the point where he presumed Crane Caller was lying. Reaching a hand against the form which lay close to the wall of the tepee, he gave a push and a low word of warning. The woman at the fire sprang up with a sudden call of suspicion.   This old lady was a dreamer of dreams, and was always hearing ghosts walking outside the lodge at night.   Now, at last, she thought that she had found her ghost.   But to her voice replied another voice, also in affright, and as he heard it Billy went cold along his

on a certain swift black horse, was riding to the lodge where Beaver Eyes was weeping. Billy had never heard of Lochinvar, but he knew how to ride.   The black horse carried the two away, figures rapidly lessening in the growing dawn.

V.

The little war was now waning.   Numbers of Indian prisoners were coming in, fresh

"THE BLACK HORSE CARRIED THE TWO AWAY."

spine.   It was not the voice of Crane Caller, but the voice of a woman—a voice which he had heard and had not forgotten, which he never could forget!

The dancing at the great lodge had now begun to spend itself.   The East was growing gray, as sometimes it grows after the white men's dances.   One by one little groups began to scatter through the village.   The howl of a dog rose here and there, and a ten-fold coyote on a neighboring hill shrilled in whining salutation. Voices sounded variously, footsteps drew nearer and passed by.   Behind the lodge Billy cowered and lay still, fearing not for himself, but for the owner of the voice that he had heard.

A little dog barked at Billy's legs.   The old woman, timorous but exultant that she had found her ghost, peered around the edge of the lodge.   But Billy mounted

from a recent round-up of the traveling bands, each charged with the murder of a few dozen settlers.   These prisoners were put in irons, to their supremest humiliation, and were confined at the Post in a great log building, where they were chained to the wall in a long row and kept under guard. In truth it must be said they did not employ their time in chanting their death songs, but seemed most concerned about tobacco.

"Tobac?" asked Yellow Horse, the chief of his band, as Billy passed near him. "Heap tobac!"

"Tobacco?   Why, sure, old man," said Billy, and dug into his pocket, bringing forth the scent and apparently the substance of the coveted weed.   Eagerly Yellow Horse filled his mouth, resolved that no portion of that piece of plug should ever return to its owner.   But he bit against it only once.   He held it before his face, a grin of rage convulsing his features. Billy grinned also, and made a pleasant gesture, a sweep of an imaginary knife at his own ear.

"Walking Dog, *your brother!*" he said.

Quick as a cat, the Indian stooped, drew back and reached forward. He had doubled the loose length of his chain and struck out with it as far as he could reach. The end of the flying iron caught Billy above the ear and felled him instantly. Private O'Brien joyfully clubbed his musket and knocked Yellow Horse also insensible. In about five minutes Billy came to his senses, borrowed a musket and shot Yellow Horse as he sat dazed in his chains. In five minutes more Billy was himself in chains, and the K. O. swore he would make an example of him this time, for he had had enough of his escapades.

One morning the corporal and three privates escorted Billy to the headquarters office under guard. The K. O., after his bath, and his libation, and his breakfast, had come down to the office early to take up the case of this scout; this half-breed who was always into trouble. He dismissed the corporal and the privates, dismissed the orderly and the quartermaster, called Billy to the table and looked him sternly and then softly in the eye. He gave Billy a rifle and a roll of blankets, and a roll of cash (which latter the K. O. could really not afford to do), and he secretly bade him goodbye as one school friend does another, and told him to go back to the guard house at once. Incidentally he mentioned that the end of the company street fronted due north.

It is all very well about discipline, but when men have often been under fire together, even though that may have been because they could not get away, the matter of an ear here or there, or even of an Indian, cuts far less figure alone in office than it does in an official report. The K. O. shook hands with Billy, and swore goodbye at him. And then Billy and Beaver Eyes disappeared. They faded away into the West, which at that time was a very large and lovable country.

VI.

Years after the time when Billy and the fugitive Arickaree maiden disappeared from view there came to be established upon a certain Indian reservation in the far North-west, many hundreds of miles from the old military post and far away from the great battle ground (where the men who made the mistakes became heroes, and the men who did the fighting became forgotten in due time), the cabin of a certain tall and not ill-looking half-breed, who always smiled, and whose name was known as Billy. He had lived for a long time here in this cabin, with his "woman," who was called Beaver Eyes. Their family had grown up about them, and all seemed happy and prosperous in their little home, in this wild corner of the mountains, tucked up under the sweeping arm of the Rockies. There had now come, all over the West, the mysterious and fascinating West of the past, the time of new things and new ways. Schools and churches had found even this far-away reservation. The buffalo were long since gone. Cattlemen tried to steal, and the Government tried to buy all of the reservation which was good for anything. The people were not permitted to worship in their own way. They dared not pray to the sun, because the white man said that was wrong. They must pray to something else, which they could not see, and must believe things which they could not understand. The priest at the Mission said that warriors must put away all their wives, or at least all of them but one; advice the justice of which it was difficult for the people to see.

Especially with the young men and the half-breeds did the priest labor, seeking to get them "legally" married to their wives. Many was the long journey the good Father made to Billy's cabin, trying to induce him to attend the Mission church, and beseeching him to stand before the altar.

All these questions seemed strange and puzzling, even to the white half of Billy. He had come of a time of war, had grown up among warriors red and white, and he could see no support for the doctrines of unselfishness, since all nature had taught him the lesson of continual contest. Yet, perhaps there was, somewhere back in the white half of Billy's brain, something of philosophy. Perhaps he remembered that Beaver Eyes, who had first known and loved him when he was a hero, had not forsaken him when he was cast down, had been faithful to him in sickness and in health, cleaving to him alone through all the years. Was there not in this some hint of that which the white priest was trying to teach? Was there not something of self-forgetfulness here, under the roof of his own cabin? Beaver Eyes was silent regarding herself through all these years, whether splitting wood in the past or fabricating pie of Governmental dried apples in the days of progress. Nor did Billy ever trouble her with philosophy.

The double current of Billy's blood served him well. One day he went to church where the white men worshipped. Then he went home, and the next morning, when the sun made first pink and then golden the visible throne of the inapproachable, the lofty and majestic peak of the Great Chief mountain, the pagan half of Billy rose in unconscious adoration. Yet it was on that day that he sent word to the priest that he was willing to be married to his wife!

VII.

The rumor of Billy's wedding had gone abroad, flying in the mysterious way of the wild land, all the people being bidden to come. It was a grand wedding, without doubt. To be sure, there was no champagne, but there was five gallons of alcohol, which is equally purposeful. The priest was near to calling it no wedding after all. For Billy stood forth clad from head to toe in the old tribal dress which was now discouraged or forbidden among the tribes; and his wife, Beaver Eyes, wore a white tunic of the skin of the mountain sheep, covered with a rattling mail of teeth of the elk; a garment which the traders would have given many cattle to possess. They made a picture from the past, as they stood before the teacher, who was trying to bring new truths into the world, regardless of the high cynicism of the Great Chief mountain, which looked down upon this ceremony as it had done upon those of the red men in centuries gone and forgotten.

It was a grand wedding, and its last scene was not done until dawn of the following day, when Billy stood at the door of his house, looking thoughtfully over many sleeping forms, and gazed out across the plain that lay before him.

Beaver Eyes had hung up her elk-tooth dress and had donned the calico of·progress. Billy absently ran his hand across the skin garment till all the teeth and the little ancient cylinders of steel that adorned it tinkled and rattled again. They sounded the music of another day, a day gone by forever. "Beaver Eyes," said Billy, laughing a little uncertainly, "come here, old girl! Put it on. Put it on again! This wedding goes. It lasts till the sun goes down behind the mountain; and till it don't come up again!" And Beaver Eyes, dutiful as always, again put on her wedding gown.

31
The Tenderfoot

H.W. MORROW

"Out of the ruck and the dust shot a lean yellow streak."

Drawing by C. M. Russell.

THE TENDERFOOT

By H. W. MORROW

THE tenderfoot sat on the rough board platform and kicking his heels, looked contemplatively out toward the bare, brown hills a mile or so away. After awhile, he took a letter from his pocket and read, punctuating occasionally with interjections of his own.

. . . . . "You've only got one life to live; what do you want to bury yourself out there for? Why not come back and live it?"

The dry winds of northwestern Nebraska gathered up sand and dust and other debris and distributed it impartially. The tenderfoot being to leeward of the little wooden station, in a sort of eddy, got his full share; the sand gritted uncomfortably in his teeth and the dried grasses found lodgment in his hair. But he only smiled a dry little smile as he put the letter back into his pocket.

The smile evoked by this part of the letter changed into a broad grin as two men in Government blue, the stripes on their arms indicating the rank of sergeant, came swinging down from the town, the one riding a diminutive, fleabit pony, the other an abnormally long-legged Government mule. It was a sight that they themselves would have been the first to find uproariously funny, except that numerous visits to a certain corner where were dispensed liquid refreshments prohibited to the red man but gloriously free to his white brother, had reduced them to a state of unnatural gravity and official dignity. The mule ran with the grace of a galloping camel and the pony looked like a rabbit by its side, taking two strides to his one.

A troop of noisy girls of from ten to sixteen years of age, riding astride their nondescript ponies, some barebacked, some in the deep men's saddles of the plains, all shouting and laughing, scampered after them across the railroad track and disappeared in a cloud of dust out toward a rough board structure that jutted up out of the prairie about a quarter of a mile to the west.

Then the Tenderfoot followed, still smiling. It amused him to think of Potter writing to him in that way. He started to whistle a little tune but the wind stopped that with a hatful of dust that it had found opportunely. The slovenly agent looked after him suspiciously. But the latter did not notice him at all. He was figuring to himself how many times it would happen that Fate, after worrying an inoffensive mortal to the verge of nervous prostration, using for that delightful purpose a branch railroad through the sandhills, would elect to strand him for six hours in the town of all others he would have selected for that event.

Indian boys dashed by on rough, uncurried ponies, vying with the white girls in the amount and variety of noise they made, their ponies' hoofs striking dully in the dust or beating a lively tattoo according as they were on the high or low ground. Statuesque old warriors, silent, dignified, blanketed to the eyes, left their tents sitting lonely or in clusters on the brown prairie, and stalked with the gliding, in-toe motion of the Indian toward the point at which the various streams of humanity were converging, apparently uninterested, looking neither to the right nor the left. The Tenderfoot wondered how many of them had been at Wounded Knee or against Custer. For profundity on a small capital there is no hope of competing with an Indian after he is fifty. Squaws with babes at their backs followed meekly and seated themselves at a respectable distance from their liege lords who saw them not at all.

It was a race week at a town near the Pine Ridge Agency and everybody was there; the Indians as ever at a race; whites of all ages, classes and conditions of soberness or otherwise; the dust and the wind over the burnt grass.

The Tenderfoot started to walk toward the lower end of the track where a race was being arranged between a sorrel colt and a black pony. He began his education at once. Many others were going the same way, treading carelessly with that free and easy swagger that becomes a man who is just as good as anyone. The Tenderfoot did likewise but with a different result. He had not gone a dozen paces when he felt a sensation not unlike that he had known when as a boy he had placed his bare foot fairly in the bosom of a vigorous Canada Thistle. "A regular cactus treading tenderfoot," quoth his mind unto him, even before he had time to raise his foot and look at the little round, wickedly barbed ball that clung so tenaciously to the inner side of his instep; and he marveled much at the immunity enjoyed by a people that strolled unconcernedly, even in moccasins, where a box calf, leather-lined shoe was no protection.

The sorrel colt was a home product; he had won barrels of money for his owner the day before, but he didn't look it; he had a stringy, washed-out look. The black pony was a stranger and looked every inch a runner from the small, nervous muzzle to the trim hind feet that set off a pair of beautifully muscled legs. He was like a wire spring and looked as though he might run the sorrel's legs off.

Back in Ohio, at the county fairs, when the Tenderfoot had such thoughts, he had been accustomed to giving them vent without serious results. He did so now, wholly unprepared for the result. "How much! Here! I'll take ten on that! Oh, well! What kind of a blanked game's that y'r givin' us! Oh, well, then don't talk. Put up or shut up!" Being totally unprepared for such a rush of language and outstretched hands, the Tenderfoot backed off, flinched and looked scaredly down toward his feet. He recovered himself quickly, but too late. They laughed, and henceforth nothing he would say would count. They had him ticketed.

He had his revenge however. It took two men to hold the black while the sorrel scored lazily. A half dozen or more times they did this, the black stubborn and vicious, the sorrel tractable and lazy. It was a three hundred and fifty yard race and the first few jumps would count. And when the start came, these first few jumps went to the black. He shot away at the crack of the pistol as though it had been the crack of a whip lash on his flank and the sorrel never lapped him after the tenth jump. "Let him go! Let him go!" yelled the sorrel's owner, but the little black running beautifully with that free, high, open gait more often pictured by the old illus-

trators than seen in a race, held his position easily to the end. And then a quiet looking man gathered in the stakes, which were not great, and the crowd straggled off toward the judge's stand where the main races were to finish, the Tenderfoot carrying his shoulders a little higher.

"Put your money on the blaze-faced sorrel mare." The shoulders came down at once. His feet were even now tingling from the cactus barbs but surely they were not so tender as that. He studied himself carefully to determine if possible just why *he* should have been selected as suitable soil for such a suggestion. Later he apologized mentally to the rough-looking young fellow who made it. He could not find him to apologize verbally. The blaze-faced sorrel looked like a horse on stilts. She looked as though nature, or art, had started to make a giraffe and then changing her mind, made the hind legs on the same plan as the front ones and attached a horse's head. The result was picturesque but not particularly horsey. The Tenderfoot feared the legs would not be able to coöperate at critical junctures. He might have saved himself all concern; at the trying out, they did seem a trifle inconsistent in their performance; the Tenderfoot and others, especially a superb woman riding a bay astride with the seat of a Diana and a man's hat, breathed the dust, the thick insistent and inquisitive dust of a Nebraska prairie and waited for the real thing. While they waited he watched the woman and read into her life a history, a wild, free, romantic history of the plains. He was probably mistaken; she may have been cook at the Henderson House.

In the meantime, they got away, the blaze-face trailing, her long legs dangling nonchalantly, the chestnut leading magnificently, the play of his superb muscles suggesting a well-oiled machine. The black-tailed bay was running a good second. It was a race of thoroughbreds and did not interest the Tenderfoot at all. He had not come out of the east to see thoroughbreds run and there was no new thrill in it. He turned to watch the woman astride just in time to see her dash out of the little crowd that surrounded her, rise in her stirrups and gaze under her leveled hand at the fleeing trio. It was grand and he forgot that a race was on; but as she continued her steady gaze, he turned to look for the reason. The chestnut had found the work too fast for him; his magnificent stride was all there was to him. The bay was pushing him muzzle for muzzle and the blaze-face still trailing. This way they made the first circuit. And then, there was nothing spectacular about it, the long legs just unraveled little by little, the white face crept up along the bay's flank, along his side, past his shoulder and they ran like a four of cavalry for awhile, the riders of the chestnut and the bay making their whips sing, the sorrel running easily. This continued till they swung into the home stretch; then there was a yellow and white awakening and the race was over. The Tenderfoot was disgusted, it was the old, old game without a redeeming feature of the picturesque. He tried to find the man who had given him the tip. It would have done him no good if he had known it was straight—he never bet anything more valuable than his opinion, but it seemed to have an originality about it that he liked.

Then he turned to see what was left. Everywhere was dust, insistent, gray, impartial dust. The superb woman on horseback lifted her bay into an easy canter and rode to talk with a patriarch in a patriarchal carriage, sitting her horse as another woman her rocking-chair Over by the judge's stand, a tall country looking fellow was flourishing ten-dollar bills and trying to get a bet on the next race. To him went the Tenderfoot; he hoped that he might be really drunk, not feigning—after the tip he felt that it might really be so. Eventually he concluded that this too was stereotyped. He began to wish his train would come.

And then he saw something. An Indian, a young Indian with the unmistakable, eagle-beak of the Sioux, with long hair floating in the wind, riding bare backed on a sway-back pony of the true buckskin, and with evident intention of entering the next race.

"What is it?" he inquired of a cattle man near by with a fine disregard for definiteness. But the man understood. "What? Oh! Next race! County against reservation! Any good! Nawh, not much; Indians aint no jockeys. There's that buckskin kin run like the devil, but they'll crowd him out one way or nuther."

The Tenderfoot turned just in time to

catch a gleam in a pair of the wickedest eyes it had been his pleasure to see; it gave him the thrill he had been looking for. There was a glint in them not unlike, in color, to the green band that circled the forehead above them and held back the thick black, horse-tail hair.

"You want to bet?" queried the owner of the eyes looking away toward where he had left his horse in the hands of another Indian. "Bet ten dollars the buckskin wins."

"Who's in it?" he started to inquire, but the cattle man was ahead of him and he found himself an involuntary stakeholder. After this important function was attended to, the Indian turned to the Tenderfoot with a sweeping gesture toward a group gathered near the judge's stand. "Them," was his sole comment as he passed on to join them.

The scoring was interesting and confusing. Not to mention the dust which made observation difficult, it is no easy matter to start twelve excitable ponies and as many more or less nervous riders and have the advantage in just the right place without palpable unfairness. The Tenderfoot picked out the winner at once. This was a little brown mare, called by courtesy a pony, but with all the earmarks of an undersized thoroughbred. She was ridden by a boy, evidently an old hand, in scarlet cap and regular jockey costume. The black victor over the sorrel colt was his next choice. His rider wore a green cap but no other jockey clothing. These scored like veterans; none of the others did. Most of the riders rode saddles but one of the white boys rode barebacked as did both Indians. Several were barefooted and nearly all bareheaded. The buckskin seemed level-headed and a likely third.

At last they were away. The race was a half mile and one circuit would finish. The track would not accommodate so many and two were crowded off almost at the outset and gave it up. Two others began to trail hopelessly. The phenomenal quickness of the black carried him well to the front but the brown was running easily and hugging his flank; the others were bunched slightly in the rear and apparently doing all they could. Before they got to the quarter the second Indian was out of it. The buckskin was well up in the bunch but crowded to the outside limit and after one glance the Tenderfoot accepted the cattle man's dictum and gave his entire attention to the leaders. It was a confusing whirl of dust, cracking whips and cries, but slowly and surely as they swept down the farther stretch, the black crept from the bunch and just as surely the brown overtook him in spite of whip and spur, ran even with him, crawled away from him and pulled in ahead and her rider threw back his head and with whip in air opened his mouth in a hearty laugh at the ease of it. It was disgusting and the Tenderfoot started to go.

But did horses hoofs ever make so much noise before? He turned to see what it meant. With rhythmical regularity came the sharp crack of a whip and then out of the ruck and the dust shot a lean yellow streak surmounted by a mass of black hair floating in the wind, an eagle-beak above which there was a flash of green, shot past the spent black and was lapping the brown's flank before her jaunty rider woke to the fact that the race was not over. The brown responded finely and accepted the challenge. Fifty yards of the remaining two hundred and fifty were covered before the crowd knew what was happening. Then there was a roar and a rush and the Tenderfoot could have hugged himself for joy. It would have been fine under any circumstances; with the memory of the cattle man's statement and the gleam in the Indian's eye, it was epic. It was not now a question of jockeying it was strength, it was speed, it was endurance. All the jockey's jauntiness was gone. His mouth that had been opened in laughter closed with a snap and his nostrils quivered almost as did those of his straining mount. With pump like regularity the Indians arm rose and fell. It almost

seemed that a straight line might have been drawn from the outstretched nose to the rapidly flying heels of the buckskin. Heedless of his reins the Indian plied the whip, leaning well forward his long legs guiltless of stirrups hanging loose, not gripping in the least, apparently. Up, up crawled the yellow, back, back slipped the brown. Would he make it! Would he make it! Would—with a final effort the yellow nose pushed a clear lead ahead as they went under the wire.

"Good for you, old man!" exclaimed the stakeholder as he turned the twenty dollars over to the winner and the cattle man laughingly added his congratulations.

A ghost of a smile flickered about the Indian's mouth as inherited stoicism struggled with acquired vanity and the desire to joke. And then he looked the Tenderfoot squarely in the eye as he replied in excellent English and with a perceptible drawl. "Yes, I didn't forget *all* they taught me while I was at Carlisle."

The Tenderfoot had a thoughtful look as he again took his seat on the platform to await his overdue train. The two sergeants loped by on the fleabit pony and the long-legged mule, keeping their seats with difficulty. The young girls shrill and noisy as always scampered homeward on their ponies apparently as free from parental restraint as so many young wolves. The old Indians stalked away across the prairie to their tents. A train whistled hoarsely in the distance. He took out the letter again and read.

"You can talk as you please, but you can't convince me that that God-forsaken country is a fit place for a civilized man to live."

"Poor old Potter," he said as he put the letter into his pocket and went into the station for his valise and coat.

32

Specimen Jones

OWEN WISTER

SPECIMEN JONES.

BY OWEN WISTER.

E PHRAIM, the proprietor of Twenty Mile, had wasted his day in burying a man. He did not know the man. He had found him, or what the Apaches had left of him, sprawled among some charred sticks just outside the Cañon del Oro. It was a useful discovery in its way, for otherwise Ephraim might have gone on hunting his strayed horses near the cañon, and ended among charred sticks himself. Very likely the Indians were far away by this time, but he returned to Twenty Mile with the man tied to his saddle, and his pony nervously snorting. And now the day was done, and the man lay in the earth, and they had even built a fence round him; for the hole was pretty shallow, and coyotes have a way of smelling this sort of thing a long way off when they are hungry, and the man was not in a coffin. They were always short of coffins in Arizona.

Day was done at Twenty Mile, and the customary activity prevailed inside that flat-roofed cube of mud. Sounds of singing, shooting, dancing, and Mexican tunes on the concertina came out of the windows hand in hand, to widen and die among the hills. A limber, pretty boy, who might be nineteen, was dancing energetically, while a grave old gentleman, with tobacco running down his beard, pointed a pistol at the boy's heels, and shot a hole in the earth now and then to show that the weapon was really loaded. Everybody was quite used to all of this—excepting the boy. He was an Eastern new-comer, passing his first evening at a place of entertainment.

Night in and night out, every guest at Twenty Mile was either happy and full of whiskey, or else his friends were making arrangements for his funeral. There was water at Twenty Mile—the only water for two score of miles. Consequently it was an important station on the road between the southern country and Old Camp Grant, and the new mines north of the Mescal Range. The stunt, liquor-perfumed adobe cabin lay on the gray floor of the desert like an isolated slab of chocolate. A corral, two desolate stable-sheds, and the slowly turning windmill were all else. Here Ephraim and one or two helpers abode, armed against Indians, and selling whiskey. Variety in their vocation of drinking and killing was brought them by the travellers. These passed and passed through the glaring vacant months —some days only one ragged fortune-hunter, riding a pony; again by twos and threes, with high-loaded burros; and sometimes they came in companies, walking beside their clanking freight-wagons. Some were young, and some were old, and all drank whiskey, and wore knives and guns to keep each other civil. Most of them were bound for the mines, and some of them sometimes returned. No man trusted the next man, and their names, when they had any, would be O'Rafferty, Angus, Schwartzmeyer, José Maria, and Smith. All stopped for one night; some longer, remaining drunk and profitable to Ephraim; now and then one staid permanently, and had a fence built round him. Whoever came, and whatever befell them, Twenty Mile was chronically hilarious after sundown—a dot of riot in the dumb Arizona night.

On this particular evening they had a tenderfoot. The boy, being new in Arizona, still trusted his neighbor. Such people turned up occasionally. This one had paid for everybody's drink several times, because he felt friendly, and never noticed that nobody ever paid for his. They had played cards with him, stolen his spurs, and now they were making him dance. It was an ancient pastime; yet two or three were glad to stand round and watch it, because it was some time since they had been to the opera. Now the tenderfoot had misunderstood these friends at the beginning, supposing himself to be among good fellows, and they therefore naturally set him down as a fool. But even while dancing you may learn much, and suddenly. The boy, besides being limber, had good tough black hair, and it was not in fear, but with a cold blue eye, that he looked at the old gentleman. The trouble had been that his own revolver had somehow hitched, so he could not pull it from the holster at the necessary moment.

"Tried to draw on me, did yer?" said the old gentleman. "Step higher! Step, now, or I'll crack open yer kneepans, ye robin's egg."

"Thinks he's having a bad time," remarked Ephraim. "Wonder how he'd like to have been that man the Injuns had sport with?"

"Weren't his ear funny?" said one who had helped bury the man.

"Ear?" said Ephraim. "You boys ought to been along when I found him, and seen the way they'd fixed up his mouth." Ephraim explained the details simply, and the listeners shivered. But Ephraim was a humorist. "Wonder how it feels," he continued, "to have—"

Here the boy sickened at his comments and the loud laughter. Yet a few hours earlier these same half-drunken jesters had laid the man to rest with decent humanity. The boy was taking his first dose of Arizona. By no means everybody was looking at his jig. They had seen tenderfeet so often. There was a Mexican game of cards; there was the concertina; and over in the corner sat Specimen Jones, with his back to the company, singing to himself. Nothing had been said or done that entertained him in the least. He had seen everything quite often.

"Higher! skip higher, you elegant calf," remarked the old gentleman to the tenderfoot. "High-yer!" and he placidly fired a fourth shot that scraped the boy's boot at the ankle and threw earth over the clock, so that you could not tell the minute from the hour hand.

"'Drink to me only with thine eyes,'" sang Specimen Jones, softly. They did not care much for his songs in Arizona. These lyrics were all, or nearly all, that he retained of the days when he was twenty, although he was but twenty-six now.

The boy was cutting pigeon-wings, the concertina played "Matamoras," Jones continued his lyric, when two Mexicans leaped at each other, and the concertina stopped with a quack.

"Quit it!" said Ephraim from behind the bar, covering the two with his weapon. "I don't want any greasers scrapping round here to-night. We've just got cleaned up."

It had been cards, but the Mexicans made peace, to the regret of Specimen Jones. He had looked round with some hopes of a crisis, and now for the first time he noticed the boy.

"Blamed if he ain't neat," he said. But interest faded from his eye, and he turned again to the wall. "'Lieb Vaterland magst ruhig sein,'" he melodiously observed. His repertory was wide and refined. When he sang he was always grammatical.

"Ye kin stop, kid," said the old gentleman, not unkindly, and he shoved his pistol into his belt.

The boy ceased. He had been thinking matters over. Being lithe and strong, he was not tired nor much out of breath, but he was trembling with the plan and the prospect he had laid out for himself. "Set 'em up," he said to Ephraim. "Set 'em up again all round."

His voice caused Specimen Jones to turn and look once more, while the old gentleman, still benevolent, said, "Yer langwidge means pleasanter than it sounds, kid." He glanced at the boy's holster, and knew he need not keep a very sharp watch as to that. Its owner had bungled over it once already. All the old gentleman did was to place himself next the boy on the off side from the holster; any move the tenderfoot's hand might make for it would be green and unskilful and easily anticipated. The company lined up along the bar, and the bottle slid from glass to glass. The boy and his tormentor stood together in the middle of the line, and the tormentor, always with half a thought for the holster, handled his drink on the wet counter, waiting till all should be filled and ready to swallow simultaneously, as befits good manners.

"Well, my regards," he said, seeing the boy raise his glass; and as the old gentleman's arm lifted in unison, exposing his waist, the boy reached down a lightning hand, caught the old gentleman's own pistol, and jammed it in his face.

"Now you'll dance," said he.

"Whoop!" said Specimen Jones, delighted. "*Blamed* if he ain't neat!" And Jones's handsome face lighted keenly.

"Hold on!" the boy sang out, for the amazed old gentleman was mechanically drinking his whiskey out of sheer fright. The rest had forgotten their drinks. "Not one swallow," the boy continued. "No, you'll not put it down either. You'll keep hold of it, and you'll dance all round this place. Around and around. And don't you spill any. And I'll be thinking what you'll do after that."

Specimen Jones eyed the boy with growing esteem. "Why, he ain't bigger than a pint of cider," said he.

"Prance away!" commanded the tenderfoot, and fired a shot between the old gentleman's not widely straddled legs.

"You hev the floor, Mr. Adams," Jones observed, respectfully, at the old gentleman's agile leap. "I'll let no man here interrupt you." So the capering began, and the company stood back to make room. "I've saw juicy things in this Territory," continued Specimen Jones, aloud, to himself, "but this combination fills my bill."

He shook his head sagely, following the black-haired boy with his eye. That youth was steering Mr. Adams round the room with the pistol, proud as a ringmaster. Yet not altogether. He was only nineteen, and though his heart beat stoutly, it was beating alone in a strange country. He had come straight to this from hunting squirrels along the Susquehanna, with his mother keeping supper warm for him in the stone farm-house

among the trees. He had read books in which hardy heroes saw life, and always triumphed with precision on the last page, but he remembered no receipt for this particular situation. Being good game American blood, he did not think now about the Susquehanna, but he did long with all his might to know what he ought to do next to prove himself a man. His buoyant rage, being glutted with the old gentleman's fervent skipping, had cooled, and a stress of reaction was falling hard on his brave young nerves. He imagined everybody against him. He had no notion that there was another American wanderer there, whose reserved and whimsical nature he had touched to the heart.

The fickle audience was with him, of course, for the moment, since he was upper dog and it was a good show; but one in that room was distinctly against him. The old gentleman was dancing with an ugly eye; he had glanced down to see just where his knife hung at his side, and he had made some calculations. He had fired four shots; the boy had fired one. "Four and one hez always made five," the old gentleman told himself with much secret pleasure, and pretended that he was going to stop his double shuffle. It was an excellent trap, and the boy fell straight into it. He squandered his last precious bullet on the spittoon near which Mr. Adams happened to be at the moment, and the next moment Mr. Adams had him by the throat. They swayed and gulped for breath, rutting the earth with sharp heels; they rolled to the floor and floundered with legs tight tangled, the boy blindly striking at Mr. Adams with the pistol-butt, and the audience drawing closer to lose nothing, when the bright knife flashed suddenly. It poised, and flew across the room, harmless, for a foot had driven into Mr. Adams's arm, and he felt a cold ring grooving his temple. It was the smooth, chilly muzzle of Specimen Jones's six-shooter.

"That's enough," said Jones. "More than enough."

Mr. Adams, being mature in judgment, rose instantly, like a good old sheep, and put his knife back obedient to orders. But in the brain of the overstrained, bewildered boy universal destruction was whirling. With a face stricken lean with ferocity, he staggered to his feet, plucking at his obstinate holster, and glaring for a foe. His eye fell first on his deliverer, leaning easily against the bar watching him, while the more and more curious audience scattered, and held themselves ready to murder the boy if he should point his pistol their way. He was dragging at it clumsily, and at last it came. Specimen Jones sprang like a cat, and held the barrel vertical and gripped the boy's wrist.

"Go easy, son," said he. "I know how you're feelin'."

The boy had been wrenching to get a shot at Jones, and now the quietness of the man's voice reached his brain, and he looked at Specimen Jones. He felt a potent brotherhood in the eyes that were considering him, and he began to fear he had been a fool. There was his dwarf Eastern revolver, slack in his inefficient fist, and the singular person still holding its barrel and tapping one derisive finger over the end, careless of the risk to his first joint.

"Why, you little son of a ——" said Specimen Jones, caressingly, to the hypnotized youth, "if you was to pop that squirt off at me, I'd turn you up and spank yu'. Set 'em up, Ephraim."

But the commercial Ephraim hesitated, and Jones remembered. His last cent was gone. It was his third day at Ephraim's. He had stopped, having a little money, on his way to Tucson, where a friend had a job for him, and was waiting. He was far too experienced a character ever to sell his horse or his saddle on these occasions, and go on drinking. He looked as if he might, but he never did; and this was what disappointed business men like Ephraim in Specimen Jones.

But now, here was this tenderfoot he had undertaken to see through, and Ephraim reminding him that he had no more of the wherewithal. "Why, so I haven't," he said, with a short laugh, and his face flushed. "I guess," he continued, hastily, "this is worth a dollar or two." He drew a chain up from below his flannel shirt-collar and over his head. He drew it a little slowly. It had not been taken off for a number of years—not, indeed, since it had been placed there originally. "It ain't brass," he added, lightly, and strewed it along the counter without looking at it. Ephraim did look at it, and being satisfied, began to uncork a new bottle, while the punctual audience came up for its drink.

"Won't you please let me treat?" said the boy, unsteadily. "I ain't likely to meet you again, sir." Reaction was giving him trouble inside.

"Where are you bound, kid?"

"Oh, just a ways up the country," answered the boy, keeping a grip on his voice.

"Well, you *may* get there. Where did you pick up that—that thing? Your pistol, I mean."

"It's a present from a friend," replied the tenderfoot, with dignity.

"Farewell gift, wasn't it, kid? Yes: I thought so. Now I'd hate to get an affair like that from a friend. It would start me wondering if he liked me as well as I'd always thought he did. Put up that money, kid. You're drinking with me. Say, what's yer name?"

"Cumnor—J. Cumnor."

"Well, J. Cumnor, I'm glad to know yu'. Ephraim, let me make you acquainted with Mr. Cumnor. Mr. Adams, if you're rested from yer quadrille, you can shake hands with my friend. Step around, you Miguels and Serapios and Cristobals, whatever yu' claim your names are. This is Mr. J. Cumnor."

The Mexicans did not understand either the letter or the spirit of these American words, but they drank their drink, and the concertina resumed its acrid melody. The boy had taken himself off without being noticed.

"Say, Spec," said Ephraim to Jones, "I'm no hog. Here's yer chain. You'll be along again."

"Keep it till I'm along again," said the owner.

"Just as you say, Spec," answered Ephraim, smoothly, and he hung the pledge over an advertisement chromo of a nude cream-colored lady with bright straw hair holding out a bottle of somebody's champagne. Specimen Jones sang no more songs, but smoked, and leaned in silence on the bar. The company were talking of bed, and Ephraim plunged his glasses into a bucket to clean them for the morrow.

"Know anything about that kid?" inquired Jones, abruptly.

Ephraim shook his head as he washed.

"Travelling alone, ain't he?"

Ephraim nodded.

"Where did yu' say yu' found that fellow layin', the Injuns got?"

"Mile this side the cañon. 'Mong them sand humps."

"How long had he been there, do yu' figure?"

"Three days anyway."

Jones watched Ephraim finish his cleansing. "Your clock needs wiping," he remarked. "A man might suppose it was nine, to see that thing the way the dirt hides the hands. Look again in half an hour and it 'll say three. That's the kind of clock gives a man the jams. Sends him crazy."

"Well, that ain't a bad thing to be in this country," said Ephraim, rubbing the glass case and restoring identity to the hands. "If that man had been crazy he'd been livin' right now. Injuns 'll never touch lunatics."

"That band have passed here and gone north," Jones said. "I saw a smoke among the foot-hills as I come along day before yesterday. I guess they're aiming to cross the Santa Catalina. Most likely they're that band from round the San Carlos that were reported as raiding down in Sonora."

"I seen well enough," said Ephraim, "when I found him that they wasn't going to trouble us any, or they'd have been around by then."

He was quite right, but Specimen Jones was thinking of something else. He went out to the corral, feeling disturbed and doubtful. He saw the tall white freight-wagon of the Mexicans, looming and silent, and a little way off the new fence where the man lay. An odd sound startled him, though he knew it was no Indians at this hour, and he looked down into a little dry ditch. It was the boy, hidden away flat on his stomach among the stones, sobbing.

"Oh, snakes!" whispered Specimen Jones, and stepped back. The Latin races embrace and weep, and all goes well; but among Saxons tears are a horrid event. Jones never knew what to do when it was a woman, but this was truly disgusting. He was well seasoned by the frontier, had tried a little of everything; town and country, ranches, saloons, stage-driving, marriage occasionally, and latterly mines. He had sundry claims staked out, and always carried pieces of stone in his pockets, discoursing upon their mineral-bearing capacity, which was apt to be very slight. That is why he was called Specimen Jones. He had exhausted all the important sensations, and did not care much for anything any more.

Perfect health and strength kept him from discovering that he was a saddened, drifting man. He wished to kick the boy for his baby performance, and yet he stepped carefully away from the ditch so the boy should not suspect his presence. He found himself standing still, looking at the dim, broken desert.

"Why, hell," complained Specimen Jones, "he played the little man to start with. He did so. He scared that old horse-thief, Adams, just about dead. Then he went to kill me, that kep' him from bein' buried early to-morrow. I've been wild that way myself, and wantin' to shoot up the whole outfit." Jones looked at the place where his middle finger used to be, before a certain evening in Tombstone. "But I never—" He glanced towards the ditch, perplexed. "What's that mean? Why in the world does he git to cryin' for *now*, do you suppose?" Jones took to singing without knowing it. "'Ye shepherds, tell me, have you seen my Flora pass this way?'" he murmured. Then a thought struck him. "Hello, kid!" he called out. There was no answer. "Of course," said Jones. "Now he's ashamed to hev me see him come out of there." He walked with elaborate slowness round the corral and behind a shed. "Hello, you kid!" he called again.

"I was thinking of going to sleep," said the boy, appearing quite suddenly. "I—I'm not used to riding all day. I'll get used to it, you know," he hastened to add.

"'Ha-ve you seen my Flo'— Say, kid, where yu' bound, anyway?"

"San Carlos."

"San Carlos? Oh. Ah. 'Flo-ra pass this way?'"

"Is it far, sir?"

"Awful far, sometimes. It's always liable to be far through the Arivaypa Cañon."

"I didn't expect to make it between meals," remarked Cumnor.

"No. Sure. What made you come this route?"

"A man told me."

"A man? Oh. Well, it *is* kind o' difficult, I admit, for an Arizonan not to lie to a stranger. But I think I'd have told you to go by Tres Alamos and Point of Mountain. It's the road the man that told you would choose himself every time. Do you like Injuns, kid?"

Cumnor snapped eagerly.

"Of course yu' do. And you've never saw one in the whole minute-and-a-half yu've been alive. I know all about it."

"I'm not afraid," said the boy.

"Not afraid? Of course yu' ain't. What's your idea in going to Carlos? Got town lots there?"

"No," said the literal youth, to the huge internal diversion of Jones. "There's a man there I used to know back home. He's in the cavalry. What sort of a town is it for sport?" asked Cumnor, in a gay Lothario tone.

"*Town*?" Specimen Jones caught hold of the top rail of the corral. "*Sport*? Now I'll tell yu' what sort of a town it is. There ain't no streets. There ain't no houses. There ain't any land and water in the usual meaning of them words. There's Mount Turnbull. It's pretty near a usual mountain, but yu' don't want to go there. The Creator didn't make San Carlos. It's a heap older than him. When he got around to it after slickin' up Paradise and them fruit trees, he just left it be as he found it, as a sample of the way they done business before he come along. He 'ain't done any work around that spot at all, he 'ain't. Mix up a barrel of sand and ashes and thorns, and jam scorpions and rattlesnakes along in, and dump the outfit on stones, and heat yer stones red-hot, and set the United States army loose over the place chasin' Apaches, and you've got San Carlos."

Cumnor was silent for a moment. "I don't care," he said. "I want to chase Apaches."

"Did you see that man Ephraim found by the cañon?" Jones inquired.

"Didn't get here in time."

"Well, there was a hole in his chest made by an arrow. But there's no harm in that if you die at wunst. That chap didn't, yu' see. You heard Ephraim tell about it. They'd done a number of things to the man before he could die. Roastin' was only one of 'em. Now your road takes you through the mountains where these Injuns hev gone. Kid, come along to Tucson with me," urged Jones, suddenly.

Again Cumnor was silent. "Is my road different from other people's?" he said, finally.

"Not to Grant, it ain't. These Mexicans are hauling freight to Grant. But what's the matter with your coming to Tucson with me?"

"I started to go to San Carlos, and I'm going," said Cumnor.

"You're a poor chuckle-headed fool," burst out Jones, in a rage. "And yu' can go, for all I care. You and your Christmas-tree pistol. Like as not you won't find your cavalry friend at San Carlos. They've killed a lot of them soldiers huntin' Injuns this season. Goodnight."

Specimen Jones was gone. Cumnor walked to his blanket-roll, where his saddle was slung under the shed. The various doings of the evening had bruised his nerves. He spread his blankets among the dry cattle-dung, and sat down, taking off a few clothes slowly. He lumped his coat and overalls under his head for a pillow, and putting the despised pistol alongside, lay between the blankets. No object showed in the night but the tall freight-wagon. The tenderfoot thought he had made altogether a fool of himself upon this first trial trip of his manhood, alone on the open sea of Arizona. No man, not even Jones now, was his friend. A stranger, who could have had nothing against him but his inexperience, had taken the trouble to direct him on the wrong road. He did not mind definite enemies. He had punched the heads of those in Pennsylvania, and would not object to shooting them here; but this impersonal, surrounding hostility of the unknown was new and bitter; the cruel, assassinating, cowardly Southwest, where prospered those jail-birds whom the vigilantes had driven from California. He thought of the nameless human carcass that lay near, buried that day, and of the jokes about its mutilations. Cumnor was not an innocent boy, either in principles or in practice, but this laughter about a dead body had burned into his young unhardened soul. He lay watching with hot, dogged eyes the brilliant stars. A passing wind turned the windmill, which creaked a forlorn minute, and ceased. He must have gone to sleep, and slept soundly, for the next he knew it was the cold air of dawn that made him open his eyes. A numb silence lay over all things, and the tenderfoot had that moment of curiosity as to where he was now which comes to those who have journeyed for many days. The Mexicans had already departed with their freight-wagon. It was not entirely light, and the embers where these early starters had cooked their breakfast lay glowing in the sand across the road. The boy remembered seeing a wagon where now he saw only chill, distant peaks, and while he lay quiet and warm, shunning full consciousness, there was a stir in the cabin, and at Ephraim's voice reality broke upon his drowsiness, and he recollected Arizona and the keen stress of shifting for himself. He noted the gray paling round the grave. Indians? He would catch up with the Mexicans, and travel in their company to Grant. Freighters made but fifteen miles in the day, and he could start after breakfast and be with them before they stopped to noon. Six men need not worry about Apaches, Cumnor thought. The voice of Specimen Jones came from the cabin, and sounds of lighting the stove, and the growling conversation of men getting up. Cumnor, lying in his blankets, tried to overhear what Jones was saying, for no better reason than that this was the only man he had met lately who had seemed to care whether he were alive or dead. There was the clink of Ephraim's whiskey-bottles, and the cheerful tones of old Mr. Adams, saying, "It's better'n brushin' yer teeth"; and then further clinking, and an inquiry from Specimen Jones.

"Whose spurs?" said he.

"Mine." This from Mr. Adams.

"How long have they been yourn?"

"Since I got 'em, I guess."

"Well, you've enjoyed them spurs long enough." The voice of Specimen Jones now altered in quality. "And you'll give 'em back to that kid."

Muttering followed that the boy could not catch. "You'll give 'em back," repeated Jones. "I seen yu' lift 'em from under that chair when I was in the corner."

"That's straight, Mr. Adams," said Ephraim. "I noticed it myself, though I hed no objections, of course. But Mr. Jones has pointed out—"

"Since when have you growed so honest, Jones?" cackled Mr. Adams, seeing that he must lose his little booty. "And why didn't you raise yer objections when you seen me do it?"

"I didn't know the kid," Jones explained. "And if it don't strike you that game blood deserves respect, why it does strike me."

Hearing this, the tenderfoot, outside in his shed, thought better of mankind and life in general, arose from his nest, and began preening himself. He had all the correct trappings for the frontier, and his toilet in the shed gave him pleasure. The sun came up, and with a stroke struck the world to crystal. The near sand hills went into rose, the crabbed yucca and the mesquite turned transparent, with lances and pale films of green, like drapery graciously veiling the desert's face, and distant violet peaks and edges framed the vast enchantment beneath the liquid exhalations of the sky. The smell of bacon and coffee from open windows filled the heart with bravery and yearning, and Ephraim, putting his head round the corner, called to Cumnor that he had better come in and eat. Jones, already at table, gave him the briefest nod; but the spurs were there, replaced as Cumnor had left them under a chair in the corner. In Arizona they do not say much at any meal, and at breakfast nothing at all; and as Cumnor swallowed and meditated, he noticed the cream-colored lady and the chain, and he made up his mind he should assert his identity with regard to that business, though how and when was not clear to him. He was in no great haste to take up his journey. The society of the Mexicans whom he must sooner or later overtake did not tempt him. When breakfast was done he idled in the cabin, like the other guests, while Ephraim and his assistant busied about the premises. But the morning grew on, and the guests, after a season of smoking and tilted silence against the wall, shook themselves and their effects together, saddled, and were lost among the waste thorny hills. Twenty Mile became hot and torpid. Jones lay on three consecutive chairs, occasionally singing, and old Mr. Adams had not gone away either, but watched him, with more tobacco running down his beard.

"Well," said Cumnor, "I'll be going."

"Nobody's stopping yu'," remarked Jones.

"You're going to Tucson?" the boy said, with the chain problem still unsolved in his mind. "Good-by, Mr. Jones. I hope I'll—we'll—"

"That'll do," said Jones; and the tenderfoot, thrown back by this severity, went to get his saddle-horse and his burro.

Presently Jones remarked to Mr. Adams that he wondered what Ephraim was doing, and went out. The old gentleman was left alone in the room, and he swiftly noticed that the belt and pistol of Specimen Jones were left alone with him. The accoutrement lay by the chair its owner had been lounging in. It is an easy thing to remove cartridges from the chambers of a revolver, and replace the weapon in its holster so that everything looks quite natural. The old gentleman was entertained with the notion that somewhere in Tucson Specimen Jones might have a surprise, and he did not take a minute to prepare this, drop the belt as it lay before, and saunter innocently out of the saloon. Ephraim and Jones were criticising the tenderfoot's property as he packed his burro.

"Do yu' make it a rule to travel with ice-cream?" Jones was inquiring.

"They're for water," Cumnor said. "They told me at Tucson I'd need to carry water for three days on some trails."

It was two good-sized milk-cans that he had, and they bounced about on the little burro's pack, giving him as much amazement as a jackass can feel. Jones and Ephraim were hilarious.

"Don't go without your spurs, Mr. Cumnor," said the voice of old Mr. Adams, as he approached the group. His tone was particularly civil.

The tenderfoot had, indeed, forgotten his spurs, and he ran back to get them. The cream-colored lady still had the chain hanging upon her, and Cumnor's problem was suddenly solved. He put the chain in his pocket, and laid the price of one round of drinks for last night's company on the shelf below the chromo. He returned with his spurs on, and went to his saddle that lay beside that of Specimen Jones under the shed. After a moment he came with his saddle to where the men stood talking by his pony, slung it on, and tightened the cinches; but the chain was now in the saddle-bag of Specimen Jones, mixed up with some tobacco, stale bread, a box of matches, and a hunk of fat bacon. The men at Twenty Mile said good-day to the tenderfoot, with monosyllables and indifference, and watched him depart into the heated desert. Wishing for a last look at Jones, he turned once, and saw the three standing, and the chocolate brick of the cabin, and the windmill white and idle in the sun.

"He'll be gutted by night," remarked Mr. Adams.

"I ain't buryin' him, then," said Ephraim.

"Nor I," said Specimen Jones. "Well, it's time I was getting to Tucson."

He went to the saloon, strapped on his pistol, saddled, and rode away. Ephraim and Mr. Adams returned to the cabin; and here is the final conclusion they came to after three hours of discussion as to who took the chain and who had it just then:

Ephraim. Jones, he hadn't no cash.

Mr. Adams. The kid, he hadn't no sense.

Ephraim. The kid, he lent the cash to Jones.

Mr. Adams. Jones, he goes off with his chain.

Both. What d—— fools everybody is, anyway!

And they went to dinner. But Mr. Adams did not mention his relations with Jones's pistol. Let it be said, in extenuation of that performance, that Mr. Adams supposed Jones was going to Tucson, where he said he was going, and where a job and a salary were awaiting him. In Tucson an unloaded pistol in the holster of so handy a man on the drop as was Specimen would keep people civil, because they would not know, any more than the owner, that it was unloaded; and the mere possession of it would be sufficient in nine chances out of ten — though it was undoubtedly for the tenth that Mr. Adams had a sneaking hope. But Specimen Jones was not going to Tucson. A contention in his mind as to whether he would do what was good for himself, or what was good for another, had kept him sullen ever since he got up. Now it was settled, and Jones in serene humor again. Of course he had started on the Tucson road, for the benefit of Ephraim and Mr. Adams.

The tenderfoot rode along. The Arizona sun beat down upon the deadly silence, and the world was no longer of crystal, but a mesa, dull and gray and hot. The pony's hoofs grated in the gravel, and after a time the road dived down and up among lumpy hills of stone and cactus, always nearer the fierce glaring Sierra Santa Catalina. It dipped so abruptly in and out of the shallow sudden ravines that, on coming up from one of these into sight of the country again, the tenderfoot's heart jumped at the close apparition of another rider quickly bearing in upon him from gullies where he had been moving unseen. But it was only Specimen Jones.

"Hello!" said he, joining Cumnor. "Hot, ain't it?"

"Where are you going?" inquired Cumnor.

"Up here a ways." And Jones jerked his finger generally towards the Sierra, where they were heading.

"Thought you had a job in Tucson."

"That's what I have."

Specimen Jones had no more to say, and they rode for a while, their ponies' hoofs always grating in the gravel, and the milk-cans lightly clanking on the burro's pack. The bunched blades of the yuccas bristled steel-stiff, and as far as you could see it was a gray waste of mounds and ridges sharp and blunt, up to the forbidding boundary walls of the Tortilita one way and the Santa Catalina the other. Cumnor wondered if Jones had found the chain. Jones was capable of not finding it for several weeks, or of finding it at once and saying nothing.

"You'll excuse my meddling with your business?" the boy hazarded.

Jones looked inquiring.

"Something's wrong with your saddle-pocket."

Specimen saw nothing apparently wrong with it, but perceiving Cumnor was grinning, unbuckled the pouch. He looked at the boy rapidly, and looked away again, and as he rode, still in silence, he put the chain back round his neck below the flannel shirt collar.

"Say, kid," he remarked, after some time, " what does J stand for?"

"J? Oh, my name! Jock."

"Well, Jock, will yu' explain to me as a friend how yu' ever come to be such a fool as to leave yer home—wherever and whatever it was — in exchange for this here God-forsaken and iniquitous hole?"

"If you'll explain to me," said the boy, greatly heartened, "how you come to be ridin' in the company of a fool, instead of goin' to your job at Tucson."

The explanation was furnished before Specimen Jones had framed his reply. A burning freight-wagon and five dismembered human stumps lay in the road. This was what had happened to the Miguels and Serapios and the concertina. Jones and Cumnor, in their dodging and struggles to exclude all expressions of growing mutual esteem from their speech, had forgotten their journey, and a sudden bend among the rocks where the road had now brought them revealed the blood and fire staring them in the face. The plundered wagon was three parts empty; its splintered, blazing boards slid down as they burned into the fiery heap on the ground; packages of soda and groceries and medicines slid with them, bursting into chemical spots of green and crimson flame; a wheel crushed in and· sank, spilling more packages that flickered and hissed; the garbage of combat and murder littered the earth, and in the air hung an odor that Cumnor knew, though he had never smelt it before. Morsels of dropped booty up among the rocks showed where the Indians had gone, and one horse remained, groaning with an accidental arrow in his belly.

" We'll just kill him," said Jones; and his pistol snapped idly, and snapped again, as his eye caught a motion—a something —two hundred yards up among the bowlders on the hill. He whirled round. The enemy was behind them also. There was no retreat. "Yourn's no good !" yelled Jones, fiercely, for Cumnor was getting out his little foolish revolver. "Oh, what a trick to play on a man ! Drop off yer horse, kid ; drop, and do like me. Shootin's no good here, even if I was loaded. *They* shot, and look at them now. God bless them ice-cream freezers of yourn, kid! Did yu' ever see a crazy man? If you 'ain't, *make it up as yu' go along!*"

More objects moved up among the bowlders. Specimen Jones ripped off the burro's pack, and the milk-cans rolled on the ground. The burro began grazing quietly, with now and then a step towards new patches of grass. The horses stood where their riders had left them, their reins over their heads, hanging and dragging. From two hundred yards on the hill the ambushed Apaches showed, their dark, scattered figures appearing cautiously one by one, watching with suspicion. Specimen Jones seized up one milk-can, and Cumnor obediently did the same.

" You kin dance, kid, and I kin sing, and we'll go to it," said Jones. He rambled in a wavering loop, and diving eccentrically at Cumnor, clashed the milk-cans together. " ' Es schallt ein Ruf wie Donnerhall,' " he bawled, beginning the song of " Die Wacht am Rhein." " Why don't you dance ?" he shouted, sternly.

CUMNOR'S AWAKENING.

The boy saw the terrible earnestness of his face, and clashing his milk-cans in turn, he shuffled a sort of jig. The two went over the sand in loops, toe and heel; the donkey continued his quiet grazing, and the flames rose hot and yellow from the freight-wagon. And all the while the stately German hymn pealed among the rocks, and the Apaches crept down nearer the bowing, scraping men. The sun shone bright, and their bodies poured with sweat. Jones flung off his shirt; his damp matted hair was half in ridges and half glued to his forehead, and the delicate gold chain swung and struck against his broad naked breast. The Apaches drew nearer again, their bows and arrows held uncertainly. They came down the hill, fifteen or twenty, taking a long time, and stopping every few yards. The milk-cans clashed, and Jones thought he felt the boy's strokes weakening. "Die Wacht am Rhein" was finished, and now it was "Ha-ve you seen my Flora pass this way?" "Yu' mustn't play out, kid," said Jones, very gently. "Indeed yu' mustn't;" and he at once resumed his song. The silent Apaches had now reached the bottom of the hill. They stood some twenty yards away, and Cumnor had a good chance to see his first Indians. He saw them move,

and the color and slim shape of their bodies, their thin arms, and their long black hair. It went through his mind that if he had no more clothes on than that, dancing would come easier. His boots were growing heavy to lift, and his overalls seemed to wrap his sinews in wet strangling thongs. He wondered how long he had been keeping this up. The legs of the Apaches were free, with light moccasins only half-way to the thigh, slenderly held up by strings from the waist. Cumnor envied their unencumbered steps as he saw them again walk nearer to where he was dancing. It was long since he had eaten, and he noticed a singing dulness in his brain, and became frightened at his thoughts, which were running and melting into one fixed idea. This idea was to take off his boots, and offer to trade them for a pair of moccasins. It terrified him—this endless molten rush of thoughts; he could see them coming in different shapes from different places in his head, but they all joined immediately, and always formed the same fixed idea. He ground his teeth to master this encroaching inebriation of his will and judgment. He clashed his can more loudly to wake him to reality, which he still could recognize and appreciate. For a time he found it a good plan

SPECIMEN JONES.

flesh. "That's good," he said, aloud. The pebble was eating the numbness away, and Cumnor drove it hard against the raw spot, and relished the tonic of its burning friction. The Apaches had drawn into a circle. Standing at some interval apart, they entirely surrounded the arena. Shrewd, half convinced, and yet with awe, they watched the dancers, who clashed their cans slowly now in rhythm to Jones's hoarse, parched singing. He was quite master of himself, and led the jig round the still blazing wreck of the wagon, and circled in figures of eight between the corpses of the Mexicans, clashing the milk-cans above each one. Then, knowing his strength was coming to an end, he approached an Indian whose war-bonnet and feathers denoted him of consequence; and Jones was near shouting with relief when the Indian shrank backward. Suddenly he saw Cumnor let his can drop, and without stopping to see why, he caught it up, and slowly rattling both, approached each Indian in turn with tortuous steps. The circle that had never uttered a sound till now receded, chanting almost in a whisper some exorcising song which the man with the feathers had begun. They gathered round him, retreating always, and the strain, with its rapid muttered words, rose and fell softly among them. Jones had supposed the boy was overcome by faintness, and looked to see where he lay. But it was not faintness. Cumnor, with his boots off, came by and walked after the Indians in a trance. They saw him, and quickened their pace, often turning to be sure he was not overtaking them. He called to them unintelligibly, stumbling up the sharp hill, and pointing to the boots. Finally he sat down. They continued ascending the mountain, herding close round the man with the feathers, until the rocks and the filmy tangles screened them from sight; and like a wind that hums uncertainly in grass, their chanting died away.

The sun was half behind the western range when Jones next moved. He called, and getting no answer, he crawled painfully to where the boy lay on the hill. Cumnor was sleeping heavily; his head was hot, and he moaned. So Jones crawled down, and fetched blankets and the canteen of water. He spread the blankets over the boy, wet a handkerchief and laid it on his forehead; then he lay down himself. The earth was again magi-

to listen to what Specimen Jones was singing, and tell himself the name of the song, if he knew it. At present it was "Yankee Doodle," to which Jones was fitting words of his own. These ran, "Now I'm going to try a bluff, And mind you do what I do"; and then again, over and over. Cumnor waited for the word "bluff"; for it was hard and heavy, and fell into his thoughts, and stopped them for a moment. The dance was so long now, he had forgotten about that. A numbness had been spreading through his legs, and he was glad to feel a sharp pain in the sole of his foot. It was a piece of gravel that had somehow worked its way in, and was rubbing through the skin into the

THE MEXICAN FREIGHT-WAGON.

cally smitten to crystal. Again the sharp cactus and the sand turned beautiful, and violet floated among the mountains, and rose - colored orange in the sky above them.

"Jock," said Specimen at length.

The boy opened his eyes.

"Your foot is awful, Jock. Can yu' eat?"

"Not with my foot."

"Ah, God bless yu', Jock ! Yu' ain't turrible sick. But *can* yu' eat?"

Cumnor shook his head.

"Eatin's what yu' need, though. Well, here." Specimen poured a judicious mixture of whiskey and water down the boy's throat, and wrapped the awful foot in his own flannel shirt. "They'll fix yu'

over to Grant. It's maybe twelve miles through the cañon. It ain't a town any more than Carlos is, but the soldiers 'll be good to us. As soon as night comes you and me must somehow git out of this."

Somehow they did, Jones walking and leading his horse and the imperturbable little burro, and also holding Cumnor in the saddle. And when Cumnor was getting well in the military hospital at Grant, he listened to Jones recounting to all that chose to hear how useful a weapon an ice-cream freezer can be, and how if you'll only chase Apaches in your stocking feet they are sure to run away. And then Jones and Cumnor both enlisted; and I suppose Jones's friend is still expecting him in Tucson.

33

The Game and the Nation

OWEN WISTER

THE GAME AND THE NATION

BY OWEN WISTER

I.

ALL America is divided into two classes—the Quality and the Equality. The latter will always recognize the former when mistaken for it. Both will be with us until our women bear nothing but kings. This is a story about both, and it begins in Colonel Cyrus Jones's Eating Palace, where I came upon the Virginian one morning.

Did you know the Palace? It stood in Omaha near the trains, and it was ten years old (which is middle-aged in Omaha) when I first saw it. It was a shell of wood, painted with golden emblems—the steamboat, the eagle, the Yosemite—and a live bear ate gratuities at its entrance. Weather permitting, it opened upon the world as a stage upon the audience. You sat in Omaha's whole sight and dined, while Omaha's dust came and settled upon the refreshments. It is gone the way of the Indian and the buffalo, for the West is growing old. You should have seen the Palace, and sat there. In front of you passed rainbows of men— Chinese, Indian chiefs, Africans, General Miles, younger sons, Austrian nobility, wide females in pink. Our continent

drained prismatically through Omaha once. So I was passing that way also, walking, for the sake of ventilation, from a sleeping-car toward a bath, when the language of Colonel Cyrus Jones came out to me. The actual Colonel I had never seen before. He stood at the rear of his Palace in gray flowery mustaches and a Confederate uniform, telling the wishes of his guests to the cook through a hole. You always bought meal-tickets at once, else you became unwelcome. Guests here had foibles at times, and a rapid exit was too easy. Therefore I bought a ticket. It was a spring and summer since I had· heard anything like the Colonel. The Missouri had not yet flowed into New York dialect freely, and his vocabulary met me like the breeze of the plains. So I went in to be fanned by it, and there sat the Virginian at a table, alone. Now this unexpected cow-puncher belonged a thousand miles beyond Omaha. I was looking to ride with him before long among the clean hills of Wyoming. His greeting was up to the code of indifference proper on the plains; but he presently remarked, "I'm right glad to see somebody," which was a good

415

deal to say. "Them that comes hyeh," he observed next, "don't eat. They feed." And he considered the guests with a sombre attention. "D'yu' reckon they find joyful di-gestion in this swallo'-an'-get-out trough?"

"What are you doing here, then?" said I.

"Oh, pshaw! When yu' can't have what yu' choose, yu' just choose what yu' have." And he took the bill of fare. I began to know that he had something on his mind, so I did not trouble him further.

Meanwhile he sat studying the bill of fare.

"Ever heard o' them?" he inquired, shoving me the spotted document.

Most improbable dishes were there —salmis, canapés, suprêmes—perfectly spelt and absolutely transparent. It was the old trick of copying some metropolitan menu to catch travellers of the third and last dimension of innocence; and whenever this is done the food is of the third and last dimension of awfulness, which the cow-puncher knew as well as anybody.

"So they keep that up here still," I said.

"But what about them?" he repeated. His finger was at a special item, *Frogs' legs à la Delmonico*. "Are they true anywheres?" he asked. And I told him, certainly. I also explained to him about Delmonico.

"There's not a little bit o' use in lyin' to me this mawning," he said, with his engaging smile. "I ain' goin' to awdeh anything's laigs."

"Well, I'll see how he gets out of it," said I, remembering the old Texas legend. (The traveller read the bill of fare, you know, and called for a *vol-au-vent*. And the proprietor looked at the traveller, and running a pistol into his ear, observed, "You'll take hash.") I was thinking of this, and wondering what would happen to me. So I took the step.

"Wants frogs' legs, does he?" said Colonel Cyrus Jones. He fixed his eye upon me, and it narrowed to a slit. "Too many brain-workers breakfasting before yu' come in, professor," said he. "Missionary ate the last leg off me just now. Brown the wheat!" he commanded through the hole to the cook, for some one had ordered hot cakes.

"I'll have fried aiggs," said the Virginian. "Cooked both sides."

"White wings!" sang the Colonel through the hole. "Let 'em fly up and down."

"Coffee an' no milk," said the Virginian.

"Draw one in the dark!" the Colonel roared.

"And beefsteak, rare."

"One slaughter in the pan, and let the blood drip!"

"I should like a glass of water, please," said I.

The Colonel threw me a look of pity. "One Missouri and ice for the professor!" he said.

"That fello's a right live man," commented the Virginian. But he seemed thoughtful. Presently he inquired. "Yu' say he was a foreigner, an' learned fancy cookin' to New York?"

That was this cow-puncher's way. Scarcely ever would he let drop a thing new to him until he had got from you your whole information about it. So I told him the history of· Augustine of Philadelphia, and of Lorenzo Delmonico and his pioneer work, as much as I knew, and the Southerner listened intently.

"Mighty inter-estin'," he said — "mighty. He could just take little old or'n'ry frawgs, an' dandy 'em up to suit the bloods. Mighty inter-estin'. I expaict, though, his cookin' would give an out-raiged stomach to a plain-raised man."

"If you want to follow it up," said I, by way of sudden experiment, "Miss Molly Wood might have some book about French dishes." I knew the Bear Creek schoolmarm lent him books.

But the Virginian did not turn a hair. "I reckon she wouldn't," he answered. "She was raised in Vermont. They don't bother overly about their eatin' up in Vermont." If you have a heart secret, speaking the precise truth does about as well as the Sphinx. "Hyeh's what Miss Wood recommended las' time I was seein' her," the cow-puncher added, bringing *Kenilworth* from his pocket. "Right fine story. That Queen Elizabeth must have cert'nly been a competent woman."

"She was," said I. But talk came to an end here. A dusty crew, most evidently from the plains, now entered and drifted to a table; and each man of them gave the Virginian about a quarter of a slouchy nod. His greeting to them was very serene. Only, *Kenilworth* went back into his pocket, and he breakfasted in silence. Presently we went together to the railway-yard.

"The Judge is doing a right smart o' business this year," he began, very casually indeed; so that I knew this was important. Besides bells and coal smoke, the smell and crowded sounds of cattle rose in the air around us. "Hyeh's our first gather o' beeves on the ranch," continued the Virginian. "The whole lot's shipped through to Chicago in two sections over the Burlington. The Judge is fighting the Elkhorn road." We passed slowly along the two trains—twenty cars, each car packed with huddled, round-eyed, gazing steers. He examined to see if any animals were down. "They 'ain't ate or drank anything to speak of," he said, while the terrified brutes stared at us through their slats. "Not since they struck the railroad they've not drank. Yu' might suppose they know somehow what they're travellin' to Chicago for." And casually, always casually, he told me the rest. Judge Henry could not spare his foreman away from the second gather of beeves. Therefore these two ten-car trains with their double crew of cowboys had been given to the Virginian's charge. After Chicago, he was to return with the men by St. Paul over the Northern Pacific; for the Judge had wished him to see the authorities in St. Paul, and explain to them how good a thing it would be for them to allow especially cheap rates to the Sunk Creek outfit henceforth. This was all the Virginian told me; and it contained the whole matter, to be sure.

"So you're acting foreman," said I.

"Why, somebody has to have the say, I reckon."

"And of course you hated the promotion."

"I don't know about promotion," he replied. "The boys have been used to seein' me one of themselves. Why don't yu' come along with us far as Plattsmouth?" Thus he shifted the subject from himself, and called to my notice the locomotives backing up to his cars, and reminded me that from Plattsmouth I had the choice of two trains returning. But he could not hide or belittle this confidence of his employer in him. It was the care of several thousand perishable dollars, and the control of men. It was a compliment. There were more steers than men to be responsible for; but none

of the steers had been suddenly picked from the herd and set above his fellows. Moreover, Chicago finished up the steers; but the new-made deputy-foreman had then to lead his six highly unoccupied brethren away from towns, and back in peace to the ranch—or disappoint the Judge, who needed their services. These things sometimes go wrong in a land where you are all born free and equal; and that quarter of a nod in Colonel Cyrus Jones's Eating Palace held more equality than any whole nod you could see. But the Virginian did not see it, there being a time for all things.

We trundled down the flopping, heavy-eddied Missouri to Plattsmouth, and there they backed us aside—the Christian Endeavor being expected to pass that way. And while the equality absorbed themselves in a deep but harmless game of poker by the side of the railway line, the Virginian and I sat on the top of a car contemplating the sandy shallows of the Platte.

"I should think you'd take a hand," said I.

"Poker? With them kittens?" One flash of the inner man lightened in his eyes and died away; and he finished in his gentle drawl, "When I play I want it to be interestin'." He took out Sir Walter's *Kenilworth* once more, and turned the volume over and over slowly, without opening it. You cannot tell if in spirit he wandered on Bear Creek with the girl whose book it was. The spirit will go one road, and the thought another, and the body its own way sometimes. "Queen Elizabeth would have played a mighty pow'ful game," was his next remark.

"Poker?" said I.

"Yes, seh. Do you expaict Europe has got any queen equal to her at present?"

I doubted it.

"Victoria 'd get pretty nigh slain sliding chips out agaynst Elizabeth. Only mos' prob'ly Victoria she'd insist on a half-cent limit. You have read this hyeh *Kenilworth*? Well, deal Elizabeth ace high, an' she could scare Robert Dudley and a full house plumb out o' the bettin'."

I said that I believed she unquestionably could.

"And," said the Virginian, "if Essex's play got next her too near, I reckon she'd

"POKER? WITH THEM KITTENS?"

have stacked the cyards. Say, Shakspere
—he wrote about that fat man?"

"Falstaff? He did."

"I saw that in San Francisco las' time.
I've saw that in Denver, Chicago, Saynt
Paul—I always go to see that. It's a
right down shame Shakspere couldn't
know about poker. He'd have had Falstaff playing all day at that Tearsheet
outfit. And the Prince would have beat
him."

"The Prince had the brains," said I.

"Brains?"

"Well, didn't he?"

"I neveh thought to notice. Like as
not he did."

"And Falstaff didn't, I suppose?"

"Oh, yes, seh! Falstaff could have
played whist."

"I suppose you know what you're talking about. I don't," said I. For he was
drawling again.

The cow-puncher's eye rested a moment
amiably upon me. "You can play whist
with your brains," he mused. "Brains
and cyards. Now cyards are only one o'
the manifestations of poker in this hyeh
world. One o' the shapes yu' fool with
it in when the day's work is oveh. If a
man is built like that Prince boy was built
(an' it's away down deep beyond brains),
he'll play winnin' poker with whatever
hand he's holdin' when the trouble begins. Maybe it will be a mean, triflin'

army, or an empty six-shooter, or a lame hawss, or maybe just nothing but his natural countenance. 'Most any old thing will do for a fellow like that Prince boy to play poker with."

"Then I'd be grateful for your definition of poker," said I.

Again the Virginian looked me over amiably. "You put up a mighty pretty game o' whist yourself," he remarked. "Don't that give yu' the contented spirit?" And before I had any reply to this, the Christian Endeavor began to come over the bridge. Three instalments crossed the Missouri from Pacific Junction, bound for Pikes Peak, every car in bright bunting, and at each window a Christian with a handkerchief, joyously shrieking. Then the cattle trains got the open signal, and I jumped off.

"Tell the Judge the steers was all right this far," said the Virginian.

That was the last of the deputy-foreman for a while.

II.

My road to Sunk Creek lay in no straight line. By rail I diverged northwest to Fort Meade, and thence, after some stay with the kind military people, I made my way on a horse. Up here in the Black Hills it sluiced rain most intolerably. The horse and I enjoyed the country and ourselves but little; and when finally I changed from the saddle into a stage-coach, I caught a thankful expression upon the animal's face, and returned the same.

"Six legs inside this jerky to-night?" said somebody, as I climbed the wheel. "Well, we'll give thanks for not havin' eight," he added, cheerfully. "Clamp your mind on to that, Shorty." And he slapped the shoulder of his neighbor. Naturally I took these two for old companions. But we were all total strangers. They told me of the new gold excitement at Rawhide, and supposed it would bring up the Northern Pacific; and when I explained the millions owed to this road's German bondholders, they were of opinion that a German would strike it richer at Rawhide. We spoke of all sorts of things, and in our silence I gloated on the autumn holiday promised me by Judge Henry. His last letter had said that an outfit would be starting for his ranch from Billings on the seventh, and he would have a horse for me.

This was the fifth. So we six legs in the jerky travelled harmoniously on over the rain-gutted road, getting no deeper knowledge of each other than what our outsides might imply.

Not that we concealed anything. The man who had slapped Shorty introduced himself early. "Scipio Le Moyne, from Gallipolice, Ohio," he said. "The eldest of us always gets called Scipio. It's French. But us folks have been white for a hundred years." He was limber and light-muscled, and fell skilfully about, evading bruises when the jerky reeled or rose on end. He had a strange long jocular nose, very wary-looking, and a bleached blue eye. Cattle was his business, as a rule, but of late he had been "looking around some," and Rawhide seemed much on his brain. Shorty struck me as "looking around" also. He was quite short, indeed, and the jerky hurt him almost every time. He was light-haired and mild. Think of a yellow dog that is lost, and fancies each new-comer in sight is going to turn out his master, and you will have Shorty.

It was the Northern Pacific that surprised us into intimacy. We were nearing Medora. We had made a last arrangement of our legs. I lay stretched in silence, placid in the knowledge it was soon to end. So I drowsed. I felt something sudden, and waking, saw Scipio passing through the air. As Shorty next shot from the jerky I beheld smoke and the locomotive. The Northern Pacific had changed its schedule. A valise is a poor companion for catching a train with. There were rutted sand and lumpy, knee-high grease-wood in our short-cut. A piece of stray wire sprang from some hole and hung caracoling about my ankle. Tin cans spun from my stride. But we made a conspicuous race. Two of us waved hats, and there was no moment that some one of us was not screeching. It meant twenty-four hours to us.

Perhaps we failed to catch the train's attention, though the theory seems monstrous. As it moved off in our faces, smooth and easy and insulting, Scipio dropped instantly to a walk, and we two others outstripped him and came desperately to the empty track. There went the train. Even still its puffs were the separated puffs of starting, that bitten-off, snorty kind, and sweat and our true natures broke freely forth.

I kicked my valise, and then sat on it, dumb.

Shorty yielded himself up aloud. All his humble secrets came out of him. He walked aimlessly round, lamenting. He had lost his job, and he mentioned the ranch. He had played cards, and he mentioned the man. He had sold his horse and saddle to catch a friend on this train, and he mentioned what the friend had been going to do for him. He told a string of griefs and names to the air, as if the air knew.

Meanwhile Scipio arrived with extreme leisure at the rails. He stuck his hands into his pockets and his head out at the very small train. His bleached blue eyes shut to slits as he watched the rear car in its smoke blur ooze away westward among the mounded bluffs. "Lucky it's out of range," I thought. But now Scipio spoke to it.

"Why, you seem to think you've left me behind," he began, easily, in fawning tones. "You're too much of a kid to have such thoughts. Age some." His next remark grew less wheedling. "I wouldn't be a bit proud to meet yu'. Why, if I was seen travellin' with yu', I'd have to explain it to my friends! Think yu've got me left, do yu'? Just because yu' ride through this country on a rail, do yu' claim yu' can find your way around? I could take yu' out ten yards in the brush and lose yu' in ten seconds, you spangle-roofed hobo! Leave *me* behind! you recent blanket-mortgage yearlin'? You plush-lined, nickel-plated, whistlin' wash-room, d'yu' figure I can't go east just as soon as west? Or I'll stay right here if it suits me, yu' dude-inhabited hot-box. Why, yu' coon-bossed face-towel—" But from here he rose in flights of novelty that appalled and held me spellbound, and which are not for me to say to you. Then he came down easily again, and finished with expressions of sympathy for it because it could never have known a mother.

"Do you expaict it could show a male parent off-hand?" inquired a slow voice behind us. I jumped round, and there was the Virginian.

"Male parent!" scoffed the prompt Scipio. "'Ain't you heard about *them* yet?"

"Them? Was there two?"

"Two? The blamed thing was sired by a whole doggone Dutch syndicate."

"Why, the piebald son of a gun!" responded the Virginian, sweetly. "I got them steers through all right," he added, to me. "Sorry to see yu' get so out o' breath afteh the train. Is your valise sufferin' any?"

"Who's he?" inquired Scipio, curiously, turning to me.

The Southerner sat with a newspaper on the rear platform of a caboose. The caboose stood hitched behind a mile or so of freight-train, and the train was headed west. So here was the deputy-foreman, his steers delivered in Chicago, his men (I could hear them) safe in the caboose, his paper in his lap, and his legs dangling at ease over the railing. He wore the look of a man for whom things are going smooth. And for me the way to Billings was smooth now, also.

"Who's he?" Scipio repeated.

But from inside the caboose loud laughter and noise broke on us. Some one was reciting "And it's my night to howl."

"We'll all howl when we get to Rawhide," said some other one; and they howled now.

"These hyeh steam-cyars," said the Virginian to Scipio, "make a man's language mighty nigh as speedy as his travel." Of Shorty he took no notice whatever—no more than of the manifestations in the caboose.

"So yu' heard me speakin' to the express," said Scipio. "Well, I guess, sometimes I— See here," he exclaimed, for the Virginian was gravely considering him, "I may have talked some, but I walked a whole lot. You didn't catch *me* squandering no speed. Soon as—"

"I noticed," said the Virginian. "Thinkin' came quicker to yu' than runnin'."

I was glad I was not Shorty, to have my measure taken merely by my way of missing a train. And of course I was sorry that I had kicked my valise.

"Oh, I could tell yu'd been enjoying us!" said Scipio. "Observin' somebody else's scrape always kind o' rests me too. Maybe you're a philosopher, but maybe there's a pair of us drawd in this deal."

Approval now grew plain upon the face of the Virginian. "By your laigs," said he, "you are used to the saddle."

"I'd be called used to it, I expect."

"By your hands," said the Southerner, again, "you 'ain't roped many steers lately. Been cookin' or something?"

"Say," retorted Scipio, "tell my future

"HAVE YOUR BOTTLE, THEN."

some now. Draw a conclusion from my mouth."

"I'm right distressed," answered the gentle Southerner. "We've not a drop in the outfit."

"Oh, drink with me uptown !" cried Scipio. "I'm pleased to death with yu'."

The Virginian glanced where the saloons stood just behind the station, and shook his head.

"Why, it ain't a bit far to whiskey from here !" urged the other, plaintively. "Step down, now. Scipio Le Moyne's my name. Yes, you're lookin' for my brass ear-rings. But there ain't no ear-rings on me. I've been white for a hundred years. Step down. I've a forty-dollar thirst."

"You're certainly white," began the Virginian. "But—"

Here the caboose resumed:

"I'm wild, and woolly, and full of fleas;
I'm hard to curry above the knees;
I'm a she-wolf from Bitter Creek, and
   It's my night to ho-o-wl—"

And as they howled and stamped, the wheels of the caboose began to turn gently and to murmur.

The Virginian rose suddenly. "Will yu' save that thirst and take a forty-dollar job?"

"Missin' trains, profanity, or what?" said Scipio.

"I'll tell yu' soon as I'm sure."

At this Scipio looked hard at the Virginian. "Why, you're talking business!" said he, and leaped on the caboose, where I was already. "I *was* thinkin' of Rawhide," he added, "but I ain't any more."

"Well, good luck!" said Shorty, on the track behind us.

"Oh, say!" said Scipio. "He wanted to go on that train, just like me."

"Get on," called the Virginian. "But as to getting a job, he ain't just like you." So Shorty came.

Our wheels clucked over the main-line switch. A train-hand threw it shut after us, jumped aboard, and returned forward over the roofs. Inside the caboose they had reached the third howling of the she-wolf.

"Friends of yourn?" said Scipio.

"My outfit," drawled the Virginian.

"Do yu' always travel outside?" inquired Scipio.

"It's lonesome in there," returned the deputy-foreman. And here one of them came out, slamming the door.

"Hell!" he said at sight of the distant town. Then, truculently, to the Virginian, "I told you I was going to get a bottle here."

"Have your bottle, then," said the deputy-foreman, and kicked him off into Dakota. (It was not North Dakota yet; they had not divided it.) The Virginian had aimed his pistol at about the same time with his boot. Therefore the man sat in Dakota quietly, watching us go away into Montana, and offering no objections. Just before he became too small to make out, we saw him rise and remove himself back toward the saloons.

III.

"That is the only step I have had to take this whole trip," said the Virginian. He holstered his pistol with a jerk. "I have been fearing he would force it on me." And he looked at empty, receding Dakota with disgust. "So nyeh back home!" he muttered.

"Known your friend long?" whispered Scipio to me.

"Fairly," I answered.

Scipio's bleached eyes brightened with admiration as he considered the Southerner's back. "Well," he stated, judicially, "start awful early when yu' go to fool with him, or he'll make you feel onpunctual."

"I expaict I've had them almost all of three thousand miles," said the Virginian, tilting his head toward the noise in the caboose. "And I've strove to deliver them back as I received them. The whole lot. And I would have. But he has spoiled my hopes." The deputy-foreman looked again at Dakota. "It's a disappointment," he added. "You may know what I mean."

I had known a little, but not to the very deep, of the man's pride and purpose in this trust. Scipio gave him sympathy. "There must be quite a balance of 'em left with yu' yet," said Scipio, cheeringly.

"I had the boys plumb contented," pursued the deputy-foreman, hurt into open talk of himself. "Away along as far as Saynt Paul I had them reconciled to my authority. Then this news about gold had to strike us."

"And they're a-dreamin' nuggets and Parisian bowleyvards," suggested Scipio.

The Virginian smiled gratefully at him. "Fortune is shining bright and blindin' to their delicate young eyes," he said, regaining his usual self.

We all listened a moment to the rejoicings within.

"Energetic, ain't they?" said the Southerner. "But none of 'em was whelped savage enough to sing himself bloodthirsty. And though they're straining mighty earnest not to be tame, they're going back to Sunk Creek with me according to the Judge's awdehs. Never a calf of them will desert to Rawhide, for all their dangerousness; nor I ain' goin' to have any fuss over it. Only one is left now that don't sing. Maybe I will have to make some arrangements about him. The man I have parted with," he said, with another glance at Dakota, "was our cook, and I will ask yu' to replace him, Colonel."

Scipio gaped wide. "Colonel! Say!" He stared at the Virginian. "Did I meet yu' at the Palace?"

"Not exackly meet," replied the Southerner. "I was praisent one mawnin' las' month when this gentleman awdehed frawgs' laigs."

"Sakes and saints but that was a mean position!" burst out Scipio. "I had to tell all comers anything all day. Stand up and jump language hot off my brain at 'em. And the pay don't near compensate for the drain on the system. I don't care how good a man is, you let him keep a-tapping his presence of mind right along, without takin' a lay-off, and you'll have him sick. Yes, sir. You'll hit his nerves. So I told them they could hire some fresh man, for I was going back to punch cattle or fight Indians, or take a rest somehow, for I didn't propose to get jaded, and me only twenty-five years old. There ain't no regular Colonel Cyrus Jones any more, yu' know. He met a Cheyenne telegraph pole in seventy-four, and was buried. But his Palace was doin' big business, and he had been a kind of attraction, and so they always keep a live bear outside, and some poor fello', fixed up like the Colonel used to be, inside. And it's a turruble mean position. Course I'll cook for yu'. Yo've a dandy memory for faces!"

"I wasn't right convinced till I kicked him off and you gave that shut to your eyes again," said the Virginian.

Once more the door opened. A man with slim black eyebrows, slim black mustache, and a black shirt tied with a white handkerchief was looking steadily from one to the other of us.

"Good-day!" he remarked, generally, and without enthusiasm; and to the Virginian, "Where's Schoffner?"

"I expaict he'll have got his bottle by now, Trampas."

Trampas looked from one to the other of us again. "Didn't he say he was coming back?"

"He reminded me he was going for a bottle, and afteh that he didn't wait to say a thing."

Trampas looked at the platform and the railing and the steps. "He told me he was coming back," he insisted.

"I don't reckon he has come, not without he clumb up ahaid somewhere. An' I mus' say, when he got off he didn't look like a man does when he has the intention o' returnin'."

At this Scipio coughed, and pared his nails attentively. We had already been avoiding each other's eye. Shorty did not count. Since he got aboard, his meek seat had been the bottom step.

The thoughts of Trampas seemed to be in difficulty. "How long's this train been started?" he demanded.

"This hyeh train?" The Virginian consulted his watch. "Why, it's been fanning it a right smart little while," said he, laying no stress upon his indolent syllables.

"Huh!" went Trampas. He gave the rest of us a final unlovely scrutiny. "It seems to have become a passenger-train," he said. And he returned abruptly inside the caboose.

"Is he the member who don't sing?" asked Scipio.

"That's the specimen," replied the Southerner.

"He don't seem musical in the face," said Scipio.

"Pshaw!" returned the Virginian. "Why, you surely ain't the man to mind ugly mugs when they're hollow!"

The noise inside had dropped quickly to stillness. You could scarcely catch the sound of talk. Our caboose was clicking comfortably westward, rail after rail, mile upon mile, while night was beginning to rise from earth into the clouded sky.

"I wonder if they have sent a search party forward to hunt Shoffner?" said the Virginian. "I think I'll maybe join their meeting." He opened the door upon them. "Kind o' dark hyeh, ain't it?" said he. And lighting the lantern, he shut us out.

"What do yu' think?" said Scipio to me. "Will he take them to Sunk Creek?"

"He evidently thinks he will," said I. "He says he will, and he has the courage of his convictions."

"That ain't near enough courage to have!" Scipio exclaimed. "There's times in life when a man has got to have courage *without* convictions—without them —or he is no good. Now your friend is that deep constitooted that you don't know and I don't know what he's thinkin' about all this."

"If there's to be any gun-play," put in the excellent Shorty, "I'll stand in with him."

"Ah, go to bed with your gun-play!" retorted Scipio, entirely good-humored. "Is the Judge paying for a car-load of dead punchers to gather his beef for him? And this ain't a proposition worth a man's gettin' hurt for himself, anyway."

"That's so," Shorty assented.

"No," speculated Scipio, as the night drew deeper round us and the caboose click-clucked and click-clucked over the rail joints; "he's waitin' for somebody else to open this pot. I'll bet he don't know but one thing now, and that's that nobody else shall know he don't know anything."

Scipio had delivered himself. He lighted a cigarette, and no more wisdom came from him. The night was established. The rolling bad-lands sank away in it. A train-hand had arrived over the roof, and hanging the red lights out behind, left us again without remark or symptom of curiosity. The train-hands seemed interested in their own society and lived in their own caboose. A chill wind with wet in it came blowing from the invisible draws, and brought the feel of the distant mountains.

"That's Montana!" said Scipio, snuffing. "I am glad to have it inside my lungs again."

"Ain't yu' getting cool out there?" said the Virginian's voice. "Plenty room inside."

Perhaps he had expected us to follow him; or perhaps he had meant us to delay long enough not to seem like a re-enforcement. "These gentlemen missed the express at Medora," he observed to his men, simply.

What they took us for upon our entrance I cannot say, or what they believed. The atmosphere of the caboose was charged with voiceless currents of thought. By way of a friendly beginning to the three hundred miles of caboose we were now to share so intimately, I recalled myself to them. I trusted no more of the Christian Endeavor had delayed them. "I am so lucky to have caught you again," I finished. "I was afraid my last chance of reaching the Judge's had gone."

Thus I said a number of things designed to be agreeable, but they met my small-talk with the smallest talk you can

have. "Yes," for instance, and "Pretty well, I guess," and grave strikings of matches and thoughtful looks at the floor. I suppose we had made twenty miles to the imperturbable clicking of the caboose when one at length asked his neighbor had he ever seen New York.

"No," said the other. "Flooded with dudes, ain't it?"

"Swimmin'," said the first.

"Leakin', too," said a third.

"Well, my gracious!" said a fourth, and beat his knee in private delight. None of them ever looked at me. For some reason I felt exceedingly ill at ease.

"Good clothes in New York," said the third.

"Rich food," said the first.

"Fresh eggs, too," said the third.

"Well, my gracious!" said the fourth, beating his knee.

"Why, yes," observed the Virginian, unexpectedly; "they tell me that aiggs there ain't liable to be so rotten as yu'll strike 'em in this country."

None of them had a reply for this, and New York was abandoned. For some reason I felt much better.

It was a new line they adopted next, led off by Trampas.

"Going to the excitement?" he inquired, selecting Shorty.

"Excitement?" said Shorty, looking up.

"Going to Rawhide?" Trampas repeated. And all watched Shorty.

"Why, I'm all adrift missin' that express," said Shorty.

"Maybe I can give you employment," suggested the Virginian. "I am taking an outfit across the basin."

"You'll find most folks going to Rawhide, if you're looking for company," pursued Trampas, fishing for a recruit.

"How about Rawhide, anyway?" said Scipio, skilfully deflecting this missionary work. "Are they taking much mineral out? Have yu' seen any of the rock?"

"Rock?" broke in the enthusiast who had beaten his knee. "There!" And he brought some from his pocket.

"You're always showing your rock," said Trampas, sulkily; for Scipio now held the conversation, and Shorty returned safely to his dozing.

"Hm!" went Scipio at the rock. He turned it back and forth in his hand,

" 'AFRAID!' HE SNEERED."

looking it over; he chucked and caught it slightingly in the air, and handed it back. "Porphyry, I see." That was his only word about it. He said it cheerily. He left no room for discussion. You could not damn a thing worse. "Ever been in Santa Rita?" pursued Scipio, while the enthusiast slowly pushed his rock back into his pocket. "That's down in New Mexico. Ever been to Globe, Arizona?" And Scipio talked away about the mines he had known. There was no getting at Shorty any more that evening. Trampas was foiled of his fish, or of learning how the fish's heart lay. And by morning Shorty had been carefully instructed to change his mind about once an hour. This is apt to discourage all

but very superior missionaries. And I too escaped for the rest of this night. At Glendive we had a dim supper, and I bought some blankets; and after that it was late, and sleep occupied the attention of us all.

We lay along the shelves of the caboose, a peaceful sight I should think, in that smoothly trundling cradle. I slept almost immediately, so tired that not even our stops or anything else waked me, save once, when the air I was breathing grew suddenly pure, and I roused. Sitting in the door was the lonely figure of the Virginian. He leaned in silent contemplation of the occasional moon, and beneath it the Yellowstone's swift ripples. On the caboose shelves the others slept sound and still, each stretched or coiled as he had first put himself. They were not untrustworthy to look at, it seemed to me—except Trampas. You would have said the rest of that young humanity was average rough male blood, merely needing to be told the proper things at the right time; and one big bunchy stocking of the enthusiast stuck out of his blanket, solemn and innocent, and I laughed at it. There was a light sound by the door, and I found the Virginian's eye on me. Finding who it was, he nodded and motioned with his hand to go to sleep. And this I did with him in my sight, still leaning in the open door, through which came the interrupted moon and the swimming reaches of the Yellowstone.

It has happened to you, has it not, to wake in the morning and wonder for a while where on earth you are? Thus I came half to life in the caboose, hearing voices, but not the actual words at first.

But presently, "Hathaway!" said some one more clearly. "Portland 1291."

This made no special stir in my intelligence, and I drowsed off again to the pleasant rhythm of the wheels. The little shock of stopping next brought me to, somewhat, with the voices still round me; and when we were again in motion, I heard: "Rosebud. Portland 1279." These figures jarred me awake, and I said, "It was 1291 before," and sat up in my blankets.

The greeting they vouchsafed and the sight of them clustering expressionless in the caboose brought last evening's uncomfortable memory back to me. Our next stop revealed how things were going to-day.

"Forsythe," one of them read on the station. "Portland 1266."

They were counting the lessening distance westward. That was the undercurrent of war. It broke on me as I procured fresh water at Forsythe and made some toilet in their stolid presence. We were drawing nearer the Rawhide station—the point, I mean, where you left the railway for the new mines. Now Rawhide station lay this side of Billings. The broad path of desertion would open ready for their feet when the narrow path to duty and Sunk Creek was still some fifty miles more to wait. Here was Trampas's great strength; he need make no move meanwhile, but lie low for the immediate temptation to front and way-

lay them and win his battle over the deputy-foreman. But the Virginian seemed to find nothing save enjoyment in this sunny September morning, and ate his breakfast at Forsythe serenely.

That meal done and that station gone, our caboose took up again its easy trundle by the banks of the Yellowstone. The mutineers sat for a while digesting in idleness.

"What's your scar?" inquired one at length, inspecting casually the neck of his neighbor.

"Foolishness," the other answered.

"Yourn?"

"Mine."

"Well, I don't know but I prefer to have myself to thank for a thing," said the first.

"I was displaying myself," continued the second. "One day last summer it was. We come on a big snake by Torrey Creek corral. The boys got betting pretty lively that I dassent make my word good as to dealing with him, so I loped my cayuse full tilt by Mr. Snake, and swung down and catched him up by the tail from the ground, and cracked him same as a whip, and snapped his head off. You've saw it done?" he said to the audience.

The audience nodded wearily.

"But the loose head flew agin me, and the fangs caught. I was pretty sick for a while."

"It don't pay to be clumsy," said the first man. "If you'd snapped the snake away from yu' instead of towards yu', its head would have whirled off into the brush, same as they do with me."

"How like a knife-cut your scar looks!" said I.

"Don't it?" said the snake-snapper. "There's many that gets fooled by it."

"An antelope knows a snake is his enemy," said another to me. "Ever seen a buck circling round and round a rattler?"

"I have always wanted to see that," said I, heartily. For this I knew to be a respectable piece of truth.

"It's worth seeing," the man went on. "After the buck gets close in, he gives an almighty jump up in the air, and down comes his four hoofs in a bunch right on top of Mr. Snake. Cuts him all to hash. Now you tell me how the buck knows that."

Of course I could not tell him. And

again we sat in silence for a while—friend-lier silence, I thought.

"A skunk 'll kill yu' worse than a snake-bite," said another, presently. "No, I don't mean that way," he added. For I had smiled. "There is a brown skunk down in Arkansaw. Kind of prairie-dog brown. Littler than our variety, he is. And he is mad the whole year round, same as a dog gets. Only the dog has a spell and dies; but this here Arkansaw skunk is mad right along, and it don't seem to interfere with his business in other respects. Well, suppose you're camping out, and suppose it's a hot night, or you're in a hurry and you've made camp late, or anyway you haven't got inside any tent, but you have just bedded down in the open. Skunk comes travel-ling along and walks on your blankets. You're warm. He likes that, same as a cat does. And he tramps with pleasure and comfort, same as a cat. And you move. You get bit, that's all. And you die of hydrophobia. Ask anybody."

"Most extraordinary!" said I. "But did you ever see a person die from this?"

"No, sir. Never happened to. My cousin at Bald Knob did."

"Died?"

"No, sir. Saw a man."

"But how do you know they're not sick skunks?"

"No, sir! They're well skunks. Well as anything. You'll not meet skunks in any State of the Union more robust than them in Arkansaw. And thick."

"That's awful true," sighed another. "I have buried hundreds of dollars' worth of clothes in Arkansaw."

"Why didn't yu' travel in a sponge-bag?" inquired Scipio. And this brought a slight silence.

"Speakin' of bites," spoke up a new man, "how's that?" He held up his thumb.

"My!" breathed Scipio. "Must have been a lion."

The man wore a wounded look. "I was huntin' owl eggs for a botanist from Boston," he explained to me.

"Chiropodist, weren't he?" said Scipio. "Or maybe a sonnabulator?"

"No, honest," protested the man with the thumb; so that I was sorry for him, and begged him to go on.

"I'll listen to you," I assured him. And I wondered why this politeness of mine should throw one or two of them

into stifled mirth. Scipio, on the other hand, gave me a disgusted look and sat back sullenly for a moment, and then took himself out on the platform, where the Virginian was lounging.

"The young feller wore knee-pants and ever so thick spectacles with a half-moon cut in 'em," resumed the narrator; "and he carried a tin box strung to a strap I took for his lunch till it flew open on him and a horn toad hustled out. Then I was sure he was a botanist—or whatever yu' say they're called. Well, he would have owl eggs—them little prairie-owl that some claim can turn their head clean around and keep a-watchin' yu', only that's nonsense. We was ridin' through that prairie-dog town used to be on the flat just after yu' crossed the south fork of Powder River on the Buffalo trail, and I said I'd dig an owl nest out for him if he was willin' to camp till I'd dug it. I wanted to know about them owls some myself—if they did live with the dogs and snakes, yu' know," he broke off, appealing to me.

"Oh, yes," I told him, eagerly.

"So while the botanist went glarin' around the town with his glasses to see if he could spot a prairie-dog and an owl usin' the same hole, I was diggin' in a hole I'd seen an owl run down. And that's what I got." He held up his thumb again.

"The snake!" I exclaimed.

"Yes, sir. Mr. Rattler was keepin' house that day. Took me right there. I hauled him out of the hole hangin' to me. Eight rattles."

"Eight!" said I. "A big one."

"Yes, sir. Thought I was dead. But the woman—"

"The woman?" said I.

"Yes, woman. Didn't I tell yu' the botanist had his wife along? Well, he did. And she acted better than the man, for he was losin' his head and shoutin' he had no whiskey and he didn't guess his knife was sharp enough to amputate my thumb and none of us chewed and the doctor was twenty miles away and if he had only remembered to bring his ammonia—well, he was screech-ing out 'most everything he knew in the world, and without arranging it any, neither. But she just clawed his pocket and burrowed and kep' yelling, 'Give him the stone, Augustus!' And she whipped out one of them Injun medi-cine-stones—first one I ever seen—and she clapped it on to my thumb, and it started in right away."

"What did it do?" said I.

"Sucked. Like blotting-paper does. Soft and funny it was, and gray. They get 'em from elks' stomachs, yu' know. And when it had sucked the poison out of the wound, off it falls of my thumb by itself! And I thanked the woman for saving my life that capable and keeping her head that cool. I never knowed how excited she had been till afterwards. She was awful shocked."

"I suppose she started to talk when the danger was over," said I, with deep silence around me.

"No; she didn't say nothing to me. But when her next child was born it had eight rattles."

Din now rose wild in the caboose. They rocked together. The enthusiast beat his knee tumultuously. And I joined them. Who could help it? It had been so well conducted from the imperceptible beginning. Fact and falsehood blended with such perfect art. And this last, an effect so new made with such world-old material! I cared nothing that I was the victim, and I joined them; but ceased, feeling suddenly somehow estranged or chilled. It was in their laughter. The loudness was too loud. And I caught the eyes of Trampas fixed upon the Virginian with exultant malevolence. Scipio's disgusted glance was upon me from the door.

Dazed by these signs, I went out on the platform to get away from the noise. There the Virginian said to me: "Cheer up! You'll not be so easy for 'em that-a-way next season."

He said no more; and with his legs dangled over the railing, appeared to resume his newspaper.

"What's the matter?" said I to Scipio.

"Oh, I don't mind if he don't," Scipio answered. "Couldn't yu' see? I tried to head 'em off from yu' all I knew, but yu' just ran in among 'em yourself. Couldn't yu' see? Kep' hinderin' and spoilin' me with askin' those urgent questions of yourn—why, I had to let yu' go your way! Why, that wasn't the ordinary play with the ordinary tenderfoot they treated you to! You ain't a common tenderfoot this trip. You're the foreman's friend. They've hit him through you. That's the way they count it. It's made them encouraged. Can't yu' see?"

Scipio stated it plainly. And as we ran by the next station, "Howard!" they harshly yelled. "Portland 1256!"

We had been passing gangs of workmen on the track. And at that last yell the Virginian rose. "I reckon I'll join the meeting again," he said. "This filling and repairing looks like the washout might have been true."

"Washout?" said Scipio.

"Big Horn bridge, they say, four days ago."

"Then I wish it came this side Rawhide station."

"Do yu'?" drawled the Virginian. And smiling at Scipio, he lounged in through the open door.

"He beats me," said Scipio, shaking his head. "His trail is turruble hard to anticipate."

We listened.

"Work bein' done on the road, I see," the Virginian was saying, very friendly and conversational.

"We see it too," said the voice of Trampas.

"Seem to be easin' their grades some."

"Roads do."

"Cheaper to build 'em the way they want 'em at the start, a man would think," suggested the Virginian, most friendly. "There go some more I-talians."

"They're Chinese," said Trampas.

"That's so," acknowledged the Virginian, with a laugh.

"What's he monkeyin' at now?" muttered Scipio.

"Without cheap foreigners they couldn't afford all this hyeh new gradin'," the Southerner continued.

"Grading! Can't you tell when a flood's been eating the banks?"

"Why, yes," said the Virginian, sweet as honey. "But 'ain't yu' heard of the improvements west of Big Timber, all the way to Missoula, this season? I'm talkin' about them."

"Oh! Talking about them. Yes, I've heard.'

"Good money-savin' scheme, ain't it?" said the Virginian. "Lettin' a freight run down one hill an' up the next as far as she'll go without steam, an' shavin' the hill down to that point." Now this was an honest engineering fact. "Better'n settin' dudes squintin' through telescopes an' cipherin' over one-per-cent. reductions," the Southerner commented.

"It's common-sense," assented Trampas. "Have you heard the new scheme about the water-tanks?"

"I ain't right certain," said the Southerner.

"I must watch this," said Scipio, "or I shall bust." He went in, and so did I.

They were all sitting over this discussion of the Northern Pacific's recent policy as to betterments, as though they were the board of directors. Pins could have dropped. Only nobody would have cared to hear a pin.

"They used to put all their tanks at the bottom of their grades," said Trampas.

"Why, yu' get the water easier at the bottom."

"You can pump it to the top, though," said Trampas, growing superior. "And it's cheaper."

"That gets me," said the Virginian, interested.

"Trains after watering can start down hill now and get the benefit of the gravity. It'll cut down operating expenses a heap."

"That's cert'nly common-sense!" exclaimed the Virginian, absorbed. "But ain't it kind o' tardy?"

"Live and learn. So they gained speed, too. High speed on half the coal this season, until the accident."

"Accident?" said the Virginian, instantly.

"Yellowstone Limited. Man fired at engine-driver. Train was flying past that quick the bullet broke every window and killed a passenger on the back platform. You've been running too much with aristocrats," finished Trampas, and turned on his heel.

"Haw, haw!" began the enthusiast, but his neighbor gripped him to silence. This was a triumph too serious for noise. Not a mutineer moved; and I felt cold.

"Trampas," said the Virginian, "I thought yu'd be afeared to try it on me."

Trampas whirled round. His hand was at his belt. "Afraid!" he sneered.

"Shorty!" said Scipio, sternly, and leaping upon that youth, took his half-drawn pistol from him.

"I'm obliged to yu'," said the Virginian to Scipio.

Trampas's hand left his belt. He threw a slight easy look at his men, and keeping his back to the Virginian, walked out on the platform and sat on the chair where the Virginian had sat so much.

"Don't you comprehend," said the Virginian to Shorty, amiably, "that this hyeh question has been discussed peaceable by civilized citizens? Now you sit down and be good, and Mr. Le Moyne will return your gun when we're across that broken bridge, if they have got it fixed for heavy trains yet."

"This train will be lighter when it gets to that bridge," spoke Trampas, out on his chair.

"Why, that's true, too!" said the Virginian. "Maybe none of us are crossin' that Big Horn bridge now, except me. Funny if yu' should end by persuadin' me to quit and go to Rawhide myself! But I reckon I'll not. I reckon I'll worry along to Sunk Creek, somehow."

"Don't forget I'm cookin' for yu'," said Scipio, gruffly.

"I'm obliged to yu'," said the Southerner.

"You were speaking of a job for me," said Shorty.

"I'm right obliged. But yu' see—I ain't exackly foreman the way this comes out, and my promises might not bind Judge Henry to pay salaries."

A push came through the train from forward. We were slowing for the Rawhide station, and all began to be busy and to talk. "Going up to the mines to-day?" "Oh, let's grub first." "Guess it's too late, anyway." And so forth; while they rolled and roped their bedding, and put on their coats with a good deal of elbow motion, and otherwise showed off. It was wasted. The Virginian did not know what was going on in the caboose. He was leaning and looking out ahead, and Scipio's puzzled eye never left him. And as we halted for the water-tank, the Southerner exclaimed, "They 'ain't got away yet!" as if it were good news to him.

He meant the delayed trains. Four stalled expresses were in front of us, besides several freights. And two hours more at least before the bridge would be ready.

Travellers stood and sat about forlorn, near the cars, out in the sage-brush, anywhere. People in hats and spurs watched them, and Indian chiefs offered them painted bows and arrows and shiny horns.

"I reckon them passengers would prefer a laig o' mutton," said the Virginian to a man loafing near the caboose.

"Bet your life!" said the man. "First lot has been stuck here four days."

"Plumb starved, ain't they?" inquired the Virginian.

"Bet your life! They've eat up their dining-cars and they've eat up this town."

"Well," said the Virginian, looking at the town, "I expaict the dining-cyars contained more nourishment."

"Say! you're about right there!" said the man. He walked beside the caboose as we puffed slowly forward from the water-tank to our siding. "Fine business here if we'd only been ready," he continued. "And the Crow agent has let his Indians come over from the reservation. There has been a little beef brought in, and game, and fish. And big money in it, bet your life! Them Eastern passengers has just been robbed. I wisht I had somethin' to sell!"

"Anything starting for Rawhide this afternoon?" said Trampas, out of the caboose door.

"Not until morning," said the man. "You going to the mines?" he resumed to the Virginian.

"Why," answered the Southerner, slowly and casually, and addressing himself strictly to the man, while Trampas, on his side, paid obvious inattention, "this hyeh delay, yu' see, may unsettle our plans some. But it 'll be one of two ways—we're all goin' to Rawhide, or we're all goin' to Billings. We're all one party, yu' see."

Trampas laughed audibly inside the door as he rejoined his men. "Let him keep up appearances," I heard him tell them. "It don't hurt us what he says to strangers."

"But I'm goin' to eat hearty either way," continued the Virginian. "And I ain' goin' to be robbed. I've been kind o' promisin' myself a treat if we stopped hyeh."

"Town's eat clean out," said the man.

"So yu' tell me. But all you folks has forgot one source of revenue that yu' have right close by, mighty handy. · If you have got a gunny sack, I'll show you how to make some money."

"Bet your life!" said the man.

"Mr. Le Moyne," said the Virginian, "the outfit's cookin' stuff is aboard, and if you'll get the fire ready we'll try how frawgs' laigs go fried." He walked off at once, the man following like a dog. Inside the caboose rose a gust of laughter.

"Frogs!" muttered Scipio. And then turning a blank face to me, "Frogs?"

"Colonel Cyrus Jones had them on his bill of fare," I said. "'*Frogs' Legs à la Delmonico.*'"

"Shoo! I didn't get up that thing. They had it when I come. Never looked at it. Frogs?" He went down the steps very slowly, with a long frown. Reaching the ground, he shook his head. "That man's trail is surely hard to anticipate," he said. "But I must hurry up that fire. For his appearance has given me encouragement," Scipio concluded, and became brisk. Shorty helped him, and I brought wood. Trampas and the other people strolled off to the station, a compact band.

Our little fire was built beside the caboose, so the cooking things might be easily reached and put back. You would scarcely think such operations held any interest, even for the hungry, when there seemed to be nothing to cook. A few sticks blazing tamely in the dust, a frying-pan, half a tin bucket of lard, some water, and barren plates and knives and forks, and three silent men attending to them— that was all. But the travellers came to see. These waifs drew near us, and stood, a sad, lorn, shifting fringe of audience; four to begin with; and then two wandered away; and presently one of these came back, finding it worse elsewhere. "Supper, boys?" said he. "Breakfast," said Scipio, crossly. And no more of them addressed us. I heard them joylessly mention Wall Street to each other, and Saratoga; I even heard the name Bryn-Mawr, which is near Philadelphia. But these fragments of home dropped in the wilderness here in Montana beside a freight caboose were of no interest to me now.

"Looks like frogs down there, too," said Scipio. "See them marshy sloos full of weeds?" We took a little turn and had a sight of the Virginian quite active among the ponds. "Hush! I'm getting some thoughts," continued Scipio. "He wasn't sorry enough. Don't interrupt me."

"I'm not," said I.

"No. But I'd 'most caught a-hold." And Scipio muttered to himself again, "He wasn't sorry enough." Presently he swore loud and brilliantly. "Tell yu'!" he cried. "What did he say to Trampas after that play they exchanged over railroad improvements and Trampas put the josh on him? Didn't he say,

'Trampas, I thought you'd be afraid to do it'? Well, sir, Trampas had better have been afraid. And that's what he meant. There's where he was bringin' it to. Trampas made an awful bad play then. You wait. Glory, but he's a knowin' man! Course he wasn't sorry. I guess he had the hardest kind of work to look as sorry as he did. You wait."

"Wait? What for? Go on, man! What for?"

"I don't know! I don't know! Whatever hand he's been holdin' up, this is the show-down. He's played for a showdown here before the caboose gets off the bridge. Come back to the fire, or Shorty'll be leavin' it go out. Grow happy some, Shorty!" he cried on arriving, and his hand cracked on Shorty's shoulder. "Supper's in sight, Shorty. Food for reflection."

"None for the stomach?" asked the passenger who had spoken once before.

"We're figuring on that too," said Scipio. His crossness had melted entirely away.

"Why, they're cowboys!" exclaimed another passenger; and he moved nearer.

From the station Trampas now came back, his herd following him less compactly. They had found famine, and no hope of supplies until the next train from the East. This was no fault of Trampas's; but they were following him less compactly. They carried one piece of cheese, the size of a fist, the weight of a brick, the hue of a corpse. And the passengers, seeing it, exclaimed, "There's Old Faithful again!" and took off their hats.

"You gentlemen met that cheese before, then?" said Scipio, delighted.

"It's been offered me three times a day for four days," said the passenger. "Did he want a dollar or a dollar and a half?"

"Two dollars!" blurted out the enthusiast. And all of us save Trampas fell into fits of imbecile laughter.

"Here comes our grub, anyway," said Scipio, looking off toward the marshes. And his hilarity sobered away in a moment.

"Well, the train will be in soon," stated Trampas. "I guess we'll get a decent supper without frogs."

All interest settled now upon the Virginian. He was coming with his man and his gunny sack, and the gunny sack hung from his shoulder heavily, as a full sack should. He took no notice of the gathering, but sat down and partly emptied the sack. "There," said he, very businesslike, to his assistant, "that's all we'll want. I think you'll find a ready market for the balance."

"Well, my gracious!" said the enthusiast. "What fool eats a frog?"

"Oh, I'm fool enough for a tadpole!" cried the passenger. And they began to take out their pocket-books.

"You can cook yours right hyeh, gentlemen," said the Virginian, with his slow Southern courtesy. "The dining-cyars don't look like they were fired up."

"How much will you sell a couple for?" inquired the enthusiast.

The Virginian looked at him with friendly surprise. "Why, help yourself! We're all together yet awhile. Help yourselves," he repeated, to Trampas and his followers. These hung back a moment, then, with a slinking motion, set the cheese upon the earth and came forward nearer the fire to receive some supper.

"It won't scarcely be Delmonico style," said the Virginian to the passengers, "nor yet Saynt Augustine." He meant Augustine of Philadelphia, whose history I had sketched him at Omaha. Scipio now officiated. His frying-pan was busy, and prosperous odors rose from it. "Run for a bucket of fresh water, Shorty," he continued, beginning his meal. "Colonel, yu' cook pretty near good. If yu' had sold 'em as advertised, yu'd have cert'nly made a name."

Several were now eating with satisfaction, but not Scipio. It was all that he could do to cook straight. The whole man seemed to glisten. His eye was shut to a slit once more, while the innocent passengers thankfully swallowed.

"Now, you see, you have made some money," began the Virginian to his assistant.

"Bet your life!" exclaimed the man. "Divvy, won't you?" And he held out half his gains.

"Keep 'em," returned the Southerner. "I reckon we're square. But I expaict they'll not equal Delmonico's, seh?" he said to a passenger.

"Don't trust the judgment of a man as hungry as I am!" exclaimed the traveller, with a laugh. And he turned to his fellow-travellers. "Did you ever enjoy supper at Delmonico's more than this?"

"Never!" they sighed.

"Why, look here," said the traveller, "what fools the people of this town are! Here we've been all these starving days, and you come and get ahead of them!"

"That's right easy explained," said the Virginian. "I've been where there was big money in frawgs, and they 'ain't been. They're all cattle hyeh. Talk cattle, think cattle, and they're bankrupt in consequence. Fallen through. Ain't that so?" he inquired of his assistant.

"That's about the way," said the man.

"It's mighty hard to do what your neighbors ain't doin'," pursued the Virginian. "Montana is all cattle, an' these folks must be cattle, an' never notice the country right hyeh is too small for a range, an' swampy, anyway, an' just waitin' to be a frawg-ranch."

At this, all wore a face of careful reserve.

"I'm not claimin' to be smarter than you folks hyeh," said the Virginian deprecatingly to his assistant. "But travellin' learns a man many customs. You wouldn't do the business they done at Tulare, California, north side o' the lake. They cert'nly utilized them hopeless swamps splendid. Of course they put up big capital and went into it scientific, gettin' advice from the government Fish Commission, an' such like knowledge. Yu' see, they had big markets for their frawgs — San Francisco, Los Angeles, and clear to New York afteh the Southern Pacific was through. But up hyeh yu' could sell to passengers every day like yu' done this one day. They would get to know yu' along the line. Competing swamps are scarce. The dining-cyars would take your frawgs, and you would have the Yellowstone Park for four months in the year. Them hotels are anxious to please, an' they would buy off you what their Eastern patrons esteem as fine eatin'. And you folks would be sellin' something instead o' nothing."

"That's a practical idea," said a traveller. "And little cost."

"And little cost," said the Virginian.

"Would Eastern people eat frogs?" inquired the man.

"Look at us!" said the traveller.

"Delmonico doesn't give yu' such a treat!" said the Virginian.

"Not exactly!" the traveller exclaimed.

"How much would be paid for frogs?" said Trampas to him. And I saw Scipio bend closer to his cooking.

"Oh, I don't know," said the traveller. "We've paid pretty well, you see."

"You're late for Tulare, Trampas," said the Virginian.

"I was not thinking of Tulare," Trampas retorted. Scipio's nose was in the frying-pan.

"Mos' comical spot you ever struck!" said the Virginian, looking round upon the whole company. He allowed himself a broad smile of retrospect. "To hear 'em talk frawgs at Tulare! Same as other folks talks hawsses or steers or whatever they're raising to sell. Yu'd fall into it yourselves if yu' started the business. Anything a man's bread and butter depends on he's going to be earnest about. Don't care if it is a frawg."

"That's so," said the assistant. "And it paid good?"

"The only money in the county was right there," answered the Virginian. "It was a dead county, and only frawgs was movin'. But that business was a-fannin' to beat four of a kind. It made yu' feel strange at first, as I said. For all the men had been cattle-men at one time or another. Till yu' got accustomed, it would give 'most anybody a shock to hear 'em speak about herdin' the bulls in a pasture by themselves." The Virginian allowed himself another smile, but became serious again. "That was their policy," he explained. "Except at certain times o' year they kept the bulls separate. The Fish Commission told 'em they'd better, and it cert'nly worked mighty well. It or something did—for, gentlemen, hush! but there was millions. You'd have said all the frawgs in the world had taken charge at Tulare. And the money rolled in! Gentlemen, hush! 'twas a gold-mine for the owners. Forty per cent. they netted some years. And they paid generous wages. For they could sell to all them French restaurants in San Francisco, yu' see. And there was the Cliff House. And the Palace Hotel made it a specialty. And the officers took frawgs at the Presidio, an' Angel Island, an' Alcatraz, an' Benicia. Los Angeles was beginnin' its boom. The corner-lot sharps wanted something by way of varnish. An' so they dazzled Eastern investors with advertising Tulare frawgs clear to N'Yol'ans an' New York. 'Twas only in Sacramento frawgs was dull. I expaict the California Legislature was too o'rn'ry for them fine-raised luxuries. They tell of one of them Senators that he raked a million out of Los Angeles real estate, and started in for a bang-up meal with champagne. Wanted to scatter his new gold thick an' quick. But he got astray among all the fancy dishes, an' just yelled right out before the ladies, 'Damn it! bring me forty dollars' worth of ham and aiggs.' He was a funny Senator, now."

The Virginian paused, and finished eating a leg. "Talkin' of Senators," he resumed, with the tone of new anecdotes in his voice, "Senator Wise—"

"How much did you say wages were at Tulare?" inquired one of the Trampas faction.

"How much? Why, I never knew what the foreman got. The regular hands got a hundred."

"A hundred a *month?*"

"Why, it was wet an' muddy work, yu' see. A man risked rheumatism some. He risked it a good deal. Well, I was goin' to tell about Senator Wise. When Senator Wise was speaking of his visit to Alaska—"

"Forty per cent., was it?" said Trampas.

"Oh, I must call my wife!" said the traveller behind me. "This is what I came West for." And he hurried away.

"Not forty per cent. the bad years," replied the Virginian. "The frawgs had enemies, same as cattle. I remember when a pelican got in the spring pasture, and the herd broke through the fence—"

"Fence?" said a passenger.

"Ditch, seh, and wire net. Every pasture was a square swamp with a ditch around, and a wire net. Yu've heard the mournful, mixed-up sound a big bunch of cattle will make? Well, seh, as yu' druv from the railroad to the Tulare frawg-ranch yu' could hear 'em a mile. Springtime they'd sing like girls in the organ-loft, and by August they were about ready to hire out for bass. And all was fit to be soloists, if I'm a judge. But in a bad year it might only be twenty per cent. The pelican rushed 'em from the pasture right into the San Joaquin River, which was close by the property. The big balance of the herd stampeded, and though of course they came out on the banks again, the news had went around, and folks below at Hemlen eat most of 'em just to spite the company. Yu' see, a frawg in a river is more hopeless than any maverick loose on the range. And

they never struck any plan to brand their stock and prove ownership."

"Well, twenty per cent. is good enough for me," said Trampas, "if Rawhide don't suit me."

"A hundred a month!" said the enthusiast. And busy calculations began to rise among them.

"It went to fifty per cent.," pursued the Virginian, "when New York and Philadelphia got to biddin' agaynst each other. Both cities had signs all over 'em claiming to furnish the Tulare frawg. And both had 'em all right. And same as cattle-trains, yu'd see frawg-trains tearing acrosst Arizona—big glass tanks with wire over 'em—through to New York, an' the frawgs starin' out."

"Why, George," whispered a woman's voice behind me, "he's merely deceiving them! He's merely making that stuff up out of his head."

"Yes, my dear, that's merely what he's doing."

"Well, I don't see why you imagined I should care for this. I think I'll go back."

"Better see it out, Daisy. This beats the geysers or anything we're likely to find in the Yellowstone."

"Then I wish we had gone to Bar Harbor as usual," said the lady; and she returned to her Pullman.

But her husband staid. Indeed, the male crowd now was a goodly sight to see, how the men edged close, drawn by a common tie. Their different kinds of feet told the strength of the bond—yellow sleeping-car slippers planted miscellaneous and motionless near a pair of Mexican spurs. All eyes watched the Virginian and gave him beautiful sympathy. Though they could not know the reason for it, what he was doing had fallen as light upon them—all except the excited calculators. These were loudly making their fortunes at both Rawhide and Tulare, drugged by their satanically aroused hopes of gold, heedless of the slippers and the spurs. Had a man given any sign to warn them, I think he would have been lynched. Even the Indian chiefs had come to see in their show war-bonnets and blankets. They naturally understood nothing of it, yet magnetically knew that the Virginian was the great man. And they watched him with approval. He sat by the fire with the frying-pan, looking his daily self—en-

THE FROG-STORY.

gaging and saturnine. And now as Trampas declared tickets to California would be dear and Rawhide had better come first, the Southerner let loose his heaven-born imagination.

"There's a better reason for Rawhide than tickets, Trampas," said he. "I said it was too late for Tulare."

"I heard you," said Trampas. "Opinions may differ. You and I don't think alike on several points."

"Gawd, Trampas!" said the Virginian, "d' yu' reckon I'd be rotting hyeh on forty dollars if Tulare was like it used to be? Tulare is broke."

"What broke it? Your leaving?"

"Revenge broke it, and disease," said the Virginian, striking the frying-pan on his knee, for the frogs were all gone. At those lurid words their untamed child minds took fire, and they drew round him again to hear a tale of blood. The crowd seemed to lean nearer.

But for a short moment it threatened to be spoiled. A passenger came along, demanding in an important voice, "Where are these frogs?" He was president of the New York Midland, they whispered me, and out for a holiday in his private car. Reaching us and walking to the Virginian, he said, cheerily, "How much do you want for your frogs, my friend?"

"You got a friend hyeh?" said the Virginian. "That's good, for yu' need care taken of yu'." And the president of the New York Midland did not further discommode us.

"That's worth my trip," whispered a New York passenger to me.

"Yes, it was a case of revenge," resumed the Virginian, "and disease. There was a man named Saynt Augustine got run out of Domingo which is a Dago island. He come to Philadelphia, an' he was dead broke. But Saynt Augustine was a live man, an' he saw Philadelphia full o' Quakers that dressed plain an' eat humdrum. So he started cookin' Domingo way for 'em, an' they caught right ahold. Terrapin, he gave 'em, an' croakeets, an' he'd use forty chickens to make a broth he called consommay. An' he got rich, and Philadelphia got well known, an' Delmonico in New York he got jealous. He was the cook that had the say-so in New York."

"Was Delmonico one of them I-talians?" inquired a fascinated mutineer.

"I don't know. But he acted like one.

Lorenzo was his front name. He aimed to cut—"

"Domingo's throat?" breathed the enthusiast.

"Aimed to cut away the trade from Saynt Augustine an' put Philadelphia back where he thought she belonged. Frawgs was the fashionable rage then. These foreign cooks set the fashion in eatin', same as foreign dressmakers do women's clothes. Both cities was catchin' and swallowin' all the frawgs Tulare could throw at 'em. So he—"

"Lorenzo?" said the enthusiast.

"Yes, Lorenzo Delmonico. He bid a dollar a tank higher. An' Saynt Augustine raised him fifty cents. An' Lorenzo raised him a dollar. An' Saynt Augustine shoved her up three. Lorenzo he didn't expaict Philadelphia would go that high, and he got hot in the collar, an' flew round his kitchen in New York, an' claimed he'd twist Saynt Augustine's Domingo tail for him and crack his ossified system. Lorenzo raised his language to a high temperature, they say. An' then quite sudden off he starts for Tulare. He buys tickets over the Santa Fe, and he goes a-fannin' and a-foggin'. But, gentlemen, hush! The very same day Saynt Augustine he tears out of Philadelphia. He travelled by the way o' Washington, an' out he comes a-fannin' and a-foggin' over the Southern Pacific. Of course Tulare didn't know nothin' of this. All it knowed was how the frawg-market was on soarin' wings, and it was feelin' like a flight o' rawckets. If only there'd been some preparation—a telegram or something—the disaster would never have occurred. But Lorenzo and Saynt Augustine was that absorbed watchin' each other—for, yu' see, the Santa Fe and the Southern Pacific come together at Mojave, an' the two cooks travelled a matter of two hundred and ten miles in the same cyar—they never thought about a telegram. And when they arruv, breathless, an' started in to screeching what they'd give for the monopoly, why, them unsuspecting Tulare boys got amused at 'em. I never heard just all they done, but they had Lorenzo singin' and dancin', while Saynt Augustine played the fiddle for him. And one of Lorenzo's heels did get a trifle grazed. Well, them two cooks quit that ranch without disclosin' their identity, and soon as they got to a safe distance they swore eternal friendship, in their foreign way. And they went home over the Union Pacific, sharing the same state-room. Their revenge killed frawgs. The disease—"

"How killed frogs?" demanded Trampas.

"Just killed 'em. Delmonico and Saynt Augustine wiped frawgs off the slate of fashion. Not a banker in Fifth Avenue 'll touch one now if another banker's around. And if ever yu' see a man that hides his feet an' won't take off his socks in company—he has worked in them Tulare swamps an' got the disease. Catch him wadin' and yu'll find he's webfooted. Frawgs are dead, Trampas, an' so are you."

"Rise up, liars, and salute your king!" yelled Scipio. "Oh, I'm in love with you!" And he threw his arms round the Virginian.

"Let me shake hands with you," said the traveller who had failed to interest his wife in these things. "I wish I was going to have more of your company."

"Thank yu', seh," said the Virginian.

Other passengers greeted him, and the Indian chiefs came, saying "How!" because they followed their feelings without understanding.

"Don't show so humbled, boys," said the deputy-foreman to his most sheepish crew. "These gentlemen from the East have been enjoying yu' some, I know. But think what a weary wait they have had hyeh. And you insisted on playing the game with me this way, yu' see. What outlet did yu' give me? Didn't I have it to do? And I'll tell yu' one thing for your consolation. When I got to the middle of the frawgs I 'most believed it myself." And he laughed out the first laugh I had heard him give.

The enthusiast came up and shook hands. That led off, and the rest followed, with Trampas at the end. The tide was too strong for him. He was not a graceful loser; but he got through this, and the Virginian eased him down by treating him precisely like the others—apparently. Possibly the most beautiful—the most American—moment of all was when word came that the bridge was open, and the Pullman trains, with noise and triumph, began to move westward at last. Every one waved farewell to every one, craning from steps and windows, so that the cars twinkled with hilarity; and in twenty minutes the whole procession in front had moved, and our turn came.

"Last chance for Rawhide," said the Virginian.

"Last chance for Sunk Creek," said a recent mutineer; and all sprang aboard. There was no question who had won his spurs now.

Our caboose trundled on to Billings along the shingly, cottonwooded Yellowstone; and as the plains and bluffs and the distant snow began to grow well known, even to me, we turned to our baggage that was to come off, since camp would begin in the morning. Thus I saw the Virginian carefully re-wrapping *Kenilworth*, that he might bring it to its owner unharmed; and I said, "Don't you think you could have played poker with Queen Elizabeth?"

"No; I expaict she'd have beat me," he replied. "She was a lady."

34

Bad-Man Mason

ANNE O'HAGAN

THE SHERIFF'S HEAVY REVOLVER SWUNG LIGHTLY UPWARD, AND
MR. MASON SAT DOWN AGAIN

BAD-MAN MASON

BY ANNE O'HAGAN

ILLUSTRATED BY GEORGE WRIGHT

"THE citizens of Copper," heavily declared Mr. Jeremy Dexter, sheriff of Sherman County, "air anxious to do the grateful thing by you, Lanky. But they air also determined to do the right thing by their fair city; an' that's why I took your gun." The sheriff's unhumorous eyes swept such part of the little, huddled, sun-baked frontier town as was visible through the window of the Palace Hotel, where he sat with his astonished captive. A long career of immunity from the results of his acts had left Lanky with no expectation of arrest after the fracas of the preceding night. "An' therefore," the sheriff continued, "I give you twelve hours to clear out, an' if you're ever caught in the confines of this county again, may God have mercy on your soul!"

Mr. John Wesley Mason, known widely, and not too favorably, as Lanky —for reasons apparent as soon as one caught a glimpse of his long, lean, sinewy body—turned from the contemplation of the Loverings' garden across the street. He met the harassed but unflinching regard of the hardly tried, conscientious sheriff. His face, browned by years of blazing sun and buffeting wind, lined deeply with the marks of alkaline air, of violent living, and of indomitable mockery, suddenly grew lugubrious. But his eyes, twinkling in their sockets like lakes in the depths of hill-recesses, gave the lie to the whimpering expression his lips assumed.

"If you was an edjicated man, Jerry, which you ain't, though it's no fault of yourn an' I'd be the last to twit you with it, you'd remember what the pote says about the favor of princes bein' vain an'——"

EVERY ONE LOOKED UP, THOUGH MORE IN DISAPPROVAL THAN INQUIRY

"I may not have had early advantages," growled the sheriff, his heavy face showing dull-red beneath its tan, "which all they does, as far as I see, is to be more blame to them as had them and yet goes wrong an' gets into

"I know, I know." Lanky's eyes were again upon the Loverings' garden, where, in the green and flowering space wrung from the desert by loving pains, a girl's figure moved. "I know, Jerry. I'd have been strung up, shot down—

A SHARP HEAT WENT STINGING THROUGH HIS BODY

trouble. But I know that's no poet-sayin'. It's the Bible. An' anyway, if you mean that Copper City is a prince an' ungrateful, you know well enough, Lanky Mason, that you'd have been food for the buzzards long ago if Copper hadn't bore in mind what you done for it. Why——"

whatever was convenient—half a dozen times, if only Copper could forget the fire an' the flood, an' if only Jerry Dexter could forget his little Alice. Well, an' now——"

"An' now the end's came," declared Mr. Dexter firmly. "You air a constant menace to the peace an' order of

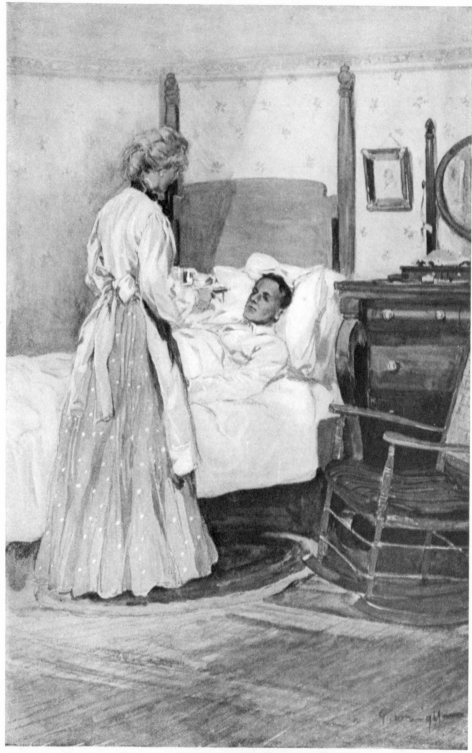

THE APPARITION WHICH HE SAW SMILING DOWN UPON HIM WITH
TENDER, DEWY EYES

Copper. You get roarin' drunk. No man's life is safe when you're rampagin'. You destroy property wilful an' wanton. You intimidate men an' you frighten women——"

"You lie!" cried Mr. Mason in virtuous rage, springing to his feet. But the sheriff's heavy revolver swung lightly upward, and Mr. Mason sat down again. "You lie," he repeated less vehemently. "I never scared no woman in my life."

"Not of purpose, Lanky, I grant you that," said the sheriff mildly. "But what lady in Copper or environs feels sure of seein' her husband come back on his own two feet when he goes out on an evenin' you're loose? I tell you, you're a lyin', gamblin', drinkin', shootin' cuss. You're a blot on the fair name of Copper. You've got to git. After that Mexican business last night —you've got to git!"

"Dirty greaser!" growled the blot on the fair name of Copper.

"Clean or dirty, greaser or white, you've got to git. It's the ultimatum. You can git either by the way I'm suggestin' to you—a horse an' an escort that'll see you outside of Sherman County—or by a rope that'll jerk you to kingdom come. Copper's got feelin's, though. It would rather you'd take the horse. It can't forget you saved it from ashes the night of the smelter fire; it can't forget how you fought for it the day of the big flood. It recollects how you reskied little Alice Dexter "—his voice broke—" from that drunken redskin. But while it's entire willin' to name you a hero an' to erect a moniment to you as such in the public square just as fast as it gits a public square, it won't stand for you in its midst another day. Now, you take your choice. On one hand is the jug, a trial for killin' that greaser last night—for he's goin' to die an' the trial 'll be before a Mexican jury, mind you—the end of a rope, an' I ain't makin' no guesses about the hereafter; on the other hand, free escort out of Sherman County, an' never another sight of you in it."

"Lord, man, to hear you talk, anybody'd think that Copper was the Venice of the Western desert; that an American gentleman couldn't take no pleasure away from its bullyvards. I'll go, an' be damned glad to leave the miser——"

He did not finish the sentence. The girl in the Loverings' garden had gone up on to the porch of the cottage across the street, and he was watching her.

"Thank God you've got so much sense," said the sheriff, wiping his forehead. "But remember—you ain't off for a visit. You're outlawed. An' if you come back, it'll be the duty of all good citizens to shoot you on sight as a menace to—— I only hope, Lanky, that you won't try it on. Turn over a new leaf, an', realizin' that the march of progress on the frontier is eliminatin' the bad man, become——"

"Aw, dry up! I ain't a Fourth of July aujence," Lanky briefly reminded his captor.

Under cover of the night Sheriff Dexter and his prisoner rode out of Copper. There was a fanfare of noise from one or two dance-halls. Through big, garishly lighted windows, here and there, the men saw from their saddles the reddish gleam of long cherry bars, the glitter of glass, the groups gathering before them and around the faro-tables. Lanky sighed a little. After all, Copper had been his abiding-place a long time, and here were his favorite diversions and the companions of them. Then the fragrance of newly watered flowers and grass was wafted to him. Through the muslin curtains of the Loverings' windows the tranquil lights shone.

"That niece of old man Lovering's that's come on to teach school out here seems a right nice young heifer." Lanky's voice was not so matter-of-fact as he had hoped to make it.

"She sure does," agreed the sheriff, cordial and indifferent.

The lights of the little town twinkled out behind them. The dim spaces of the desert, shadowy outlines of mesa, dark bulk of scanty growths indistinct in the night, broad stretches of emptiness, engulfed them. They rode in silence beneath the velvety blackness of the sky, pierced by large, luminous, low-hanging stars. By and by the sheriff drew rein.

"Our ways part here, Lanky," he announced. "This here's the line between Sherman an' Annunciata County."

Lanky sat his horse, speechless at the last.

"I—I—damn it all," cried the sheriff. "Never, so long's I live, will I forget what you done for me an' mine, Lank Mason! An' Alice—every night —her prayers—she says 'em to her mother—whatever you do, don't never come back," he quavered.

"I won't," said Lank with unwonted gentleness. "Unless I'm hot-foot after suicide. Oh, by the way, Jerry—that Fanny Lovering—I—somehow I could wish—a garden an' a lamp at home an' —oh, well, I ain't been fittin' myself for that sort of thing so's you could notice it, have I? But—make the best of me to her, will you?"

The sheriff wrung his hand painfully.

"I'll pound it into her head that you was the best man an' the blamedest fool Copper ever seen," he declared manfully. And with the comfort of that promise the bad man of Copper City rode on.

II

A WEEK out of Sherman County, Lanky rode gaily and valorously into La Sonora. He had banished sentiment; he had banished resentment against the town to which he had at least twice been of such signal and of such unrewarded service. Negligibly small as was the pack upon his pommel, dismally faint as was the jingle when his hands played in his pockets, he faced the future cheerfully.

As for Fanny Lovering, with her shining, expectant eyes and her frank, smiling mouth, she was nothing to him except the momentary personification of all that he had flung away in the world. He waved the thought of her a wide farewell with his sombrero as he dug spurs into his horse and pranced and curveted up to the entrance of Riley's Pink Poodle Hotel. He was something of an actor, Lanky, as your true sentimentalist is, and he loved an impressive entrance. Within half an hour he had a sufficient acquaintance to insure him against the boredom of loneliness, and within an hour he was deep at his evening's occupation of poker.

It was at a smallish table in the corner of the room that he sat down to his game with confiding gentlemen who did not demand a man's family history before entering into recreation with him. Nearer the bar was the faro-table, and at it the dealer's voice croaked with a dull lack of inflection as the bettors monotonously placed their bets. One voice, by its high pitch of excitement, separated itself from the other noises of the place. It declared its owner's wagers almost shrilly. It flung demands for drinks between plays. It took the game, not with the calm, almost bored, matter-of-factness of the habitual player, but with a nervousness that proclaimed the novice. Lanky was disagreeably conscious of it, as he would have been of any disturbing noise. Still he did not look from his own hand and his growing pile, until, suddenly, a laugh rang upon the air with the effect of a pistol-shot, hollow, boisterous, despairing. Every one looked up, though more in disapproval than inquiry.

"It's that damned tenderfoot," announced Mr. Reddy Allen, one of Lank's companions. "Been here losin' his money an' fillin' hisself plumb full of Riley's booze for three days."

Lanky looked frowningly at the disturber of the peace, a tall youth, with yellow hair and bloodshot, wretched eyes.

"That winds me up, gentlemen," he was announcing in tones that shook despite the evident bravado of his intention. "Six hundred gone in three days. Nothing left but my cuff-buttons and my revolver. I won't let my revolver go; I may need it. But my buttons—say, barkeep, will you advance anything on these links?"

He tore the gold trifles from his sleeves. Lanky scowled.

"He'll be shootin' himself here next," he remarked with the distaste of the old resident and the conservative. "I know that kind. Hey, you, there, stranger."

The boy turned and met the searching regard of the deep-set, lambent blue eyes. He laughed again, more vacantly, and swayed toward Lanky.

Within five minutes the magic that Copper City had known so long was exerted. The younger man had unresentfully heard a few home truths concerning the ways of the Eastern greenhorn, and was sitting, slightly cowed, entirely hopeful, waiting for his new acquaintance to finish the evening's poker and to assume the direction of his tenderfoot existence.

"You're a plumb fool," declared Lanky to him later, in the seclusion of his room. "When you play faro, play faro. When you drink, drink. I myself ain't no temperance society"—he spoke with complete solemnity—"but when I'm playin' cards I ain't imbibin', nor vicy-versy. Now, you ain't no ways fit for this kind of life. You air too excitable, an' you ain't quick enough in the eye. What you doin' here?"

"I made a mistake and got on the wrong train at Lamy Junction," confessed the youth sullenly. "I was bound for Copper City, but I took the southern branch instead of the western. And then—oh, then I thought I'd stay on it and see what came of it. I—I don't know. It just happened, that's all."

"First time away from home?"

"No, I'm a college man."

"Oh-h-h! A college man. An' what was you thinkin' of doin' in the West?"

"Ranching, maybe, or maybe mining a little, or getting into the cattle business. I don't know. I just came into a little money. And what blamed business is it of yours, anyway?"

"It ain't none," agreed Lank composedly. "An' as a usual thing I make money on mindin' my own business an' lettin' others do the same by theirs. I ain't keen on missionarin'. But—I always kinder take to the under dog, an' if ever I seen an under dog it was you talkin' to them grown men about cuff-buttons an' revolvers."

The boy began to blubber.

"The worst of it all is," he confessed maudlinly, "there's a girl. I came to see her. I'm—we're engaged, in a way. That is, she said for me to prove myself a man—that's what she called it; she meant for me to walk the chalk-line and earn my own living. But I wanted to see her, and when I had the money left me I started after her."

"What's her name?" asked Lanky in a flat voice. He knew it well enough before it was spoken. Of course; that accounted for his interest in this weak, flushed fool. Of course it was the shadowy presence of Fanny Lovering that made the bond between them.

"Um-m-m," he said when he heard. "You air an ungrateful fool." Most offensively he bade his charge be quiet; most truculently he refused to listen to the young egoist's self-excusings and pratings. Bitterly he consigned the newcomer to torment.

Three days later, however, they rode side by side out of La Sonora. Lanky had discovered that there was but one way in the world to keep Ned Caldwell sober and sane. That was to mount perpetual watch over him. Wherefore he charged himself with the guardianship of the boy into Copper—up to Fanny Lovering's door.

"It ain't right," he told himself half a dozen times a day. "The poor jumpin' jack-rabbit ain't worth her notice. But if she wants him like he says she does, she's goin' to have him, delivered in good condition. An' she can make a man of him, if anything on God Almighty's earth can. She could make a man of a sneakin' fox, she could."

Very grim and silent, he rode the wastes. His companion talked and talked. Lanky did not trouble to hear him. He was occupied with his own thoughts. Of course he'd try to escape again, he told himself. But if he didn't—ah, how much better to throw away his worthless life saving Fanny Lovering's happiness for her than if he had lost it in any of his dozen daredevil heroisms, any of his score of reckless affrays!

III

DAWN, a wonderful sudden fire, blazed upon Copper. The two men had broken their camp very early and had ridden through the pearly grayness in which the last star throbbed itself out into the huddled little town.

"I ain't goin' to ride clear in with you," said Lank stolidly. "This here climate ain't none too healthy for my complaint. But you'll go straight to your lady friend?"

"I certainly shall," said Caldwell, "as soon as the conventions will permit me to call. This isn't much of a place, is it?"

"That depends on what you're lookin'

for in a place," answered Lanky with some bruskness. " Well, I'll be ridin' back. You can tell her I brought you— if you want to. Come to think of it, you won't want to; won't want to talk much of Sonora. Well, she's a nice young lady. Some time you might mention casual that I friended you once. You'll know her uncle's house by the garden. It's the best in town, and it's opposite the Palace. She's got—they've got—oleanders in tubs, an' climbin' roses, an' some greeny stuff that smells good they call mignonette. I've got a mind to ride a little nearer to show you for sure——"

" Oh, I guess I can find it," remarked the young man lightly.

" I'd kinder like to see the place myself," confessed Mr. Mason with unwonted wistfulness.

" Oh, in that case," conceded Mr. Caldwell.

They rode gently down the slight declivity of the street into the still little town, bathed in the first freshness of morning light. Suddenly, from the direction of the big smelting works on the edge of the town a dark stream of workmen flowed across the street at the foot of the incline; the night-shift was going home.

Lanky drew his rein taut and whistled between his clenched teeth. The men looked up the slope at the two horsemen, outlined like targets against the open gold of the eastern sky, ablaze behind the plain. Lanky heard a sudden sibilant cry, the whir of a bullet. A sharp heat went stinging through his body. He had a second's consciousness of his companion's scream of horror. Then he knew no more.

IV

THERE were muslin curtains at the window. They stirred softly in a breeze that exhaled the sweetness of rose and mignonette. Lanky surveyed the room in its cool exquisiteness. Finally his slow-traveling gaze rested upon the sheriff, seated, large and solemn, in an armchair near the foot of the bed.

" Didn't he do for me—the greaser?" Lanky whispered. He had had no intention of whispering, but his voice was lurking in unaccountable distances and did not come at his summons.

" Luis's brother? The brother of the fellow you shot the night before you was banished from Copper? No, he didn't do for you—quite. You're livin' yet, Lanky, an' the same blamed fool you always was."

" Where's young—young—I forget his name—that was with me?" Again it was a painful whisper that issued from Lanky's lips.

" Sent back East, where he belongs, for a poor, helpless idjit," said the sheriff briefly—" sent back by Miss Fanny Lovering."

" Oh!" said Lanky. His voice was stronger now.

" Yes. An' I may say there's no more price on your good-for-nothin' head, Lank. The committee of public safety, it holds that things has been evened up enough by the greaser's brother shootin' you. An' a lady in good standin'—she fired up somethin' hot about drivin' you out of town, an' she's made herself surety for your good behavior."

Lanky's eyes lost the dull glaze of fever.

" Jerry," he said entreatingly.

" Women beat the devil," remarked the sheriff in tones of pure philosophy. " Here she sends that long-legged dude back to where he come from because he owned up to some drinkin' an' carousin' around in Sonora. An' here you, that'd make him look like a Easter lily for virtue, here you, a gamblin', drinkin' outlaw—she will have you brought here. You're a man, she says. Lanky——"

" Damn you!" cried Lanky with sudden vigor. " How long have I got to listen to you, you old gas-bag? I want to see her—her!"

Then, as Jerry Dexter, with a friendly grin upon his face, rose ponderously and moved toward the door, a spasm of shyness seized the bad man.

" No, no," he cried. " Don't. I ain't fit." And he closed his eyes lest blindness should follow the apparition which he knew was entering the room— which he heard gently coming toward him—which, when at last he dared to look, he saw smiling down upon him with tender, dewy eyes.

35

Carruthers for Sheriff

RILEY H. ALLEN

"NEBRASKY, ARE YOU GOIN' TO SHY AT A LITTLE FELLER LIKE HIM?"

CARRUTHERS FOR SHERIFF.

BY RILEY H. ALLEN.

I.

CARRUTHERS rode down from the eastern hills and out upon the red desert in the sunlight of an August morning. Ahead of him stretched the silent San Jacinto plains, already beginning to shimmer in the heat-waves. On the very edge of the western horizon, seemingly at the end of the world, rose the Hermosa Mountains, a blur of purple in the distance.

Carruthers sat his pinto cow-pony with the grace that comes from spending nine months out of every year in the saddle. One casual hand rested on his hip; his body swayed easily with the tireless lope of the pony. He wore the fringed leathern chaps of the cow-puncher, and a gay red handkerchief was knotted around his neck. His mouth was good-humored, but there was strength in the square jaw and straight nose, and he looked across the desert to the far blue hills with the level gaze of the frontier.

"You, Nebrasky," he said to the horse, "I reckon you've got to travel some to-day. It's sixty miles to them mountains. I've got to get there sure." He swore lazily, affectionately, and slapped the pony's flank with a gentle hand. "You old stump-sucker, I'm expectin' you to hit the high places to Rawhide. I'm runnin' for sheriff, Nebrasky; what do you think o' that? And you got to pike into Rawhide City to-night if you bust a leg a-tryin'. Me a sheriff! I reckon that'll make Kenard kinder sore. Didn't see him as I passed the ranch this mornin'. He'll be over at Rawhide City, Nebrasky, and we better be makin' it, too!"

A quick, silent shadow crossed the trail. Looking up, Carruthers saw a buzzard skimming along on motionless wings. Idly he watched its course. The wings quivered, drooped a little, and a moment later it circled downward, more and more slowly, till it dropped into an arroyo a hundred yards to the left. It was a common sight on those plains, and Carruthers turned back in the saddle.

And then, as silent and quick as the shadow of the buzzard, a coyote loped across the trail so close before that the cow-pony threw up its head. Half-mechanically, Carruthers saw the coyote stop at the gully where the buzzard had disappeared and crouch forward to the edge. Then it whirled in a startled flash of yellow-gray fur, and loped silently away across the desert, fading imperceptibly among the sage-bushes.

"The dern kangaroo!" said Carruthers reflectively. "Nebrasky, I sure guess there's somethin' in that waller."

He turned the pony's head and rode to the edge of the arroyo. At the bottom, on the loose red sand, crouched a forlorn little figure in a very dusty pair of blue kilts and torn blouse-waist. It sat up and looked at Carruthers out of frightened eyes.

He leaped from his horse and clambered down into the gully. The buzzard rose from a near-by rock and floated away on silent pinions. The child tried to run in a tottering, weak way, but fell at the first step. Carruthers picked him up and held him in careful arms.

"You pore lost little maverick!" he said. "Where did you come from?"

He wiped the dirty face with his big red handkerchief. The small, grimy hands were bruised, and Carruthers knew that the boy had been crawling on the rough sand.

"Been lost since yesterday mornin', I reckon. Too scared to speak," said the cow-boy impersonally. "And now let's get out o' this."

He scrambled up the arroyo with the child on one arm, and walked toward the pony. His hand was stretched out for the bridle when the animal suddenly reared, snorting loudly.

"Nebrasky," said the cowboy, "are you goin' to shy at a little feller like him? I reckon you ain't often seen me with a kid; but I'm sure ashamed of you, actin' like this!"

He tried to seize the bridle. The horse jerked up his head, trotted back to the trail, stopped till the pursuing cowboy was ten feet away, then swung about and cantered off to the eastward. Carruthers swore at him.

"Nebrasky," he said, "I must be locoed, fergettin' to drop that bridle over your mule head! I might 'a' expected it of you—a horse that would shy at a little maverick like this!"

He regarded the boy with curious eyes. He noticed that the baby lips were drawn, the temples hot and feverish. He took a bottle from his pocket, forced a few drops into the dry mouth, and sat down on the ground with the child in his arms.

The air grew perceptibly hotter, the heat waves shimmered above the greasewood and stunted sahuaros. Carruthers shook himself; watching the color come into the child's face, he had forgotten the desert.

"Little maverick," he said gently, " it's goin' to be mighty hot to-day. Let's be hittin' the trail." He stood up, looking over the red plain. Behind him lay the hills he had left in the morning. To the west were the Hermosas. "I'm mighty sorry, little maverick," he said. "I cain't go back; no, I just cain't. It ain't far across, and there ain't no water back there. I got to be at Rawhide to-morrow. I said I'd come, and I reckon I ain't goin' to let Kenard scare me out!"

The child looked at him gravely, out of steady, unwinking eyes. Carruthers gulped a mouthful of brandy and went forward.

Higher rose the sun. Behind the plodding cowboy the sage-bushes and cactus passed in dull, unending rows, and the trail stretched on. In his arms the child dozed, waking up at short intervals with low cries of fear, then dropping back into uneasy slumber.

At noon they stopped under the scant shade of a huge thorn-cactus and rested for an hour; then on again. The afternoon sun struck blindingly upon Carruthers' face, and the long rows of sagebrush seemed to move more slowly; but by night the eastern hills were far distant, and he calculated he had covered twenty miles. The child slept heavily in his arms as he lay down under the greasewood to sleep.

In the night Carruthers woke, thirsty. The moonlight fell upon the face of the boy.

"Pore little feller!" he said softly. "You must be mighty near tired. You got to be brave, little feller," he whispered; then he went back to sleep in spite of his thirst, for he was very tired.

In the morning, before the sun had topped the hills to the eastward, he started on. The child was awake now, and still it never spoke, only stared at him out of red, frightened eyes. His own

felt strangely blurred, and his limbs were shot with pangs, for the western cowboy spends his life in the saddle.

As the white-hot sun burned its course higher up the sky, the boy panted in his arms, and his own brain swam in the fierce air. About eleven o'clock, as he guessed, he had to stop under a cactus to ease the pain in his shoulders. He stayed there all the afternoon, now and then giving the precious brandy to the boy, drop by drop. When the shadows slanted in long rows to the east, he started forward again, looking steadily at the blue foothills of the Hermosas.

The child seemed weaker, Carruthers thought, and then a feeling struck him that the baby understood everything he said, and was reproaching him.

"It's like this," Carruthers explained. "There's a man in Rawhide City who says I cain't be sheriff. He's a mighty mean man, little maverick, Kenard is. I says to him, 'I'll be there at the election, Kenard,' and he says, 'I'll shoot you if you come.' I ain't that kind of a man. But I says to him, 'I'll be there,' and I will. It was hard luck of Nebrasky to run away. Yes, that cert'nly was mighty hard luck, but it's only twenty miles now, maverick!"

The full moon rose over the wide desert, turning the ragged greasewood and chaparral into tawny sprays of strange beauty. After a while the dry air grew cooler. Carruthers gave the last of the brandy to the boy, and smiled as he did so, though his own mouth was harsh and dry. He went on over the arid plain.

The moon sank lower and lower, one by one the stars paled, and a gray light shot out of the east. The gray glowed, crimsoned; day dawned. Up over the eastern hills sprang the sun and shone hotter and hotter on the San Jacinto desert. The dry sand slipped under Carruthers' feet. The child in his arms panted in hoarse, short sobs.

Carruthers dared not stop. He could see the distant Hermosas, blue and inviting in the west, with cool, dark canyons and green valleys. His throat felt caked and his lips split open. The trail blurred before him; red dust filled his lungs. His arms and back ached with intolerable surges of pain from the weight of the child, but he set his teeth and kept his eyes on the Hermosas. Somewhere at the foot of those hills lay the gray walls of Rawhide City, and at the thought of his mission he set his teeth afresh.

"Little maverick," he said, "I got to do it. There ain't no other way. I told Kenard I'd be there. To-day's election day, and they're expectin' me to come."

So he went forward toward Rawhide City and the man who would kill him on sight. It was the thought of his word that kept him on the trail—that, and the child in his arms. He felt a strange companionship with the boy, intangible, yet real.

"Little maverick," he muttered, "I got to keep goin', keep goin'—to—Rawhide—City."

He laid the child gently under a chaparral bush, stumbled, and fell beside it.

After a while the scant shade of the chaparral revived him. He looked across the grim desert—down the faint white line of the trail—back over the route he had come. He saw not one living thing, not even a skulking coyote. He looked up at the burnished sky and saw a dark buzzard, wheeling in languid circles, lower and lower over the chaparral.

He tried to shout—his voice was rusty and hoarse. He lifted his arms to the sky and cried aloud. He swore, but there was prayer in the despairing tones. The child panted heavily; its eyes, unwinking as ever, were haunted with fever.

Carruthers looked wildly across the desert to the cool Hermosas.

"Little feller," he said, "I got to leave you. There ain't no other way. But I'll come back right soon. Yes, I'll cert'nly come back. You got to be mighty brave, and I'll go as fast as I can. I—I'm mighty near tired out."

He covered the face of the motionless child with the sombrero, and, taking out his red handkerchief, tied it to the chaparral bush.

"Good-by, little feller!" he called. "I'll sure be back soon." Then he started toward Rawhide City, ten miles away across the burning sands, and the buzzard circled lower and lower above the chaparral.

II.

Where the desert died away in a last endeavor to encroach upon the caked adobe huts of Rawhide City, stood the schoolhouse—bare, hot walls painted on a grimy canvas. Inside, the election for sheriff of Paloma County was being held, and the sound of rude laughter, oaths, and incipient quarrels came to a dark-faced man outside, sitting heavily upon his calico cow-pony, with a Winchester

across the pommel of his fringed Mexican saddle.

A cowboy came out of the schoolhouse and lounged toward the rider.

"Bill," he said, "better come on in and vote."

The man on the horse swore.

"I'm goin' to stay here till them polls close. It ain't long now."

"Sundown, I reckon," answered the other. "And Carruthers ain't showed up yet."

"How's the election goin', Charlie?" asked the watcher.

"They's a lot of fellers waitin' to see whether Carruthers 'll come before they vote. He told 'em he'd be here by sundown. If he ain't, he'll never be no sheriff in God's world. Oh, no, they won't vote for a coward. It ain't long now," he concluded, looking judicially at the western sun.

The man on the horse spoke fiercely.

"I'll kill the hound if he does come! I'll show Carruthers they won't be no dude sheriff of Paloma County. I've been layin' for him ever since he come into the cattle country, and he's got to leave the law alone!"

"You goin' home to-night, Bill?" asked the other.

"Yes, I reckon so. Been gone four days now. Told my wife I'd be home yeste'day. She and the kid are all alone. The kid rode part way down to the Jacinto with me." He spoke as if ashamed. "When I put him down he ran up the trail mighty lively." Then the man's face hardened again. "I've been hangin' round here waitin' to finish with Carruthers and this confounded election business."

"It ain't long till sundown now," said Charlie.

Out on the San Jacinto trail a figure came into view. As they watched, it reeled and fell, then rose again and staggered on.

"Some drunk, I reckon," said Bill.

They watched it indifferently. The man fell again, got upon his hands and knees, and crawled along the red trail. They could see his upturned face.

"Bill," said Charlie, "it's Carruthers!"

He started forward. The man on the horse raised his rifle with an oath.

"Stop that!" said Charlie. "You let him come—if he can."

Carruthers got to his feet again, and came unsteadily forward, fell, and once more began crawling upon his knees. His mouth opened and showed the tongue, black and swollen. His eyes were red-rimmed and ghastly. His sombrero was gone, and the setting sun glowed redly upon his face as he came to the man on the horse.

Kenard cocked his rifle, leveling it steadily at the distorted face below him. Carruthers tried to speak, but the words came slow and uncertainly, as if from long disuse.

"The little feller," he said. "Out on—the San Jacinto. Found him—Nebrasky—locoed—tried to make it—out there."

"You dirty hound!" said Kenard. "What did you find?"

"Baby—boy—maverick," came from the cowboy's black lips. "Just after Storcher's Canyon. Little feller—yellow curls—blue—blue clothes." He raised his arm and swept it to the east. "Kenard, cain't you go? He's dyin' out there."

"Where did you find him?" Kenard was beside the muttering cowboy, forcing whisky between his lips. "Charlie, it must be Tim—and he never went home!"

Carruthers wandered into delirium.

"Little maverick," he murmured, "I'll come back soon. Yes, I'll cert'nly come back right away!" The whisky brought him once more from his stupor. "That wagon," he whispered. "I'll go back to him."

The two men carried him to the wagon and laid him on the floor.

"He's a scoundrel," said Kenard fiercely. "It ain't the truth, I tell you!"

And yet he took the reins. Charlie, in the rear, sat beside Carruthers, again in delirium, while Kenard lashed the ponies forward. Men poured out of the schoolhouse. To them Charlie shouted back the news—Kenard's boy lay dying somewhere on the desert; Carruthers was dying, too, and he was the only one who could find the boy.

As for Carruthers, he felt the rush of the wagon dimly. He heard Kenard raging at the horses, and at intervals threatening the man who had deserted his child. Somewhere there was a boy—a maverick—lying under the chaparral, with a red rag to point him out. Carruthers' throat was burning up, his head throbbed intolerably, but he knew he must not faint. The wheels ground out the same pulsing refrain, "A red—a red—a red," and his brain mocked him with the fantastic images of a thousand red, red banners floating above the sentinel yuccas.

He raised himself on his arm and pointed to the right.

"Across—across!" he cried. "The red handkerchief!"

Kenard turned the plunging buckboard. As they drove up to the bush a buzzard floated away and circled above their heads.

"I've come, little feller!" said Carruthers.

Kenard turned upon him fiercely.

"Curse you for deserting him!"

Then he bent over the baby face beneath the sombrero.

III.

THE foremost men from Rawhide City, running down the trail, met the returning buckboard, with Charlie driving the galloping ponies. The men turned, running along with the wagon, calling to Charlie: "Is the kid dead?" And then: "Is *he* dead?"

Kenard sat in the rear, the child in his arms. Beside him lay Carruthers. The crowd thickened. The schoolhouse came in sight, with all Rawhide City before it. Charlie stood up on the seat.

"They're alive!" he shouted, while the men around him cheered.

The echo was taken up along the trail; the men at the schoolhouse cheered. It was to the sound of cheering that Carruthers and the child were carried into the grimy building. The men worked over them.

Kenard laughed brokenly when they told him the baby would live. They trickled cool water into Carruthers' mouth drop by drop and dashed pailful after pailful over his quivering body.

He lifted his head and looked at the child.

"Little maverick," he said anxiously, "cain't you speak to me?"

"He's all right, Jim," said Charlie.

Carruthers smiled.

"Hello, Charlie!" he murmured. "I sure reckon I called the bluff!"

Kenard came over, holding out his hand.

"Jim," he said, "they say you're sheriff all right."

The cowboy took Kenard's hand.

"Aw now, Kenard," he stammered, embarrassed. He stopped, and looked guiltily around him. "Well, Bill," he said finally. Then he stopped again. Apparently he could think of nothing to say. Once more he stared deprecatingly at Charlie. "Say, Charlie," he murmured sheepishly, "cain't you stop them men makin' that fool noise? I ain't no derned Indian massacre!"

36

A Pilgrim on the Gila

OWEN WISTER

A PILGRIM ON THE GILA.

BY OWEN WISTER.

PART I.

MIDWAY from Grant to Thomas comes Paymaster's Hill, not much after Cedar Springs and not long before you sight the valley where the Gila flows. This lonely piece of road must lie three thousand miles from Washington; but in the holiday journey that I made they are near together among the adventures of mind and body that overtook me. For as I turned southward, our capital was my first stopping-place, and it was here I gathered the expectations of Arizona with which I continued on my way.

Arizona was the unknown country I had chosen for my holiday, and I found them describing it in our National House of Representatives where I had strolled for sight-seeing, but staid to listen. The Democrats were hot to make the Territory a State, while the Republicans objected that the place had about it still too much of the raw frontier. The talk and replies of each party were not long in shaking off restraint, and in the sharp exchange of satire the Republicans were reminded that they had not thought Idaho and Wyoming unripe at a season when those Territories were rumored to be Republican. Arizona might be Democratic, but neither cattle wars nor mine revolutions flourished there. Good order and prosperity prevailed. A member from Pennsylvania

presently lost his temper, declaring that gigantic generalities about milk and honey and enlightenment would not avail to change his opinion. Arizona was well on to three times the size of New York, had a hundred and thirteen thousand square miles. Square miles of what? The desert of Sahara was twice as big as Arizona, and one of the largest misfortunes on the face of the earth. Arizona had sixty thousand inhabitants, not quite so many as the town of Troy. And what sort of people? He understood that cactus was Arizona's chief crop, stage-robbing her most active industry, and the Apache her leading citizen.

And then the Boy Orator of the Rio Grande took his good chance. I forgot his sallow face and black unpleasant hair, and even his single gesture—that straining lift of one hand above the shoulder during the suspense of a sentence and that cracking it down into the other at the full stop, endless as a pile-driver. His facts wiped any trick of manner from my notice. Indians? Stage-robbers? Cactus? Yes. He would add famine, drought, impotent law, daily murder; he could add much more, but it was all told in Mr. Pumpelly's book, true as life, thirty years ago—doubtless the latest news in Pennsylvania! Had this report discouraged the gentleman from visiting Arizona? Why, he could go there to-day in a Pullman car by two great roads, and eat his three meals in security. But Eastern statesmen were too often content with knowing their particular corner of our map while a continent of ignorance lay in their minds.

At this stroke applause sounded beside me, and turning, I had my first sight of the yellow duster. The bulky man that wore it shrewdly and smilingly watched the orator, who now dwelt upon the rapid benefits of the railways, the excellent men and things they brought to Arizona, the leap into civilization that the Territory had taken. " Let Pennsylvania see those blossoming fields for herself," said he ; "those boundless contiguities of shade." And a sort of cluck went off down inside my neighbor's throat, while the speaker with rising heat gave us the tonnage of plums exported from the Territory during the past fiscal year. Wool followed.

"Sock it to 'em, Limber Jim!" murmured the man in the duster, and executed a sort of step. He was plainly a personal acquaintance of the speaker's.

Figures never stick by me, nor can I quote accurately the catalogue of statistic abundance now recited in the House of Representatives; but as wheat, corn, peaches, apricots, oranges, raisins, spices, the rose, and the jasmine flowered in the Boy Orator's eloquence, the genial antics of my neighbor increased until he broke into delighted mutterings, such as " He's a stud-horse," and " Give 'em the kybosh," and many more that have escaped my memory. But the Boy Orator's peroration I am glad to remember, for his fervid convictions lifted him into the domain of metaphor and cadence; and though to be sure I made due allowance for enthusiasm, his picture of Arizona remained vivid with me, and I should have voted to make the Territory a State that very day.

"With her snow-clad summits, with the balm of her Southern vineyards, she loudly calls for a sister's rights. Not the isles of Greece, nor any cycle of Cathay, can compete with her horticultural resources, her Salt River, her Colorado, her San Pedro, her Gila, her hundred irrigated valleys, each one surpassing the shaded Paradise of the Nile, where thousands of noble men and elegantly educated ladies have already located, and to which thousands more, like patient monuments, are waiting breathless to throng when the

franchise is proclaimed. And if my death could buy that franchise, I would joyfully boast such martyrdom."

The orator cracked his hands together in this supreme moment, and the bulky gentleman in the duster drove an elbow against my side, whispering to me at the same time behind his hand in a hoarse confidence: "Deserted Jericho! California only holds the record on stoves now."

"I'm afraid I do not catch your allusion," I began. But at my voice he turned sharply, and giving me one short ugly stare, was looking about him, evidently at some loss, when a man at his farther side pulled at his duster, and I then saw that he had all along been taking me for a younger companion he had come in with, and with whom he now went away. In the jostle we had shifted places while his eyes were upon the various speakers, and to him I seemed an eavesdropper. Both he and his friend had a curious appearance, and they looked behind them, meeting my gaze as I watched them going; and then they made to each other some laughing comment, of which I felt myself to be the inspiration. I was standing absently on the same spot, still in a mild puzzle over California and the record on stoves. Certainly I had overheard none of their secrets, if they had any; I could not even guess what might be their true opinion about admitting Arizona to our Union.

With this last memory of our Capitol and the statesmen we have collected there to govern us, I entered upon my holiday, glad that it was to be passed in such a region of enchantment. For peaches it would be too early, and with roses and jasmine I did not importantly concern myself, thinking of them only as a pleasant sight by the way. But on my gradual journey through Lexington, Bowling Green, Little Rock, and Fort Worth I dwelt upon the shade of the valleys, and the pasture-hills dotted with the sheep of whose wool the Boy Orator had spoken ; and I wished that our cold Northwest could have been given such a bountiful climate. Upon the final morning of railroad I looked out of the window at an earth which during the night had collapsed into a vacuum, as I had so often seen happen before upon more northern parallels. The evenness of this huge nothing was cut by our track's interminable scar, and broken to the eye by the towns which now and again rose and littered the horizon like boxes dumped by emigrants. We were still in Texas, not distant from the Rio Grande, and I looked at the boxes drifting by, and wondered from which of them the Boy Orator had been let loose. Twice or three times upon this day of sand I saw green spots shining sudden and bright and biblical in the wilderness. Their isolated loveliness was herald of the valley land I was nearing each hour. The wandering Mexicans, too, bright in rags and swarthy in nakedness, put me somehow in mind of the Old Testament.

In the evening I sat at whiskey with my first acquaintance, a Mr. Mowry, one of several Arizona citizens whom my military friend at San Carlos had written me to look out for on my way to visit him. My train had trundled on to the Pacific, and I sat in a house once more—a saloon on the platform, with an open door through which the night air came pleasantly. This was now the long-expected Territory, and time for roses and jasmine to begin. Early in our talk I naturally spoke to Mr. Mowry of Arizona's resources, and her chance of becoming a State.

"We'd have got there by now," said he, "only Luke Jenks ain't half that interested in Arizona that he is in Luke Jenks."

I reminded Mr. Mowry that I was a stranger here and unacquainted with the prominent people.

"Well, Luke's as near a hog as you kin be and wear pants. Be with you in a minute," added Mr. Mowry, and shambled from the room. This was because a shot had been fired in a house across the railroad tracks. "I run two places," he explained, returning quite soon from the house and taking up the thread of his whiskey where he had dropped it. "Two outfits. This side for toorists. Th'other pays better. I come here in sixty-two."

"I trust no one has been—hurt?" said I, inclining my head towards the further side of the railroad.

"Hurt?" My question for the moment conveyed nothing to him, and he repeated the word, blinking with red eyes at me over the rim of his lifted glass. "No, nobody's hurt. I've been here a long while, and seen them as was hurt, though." Here he nodded at me depreciatingly, and I felt how short was the time that I had been here. "Th'other side pays better,"

he resumed, "as toorists mostly go to bed early. Six bits is about the figger you can reckon they'll spend, if you know anything." He nodded again, more solemn over his whiskey. "That kind's no help to business. I've been in this Territory from the start, and Arizona ain't what it was. Them mountains are named from me." And he pointed out of the door. "Mowry's Peak. On the map." With this last august statement his mind seemed to fade from the conversation, and he struck a succession of matches along the table and various parts of his person.

"Has Mr. Jenks been in the Territory long?" I suggested, feeling the silence weigh upon me.

"Luke? He's a hog. Him the people's choice! But the people of Arizona ain't what they was. Are you interested in silver?"

"Yes," I answered, meaning the political question. But before I could say what I meant he had revived into a vigor of attitude and a wakefulness of eye of which I had not hitherto supposed him capable.

"You come here," said he; and catching my arm he took me out of the door and along the track in the night, and round the corner of the railroad hotel into view of more mountains that lay to the south. "You stay here to-morrow," he pursued, swiftly, "and I'll hitch up and drive you over there. I'll show you some rock behind Helen's Dome that 'll beat any you've struck in the whole course of your life. It's on the wood reservation, and when the government abandons the post, as they're going to do—"

There is no need for my entering at length into his urgence, or the plans he put to me for our becoming partners, or for my buying him out and employing him on a salary, or buying him out and employing some other, or no one, according as I chose—the whole bright array of costumes in which he presented to me the chance of making my fortune at a stroke. I think that from my answers he gathered presently a discouraging but perfectly false impression. My Eastern hat and inexperienced face (I was certainly young enough to have been his grandchild) had a little misled him; and although he did not in the least believe the simple truth I told him, that I had come to Arizona on no sort of business, but for the pleasure of seeing the country, he now overrated my brains as greatly as he had in the beginning despised them, quite persuaded I was playing some game deeper than common, and either owned already or had my eye upon other silver mines.

"Pleasure of seeing the country, ye say?" His small wet eyes blinked as he stood on the railroad track bareheaded, considering me from head to foot. "All right. Did ye say ye're going to Globe?"

"No. To San Carlos to visit an army officer."

"Carlos is on the straight road to Globe," said Mr. Mowry, vindictively. "But ye might as well drop any idea of Globe, if ye should get one. If it's copper ye're after, there's parties in ahead of you."

Desiring, if possible, to shift his mind from its present unfavorable turn, I asked him if Mr. Adams did not live between here and Solomonsville, my route to Carlos. Mr. Adams was another character of whom my host had written me, and at my mention of his name the face of Mr. Mowry immediately soured into the same expression it had taken when he spoke of the degraded Jenks.

"So you're acquainted with him! He's got mines. I've seen 'em. If you represent any Eastern parties, tell 'em not to drop their dollars down old Adams's hole in the ground. He ain't the inexperienced juniper he looks. Him and me's been acquainted these thirty years. People claim it was Cyclone Bill held up at the Ehrenberg stage. Well, I guess I'll be seeing how the boys are getting along."

With that he moved away. A loud disturbance of chairs and broken glass had set up in the house across the railroad, and I watched the proprietor shamble from me with his deliberate gait towards the establishment that paid him best. He had left me possessor of much incomplete knowledge, and I waited for him, pacing the platform; but he did not return, and as I judged it inexpedient to follow him, I went to my bed on the tourist side of the track.

In the morning the stage went early, and as our road seemed to promise but little variety—I could see nothing but an empty plain—I was glad to find my single fellow-passenger a man inclined to talk. I did not like his mustache, which was too large for his face, nor his too

careful civility and arrangement of words; but he was genial to excess, and thoughtful of my comfort.

"I beg you will not allow my valise to incommode you," was one of his first remarks; and I liked this consideration better than any Mr. Mowry had shown me. "I fear you will detect much initial primitiveness in our methods of transportation," he said, soon.

This again called for gracious assurances on my part, and for a while our polite phrases balanced to corners until I was mentally winded keeping up such a pace of manners. The train had just brought him from Tucson, he told me, and would I indulge? On this we shared and complimented each other's whiskey.

"From your flask I take it that you are a Gentile," said he, smiling.

"If you mean tenderfoot," said I, "let me confess at once that flask and owner are from the East, and brand-new in Arizona."

"I mean you're not a Mormon. Most strangers to me up this way are. But they carry their liquor in a plain flat bottle, like this."

"Are you a—a—" Embarrassment took me as it would were I to check myself on the verge of asking a courteously disposed stranger if he had ever embezzled.

"Oh, I'm no Mormon," my new friend said, with a chuckle, and I was glad to hear him come down to reasonable English. "But Gentiles are in the minority in this valley."

"I didn't know we'd got to the valleys yet," said I, eagerly, connecting Mormons with fertility and jasmine. And I lifted the flaps of the stage, first one side and then the other, and saw the desert everywhere flat, treeless, and staring like an eye without a lid.

"This is the San Simon Valley we've been in all the time," he replied. "It goes from Mexico to the Gila, about a hundred and fifty miles."

"Like this?"

"South it's rockier. Better put the flap down."

"I don't see where people live," I said, as two smoky spouts of sand jetted from the tires and strewed over our shoes and pervaded our nostrils. "There's nothing —yes, there's one bush coming." I fastened the flaps.

"That's Seven-Mile Mesquite. They

held up the stage at this point last October. But they made a mistake in the day. The money had gone down the afternoon before, and they only got about a hundred."

"I suppose it was Mormons who robbed the stage?"

"Don't talk quite so loud," the stranger said, laughing. "The driver's one of them."

"A Mormon or a robber?"

"Well, we only know he's a Mormon."

"He doesn't look twenty. Has he many wives yet?"

"Oh, they keep that thing very quiet in these days, if they do it at all. The government made things too hot altogether. The Bishop here knows what hiding for polygamy means."

"Bishop who?"

"Meakum," I thought he answered me, but was not sure in the rattle of the stage, and twice made him repeat it, putting my hand to my ear at last. "Meakum! Meakum!" he shouted.

"Yes, sir," said the driver.

"Have some whiskey?" said my friend, promptly; and when that was over and the flat bottle passed back, he explained in a lower voice, "A son of the Bishop's."

"Indeed!" I exclaimed.

"So was the young fellow who put in the mail-bags, and that yellow-headed duck in the store this morning." My companion, in the pleasure of teaching new things to a stranger, stretched his legs on the front seat, lifted my coat out of his way, and left all formality of speech and deportment. "And so's the driver you'll have to-morrow if you're going beyond Thomas, and the stock-tender at the sub-agency where you'll breakfast. He's a yellow head too. The old man's postmaster, and owns this stage line. One of his boys has the mail contract. The old man runs the hotel at Solomonsville and two stores at Bowie and Globe, and the store and mill at Thacher. He supplies the military posts in this district with hay and wood, and a lot of things on and off through the year. Can't write his own name. Signs government contracts with his mark. He's sixty-four, and he's had eight wives. Last summer he married number nine—rest all dead, he says, and I guess that's so. He has fifty-seven recorded children, not counting the twins born last week. Any yellow-heads you'll see in the valley 'll

answer to the name of Meakum as a rule, and the other type's curly black, like this little driver specimen."

"How interesting there should be only two varieties of Meakum!" said I.

"Yes, it's interesting. Of course the whole fifty-seven don't class up yellow or black curly, but if you could take account of stock you'd find the big half of 'em do. Mothers don't seem to have influenced the type appreciably. His eight families, successive and simultaneous, cover a period of forty-three years, and yellow and black keep turning up right along. Scientifically, the suppression of Mormonism is a loss to the student of heredity. Some of the children are dead. Get killed now and then, and die too—die from sickness. But you'll easily notice Meakums as you go up the valley. Old man sees all get good jobs as soon as they're old enough. Places 'em on the railroad, places 'em in town, all over the lot. Some don't stay; you couldn't expect the whole fifty-seven to be steady; but he starts 'em all fair. We have six in Tucson now, or five, maybe. Old man's a good father."

"They're not all boys?"

"Certainly not; but more than half are."

"And you say he can't write?"

"Or read, except print, and he has to spell out that."

"But, my goodness, he's postmaster!"

"What's that got to do with it? Young Meakums all read like anything. He don't do any drudgery."

"Well, you wouldn't catch me signing any contracts I couldn't read."

"Do you think you'd catch anybody reading a contract wrong to old Meakum? Oh, momma! Why, he's king round here. Fixes the county elections and the price of tomatoes. Do you suppose any Tucson jury 'll convict any of his Mormons if he says nay? No, sir! It's been tried. Why, that man ought to be in Congress."

"If he's like that I don't consider him desirable," said I.

"Yes, he is desirable," said my friend, roughly. "Smart, can't be fooled, and looks after his people's interests. I'd like to know if that don't fill the bill?"

"If he defeats justice—"

"Oh, rats!" This interruption made me regret his earlier manner, and I was sorry the polish had rubbed through so quickly and brought us to a too precipitate familiarity. "We're Western out here," he continued, "and we're practical. When we want a thing, we go after it. Bishop Meakum worked his way down here from Utah through desert and starvation, mostly afoot, for a thousand miles, and his flock to-day is about the only class in the Territory that knows what prosperity feels like, and his laws are about the only laws folks don't care to break. He's got a brain. If he weren't against Arizona's being admitted—"

"He should know better than that," said I, wishing to be friendly. "With your fruit exports and high grade of citizens you'll soon be another California."

He gave me an odd look.

"I am surprised," I proceeded, amiably, "to hear you speak of Mormons only as prosperous. They think better of you in Washington."

"Now see here," said he, "I've been pleasant to you, and I've enjoyed this ride. But I like plain talk."

"What's the matter?" I asked.

"And I don't care for Eastern sarcasm."

"There was no intention—"

"I don't take offence where offence is not intended. As for high-grade citizens, we don't claim to know as much as—I suppose it's New York you come from?—gold-bugs and mugwumps—"

"If you can spare the time," said I, "and kindly explain what has disturbed you in my remarks, we'll each be likely to find the rest of these forty miles more supportable."

"I guess I can stand it," said he, swallowing a drink. He folded his arms and resettled his legs; and the noisome hatefulness of his laugh filled me with regret for the wet-eyed Mowry. I would now gladly have taken any amount of Mowry in exchange for this; and it struck me afresh how uncertainly one always reckons with those who suspect their own standing.

"Till Solomonsville," said I, "let us veil our estimation of each other. Once out of this stage and the world will be large enough for both of us." I was wrong there; but presentiments do not come to me often. So I too drank some of my own whiskey, lighted a cigar, and observed with pleasure that my words had enraged him.

Before either of us had devised our next remark, the stage pulled up to change horses at the first and last water in forty miles. This station was kept by Mr. Adams, and I jumped out to see the man Mr. Mowry had warned me was not an inexperienced juniper. His appearance would have drawn few but missionaries to him, and I should think would have been warning enough to any but an over-trustful child of six.

"Are you the geologist?" he said at once, coughing heavily; and when I told him I was simply enjoying a holiday, he looked at me sharply and spat against the corner of the stable. "There's one of them fellers expected," he continued, in a tone as if I need not attempt to deny that, and I felt his eye watching for signs of geology about me. I told him that I imagined the geologist must do an active business in Arizona.

"I don't hire 'em!" he exclaimed. "They can't tell me nothing about mineral."

"I suppose you have been here a long while, Mr. Adams?"

"There's just three living that come in ahead of—" The cough split his last word in pieces.

"Mr. Mowry was saying last night—"

"You've seen that old scamp, have you? Buy his mine behind Helen's Dome?"

My mirth at this turned him instantly confidential, and rooted his conviction that I was a geologist. "That's right!" said he, tapping my arm. "Don't you let 'em fool you. I guess you know your business. Now, if you want to look at good paying rock, thousands in sight, in sight, mind you—"

"Are you coming along with us?" called the little Meakum driver, and I turned and saw the new team was harnessed and he ready on his box, with the reins in his hands. So I was obliged to hasten from the disappointed Adams and climb back in my seat. The last I saw of him he was standing quite still in the welter of stable muck, stooping to his cough, the desert sun beating on his old body, and the desert wind slowly turning the windmill above the shadeless mud hovel in which he lived alone.

"Poor old devil!" said I to my enemy, half forgetting our terms in my contemplation of Adams. "Is he a Mormon?"

My enemy's temper seemed a little improved. "He's tried 'most everything except jail," he answered, his voice still harsh. "You needn't invest your sentiment there. He used to hang out at Twenty Mile in Old Camp Grant days, and he'd slit your throat for fifty cents."

But my sentiment was invested somehow. The years of the old-timers were ending so gray. Their heyday and carousals and happy-go-luckiness all gone, and in the remaining hours—what? Empty youth is such a grand easy thing, and empty age so grim!

"Has Mowry tried everything too?" I asked.

"Including jail," said my companion; and he gave me many entertaining incidents of Mowry's career, with an ill-smelling saloon cleverness that put him once more into favorable humor with me, while I retained my opinion of him. "And that uneducated sot," he concluded, "that hobo with his record of cattle-stealing and claim-jumping, and his acquittal from jail through railroad influence, actually undertook to run against me last elections. My name is Jenks—Luke Jenks, Territorial Delegate from Arizona." He handed me his card.

"I'm just from Washington," said I.

"Well, I've not been there this session. Important law business has detained me here. Yes, they backed Mowry in that election. The old spittoon had quite a following, but he hadn't the cash. That gives you some idea of the low standards I have to combat. But I hadn't to spend much. This Territory's so poor they come cheap. Seventy-five cents a head for all the votes I wanted in Bisbee, Nogales, and Yuma; and up here the Bishop was my good friend. Holding office booms my business some, and that's why I took it, of course. But I've had low standards to fight."

The Territorial Delegate now talked freely of Arizona's frontier life. "It's all dead," he said, forgetting in his fluency what he had told me about Seven-Mile Mesquite and last October. "We have a community as high toned as any in the land. Our monumental activity—" And here he went off like a cuckoo clock, or the Boy Orator, reciting the glories of Phœnix and Salt River, and the future of silver, in that special dialect of platitudes which is spoken by our more talkative statesmen, and is not quite Latin, quite grammar, or quite falsehood. "We're not all Mowrys and Adamses," said he, landing from his flight.

"In a population of fifty-nine thousand," said I, heartily, "a stranger is bound to meet decent people if he keeps on."

Again he misinterpreted me, but this time the other way, bowing like one who acknowledges a compliment; and we came to Solomonsville in such peace that he would have been astonished at my private thoughts. For I had met no undisguised vagabond nor out-and-out tramp whom I did not prefer to Luke Jenks, vote-buyer and politician. With his catch-penny plausibility, his thin-spread good-fellowship, and his New York clothes, he mistook himself for a respectable man, and I was glad to be done with him.

I could have reached Thomas that evening, but after our noon dinner let the stage go on, and delayed a night for the sake of seeing the Bishop hold service next day, which was Sunday, some few miles down the valley. I was curious to learn the Mormon ritual and what might be the doctrines that such a man as the Bishop would expound. It dashed me a little to find this would cost me forty-eight hours of Solomonsville, no Sunday stage running. But one friendly English-speaking family—the town was chiefly Mexican—made some of my hours pleasant, and others I spent in walking. Though I went early to bed I slept so late that the ritual was well advanced when I reached the Mormon gathering. From where I was obliged to stand I could only hear the preacher, already in the middle of his discourse.

"Don't empty your swill in the dooryard, but feed it to your hogs," he was saying; and any one who knows how plainly a man is revealed in his voice could have felt instantly, as I did, that here was undoubtedly a leader of men. "Rotten meat, rotten corn, spoiled milk, the truck that thoughtless folks throw away, should be used. Their usefulness has not ceased because they're rotten. That's the error of the ignorant, who know not that nothing is meant to be wasted in this world. The ignorant stay poor because they break the law of the Lord. Waste not, want not. The children of the Gentiles play in the dooryard and grow sickly and die. The mother working in the house has a pale face and poison in her blood. She cannot be a strong wife. She cannot bear strong sons to the man. He stays healthy because he toils in the field. He does not breathe the tainted air rising from the swill in the door-yard. Swill is bad for us, but it is good for swine. Waste it by the threshold it becomes deadly, and a curse falls upon the house. The mother and children are sick because she has broken a law of the Lord. Do not let me see this sin when I come among you in the valley. Fifty yards behind each house, with clean air between, let me see the well-fed swine receiving each day, as was intended, the garbage left by man. And let me see flowers in the door-yard, and stout blooming children. We will sing the twenty-ninth hymn."

The scales had many hours ago dropped from my eyes, and I saw Arizona clear, and felt no repining for roses and jasmine. They had been a politician's way of foisting one more silver State upon our Senate, and I willingly renounced them for the real thing I was getting; for my holiday already far outspangled the motleyest dream that ever visited me, and I settled down to it as we settle down in our theatre chairs, well pleased with the flying pantomime. And when, after the hymn and a blessing—the hymn was poor stuff about wanting to be a Mormon and with the Mormons stand—I saw the Bishop get into a wagon, put on a yellow duster, and drive quickly away, no surprise struck me at all. I merely said to myself: Certainly. How dull not to have foreseen that! And I knew that we should speak together soon, and he would tell me why California only held the record on stoves.

But, oh, my friends, what a country we live in, and what an age, that the same stars and stripes should simultaneously wave over this and over Delmonico's! This too I kept thinking as I killed more hours in walking the neighborhood of Solomonsville, an object of more false hope to natives whom I did not then observe. I avoided Jenks, who had business clients in the town. I went among the ditches and the fields thus turned green by the channelled Gila; and though it was scarce a paradise surpassing the Nile, it was grassy and full of sweet smells until after a few miles each way, when the desert suddenly met the pleasant verdure full in the face and corroded it to death like vitriol. The sermon came back to me as I passed the

little Mormon homes, and the Bishop rose and rose in my esteem, though not as one of the children of light. That sagacious patriarch told his flock the things of week-day wisdom down to their level, the cleanly things next to godliness, to keep them from the million squalors that stain our Gentile poor; and if he did not sound much like the Gospel, he and Deuteronomy were alike as two peas. With him and Moses thus in my thoughts, I came back after sunset, and was gratified to be late for supper. Jenks had left the dining-room, and I ate in my own company, which had become lively and full of intelligent impressions. These I sat recording later in my journal, when a hesitating knock came at my bedroom, and two young men in cowboy costume entered like shy children, endeavoring to step without creaking.

" Meakums!" my delighted mind exclaimed inwardly; but the yellow one introduced the black curly one as Mr. Follet, who in turn made his friend Mr. Cunningham known to me, and at my cordial suggestion they sat down with increasing awkwardness, first leaving their hats outside the door.

"We seen you walking around," said one.

"Lookin' the country over," said the other.

"Fine weather for travelling," said the first.

"Dusty, though," said the second.

Perceiving them to need my help in coming to their point, I said, "And now about your silver-mine."

"You've called the turn on us!" exclaimed yellow, and black curly slapped his knee. Both of them sat looking at me, laughing enthusiastically, and I gathered they had been having whiskey this Sunday night. I confess that I offered them some more, and when they realized my mildness they told me with length and confidence about the claims they had staked out on Mount Turnbull. "And there's lots of lead too," said yellow.

"I do not smelt" said I, "or deal in any way with ore. I have come here without the intention of buying anything."

"You ain't the paymaster?" burst out black curly, wrinkling his forehead like a pleasant dog.

Yellow touched his foot.

"Course he ain't!" said curly, with a

swerve of his eye. "He ain't due. What a while it always is waitin'!"

Now the paymaster was nothing to me, nor whom he paid. For all I knew, my visitors were on his roll; and why yellow should shy at the mention of him and closely watch his tipsy mate I did not try to guess. Like every one I had met so far in Arizona, these two evidently doubted I was here for my pleasure merely; but it was with entire good-humor that they remarked a man had the right to mind his own business; and so, with a little more whiskey, we made a friendly parting. They recommended me to travel with a pistol in this country, and I explained that I should do myself more harm than good with a weapon that any one handled more rapidly than I, with my inexperience.

"Good-night, Mr. Meakum," I said.

"Follet," corrected black curly.

"Cunningham," said yellow, and they picked up their hats in the hall and withdrew.

I think now those were their names— the time was coming when I should hear them take oath on it—yet I do not know. I heard many curious oaths taken.

I was glad to see black curly in the stage next day, not alone for his company, but to give him a right notion of what ready money I had about me. Thinking him over, and his absence of visible means of support, and his interest in me, I took opportunity to mention quite by the way that five or six dollars was all that I ever carried on my person, the rest being in New York drafts, worthless in any hands but mine. And I looked at the time once or twice for him to perceive the cheapness of my nickel watch. That the Bishop was not his father I had indirect evidence when we stopped at Thacher to change horses and drop a mail-sack, and the Mormon divine suddenly lifted the flap and inspected us. He nodded to me and gave Follet a message.

"Tell your brother" (wouldn't a father have said Tom or Dick?) "that I've given him chances enough and he don't take 'em. He don't feed my horses, and my passengers complain he don't feed them —though that's not so serious!" said he to me, with a jovial wink. "But I won't have my stock starved. You'll skip the station and go through to Thomas with this pair," he added to the driver in his voice of lusty command. "You'll get

supper at Thomas. Everything's moved on there from to-day. That's the rule now." Then he returned to black curly, who, like the driver, had remained cowed and respectful throughout the short harangue. "Your brother could have treated me square and made money by that station. Tell him that, and to see me by Thursday. If he's thinking of peddling vegetables this season, I'll let him sell to Fort Bowie. Safford takes Carlos, and I won't have two compete in the same market, or we'll be sinking low as Eastern prices," said he to me, with another wink. "Drive on now. You're late."

He shut the flap, and we were off quickly—too quickly. In the next few moments I could feel that something all wrong went on; there was a jingle and snapping of harness, and such a voice from the Bishop behind us that I looked out to see him. We had stopped, and he was running after us at a wonderful pace for a man of sixty-four.

"If you don't drive better than that," said the grizzled athlete, arriving cool and competent, "you'll saw wood for another year. Look how you've got them trembling."

It was a young pair, and they stood and steamed while the broken gear was mended.

"What did California hold the record in before the Boy Orator broke it?" said I, getting out.

He shot at me the same sinister look I had seen in the Capitol, the look he must always wear, I suppose, when taken aback. Then he laughed broadly and heartily, a strong pleasant laugh that nearly made me like him. "So you're that fellow! Ho, ho! Away down here now! Oh, ho, ho! What's your business?"

"You wouldn't believe if I told you," said I, to his sudden sharp question.

"Me? Why, I believe everything I'm told. What's your name?"

"Will you believe I haven't come to buy anybody's silver-mine?"

"Silver! I don't keep it. Unloaded ten years ago, before the rabbit died."

"Then you're the first anti-silver man I've met."

"I'm anti anything I can't sell, young man. Here's all there is to silver: Once upon a time it was hard to get, and we had to have it. Now it's easy. When it gets as common as dirt it 'll be as cheap as dirt. Same as watermelons when it's a big crop. D'you follow me? That's silver for you, and I don't want it. So you've come away down here. Well, well! What did you say your name was?"

I told him.

"Politician?"

"God forbid!"

"Oh, ho, ho! Well, yes. I took a look at those buzzards there in Washington. Our Senate and Representatives. They were screeching a heap. All about ratios. You'll be sawing wood yet!" he shouted to the driver, and strode up to help him back a horse. "Now ratio is a good-sounding word too, and I guess that's why they chew on it so constant. Better line of language than they get at home. I'll tell you about Congress. Here's all there is to it: You can divide them birds in two lots. Those who know better and those who don't. D'you follow me?"

"And which kind is the Boy Orator?"

"Limber Jim? Oh, he knows better. I know Jim. You see, we used to have a saying in Salt Lake that California had the smallest stoves and the biggest liars in the world. Now Jim—well, there's an old saying busted. But you'll see Arizona 'll go back on the Democrats. If they put wool on the free list she'll stay Republican, and they won't want her admitted, which suits me first rate. My people here are better off as they stand."

"But your friend Mr. Jenks favors admission!" I exclaimed.

"Luke? He's been talking to you, has he? Well, now, Luke. Here's all there is to him Natural gas. That's why I support him, you see. If we sent a real smart man to Washington he might get us made a State. Ho, ho! But Luke stays here most of the time, and he's no good anyway. Oh, ho, ho! So you're buying no mines this season?"

Once more I found myself narrating the insignificance of my visit to Arizona —the Bishop must have been a hard inquisitor for even the deeply skilful to elude—and for the first time my word was believed. He quickly took my measure, saw that I had nothing to hide, and after telling me I could find good hunting and scenery in the mountains north, paid me no further attention, but masterfully laid some final commands on the intimidated driver. Then I bade good-by to the Bishop, and watched that old loco-

motive moving vigorously back along the road to his manifold business.

The driver was ill pleased to go hungry for his supper until Thomas, but he did not dare complain much over the new rule, even to black curly and me. This and one other thing impressed me. Some miles further on we had passed out of the dust for a while, and rolled up the flaps.

"She's waiting for you," said the driver to black curly, and that many-sided youth instantly dived to the bottom of the stage, his boots and pistol among my legs.

"Throw your coat over me," he urged.

I concealed him with that and a mail-sack, and stretched my head out to see what lioness stood in his path. But it was only a homelike little cabin, and at the door a woman, comely and mature, eying the stage expectantly. Possibly wife, I thought, more likely mother, and I asked, "Is Mrs. Follet strict?" choosing a name to fit either.

The driver choked and chirruped, but no sound came from under the mail-sack until we had passed the good-day to the momentous female, whose response was harsh with displeasure as she wheeled into her door. A sulky voice then said, "Tell me when she's gone, Bill." But we were a safe two hundred yards on the road before he would lift his head, and his spirits were darkened during the remainder of the journey.

"Come and live East," said I, inviting him to some whiskey at the same time. "Back there they don't begin sitting up for you so early in the evening."

This did not enliven him, although upon our driver it seemed to bring another fit as much beyond the proportion of my joke as his first had been. "She tires a man's spirit," said black curly, and with this rueful utterance he abandoned the subject; so that when we reached Thomas in the dim night my curiosity was strong, and I paid little heed to this new place where I had come or to my supper. Black curly had taken himself off, and the driver sat at the table with me, still occasionally snickering in his plate. He would explain nothing that I asked him until the gaunt woman who waited on us left us for the kitchen, when he said, with a nervous, hasty relish, "The widow Sproud is slick," and departed.

Consoled by no better clew than this I went to bed in a downstairs room, and in my strange rising next day I did not see the driver again. Callings in the air awaked me, and a wandering sound of wheels. The gaunt woman stood with a lamp in my room saying the stage was ready, and disappeared. I sprang up blindly, and again the callings passed in the blackness outside, long cries, inarticulate to me. Wheels heavily rolled to my door, and a whip was struck against it, and there loomed the stage, and I made out the calling. It was the three drivers, about to separate before the dawn on their three diverging ways, and they were wailing their departure through the town that travellers might hear, in whatever place they lay sleeping. "Boo-wie! All aboa-rd!" came from somewhere, dreary and wavering, met at further distance by the floating antiphonal, "Aboa-rd, aboa-rd for Grant!" and in the chill black air my driver lifted his portion of the strain, chanting, "Car-los! Car-los!" One last time he circled in the nearer darkness with his stage to let me dress. Mostly unbuttoned, and with not even a half-minute to splash cold water in my eyes, I clambered solitary into the vehicle and sat among the leather mail-bags, some boxes, and a sack of grain, having four hours yet till breakfast for my contemplation. I heard the faint reveille at Camp Thomas, but to me it was a call for more bed, and I pushed and pulled the grain-sack until I was able to distribute myself and in a manner doze shivering in my overcoat. Not the rising of the sun upon this blight of sand, nor the appearance of a cattle herd, and both black curly and yellow driving it among its dust clouds, warmed my frozen attention as I lay in a sort of spell. I saw with apathy the mountains extraordinary in the crystal prism of the air, and soon after the strangest scene I have ever looked on by the light of day. For as we went along the driver would give a cry, and when an answering cry came from the thorn-bush we stopped, and a naked Indian would appear, running, to receive a little parcel of salt or sugar or tobacco he had yesterday given the driver some humble coin to buy for him in Thomas. With changeless pagan eyes staring a moment at me on my sack of grain, and a grunt when his purchase was set in his hand, each black-haired desert figure turned away, the bare feet moving silent and the copper body, stark naked except the breech-clout, receding to dimness in

the thorn-bush. But I lay incurious at this new vision of what our wide continent holds in fee under the single title United States, until breakfast came. This helped me, and I livened somewhat at finding the driver and the breakfast man were both genuine Meakums, as Jenks had told me they would be.

It surprised me to discover now that I was looked for along the Gila, and my name approximately known, and when I asked if my friend Captain Stirling had spoken of my coming, it was evidently not he, but the news was in the air. This was a prominence I had never attained in any previous part of the world, and I said to the driver that I supposed my having no business made me a curiosity. That might have something to do with it, he answered (he seemed to have a literal mind), but some had thought I was the paymaster.

"Folks up here," he explained, "are liable to know who's coming."

"If I lived here," said I, "I should be anxious for the paymaster to come early and often."

"Well, it does the country good. The soldiers spend it all right here, and us civilians profit some by it."

Having got him into conversation, I began to introduce the subject of black curly, hoping to lead up to the widow Sproud; but before I had compassed this we reached San Carlos, where a blow awaited me. Stirling, my host, had been detailed on a scout this morning! I was stranded here, a stranger, where I had come thousands of miles to see an old friend. His regret and messages to make myself at home, and the quartermaster's hearty will to help me to do so, could not cure my blankness. He might be absent two weeks or more. I looked round at Carlos and its staring sand. Then I resolved to go at once to my other friends, now stationed at Fort Grant. For I had begun to feel myself at an immense distance from any who would care what happened to me for good or ill, and I longed to see some face I had known before. So in gloom I retraced some unattractive steps. This same afternoon I staged back along the sordid incompetent Gila River, and to kill time pushed my Sproud inquiry, at length with success. To check the inevitably slipshod morals of a frontier commonwealth, Arizona has a statute that in reality only sets in writing a presumption of the common law, the ancient presumption of marriage, which is that when a man and woman go to housekeeping for a certain length of time, they shall be deemed legally married. In Arizona this period is set at twelve months, and ten had run against Mrs. Sproud and young Follet. He was showing signs of leaving her. The driver did not think her much entitled to sympathy, and certainly she showed later that she could devise revenge. As I thought over these things we came again to the cattle herd, where my reappearance astonished yellow and black curly. Nor did the variance between my movements and my reported plans seem wholly explained to them by Stirling's absence, and at the station where I had breakfasted I saw them question the driver about me. This interest in my affairs heightened my desire to reach Fort Grant; and when next day I came to it after another waking to the chanted antiphonals and another faint reveille from Camp Thomas in the waning dark, extreme comfort spread through me. I sat in the club with the officers, and they taught me a new game of cards called Solo, and filled my glass. Here were lieutenants, captains, a major, and a colonel, American citizens with a love of their country and a standard of honor; here floated our bright flag serene against the lofty blue, and the mellow horns sounded at guard mounting, bringing moisture to the eyes. The day was punctuated with the bright trumpet, people went and came in the simple dignity of duty, and once again I talked with good men and women. God bless our soldier people! I said it often.

They somewhat derided my uneasiness in the Gila Valley, and found my surmisings sensational. Yet still they agreed much ready money was an unwise thing on a stage journey, although their profession (I suppose) led them to take being "held up" less seriously than I with my peaceful traditions of elevators and the downtown lunch. In the wide Sulphur Springs Valley, where I rode at large, but never so long or so far that Fort Grant lay not in sight across that miracle of air, it displeased me to come one morning upon yellow and black curly jogging along beneath the government telegraph line.

"You cover a wide range," said I.

"Cowboys have to," they answered. "So you've not quit us yet?"

"I'm thinking of taking a hunt and fish towards Fort Apache."

"We're your men, then. You'll find us at Thomas any time. We're gathering stock up these draws, but that 'll be through this week."

They spurred their horses and vanished among the steep little hills that run up to Mount Graham. But indeed they should be no men of mine! Stirling had written me his scout was ended, and San Carlos worth a longer visit than I had made there, promising me an escort should I desire to camp in the mountains. An escort it should be, and no yellow or black curly, over-curious about my private matters! This fell in excellently with the coming paymaster's movements. Major Pidcock was even now on his way to Fort Grant from Fort Bowie; and when he went to Thomas and Carlos I would go too, in his ambulance; and I sighed with pleasure at escaping that stage again.

Major Pidcock arrived in a yellow duster, but in other respects differed from the Bishop, though in his body a bulky man. We were introduced to each other at the club.

"I am glad, sir, to meet you at last," I said to him. "The whole Gila Valley has been taking me for you."

"Oh—ah!" said Pidcock, vaguely, and pulling at some fat papers in his coat; "indeed. I understand that is a very ignorant population. Colonel Vincent, a word with you. The Department Commander requests me—" And here he went into some official talk with the Colonel.

I turned among the other officers, who were standing by an open locker having whiskey, and Major Evlie put his hand on my shoulder. "He doesn't mean anything," he whispered, while the rest looked knowingly at me. Presently the Colonel explained to Pidcock that he would have me to keep him company to Carlos.

"Oh—ah, Colonel. Of course we don't take civilians not employed by the government, as a rule. But exceptions—ah—can be made," he said to me. "I will ask you to be ready immediately after breakfast to-morrow." And with that he bowed to us all and sailed forth across the parade-ground.

The Colonel's face was red, and he

THE RED MAN'S PARCEL POST.

swore in his quiet voice; but the lips of the lieutenants by the open locker quivered fitfully in the silence.

"Don't mind Pidcock," Evlie remarked. "He's a paymaster." And at this the line officers became disorderly, and two lieutenants danced together; so that, without catching Evlie's evidently military joke, I felt pacified.

"And I've got to have him to dinner," sighed the Colonel, and wandered away.

"You'll get on with him, man—you'll get on with him in the ambulance," said my friend Paisley. "Flatter him, man. Just ask him about his great strategic stroke at Cayuse Station that got him his promotion to the pay department."

Well, we made our start after breakfast, Major Pidcock and I, and another passenger too, who sat with the driver—a black cook going to the commanding officer's at Thomas. She was an old plantation mammy, with a kind but bewildered face, and I am sorry that the noise of our driving lost me much of her conversation; for whenever we slowed, and once when I walked up a hill, I found her remarks to be steeped in a flighty charm.

"Fo' Lawd's sake!" said she. "W'at's dat?" And when the driver told her that it was a jack-rabbit, "You go 'long!" she cried, outraged. "I's seed rabbits earlier 'n de mawnin' dan yo'self." She watched the animal with all her might, muttering, "Law, see him squot!" and "Hole on, hole on!" and "Yasser, he done gone fo' sho. My grashus, you lemme have a scatter shoot gun an' a spike-tail smell-dog, an' I'll git one of day narrah-gauge mules."

"I shall not notice it," said Major Pidcock to me, with dignity. "But they should have sent such a creature by the stage. It's unsuitable, wholly."

"Unquestionably," said I, straining to catch the old lady's song on the box.

"'Don't you fo'git I'm a-comin' behind you—
Lam slam de lunch ham.'"

"This is insufferable," said Pidcock. "I shall put her off at Cedar Springs."

I suppose the drive was long to him, but to me it was not. Noon and Cedar Springs prematurely ended the first half of this day most memorable in the whole medley of my excursion, and we got down to dine. Two travellers bound for Thomas by our same road were just setting out, but they firmly declined to transport our cook, and Pidcock moodily saw them depart in their wagon, leaving him burdened still; for this was the day the stage made its down trip from Thomas. Never before had I seen water paid for. When the Major, with windy importance, came to settle his bill, our dozen or fourteen escort horses and mules made an item, the price of watering two head being two bits, quite separate from the feed; and I learned that water was thus precious over most of the Territory.

Our cook remounted the box in high feather, and began at once to comment upon Arizona. "Dere ain't no winter, nor no spring, nor no rain de whole year roun'. My! what a country fo' to gib de chick'ns courage! Dey hens must jus' sit an' lay an' lay. But de po' ducks done have a mean time.

"'O—Lawd!
Sinner is in my way, Daniel.'"

"I would not permit a cook like that inside my house," said Major Pidcock.

"She may not be dangerous," I suggested.

"Land! is dey folks gwineter shoot me?" Naturally I looked, and so did the Major; but it was two of our own mounted escort that she saw out to the right of us among the hills. "Tell dem nigger jockeys I got no money. Why do dey triflin' chillun ride in de kerridge?" She did not mean ourselves, but the men with their carbines in the escort wagon in front of us. I looked out at them, and their mouths were wide open for joy at her. It was not a stately progress for twenty-eight thousand dollars in gold and a paymaster to be making. Major Pidcock unbuttoned his duster and reclined to sleep, and presently I also felt the after-dinner sloth shutting my eyes pleasantly to this bleak road.

"Heave it, chillun! can't you heave?" I heard our cook say, and felt us stop.

"What's that?" I asked, drowsily.

"Seems to be a rock fallen down," the Major answered. "Start it, men; roll it!"

I roused myself. We were between rocks and banks on the brow of a hill, down which the narrow road descended with a slight turn. I could see the escort wagon halted ahead of us, and beyond it the men stooping at a large stone, around which there was no possible room to drive. This stone had fallen, I reflected, since those travellers for Thomas—

There was a shot, and a mule rolled over.

I shall never forget that. Why, it was like the theatre for one paralyzed second! The black soldiers, the mule, the hill, all a clear picture seen through an opera-glass, stock-still, and nothing to do with me—for a congealed second. And, dear me, what a time we had then!

Crackings volleyed around us, puffs of smoke jetted blue from rock ramparts which I had looked at and thought natural—or rather, not thought of at all—earth and gravel spattered up from the ground, the bawling negress spilled off her box and ran in spirals, screaming, "Oh, bless my soul, bless my soul!" and I saw a yellow duster flap out of the ambulance. "Lawd grashus, he's a-leavin' us!" screeched the cook, and she changed her spirals for a bee-line after him. I should never have run but for this example, for I have not naturally the presence of mind, and in other accidents through which I have passed there has never been promptness about me; the reasoning and all have come when it was over, unless it went on pretty long, when I have been sometimes able to leap to a conclusion. But yes, I ran now, straight under a screen of rocks, over the top of which rose the heads of yellow and black curly. The sight of them sent rushing over me the first agreeable sensation I had felt—shapeless rage—and I found myself shouting at them, "Scoundrels! scoundrels!" while shooting continued briskly around me. I think my performance would have sincerely entertained them could they have spared the time for it; and, as it was, they were regarding me with obvious benevolence, when Mr. Adams looked evilly at me across the stones, and black curly seized the old devil's rifle in time to do me a good turn. Mr. Adams's bullet struck short of me ten feet, throwing the earth in my face. Since then I have felt no sympathy for that tobacco-running pioneer. He listened, coughing, to what black curly said as he pointed to me, and I see now that I have never done a wiser thing than to go unarmed in that country. Curly was telling Mr. Adams that I was harmless. Indeed, that was true! In the bottom of this cup, target for a circled rim of rifles, separated from the widely scattered Major and his men, aware of nothing in particular, and seeing nothing in particular but smoke and rocks and faces peering everywhere, I walked to a stone and sat upon it, hypnotized again into a spectator. From this undisturbed vantage I saw shape itself the theft of the gold. The first theft, that is; for it befell me later to witness a ceremony by which these eagles of Uncle Sam again changed hands in a manner that stealing is as good a name for as any.

They had got two mules killed, so that there could be no driving away in a hurry, and I saw that killing men was not a part of their war, unless required as a means to their end. Major Pidcock had spared them this necessity; I could see him nowhere; and with him to imitate I need not pause to account for the members of our dismounted escort. Two soldiers, indeed, lay on the ground, the sergeant and another, who had evidently fired a few resisting shots; but let me say at once that these poor fellows recovered, and I saw them often again through this adventure that bound us together, else I could not find so much hilarity in my retrospect. Escort wagon and ambulance stood empty and foolish on the road, and there lay the ingenious stone all by itself, and the carbines all by themselves foolish in the wagon, where the innocent soldiers had left them on getting out to move the stone. Smoke loitered thin and blue over this now exceedingly quiet scene, and I smelt it where I sat. How secure the robbers had felt themselves, and how reckless of identification! Mid-day, a public road within hearing of a ranch, an escort of a dozen regulars, no masks, and the stroke perpetrated at the top of a descent, contrary to all laws of road agency. They swarmed into sight from their ramparts. I cannot tell what number, but several I had never seen before and never saw again; and Mr. Adams and yellow and black curly looked so natural that I wondered if Jenks and the Bishop would come climbing down too. But no more old friends turned up that day. Some went to the ambulance swift and silent, while others most needlessly stood guard. Nothing was in sight but my seated inoffensive form, and the only sound was, somewhere among the rocks, the voice of the incessant negress speeding through her prayers. I saw them at the ambulance, surrounding, passing, lifting, stepping in and out, ferreting, then moving slowly up with their

HOLDING UP THE PAY ESCORT.

booty round the hill's brow. Then silence; then hoofs; then silence again, except the outpouring negress, scriptural, melodious, symbolic:

"Oh—Lawd!
Sinner is in my way, Daniel."

PART II.

ALL this while I sat on the stone. "They have done us brown," I said aloud, and hearing my voice waked me from whatever state I had been in. My senses bounded, and I ran to the hurt soldiers. One was very sick. I should not have known what to do for them, but people began to arrive, brought from several quarters by the fusillade—two in a wagon from Cedar Springs, two or three on horses from the herds they were with in the hills, and a very old man from somewhere, who offered no assistance to any one, but immediately seated himself and began explaining what we all should have done. The negress came out of her rocks, exclamatory with pity over the wounded, and, I am bound to say, of more help to them than any of us, kind and motherly in the midst of her ceaseless discourse. Next arrived Major Pidcock in his duster, and took charge of everything.

"Let yer men quit the'r guns, did ye, general?" piped the very old man. "Escort oughtn't never to quit the'r guns. I seen that at Molino del Rey. And ye should have knowed that there stone didn't crawl out in the road like a turtus to git the sunshine."

"Where were you?" thundered the Major to the mounted escort, who now appeared, half an hour after the event, from our flanks, which they had been protecting at an immense distance. "Don't you know your duty's to be on hand when you hear firing?"

"Law, honey!" said the cook, with a guffaw, "lemme git my han's over my mouf."

"See them walls they fooled yer with," continued the old man, pointing with his stick. "I could have told yer them wasn't natural. Them doesn't show like country rock," by which I found that he meant their faces were new-exposed and not weather-beaten.

"No doubt you could have saved us, my friend," said the Major, puffing blandly.

But one cannot readily impress ninety summers. "Yes, I could have told yer that," assented the sage, with senile complacence. "My wife could have told yer that. Any smart girl could have told yer that."

"I shall send a despatch for re-enforcements," announced Pidcock. "Tap the telegraph wire," he ordered.

"I have to repawt to the Major," said a soldier, saluting, "dat de line is cut."

At this I was taken with indecent laughter, and turned away, while ninety summers observed, "Of course them boys would cut the wire if they knew their business."

Swearing capably, the Major now accounted clearly to us for the whole occurrence, striding up and down, while we lifted the hurt men into the ranch wagon, and arranged for their care at Cedar Springs. The escort wagon hurried on to Thomas for a doctor. The ambulance was of course crippled of half its team, and the dead mules were cleared from their harness and got to the road-side. Having satisfactorily delivered himself of his explanation, the Major now organized a party for following the trail of the robbers, to learn into what region they had betaken themselves. Incredible as it may seem, after my late unenterprising conduct, I asked one of the riders to lend me his horse, which he did, remarking that he should not need it for an hour, and that he was willing to risk my staying absent longer than that.

So we rode away. The trail was clear, and we had but little trouble to follow it. It took us off to the right through a mounded labyrinth of hillocks, puny and gray like ash-heaps, where we rose and fell in the trough of the sullen landscape. I told Pidcock of my certainty about three of the robbers, but he seemed to care nothing for this, and was something less than civil at what he called my suggestions.

"When I have ascertained their route," he said, "it will be time enough to talk of their identity."

In this way we went for a mile or so, the trail leading us onward, frank and straight, to the top of a somewhat higher hill, where it suddenly expired off the earth. No breath vanishes cleaner from glass, and it brought us to a dead halt. We retraced the tracks to make sure we had not lost them before, but there was no mistake, and again we halted dead at the vanishing-point. Here were signs that something out of the common had happened. Men's feet and horseshoe prints, aimless and superimposed, marked a trodden frame of ground, inside which was nothing, and beyond which nothing lay but those faint tracks of wandering cattle and horses that scatter everywhere in this country. Not one defined series, not even a single shod horse, had gone over this hill, and we spent some minutes vainly scouring in circles wider and wider. Often I returned to stare at the trodden imperturbable frame of ground, and caught myself inspecting first the upper air, and next the earth, and speculating if the hill were hollow; and mystery began to film over the hitherto sharp figures of black curly and yellow, while the lonely country around grew so unpleasant to my nerves that I was glad when Pidcock decided that he must give up for to-day. We found the little group of people beginning to disperse at the ambulance.

"Fooled yer ag'in, did they?" said the old man. "Played the blanket trick on yer, I expect. Guess yer gold's got pretty far by now." With this parting, and propped upon his stick, he went as he had come. Not even at any time of his youth, I think, could he have been companionable, and old age had certainly filled him with the impartial malevolence of the devil. I rejoice to say that he presided at none of our further misadventures.

Short twenty-eight thousand dollars and two mules, we set out anew, the Major, the cook, and I, along the Thomas road, with the sun drawing closer down upon the long steel saw that the peaks to our westward made. The site of my shock lay behind me—I knew now well enough that it had been a shock, and that for a long while to come I should be able to feel the earth spatter from Mr. Adams's bullet against my ear and sleeve whenever I might choose to conjure that moment up again—and the present comfort in feeling my distance from that stone in the road increase continually put me in more cheerful spirits. With the quick rolling of the wheels many subjects for talk came into my mind, and had I been seated on the box beside the cook we should have found much in common. Ever since her real tenderness to those wounded men, I had wished to ask the poor old creature how she came in this

weary country, so far from the pleasant fields of cotton and home. Her hair was gray, and she had seen much, else she had never been so kind and skilful at bandaging. And I am quite sure that somewhere in the chambers of her incoherent mind and simple heart abided the sweet ancient fear of God and love of her fellow-men—virtues I had met but little in Arizona.

"De whole family, scusin' two," she was saying, "dey bust loose and tuck to de woods." And then she moralized upon the two who staid behind and were shot. "But de Gennul, he 'low dat wuz mighty pore reasonin'."

I should have been glad to exchange views with her, for Major Pidcock was dull company. This prudent officer was not growing distant from his disaster, and as night began to come, and we neared Thomas, I suppose the thought that our ambulance was driving him perhaps to a court martial was enough to submerge the man in gloom. To me and my news about the robbers he was a little more considerate, although he still made nothing of the fact that some of them lived in the Gila Valley, and were of the patriarchal tribe of Meakum.

"Scoundrels like that," he muttered, lugubriously, "know every trail in the country, and belong nowhere. Mexico is not a long ride from here. They can get a steamer at Guaymas and take their choice of ports down to Valparaiso. Yes, they'll probably spend that money in South America. Oh, confound that woman!"

For the now entirely cheerful negress was singing:

> "'Dar's de gal, dar's my Susanna.
> How by gum you know?
> Know her by de red bandanna,
> An' de shoestring hangin' on de flo'—
> Dad blam her!—
> An' de shoestring hangin'—'"

"Goodness grashus w'at *you* gwineter do?"

At this sudden cry and the stopping of the ambulance I thought more people were come for our gold, and my spirit resigned itself. Sit still was all I should do now, and look for the bright day when I should leave Arizona forever. But it was only Mrs. Sproud. I had clean forgotten her, and did not at once take in to what an important turn the affairs of some of us had come. She stepped out of the darkness, and put her hand on the door of the ambulance.

"I suppose you're the paymaster?" Her voice was soft and easy, but had an ample volume. As Pidcock was replying with some dignity that she was correct, she caught sight of me. "Who is this man?" she interrupted him.

"My clerk," said Pidcock; and this is the promptest thing I can remember of the Major, always excepting his conduct when the firing began on the hill. "You're asking a good many questions, madam," he added.

"I want to know who I'm talking to," said she, quietly. "I think I've seen property of yours this evening."

"You had better get in, madam; better get in."

"This is the paymaster's team from Fort Grant?" said Mrs. Sproud to the driver.

"Yes, yes, madam. Major Pidcock— I am Major Pidcock, Paymaster to the United States Army in the Department of the Colorado. I suppose I understand you."

"Seven canvas sacks," said Mrs. Sproud, standing in the road.

"Get in, madam. You can't tell who may be within hearing. You will find it to your advantage to keep nothing—"

Mrs. Sproud laughed luxuriously, and I began to discern why black curly might at times have been loath to face her.

"I merely meant, madam—I desired to make it clear that—a—"

"I think I know what you meant. But I have no call to fear the law. It will save you trouble to believe that before we go any farther."

"Certainly, madam. Quite right." The man was sweating. What with court martial and Mrs. Sproud, his withers were wrung. "You are entirely sure, of course, madam—"

"I am entirely sure I know what I am about. That seems to be more than some do that are interested in this gold—the folks, for instance, that have hid it in my hay-stack."

"Hay-stack! Then they're not gone to Mexico!"

"Mexico, sir? They live right here in the valley. Now I'll get in, and when I ask you, you will please to set me down." She seated herself opposite us and struck a match. "Now we know what we all look like," said she, holding the light up, massive and handsome. "This young

man is the clerk, and we needn't mind him. I have done nothing to fear the law, but what I am doing now will make me a traveller again. I have no friends here. I was acquainted with a young man." She spoke in the serenest tone, but let fall the match more quickly than its burning made needful. "He was welcome in my home. He let them cook this up in my house and never told me. I live a good ways out on the road, and it was a safe place, but I didn't think why so many met him, and why they sat around my stable. Once in a while this week they've been joking about winning the soldiers' pay—they often win that— but I thought it was just cowboy games, till I heard horses coming quick at sundown this afternoon, and I hid. Will hunted around and said—and said I was on the stage coming from Solomonsville, and so they had half an hour yet. He thought so. And, you see, nobody lives in the cabin but—but me." Mrs. Sproud paused a moment here, and I noticed her breathing. Then she resumed: "So I heard them talk some; and when they all left, pretty soon, I went to the hay-stack, and it was so. Then the stage came along and I rode to Thomas."

"You left the gold there!" groaned the wretched Major, and leaned out of the ambulance.

"I'm not caring to touch what's none of mine. Wait, sir, please; I get out here. Here are the names I'm sure of. Stop the driver, or I'll jump." She put a paper in the Major's hand. "It is Mrs. Sproud's hay-stack," she added.

"Will you—this will never—can I find you to-morrow?" he said, helplessly, holding the paper out at her.

"I have told you all I know," said Mrs. Sproud, and was gone at once.

Major Pidcock leaned back for some moments as we drove. Then he began folding his paper with care. "I have not done with that person," said he, attempting to restore his crippled importance. "She will find that she must explain herself."

Our wheels whirled in the sand and we came quickly to Thomas, to a crowd of waiting officers and ladies; and each of us had an audience that night—the cook, I feel sure, while I myself was of an importance second only to the Major's. But he was at once closeted with the commanding officer, and I did not learn their counsels, hearing only at breakfast that the first step was taken. The detail sent out had returned from the hay-stack, bringing gold, indeed—one half-sackful. The other six were gone, and so was Mrs. Sproud. It was useless to surmise, as we, however, did that whole forenoon, what any of this might mean; but in the afternoon came a sign. A citizen of the Gila Valley had been paying his many debts at the saloon and through the neighborhood, in gold. In one well known for the past two years to be without a penny, it was the wrong moment to choose for honest affluence, and this citizen was the first arrest. This further instance of how secure the robbers felt themselves to be outdid anything that had happened yet, and I marvelled until following events took from me the power of astonishment. The men named on Mrs. Sproud's paper were fewer than I think fired upon us in the attack, but every one of them was here in the valley, going about his business. Most were with the same herd of cattle that I had seen driven by yellow and black curly near the subagency, and they too were there. The solvent debtor, I should say, was not arrested this morning. Plans that I, of course, had no part in delayed matters, I suppose for the sake of certainty. Black curly and his friends were watched, and found to be spending no gold yet; and since they did not show sign of leaving the region, but continued with their cattle, I imagine every effort was being made to light upon their hidden treasure. But their time came, and soon after it mine. Stirling, my friend, to whom I had finally gone at Carlos, opened the wire door of his quarters where I sat one morning, and with a heartless smile introduced me to a gentleman from Tucson.

"You'll have a chance to serve your country," said Stirling.

I was subpœnaed!

"Certainly not!" I said, with indignation. "I'm going East. I don't live here. You have witnesses enough without me. We all saw the same thing."

"Witnesses never see the same thing," observed the man from Tucson. "It's the government that's after you. But you'll not have to wait. Our case is first on the list."

"You can take my deposition," I began; but what need to dwell upon this interview? "When I come to visit you again," I said to Stirling, "let me know." And that pink-faced, gray-haired captain still shouted heartlessly.

"You're an egotist," said he. "Think of the scrape poor old Pidcock has got himself into."

"The government needs all the witnesses it can get," said the man from Tucson. "Luke Jenks is smart in some ways."

"Luke Jenks?" I sat up in my canvas extension chair.

"Territorial Delegate; firm of Parley and Jenks, Tucson. He's in it."

"By heavens!" I cried, in unmixed delight. "But I didn't see him when they were shooting at us."

The man from Tucson stared at me curiously. "He is counsel for the prisoners," he explained.

"The Delegate to Washington defends these thieves who robbed the United States?" I repeated.

"Says he'll get them off. He's going to stay home from Washington and put it through in shape."

It was here that my powers of astonishment went into their last decline, and I withheld my opinion upon the character of Mr. Jenks as a public man. I settled comfortably in my canvas chair.

"The prisoners are citizens of small means, I judge," said I. "What fee can they pay for such a service?"

"Ah!" said Stirling.

"That's about it, I guess," said the man from Tucson. "Luke is mighty smart in his law business. Well, gents, good-day to you. I must be getting after the rest of my witnesses."

"Have you seen Mrs. Sproud?" I asked him.

"She's quit the country. We can't trace her. Guess she was scared."

"But that gold!" I exclaimed, when Sterling and I were alone. "What in the world have they done with those six other bags?"

"Ah!" said he, as before. "Do you want to bet on that point? Dollars to doughnuts Uncle Sam never sees a cent of that money again. I'll stake my next quarter's pay—"

"Pooh!" said I. "That's poor odds against doughnuts if Pidcock has the paying of it." And I took my turn at laughing at the humorous Stirling.

"That Mrs. Sproud is a sensible woman to have gone," said he, reflectively.

"They would know she had betrayed them, and she wouldn't be safe in the valley. Witnesses who know too much sometimes are found dead in this country—but you'll have government protection."

"Thank you kindly," said I. "That's what I had on the hill."

But Stirling took his turn at me again with freshened mirth.

Well, I think that we witnesses were worth government protection. At seasons of especial brightness and holiday, such as Christmas and Easter, the theatres of the variety order have a phrase which they sometimes print in capitals upon their bills—Combination Extraordinary; and when you consider Major Pidcock and his pride, and the old plantation cook, and my reserved Eastern self, and our coal-black escort of the hill, more than a dozen, including Sergeant Brown and the private, both now happily recovered of their wounds, you can see what appearance we made descending together from the mean Southern Pacific train at Tucson, under the gaze of what I take to have been the town's whole population, numbering five thousand.

Stirling, who had come to see us through, began at his persiflage immediately, and congratulated me upon the house I should play to, speaking of box-office receipts and a benefit night. Tucson is more than half a Mexican town, and in its crowd upon the platform I saw the gaudy shawls, the ear-rings, the steeple straw hats, the old shrivelled cigarette-rolling apes, and the dark-eyed girls, and sifted with these the loungers of our own race, boots, overalls, pistols, hotel clerks, express agents, freight hands, waitresses, red shirts, soldiers from Lowell Barracks, and officers, and in this mass and mess of color and dust and staring, Bishop Meakum, in his yellow duster, by the door of the Hotel San Xavier. But his stare was not, I think now, quite of the same idleness with the rest. He gave me a short nod, yet not unfriendly, as I passed by him to register my name. By the counter I found the wet-eyed Mowry standing.

"How's business on the other side of the track?" I said to him.

"Fair to middlin'. Get them mines ye was after at Globe?"

"You've forgotten I told you they're a property I don't care for, Mr. Mowry. I suppose it's interest in this recent gold discovery that brings you to Tucson." He had no answer for me but a shrewd shirking glance that flattered my sense of acumen, and adding, pleasantly, "So many of your Arizona citizens have forsaken silver for gold just now," I wrote my name in the hotel book, while he looked to remind himself what it was.

"Why, you're not to stay here," said Stirling, coming up. "You're expected at the barracks."

He presented me at once to a knot of officers, each of whom in turn made me known to some additional bystander, until it seemed to me that I shook a new hand sixty times in this disordered minute by the hotel book, and out of the sixty caught one name, which was my own.

These many meetings could not be made perfect without help from the saloon-keeper, who ran his thriving trade conveniently at hand in the office of the San Xavier. Our group remained near him, and I silently resolved to sleep here at the hotel, away from the tempting confusion of army hospitality upon this eve of our trial. We were expected, however, to dine at the post, and that I was ready to do. Indeed, I could scarcely have got myself out of it without rudeness, for the ambulance was waiting us guests at the gate. We went to it along a latticed passage at the edge of a tropical garden, only a few square yards in all, but how pretty! and what an oasis of calm in the midst of this teeming desolation of unrest! It had upon one side the railway station, wooden, sordid, congesting with malodorous packed humanity; on the next the rails themselves and the platform, with steam and bells and baggage-trucks rolling and bumping; the hotel stood on the third, a confusion of tongues and trampings; while a wide space of dust, knee-deep, and littered with manœuvring vehicles, hemmed in this silent garden on the fourth side. A slender slow little fountain dropped inaudibly among some palms, a giant cactus, and the broad-spread shade of trees I did not know. This was the whole garden, and a tame young antelope was its inhabitant. He lay in the unchanging shade, his large eyes fixed remotely upon the turmoil of this world, and a sleepy charm touched my senses as I looked at his domain. Instead of going to dinner, or going anywhere, I should have liked to recline indefinitely beneath those palms and trail my fingers in the cool fountain. Such enlightened languor, however, could by no happy chance be the lot of an important witness in a Western robbery trial, and I dined and wined with the jovial officers, at least talking no business.

With business I was sated. Pidcock and the attorney for the United States—I can remember neither his name nor the proper title of his office, for he was a nobody, and I had forgotten his features each new time that we met—had mapped out the trial to me, preparing and rehearsing me in my testimony until they had pestered me into a hatred of them both. And when word was brought me here, dining at Lowell Barracks, where I had imagined myself safe from justice, that this same attorney was waiting to see me, I rose and I played him a trick. Possibly I should not have done it but for the saloon-keeper in the afternoon and this sustained dining now; but I sent him word I should be with him directly—and I wandered into Tucson by myself.

Faithful to my last strong impression there, I went straight to the tiny hotel garden, and in that darkness lay down in a delicious and torpid triumph. The attorney was most likely waiting still. No one on earth knew where I was. Pidcock could not trace me now. I could see the stars through the palms and the strange trees, the fountain made a little sound, somewhere now and then I could hear the antelope, and, cloaked in this black serenity, I lay smiling. Once an engine passed heavily, leaving the station utterly quiet again, and the next I knew it was the antelope's rough tongue that waked me, and I found him nibbling and licking my hand. People were sitting in the latticed passage, and from the light in the office came Mr. Mowry, untying a canvas sack that he held. At this sight my truancy to discretion was over, and no head could be more wakeful or clear than mine instantly became.

"How much d'yer want this time, Mr. Jenks?" inquired Mowry.

I could not hear the statesman's reply, but thought, while the sound of clinking came to me, how a common cause will often serve to reconcile the most bitter opponents. I did not dare go nearer to catch all their talk, and I debated a little upon my security even as it was, until my own name suddenly reached me.

"Him?" said Mowry; "that there tai-lor-made boy? They've got him sleepin' at the barracks."

"Nobody but our crowd's boarding here," said some one.

"They think we're laying for their witnesses," said the voice of Jenks. And among the various mingled laughs rose distinct a big one that I knew.

"Oh, ho, ho! Well, yes. Tell you about witnesses. Here's all there is to them: spot cash to their figure, and kissing the Book. You've done no work but what I told you?" he added, sharply.

"We haven't needed to worry about witnesses in any shape, Bishop."

"That's good. That's economy. That little Eastern toorist is harmless."

"Leave him talk, Bishop. Leave 'em all tell their story."

"It's going to cost the whole stake, though," said Jenks.

"Deserted Jericho!" remarked old Meakum.

"I don't try cases for nothing, Bishop. The deal's covered. My clients have publicly made over to me their horses and saddles."

"Oh, ho, ho!" went the Bishop. But this last word about the horses was the only part of the talk I could not put a plain meaning upon.

Mr. Mowry I now saw re-enter the lighted door of the office, with his canvas sack in his hand. "This'll be right here in the safe," said he.

"All right," answered Jenks. "I'll not be likely to call on you any more for a day or so."

"Hello!" said the office clerk, appearing in his shirt sleeves. "You fellows have made me forget the antelope." He took down a lantern, and I rose to my feet.

"Give us a drink before you feed him," said Jenks. Then I saw the whole of them crowd into the door for their nightcap, and that was all I waited for.

I climbed the garden fence. My thoughts led me at random through quantities of soft dust, and over the rails, I think, several times, until I stood between empty and silent freight trains, and there sat down. Harmless! It seemed to me they would rate me differently in the morning. So for a while my mind was adrift in the turbulent cross-currents of my discovery; but it was with a smooth innocent surface that I entered the hotel office and enjoyed the look of the clerk when he roused and heard me, who, according to their calculations, should have been in slumber at the barracks, asking to be shown my room here. I was tempted to inquire if he had fed the antelope—such was the pride of my elation—and I think he must have been running over questions to put me; but the two of us marched up the stairs with a lamp and a key, speaking amiably of the weather for this time of year, and he unlocked my door with a politeness and hoped I would sleep well with a consideration that I have rarely met in the hotel clerk. I did not sleep well. Yet it seemed not to matter. By eight I had breakfast, and found the attorney—Rocklin I shall name him, and that will have to answer—and told him how we had become masters of the situation.

He made me repeat it all over, jotting memoranda this second time; and when my story was done, he sat frowning at his notes, with a cigar between his teeth. "This ain't much," he said. "Luckily I don't need anything more. I've got a dead open-and-shut case without it."

"Why don't you make it deader, then?" said I. "Don't you see what it all means?"

"Well, what does it all mean?"

Either the man was still nettled at my treatment of him last evening, or had no liking for amateur opinions and help; otherwise I see no reason for the disparagement with which he regarded me while I interpreted what I had overheard, piece by piece, except the horse and saddle remark.

"Since that don't seem clear, I'll explain it to you," he said, "and then you'll know it all. Except their horses and saddles, the accused haven't a red cent to their names—not an honest one, that is. So it looks well for them to be spending all they've apparently got in the world to pay counsel fees. Now I have this case worked up," he pursued, complacently, "so that any such ambiguous stuff as yours is no good to me at all—would be harmful, in fact. It's not good policy, my friend, to assail the character of opposing counsel. And Bishop Meakum! Are you aware of his power and standing in this section? Do you think you're going to ring him in?"

"Great goodness!" I cried. "Let me testify, and then let the safe be opened."

Rocklin looked at me a moment, the cigar wagging between his teeth, and then he lightly tossed his notes in the waste-paper basket.

"Open your safe," said he, "and what then? Up steps old Mowry and says, 'I'll thank you to let my property alone.' Where's your proof? What word did any of them drop that won't bear other constructions? Mowry's well known to have money, and he has a right to give it to Jenks."

"If the gold could be identified?" I suggested.

"That's been all attended to," he answered, with increasing complacence. "I'm obliged to you for your information, and in a less sure case I might risk using it, but— Why, see here; we've got 'em hands down!" And he clapped me on the knee. "If I had met you last evening I was going to tell you our campaign. Pidcock 'll come first, of course, and his testimony 'll cover pretty much the whole ground. Then, you see, the rest of you I'll use mainly in support. Sergeant Brown — he's very strong, and the black woman, and you—I'll probably call you third or fourth. So you'll be on hand sure now?"

Certainly I had no thought of being anywhere else. The imminence of our trial was now heralded by the cook's coming to Rocklin's office punctually to his direction, and after her Pidcock almost immediately. It was not many minutes before the more important ones of us had gathered, and we proceeded to court, once again a Combination Extraordinary—a spectacle for Tucson. So much stir and prosperity had not blossomed in the town for many years, its chief source of life being the money that Lowell Barracks brought to it. But now its lodgings were crowded and its saloons and Mexican dens of entertainment waked to activity. From a dozing sunburnt village of adobe walls and almond-trees, it was become something like those places built in a single Western day of riot extravagance, where corner lots are clamored for, and men pay a dollar to be shaved.

Jenks was before us in the room with his clients. He was practising what I always think of as his celluloid smile, whispering and all-hail with everybody. One of the prisoners had just such another mustache as his own, too large for his face; and this has led me since to notice a type of too large mustaches through our country in all ranks, but of similar men, who generally have either stolen something or lacked the opportunity. Catching sight of me, Jenks came at once, friendly as you please, shaking my passive hand, and laughing that we should meet again under such circumstances.

"When we're through this nuisance," said he, "you must take dinner with me. Just now, you understand, it wouldn't look well to see me hobnobbing with a government witness. See you again!" And he was off to some one else.

I am confident this man could not see himself as others—some others, at least—saw him. To him his whole performance was natural and professional, and my view that he was more infamous by far than the thieves would have sincerely amazed him. Indeed, for one prisoner I felt very sorry. Black curly was sitting there, and in contrast to Mr. Adams, down whose beard the tobacco forever ran, he seemed downcast and unhardened, I thought. He was getting his deserts through base means. It was not for the sake of justice but from private revenge that Mrs. Sproud had moved; and, after all, had the boy injured her so much as this? Yet how could I help him? They were his deserts. My mood was abruptly changed to diversion when I saw among our jury specimens of both types of Meakum, and prominent among the spectator throng their sire, that canny polygamist, surveying the case with the same forceful attention I had noticed first in the House of Representatives, and ever since that day. But I had a true shock of surprise now. Mrs. Sproud was in court. There could be no mistake. No one seemed to notice her, and I wondered if many in the town knew her face, and with what intent she had returned to this dangerous neighborhood. I was so taken up with watching her and her furtive appearance in the almost concealed position she had chosen that I paid little heed to the government's opening of its case. She had her eyes upon black curly, but he could not see her. Pidcock was in the midst of his pompous recital when the court took its noon intermission. Then I was drawn to seek out black curly, as he was conducted to his dinner.

"Good-day," said he, as I came beside him.

"I wish I didn't have to go on oath about this," I said.

"Oath away," he answered, doggedly. "What's that got to do with me?"

"Oh, come!" I exclaimed.

"Come where?" He looked at me defiantly.

"When people don't wish to be trailed," I went on, "do I understand they sometimes spread a blanket and lead their horses on it and take off their shoes? I'm merely asking out of a traveller's curiosity."

"I guess you'll have to ask them that's up on such tricks," he answered, grinning.

I met him in the eyes, and a strong liking for him came over me. "I probably owe you my life," I said, huskily. "I know I do. And I hate— You must consider me a poor sort of bird."

"Blamed if I know what you're drivin' at," said black curly. But he wrinkled his forehead in the pleasant way I remembered. "Yer whiskey was good all right," he added, and gave me his hand.

"Look here," said I. "She's come back."

This took the boy unguarded, and he swore with surprise. Then his face grew sombre. "Let her," he remarked; and that was all we said.

At the afternoon sitting I began to notice how popular sympathy was not only quite against the United States, but a sentiment amounting to hatred was shown against all soldiers. The voice of respectability seemed entirely silent; decent citizens were there, but not enough of them. The mildest opinion was that Uncle Sam could afford to lose money better than poor people, and the strongest was that it was a pity the soldiers had not been killed. This seemed inappropriate in a Territory desiring admission to our Union. I supposed it something local then, but have since observed it to be a prevailing Western antipathy. The unthinking sons of the sage-brush ill tolerate a thing which stands for discipline, good order, and obedience, and the man who lets another command him they despise. I can think of no threat more evil for our democracy, for it is a fine thing diseased and perverted—namely, independence gone drunk.

Pidcock's examination went forward, and the half-sack of gold from the haystack brought a great silence in court. The Major's identification of the gold was conducted by Rocklin with stage effect, for it was an undoubted climax; but I caught a most singular smile on the face of Bishop Meakum, and there sat Mrs. Sproud, still solitary and engulfed in the throng, her face flushed and her eyes blazing. And here ended the first day.

In the morning came the Major's cross-examination, with the room more crowded than before, but I could not find Mrs. Sproud. Rocklin did not believe I had seen her, and I feared something had happened to her. The Bishop had walked to the court with Jenks, talking and laughing upon general subjects, so far as I could hear. The counsel for the prisoners passed lightly over the first part of the evidence, only causing an occasional laugh on the score of the Major's military prowess, until he came to the gold.

"You said this sack was one of yours, Major?" he now inquired.

"It is mine, sir."

A large bundle of sacks was brought. "And how about these? Here are ten, fifteen—about forty. I'll get some more if you say so. Are they all yours?"

"Your question strikes me as idle, sir." The court rapped, and Jenks smiled. "They resemble mine," said Pidcock. "But they are not used."

"No; not used." Jenks held up the original, shaking the gold. "Now I'm going to empty your sack for a moment."

"I object," said Rocklin, springing up.

"Oh, it's all counted," laughed Jenks; and the objection was not sustained. Then Jenks poured the gold into a new sack and shook that aloft. "It makes them look confusingly similar, Major. I'll just put my card in your sack."

"I object," said Rocklin, with anger, but with futility. Jenks now poured the gold back into the first, then into a third, and thus into several, tossing them each time on the table, and the clinking pieces sounded clear in the room. Bishop Meakum was watching the operation like a wolf. "Now, Major," said Jenks, "is your gold in the original sack, or which sack is my card in?"

This was the first time that the room broke out loudly; and Pidcock, when the people were rapped to order, said, "The sack's not the thing."

"Of course not. The gold is our point. And of course you had a private mark on it. Tell the jury, please, what the private mark was."

He had none. He spoke about dates, and new coins, he backed and filled, swelled importantly, and ended like a pricked bladder by recanting his identification.

"That is all I have to say for the present," said Jenks.

"Don't complicate the issue by attempting to prove too much, Mr. Rocklin," said the judge.

Rocklin flushed, and called the next witness, whispering sulkily to me, "What can you expect if the court starts out against you?" But the court was by no means against him. The judge was merely disgusted over Rocklin's cardinal folly of identifying coin under such loose conditions.

And now came the testimony of Sergeant Brown. He told so clear a story as to chill the enthusiasm of the room. He pointed to the man with the mustache, black curly, and yellow. "I saw them shooting from the right of the road," he said. Jenks tried but little to shake him, and left him unshaken. He was followed by the other wounded soldier, whose story was nearly the same, except that he identified different prisoners.

"Who did you say shot you?" inquired Jenks. "Which of these two?"

"I didn't say. I don't know."

"Don't know a man when he shoots you in broad daylight?"

"Plenty was shooting at me," said the soldier. And his testimony also remained unshaken.

Then came my own examination, and Jenks did not trouble me at all, but, when I had likewise identified the men I knew, simply bowed smilingly, and had no questions to ask his friend from the East.

Our third morning began with the negress, who said she was married, told a scattered tale, and soon stated that she was single, explaining later that she had two husbands, and one was dead, while the other had disappeared from her ten years ago. Gradually her alarm subsided and she achieved coherence.

"What did this gentleman do at the occurrence?" inquired Jenks, indicating me.

"Dat gemman? He jes flew, sir, an' I don' blame him fo' bein' no wusser skeer'd dan de whole party. Yesser, we all flew scusin' dey two pore chillun; an' we staid till de 'currence was ceased."

"But the gentleman says he sat on a stone, and saw those men firing."

"Land! I seed him goin' like he was gwineter Fo't Grant. He run up de hill, an' de Gennul he run down like de day of judgment."

"The General ran?"

"Lawd grashus, honey, yo' could have played checkers on dey coat tails of his."

The court rapped gently.

"But the gold must have been heavy to carry away to the horses. Did not the General exert his influence to rally his men?"

"No, sah. De Gennul went down de hill, an' he took his inflooence with him."

"I have no further questions," said Jenks. "When we come to our alibis, gentlemen, I expect to satisfy you that this good lady saw more correctly, and when she is unable to recognize my clients it is for a good reason."

"We've not got quite so far yet," Rocklin observed. "We've reached the hay-stack at present."

"Aren't you going to make her describe her own confusion more?" I began, but stopped, for I saw that the next witness was at hand, and that it was Mrs. Sproud.

"How's this?" I whispered to Rocklin. "How did you get her?"

"She volunteered this morning, just before trial. We're in big luck."

The woman was simply dressed in something dark. Her handsome face was pale, but she held a steady eye upon the jury, speaking clearly and with deliberation. Old Meakum, always in court and watchful, was plainly unprepared for this, and among the prisoners, too, I could discern uneasiness. Whether or no any threat or constraint had kept her invisible during these days, her coming now was a thing for which none of us were ready.

"What do I know?" she repeated after the counsel. "I suppose you have been told what I said I knew."

"We'd like to hear it directly from you, Mrs. Sproud," Rocklin explained.

"Where shall I start?"

"Well—there was a young man who boarded with you, was there not?"

"I object to the witness being led," said Jenks. And Bishop Meakum moved up beside the prisoners' counsel and began talking with him earnestly.

"Nobody is leading me," said Mrs.

Sproud, imperiously, and raising her voice a little. She looked about her. "There was a young man who boarded with me. Of course that is so."

Meakum broke off in his confidences with Jenks, and looked sharply at her.

"Do you see your boarder anywhere here?" inquired Rocklin, and from his tone I perceived that he was puzzled by the manner of his witness.

She turned slowly, and slowly scrutinized the prisoners one by one. The head of black curly was bent down, and I saw her eyes rest upon it while she stood in silence. It was as if he felt the summons of her glance, for he raised his head. His face was scarlet, but her paleness did not change.

"He is the one sitting at the end," she said, looking back at the jury. She then told some useless particulars, and brought her narrative to the afternoon when she had heard the galloping. "Then I hid. I hid because this is a rough country."

"When did you recognize that young man's voice?"

"I did not recognize it."

Black curly's feet scraped as he shifted his position.

"Collect yourself, Mrs. Sproud. We'll give you all the time you want. We know ladies are not used to talking in court. Did you not hear this young man talking to his friends?"

"I heard talking," replied the witness, quite collected. "But I could not make out who they were. If I could have been sure it was him and friends, I wouldn't have staid hid. I'd have had no call to be scared."

Rocklin was dazed, and his next question came in a voice still more changed and irritable.

"Did you see any one?"

"No one."

"What did you hear them say?"

"They were all talking at once. I couldn't be sure."

"Why did you go to the hay-stack?"

"Because they said something about my hay-stack, and I wanted to find out, if I could."

"Did you not write their names on a paper and give it to this gentleman? Remember you are on oath, Mrs. Sproud."

By this time a smile was playing on the features of Jenks, and he and Bishop Meakum talked no longer together, but sat back to watch the woman's extraordinary attempt to undo her work. It was shrewd, very shrewd, in her to volunteer as our witness instead of as theirs. She was ready for the paper question, evidently.

"I wrote—" she began, but Rocklin interrupted.

"On oath, remember!" he repeated, finding himself cross-examining his own witness. "The names you wrote are the names of these prisoners here before the court. They were traced as the direct result of your information. They have been identified by three or four persons. Do you mean to say you did not know who they were?"

"I did not know," said Mrs. Sproud, firmly. "As for the paper, I acted hasty. I was a woman, alone, and none to consult or advise me. I thought I would get in trouble if I did not tell about such goings on, and I just wrote the names of Will—of the boys that came round there all the time, thinking it was most likely them. I didn't see him, and I didn't make out surely it was his voice. I wasn't sure enough to come out and ask what they were up to. I didn't stop to think of the harm I was doing on guess-work."

For the first time the note of remorse conquered in her voice. I saw how desperation at what she had done when she thought her love was cured was now bracing the woman to this audacity.

"Remember," said Rocklin, "the gold was also found as the direct result of your information. It was you who told Major Pidcock in the ambulance about the seven sacks."

"I never said anything about seven sacks."

This falsehood was a master-stroke, for only half a sack had been found. She had not written this down. There was only the word of Pidcock and me to vouch for it, while against us stood her denial, and the actual quantity of gold.

"I have no further questions," said Rocklin.

"But I have," said Jenks. And then he made the most of Mrs. Sproud, although many in the room were laughing, and she herself, I think, felt she had done little but sacrifice her own character without repairing the injury she had done black curly. Jenks made her repeat that she was frightened; not calm enough to be sure of voices, especially many speaking together; that she had seen no one

throughout. He even attempted to show that the talk about the hay-stack might have been purely about hay, and that the half-sack of gold might have been put there at another time—might belong to some honest man this very moment.

"Did you ever know the young man who boarded with you to do a dishonorable thing?" inquired Jenks. "Did you not have the highest opinion of him?"

She had not expected a question like this. It nearly broke the woman down. She put her hand to her breast, and seemed afraid to trust her voice. "I have the highest opinion of him," she said, word painfully following word. "He — he used to know that."

"I have finished," said Jenks.

"Can I go?" asked the witness, and the attorneys bowed. She stood one hesitating moment in the witness-stand, and she looked at the jury and the court; then, as if almost in dread, she let her eyes travel to black curly. But his eyes were sullenly averted. Then Mrs. Sproud slowly made her way through the room, with one of the saddest faces I have ever seen, and the door closed behind her.

We finished our case with all the prisoners identified, and some of them doubly. The defence was scarcely more than a sham. The flimsy alibis were destroyed even by the incompetent, unready Rocklin, and when the charge came, blackness fell upon the citizens of Tucson. The judge's cold statements struck them as partisan, and they murmured and looked blackly at him. But the jury, with its Meakums, wore no expression at all during any of his remarks. Their eyes were upon him, but entirely fishlike. He dismissed the cumbersome futilities one by one. "Now three witnesses have between them recognized all the prisoners but one," he continued. "That one, a reputed pauper, paid several hundred dollars of debts in gold the morning after the robbery. The money is said to be the proceeds of a cattle sale. No cattle have ever been known to belong to this man, and the purchaser had never been known to have any income until this trial began. The prisoner's name was on Mrs. Sproud's paper. The statement of one witness that he sat on a stone and saw three other of the prisoners firing has been contradicted by a woman who described herself as having run away at once; it is supported by two men who are admitted by all to have remained, and in consequence been shot. Their statements have been assailed by no one. Their testimony stands on the record unimpeached. They have identified five prisoners. If you believe them —and remember that not a word they said has been questioned—" Here the judge emphasized more and more clearly. He concluded with the various alternatives of fact according to which the jury must find its several possible verdicts. When he had finished, the room sat sullen and still, and the twelve went out. I am told that they remained ten minutes away. It seemed one to me.

When they had resumed their seats I noticed the same fishlike oracular eye in most of them unchanged.

"Not guilty," said the foreman.

"What!" shouted the judge, startled out of all judicial propriety. "None of 'em?"

"Not guilty," monotonously repeated the foreman.

We were silent amid the din of triumph now raised by Tucson. In the laughter, the hand-shaking, the shouting, and the jubilant pistol-shots that some particularly free spirit fired in the old Cathedral Square, we went to our dinner; and not even Stirling could joke. "There's a certain natural justice done here in spite of them," he said. "They are not one cent richer for all their looted twenty-eight thousand. They come out free, but penniless."

"How about Jenks and that jury?" said I. And Stirling shrugged his shoulders.

But we had yet some crowning impudence to learn. Later, in the street, the officers and I met the prisoners, their witnesses, and their counsel emerging from a photographer's studio. The Territorial Delegate had been taken in a group with his acquitted thieves. The Bishop had declined to be in this souvenir.

"That's a picture I want," said I. "Only I'll be sorry to see your face there," I added to black curly.

"Indeed!" put in Jenks.

"Yes," said I. "You and he do not belong in the same class. By-the-way, Mr. Jenks, I suppose you'll return their horses and saddles now?"

Too many were listening for him to lose his temper, and he did a sharp thing. He took this public opportunity for breaking some news to his clients. "I had hoped to," he said; "that is, as many as were not needed to defray necessary costs. But it's been an expensive suit, and I've found myself obliged to sell them all. It's little enough to pay for clearing your character, boys."

They saw through his perfidy to them, and that he had them checkmated. Any protest from them would be a confession of their theft. Yet it seemed an unsafe piece of villany in Jenks.

"They look disappointed," I remarked. "I shall value the picture very highly."

"If that's Eastern sarcasm," said Jenks, "it's beyond me."

"No, Mr. Jenks," I answered. "In your presence sarcasm drops dead. I think you'll prosper in politics."

But there I was wrong. There is some natural justice in these events, though I wish there were more. The jury, it is true, soon seemed oddly prosperous, as Stirling wrote me afterwards. They painted their houses; two of them, who had generally walked before, now had wagons; and in so many of their gardens and small ranches did the plants and fruits increase that, as Stirling put it, they had evidently sowed their dollars. But upon Jenks Territorial displeasure did descend. He had staid away too much from Washington. A pamphlet appeared with the title, "What Luke Jenks has done for Arizona." Inside were twenty blank pages, and he failed of re-election.

Furthermore, the government retaliated upon this district by abandoning Camp Thomas and Lowell Barracks, those important sources of revenue for the neighborhood. The brief boom did not help Tucson very long, and left it poorer than ever.

At the station I saw Mrs. Sproud and black curly, neither speaking to the other. It was plain that he had utterly done with her, and that she was too proud even to look at him. She went West, and he as far East as Willcox. Neither one have I ever seen again.

But I have the photograph, and I sometimes wonder what has happened to black curly. Arizona is still a Territory; and when I think of the Gila Valley and of the Boy Orator, I recall Bishop Meakum's remark about our statesmen at Washington: "You can divide them birds in two lots—those who know better, and those who don't. D'you follow me?"

37

Red Saunders at Big Bend

HENRY WALLACE PHILLIPS

McCLURE'S MAGAZINE

JANUARY, 1904

RED SAUNDERS AT BIG BEND

I

ENTER MR. SETT AND EXIT THE DOG

BY

HENRY WALLACE PHILLIPS

AUTHOR OF ''RED SAUNDERS''

ILLUSTRATED BY A. B. FROST

"F all the worlds I ever broke into, this one's the most curious," said Red. "And one of the curiousest things in it is that I think it's queer. Why should I, now? What puts it into our heads that affairs ought to go so and so and so, when they never do anything of the sort? Take any book you read, or any story a man tells you : it runs along about how Mr. Smith made up his mind to do this or that, and proceeded to do it. And that never happened. What Mr. Smith calls making up his mind is, when you come down to bed-rock, nothing more nor less than what Mr. Smith pleasantly calls his mind dodging to cover under pressure of circumstances. That's straight. Old lady Luck comes for Mr. Smith's mind, swinging both hands ; she gives it a stem-winder on the ear ; lams it for keeps on the smeller ; chugs it one in the short ribs, drives right and left into its stummick, and Mr. Smith's mind breaks for cover ; then Mr. Smith tells his wife that — he's made up his mind — He, mind you. Wouldn't that stun you?

"Some people would say, 'Mr. Sett and Mr. Burton made up their minds to start the Big Bend Ranch.' All right ; perhaps

"HE WAS A LOVELY PET"

"'HERE COMES A FUNNY LITTLE CUSS'"

they did, but let me give you an inside view of the factory.

"First off, Billy Quinn, Wind-River Smith, and me were putting up hay at the lake beds. It was a God-forsaken, lonesome job, to say the best of it, and we took to collecting pets, to make it seem a little more like home.

"Billy shot a hawk, breaking its wing. That was the first in the collection. He was a lovely pet. When you gave him a piece of meat he said 'Cree,' and clawed chunks out of you, but most of the time he sat in the corner with his chin on his chest, like a broken-down lawyer. We didn't get the affection we needed out of him. Well, then Wind-River found a bull-snake asleep and lugged him home, hanging over his shoulder. We sewed a flannel collar on the snake and picketed him out until he got used to the place. And around and around and around squirmed that snake until we near got sick at our stummicks watching him. All day long, turning and turning and turning.

"'Darn it,' says I; 'I like more variety.' So that day, when I was cutting close to a timbered slew, out pops an old bob-cat and starts to open my shirt to see if I am her long-lost brother. By the time I got her strangled I had parted with most

of my complexion. Served me right for being without a gun. The team run away as soon as I fell off the seat and I was booked to walk home. I heard a squeal from the bushes, and here comes a funny little cuss. I liked the look of him from the jump-off, even if his mother did claw delirious delight out of me. He balanced himself on his stubby legs and looked me square in the eye, and he spit and fought as though he weighed a ton when I picked him up — never had any notion of running away. Well, that was Robert — long for Bob.

"The style that cat spread on in the matter of growing was simply astonishing ; he grew so's you could notice it overnight. At the end of two months he was that big he couldn't stand up under our sheet-iron cook-stove, and this was about the beginning of our family troubles. Tommy, the snake, was a good deal of a nuisance from the time he settled down. You'd have a horrible dream in the night — be way down under something or other, gasping for wind, and, waking up, find Tommy nicely coiled on your chest. Then you'd slap Tommy on the floor like a section of large rubber hose. But he bore no malice. Soon's you got asleep he'd be right back again. When the weather got cool he was always under foot. He'd roll beneath you and land you on your scalp-lock, or you'd ketch your toe on him and get a dirty drop. I don't think I ever laughed more in my life than one day when Billy come in with an armful of wood, tripped on Tommy, and come down with a clatter right where Judge Jenkins, the hawk, could reach him. The Judge fastened one claw in Billy's hair and scratched his whiskers with the other. Gee ! The hair and feathers flew ! Bill had a hot temper and he went for the hawk like it was a man. The first thing he laid his hand on was Tommy, so he used the poor snake for a club. Wind-River and me were so weak from laughing that we near lost two pets before we got strength to interfere.

"But, as I was saying, the cold nights played Keno with our happy home. Neither Tommy nor Bob dared monkey with the Judge — he was the only thing on top of the earth the cat was afraid of. Bob used to be very anxious to sneak a hunk of meat from His Honor at times, yet, when the Judge stood on one foot, cocked his head sideways, snapped his bill and said 'Cree,' Robert reconsidered. On the other hand, Tommy and Bob were forever scrapping. Lively set-to's, I want to tell you. The snake butted with his head like a young streak of lightning. I've seen him knock the cat ten foot. And while a cat doesn't grow moldy in the process of

the corner of the house to bait 'em, and Bob would watch there hour on end until one got within range. It was a dead coyote in ten seconds by the watch, if the jump landed. If it didn't, Bob had learned there was no use wasting his young strength trying to ketch him. He used to sit still and gaze after them flying streaks of hair and bones as

''WE NEAR LOST TWO PETS''

making a move, yet the snake is there about one seventeen-hundredth-millionth part of a second sooner. And that's a good deal where those parties are concerned. Now, on cold nights, they both liked to get under the stove, where it was warm, and there wasn't room for more'n one. Hence, trouble; serious trouble. Bob hunted coyotes on moonlight nights. We threw scraps around

though he was thinking 'I wisht somebody'd telegraph that son-of-a-gun for me.'

"Well, then he'd be chilly and reckon he'd climb under the stove. But Thomas 'ud be there.

"'H-h-h-h-hhhh!' says Tom, in a whisper.

"'Er-raow-pht!' says Robert. 'Mmm-mmmm—errrrr—pht!' And so on for some

"'I WISHT SOMEBODY'D TELEGRAPH THAT SON-OF-A-GUN FOR ME'"

time, the talk growing louder, then, with a yell that would stand up every hair on your head, Bob 'ud hop him. Over goes the cook-stove. Away rolls the hot coals on the floor. Down comes the stove-pipe and the frying-pans and the rest of the truck, whilest the old Judge in the corner hollered decisions, heart-broke because he was tied by the leg and could not get a claw into the dispute.

"By the time we had 'em separated— Bob headed up in his barrel and Tom tied up in his sack—put the fire out, and fixed things generally, there wasn't a great deal left of that night's rest.

"But children will be children. We swore awful, still we wouldn't have missed their company for a fair-sized farm.

"And now comes in the first little twist of the Big Bend Ranch, proper—all these things I'm telling you were the eggs. Here's where the critter pipped.

"'Twas November, and such a November as you don't get outside of Old Dakota, a regular mint-julep of a month, with a dash of summer, a sprig of spring, a touch of fall, and a sniff or two of winter to liven you up. If you'd formed a committee to furnish weather for a month, and they'd turned out a month like that, not even their best friends would have kicked. And here we'd been makin' hay, and makin' hay, the ranch people thanking Providence that prairie grass cures on the stem, while we cussed, for we were sick of the sight of hay. I got so the rattle of a mower give me hysterics. We were picked because we were steady and reliable, but one day we bunched the job. Says I, 'Here; we've cut grass for four solid months includin' Sundays and legal holidays, although the Lord knows where they come in, for I haven't the least suspicion what day of the month it may be, but anyhow, let's knock off one round.'

"So we did. I sat outside in the afternoon, while the other two boys and the rest of the family took a snooze. Here comes a man across the south flat a-horseback.

"I watched him, much interested: first place, he was the first strange human animal we'd laid eye on for six weeks; next place, his style of riding attracted attention. I thought at the time he must have invented it, him being the kind of man that hated horses, and wanted to keep as far away from them as possible, yet forced by circumstances to climb upon their backs.

"His mount was a big American horse, full sixteen hand high, trotting in twenty-foot jumps. If I had anything against a person, just short of killing, I'd tie him on the back of a horse trotting like that. It's a great gait to sit out. Howsomever, this man didn't sit it out ; what he wanted of a saddle beyond the stirrups was a mystery, for he never touched it. He stood up on his stirrups, bent forward like he was going to bite the horse in the ear, soon's the strain got unendurable.

"Well, here he come, straight for us. I'd a mind to wake the other boys up, to let 'em see something new in the way of mishandling a horse, but they snored so peaceful, I refrained.

"'How-de-do ?' says he.

"I said I was worrying along, and sized him up, on the quiet. He was a queer pet. Not a bad set-up man, and rather good-looking in the face. Light yellow hair, little yellow mustache, light blue eyes. And clean ! Say, I never saw anybody that looked so aggravating clean in all my life. It seemed kind of wrong for him to be outdoors ; all the prairie and the cabin and everything looked mussed up beside him.

"As soon as he opened up, I noticed he had a little habit of speaking in streaks, that bothered me. I missed the sense of his remarks.

"'Would you mind walking over that trail again ?' I asked him. 'I do most of my thinking at a foot-step and your ideas is over the hill and far away before I can recognize the cut of their scalp-lock.'

"'Haw !' says he and stared at me. I was just on the point of askin' him if red hair was a new thing to him, when all of a sudden he begun to laugh. 'Haw-haw-haw !' says he. 'Not bad at all, ye know.'

"'Of course not,' says I. 'Why should it be ?'

"This got him going. I saw him figuring away to himself, and then I had to smile so you could hear it.

"'Well,' says I, better humored, 'tell us it again — I caught the word sheep in the hurricane.'

"So he went over it, talking slow. I listened with one ear, for he had a white bulldog with him ; a husky, bandy-legged brute with a black eye, and he was sniffing, dog fashion, around the door, while I blocked him out with my legs. Doggy was in a frame of mind, puzzling out bull-snake trail, and hawk trail, and bob-cat trail. He foresaw much that was entertaining the other side of the door, and wanted it, powerful.

"'Here,' says I, 'call your dog. I can't pay attention to both of you.'

"'He won't hurt anything, you know,' says the man.

"'Well, we've got a cat in there that'll hurt *him*,' I says. 'You'd better whistle him off before old Bob wakes up and scatters him around the front yard.'

"'BOB 'UD HOP HIM'"

"Gee ! That man sat up straight on his horse ! Cat hurt that dog? Nonsense ! Of course, he wouldn't let the dog hurt the cat, and as long as I was afraid ——

"I looked into that peaceful cabin. Billy was lying on his back, his fine manly nose vibrating with melody ; Wind-River was cooing in a gentle, choked-to-death sort of fashion, on the second bunk ; Tom was coiled in the corner, the size of half a barrel ; the Judge slept on his perch ; Robert reposed under the cook-stove with just a front paw sticking out. It was one of them restful scenes our friends the poets sing about. It did appear wicked to disturb it but——

"'Will you risk your dog?' I asked that man, very softly and politely.

"'Certainly!' says he.

"Says I, 'His blood be on your shirt-front,' and I moved my leg.

"Well, sir, Billy landed on the grocery shelf. Wind-River grabbed his gun and sat up paralyzed. It really was a most surprising noise. I've had hard luck in my life, but all the things that ever happened to me would seem like a recess to that bull-dog. Our domestic difficulties was forgotten. 'United We Stand,' waved the motto of the lake-bed cabin. Jerusalem! That dog was snake-bit, and hawk-scratched-and-bit-and-clawed, and bob-cat-scratched-and-bit-and-clawed, till you couldn't see a cussed thing in that cabin but blur. And of all the hissing and squawking and screech-ing and yelling and snapping and roaring and growling you or any other man ever heard, that was the darnedest. I took a look at the visitor. He'd got off his horse and was stand-ing in the doorway with his hands spread out. His face expressed nothing at all, very forcible. Meanwhile, things were boilin' for fair; cook-stove, frying-pans, stools, boxes, saddles, tin cans, bull-snakes, hawks, bob-cats, and bulldogs simply floated in the air.

"HIS STYLE OF RIDING ATTRACTED ATTENTION"

"'SEARCHING HIS SOUL FOR SOUNDS TO TELL HOW SCART HE WAS''

"'I wish you'd tell me what in all perdition has busted loose in this cabin, Red Saunders !' howls old Wind-River in an injured tone of voice ; 'and whether I shell shoot or sha'n't I.'

"There come a second's lull. I see Judge Jenkins on the dog's back, his talents sunk to the hock, whilest he had hold of an ear with his bill, pullin' manfully. Tommy had swallered the dog's stumpy tail, and Bob was dragging hair out of the enemy like an Injun dressing hides.

"A bulldog is like an Irishman ; he's brave because he don't know any better, and you can't get any braver than that, but there's a limit, even to lunk-headedness. It bored through that dog's thick skull that he had butted into a little bit the darnedest hardest streak of petrified luck that anything on legs could meet with.

"'By-by,' says he to himself. 'Out doors will do for me !' And here he comes ! Neither the visitor nor me was expecting him. He knocked the feet out from under us and sat his master on top. We got up in time to see a winged bulldog, with a tail ten foot long, bounding merrily over the turf, searching his soul for sounds to tell how scart he was, whilest a desperate bob-cat, spitting fire and brimstone, threw dirt fifty foot in the air trying to lay claws on him.

"As they disappeared over the first rise I rolls me a cigarette and lights it slowly.

"'Just by way of curiosity,' says I ; 'how much will you take for your dog ?'

"'My Heavens !' says he, recovering the power of speech. 'What kind of animal was that ?'

"'Come in,' says I, 'and take a drink — you need it.'

"So we gathered up the ruins and tidied things some, while the new man sipped his whisky.

"'My !' says he, of a sudden. 'I must go after my poor dog.'

"I sort of warmed to him at that. 'Dog's all right,' says I. 'He'll shake 'em loose and be home in no time. Now you tell me about them sheep.'

"'Sheep?' says he, putting his hand to his head. 'What was it about sheep?'

"'Hello in the house !' sings out Billy. 'The children's comin' home !'

"We tumbled out. Sure enough, the warriors was returning. First come the Judge, tougher than rawhide, half walking and half flying, his wings spread out, 'cree-ing' to himself about bulldogs and their ways ; next come Bobby, still sputtering and swearing, and behind ambled Thomas at a lively wriggle, a coy, large smile upon his face.

"'Ur-r-roup ! Roup !' sounds from the top of the rise. The family halted and turned around, expectin' more pleasure, for there on the top of the hill stood the terrible scart but still faithful bulldog calling for his master to come away from that place quick, before he got killed. But he had one eye open for safety, and when the

"CALLING FOR HIS MASTER TO COME
AWAY FROM THAT PLACE QUICK,
BEFORE HE GOT KILLED"

family stopped, he ducked down behind the hill surprisin'.

"'Well, I must be going,' says the visitor. 'My name's Sett — Algernon Alfred Sett—and I shall be over next week to talk to you about those sheep.'

"'Any time,' says I. 'We'll be here till we have to shovel snow to get at the hay, from the look of things.'

"'Well, I'm very anxious to have a good long talk with you about sheep,' says he. 'I've been informed that you had a long experience in that line in — er — Nevverdah——'

"'Nevverdah?' says I. 'Oh! — Nevada. I beg your pardon — I've got in the habit of pronouncing in that way. It wasn't Nevada, by the way — it was Texas

—but that's only a matter of a Europe or so. Yes, I met a sheep or two in that country, I'm sorry to say.'

"'I — er — think of engaging in the business, dontcher know,' says he, relaxing into his first method of speech ; 'and should like to consult you professionally.'

"'All right, sir!' says I. 'I'm one of the easiest men to consult west of any place east. Can't you stay now and get the load off your mind?'

"'Well — *no*,' he says to me very confidentially. 'You see, that dog is a great pet of my wife's, and I'm also afraid she will be a little worried by my long absence, so——'

"'I see, sir — I see,' I answered him. 'Well, come around again and we'll talk sheep.'

"'Thank you — thank you *so* much,' says he, and pops up on his horse. Then again, without any warning, he broke into a haw-haw-haw ! as he threw a glance at the family, who sat around eyeing him. 'You were quite right about that *cat*, you know,' says he. 'Capital ! Capital ! But a *little* rough on the dog.' And off he goes, bobbity-bob, bobbity-bob.

"'Where'd you tag that critter, Red?' says Wind-River. 'My mind's wanderin'.'

"'He comes down the draw much the graceful way he's going up it,' says I. 'From where, and why how, I dunno. But I kind of like him against my better instincts, Windy.'

"Windy spit thoughtfully at a fly fifteen foot away. 'I shouldn't have time to hate him much myself,' says he.

"And there you are. That's how I met Brother Sett, and the Big Bend Ranch stuck her head out of the shell."